THE SCOUTING
REPORT: 1986

THE SCOUTING REPORT: 1986

An in-depth analysis of the strengths
and weaknesses of every
active major league baseball player

by
Dave Campbell
Harmon Killebrew
Brooks Robinson
and
Duke Snider

Edited by
Marybeth Sullivan

1817

HARPER & ROW, PUBLISHERS, New York
Cambridge, Philadelphia, San Francisco, London,
Mexico City, São Paulo, Singapore, Sydney

The player photographs which appear in THE SCOUTING REPORT were furnished individually by the twenty-six teams that comprise Major League Baseball. Their cooperation is gratefully acknowledged: Baltimore Orioles, Boston Red Sox, California Angels, Chicago White Sox, Cleveland Indians, Detroit Tigers, Kansas City Royals, Milwaukee Brewers, Minnesota Twins, New York Yankees, Oakland A's, Seattle Mariners, Texas Rangers, Toronto Blue Jays, Atlanta Braves, Chicago Cubs, Cincinnati Reds, Houston Astros, Los Angeles Dodgers, Montreal Expos, New York Mets, Philadelphia Phillies, Pittsburgh Pirates, St. Louis Cardinals, San Diego Padres and San Francisco Giants.

EDITORIAL STAFF

Gordon Edes, Los Angeles Times
Tom Flaherty, Milwaukee Journal
Joe Giuliotti, Boston Herald
Paul Hagan, Ft. Worth Star-Telegram
Jim Henneman, Baltimore Evening Sun
Bob Hertzel, Pittsburgh Press
Greg Hoard, Cincinnati Enquirer
Paul Hoynes, Horvitz Newspapers
Rick Hummel, St. Louis Post-Dispatch
Bruce Jenkins, San Francisco Chronicle
Neil MacCarl, Toronto Star
Bob Markus, Chicago Tribune

Marty Noble, Newsday
Tom Pedulla, Westchester-Rockland Newspapers
Nick Peters, Oakland Tribune
Vern Plagenhoef, Booth Group
Rusty Pray, Camden Courier Post
Tracy Ringolsby, Kansas City Star
Terry Scott, AP
Harry Shattuck, Houston Chronicle
Howard Sinker, Minneapolis Star and Tribune
Tim Tucker, Atlanta Journal
Dave van Dyck, Chicago Sun-Times

THE SCOUTING REPORT: 1986

Copyright © 1986 by TeamWork Enterprises, Inc.

Designer: Marybeth Sullivan

ISSN: 0743-1309
ISBN: 0-06-096050-7

86 87 88 89 90 MVP 10 9 8 7 6 5 4 3 2 1

CONTENTS

Some things you should know:

You know what? I like this book. It's been around for a few years (this is the fourth edition) and it feels good to say right here in print that I like this book.

When I began to develop the concept of publishing scouting reports in the summer of 1981, I was met in baseball circles with varying degrees of astonishment. Scouting reports have always been private documents held closely to the bosom of major league teams. Nobody would let anything out of the bag and most clubs were aghast at the thought of their publication. Professional scouts themselves have a unique camaraderie and rarely discuss their reports with each other. Yet, how each player actually performs and what he is especially good or not-so-good at is the most important aspect of the game! Most major league managers don't develop strategy based on reams of numbers. While percentages do play a role, managers rely on experience, a sense of their own players' strengths and weaknesses and the scouting reports on the opposition.

This is the only book that baseball fans can use to know what professional baseball thinks about each player in a scouting fashion.

THE SCOUTING REPORT is easy to read. It has heart and soul in it. It is human. It is honest and straightforward. You can pick it up for five minutes as easily as you can spend the entire season with it. It is a big book but you don't have to read it all to get the picture.

It makes me nervous to see too many actions broken down into numbers. My electronic banking card once gave a printout of all of the minutiae associated with my account: frequency of use, frequency of use at night, cash allowed, withdrawals on the road---my eyes went wide and I wanted to head for the hills. To me, baseball is an enjoyable game that everybody plays when the weather is nice. Why does the bank keep track of how many withdrawals I make at 2 AM? It must be important to them. As for me, just show me the balance. Not coincidentally, this book feels the same way. This book will not overwhelm you with numbers--there's nothing here on how well certain players do in day games following night games, or when the moon is full. Instead, the numbers presented here were chosen for their applicability in an overall sense to each player's strengths and weaknesses.

What you will find is keen analysis by four men who have massive amounts of baseball knowledge under their caps. THE SCOUTING REPORT: 1986 gives you player-by-player analysis of over 680 major league baseball players. Following the format used by professional scouts, each player is evaluated by men who know how the game should be played. Everything has been covered: hitting, pitching, fielding, baserunning. There's plenty here to keep you going from February through October.

So, here you have it. If this is your first trip with us, come on in and enjoy yourself. If you have had our book in the past, nice to see you again. Sit down, have a report.

Marybeth Sullivan

Managing Editor

The format:

THE SCOUTING REPORT: 1986 is divided into two sections: first, the fourteen teams of the American League, followed by the twelve teams of the National League. Player reports are located alphabetically with their team, with the exception of some players who are used on a limited basis; these players appear at the end of their team's section.

Free agency and trades make it impossible to keep up with all of the players' movements--use the index located on page 657 to locate players who have been traded to or signed by other teams since this book went to press.

One of the most popular features of THE SCOUTING REPORT is the batter's chart; reviewing the diagrams before each game could help you follow the pitcher's strategy to a particular batter and pick up the subtleties of defensive alignments:

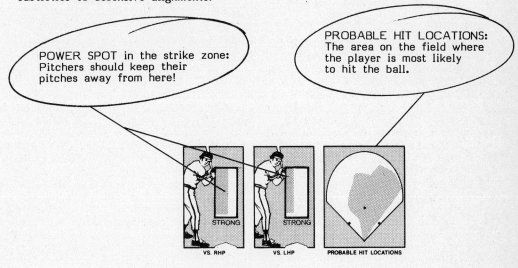

POWER SPOT in the strike zone: Pitchers should keep their pitches away from here!

PROBABLE HIT LOCATIONS: The area on the field where the player is most likely to hit the ball.

VS. RHP   VS. LHP   PROBABLE HIT LOCATIONS

Acknowledgments

It is the intention of this book to make baseball a more enjoyable game for fans by providing information in a scouting format unavailable anywhere else. If you enjoy THE SCOUTING REPORT: 1986, it is because a lot of people want to bring you the best information possible. Dave Campbell, Harmon Killebrew, Brooks Robinson and Duke Snider keep a watchful eye on the strengths and weaknesses of each ballplayer throughout the season and report their findings to you. The baseball beat writers whose names appear on page 4 give this book its color and texture. Jim Armstrong and Rick Rennert make certain that the text is clear and concise. Buz Wyeth and Dan Bial of Harper & Row see to it that there is any book at all. Mary Kay Fama and Rose Petersons piece the puzzle together and Eileen Sullivan does a little bit of everything--including keeping the Managing Editor smiling.

THE AUTHORS

Harmon Killebrew

In 1954, a scout for the Washington Senators traveled to the Idaho-Oregon border to take a look at a big, young man play ball. The powerful 17-year-old prospect, Harmon Killebrew, went 14-for-14 (including five home runs and four triples) that day. He shot one of the home runs over a fence 435 feet away. The otherwise-tightfisted Senators quickly unfolded their bankroll and gave him $30,000 to make him their first bonus player.

During his 22-year career, Killebrew continued to tear up big league pitching. He led the league in home runs six times and hit over 40 home runs in a season eight times. He played at third base, first base and the outfield and was elected to the All-Star team eleven times. Killebrew approached each at-bat calmly and deliberately, intent on his job. He would move into the on-deck circle, take three or four swings and then kneel motionless, staring at the pitcher. Once in the batter's box, he took just a single swing between pitches. Waiting for the pitch, Killebrew stood still, a huge boulder of a man, with his bat resting on his shoulder. Every pitcher knew that any moment the "Killer" could take them downtown.

Most pitchers had no idea how to pitch to Harmon Killebrew: they dared not pitch him inside lest he get even more power to pull the ball and they were afraid to pitch him outside because he could lash that pitch as well. His scouting report: "A righthanded power hitter with switch-hitting effects. Good luck."

Killebrew was inducted into the Hall of Fame in 1984 and is in his first season providing the reports on the players of the American League West for THE SCOUTING REPORT.

Brooks Robinson

Brooks Robinson was the first to believe in the merits of bringing scouting reports to baseball fans--he's always been ahead of his time. Brooks was the man who brought third base out of the closet. Before he set the standard for everyone to follow, the importance of third base, or spectacular defense in general, was an overlooked commodity in baseball.

Casey Stengel once offered this succinct scouting report to his players on Brooks Robinson: "Don't hit it to that feller." In his 23-year career, he was an All-Star for 18 consecutive seasons. He won 16 Gold Gloves. He was the MVP of the All-Star game in 1966; the MVP of the American League in 1964 and the MVP of the World Series in 1970. After seeing him dive, jump, roll and stretch all over the left side of the infield during the 1970 World Series, Pete Rose grumbled, almost to himself, "That guy can field a ball with a pair of pliers." Brooks probably could have.

Inducted into the Hall of Fame in 1983, Brooks Robinson is now in his ninth season as color commentator for the Baltimore Orioles. He is the Executive Vice President and Director of Personal Management Associates, a Baltimore-based player management firm. He also works as Special Assistant for the Crown Petroleum Company and is in his fourth season reporting on the players in the American League East for THE SCOUTING REPORT.

Dave Campbell

Dave Campbell has been reviewing the players of the National League West for THE SCOUTING REPORT since 1984. Now entering his ninth season as a member of the San Diego Padres' broadcast team, Dave began his eight-year playing career with the Detroit Tigers in 1967. He was a speedy second baseman who could also sting the opposition with a home run. Dave holds the current Padre record for most home runs in a season by a second baseman with 12, which he hit in 1970.

Playing mostly as a second baseman, he also appeared at third base, first base and shortstop as well as the outfield. Dave went on to play for two other teams during his career: the St. Louis Cardinals and the Houston Astros.

While attending the University of Michigan, Dave played on the 1962 NCAA Championship team and captained the 1964 club. He ended his major league playing days in 1974, then sandwiched his San Diego broadcasting career around one season of minor league managing in the Padres farm system.

Dave Campbell is the host of the popular San Diego radio show, "10th Inning," and has earned the respect of his peers and Padres fans for his keen insights and thorough game analysis.

Duke Snider

Elected to the Hall of Fame in 1980, Duke Snider ended his 18-year major league career in 1964, but remains as popular today as he was when he was a member of the Brooklyn Dodgers. During his career, he also played for the Los Angeles Dodgers, the San Francisco Giants and the New York Mets. He appears at numerous baseball memorabilia shows throughout the year and is a much sought-after batting instructor at "Dream Week" vacations, where fans have the chance to play alongside big leaguers and get tips from the pros.

And Duke has been a pro since he was 17 years old, but even from his younger years, he assured his parents that he would be a major leaguer. His earliest days as a ballplayer, however, were not easy. By everyone's admission, Duke was one of a few in the game's history to be labeled a future great at first glance because of his speed, the uninhibited swing of his bat, his leaping catches and his irrepressible eagerness to play. But he was also temperamental; it was the patience of Branch Rickey and the batting instruction of George Sisler that guided Duke to stardom. Together, they taught him the strike zone, how to hit the change-up and how to hit to the opposite field.

The result was Duke Snider, the player many consider to be the greatest Dodger center fielder of all time. He appeared in seven All-Star games, is the Dodgers' all-time home run leader (407 career home runs) and has more home runs (11) and RBIs (26) in World Series competition than any other National Leaguer in history.

This season marks his thirteenth season of broadcasting for the Montreal Expos and his third season offering his evaluations of the players in the National League East for THE SCOUTING REPORT.

THE SCOUTS' CHOICE

Each baseball season brings a fresh package of surprises. New stars emerge and old records are broken. Some teams clinch their pennant early, while other races go down to the wire. Players are sold and swapped and managers are hired and fired with regularity. And each day, news of the feats of players who are the best at what they do screams across headlines. THE SCOUTING REPORT reports ballplayers' progress in a different way. By describing each player's skills, it becomes clear that there are very good players who do not get the opportunity to showcase their talents before a large audience either because they play for weak teams or there are other, more spectacular performers ahead of them.

THE SCOUTS' CHOICE highlights some of these players. Each was chosen for his ability at his position in relation to the rest of the players in the league. This is not a record of the best players at each position, rather THE SCOUTS' CHOICE is a list of players who, for an assortment of reasons, are underrated. Keep your eye on them; some will move on to become stars--and grab headlines of their own.

THE AMERICAN LEAGUE

CATCHER:

MARK SALAS-Minnesota Twins
. . . the type of hitter whose style should keep him from falling into extended slumps . . . has worked hard on his defensive shortcomings . . . others at his position could learn from his fearless way behind the plate. page 232.

MICKEY TETTLETON-Oakland A's
. . . Don Sutton praised his "quiet confidence" . . . good range and agility for a big man . . . will move along more quickly as he improves his hitting. page 288.

FIRST BASEMAN:

PETER O'BRIEN-Texas Rangers
. . . has one of the most textbook swings in baseball . . . great confidence . . . could win a Gold Glove someday . . . one of the best at starting a double play. page 329.

SECOND BASEMAN:

DONNIE HILL-Oakland A's
. . . an opposite field hitter with a good eye . . . has what may be one of the strongest arms among AL second basemen . . . became steady on everything from turning the DP to running down pop-ups. page 277.

HAROLD REYNOLDS-Seattle Mariners
. . . has the defensive potential to be a star . . . what he needs is a real chance . . . is quick to both his left and right . . . not intimidated by oncoming runners . . . will get the most out of his ability. page 309.

THE NATIONAL LEAGUE

CATCHER:

DARREN DAULTON-Philadelphia Phillies
. . . it is expected that he will become more relaxed and aggressive in 1986 . . . shows a keen ability to set up the hitters . . . the catcher of the Phils' future. page 541.

FIRST BASEMAN:

TIM CORCORAN-Philadelphia Phillies
. . . good range to either side . . . digs balls out of the dirt well . . . well-schooled in the fundamentals. page 540.

SECOND BASEMAN:

RON OESTER-Cincinnati Reds
. . . has become more aware of the strike zone . . . has a better arm than anyone else . . . will take his knocks. page 428.

JOHNNY RAY-Pittsburgh Pirates
. . . seldom makes a bad throw . . . made a dramatic improvement in his ability to turn the double play pivot . . . did not have as good a year as he is capable of. page 578.

SHORTSTOP:

SPIKE OWEN-Seattle Mariners
. . . not flashy, but he is steady . . . he
grows on you . . . plays hard and does the
little things to help a team. page 304.

DICK SCHOFIELD-California Angels
. . . is as sure-handed as any shortstop in
the American League . . . good initial reactions . . . is young enough that it is
reasonable to expect him to become more of an
offensive force. page 80.

THIRD BASEMAN:

FLOYD RAYFORD-Baltimore Orioles
. . . To classify him as a surprise would be
putting it mildly . . . his defensive play
is much better than adequate. page 29.

MIKE PAGLIARULO-New York Yankees
. . . is coming along . . . has to stick with
it and the organization has to stick with
him . . . he has a lot of talent. page 255.

RIGHT FIELDER:

MIKE DAVIS-Oakland A's
. . . still not the best he is capable
of being . . . strong and accurate arm
ranks up there with the best. page 272.

CENTER FIELDER:

REID NICHOLS-Chicago White Sox
. . . has never been a regular . . . is an
above-average fielder . . . arm is strong
and accurate . . . only deficiency is a lack of
home run power. page 104.

LEFT FIELDER:

MEL HALL-Cleveland Indians
. . . aggressive hitter . . . strong arm,
can make the difficult catch . . . so much
depends on his health. page 122.

STARTING PITCHER:

JOSE RIJO-Oakland A's
. . . strikes out batters with cool
regularity . . . raw talent. page 287.

SHORT RELIEVER:

JERRY REED-Cleveland Indians
. . . a two-pitch pitcher . . . can pitch on
short notice . . . works hard. page 127.

SHORTSTOP:

SAM KHALIFA-Pittsburgh Pirates
. . . can only get better and better on
defense . . . has soft, sure hands . . .
showed surprising power. page 570.

THIRD BASEMAN:

RICK SCHU-Philadelphia Phillies
. . . has excellent reflexes and an accurate
arm that should get stronger . . . is several
years away from his peak . . . a gutty
player who plays hurt. page 557.

CHRIS BROWN-San Francisco Giants
. . . surpassed all expectations with his bat
and glove . . . played third base as well as
anyone in the NL . . . page 636.

RIGHT FIELDER:

JOEL YOUNGBLOOD-San Francisco Giants
. . . not a happy player in 1985 . . . his
strong throwing arm makes him an above-
average outfielder . . . he can do an
awful lot of things. page 651.

CENTER FIELDER:

LEN DYKSTRA-New York Mets
. . . has all the qualities of a good leadoff
hitter . . . charges the ball well . . . his
arm is extraordinarily strong. page 517.

LEFT FIELDER:

JEFF LEONARD-San Francisco Giants
. . . continued his development into becoming
one of the better outfielders . . . uses good
judgment . . . natural ability. page 646.

STARTING PITCHER:

DENNIS ECKERSLEY-Chicago Cubs
. . . not short on nerve or desire . . .
seems to take the game more seriously now
. . . has worked harder than ever. page 398.

SHORT RELIEVER:

DON ROBINSON-Pittsburgh Pirates
. . . has come up with a palmball . . . he
is a strikeout pitcher . . . needs to be
healthy . . . has a lot of guts. page 582.

1985 American League Leaders

BATTING AVERAGE:

Wade Boggs, Boston, .368
George Brett, Kansas City, .335

HOME RUNS:

Darrell Evans, Detroit, 40
Carlton Fisk, Chicago, 37

HITS:

Wade Boggs, Boston, 240
Don Mattingly, New York, 211

DOUBLES:

Don Mattingly, New York, 48
Bill Buckner, Boston, 46

TRIPLES:

Willie Wilson, Kansas City, 21
Brett Butler, Cleveland, 14

RUNS:

Rickey Henderson, New York, 146
Cal Ripken, Baltimore, 116

RUNS BATTED IN:

Don Mattingly, New York, 145
Eddie Murray, Baltimore, 124

GAME-WINNING RBI:

Don Mattingly, New York, 21
Dave Winfield, New York, 19

WALKS:

Dwight Evans, Boston, 114
Toby Harrah, Texas, 113

STOLEN BASES:

Rickey Henderson, New York, 80
Gary Pettis, California, 56

WON-LOST:

Ron Guidry, New York, 22-6
Bret Saberhagen, Kansas City, 20-6

ERA:

Dave Stieb, Toronto, 2.48
Charlie Leibrandt, Kansas City, 2.69

GAMES:

Dan Quisenberry, Kansas City, 84
Ed Vande Berg, Seattle, 76

COMPLETE GAMES:

Bert Blyleven, Minnesota, 24
Charlie Hough, Texas, 14
Mike Moore, Seattle, 14

INNINGS PITCHED:

Bert Blyleven, Minnesota, 293.2
Dennis Boyd, Boston, 272.1

STRIKEOUTS:

Bert Blyleven, Minnesota, 206
Floyd Bannister, Chicago, 198

SHUTOUTS:

Bert Blyleven, Minnesota, 5
Britt Burns, Chicago, 4
Jack Morris, Detroit, 4

SAVES:

Dan Quisenberry, Kansas City, 37
Bob James, Chicago, 32

THE AMERICAN LEAGUE

BALTIMORE ORIOLES

PITCHING:

No deception.
No finesse.
Nothing soft.
A two-pitch pitcher.
Throws over-the-top.
And everything is hard.

Don Aase was signed as a free agent prior to the 1985 season to bolster the Orioles' bullpen and team officials were initially concerned about the health of his elbow. An operation sidelined him for most of the 1984 season; Aase did not pitch at all during 1983 and pitched in pain for parts of 1982.

He was used guardedly in the early part of last season, but seemed to come into his own in the second half. He had some control problems during the first half of 1985, but took over as the O's number one late-inning stopper after the All-Star break. It looks as though his elbow is healthy.

In 1985, Aase was most effective in his last 26 appearances, posting a 6-3 record with 12 saves and a 1.94 ERA. He had a career high of 14 saves.

Aase has an impressive arsenal. He throws a fastball that is consistently in the 90 MPH range and a curve that is not much slower than the fastball. His curveball can be devastating. He also has a slider and a change-up; he will use the slider sparingly and show his change-up even less often.

A fast worker, Aase believes in going right to the hitter, pitting strength against strength. Now that he appears to be injury-free, he is able to throw his fastball at full speed. On days when he has the velocity on his fastball and total command of his breaking pitch, Aase borders on the unhittable. His control can be spotty, however, and when he is struggling, he gets his pitches up in the strike zone. Maintaining control is

DON AASE
RHP, No. 41
RR, 6'3", 210 lbs.
ML Svc: 8 years
Born: 9-8-54 in
Orange, CA

1985 STATISTICS													
W	L	ERA	G	GS	CG	SV	IP	H	R	ER	BB	SO
10	6	3.78	54	0	0	14	88	83	44	37	35	67
CAREER STATISTICS													
W	L	ERA	G	GS	CG	SV	IP	H	R	ER	BB	SO
55	47	3.46	259	91	22	41	875	877	399	371	343	485

the part of his game that needs the most improvement.

Basically, Aase likes to work the outside half of the plate and will come inside only occasionally.

FIELDING:

In the role of short reliever, Aase generally finds himself fielding only bunts. His delivery leaves him in good position and he is, at least, an average fielder.

There is nothing special about his move to first, but he throws over often enough to keep runners honest. Because he is a fast worker and hard thrower, it is difficult for a runner to get a good jump on him.

OVERALL:

Robinson: "Don seemed to reach his peak in the second half of last year. He is the kind of power pitcher the Orioles need in the bullpen. He has got to work on his control in order to make his fastball as overpowering as possible as often as he can. He has all the tools and will have the opportunity this season to be a top-notch reliever.

PITCHING:

Mike Boddicker and Scott McGregor were the two biggest mysteries of the pitching staff last year. Boddicker had no physical problems until late in the season, when a case of tendinitis in his knee restricted him and finally forced him to miss his last two starts.

Boddicker entered the 1985 season with impressive numbers: he had compiled a 36-19 record over his first two years, had led the league in shutouts as a rookie (5 in 1983) was the AL's only 20-game winner and led the league in ERA in 1984. Last season, things started off just as well--he won six of his first seven games. Suddenly, everything began to unravel--he was getting shellacked.

By the time he realized what a large part of his problem was, it was too late--he ended the season losing 16 of his last 22 decisions. He discovered that he was tipping off his change-up, a key pitch for him. Hitters were able to tell when it was coming--but he didn't know it. It partially explained his slump.

He uses a variety of deliveries and throws his four pitches from different positions, sometimes changing the release point on each pitch. He can throw up to 87 MPH, but is a control pitcher who relies on a curveball that breaks wide rather than down and a change-up that reacts like a combination of a forkball and screwball.

Boddicker doesn't follow any set pattern. He will move the ball all around and will come in with the fastball on hitters who crowd the plate. Like many on the Orioles' staff, he appeared to pitch very timidly at times in 1985, and his control wasn't as sharp as it had been his two previous years.

He was very effective in games when he had a good fastball, but sometimes didn't have enough to keep hitters from waiting on his breaking ball. Boddicker

MIKE BODDICKER
RHP, No. 52
RR, 5'11", 182 lbs.
ML Svc: 3 years
Born: 8-23-57 in
   Cedar Rapids, IA

1985 STATISTICS

W	L	ERA	G	GS	CG	SV	IP	H	R	ER	BB	SO
12	17	4.07	32	32	9	0	203.1	227	104	92	89	135

CAREER STATISTICS

W	L	ERA	G	GS	CG	SV	IP	H	R	ER	BB	SO
49	37	3.24	103	93	35	0	682.1	623	284	246	241	409

will change speeds effectively on all of his pitches, but has to rely on pinpoint control to put the pitches right.

FIELDING:

Boddicker ranks with Bret Saberhagen and Ron Guidry as one of the best fielding pitchers in the game. His perfect follow-through always has him in excellent position and he has cat-like quickness on the mound. He led AL pitchers in chances for the third straight year.

His problem, however, is that he continues to make far too many throwing errors on attempted pickoff plays. Yet, he hasn't made an error on a batted ball in the big leagues.

OVERALL:

Boddicker pitched better than his 1985 record indicates and is at an age when he really should be coming on.

Robinson: "I see no reason why he cannot bounce back and pitched the way he did in 1983 and 1984. Mike's fastball is just average, but his breaking ball and change-up are excellent.

"A pitcher with his kind of stuff should be a consistent winner."

PITCHING:

Storm Davis struggled through an inconsistent 1985 season. But with four years of experience at the age of 24, his best years are ahead of him.

Davis is the only real power pitcher in the Baltimore rotation. He has a fastball that can climb as high as 93 MPH. He uses all of the standard pitches and, in general, has good control, although periods of wildness hurt him often during the first half of 1985 (especially in the early innings).

He has a very methodical overhand-to-three-quarters delivery, which can be overpowering, but it is not deceptive to the hitter. His control problems might have been the result of relinquishing some of his power and trying to be too much of a finesse pitcher; Davis is at his best when he challenges the hitters.

He has a good curveball, which he can throw over for strikes, but he has been hurt by hanging too many breaking balls. Davis uses his slider sparingly and then usually only against righthanded hitters.

Over the past two years, he has been working on a forkball as an off-speed pitch. It peaks and then declines in effectiveness. His bread-and-butter pitch will probably always be his out pitch, the fastball.

Because his style is remindful of Jim Palmer, Davis has labored somewhat in the shadow of the Orioles' former ace. Last year was a disappointment for him, even though it was his fourth straight winning season. The Orioles, however, feel that Davis has the ability to be a take-charge type with the ability to win 20 games.

FIELDING:

His motion is such that Davis doesn't

STORM DAVIS
RHP, No. 34
RR, 6'4", 194 lbs.
ML Svc: 4 years
Born: 12-26-61 in
Dallas, TX

1985 STATISTICS

W	L	ERA	G	GS	CG	SV	IP	H	R	ER	BB	SO
10	8	4.53	31	28	8	0	175	172	92	88	70	93

CAREER STATISTICS

W	L	ERA	G	GS	CG	SV	IP	H	R	ER	BB	SO
45	28	3.66	129	96	25	1	701	653	308	285	233	390

finish in the classic fielding position, but his quickness helps make up for it. He is a good fielder who handles bunts and covers first very well.

He does not have a good move and runners will take some liberties with him. He tries to keep them close by throwing over often.

OVERALL:

Davis still has his peak years ahead of him and should improve in the next few seasons. He was very inconsistent in 1985, but appeared to be putting it all together during the second half, when he had some overpowering stretches.

Robinson: "He has performed well in some big games during his brief career. Even though he's still relatively inexperienced, Davis has the most ability on the Orioles' staff and could easily be the leader in the years ahead.

"He has outstanding stuff, but his greatest weakness is that he is still learning. However, he did seem to get his act together in the second half and should be a big winner in 1986."

HITTING:

Over the past 13 seasons, the only changes in the hitting style of the O's spirited catcher have been born of experience. And that has been good.

Last season, Rick Dempsey hit a career high 12 home runs and 52 RBIs while hitting .254. Dempsey has not changed his hitting style per se, but he is making better contact with the ball. He is still a fastball hitter and continues to pull the ball the way he always has-- and, as always, pulling the ball is not necessarily a good thing for him. But his increased home run total (he hit 11 in 1984) indicates that he's making better contact now than in the past.

Control pitchers who can throw a steady diet of pitches on the outer half of the plate--especially breaking stuff --give Dempsey a lot of trouble. He can handle the fastball, either up or down, but needs it on the inner half to be successful.

BASERUNNING:

For a catcher, Dempsey has good speed, though that, of course, does not mean he is fast. He is, however, very aggressive on the basepaths.

He keeps the bunt in his back pocket and will occasionally pull it out to get a base hit.

FIELDING:

Dempsey has been one of the top defensive catchers throughout his entire career.

His throwing arm is not as strong as it once was (shoulder injuries having taken their toll), but he still has a quick release and is accurate with his throws. He is agile behind the plate,

RICK DEMPSEY
C, No. 24
RR, 6'0", 184 lbs.
ML Svc: 13 years
Born: 9-13-49 in
Fayetteville, TN

1985 STATISTICS

AVG	G	AB	R	H	2B	3B	HR	RBI	BB	SO	SB
.254	132	362	54	92	19	0	12	52	50	87	0

CAREER STATISTICS

AVG	G	AB	R	H	2B	3B	HR	RBI	BB	SO	SB
.240	1297	3622	396	871	168	11	65	351	421	497	16

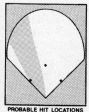

VS. RHP   VS. LHP   PROBABLE HIT LOCATIONS

fields bunts extremely well and holds his ground on tag plays better than anybody.

OVERALL:

At age 36, Dempsey no doubt is beyond his peak years, but the experience seems to be helping him as a hitter. He still has great enthusiasm for the game and figures to be around for a few more years.

Robinson: "For the first time in his career, Rick has realized that he has to take a day off now and then. When he is rested, he is a better overall player.

"He doesn't gun down as many runners as he used to, but, for the most part, that stems from the Orioles pitchers' inability to hold runners close."

KEN DIXON
LHP, No. 39
SR, 5'11", 166 lbs.
ML Svc: 1 year
Born: 10-17-60 in
Monroe, VA

PITCHING:

Although he started only 18 games, the rookie righthander was the Orioles' most consistent, and effective, starter last year. Ken Dixon's fastball is in the 88-91 MPH range and he also features a sharp curveball. His curve was a very effective out pitch. He doesn't use the slider and is still trying to develop a change-up, which could be the extra pitch he needs.

After an excellent start, Dixon slipped into a rut where he kept falling behind in the count. He struggled for a while, then became effective in long relief, then he was given a few starts in the last month of the season. The only thing that kept him out of the regular rotation was manager Earl Weaver's style of breaking in pitchers slowly.

Dixon uses all of the plate and will not hesitate to come inside on a hitter. Last season, he often had trouble putting hitters away after he got ahead of them in the count. His mistakes were rookie gaffes: he would give the hitter too much credit or simply make bad pitches after two strikes.

At one point, Dixon's confidence may have been shaken a little bit, but in general, he proved himself to be a cool, confident operator who has good stuff and will get better. At this point he is nowhere near his potential; he figures to make a strong bid for a regular starting job in 1986.

FIELDING:

He and Mike Boddicker are the best fielding pitchers on the staff. Dixon

1985 STATISTICS												
W	L	ERA	G	GS	CG	SV	IP	H	R	ER	BB	SO
8	4	3.67	34	18	3	1	162	144	68	66	64	108

CAREER STATISTICS												
W	L	ERA	G	GS	CG	SV	IP	H	R	ER	BB	SO
8	5	3.70	36	20	3	1	175	158	74	72	68	116

is an excellent athlete, very agile, with great quickness off the mound.

He does, however, have trouble with baserunners. He has been working to develop a quicker move to first. Last year, runners were able to distract him by taking good jumps. His pickoff is one area that definitely needs work.

OVERALL:

After working as both a starter and a reliever in 1985, Dixon seems destined to move in permanently as a starter. He has a good fastball and an excellent curve and his control is above average for a young pitcher.

Robinson: "He needs to develop a change-up, which would give him three solid pitches. He has the equipment to be a solid starter once he gets the necessary experience."

PATENT HITTER

HITTING:

Coming off a knee operation that sidelined him for six weeks in 1984, this veteran outfielder was used more extensively last season than at any other time in the five years he's been with the Orioles. Primarily a spot player throughout his career, Jim Dwyer was a regular platoon player throughout most of the first half of the season and hit close to .300 while being used on a steady basis. In the second half (after Earl Weaver replaced Joe Altobelli as manager), Dwyer reverted to his more familiar role of pinch-hitter.

Basically a low-ball, fastball hitter, he has been very effective coming off the bench. He has good power for the role he plays, but is basically a line drive pull hitter. He also has been the best bunter on the team.

Pitchers have their greatest success against him using off-speed breaking pitches. Dwyer is a patient hitter with a good eye, yet he is still aggressive enough to go after the first pitch if it's one he is looking for.

He is used exclusively against right-handed pitching and only rarely hits to the opposite field. His power is as a pull hitter fron his conventional square stance fairly close to the plate.

Although he has played on a daily basis only in emergencies during his career, Dwyer is a steady performer who doesn't have any major flaws. In the past, has been very successful scoring runners from third base with less than two outs.

BASERUNNING:

He has never been a basestealing threat, but has above-average speed and knows how to run the bases. He will not take foolish gambles, but has good instincts and is aggressive when it comes to breaking up the double play. He gets out of the batter's box quickly.

FIELDING:

Dwyer can play all three outfield po-

JIM DWYER
RF, No. 9
LL, 5'10", 182 lbs.
ML Svc: 11 years
Born: 1-3-50 in
    Evergreen Park, IL

1985 STATISTICS
AVG	G	AB	R	H	2B	3B	HR	RBI	BB	SO	SB
.249	101	233	35	58	8	3	7	36	37	31	0

CAREER STATISTICS
AVG	G	AB	R	H	2B	3B	HR	RBI	BB	SO	SB
.256	949	1968	286	504	82	15	48	237	276	264	20

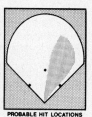

VS. RHP VS. LHP PROBABLE HIT LOCATIONS

sitions, though he's most comfortable in right field. He has quick reactions to the ball, especially on ones hit directly in front of him. He has good overall range. His arm is average, but it is extremely accurate.

A good, but not spectacular, defensive player, Dwyer can also play first base, a position where the Orioles need little help.

OVERALL:

Dwyer has been a valuable contributor to the Orioles for five years as a part-time performer. He is ideally suited to be a role player, understands his job and comes prepared.

Robinson: "When he got a chance to play semiregularly in 1983 and again last year, he did very well. Still, his forte is pinch-hitting and he is one of the best in the AL in that role."

MIKE FLANAGAN
LHP, No. 46
LL, 6'0", 195 lbs.
ML Svc: 10 years
Born: 12-16-51 in
   Manchester, NH

1985 STATISTICS
W	L	ERA	G	GS	CG	SV	IP	H	R	ER	BB	SO
4	5	5.13	15	15	1	0	86	101	49	49	28	42

CAREER STATISTICS
W	L	ERA	G	GS	CG	SV	IP	H	R	ER	BB	SO
129	92	3.80	299	283	92	1	1917.2	1911	871	811	590	1079

PITCHING:

Over the last few seasons, Mike Flanagan has made the transition from a power pitcher to one who relies more and more on finesse. He can still throw the fastball in the high 80s, but most of the time it is around 85 MPH. As a result, Flanagan relies on a variety of pitches.

He uses a three-quarters delivery and often drops down to sidearm against lefthanded hitters. His trademark is a big breaking curveball, but his fastball, which he throws at varying speeds, remains his out pitch. Flanagan has also developed an outstanding change-up, which he will throw at any time, mostly to righthanders.

Last year was almost a lost season for the lefthander because of a ruptured Achilles tendon that sidelined him for the first four months. He might have been brought back too quickly. The second half of the season was like spring training for him, although he had several good outings.

Flanagan will turn over his fastball, giving it a sinkerball effect. It has been an effective pitch for him. He is much more of a pitcher now than when he won Cy Young Award in 1979, when he relied mostly on the fastball and curveball.

He is especially tough on lefthanded hitters because of his breaking ball and the fact that he will drop down with both the fastball and the curve.

He does not follow a particular pattern and when he is on top of his game, he will induce a lot of ground ball outs. If he is too strong, he loses his sinker, and when he tires, he will come up in the strike zone.

FIELDING:

Despite his good position as he ends his follow-through, Flanagan is not a good fielder. He is slow covering first, more so perhaps because of his Achilles tendon injury.

Baserunners, however, do not distract him because he has one of the best moves in the business. He will throw to first often, sometimes as a decoy, and even though his motion is very deliberate, he is very difficult to steal on unless the runner guesses right.

OVERALL:

Although he has probably leveled off at the age of 34, Flanagan still has the ability to win because he is a complete pitcher.

Robinson: "You can throw last year out the window because of his operation. His biggest strength is his knowledge of pitching, while his chief weakness is the fact that he no longer is overpowering. If he is healthy, Flanagan will win again in 1986. Last year, he just never caught up, and the Orioles found out how important he is to the staff."

HITTING:

Nothing would make Wayne Gross happier than if he could hit a home run every time he made contact. He has the long ball on his mind during each plate appearance, and when he is on top of his game, his home run to at-bat ratio is among the league's best.

Gross' all-or-nothing theory seems to work fine when he is playing every day, but last season, he found himself buried on the Oriole bench as Floyd Rayford emerged both offensively and defensively to replace Gross in the hot corner during the second half of the season.

Gross is a one-dimensional hitter. If the pitch is not a fastball and if he cannot pull it, no damage can be done. He is very aggressive and will swing at the first pitch, hoping for a fastball. He is strong enough to hit the ball out of any part of any park in the league, but his power is mainly as a pull hitter. When Gross is hitting well, even the hardest throwers in the American League have trouble pitting their power against his.

But Gross' greatest strength is also his greatest weakness. Any pitch other than a fastball--especially off-speed breaking pitches--will render him helpless. Last year he managed 11 home runs in 217 at-bats, but drove in only 18 runs, which was easily a career low. He was all but phased out of the lineup after Earl Weaver took over as manager.

BASERUNNING:

Because he has below-average speed, Gross must be considered a below-average runner. Never a threat to steal, he is nevertheless aggressive and goes hard into second on the double play. He does not take foolish chances, but the home run is the only "extra" base he can take.

FIELDING:

Gross' defense is not good enough to

WAYNE GROSS
INF, No. 14
LR, 6'2", 215 lbs.
ML Svc: 10 years
Born: 1-14-52 in
Riverside, CA

1985 STATISTICS

AVG	G	AB	R	H	2B	3B	HR	RBI	BB	SO	SB
.235	103	217	31	51	8	0	11	18	46	48	1

CAREER STATISTICS

AVG	G	AB	R	H	2B	3B	HR	RBI	BB	SO	SB
.233	1216	3123	374	727	126	9	121	396	481	495	24

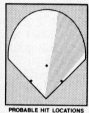

VS. RHP   VS. LHP   PROBABLE HIT LOCATIONS

justify an everyday role. As a third baseman, he is average, at best, in all aspects of the position. He doesn't have much range, though he is better going to his right than to his left.

His throwing arm, for the most part, is strong and accurate, but, defensively, Floyd Rayford opened a lot of eyes last season with his quickness at third and versatility as a catcher. In short, Gross does not offer as much as Rayford does.

OVERALL:

The Orioles' tune is changing; the team has recently begun to import (read: traded for) and groom new talent to fill offensive and defensive holes.

Gross is one of the players whose time may have come to move on.

Robinson: "There is no question that Wayne has power in his bat, but his defense hurts him to the point where he will have difficulty fitting into the Orioles' plans."

HITTING:

Lee Lacy is a very aggressive line drive hitter who did the most to change the complexion of the top of the Birds' batting order last season. Despite missing the first five weeks of the season, he was a big offensive contributor.

After a brief trial as the leadoff hitter, Lacy settled in nicely in the number two spot and was an ideal batter in front of Cal Ripken and Eddie Murray.

Primarily a fastball hitter, Lacy likes the ball out over the plate and has good line drive power to right field. He has a big swing and pitchers will try to come up and in with the fastball. He has the most trouble with righthanders who throw breaking balls away, out of the strike zone.

Lacy is not a patient or selective hitter and he strikes out more often than is expected of a contact hitter. Still, he made his point last year and got himself on base when it counted. He was especially effective in the middle three months of the year when his thumb was injury-free.

BASERUNNING:

Lacy gets out of the box quickly and will, on occasion, bunt for the base hit. He is a hard slider who can break up the double play and he would steal more bases than he does if he weren't hitting in front of Ripken and Murray.

He is an aggressive baserunner who sometimes gets carried away, but overall his speed more than makes up for any deficiencies in judgment.

FIELDING:

In the outfield, Lacy shows good reactions to the ball and has a better-than-average arm. His throwing can be erratic, but he has good range and is better than average either coming in or going back on the ball.

Given the chance to play every day,

LEE LACY
OF, No. 27
RR, 6'1", 185 lbs.
ML Svc: 13 years
Born: 4-10-49 in
Longview, TX

```
1985 STATISTICS
AVG   G    AB    R    H    2B  3B HR  RBI  BB  SO  SB
.293 121   492  69  144   22   4  9   48  39  95  10
CAREER STATISTICS
AVG   G    AB    R    H    2B  3B HR  RBI  BB  SO  SB
.289 1306 3800 538 1099  176  39 73  383 303 537 178
```

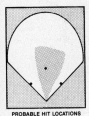

STRONG   STRONG

VS. RHP   VS. LHP   PROBABLE HIT LOCATIONS

Lacy developed into a much better defensive player last season than had been generally suspected.

OVERALL:

Age-wise, Lacy is past his peak, but after two seasons as a regular, he has established himself as a bonafide major league hitter. Now that he has a season in the American League under his belt, he should be able to improve on his 1985 numbers.

Robinson: "Lee impressed me a great deal last season. His thumb was injured for some of the season and affected his hitting. But his finger should be better right from the start of this season and that should give him the opportunity to show what he can really do at the plate.

"Defensively, he seems to be improving in each outing and his speed could be a big asset for the Orioles. This should be a very good season for him."

HITTING:

Fred Lynn has a picture-perfect swing, one whose style hasn't changed much since he first came into the American League in 1975. He was off to a terrific start last season and continued to have a good year until his ankle began to bother him and caused his average to suffer. Still, he gave the Orioles what they wanted from their number five hitter.

Lynn likes the fastball out over the plate and has good power to straightaway center field. He will swing at a lot of first pitches against lefthanders and is sometimes impatient against them because he doesn't like to get behind in the count. He is a more selective hitter against righthanders.

BASERUNNING:

Lynn has better-than-average speed and gets out of the box well. He is not much of a basestealer, but he is always watching for a pitcher's indiscretion of neglecting him as a baserunner.

He doesn't make mistakes on the basepaths and is a good-to-excellent runner with a gliding style who can look more nonchalant and slower than he really is.

FIELDING:

Lynn has always been a very good outfielder with a strong and accurate arm. He has good instincts and good range to both his left and his right. He plays center field aggressively.

He gets to the ball quickly and keeps his head in the game; he does not misjudge his throws to the infield. He has been around long enough to know how to play his position.

OVERALL:

Assorted minor injuries have bothered

FRED LYNN
CF, No. 19
LL, 6'1", 190 lbs.
ML Svc: 12 years
Born: 2-3-52 in
Chicago, IL

1985 STATISTICS

AVG	G	AB	R	H	2B	3B	HR	RBI	BB	SO	SB
.263	124	448	59	118	12	1	23	68	53	100	7

CAREER STATISTICS

AVG	G	AB	R	H	2B	3B	HR	RBI	BB	SO	SB
.292	1425	5192	839	1518	323	39	218	859	663	788	62

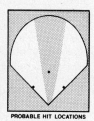

VS. RHP   VS. LHP   PROBABLE HIT LOCATIONS

Lynn throughout his career, though rarely have his ailments affected his play. He has been a reliable and steady performer for years.

Lynn has enough power to bat in the number five spot and is even a good enough hitter to be used as the number three man. He is probably a step or two beyond his peak, but he can still be counted on to give his best effort all of the time.

Robinson: "I think that the back and ankle injuries have started to take their toll on Fred; he is not really able to play 150 games each season and still be as consistently good as he has been. But if he is used properly, he will give the Orioles good, solid hitting and steady, heads-up defense."

PITCHING:

If there is one word to describe the career of Dennis Martinez it is likely to be: inconsistent. He is somewhere between a power pitcher who doesn't always have his power and a control pitcher who does not always have good control. Although he doesn't walk many batters (less than two per game), it is the location of his pitches which often does him in. Walks won't kill Martinez; home runs will: he gave up 29 in 180 innings last year.

He has a very good arm, but there were times last year when his fastball dropped to the low 80s and other times when it was in the upper 80s. He has good breaking pitches, but must have his fastball in place to make anything happen. Unfortunately, he has been too inconsistent with his money pitch. When his fastball slows down he can really get hurt because then his pitches are all about the same speed.

Martinez is a very deliberate worker, yet his lack of concentration continually gets him into trouble. When that happens, his control usually leaves him, marking a sure point that he is starting to lose it.

He was in the starting rotation most of the 1985 season, but even though his record was an improvement over his 6-9 and 7-16 records of the previous two years, he still seemed to be feeling his way back from his rehabilitation from alcohol abuse, which he underwent following the 1983 season.

Even though Martinez has won 14 or more games in five of the seven previous seasons, he has yet to reach what many feel is his potential. He made some strides last year and at the age of 30 is still young enough, but there is some feeling he might need a change of scenery and a fresh start to get something going for himself.

DENNIS MARTINEZ
RHP, No. 30
RR, 6'1", 182 lbs.
ML Svc: 9 years
Born: 5-14-55 in
Granada, NIC

1985 STATISTICS

W	L	ERA	G	GS	CG	SV	IP	H	R	ER	BB	SO
13	11	5.15	33	31	3	0	180	203	110	103	63	68

CAREER STATISTICS

W	L	ERA	G	GS	CG	SV	IP	H	R	ER	BB	SO
108	93	4.15	315	243	69	5	1768.2	1811	894	815	581	856

FIELDING:

Martinez is an above-average fielder with good reactions and quickness. He gets off the mound consistently to cover first base. He now has a much better move to first base than he used to and led the club in pickoffs last year.

Still, baserunners can take liberties with him because he is slow in delivering the ball to the plate. The improved move, however, has made runners less of a distraction to him.

OVERALL:

Robinson: "His fastball has to be more consistent and he needs to challenge the hitters more. He uses all of his pitches to all hitters, but there are times when it looks as if he would be better off just to stick with his fastball and slider, while mixing in an occasional change-up. Then there are other times when it looks as though he needs to use his change-up more often; it's almost as if he has forgotten that he has one.

"Last year I said he'd win 15 games and I feel the same way this year. He still has the ability."

PITCHING:

Tippy Martinez had his career year three seasons ago. This year, he is coming off his second straight sub-par year. He could be at a crossroads.

Bothered by shoulder trouble, he is hoping that an off-season strength program can help him come back.

Martinez is strictly a two-pitch pitcher: fastball and curve. He pitches overhand and is a power type of pitcher whose fastball is underrated. When he's right, his fastball is deceptive and will coax the radar to read in the high 80s.

His curveball has been his out pitch over the years, but this lefthanded reliever has struggled with it for the past two seasons. When he was at his peak, his curve was one of the best, and dropped sharply. He still gets a lot of strikes on breaking balls down and out of the strike zone. Since 1983, however, the bite has been missing.

His control has been spotty, perhaps because of his various injuries, and led to his two-year inconsistent stretch. In his 70 innings pitched, he was able to log only four saves last year. He was used sparingly in the second half and not at all in the final two weeks of the season.

Until 1984, he had been one of the most durable relievers in the game, but the wear and tear might have extracted a heavy toll. Because of injuries over the last two years, he is questionable for 1986, even though he's the only proven lefthander in the bullpen.

FIELDING:

At best, he is an average fielder and is sometimes slow getting from the mound

TIPPY MARTINEZ
LHP, No. 23
LL, 5'10", 180 lbs.
ML Svc: 10 years
Born: 5-31-50 in
    La Junta, COLUM

1985 STATISTICS												
W	L	ERA	G	GS	CG	SV	IP	H	R	ER	BB	SO
3	3	5.40	49	0	0	4	70	70	48	42	37	47

CAREER STATISTICS												
W	L	ERA	G	GS	CG	SV	IP	H	R	ER	BB	SO
55	40	3.34	529	2	0	114	814.2	706	338	302	409	617

to first base. He has developed a decent move to first and throws over more now than he ever did before. He once picked three men off in one inning during a game against Toronto (1983) and has been better at holding runners since then.

OVERALL:

He may be the toughest Oriole pitcher to try to figure out for 1986. He will be 36 years old in May and has to be considered beyond his peak. Everything will depend on whether or not he's healthy. If he is, this lefthander will give the Orioles excellent balance in the bullpen. If his shoulder doesn't respond, however, his career will be in jeopardy. He is entering the final year of his contract, so this season is vital to his future.

Robinson: "He needs to find the real curve of his curveball again and to maintain better control overall. The curveball has been rolling instead of biting, and Tippy will have to work hard if he's going to be a factor this year."

PITCHING:

Scott McGregor is coming off the worst year of his career--which seemed to be the pattern for most of the Birds' starters in 1985. Most of McGregor's troubles can be traced to the loss of his fastball (which was never really that fast, but at least it was always effective enough to set up everything else).

Even though McGregor is classified as a finesse (some might say junkball) type of pitcher, he has always relied heavily on his fastball, which he can throw at varying speeds. But there were only a couple of games last year when he threw it effectively. The result was that all of his pitches arrived at roughly the same speed, a deadly situation unless the pitcher is overpowering.

In the last few years, McGregor has used an excellent change-up to keep hitters off stride, but it was still the fastball, modest as it was velocity-wise, that kept everything together. A year ago the hitters seemed to wait on his off-speed stuff.

He has a big, breaking curveball that he throws to both righthanded and left-handed hitters. Generally a fast worker, he has an unorthodox across-the-body delivery, which occasionally breaks down when his mechanics go haywire.

Despite his style, McGregor was always an aggressive pitcher during his successful years with the Orioles--a characteristic, however, that was not in evidence last season.

The 34 home runs he allowed (in 204 innings) are testimony enough that he did not get hitters to hit his pitch last year. The rediscovery of both his control and his fastball will be the key in 1986.

FIELDING:

He has good reactions and is quick to

SCOTT McGREGOR
LHP, No. 16
SL, 6'1", 186 lbs.
ML Svc: 9 years
Born: 1-18-54 in
    Inglewood, CA

1985 STATISTICS

W	L	ERA	G	GS	CG	SV	IP	H	R	ER	BB	SO
14	14	4.81	35	34	8	0	204	226	118	109	65	86

CAREER STATISTICS

W	L	ERA	G	GS	CG	SV	IP	H	R	ER	BB	SO
125	83	3.76	292	257	78	5	1835.1	1890	834	767	419	760

move from the mound to cover first base. A fine athlete, McGregor is an adept good fielder who doesn't throw to the wrong base and who is always alert to his positioning as a backup man.

OVERALL:

Part of his struggle last season might be traced to the fact that his control, an important element to his success, wasn't nearly as sharp as it had been in the past. His control was off because he lost confidence in his fastball. But for such a finely tuned athlete as McGregor, it becomes a chicken-or-egg type of circle: which came first?

He is the biggest question mark on a staff loaded with disappointments from last year. An off-season workout program to build up his strength might juice up his fastball.

Robinson: "Last year, he became more of a defensive pitcher than ever before. I'm certain that he can bounce back if he regains his fastball. He is not a young pitcher; Scott has been through it all before and is very competitive--that should help him."

HITTING:

Eddie Murray has played major league baseball for nine years without an off season. Many observers feel that he is just now reaching his peak performance level. There are about 130 pitchers and exactly 13 big league managers who are not very happy about that.

Offensively, Murray has no major weaknesses. Remembering his earlier years when he was not a selective hitter, most pitchers try to work around Murray in key situations. That tactic no longer keeps him off base: he has become a choosey hitter and has drawn 191 walks over the last two years.

Murray wants to see the fastball, though he can crush just about anything thrown his way. A switch-hitter, he has power to all fields from both sides of the plate and his average and home run ratio are about the same as a righty as they are as a lefty. He pulls the ball a little more as a righthander, which is his natural side, and hits the ball to the opposite field with power more consistently from the left side.

He is very deliberate in the batter's box and hits from a slightly open and crouched stance from both sides. His mannerisms are a little more pronounced from the left side. Pitchers will throw him low and away as a righthanded hitter and up and in as a lefty. A pitcher's best chance for success is never to throw him the same pitch twice in a row.

Murray has averaged over 100 RBIs and almost 30 home runs a year, has never hit lower than .283 (in his rookie year) or less than 22 home runs (during the strike-shortened 1981 season).

BASERUNNING:

Once Murray gets on base, most pitchers are so grateful he did not take them downtown that they tend to forget about him on the bases. Murray will steal a base if the pitcher really naps. He is not a good slider and will not gamble on the basepaths unless the game is on the line.

EDDIE MURRAY
1B, No. 33
SR, 6'2", 216 lbs.
ML Svc: 9 years
Born: 2-24-56 in
Los Angeles, CA

1985 STATISTICS

AVG	G	AB	R	H	2B	3B	HR	RBI	BB	SO	SB
.297	156	583	111	173	37	1	31	124	84	68	5

CAREER STATISTICS

AVG	G	AB	R	H	2B	3B	HR	RBI	BB	SO	SB
.298	1362	5129	823	1528	271	19	258	931	630	719	52

  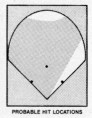

VS. RHP   VS. LHP   PROBABLE HIT LOCATIONS

FIELDING:

Last season was easily Murray's poorest in the field as he made 19 errors. Though he might not be rated as a great defensive performer, he can make the spectacular play. Murray is particularly adept at getting the force-out at second base and no first baseman in the AL can play the bunt better than he does. He is always alert to put on the pickoff and has a powerful and accurate arm.

OVERALL:

The Orioles gave away the vault to Eddie Murray last season and signed him to a contract that will pay him a reported $12 million for five years.

Robinson: "Eddie is an Orioles type of player; he has been in the organization for his whole career and looks as if he's going to stay a while longer. He improves each season and it is only a matter of time before Murray will be the American League MVP."

HITTING:

After a vagabond minor league career that took him from one coast to the other and brief flings with both the Orioles and Cardinals, Floyd Rayford finally got a chance to play regularly during the second half of last year. To classify him as a surprise would be putting it mildly.

In 1985 Rayford found two jobs: third base and catcher. He did well at both. He played 105 games, primarily as the regular third baseman after the All-Star break. He also was pressed into service behind the plate when Rick Dempsey was sidelined.

A high-fastball, straightaway hitter, Rayford may also have been a victim of his own overanxiousness early in his career. He seldom walks (22 times in 609 at-bats over the last two years), an indication that he isn't as patient or selective a hitter as he could be. Not much changed last year, except that he played regularly.

He has a slightly closed stance and his power tends to be between the gaps in left field and right field. He has trouble with breaking balls away and sometimes chases pitches that are up and out of the strike zone.

Rayford had the highest average on the team last year and, for the first time, displayed some consistent power. Forty of his hits were for extra bases, 18 for home runs. He is very aggressive at the plate, as his high strikeout total will testify. Still, the only difference seemed to be that he was playing every day, whereas before he was severely limited because his role as the third catcher kept him chained to the bench.

BASERUNNING:

Because of his build, Rayford's speed is very deceptive, but he will still not be mistaken as a basestealing threat. He gets to first base in about average time and runs the bases well enough, but it wasn't his running ability that finally got him a steady job.

FLOYD RAYFORD
3B/C, No. 6
RR, 5'10", 216 lbs.
ML Svc: 4 years
Born: 7-27-57 in Memphis, TN

1985 STATISTICS

AVG	G	AB	R	H	2B	3B	HR	RBI	BB	SO	SB
.306	105	359	55	110	21	1	18	48	10	69	3

CAREER STATISTICS

AVG	G	AB	R	H	2B	3B	HR	RBI	BB	SO	SB
.264	289	784	92	207	39	1	28	95	38	166	4

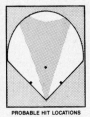

VS. RHP   VS. LHP   PROBABLE HIT LOCATIONS

FIELDING:

He has surprising quickness at third base and his defensive play there is much better than adequate. He made all the plays and his arm is strong enough to make all the throws.

Behind the plate, it is much the same as his quickness allows him to block pitches in the dirt. He has a good release to go with adequate arm strength. All in all, he is a better-than-average defensive player.

OVERALL:

Undoubtedly, Rayford suffered in the past because he does not have the classic build of a big league player. But he is strong and quick and last year showed that he had some pop.

Robinson: "When he got the chance to play, he was unbelievable. He did the job at the plate and in the field. He will be the regular third baseman in 1986."

HITTING:

Just when you think that Cal Ripken couldn't possibly get any better, he finds a way to improve. In many ways, he is much like teammate Eddie Murray: durable, powerful and consistent. And like Murray, Ripken has not yet reached his prime years.

The most marked change in Ripken since his rookie year (1982) has been his increased patience at the plate; he now hits for a higher average.

He stands as far off the plate as any hitter in the game, yet is still able to cover the strike zone from deep in the batter's box. He could probably hit more home runs if he stood closer to the plate, but then he would sacrifice his average for the added power.

It's hard to get a beat on Ripken's hitting pattern: one day he will hit the first pitch he sees, then the next day he will wait the pitcher out, preferring to get a good, long gander. He will look for pitches in certain situations and has been an especially good breaking ball hitter for a young player.

Pitchers try to work the outside corner with breaking balls, but have to come inside with hard stuff occasionally to make that tactic work. Ripken is a very aggressive hitter, but is selective enough to take a strike if it is not the pitch he is looking for in the area he wants.

BASERUNNING:

Because Ripken takes a big cut, he doesn't get out of the batter's box very quickly. He is a strong, well-built young man with just average speed, yet he is one of the Orioles' best baserunners. He has excellent instincts on the basepaths and is always aware of the game situation. He is a good, hard slider who will break up the double play.

FIELDING:

Physically, Ripken is much bigger than any other shortstop in the majors,

CAL RIPKEN
SS, No. 8
RR, 6'4", 215 lbs.
ML Svc: 4 years
Born: 8-24-60 in
  Havre de Grace, MD

1985 STATISTICS

AVG	G	AB	R	H	2B	3B	HR	RBI	BB	SO	SB
.282	161	642	116	181	32	5	26	110	67	68	2

CAREER STATISTICS

AVG	G	AB	R	H	2B	3B	HR	RBI	BB	SO	SB
.280	668	2583	431	750	148	19	108	391	243	357	7

  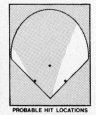

VS. RHP VS. LHP PROBABLE HIT LOCATIONS

and his size dictates less-than-average quickness. To compensate, he has developed an excellent knowledge of hitters' tendencies in light of the style of each Oriole pitcher. As a result, he is rarely out of position and he has the sure hands which enable him to make all of the plays.

He has one of the strongest throwing arms among infielders in the game and is especially effective on relay throws. Last year was not his best defensive season, but he is consistently among the leaders in successful chances and double plays.

OVERALL:

Robinson: "The Orioles have a lot going for them with Murray and Ripken back-to-back in the lineup. Both are durable players who are always there.

"Cal is underrated defensively, and offensively he is just coming into his own. He plays 'smart' at short, and at the plate he is picking his pitches much better now."

HITTING:

Gary Roenicke has never been an everyday player for an entire season, though, in general, he has been a productive platoon player for most of his eight-year career. He begins the 1986 season, however, with his future in question, having had two straight off-years. Despite hitting 15 home runs in only 225 at-bats, he hit .218 last year, which came on the heels of a .224 year in 1984.

Roenicke's hitting style has not changed much since he came to the American League in 1978 (he was the Expos' first-round draft pick in 1973). He continues to hit home runs against left-handers but has struggled more and more with his average against them. Right-handers are nearly impossible for him to hit--he is strictly a platoon player.

Obviously, there are still some home runs in his bat, but his declining average indicates there may not be much more than occasional power left. He is a high fastball hitter and stands right up on the plate. Roenicke is always looking to pull and likes the ball on the inside half of the plate. A pitcher can show him something hard inside and then stay away from his power and pitch him almost exclusively outside. Roenicke gets hurt because he tries to pull everything.

Since the Orioles have three regular outfielders in Fred Lynn, Mike Young and Lee Lacy, with the switch-hitting John Shelby to back them up, Roenicke's role figures to be severely limited if he is still with the Orioles in spring training.

BASERUNNING:

Despite only average speed, Roenicke is a very good baserunner. He has good instincts and will take the extra base if given the chance. He is an aggressive runner and will come in hard to break up the double play.

FIELDING:

Roenicke is a dependable outfielder.

GARY ROENICKE
LF, No. 35
RR, 6'3", 200 lbs.
ML Svc: 8 years
Born: 12-5-54 in
Covina, CA

```
1985 STATISTICS
AVG  G   AB    R    H   2B  3B  HR  RBI  BB   SO   SB
.218 113 225   36   49  9   0   15  43   44   36   2
CAREER STATISTICS
AVG  G   AB    R    H   2B  3B  HR  RBI  BB   SO   SB
.249 878 2307 320  575 117 4   108 357  339  360  15
```

  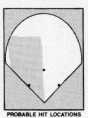

VS. RHP   VS. LHP   PROBABLE HIT LOCATIONS

He has played the three outfield positions, and is at least acceptable at all of them, though left field is his best spot.

He covers a lot of ground, is sure-handed and has an accurate throwing arm with above-average strength. He is quick and has good reactions to non-routine plays. He does not miss the cutoff man.

OVERALL:

At one point, it was thought Roenicke could be an everyday player, but his difficulty with righthanded pitching precludes that role.

Robinson: "Gary was most successful when he played part-time in left field, but the outfield platoon system has passed through Baltimore already. He is a solid defensive player, but for the past two seasons, he has only hit with occasional power against lefthanders."

POWER POTENTIAL

LARRY SHEETS
OF, No. 18
LR, 6'3", 220 lbs.
ML Svc: 1 year plus
Born: 12-6-59 in
Staunton, VA

HITTING:

Last year was a transition period from the minor leagues to the majors for this promising lefthanded hitter. Larry Sheets was a straightaway hitter in his rookie year, but should become more of a pull hitter as he gains experience. A low-fastball hitter who stands about midway in the batter's box, he has to become a little more patient as a hitter. Last year, he became too anxious when behind in the count, especially with men on base.

He has a tendency to chase some bad pitches with two strikes on him, but when he hits it, the ball jumps off his bat. Pitchers had success against him by throwing off-speed pitches and by getting ahead in the count.

Sheets has only begun to scratch the surface of his potential. With increased playing time, his home run and RBI totals will improve. He was used almost exclusively as a designated hitter last season and will probably remain in that role.

He is a fast learner and takes instruction well, two assets that should help him in the future. Bunting is not part of his game. He had a checkered career in the minor leagues, but showed enough to indicate he will be a good hitter. As he gains confidence, his natural ability should make him a legitimate home run threat.

BASERUNNING:

Sheets is a slow runner, which restricts him in just about all phases of baserunning. He doesn't get away from the plate fast and is no threat to steal once he reaches base. He doesn't make mistakes and is a hard slider, but his lack of speed makes him below average on the bases.

FIELDING:

Again, the lack of speed restricts

1985 STATISTICS											
AVG	G	AB	R	H	2B	3B	HR	RBI	BB	SO	SB
.262	113	328	43	86	8	0	17	50	28	52	0

CAREER STATISTICS											
AVG	G	AB	R	H	2B	3B	HR	RBI	BB	SO	SB
.270	121	344	46	93	9	0	18	52	29	55	0

VS. RHP

VS. LHP

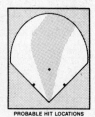
PROBABLE HIT LOCATIONS

his range. However, in spring training and during brief stints in the outfield, he showed good hands and at least an average arm. He gets rid of the ball quickly and is accurate, but had only a few defensive opportunities last year. At the moment, he seems locked in as DH.

OVERALL:

Sheets is still learning and needs more experience against major league pitching, but he definitely has the potential to be a good hitter. His power is still untapped.

He played almost exclusively against righthanders, but has indicated he can hold his own against lefthanders.

Robinson: "Larry is going to get a lot better. He figures to play every day against righthanders and will probably see some lefthanders too. He has a good bat and will eventually learn to pull the ball with authority."

HITTING:

John Shelby may still have a bright future ahead of him, though, admittedly, his light has dimmed in Baltimore. He became expendable last season when the Orioles added Fred Lynn and Lee Lacy to the roster. Shelby started the 1985 season in the minor leagues. He was called to the parent club earlier than planned last year when injuries began to deplete the O's ranks. Although he played in only 69 games last season, a solid .283 performance returned him to good standing with the Orioles.

A switch-hitter, Shelby is a high-ball hitter from both sides of the plate and hits to all fields. He will occasionally show power when he pulls a pitch.

One of his weaknesses as a hitter has been that he is not patient; late last season, Shelby began to show signs of improvement in this regard. He would be likely to become a more selective hitter if he got more playing time, but at this point, it will be tough for him to crack the Orioles' outfield as a starter.

Still, Shelby is a more impressive player now than at anytime in his brief major league career. It appears that he has become accustomed to major league pitching and, as a result, is a more confident hitter. In particular, last season he was a good hitter from the left side of the plate (.309) and developed his skill as a bunter.

BASERUNNING:

Shelby bursts from the batter's box quickly, which helps him to leg out bunts.

In 1983, he appeared in 126 games and led the Orioles with 15 stolen bases. He is not, however, as good a basestealer as his above-average speed might suggest. He does not pick his spots well and does not get a good jump.

FIELDING:

Shelby's opportunity in the major

JOHN SHELBY
OF, No. 37
SR, 6'1", 180 lbs.
ML Svc: 3 years
Born: 2-23-58 in
   Lexington, KY

1985 STATISTICS

AVG	G	AB	R	H	2B	3B	HR	RBI	BB	SO	SB
.283	69	205	28	58	6	2	7	27	7	23	7

CAREER STATISTICS

AVG	G	AB	R	H	2B	3B	HR	RBI	BB	SO	SB
.245	356	950	134	233	36	9	19	86	45	119	7

STRONG   STRONG

VS. RHP   VS. LHP   PROBABLE HIT LOCATIONS

leagues is based on his ability as an outfielder. He uses his speed well: he has good range and gets a good jump on the ball. He has a strong and accurate arm. Last season, his defensive prowess seemed to improve as he began to find himself at the plate. Like many players, he would get better if he were given more playing time.

OVERALL:

The Orioles could be tempted to use Shelby as trade-bait because of the presence of Fred Lynn, but have held back because they like the idea of using Shelby as a fourth outfielder who gives them speed and defensive protection.

Robinson: "John is giving the team something to think about right now. He is starting to play up to his potential.

"He has not been consistent and has had one good year (1983) followed by a poor one (1984). After his trip to the minors last season, he came back up and played well--it looks as if he could be a late bloomer."

PITCHING:

The most pleasant surprise on the Orioles' pitching staff last year was Nate Snell, a 32-year-old rookie. He was also the club's most effective pitcher, despite his late-season slump.

He is not an overpowering type of pitcher--rather, the slender righthander relied on an excellent sinker and good control while compiling the team's best earned run average.

He was used almost exclusively in long relief. The velocity on his fastball is only in the mid-80s, but his sinker was very effective (though it lost something during the second half of 1985).

During the second half, Snell was only an average pitcher. He didn't seem to recover from a broken rib suffered when he was hit by a line drive earlier in the year.

He is one of those pitchers who is better off when he's a little tired. If he's too strong, he loses the sinker: the ball stays up and he gets lit up. Snell is at his best when he is working the outer part of the plate and hitting his spots near the hitter's knees. He will rarely come inside on a hitter.

His sinker produces a lot of ground balls which result in double plays, enabling him to get out of inherited jams. There is nothing tricky or fancy about Snell; he doesn't change speeds much, but he is a fast worker who likes to go out and just pitch.

FIELDING:

He falls off to the first-base side on his follow-through, which leaves him

NATE SNELL
RHP, No. 36
RR, 6'4", 190 lbs.
ML Svc: 1 year plus
Born: 9-2-52 in
  Orangeburg, SC

1985 STATISTICS

W	L	ERA	G	GS	CG	SV	IP	H	R	ER	BB	SO
3	2	2.69	43	0	0	5	100.1	100	44	30	30	41

CAREER STATISTICS

W	L	ERA	G	GS	CG	SV	IP	H	R	ER	BB	SO
4	3	2.67	48	0	0	5	108	108	46	32	31	48

in a poor fielding position. He doesn't get over to first base all of the time as quickly as he should.

Snell has a good move with runners on base and is not distracted by anyone in spite of the fact that he throws over to first base often.

OVERALL

Snell is an example of someone who gets everything out of his ability. He was a real suprise for both the Orioles and the hitters in the American League last season. He was the ninth pitcher on the staff when the team left spring training, but blossomed to become a dependable reliever.

Robinson: "Snell is resilient; he bounces back quickly even after long stints of sitting in the pen. His sinker is the key for him and could take him a long way if he can keep it low; he makes the hitter put the ball in play.

"He made the most out of the opportunity he had last year."

PITCHING:

Sammy Stewart is a power pitcher who has been used every which way by the Orioles--his role has never been clearly defined. It is generally conceded that he is best suited to long relief, but he has also been used in the short role and even as a starter.

Stewart uses a variety of pitches and deliveries, but is most effective as a hard thrower from a three-quarters position. He can hit the low 90s with his fastball. He also has an explosive slider, which has a very quick break. He likes to throw an overhand curveball to righthanded hitters, and when his control is on, it's a very effective pitch. He does not rely on his change-up too often.

The velocities of Stewart's fastball and slider are very similar, which can make him extremely difficult to hit (especially for righthanded batters).

He has been a durable performer who bounces back quickly. Stewart has been used mostly to keep a game from getting out of hand early and his ability to work five or six innings in that role keeps the bullpen intact.

He is at his best when he is challenging the hitters, going inside with hard stuff on those who crowd the plate. Stewart can be overpowering at times, but hasn't always been consistent, a fact usually traced to faulty control.

His walks-strikeouts ratio is not as good as it should be. His relatively modest won-lost and save records generally reflect the role he has most often played--that of set-up man for the late men. Stewart consistently ranks among the league leaders for relievers in innings pitched.

For the most part, he pitched well in 1985, but was hurt by walks (66) and home runs (15) in the 129 2/3 innings he worked.

SAMMY STEWART
RHP, No. 53
RR, 6'3", 219 lbs.
ML Svc: 7 years
Born: 10-28-54 in
Asheville, NC

1985 STATISTICS

W	L	ERA	G	GS	CG	SV	IP	H	R	ER	BB	SO
5	7	3.61	56	1	0	9	129.2	117	60	52	66	77

CAREER STATISTICS

W	L	ERA	G	GS	CG	SV	IP	H	R	ER	BB	SO
51	45	3.47	307	25	4	42	866	774	366	334	433	514

FIELDING:

His delivery leaves him in a good position for balls hit back to the mound, but he is below average in most defensive categories. He is much better holding runners on base and has an especially good move to second base.

Stewart throws over to first base quite often, sometimes to the point of disrupting his concentration, but as a whole, he is better than average.

OVERALL:

Stewart has not always been enamored of his role with the Orioles and his situation this year is further complicated by contractual differences.

He has one year left on his contract and, with the club and him apparently far apart on his dollar value, there is a strong possibility he could be traded.

Robinson: "Though he still needs to maintain better control, Sammy is at his peak. He has one of the strongest and most durable arms in the game. He can pitch anywhere, anytime, and he likes to take the ball. In the right situation, he is a valuable asset."

HITTING:

Alan Wiggins is an opposite field hitter whose speed puts a lot of pressure on the defense. This switch-hitting second baseman slaps the ball from both sides of the plate.

Wiggins is primarily a high-ball hitter from the right side and a low-ball hitter from the left side.

He likes the ball out over the plate; pitchers try to throw him fastballs in and mix in slow breaking balls.

Wiggins is a good leadoff hitter: he is patient and draws his share of walks. He knows that he has to use every offensive weapon available to get on base. He is not afraid to try to bunt his way on and is very good at it. Knowing that he can bunt at any time puts even more pressure on the infielders. So, his offensive tools do exactly what they are supposed to: keep the infielders guessing.

BASERUNNING:

Wiggins is an extremely fast runner and a very good basestealer. He led the Orioles with 30 stolen bases in less than half a season and should be even more of a threat when he's acclimated to the league.

He is a disrupter on the bases and his speed, combined with the power hitting of Lee Lacy, Cal Ripken and Eddie Murray batting behind him, should create a lot of Orioles runs in 1986.

Wiggins does, however, have a tendency to get picked off base too often--especially against lefthanded pitchers. That is a part of his game the Orioles will undoubtedly try to improve upon.

FIELDING:

Wiggins is a converted outfielder and sometimes it shows. His speed gives him excellent range and his arm is strong, especially on the double play. But his play in the field is often erratic, and last year nonchalance hurt him on a few occasions.

ALAN WIGGINS
2B, No. 2
SR, 6'2", 164 lbs.
ML Svc: 4 years
Born: 2-17-58 in
   Los Angeles, CA

1985 STATISTICS

AVG	G	AB	R	H	2B	3B	HR	RBI	BB	SO	SB
.285	76	298	43	85	11	4	0	21	29	16	30

CAREER STATISTICS

AVG	G	AB	R	H	2B	3B	HR	RBI	BB	SO	SB
.269	465	1665	276	448	53	16	4	92	183	135	201

VS. RHP   VS. LHP   PROBABLE HIT LOCATIONS

Wiggins is one of the Orioles' "imports," that is, he has not been trained to make infield plays in the Baltimore style. Crossed signals and confusion over infield procedure led to quite a few errors when he first arrived. He has the physical tools to play second base, but he will need to conform to the way the infield is played in Crabcake City.

OVERALL:

Wiggins gives the Orioles a dimension they haven't had for a long time--speed at the top of the batting order. He might not get the green light to steal as often as he is used to (especially if his pickoff ratio doesn't improve) because he has such sure bets batting behind him now.

Robinson: "Alan is a much better overall player than I was expecting him to be; he is definitely going to be an asset to the club's offense. Now that he knows something about the league, I'm looking forward to what is going to develop on the bases this year."

POWER POTENTIAL

MIKE YOUNG
LF, No. 43
SR, 6'2", 195 lbs.
ML Svc: 2 years
Born: 3-20-60 in
Oakland, CA

HITTING:

For the second consecutive season, Mike Young came into his own during the second half of the year. As in 1984, he was a much better offensive player in the latter portion of 1985. If he does not put together a good full year this season, he will have an uphill battle to fight the tag of "half-season player." If he puts two good halves together, however, he will be something special.

After hitting 17 home runs (11 in the last two months) as a rookie in 1984, Young had an unimpressive spring and had trouble getting into the lineup early last year. After the All-Star break, however, he simply exploded: he hit 20 home runs and drove in 50 runs in a 51-game span from July to September. He finished second on the club with 28 home runs and set a team record for RBIs in a month with 32 in August.

He has changed his stance somewhat and he has moved off the plate; he now favors a slightly open, crouched stance. He continues to strike out a lot, but has begun to show signs of becoming a more disciplined hitter. After hitting only .195 from the right side in 1984, Young picked his average up to .293 as a righthander last year, the result of laying off low breaking pitches out of the strike zone.

As a righthanded hitter, Young likes the high fastball, and from the left side, he wants the low one. His power has been primarily straightaway, but with experience, he is now becoming more of a pull hitter.

BASERUNNING:

Young has good speed out of the box and on the basepaths, but he is not a good basestealer at this point. This is an area where he should improve. There are times when he is too tentative on the bases. He does not take a good, aggressive, I-mean-business kind of lead.

FIELDING:

After playing mostly in right field,

1985 STATISTICS

AVG	G	AB	R	H	2B	3B	HR	RBI	BB	SO	SB
.273	139	450	72	123	22	1	28	81	48	104	1

CAREER STATISTICS

AVG	G	AB	R	H	2B	3B	HR	RBI	BB	SO	SB
.259	292	889	138	230	41	4	45	135	108	223	8

  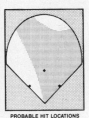

VS. RHP   VS. LHP   PROBABLE HIT LOCATIONS

Young was switched to left last year and seemed to make the adjustment. He had been previously considered an average fielder until last year, when his offensive contributions appeared to lift his confidence in the field. Again, however, this is an area which shows potential only when he is hitting well. He doesn't have a strong arm and will overthrow the ball.

OVERALL:

Young is improving as a hitter and in the field and is a very intense player.

Robinson: "I have a lot of faith in Mike; he could be a bit more patient at the plate, but he has all the raw ability in the world. When he is hitting the ball well, it just seems to rocket off his bat.

"He still has some things to learn, but he seems to have what it takes; I think he has only shown us a bit of his power to date."

RICH DAUER
2B, No. 25
RR, 6'0", 190 lbs.
ML Svc: 9 years
Born: 7-27-52 in
San Bernardino, CA

HITTING, BASERUNNING, FIELDING:

Last season was Rich Dauer's worst professional season to date. His future is in jeopardy. After the team acquired Alan Wiggins, Dauer sat on the bench and made only occasional appearances during the second half of the season.

Dauer likes hard stuff on the inside half of the plate and up. He is a strong player and at one time ranked among the team leaders in doubles, but his extra-base output declined by a very large degree last season. Dauer is a pull hitter, though in the past he has been successful working the hit-and-run.

He has below-average speed and is no threat to steal or take the extra base.

Despite what is considered mediocre range at second base, Dauer has been highly consistent in the field. He needs to play only 10 more games to qualify for the highest fielding percentage in history for second basemen with at least 1000 games. He is a heady defensive player and can turn the double play.

OVERALL:

His career has been in a tailspin over the last two years and the Orioles have no interest in bringing him back. He will have to move on if he's going to continue to play.

LENN SAKATA
2B, No. 12
RR, 5'9", 160 lbs.
ML Svc: 7 years
Born: 6-8-53 in
Honolulu, HI

HITTING, BASERUNNING, FIELDING:

Lenn Sakata is yet another high-ball, fastball, pull hitter who has never had much of an average. He is much stronger than his 5'9", 160-pound frame would indicate and can hit an occasional home run. But he has never hit consistently enough to get into the lineup on a daily basis.

He is not a very patient hitter and will chase breaking balls away.

Sakata has above-average speed, but he isn't a threat to steal. He does run the bases well, however. He doesn't bunt often, but has good instincts on the bases and won't make foolish mistakes.

If defense was all he had to do, Sakata could play regularly for most of the teams in the major leagues. Second base is easily his best position, though he has played shortstop and third on occasion. He has very quick hands which enable him to turn the double play with the best of them. His arm is not overpowering, though it is strong enough and accurate enough for second base. He is an excellent defensive player in just about every phase of the game.

OVERALL:

Sakata was another victim of the O's infield shakeup last year and will not return in 1986.

Robinson: "Lenn has always been an excellent utility infielder who has always been a dependable replacement, but right now it appears that he will be hard-pressed to stay in the majors."

BOSTON RED SOX

HITTING:

Tony Armas will go for two weeks and look like the worst hitter in baseball. Then he'll spend the next two weeks hitting balls out of sight, into the parking lot or over the roof.

Armas is a great mistake hitter. If a pitcher uses the wrong strategy or is unable to place the pitch just right, it is gone. Armas is a challenging type of hitter and stands up at the plate with the bat held high in an almost threatening position.

Because he stands so far away from the plate, he can be made to look bad on outside breaking balls. A hard thrower can also get him out high and inside-- but even the league's flamethrowers had better make sure the pitch is in and hard.

Armas is strictly a power hitter and like all power hitters, he is not going to hit for much of an average. But last year, he began to work on hitting the ball up the middle to cut down on his strikeouts and hit for a better average.

He was hitting close to .270 with 14 home runs in early June, when he tore a calf muscle which all but ended his season. He missed two important months.

Even though he returned to the lineup late in the year, he was far from 100% and his hitting suffered.

BASERUNNING:

Armas is not a single-threat player; he is, without question, the best baserunner on the Red Sox. He does not have blinding speed, but he knows how to run the bases and when to take the extra base. He runs as hard after grounding a ball back to the pitcher as he does in trying to stretch a single.

FIELDING:

Until his leg injuries cut down his

TONY ARMAS
CF, No. 20
RR, 6'1", 200 lbs.
ML Svc: 9 years
Born: 7-2-53 in
Anzoatequi, VEN

1985 STATISTICS

AVG	G	AB	R	H	2B	3B	HR	RBI	BB	SO	SB
.265	103	385	50	102	17	5	23	64	18	90	0

CAREER STATISTICS

AVG	G	AB	R	H	2B	3B	HR	RBI	BB	SO	SB
.250	1103	4088	502	1022	153	31	213	669	206	978	16

VS. RHP   VS. LHP   PROBABLE HIT LOCATIONS

range, Armas had been vastly underrated as an outfielder. He became one of the league's better center fielders once the Red Sox gave him the job. He had been a right fielder in Oakland.

He has a good arm but leg problems have begun to cut down on his range.

OVERALL:

Tony Armas is a key for the Red Sox, a point made even more clear when he was out of the lineup last season. His absence hurt the entire team and was one of the big reasons the Red Sox were only a .500 team. The Red Sox can't lose a run producer like Armas and hope to be in contention.

Robinson: "Tony is the kind of hitter who can carry just about an entire team. He is such a presence as a hitter that he helps everyone else in the lineup just by being in it."

HITTING:

For the second year in a row, Marty Barrett did a solid job both offensively and defensively for the Red Sox.

He's not fast, not quick, not spectacular and seldom noticed. But when it's over and the numbers are in, one quick look shows just a few errors (11 last year) and a decent average (.266).

Barrett is an good contact hitter with a quick bat. Normally, he will try and go up the middle or to right field but, occasionally, he can turn on an inside pitch.

In 1984, Barrett hit .303 by dropping a lot of singles into right field. Last year, however, defenses played him shallow and caught a lot of his bloopers.

BASERUNNING:

Barrett is an aggressive baserunner, but he is far from fast. However, he knows how to run the bases and many times that makes up for his lack of speed.

FIELDING:

Barrett does not have good range at second base, but if he can get his glove on the ball, he will make the play. He is not good at making the pivot on the double play. He's not the best defensive second baseman by a long shot but he is not the worst either.

He pulled the hidden ball trick twice last year, both times against the California Angels. The ploy is something he

MARTY BARRETT
2B, No. 17
RR, 5'10", 175 lbs.
ML Svc: 3 years
Born: 6-23-58 in
  Arcadia, CA

1985 STATISTICS

AVG	G	AB	R	H	2B	3B	HR	RBI	BB	SO	SB
.266	156	534	59	142	26	0	5	56	56	50	7

CAREER STATISTICS

AVG	G	AB	R	H	2B	3B	HR	RBI	BB	SO	SB
.277	336	1071	122	297	50	4	8	103	101	77	12

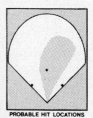

STRONG   STRONG   PROBABLE HIT LOCATIONS

VS. RHP   VS. LHP

was very good at in the minors and it just gives the baserunner something to think about at second.

OVERALL:

Barrett is a steady performer who will go out game after game and give a 100% effort.

Robinson: "He's a decent contact hitter but he has no power. Defensively, he is adequate and might get a little better. He's a journeyman type player."

HITTING:

When it comes to hitting, Wade Boggs doesn't have a weakness and is most dangerous when he has two strikes on him. In 1985, he hit .390 on 0-2 counts.

Boggs read Ted Williams' book when he was a youngster and it has been his guide ever since. He rarely swings at a pitch out of the strike zone, and he watches the ball through its entire flight right to the instant it lands in the catcher's mitt.

Boggs has won two major league batting titles in three years and has a lifetime .351 average in four years. Bill Fischer, Red Sox pitching coach, after watching Boggs for three-quarters of a season, can offer no advice: "If I had to pitch to him, I would have no idea how to get him out or where to put the ball."

Boggs uses the entire field; there is only one way to defense him and that is to just "be ready." He has power, but does not use it. He could hit 25-30 homers a year but won't try. "That's not what got me to the big leagues," he claims, neglecting to mention that it is not what made him a millionaire, either.

BASERUNNING:

Boggs is not fast, but he has has worked hard to develop excellent speed out of the batter's box. He has turned what used to be a flaw into another asset.

However, he is not a very good baserunner nor is he a very aggressive one, except when he's running to first.

FIELDING:

Boggs may be the most improved third baseman in baseball. It is not by accident. He is an extremely hard worker and on most days, he takes 100 ground balls before batting practice.

Like Glenn Hoffman, Boggs rarely

WADE BOGGS
3B, No. 26
LR, 6'2", 190 lbs.
ML Svc: 4 years
Born: 6-15-58 in
Omaha, NE

1985 STATISTICS

AVG	G	AB	R	H	2B	3B	HR	RBI	BB	SO	SB
.368	161	653	107	240	42	3	8	78	96	61	2

CAREER STATISTICS

AVG	G	AB	R	H	2B	3B	HR	RBI	BB	SO	SB
.351	576	2198	367	771	131	15	24	251	312	162	9

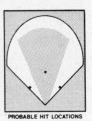

VS. RHP   VS. LHP   PROBABLE HIT LOCATIONS

makes a bad throw and has a strong arm. He has developed what it takes to become a Gold Glove third baseman. That award may come, too.

OVERALL:

Boggs, who could always hit, has made himself into a very good all-around ballplayer. He may be a bit selfish in some areas (such as not trying for the long ball when his team could really use a home run to drive in some runs) but he's a fierce competitor and a valuable performer for the Red Sox.

Robinson: "Boggs loves the ball over the middle of the plate. He doesn't like to pull the ball--still, he's almost impossible to pitch to.

"As a third baseman, he's made giant strides since coming up because he works hard at it. He has developed from being a below-average fielder to an above-average one."

PITCHING:

Last season, Oil Can Boyd said that he wanted to improve his 1984 record of 12 victories and win between 15-18 games in 1985: mission accomplished.

He became the winningest Red Sox pitcher since 1979 when Dennis Eckersley had 17 wins and Bob Stanley had 16. Had it not been for a horrendous six-week period in the middle of the summer last year, Boyd might well have won 20 games; he did not register even one win from July 14 to September 5.

In the past, one of Boyd's big problems had been a lack of consistent concentration; he failed to think about every pitch to each batter. Determined to bear down last season, Boyd did well during the first half of the season, but lost his concentration when he was passed over for the All-Star team. He was unable to get his mind and his pitching back on track until September.

He continues to be a pitcher who is overly affected by circumstances unrelated to his pitching. He has a lot of highs as well as lows and speaks his mind quickly, though not always at the most appropriate times.

It appears as though while the pitcher in him has learned how to pitch, The Can alternately holds him back and pushes him to the limits.

Boyd throws a 90 MPH fastball as his out pitch and uses a slider and curveball to set up the heater. He uses a quick delivery and is a fast worker. He pitches overhand to three-quarters and can drop down even lower to some right-handed hitters.

He gets hurt by the long ball and gave up 26 home runs last season, but his overall control improved remarkably in 1985.

Boyd always wants the ball; he finished second in the league last year in innings pitched (to Bert Blyleven), fourth in shutouts and fourth in complete games.

DENNIS BOYD
RHP, No. 23
RR, 6'1", 155 lbs.
ML Svc: 3 years
Born: 10-6-59 in
Meridian, MS

1985 STATISTICS

W	L	ERA	G	GS	CG	SV	IP	H	R	ER	BB	SO
15	13	3.70	35	35	13	0	272.1	273	117	112	67	154

CAREER STATISTICS

W	L	ERA	G	GS	CG	SV	IP	H	R	ER	BB	SO
31	34	3.88	82	75	28	0	577.1	594	277	249	145	333

FIELDING:

Sometimes it appears as though Boyd wants to be everywhere on the field; he is quick off the mound and loves helping his own cause by fielding balls hit back to him. He covers first well and seems to be a better fielder when he is pitching a good game.

OVERALL:

Boyd is emotional, controversial and nowhere near his potential. He is one of the most entertaining pitchers to watch in all of baseball; there is no pitcher more consistently demonstrative of his elation or disgust than Boyd. Yet it is possible that his exuberance is getting in the way of his overall pitching; his high moments make him soar, but his low spots bring him down.

Robinson: "The Red Sox did not give him much help last season and Boyd sometimes defeats himself as well. If he can continue to learn from his mistakes, he should have the chance to win 20 games very soon."

GOOD CLUTCH HITTER

HITTING:

One of the better trades the Boston Red Sox have made in recent years was the one which brought Bill Buckner from the Chicago Cubs for Dennis Eckersley.

Buckner not only solidified the Red Sox infield, but he turned out to be a quality hitter and a man who could hit in the clutch. He does not walk much, nor does he strike out much. All he does is hit and, occasionally, hit with power, as his 16 home runs last year will attest.

He stands in the middle of the box in a slight crouch with the bat off his shoulder and makes good contact.

Buckner will kill a fastball, especially if it is over the middle of the plate. Sidewinding lefthanders can give him trouble, especially with a sweeping breaking ball. But Buckner is a pure hitter and will not be fooled by the same pitch or the same delivery very often.

Last season, he led the Red Sox with 110 RBIs, which was a career high for him.

BASERUNNING:

Buckner takes treatment before and after every game for his bad ankle, yet he may be the most reckless baserunner in baseball. He subscribes to the theory "Run until someone tags you out."

He led the Sox in stolen bases with 18 but also led the club in being thrown out on the bases (22). He is too aggressive in the same manner Yaz was.

FIELDING:

Buckner does not have great range, but catches anything he gets his hand on and picks low throws out of the dirt as well as anyone in baseball.

BILL BUCKNER
1B, No. 6
LL, 6'1", 185 lbs.
ML Svc: 16 years
Born: 12-14-49 in
     Vallejo, CA

1985 STATISTICS

AVG	G	AB	R	H	2B	3B	HR	RBI	BB	SO	SB
.299	162	673	89	201	46	3	16	110	30	36	18

CAREER STATISTICS

AVG	G	AB	R	H	2B	3B	HR	RBI	BB	SO	SB
.295	2023	7795	935	2296	423	44	146	970	362	370	169

  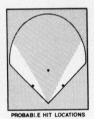

VS. RHP   VS. LHP   PROBABLE HIT LOCATIONS

Because his arm is very weak and his ankle is bad, Buckner always lets the pitcher cover the bag on ground balls to first. As a result, he set a big league record for assists last season.

OVERALL:

Buckner shows no signs of slowing down; there's no reason why he cannot have the same type of season he's had in Boston the last two years, even at age 36.

Robinson: "He has always been one of the better hitters in the game and has proved he still is. Last season, he was the team's clutch performer and continued to do his usual, competent defensive job."

BIG, BREAKING CURVEBALL

PITCHING:

For the second straight year, Mark Clear was able to retire hitters in spring training, but once the season began, he fell back into his old problem of being plagued by wildness. It is bad enough that he walks hitters, but because he has absolutely no move to first base, the runner he walked is a sure bet to steal second base. At one point last year, opponents stole 57 consecutive times against him before one was thrown out.

Clear has a major league arm, a curve ball which is second to none and a good fastball. But when he is unable to get them over the plate, he might as well be throwing underhand. When he can't find the strike zone with his big curveball, hitters can sit on his fastball.

He doesn't give up too many home runs, but the walks and the automatic steals which follow bury him. He worked hard to develop a new motion last year. Clear tried to lower his leg kick and adjust his arm speed to help his control; for a two-week period in July, the altered motion worked, but it was all downhill after that. He was hardly used during the final month of the season.

FIELDING:

Clear may be among the worst fielding pitchers in baseball. He has a very slow reaction time to balls hit toward the mound and sometimes handles bunts as though they were live grenades.

MARK CLEAR
RHP, No. 25
RR, 6'4", 215 lbs.
ML Svc: 7 years
Born: 5-27-56 in
Los Angeles, CA

1985 STATISTICS

W	L	ERA	G	GS	CG	SV	IP	H	R	ER	BB	SO
1	3	3.72	41	0	0	3	55.2	45	26	23	50	55

CAREER STATISTICS

W	L	ERA	G	GS	CG	SV	IP	H	R	ER	BB	SO
57	39	3.99	335	0	0	61	615.2	523	309	273	433	606

OVERALL:

Mark Clear doesn't figure very high in the Red Sox' plans. He will be a mop-up man who will never be brought in with the game on the line unless there's no one else available or unless he turns things around. However, it does not appear as if he will improve enough to get that opportunity.

Robinson: "Mark has certainly has had his ups-and-downs; I believe that a change of scenery would be the best thing for him.

"Clear has a terrific curveball--it was voted one of the best in the league by the players, so you know how hard it can be to hit. But he really hurts himself by putting so many runners on base. A short reliever simply cannot do that."

PITCHING:

Roger Clemens has been touted as the Red Sox' best pitching prospect in many, many years, but he was hampered by an injury last season for the second year in a row. A torn forearm muscle side-lined him in the final month of the 1984 season, but a much more serious shoulder ailment, which ultimately required surgery, was the culprit last year.

When he is healthy, Clemens is the hardest thrower in the league and has the ability to be a 25-game winner.

There is nothing fancy about Clemens. He just stares at the hitter, rears back and fires. And when he's on, a hitter has no chance whatsoever.

He continues to work on a curveball, a change-up and a forkball. When he comes close to perfecting those pitches, and provided he can bounce back from the surgery, Clemens should fulfill his pro-mise of becoming one of the top pitchers in baseball for years to come.

There aren't many pitchers who have his confidence. He is much more mature than his 23 years. He also has the grit of a veteran, and if he catches a hitter leaning too far inside, Clemens will buzz a pitch in close.

FIELDING:

Clemens is a good, all-around athlete and is a fine fielder. He is quick off the mound and always has his head in the

ROGER CLEMENS
RHP, No. 21
RR, 6'4", 205 lbs.
ML Svc: 2 years
Born: 8-4-62 in
Dayton, OH

1985 STATISTICS

W	L	ERA	G	GS	CG	SV	IP	H	R	ER	BB	SO
7	5	3.29	15	15	3	0	98.1	83	38	36	37	74

CAREER STATISTICS

W	L	ERA	G	GS	CG	SV	IP	H	R	ER	BB	SO
16	9	3.89	36	35	8	0	231.2	229	105	100	66	86

game. One thing he lacks, however, is a good move to first base.

OVERALL:

If. If. If.

When? When? When?

Clemens has all the talent and abil-ity in the world, with the confidence to match. His fastball is dazzling heat. Two questions remain unanswered.

Robinson: "Clemens throws that true rising type of fastball that hitters just can't lay off but can't hit. The pitch reminds me a lot of Jim Palmer's rising fastball; there weren't a lot of batters who could hit Palmer's and there won't be many to hit Roger's."

PITCHING:

Ask manager John McNamara who was one of the big surprises of 1985, and he'll quickly tell you that it was Steve Crawford. The reports on this righthander weren't very favorable when spring training started last year, but he went out and won a job the old fashioned way--he earned it.

When the season ended, Crawford was the Red Sox' top reliever and had done everything he was asked: spot-start, long relief and middle relief. He was, however, handicapped by injuries. He was disabled twice: first when he tore a forearm muscle and when he hurt his back.

Crawford uses a cross-seam, rising fastball taught to him by Red Sox pitching coach Bill Fischer. The riser complements his sinking fastball well.

A big, tough competitor, Crawford is a nasty-looking figure on the mound and becomes just as ferocious when it comes to making sure nobody is going to lean in and jump at his pitches. Whenever he starts to believe just how good he can be, look out.

FIELDING:

Crawford is an average fielder who tends to rush himself on balls hit back to the mound. But that's part of his intense nature. He would rather field "fast" than "slow and lazy."

STEVE CRAWFORD
RHP, No. 28
RR, 6'5", 225 lbs.
ML Svc: 2 years
Born: 4-29-58 in Pryor, OK

1985 STATISTICS

W	L	ERA	G	GS	CG	SV	IP	H	R	ER	BB	SO
6	5	3.76	44	1	0	12	91	103	47	38	28	58

CAREER STATISTICS

W	L	ERA	G	GS	CG	SV	IP	H	R	ER	BB	SO
14	10	3.86	104	16	2	13	252	296	133	108	75	120

OVERALL:

Despite his figures last year, he will attend spring training without a defined position. He will probably start as a middle long man and, if the bullpen fails again, wind up as the short reliever.

Robinson "No one was really expecting Steve to help the Red Sox as much as he did last year. They could use more surprises like him.

"He throws hard and has the right attitude. He may have lacked enough confidence in himself, but last year's success should have cured that. He has a good sinker and an effective rising fastball that, if he can keep both of them in control, should enable him to do even more this year."

HITTING:

Mike Easler has always been known as the "Hit Man" and he's more than fulfilled his contract in Boston.

Easler slipped a bit last year when he had to hit full time against southpaws for the first time in his career. He dropped from .313 with 27 homers and 91 RBIs in 1984 to .262 with 16 homers and 74 RBIs in 1985. Pitchers had a better idea of how to pitch him in his second year in the league.

Easler still has the severe crouch with the bat cocked high over his head. He's not as quick as he once was.

Last season, he had trouble with both the high fastball and the breaking ball. But if the fastball wasn't high enough or the breaking ball hung a bit, he could still hit it and hit it far.

Lefthanders give him fits with the breaking ball and off-speed pitches.

BASERUNNING:

In one game, it took three singles to score Easler from second base. That best describes his baserunning. His top speed is slower than slow.

FIELDING:

Last year, Easler had the opportunity to prove why he is a designated hitter. He was forced to play in the outfield a few times and catching routine fly balls was a supreme adventure. He was a terrible replacement for Jim Rice in left field.

MIKE EASLER
DH/OF, No. 7
LR, 6'1", 196 lbs.
ML Svc: 8 years
Born: 11-29-50 in
Cleveland, OH

1985 STATISTICS

AVG	G	AB	R	H	2B	3B	HR	RBI	BB	SO	SB
.262	155	568	71	149	29	4	16	74	53	129	0

CAREER STATISTICS

AVG	G	AB	R	H	2B	3B	HR	RBI	BB	SO	SB
.293	907	2910	381	852	153	23	99	413	252	557	16

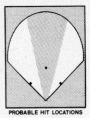

VS. RHP   VS. LHP   PROBABLE HIT LOCATIONS

OVERALL:

Easler can still hit righthanded pitching but will be a liability for the Red Sox if he has to be a full-time DH.

Robinson: "He was not as good a hitter last year as he was in 1984 and I think what you saw last year is what he will settle in at. He had the advantage in 1984, as it was his first year in the league, but now a lot of pitchers have his number. He benefits from hitting in Fenway Park."

HITTING:

It seems as though Dwight Evans gets off to a slow start every year, and last season was no exception. He didn't even begin to look like the real Dwight Evans until mid-July. Evans is perhaps the number one pupil of batting coach Walter Hriniak; the two worked many long hours trying to figure out what was wrong.

Evans hits out of a crouch and keeps his weight on his back foot and does a little tap dance with his front one as the pitcher goes into his windup. He can hit the ball to all fields and has good power. He is one of the strongest men on the Red Sox.

Because he is one of the league's best 3-0 hitters, he almost always has the green light. He will not swing, however, unless the ball is exactly where he wants it.

Righthanded pitchers try to work him down and away while lefthanders like to give him breaking balls down and in and fastballs down and away.

One of the right fielder's biggest problems last season was hitting with runners in scoring position and getting the runner home from third with less than two outs.

Evans swings through many pitches and annually records a lot of strikeouts. Last season, he had the second highest number of strikeouts on the team (105) behind Mike Easler's 129.

BASERUNNING:

Evans fits the mold of all the Red Sox' baserunners--slow. He has had knee problems over the last few years and does not take many chances on the bases. He is one of the worst sliders in the league.

FIELDING:

Evans does not record many assists because it's a rare day when a runner

DWIGHT EVANS
RF, No. 24
RR, 6'3", 205 lbs.
ML Svc: 13 years
Born: 11-3-51 in
Santa Monica, CA

1985 STATISTICS

AVG	G	AB	R	H	2B	3B	HR	RBI	BB	SO	SB
.263	159	617	110	162	29	1	29	78	114	105	7

CAREER STATISTICS

AVG	G	AB	R	H	2B	3B	HR	RBI	BB	SO	SB
.269	1781	6132	996	1648	328	55	265	852	892	1172	58

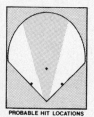

VS. RHP   VS. LHP   PROBABLE HIT LOCATIONS

tests his arm by attempting to take an extra base. He is still one of the game's best right fielders.

He has a bad knee which bothers him from time to time, but it does not hinder his ability to race down anything hit into right field. He does an excellent job at catching bloopers.

OVERALL:

This year, Evans begins his 15th season with the Red Sox. At age 34, he is beginning to test the clock, but if he can stay healthy and get an occasional day or two off during the year, he can still play solid, all-around baseball.

Robinson: "Dwight struggled early last season and wasn't able to start to put things together until the year was almost over. He's getting to the point where age may be catching up with him."

HITTING:

Rich Gedman is a manager's dream. He is a lefthanded hitter who can hit, hit with power and also catch.

Gedman has worked long hours to make himself into a good hitter. He can still be made to look bad at the plate, but he also has the ability to turn a ballgame around. He is a student of hitting coach Walter Hriniak, who subscribes to the Charlie Lau theory of hitting.

Gedman has an open stance and keeps his head down and his chin tucked in. Many times, he looks more as though he's lining up a putt (he keeps his head down long after contact has been made) than hitting a baseball.

Gedman has power to all parts of the field. He prefers the ball out over the plate and likes to shoot it into left field and left-center field. He also has the ability to turn on an inside pitch and hit it with authority.

Last season, Gedman played full-time against lefthanded pitching for the first time in his career. Naturally, he had a hard time. Lefthanders would put him away with high, hard stuff and breaking balls low and away. Righthanders try to fool Gedman with an abundance of off-speed pitches. At one time, he had little chance against that type of strategy, but in the past two years, he has become a much better hitter against righthanders' off-speed offerings.

BASERUNNING:

Gedman may be the slowest player on the Red Sox, yet he tied Tony Armas for the team lead in triples with five.

He will rarely attempt to steal a base and collected only the first two steals of his professional career last season.

FIELDING:

Gedman was among the better defensive catchers in the league last year. He has

RICH GEDMAN
C, No. 10
LR, 6'0", 215 lbs.
ML Svc: 5 years
Born: 9-26-59 in
Worcester, MA

1985 STATISTICS

AVG	G	AB	R	H	2B	3B	HR	RBI	BB	SO	SB
.295	144	498	66	147	30	5	18	80	50	79	2

CAREER STATISTICS

AVG	G	AB	R	H	2B	3B	HR	RBI	BB	SO	SB
.278	521	1669	195	464	104	12	53	223	113	261	2

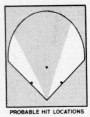

VS. RHP   VS. LHP   PROBABLE HIT LOCATIONS

a rifle-like arm and a quick release. He threw out over 40% of the runners who tried to steal against him. That 40% mark would be even higher were he working with a pitching staff that was any good at keeping runners close.

He has also vastly improved his ability of keeping the ball in front of him.

OVERALL:

Last season was the first year that Gedman was not platooned. He showed that he was ready, willing and able to take charge and to catch every day. It looks as though he is going to be the Red Sox catcher for many years.

Robinson: "Right now, I think that Rich is close to being the best catcher in baseball at throwing out runners. He has improved more than anyone I've ever seen at that position. He is a good defensive catcher, calls a good game, works well with his pitchers and, as an added bonus, he can also hit."

HITTING:

Jackie Gutierrez started the season as the Red Sox' number one shortstop, suffered a slight injury behind his right knee in May and was never able to reclaim his job. Glenn Hoffman took over and seized the opportunity by playing well. Gutierrez, the Red Sox' Rookie of the Year in 1984, performed poorly.

At times last season, he became almost an automatic out and was slumping at .218. Gutierrez was told he tried to pull the ball too much, so he decided to go to right field. It was a bad mistake.

In his efforts to hit to the opposite field, he stood too far off the plate and pitchers found it easy to simply pitch him outside, outside, outside. His entire game fell apart: he wasn't able to execute the sacrifice bunt and by September, he was barely making any kind of solid contact.

By the end of the year, this young player was a very confused hitter and was hoping to get straightened out in winter ball.

BASERUNNING:

Gutierrez stole 10 bases last year and would have been able to take much more if he had been able to get himself to first base more often. He has worked to improve his baserunning and now gets a much better jump off first base than he did in his rookie season.

FIELDING:

He has the talent to become one of the better shortstops in the league. He can go behind second base to make the spectacular play to win a game. But he can also be very careless and will make many more errors than he should.

Gutierrez has an outstanding arm, but

JACKIE GUTIERREZ
SS, No. 41
RR, 6'1", 175 lbs.
ML Svc: 2 years
Born: 6-27-60 in
   Cartagena, COL

1985 STATISTICS

AVG	G	AB	R	H	2B	3B	HR	RBI	BB	SO	SB
.218	103	275	33	60	5	2	2	21	12	37	10

CAREER STATISTICS

AVG	G	AB	R	H	2B	3B	HR	RBI	BB	SO	SB
.246	259	734	90	181	17	5	4	50	28	87	22

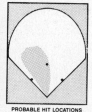

STRONG VS. RHP
STRONG VS. LHP
PROBABLE HIT LOCATIONS

has trouble making routine throws and double play relays.

OVERALL:

He lost his regular job last season and will have a battle on his hands if he hopes to win it back. When he returned in September, he was trying to make up for lost time and was pressing to excess. Instead of doing well, his fielding and hitting were awful. Many feel that a winter of baseball in a less pressured atmosphere will do wonders for him.

Robinson: "He was very erratic and couldn't even make the routine plays. He was overpowered at the plate and had a miserable season. He will have to come back and produce very quickly if he is to get another chance to crack the starting lineup."

HITTING:

Glenn Hoffman lost his starting job in 1984 when he was still feeling the effects of his 1983 knee surgery. Last season, he was fully recovered and marched in to take back his old position as the Sox' number one shortstop.

He stands straight up in the box and can be fooled on breaking balls down and away and has a hard time with a good, high inside fastball. Both lefthanders and righthanders can get him with good, low breaking balls.

He ended the season with a .276 average, his best since his rookie season of 1980. Hoffman is not a power hitter but he is strong enough to (occasionally) hit one over the fence.

FIELDING:

Hoffman has an excellent pair of hands, a strong, accurate arm, and rarely makes a bad throw. He will make every routine play and, despite his lack of speed and range, can go into the hole to his right to make the big plays.

BASERUNNING:

He has never had outstanding speed and is even slower since his knee surgery. He compensates for a lack of speed with smart, heads-up baserunning. He is seldom thrown out going from first to third or to second to home. He knows when to take the extra base.

GLENN HOFFMAN
SS, No. 18
RR, 6'2", 190 lbs.
ML Svc: 6 years
Born: 7-7-58 in
    Orange, CA

1985 STATISTICS

AVG	G	AB	R	H	2B	3B	HR	RBI	BB	SO	SB
.276	96	279	40	77	17	2	6	34	25	40	2

CAREER STATISTICS

AVG	G	AB	R	H	2B	3B	HR	RBI	BB	SO	SB
.247	.645	1849	222	457	93	9	22	190	121	261	5

VS. RHP VS. LHP PROBABLE HIT LOCATIONS

OVERALL:

Hoffman has re-established himself as the regular shortstop and opened the door for a possible trade of Jackie Gutierrez.

Robinson: "Hoffman is a very steady performer with a strong and accurate arm. He doesn't swing at as many bad pitches as he once did."

PITCHING:

For years, baseball people have been waiting for Bruce Hurst to develop into a big winner. And for years, he has finished at .500 or below. He is 42-46 lifetime. In 1983 and 1984, he ended at 12-12. He missed finishing with that record last year when he lost on the final day of the season to end at 11-13.

Hurst turned into a strikeout pitcher last year, and is using a forkball to go along with his good fastball.

Last season, he started out by losing seven of his first nine decisions, found himself in the bullpen and couldn't understand why. Despite his good stuff, Hurst was simply not tough on the mound. He let all kinds of little things bother him and at the slightest bit of adversity he would blow up.

But after his stint in the bullpen, he came back a different pitcher. He was all business, worked fast, used his compact delivery and, for the first time in his career, took charge of the game.

The result was five straight wins and eight of eleven thereafter, lending hope (again) that this year may be the year.

FIELDING:

Hurst is not a cat off the mound on bunts and dribblers, but he does an adequate job fielding his position. He has one of the better pickoff moves in baseball. He had 15 pickoffs in 1984 and recorded 13 last season.

BRUCE HURST
LHP, No. 47
LL, 6'3", 215 lbs.
ML Svc: 4 years
Born: 3-24-58 in
     St. George, UT

1985 STATISTICS
W	L	ERA	G	GS	CG	SV	IP	H	R	ER	BB	SO
11	13	4.51	35	31	6	0	229.1	243	123	115	70	189

CAREER STATISTICS
W	L	ERA	G	GS	CG	SV	IP	H	R	ER	BB	SO
42	46	4.59	146	127	21	0	829.1	939	462	423	288	520

OVERALL:

It appears that Hurst will never become the pitcher that many felt he might. He throws too many home run balls and is consistently inconsistent.

He gets upset when his potential is mentioned and says that he does not want to be a leader. Hurst will begin the 1986 season as he ended the 1985 season: the number five pitcher in the starting rotation.

Robinson: "Bruce is hard to figure out. He will pitch a great game one day, but then for the next two, he'll pitch poorly. To me, the answer is that he has got to continue to have that same kind of aggressiveness and determination he showed late last year."

PITCHING:

Tim Lollar was obtained last August from the Chicago White Sox. The Red Sox management have crossed their toes, fingers and eyes hoping he will turn out to be the lefthanded short man they have been desperately seeking.

Originally placed in the starting rotation, Lollar was a disaster there.

He is a hard thrower who comes over the top, and he has a good slider. His problem, however, is controlling it. When he can't get his slider over, he is in big trouble and gets hit hard by lefthanders and righthanders alike.

When Lollar does have control, he is extremely tough on the lefthanded hitters--and that's all the Red Sox will be looking for him to do this year.

FIELDING:

The Red Sox didn't have much of an opportunity to see Lollar as a fielder but he has the reputation of being just adequate. He does have a decent move to first base and can keep runners close.

OVERALL:

Lefthanded pitchers who can throw hard always have a chance. Lollar won't have to worry about starting nor will he have to be concerned about facing many

TIM LOLLAR
LHP, No. 46
LL, 6'3", 195 lbs.
ML Svc: 6 years
Born: 3-17-56 in
  Poplar Bluff, MO

1985 STATISTICS

W	L	ERA	G	GS	CG	SV	IP	H	R	ER	BB	SO
8	10	4.62	34	23	1	1	150	140	85	77	98	105

CAREER STATISTICS

W	L	ERA	G	GS	CG	SV	IP	H	R	ER	BB	SO
45	52	4.19	167	130	9	1	853.1	790	424	397	446	572

righthanded hitters. His job will be very simple and very quick: to come in and get one or two lefties out. Bang.

However, the Red Sox may also occasionally call on him as a lefthanded pinch-hitter. He was known as a good-hitting pitcher when he was in the National League and might keep himself in a game or two with his bat.

Robinson: "His problem always has been control; he has not been able to get the ball over consistently enough. With Lollar, it is simple: he doesn't have enough stuff to win in the majors without his control. He has to throw strikes."

HITTING:

Steve Lyons tore up the International League for the first half of the 1984 season before he started to tail off. But he came to spring training last year and showed manager John McNamara enough to make the club as a utility player.

He got his chance to play when Tony Armas was cut down with injuries and, in his first start, was as impressive as he could be: he hit two home runs.

Lyons is a very aggressive player-- and the opposing pitchers found that they could use that aggressiveness to their own advantage last season. He saw a steady diet of off-speed pitches and had trouble with all kinds of breaking balls. But his biggest problem was with the change-up. Hard-throwing lefthanders found him pretty easy pickings, too. Still, Lyons managed to hit .264 and was willing to work on his shortcomings at the plate; he should improve this year.

Lyons is a better-than-average bunter and had ten bunt singles on the season.

BASERUNNING:

Lyons' aggressiveness was his Achilles heel on the bases just as it was at the plate. He has good speed, gets a decent jump and was able to steal 12 bases. But he sometimes wandered too far off base in his attempt to get a jump and was picked off. In addition, he was hurt a few times trying to go from second to third on balls hit to the shortstop.

FIELDING:

Lyons' speed and quickness enable him to run down a lot of balls. They also help him to overcome his bad habit of either breaking the wrong way or not getting a good jump on the ball. On more than one occasion last year, Lyons

STEVE LYONS
3B, No. 12
LR, 6'3", 190 lbs.
ML Svc: 1 year
Born: 6-3-60 in
Tacoma, WA

1985 STATISTICS

AVG	G	AB	R	H	2B	3B	HR	RBI	BB	SO	SB
.264	133	371	52	98	14	3	5	30	32	64	12

CAREER STATISTICS

AVG	G	AB	R	H	2B	3B	HR	RBI	BB	SO	SB
.264	133	371	52	98	14	3	5	30	32	64	12

  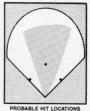

VS. RHP   VS. LHP   PROBABLE HIT LOCATIONS

initially misjudged a ball but was able to recover and make the play.

He has a decent arm, but needs more experience and work in the outfield. In the minors, he was a third baseman, but he will be a utility outfielder with the Red Sox.

OVERALL:

Lyons is the type of player who can help a ballclub. He can fill in at all of the outfield positions and, in an emergency, play a decent third base. He is enthusiastic but must learn to harness his energy during a game.

Robinson: "Steve has great ability but made a lot of rookie mistakes--not the least of which was trying to do more than he was able to do. The key for him will be to keep his average as high as his energy level. His lack of power hurts him."

PITCHING:

Al Nipper's season began going down-hill long before it started. In the early days of spring training last season, a routine physical exam disclosed a problem with his blood. Eventually, it was diagnosed as anemia caused by a stomach ulcer. Nipper, who was the Red Sox' most consistent pitcher during his rookie season (1984), missed most of the training period and then was hit with a succession of injuries that turned his year into a nightmare.

In May and June, when he was healthy, Nipper was 6-1, allowing only 12 earned runs in those victories. During his two injury-free months, Nipper showed that he had not lost the pinpoint control he needs to be an effective pitcher.

Nipper is not an overpowering type of pitcher. He doesn't have a fastball that lights up radar guns, and if he isn't on the corners with almost perfect pitches, he will not get anyone out.

What Nipper does have is an excellent breaking ball and slider. And what he does is move them around. He is extremely tough when he has his pitches working. He can drive a manager crazy because he's constantly behind hitters, 2-0 or 3-1. But when he misses the strike zone, he misses it by a hair.

Nipper, who made the team as the 10th pitcher in his rookie year, quickly developed into a top starter and drew attention from rivals with his maturity. Despite his relative inexperience, he was in charge when he took the mound, always had the poise of a veteran and always knew what he was doing.

AL NIPPER
RHP, No. 49
RR, 6'0", 188 lbs.
ML Svc: 2 years
Born: 4-2-59 in
San Diego, CA

1985 STATISTICS

W	L	ERA	G	GS	CG	SV	IP	H	R	ER	BB	SO
9	12	4.06	25	25	5	0	162	157	83	73	82	85

CAREER STATISTICS

W	L	ERA	G	GS	CG	SV	IP	H	R	ER	BB	SO
21	19	3.89	57	51	12	0	360.2	357	173	156	141	174

FIELDING:

Nipper is one of the better fielders among American League pitchers. He is quick off the mound, does an excellent job of fielding bunts and always knows what base he's going to throw to. He works on his fielding and it shows.

OVERALL:

A healthy Nipper could easily be a 15-game winner, especially with a good bullpen behind him. He is a durable pitcher, and in the majority of his starts pitches into the seventh inning. He always keeps the team in the game.

Robinson: "He started the year by being hospitalized and never really got straightened out. He finished under .500, but he's a much better pitcher than that and if he stays healthy he will prove it."

HITTING:

For most players, a .291, 27-home-run, 103-RBI year would be a satisfying season. But for Jim Rice, it was far from satisfactory. He called it embarrassing and came down hard on himself as the major reason the Red Sox' failure last year.

For most of the season, he struggled around the .260 mark, and by the end of August, he had grounded into 33 double plays, three shy of the record he set in 1984.

It was the second straight year he had not hit well. Then, in the final month, he went back to swinging the bat the way he did during his first nine years in the big leagues--and became a completely different hitter.

Rice, who rarely steps out of the batter's box between pitches, had been "feeling" for the ball and as a result hit a lot of ground balls. To be effective, Rice has to turn the bat loose.

Pitchers can get a high, hard fastball by him and he goes fishing for low, outside breaking pitches, although not as much as he did earlier in his career.

He has become a little more patient and uses all fields. Actually, when he's in a groove, Rice hits balls hard to right and right-center. He can be jammed on a pitch yet still muscle the ball the other way.

He played the second half of the season with a knee injury--an injury which eventually forced him to the sidelines in the final two weeks and then led to off-season arthroscopic surgery.

BASERUNNING:

Rice was a track star in high school, but somewhere along the way something happened to his speed. He is slow getting down the first base line and often has trouble with his feet going from first to third. He rarely attempts a steal but will always slide hard trying to break up the double play at second and into the plate trying to score.

JIM RICE
LF, No. 14
RR, 6'2", 205 lbs.
ML Svc: 12 years
Born: 3-8-53 in
   Anderson, SC

1985 STATISTICS
AVG	G	AB	R	H	2B	3B	HR	RBI	BB	SO	SB
.291	140	546	85	159	20	3	27	103	51	75	2

CAREER STATISTICS
AVG	G	AB	R	H	2B	3B	HR	RBI	BB	SO	SB
.302	1633	6509	1006	1963	292	72	331	1179	502	1140	55

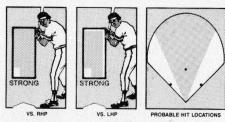

STRONG   STRONG

VS. RHP   VS. LHP   PROBABLE HIT LOCATIONS

FIELDING:

Rice has mastered playing the Green Monster in Fenway Park. He can now barehand the ball off the wall and make a strong throw to second base.

Strangely, however, he has trouble throwing to third and home, even from shallow left field. Rice has made himself into a decent defensive player and is able to make the tough catch coming in on balls or going down the left-field line.

OVERALL:

Rice feels that he learned a valuable lesson last season. He tried to carry the team by himself, altered his thinking at the plate and was hurt by it.

Robinson: "Look for a big year from him--a very big year. Offensively, he had a good season, though 1985 wasn't his kind of year. Jim got caught in the trap of trying to do too much to save a sinking ship, but I doubt that will happen again."

PITCHING:

It was another off year for Bob Stanley, but this time there may have been a reason. In early May last year, he began feeling discomfort at the base of the index finger of his pitching hand. By August, it felt as though there was a steel ball under his skin, and in September he underwent surgery for the removal of a growth. Stanley, whose record fell from 33 saves in 1983 to 22 in 1984, had only 10 last season, with the last coming June 26.

The growth prevented Stanley from gripping the ball properly, but whether that was the reason he didn't pitch well or it was the fact his sinker is not sinking as it used to is a question to be answered this year. Stanley has one of the best sinkers in baseball, yet he began a love affair with the slider last year and was hurt by it.

His ERA last year was a respectable, but misleading, 2.87. Stanley's problem was that he consistently was unable to get the first hitter he faced: 24 of his 48 inherited runners last year scored.

He is always looking for another pitch: he now has a palmball, a change-up and a slider to go along with his hard sinker.

FIELDING:

Hard work has made Stanley a good fielding pitcher. There was a time when a routine ball grounded back at him was

BOB STANLEY
RHP, No. 46
RR, 6'4", 220 lbs.
ML Svc: 9 years
Born: 11-10-54 in
  Portland, ME

1985 STATISTICS											
W	L	ERA	G	GS	CG	SV	IP	H	R	ER	BB	SO
6	6	2.87	48	0	0	10	87.2	76	30	28	30	46

CAREER STATISTICS											
W	L	ERA	G	GS	CG	SV	IP	H	R	ER	BB	SO
94	70	3.39	437	64	17	107	1291	1359	558	486	352	483

never a routine play. That is no longer the case, although he is not a solid candidate to win a Gold Glove.

OVERALL:

Stanley's outlook is positive. He knows that he is a better pitcher than he showed last year and he is anxious to prove it. He will probably begin this season as a long reliever. Look for him to rebound.

Robinson: "It looked to me as though his sinker wasn't sinking very much last year. He was fooling around with too many pitches and it hurt him; if Stanley is going to have any kind of success, he is going to have to stop throwing so many less effective kinds of pitches and go back to his strength, the sinker."

PITCHING:

Before the 1985 season began, Muke Trujillo was drafted by the Red Sox off the Triple-A roster of the San Francisco Giants. Under the rules of the transaction, Trujillo had to remain with the Red Sox on their major league roster for the entire season or be returned to the Giants' Triple-A club. Some members of the Red Sox management feel he would have been better off pitching every fifth day (as he would have in the minors), but others, Trujillo included, believe that having the opportunity to observe at the big league level and getting a chance to pitch now and then is much more beneficial.

Nonetheless, at times last season he showed he may, one day, develop into a decent pitcher, but there is little question that he needs much more experience.

Trijullo is not overpowering, but he does have a good breaking ball. The biggest thing he has going for him is that he throws strikes.

Like Al Nipper, he has the poise of a veteran, and when he had a chance to pitch on a semiregular basis late in the season, he did a respectable job.

FIELDING:

Trujillo is a good athlete, is quick and showed he is a competent fielder who has excellent reactions on balls hit straight back at him.

MIKE TRUJILLO
RHP, No. 45
RR, 6'1", 180 lbs.
ML Svc: 1 year
Born: 1-12-60 in
Denver, CO

1985 STATISTICS

W	L	ERA	G	GS	CG	SV	IP	H	R	ER	BB	SO
4	4	4.82	27	7	1	1	84	112	55	45	23	19

CAREER STATISTICS

W	L	ERA	G	GS	CG	SV	IP	H	R	ER	BB	SO
4	4	4.82	27	7	1	1	84	112	55	45	23	19

OVERALL:

It was hard to tell just what kind of a pitcher Trujillo can be. He has the confidence and poise that is needed to pitch at the major league level and the hard-work attitude that goes with it. Throwing strikes is going to help him get by.

Robinson: "I only got the chance to see Mike pitch a few times. But he was able to show me a few little things that I liked. He's not going to blow his fastball by anyone, but he certainly looks as though he knows how to pitch. I think he can be the ninth or tenth pitcher on the staff this year."

ED JURAK
INF, No. 22
RR, 6'2", 185 lbs.
ML Svc: 3 years
Born: 10-24-57 in
Los Angeles, CA

HITTING, FIELDING:

Ed Jurak is a utility infielder who has seen less, not more, action in his first three full big league seasons. His number of at-bats per season has decreased from 159 in 1983 to 66 in 1984 to 26 last year. Offensively, his forte has been driving in the runner on third with less than two outs, but his chances to do that were few and far between in 1985.

Jurak makes contact with the ball and hits into right field. He has trouble with outside breaking balls and inside fastballs from both right- and lefthanded pitchers.

Defensively, Jurak is versatile. He can fill in at all four infield positions, but last season, he was called on to play in only 26 games.

OVERALL:

Jurak is a capable fielder anywhere he is asked to play and is a good insurance policy around the infield. He could also step in behind the plate in an emergency.

Robinson: "Eddie is one of those players who can play enough positions to stick with a major league club in a utility role but who does not have the tools to be an everyday player on a good team."

BRUCE KISON
RHP, No. 29
RR, 6'4", 175 lbs.
ML Svc: 14 years
Born: 2-18-50 in
Pasco, WA

PITCHING:

The Red Sox took a chance last season when they signed Bruce Kison as a free agent. The club hoped that the 35-year-old veteran could provide some long relief help, but that was not to be.

Kison suffered several nagging injuries during the year that limited him to just 22 appearances and 92 innings. He ended the season with a record of 5-3 with a 4.11 ERA.

He got off a bad start when he was thrust in to the role of starter by the illness of Al Nipper. Kison was not cut out for the role and did not perform well.

He fared better as a reliever and was able to get hitters out with his off-speed breaking balls.

Kison was not protected on the Red Sox 40-man roster last season, but he was promised an invitation to spring training this season as a non-roster player if he was unsigned by another club.

OVERALL:

Kison is a tenacious, gritty pitcher who has been plagued by back problems for a few seasons. His overall major league record of 115-88 is more impressive than most. He has learned how to pitch with his ailments and is the kind of pitcher that a manager wants to have on his club because he has a never-say-die attitude. His career, however, hangs in the balance.

RICK MILLER
1B/OF, No. 3
LL, 6'0", 180 lbs.
ML Svc: 14 years
Born: 4-19-48 in
    Grand Rapids, MI

HITTING, BASERUNNING, FIELDING:

Rick Miller was an outstanding pinch-hitter for the Red Sox in 1983, when he led the American League with a .457 average and was second in the league with 16 pinch-hits.

He hasn't been as adept at pinch-hitting over the last two years and was used sparingly last season, coming to the plate only 45 times (15 hits). Most of his at-bats came at the end of the season.

Miller was not given the opportunity to play in the field and that bothered him. He felt he had a season or two left in his 37-year-old body and declared himself a free agent at the end of the season.

OVERALL:

Miller's ability to make contact was what made him such a good pinch-hitter in 1983. But he hasn't been getting his bat on the ball the last two years and has struck out a lot. Nevertheless, a lefthanded bat on the bench is always in demand.

Robinson: "Age catches up to all of us. I'm afraid that that is the case with Rick, as well."

CALVIN SCHIRALDI
RHP, No. 40
RR, 6'4", 200 lbs.
ML Svc: 1 year
Born: 6-16-62 in
    Houston, TX

PITCHING, FIELDING:

Calvin Schiraldi was rushed to the major leagues last year when injuries and ineffectiveness began to deplete the pitching staff of the New York Mets.

He showed some encouraging signs, but for the most part, he was a very hittable pitcher. His slider, which is supposed to be his best off-speed pitch, was mediocre last season.

He has developed a curve--perhaps in doing so he has hurt his slider--but it is nothing special. And he just does not have enough movement or velocity on his fastball.

He is not a gifted defensive player and no one is going to ask him to pinch-run. His delivery invites runners to steal. His move is so-so.

OVERALL:

Schiraldi does a little of everything but nothing particularly well.

Snider: "He was a successful pitcher in the minor leagues but does not appear to have the same touch with his slider or his curveball against the more savvy and powerful major league hitters."

DAVE STAPLETON
INF, No. 11
RR, 6'1", 185 lbs.
ML Svc: 6 years
Born: 1-16-54 in
Fairhope, AL

HITTING, BASERUNNING, FIELDING:

Dave Stapleton, the runner-up to Joe Charboneau as the American League Rookie of the Year in 1980, has fallen on hard times. He never fully recovered from a knee injury and the subsequent surgery that limited him to 13 games in 1984.

Last season he appeared in 30 games and only came to the plate 66 times.

The ball does not jump off his bat as it once did and he has trouble with balls high and tight and low and away. He is not the good right field hitter of his healthier years.

As a baserunner, he is absolutely devoid of speed.

In the few games he played at second base in 1985, he acquitted himself well but his knee couldn't stand the wear and tear of playing more than a few games in a row.

OVERALL:

Stapleton will be, at best, a sparely used utility player and his career could be nearing the end.

Robinson: "He was a versatile player at one time, but his knee injury has kept him pretty much out of the lineup and is likely to do so again."

MARC SULLIVAN
C, No. 15
RR, 6'4", 205 lbs.
ML Svc: 1 year plus
Born: 7-25-58 in
Quincy, MA

HITTING, BASERUNNING, FIELDING:

Marc Sullivan was the backup catcher to Rich Gedman and saw little playing time last season. Throughout his minor league career he never was much of a hitter for average, although he did crack out 15 home runs and knock in 63 at Pawtucket in 1984.

Sullivan has trouble with breaking balls and off-speed pitches. He can hit a fastball—but he rarely saw one last season.

He is an excellent defensive catcher with a very strong throwing arm and a quick release. But because Rich Gedman had such a great year and is the ironman type of catcher, Sullivan apppeared in only 32 games. He hit .174 with two home runs and three RBIs.

OVERALL:

Unless Gedman gets hurt, Sullivan can plan on only occasional use to give the first-stringer a rest. But the Sox do not lose anything defensively with him as the backstop.

Robinson: "He has a strong arm but he certainly doesn't seem to be much of a hitter. He has the chance to hit a few home runs, simply because he plays at Fenway Park."

CALIFORNIA ANGELS

HITTING:

Juan Beniquez fits well in the role of a fourth outfielder. He has become a consistent offensive player and has hit better than .300 in each of the last three years. Beniquez does the bulk of his offensive damage against lefthanders (.355 last year and .361 over the last two combined), but has gotten better against righthanders with spot appearances (his .269 in 1985 was 22 points higher than his career average).

Beniquez is still a free-swinger who goes up to the plate ready to attack the first fastball thrown to him. He is beginning to become a bit more selective and has cut down on his strikeouts (47 Ks in 411 at-bats) and has increased his walks (34).

He can make contact and is an excellent hit-and-run candidate. On the advice of teammate Rod Carew, Beniquez developed an inside-out swing that helped him handle breaking pitches better, although when he is in a slump he will still swing wildly at curveballs. He will crowd the plate, hoping that a pitcher will bust him inside, where he can turn on the ball and drive it.

With the development of his inside-out swing, Beniquez also began to drive the ball the opposite way last season which is a big part of why he has become a more consistent average hitter.

Beniquez does not bunt for base hits, although he could open some things up offensively if he did, but he is good at laying down the sacrifice bunt.

BASERUNNING:

Earlier in his career, Beniquez was a good basestealer but he never seemed motivated to really push himself. He has lost some of that speed the last few seasons and is no threat to steal now.

Beniquez does have good instincts as far as taking the extra base and--when he is motivated--will go hard into a base.

FIELDING:

Beniquez is a defensive asset to any

JUAN BENIQUEZ
OF, No. 12
RR, 5'11", 175 lbs.
ML Svc: 13 years
Born: 5-13-50 in
   San Sebastian, DR

1985 STATISTICS

AVG	G	AB	R	H	2B	3B	HR	RBI	BB	SO	SB
.304	132	411	54	125	13	5	8	42	34	47	4

CAREER STATISTICS

AVG	G	AB	R	H	2B	3B	HR	RBI	BB	SO	SB
.273	1264	3995	533	1090	161	29	64	385	285	458	102

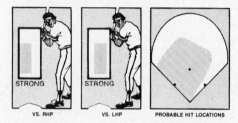

VS. RHP   VS. LHP   PROBABLE HIT LOCATIONS

outfield. Signed as a shortstop in 1969, he made a solid transition to the outfield in 1974, winning a Gold Glove in 1977 when he was with the Texas Rangers.

He can play all three outfield positions and play them well, but at times he gets lazy and will botch routine plays. He has a strong and accurate arm but his mind has a tendency to wander and he throws to the wrong base.

OVERALL:

Over the last couple of seasons, Beniquez has mellowed. The tantrums of his younger days have become history. His new demeanor has made him a valuable asset to the team as a fourth outfielder and as a bat off the bench.

Killebrew: "Beniquez is getting up there in years, but can contribute to a team as a backup outfielder, designated hitter or pinch-hitter. He is doing a better job as a backup than he did when played every day."

HITTING:

Just when it appeared Bob Boone's baseball days were coming to an end, he found the fountain of youth and, at age 37, had a solid season, bouncing back from a career-worst .202 in 1984.

Boone does all the little things that make him an asset at the bottom of the order for the Angels. He has excellent bat control (he has never struck out more than 49 times in a season, and only 35 times last year). He can hit-and-run, give himself up to get runners over and is an excellent bunter. He will surprise with a squeeze bunt--and he will get a piece of the ball no matter where it is thrown in squeeze situations.

He wants to get his bat on the ball-- he spreads out at the plate, trying to get as much coverage as possible. He fights off the inside pitch, looking for a ball he can punch up the middle. He will do damage with the high fastball, but only if the pitch doesn't have much on it. Pitchers try to jam him and then throw breaking balls away, but they will not get him to chase a pure waste pitch.

BASERUNNING:

Boone was never a threat on the bases, even when he was young. He does not take chances and goes only for the sure base. He will go in hard if he gets to the base fast enough to create a problem for the fielder making the relay throw.

FIELDING:

Boone is still one of the best catchers in the game. He is agile, adjusts well to block balls in the dirt and is quick enough with the glove to avoid looking as though he ever gets crossed up by pitches.

Not only does Boone have a strong arm, but he has a quick release and throws on the money. As long as a pitcher gives him a chance, he can throw out any runner. His presence makes most

BOB BOONE
C, No. 8
RR, 6'2", 202 lbs.
ML Svc: 14 years
Born: 11-19-47 in
    San Diego, CA

1985 STATISTICS

AVG	G	AB	R	H	2B	3B	HR	RBI	BB	SO	SB
.248	150	460	37	114	17	0	5	55	37	35	1

CAREER STATISTICS

AVG	G	AB	R	H	2B	3B	HR	RBI	BB	SO	SB
.253	1699	5540	607	1403	240	22	89	653	490	467	31

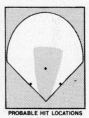

STRONG VS. RHP   STRONG VS. LHP   PROBABLE HIT LOCATIONS

baserunners less aggressive than they would be against a catcher of lesser ability.

Boone anticipates running situations well and calls his own pitch-outs. He is an excellent handler of pitchers; he adjusts his pitch selection to what a pitcher has going well on a particular day. He knows how to nurse a pitcher through the early innings and how to get a pitcher going.

OVERALL:

Defensively, the only knock on Boone is that he doesn't block the plate aggressively. Maybe not, but he keeps himself healthy enough to catch every day despite his age. Having him behind the plate is more important than one dramatic play that knocks him out for a week.

Killebrew: "Boone is an excellent field general. Physically, he has leveled off, but mentally, his skills are as sharp as ever. His offensive production is a bonus."

PITCHING:

Last season, when the Angels needed a quick fix for their pitching rotation down the stretch, they mortgaged the future (again) and got John Candelaria and Al Holland and George Hendrick in return. Candelaria did a strong job--but not strong enough (he won 7 of 10 decisions) but got rocked by Kansas City late in the year.

Candelaria is especially tough on lefthanders because his deceptive three-quarters delivery disguises his pitches. Only 15 of the 161 career home runs he has allowed have been hit by lefthanded batters.

He is a power pitcher who has the rare distinction of also being considered a control pitcher. This is a guy who thought himself a bit on the wild side because he walked 24 batters in 71 innings after joining the Angels last season.

His fastball is consistently in the upper 80s and occasionally breaks the 90 MPH mark. What makes it such a devastating pitch is his late-breaking curveball; it has a tight rotation, and he can get it over for strikes almost all the time.

His fastball tails away from left-handed hitters, which is the reason for his success against them. He will spot his slider to jam righthanded hitters and to set up the fastball.

He has thrown his change-up more and more over the past few seasons and now has enough confidence in the pitch to throw it when he is behind in the count.

Candelaria has a history of back ailments. When he gets in trouble, it usually looks as though his back is bothering him. His pitches get up in the strike zone and he doesn't seem to be bending over smoothly to finish off his delivery.

JOHN CANDELARIA
LHP, No. 45
SL, 6'7", 250 lbs.
ML Svc: 11 years
Born: 11-6-53 in
New York, NY

1985 STATISTICS
W	L	ERA	G	GS	CG	SV	IP	H	R	ER	BB	SO
9	7	3.73	50	13	1	9	125.1	127	56	52	38	100

CAREER STATISTICS
W	L	ERA	G	GS	CG	SV	IP	H	R	ER	BB	SO
131	87	3.16	334	284	46	15	1925	1808	745	675	451	1195

FIELDING:

For a lefthanded pitcher, Candelaria is nonchalant about his move to first. He'll throw over to try and keep a runner close, but he doesn't come with a good move very often and runners can get a good jump on him. He is big and is not always smooth in ending his delivery, but he does a decent job fielding his position. He is slow to cover first.

OVERALL:

Candelaria loves to compete. He was burned out by the no-win situation with the Pirates and it showed in his stats. The move to California got Candelaria going again. He gives the Angels a proven lefthanded starter to complement Geoff Zahn.

Killebrew: "He's a lefthander who knows how to pitch and has four pitches. He was a short-man in Pittsburgh but I believe that he is more suited to a starting role."

HITTING:

The numbers tell the story of Rod Carew, whose final chapters are now being written. After 15 years in a row at or above the .300 level, Carew failed to reach that magical mark for the second straight year, even though he did surpass the 3,000-hit plateau. And when he did hit, he didn't drive the ball the way he once did.

Carew's career has been built on the fact that he is a contact hitter: he uses the whole field. He can put the ball in play no matter what pitch he is thrown--fastball, breaking ball or off-speed pitch--although power pitchers now can overpower him.

Carew once said the key to pitching to him is to "throw the ball down the middle and have the fielders move at the last second to try to get in the way of where I'm going to hit it." Carew has great eye-hand coordination and is constantly making adjustments at the plate; the opposition's defensive alignment has to be ready for anything.

Infielders have to be careful. Carew doesn't bunt as much as he once did, but it is still a big part of his game. He can avoid hurting his batting average by putting a bunt down in a sacrifice situation (which he does on his own) and is not hesitant at all about doing it.

BASERUNNING:

Once a feared basestealer (he was the best at stealing home), Carew really doesn't run much any more. Now, he measures his lead carefully--just to give the pitcher something to think about. He really doesn't run much.

When he does run, it almost looks as if he's gliding. His running style has such an easy appearance that he never looks as though he is going full speed.

FIELDING:

Carew always has complained of being

ROD CAREW
1B, No. 29
LR, 6'0", 180 lbs.
ML Svc: 19 years
Born: 10-1-45 in
Gatun, PAN

1985 STATISTICS
AVG	G	AB	R	H	2B	3B	HR	RBI	BB	SO	SB
.280	127	443	69	124	17	3	2	39	64	47	5

CAREER STATISTICS
AVG	G	AB	R	H	2B	3B	HR	RBI	BB	SO	SB
.328	2469	9315	1424	3053	445	112	92	1015	1018	1028	353

VS. RHP   VS. LHP   PROBABLE HIT LOCATIONS

slighted for his defensive ability. The truth is that he has always been a decent fielder--no more, no less. He has adequate range, but doesn't do much to help out other infielders with their errant throws.

OVERALL:

Probably nothing speaks so clearly about the decline of Carew than the fact that he failed to be selected to the All-Star team last summer for the first time in 19 years.

Killebrew: "He will make changes during the course of a game, not only based on the pitcher but also based on how he is swinging the bat that day.

"As long as he stays healthy he will probably play as long as he wants to."

90+ FASTBALL

PITCHING:

While it was Donnie Moore who got most of the attention for the Angels' rebuilt bullpen last year, Stew Cliburn was the silent partner. Any stopper has to have a solid set-up man, and Cliburn provided just that in his rookie season last year. As well as a 9-3 record, 6 saves and 2.09 ERA, he gave up only 87 hits in 99 innings and struck out 48 while walking 26.

Like Moore, Cliburn relies on power. He is basically a two-pitch pitcher with a fastball that hits near 90 MPH and a hard-breaking slider.

Nothing he throws is straight.

He challenges hitters and will throw inside often enough and hard enough to keep them from crowding the plate and getting too comfortable.

Despite his lack of major league experience, Cliburn never seem intimidated by the surroundings last season, even in the pressure of the late-season pennant race.

If Cliburn is going to develop into more than a set-up man, he will have to come up with--at least--an off-speed pitch. But the Angels might not want to upset the winning formula that the mixture of Cliburn & Moore found so successful last season.

FIELDING:

Cliburn works hard at holding runners close, a necessity for a relief pitcher, who usually comes into a game with men on base. He has a quick move to first and will throw over often. He varies his delivery to the plate to keep runners off balance, giving the catcher an edge in thwarting basestealing threats.

STEW CLIBURN
RHP, No. 33
RR, 6'0", 187 lbs.
ML Svc: 1 year
Born: 12-19-56 in
   Jackson, MS

1985 STATISTICS

W	L	ERA	G	GS	CG	SV	IP	H	R	ER	BB	SO
9	3	2.09	44	0	0	6	99	87	25	23	26	48

CAREER STATISTICS

W	L	ERA	G	GS	CG	SV	IP	H	R	ER	BB	SO
9	3	2.32	45	0	0	6	101	90	28	26	27	49

Cliburn has a quick, easy motion and his follow-through leaves him in a good position to field balls hit back up the middle. He is in control of himself when he has to make a throw and is not afraid to try to get the lead runner in a force situation.

OVERALL:

The Angels are beginning to find out that they can get help from their farm system. Cliburn is another example that young talent can sometimes provide better results than castoffs from other teams.

Killebrew: "He will certainly get better with more experience. He is in a fortunate situation: he has the type of arm which could eventually lead him from the set-up role to that of the stopper, or he could develop an off-speed pitch at some point and try his hand in the starting rotation."

PITCHING:

Doug Corbett's "fastball" is a misnomer. It's consistently in the low 80 MPH range.

As for his breaking pitches, all he has is a big, breaking slider that is flat and usually runs out of the strike zone. It's just a little something he likes to show the hitters.

Corbett doesn't even try to throw a curveball. His only strong pitch other than his sinker is a change-up. He throws it to lefthanded hitters when he is ahead in the count. It runs away from them, but to make it truly effective, Corbett has to be willing to pitch inside more than he has to date. Corbett has been known to experiment with a lot of different pitches, but when it is bottom-line time, he goes back to the sinker.

When he was with the Minnesota Twins (1980-82), the ball had so much sinking action that folks around the American League created a stink that Corbett was doctoring the ball. When he has the sinker going, he gets a lot of ground balls. Hitters, however, have made some adjustments to him. They lay off that pitch, which often sinks out of the strike zone, and force him to bring the ball up. When he does that, it straightens out and he is in trouble. It's easy to see when that time comes because so many balls get hit in the air.

FIELDING:

For a relief pitcher, Corbett's move to first base is below average. He will throw over to first a lot but it doesn't do much good because the move is not de-

DOUG CORBETT
RHP, No. 23
RR, 6'1", 185 lbs.
ML Svc: 6 years
Born: 11-4-52 in
  Sarasota, FL

1985 STATISTICS												
W	L	ERA	G	GS	CG	SV	IP	H	R	ER	BB	SO
3	3	4.89	30	0	0	0	46	49	33	25	20	24

CAREER STATISTICS												
W	L	ERA	G	GS	CG	SV	IP	H	R	ER	BB	SO
20	26	3.03	256	1	0	55	451.1	406	170	152	165	290

ceptive. As a sinkerballer, he knows there a good chance for contact and for the ball to be hit back up the middle. He gets himself in position quickly to field the ball and breaks well for first base.

OVERALL:

His stock has dropped dramatically in his three years with the Angels. He can no longer can be considered a late-inning stopper. All he can be asked to do is come in as a middle reliever against a righthanded-hitting lineup either to try to force the opposing manager to use up his bench or to try and keep the Angels close.

Killebrew: "Corbett's best years are behind him. He does not have the bite in his sinker that he did during his days with the Twins. His control is erratic, he nibbles around the plate and tries to trick the hitters."

HITTING:

Don't give Doug DeCinces a break or he's liable to break open the game. Age and ailments (particularly a bad back) have slowed him down, but he still has that ability to come up with the big hit in a crucial situation. He stands on top of the plate, looking for the pitch away. Pitchers can tie DeCinces up by coming inside: he overreacts to an inside pitch. But if a pitcher leaves the ball out over the plate, he will drive it deep (20 home runs in 120 games last year). He lives off hard stuff, and adjusts to the slider well.

Pitchers have to mix up their pitches to him. Pitching inside puts the idea in his mind to back off the plate-- coming back with breaking pitches and off-speed stuff away might bring the pitcher to an advantage in the count. If DeCinces gets the edge, he will sit on the fastball; if he then gets a fastball down, he will take care of things in a hurry.

Bunting may be a big part of the Angels' game under Gene Mauch but DeCinces is one of the few Angels who isn't asked to play "little ball." The Angels need him for big hits.

BASERUNNING:

When he was young, DeCinces was a below-average runner--and he doesn't move as well now as he used to. There's little threat of DeCinces stealing. He will go for the extra base, but doesn't take too many chances. With his back problems, he knows he can't afford to be too daring.

FIELDING:

DeCinces has the quick reactions a third baseman needs and can charge the slow roller well. When he is healthy, he has above-average range. But when his back problem flares up, his fielding ability is the first place it is noticeable. His movements become stiff and his ability to move quickly to his side disappears.

DOUG DeCINCES
3B, No. 11
RR, 6'2", 195 lbs.
ML Svc: 11 years
Born: 8-29-50 in
    Burbank, CA

1985 STATISTICS
AVG	G	AB	R	H	2B	3B	HR	RBI	BB	SO	SB
.244	120	427	50	104	22	1	20	78	47	71	1

CAREER STATISTICS
AVG	G	AB	R	H	2B	3B	HR	RBI	BB	SO	SB
.262	1372	4835	643	1266	267	26	195	719	496	742	54

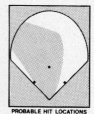

STRONG VS. RHP — STRONG VS. LHP — PROBABLE HIT LOCATIONS

He has a strong and accurate arm. The Angels have kicked around the idea of moving him to first base, figuring it might take some of the demand off his back, though that line of reasoning is flawed. Playing first base requires a lot of bending and there is a lot more involvement in the course of a game for a first baseman than there is for a third baseman.

OVERALL:

DeCinces is a solid player (health permitting) who knows what he has to do to win. He has excellent baseball instincts, but still suffers from his early years in Baltimore when he was constantly compared to Brooks Robinson. His long-harbored feelings of inferiority become obvious when he is questioned on his judgment at third base.

Killebrew: "Like so many of the California players, he is not getting any younger and must stay healthy to remain productive."

HITTING:

Aggressive and selective.

Brian Downing will aggressively select almost any pitch from the belt to
his eyes. He attacks pitches--and as
long as they are up, they don't have to
be in the strike zone.

He doesn't swing wildly, however
(last season, he had 78 walks and 60
strikeouts). Pitchers have to be careful in pitching to him. Downing is primarily a fastball hitter, but he is notorious as a guess hitter.

Downing stays on the offensive; he
sets up the pitcher. He will be very patient early in a game, but in the later
innings, if he sees that a pitcher is
giving him first-pitch strikes, Downing
will jump on it in a hurry. With his
aggressive approach, pitchers who have a
good change-up have the most consistent
success with him.

He is quick enough and strong enough
to handle the pitch inside and is disciplined enough to go the other way with
outside pitches.

Downing feels that his open stance
negates the advantage that righthanded
pitchers have against him. Who's to
argue? He hit .265 against lefties last
year and .263 against righthanders. And
when he has to, Downing can put down a
bunt.

BASERUNNING:

In another life, Downing might have
been a kamikaze pilot. He has an all-
or-nothing approach on the bases and
anybody who gets in his way is fair
game. He has average speed, but his
throttle is always open.

He is not a basestealing threat, but
he can be a downright frightening sight
to infielders covering a base.

FIELDING:

What Downing lacks in speed he makes
up for in hustle. Downing has never met

BRIAN DOWNING
LF, No. 5
RR, 5'10", 200 lbs.
ML Svc: 13 years
Born: 10-9-50 in
Los Angeles, CA

1985 STATISTICS											
AVG	G	AB	R	H	2B	3B	HR	RBI	BB	SO	SB
.263	150	520	80	137	23	1	20	85	78	60	5

CAREER STATISTICS											
AVG	G	AB	R	H	2B	3B	HR	RBI	BB	SO	SB
.266	1434	4688	673	1245	208	13	146	639	694	634	36

  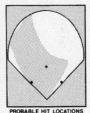

STRONG	STRONG	
VS. RHP	VS. LHP	PROBABLE HIT LOCATIONS

a wall he didn't like and some say the
wall looks worse than Downing does after
he crashes into it.

He is a sure-handed fielder. He comes
up with the ball ready to throw and anticipates the play well when he gets rid
of it, making what is merely average arm
strength get above-average results.

OVERALL:

A lot of people talk about the way
baseball used to be, and Downing reminds
folks how they used to play: always at
full speed, never a fear of injury. He
is a leader by example and has made himself into a legitimate major leaguer after not even making the varsity baseball
team in high school.

Killebrew: "Downing certainly gets
the most out of his ability. He puts up
solid numbers and gives more than a good
effort."

HITTING:

Time may be catching up with Bobby Grich. His average dropped to a career-low .242 in 1985. But he still showed enough ability to be considered an offensive threat.

Grich has made some refinements to his stance over the last couple of years and now hits from a crouch instead of the straight-up stance that had been his trademark. He wraps the bat a bit behind his head and keeps it going in a circular motion waiting for the pitch.

Grich likes the fastball up and over the plate, and when he gets that pitch he will drive it. He has as much power to right-center as he does left-center and is programmed to go that way with everything. Pitchers try to keep the ball down in the strike zone: he takes a lot of low pitches.

He does not chase bad pitches, except an occasional fastball up. Grich can be jammed and has to cheat a little bit on inside pitches. If he isn't guessing inside, he no longer has the bat speed to get around and jerk the ball.

He can bunt, and if he notices the infielders cheating back will at least show the bunt to draw them in and, as a result, open some holes.

BASERUNNING:

Grich gets a good lead off the base but he is not a threat to steal. He wants to get as good a start as possible because, despite his slightly below-average speed, he is an aggressive baserunner with excellent instincts. He is always looking for some type of an edge to try to steal a run and he never backs down from contact. Grich is one of the hardest sliders in the AL.

FIELDING:

There is nothing flashy about Grich—even with a loss of some range over the years he is still one of the more solid defensive second basemen around. He does not move as well as he used to, his left

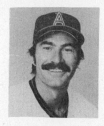

BOBBY GRICH
1B/2B, No. 4
RR, 6'2", 190 lbs.
ML Svc: 15 years
Born: 1-15-49 in
Muskegon, MI

1985 STATISTICS

AVG	G	AB	R	H	2B	3B	HR	RBI	BB	SO	SB
.242	144	479	74	116	17	3	13	53	81	77	3

CAREER STATISTICS

AVG	G	AB	R	H	2B	3B	HR	RBI	BB	SO	SB
.266	1910	6577	991	1749	302	47	215	834	1048	1224	103

  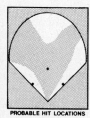

STRONG — VS. RHP   STRONG — VS. LHP   PROBABLE HIT LOCATIONS

or right, but he makes up for that with a great knowledge of how to position himself for hitters and pitches.

He has a strong arm and comes over-the-top on the double play, having maintained the strong throwing mechanics from his early days as a shortstop.

Grich looks for little edges, like blocking the bag on pickoff attempts, and is one of the better infielders at fake-fielding on hit-and-run plays, leaving baserunners confused about what they should do. He has played a bit at third base as well as at first base recently and could find himself playing more of a utility role in the future.

OVERALL:

Grich is not the stellar player he once was, but he still has a win-at-all-costs approach to the game.

Killebrew: "Grich is not afraid to mix it up. He can do all the little things to help a team win. If he stays healthy, he can help a team as a utility infielder who could play often."

HITTING:

Reggie is still a power threat to righthanded pitchers (.267 with 24 home runs in 348 at-bats), but against left-handers, he is a considerably lesser hitter. Last season, he had 112 at-bats against southpaw pitching and hit just .205 with three home runs.

Jackson has made some concessions to Father Time. He is still basically a pull hitter, looking for that awesome home run, but in recent seasons, he has learned to go to left field occasionally to drive the ball deep.

He remains a low-ball hitter and he still loves the hard stuff. Despite all of his experience, Jackson still chases the fastball up and has a hard time catching up to it if the pitch is a good one. Pitchers can make him chase breaking balls, but if he sees a hanging one, well . . . you know what he'll do to it by now.

Jackson will adjust during a game. He'll take his strikeouts, but knows pitchers' patterns and if the pitcher tries to get him the same way twice, Reggie can usually get the edge. He did not move into the number eight spot on the all-time home run list (530) and 16th in RBIs (1601) by missing mistakes.

BASERUNNING:

His power and his personality have always been the most obvious aspects of Jackson's game, but he has been a solid baserunner throughout his career. He is one of only four players who has hit 400 or more home runs and stolen 200 or more bases during his career.

He doesn't run much anymore, but he still likes to surpise a defense. He gets a good lead, looks for the extra base and will do whatever he can to create havoc for the fielders. At times, he does get too aggressive and will get thrown out trying to do too much.

FIELDING:

The most noticeable dropoff in his

REGGIE JACKSON
DH/RF, No. 44
LL, 6'0", 208 lbs.
ML Svc: 19 years
Born: 5-18-46 in
Wyncote, PA

1985 STATISTICS

AVG	G	AB	R	H	2B	3B	HR	RBI	BB	SO	SB
.252	143	460	64	116	27	0	27	85	78	138	1

CAREER STATISTICS

AVG	G	AB	R	H	2B	3B	HR	RBI	BB	SO	SB
.265	2573	9109	1444	2409	437	46	530	1601	1251	2385	225

  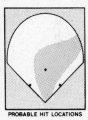

VS. RHP   VS. LHP   PROBABLE HIT LOCATIONS

skills has been in the field. At one time, he was a decent right fielder, but now he is really best suited as a DH. His considerable pride pushes him to fight for a chance to play in the field. He does not move well and his arm is barely adequate. He never has been a good fundamental thrower. Even when he had a strong arm he missed cutoff men and threw to the wrong base.

OVERALL:

Jackson is still very much a contributor. However, he has to accept the fact that is not an everyday big man in the lineup. He grumbles about his reduced role and creates friction in the clubhouse when what he says is caring is interpreted as a selfish attitude.

Killebrew: "Reggie is still a very dangerous hitter--he is just not as consistent as he used to be. Pitchers have to mix things up on him because the threat is there any time Jackson has a bat in his hand. His career is entering its final stage."

HITTING:

For a guy who had nowhere to go just two years ago, Ruppert Jones is now the man everyone wants at their party. He's a platoon left fielder and a lefthanded pinch-hitter, and while his average is not much to speak of, he did hit 21 home runs last year.

Jones likes the ball on the outside portion of the plate. He has disciplined himself and shows just as much power driving the ball to left field as he has pulling it to right. Last season, he hit a home run to left field at Royals Stadium, which is one of the tougher parks in the AL in which to do that.

Jones is an aggressive hitter who goes up to the plate ready to attack the first fastball he sees. Pitchers have to try to keep the ball inside so Jones does not get the full extension of his muscular arms. They then should come back with breaking pitches--preferably down and in.

While his playing has become a part-time affair over the last two years, Jones seems to have become a more valuable player. He has adjusted to the role and has made hitting adjustments that come from knowing what he has to do to get his job done.

Jones has the ability to bunt and, against pitchers who run the ball in on him hard, he might do well to drop the bunt more to bring the infielders in.

BASERUNNING:

When he was younger, Jones was a big basestealing threat (he was the first Seattle Mariner to reach the 20 home runs/20 stolen bases mark). He can still come up with an occasional theft, but he no longer runs as often. When he pushes himself, he is an aggressive baserunner. He is strong and can make life miserable for an infielder trying to make a relay throw.

FIELDING:

Originally a center fielder who

RUPPERT JONES
OF, No. 19
LL, 5'10", 175 lbs.
ML Svc: 10 years
Born: 3-12-55 in
Dallas, TX

1985 STATISTICS

AVG	G	AB	R	H	2B	3B	HR	RBI	BB	SO	SB
.231	125	389	66	90	17	2	21	67	57	82	7

CAREER STATISTICS

AVG	G	AB	R	H	2B	3B	HR	RBI	BB	SO	SB
.252	1120	3830	545	966	186	33	122	502	477	725	131

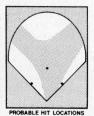

VS. RHP   VS. LHP   PROBABLE HIT LOCATIONS

could go back on the ball with ease, Jones lost one too many battles with an outfield fence; he is now a left fielder--a solid one. He has excellent range for that position as well as a better arm than most left fielders. His throws however, can be erratic and he often bypasses the cutoff man.

OVERALL:

Jones is one of the better part-time lefthanded hitters around. He is a definite power threat and has better-than-average speed.

Killebrew: "Over the past few years, Jones has become a more dangerous hitter than ever. He should get even better as he becomes more comfortable in his new role as pinch-hitter. He keeps himself in good shape and always hustles."

PITCHING:

Manager Gene Mauch is not known for his patience with young pitchers. Yet last season, the Angels were forced to give a lot of youngsters a chance (there were a total of seven rookie pitchers who were on the roster at different points). Urbano Lugo was the one who was given the least opportunity to show what he could do.

But then, Lugo was the least intimidating of the group, although he had been a winner at every level in the minor leagues. His fastball is average. He has a curveball that is average as well as an average slider. Lugo can throw a change-up, but it is nothing special.

So, what is it with this kid?

A forkball. With good control.

He keeps the pitch down and can move it in and out. He is not going to get a lot of strikes, but the infield will be busy all day long with ground balls.

When Lugo gets in trouble, it is because he is getting wild with the placement of the forkball. However, it does not necessarily mean that he is not throwing strikes--it's just that the quality of his strikes is debatable. He will get the ball up and right over the middle of the plate. Because he doesn't throw hard, hitters are able to drive a pitch like that far. Lugo cannot afford any mistakes.

Last season, he pitched well as both a starter (one complete game in ten starts) and as a reliever. With the type of stuff he has, Lugo's main use out of the bullpen is as a long man. He can come into a game and keep it close. He cannot, however, come in with a big jam and get the strikeout to put an end to the rally.

Like a lot of young pitchers who do not have overpowering stuff, Lugo does not pitch inside as often as he needs to in order to keep hitters honest. He cannot survive pitching away. Hitters will

URBANO LUGO
RHP, No. 18
RR, 6'0", 185 lbs.
ML Svc: 1 year
Born: 8-12-62 in
Caracas, VEN

1985 STATISTICS
W	L	ERA	G	GS	CG	SV	IP	H	R	ER	BB	SO
3	4	3.69	20	10	1	0	83	86	36	34	29	42

CAREER STATISTICS
W	L	ERA	G	GS	CG	SV	IP	H	R	ER	BB	SO
3	4	3.69	20	10	1	0	83	86	36	34	29	42

lean over the plate and watch for what he offers on the outside corner.

FIELDING:

Lugo's heart does not appear to be into the fielding aspects of the game: his move to first base is only adequate. He does an acceptable job of fielding his position, though he does need to work at getting into a better position more quickly after his follow-through.

OVERALL:

Lugo is the type of pitcher a manager has to have faith in. He is not going to make a big impression by overpowering hitters, but he has shown he can get hitters out if he gets regular work.

Killebrew: "Lugo could use some more experience and I wouldn't be surprised if he begins this season in the minor leagues. Because he has to be so accurate with his forkball, he needs to develop better concentration and more command of his repertoire. He has definitely indicated his abilities to pitch at the major league level, but he is not completely ready just yet."

PITCHING:

Kirk McCaskill is a true diamond in the rough. He showed signs of his potential last year, but had trouble maintaining consistency. But then, until April of 1984, McCaskill wasn't sure he even wanted to play baseball. Having quit the Angels (after being signed out of high school) to play pro hockey, he bought out his own contract with the Winnipeg Jets of the NHL in the spring of 1984 and returned to California.

The Angels are glad he did. Despite his limited experience, he found himself as a regular member of the Angels' rotation in 1985 and tied Mike Witt for the Angels' lead in complete games with six.

McCaskill promises to do nothing but get better with experience and the consistency that should come with it. He has the raw ability that made the Angels comfortable with him in 1985 after they suffered through his growing pains the year before.

McCaskill's fastball is consistently in the upper 80 MPH range and has outstanding movement. He will run it in to righthanded hitters and away from lefthanded hitters. He also has a slider that makes a late--but not very hard--break.

What McCaskill needs is some refinement in his curveball--it has a tendency to flatten out. He also would benefit from a change-up, which would set up his hard stuff. He needs to become more confident with pitching inside to lefthanded hitters.

As impressive as any aspect of his performance in his rookie season last year was the way he maintained his composure. He does not panic in tight situations and when he gets knocked around, he leaves it behind; he does not allow a beating to effect his next outing. He has the type of confidence that big winners have to have.

KIRK McCASKILL
RHP, No. 15
RR, 6'1", 195 lbs.
ML Svc: 1 year
Born: 4-9-61 in
  Burlington, VT

| 1985 STATISTICS | | | | | | | | | | | | |
W	L	ERA	G	GS	CG	SV	IP	H	R	ER	BB	SO
12	12	4.70	30	29	6	0	189.2	189	105	99	0	0

| CAREER STATISTICS | | | | | | | | | | | | |
W	L	ERA	G	GS	CG	SV	IP	H	R	ER	BB	SO
12	12	4.70	30	29	6	0	189.2	189	105	99	0	0

FIELDING:

Remember, McCaskill is a good enough athlete that he was a pro hockey player with just as bright a future in that sport as he has in baseball. He has excellent reactions and has a smooth motion that leaves him in a good position to field the ball. He holds runners fairly well for a young pitcher, though he could still use some more work in that area. With his compact motion, he has a good delivery time to the plate.

OVERALL:

McCaskill has an excellent understanding of how to pitch. Watching him pitch on a regular basis gives one the feeling that he is going to continue to improve during the next couple of years and will eventually become a big strike-out pitcher.

Killebrew: "He's just a young guy, but McCaskill doesn't run scared. He takes it right to the hitters and has poise and confidence in his ability. He has already had the experience of being in a pennant race, which is will help in his development."

HITTING:

Darrell Miller has taken advantage of the opportunities that have been offered him. With only 48 plate appearances in 51 games for the Angels, he hit .394 against lefthanders and .333 against righthanders. He is versatile enough that it would seem likely that he will have the chance to see more playing time this season.

Miller is an aggressive hitter and goes up to the plate swinging at the first pitch with the hope that it will be a fastball. Pitchers try to keep him off balance with breaking balls and change-ups. They come inside with the fastball, but Miller has a quick enough bat to react and handle that pitch. He will chase the ball away, but if the pitch is not far enough away, he can drive it to the opposite field.

For an inexperienced player, he shows good discipline and a sharp realization of what he has to do to stay in the big leagues.

BASERUNNING:

For a catcher of his size, Miller has surprising speed, a byproduct of his overall athletic excellence. He is not afraid to steal a base when he is given the green light. He gets a good lead and is an aggressive player who pushes himself to take the extra base. Miller slides hard and looks for the chance to break up the double play.

FIELDING:

One of the keys to Miller's major league future is his versatility. He is average to better-than-average at three positions: right field, first base and catching. Miller gave up catching for a couple of years in the minors because of a sight problem that was taken care of by corrective lenses.

He is fairly agile for a big man and will get better if he gets more playing time. His arm is above average, but his

DARRELL MILLER
C, No. 32
RR, 6'2", 200 lbs.
ML Svc: 1 year plus
Born: 2-26-59 in
    Washington, D.C.

1985 STATISTICS

AVG	G	AB	R	H	2B	3B	HR	RBI	BB	SO	SB
.375	51	48	8	18	2	1	2	7	1	10	0

CAREER STATISTICS

AVG	G	AB	R	H	2B	3B	HR	RBI	BB	SO	SB
.280	68	89	13	25	2	1	2	8	5	19	0

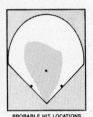

VS. RHP VS. LHP PROBABLE HIT LOCATIONS

footwork on throwing out baserunners needs a little more work. He has good range at first base, and the soft hands of a catcher are an asset on his coming up with throws in the dirt. Miller moves well in the outfield and has a strong and accurate arm.

OVERALL:

Athletic ability runs in his family. Brother Reggie plays basketball at USC and sister Cheryl was an All-American basketball player at UCLA. Darrell is no slouch either. An even bigger attribute than his physical ability is his attitude. Miller has a bubbly personality and is a positive thinker.

Killebrew: "For a young player who is having to adapt to a very limited role, Miller has an outstanding attitude. He is not afraid to put out the extra effort. He is ticketed as a backup player, but could be better with more playing time."

CALIFORNIA ANGELS

PITCHING:

Before the 1985 season began, a desperate situation was unfolding in the Angels' bullpen. It was practically empty. They took a gamble and selected Donnie Moore from Atlanta as compensation for having lost free agent Fred Lynn. They hit the jackpot. More than any other player, Moore was the reason the Angels were a factor in the divisional title race into the final weekend.

Moore flourished as the late-inning workhorse for California. He set a club record for saves in a single season—31 (6 more than he had over 5 major league seasons).

He goes right after hitters and challenges them with a legitimate big league fastball. His fastball is consistently in the upper 80 MPH range and occasionally gets faster. The pitch also has excellent movement and stays low, which makes it tough for hitters to make solid contact.

Moore will come inside to righthanded and lefthanded hitters; just to keep the batters honest, he will also mix in a breaking ball (which is a blend of a slider and a curve) and a change-up from time to time. When the game is on the line, however, there is only one pitch on everyone's mind: the heater.

Moore has the perfect makeup for a short reliever: he gets loose in a hurry, can pitch often (with 65 appearances, he was in 21 games more than any other Angel pitched) and he throws strikes. Perhaps his best quality, however, is that the tighter the jam, the tougher he gets.

Last season, he allowed only 91 hits in 103 innings and had better than a 3-to-1 strikeouts-to-walks ratio (striking out 72 and walking 21), indicating that he did little to contribute to whatever problems already existed when he came into the game.

DONNIE MOORE
LHP, No. 37
LR, 6'0", 185 lbs.
ML Svc: 8 years
Born: 2-13-54 in
Lubbock, TX

1985 STATISTICS

W	L	ERA	G	GS	CG	SV	IP	H	R	ER	BB	SO
8	8	1.92	65	0	0	31	103	91	28	22	21	72

CAREER STATISTICS

W	L	ERA	G	GS	CG	SV	IP	H	R	ER	BB	SO
32	31	3.72	286	4	0	59	524.2	562	248	217	143	324

FIELDING:

Moore has a quick move to first base and to second base as well, keeping runners from getting a big jump. He will throw over a lot, but never loses his concentration on the batter. He falls off the mound a little on his follow-through, but regains his balance quickly and has that initial quickness necessary to field his position or break to first base.

OVERALL:

It is hard to imagine Moore getting much better, although the suddenly economy-minded Angels want him to prove his consistency by repeating his success this season before they will unlock the bank for him.

Killebrew: "For ten years, Donnie has bounced around the majors. He has come into his own over the last two seasons. He has developed a good knowledge of pitching and has the poise and bear-down attitude of a good short man. Everything will pay off for him if he keeps himself in shape and maintains the level of success he had in 1985."

HITTING:

Gary Pettis' greatest asset is his speed. But to make it work for him, he has to work harder to make contact. A slap-and-run hitter, Pettis struck out 125 times last year, giving him 240 Ks in two full major league seasons. He walked only 62 times last season, making it impossible for him to outrun his swings and misses.

His hitting did pick up a bit last year. His overall average rose 30 points over his 1984 figure. He had almost identical increases from both sides, raising his average to .242 as a left-handed hitter and to .293 as a righty.

Pettis likes the ball up from the right side, but is a low-ball hitter lefthanded. He will do his damage on fastballs out over the plate. Pettis is not strong enough to handle the fastball in on his fists, especially from right-handed pitchers who can overpower him.

Lefthanders do their damage against Pettis with breaking balls, especially if they change speeds. What Pettis can do as well as anyone in the AL is bunt. It is a tool of speed and he recognizes that. He gets sacrifice bunts, but even in those situations Pettis is looking to leg them out for hits.

BASERUNNING:

Pettis is a legitimate threat once he reaches base. He can quickly take advantage of any infielder who gets lax in fielding what should be a routine ground ball. Pettis always goes at full speed, stretching base hits and taking the extra base, but he is too frail to slide too hard into a base. He creates havoc when he is on first. Not only does he get a good lead, but he reads pitchers well.

Pettis has 41 stolen bases against righthanders on the mound, but he is not intimidated by lefties. He was 15 for 16 stealing bases with a southpaw working last year.

FIELDING:

Pettis already has reached a point

GARY PETTIS
CF, No. 20
SR, 6'1", 159 lbs.
ML Svc: 3 years
Born: 4-3-58 in
   Oakland, CA

1985 STATISTICS

AVG	G	AB	R	H	2B	3B	HR	RBI	BB	SO	SB
.257	125	443	67	114	10	8	1	32	62	125	56

CAREER STATISTICS

AVG	G	AB	R	H	2B	3B	HR	RBI	BB	SO	SB
.247	297	930	154	230	23	17	7	68	129	257	112

VS. RHP   VS. LHP   PROBABLE HIT LOCATIONS

where other center fielders are being compared to him. He plays shallow, cutting off a lot of balls that would otherwise drop in for hits. He goes back on the ball exceptionally well. He has that ability to leap at the fence to rob hitters of home runs. He fills the gaps well on line drives to the alleys.

Pettis has that instinctive ability to make diving and sliding catches. He is, however, intimidated by artificial surfaces, afraid of balls getting by him or bouncing over his head.

Pettis has a stronger arm than would be expected from a speedy center fielder. He also helps himself by getting rid of the ball quickly.

OVERALL:

Killebrew: "The more Pettis hits and the less often he strikes out, the better player he will become. He is already as good a center fielder as there is in the American League."

PITCHING:

Ron Romanick took a lot of heat for the falling Angels in the final days of the 1985 season. He won just once after July 31. After the season, the club discovered he had been pitching with a broken bone in his foot during the final two months of the season. Despite all the moaning, Romanick did wind up tied for the Angels' lead with six complete games, and his 14 victories were one short of staff-leader Mike Witt.

Romanick is one of the bright young hopes for the future of the Angels. He is a quality pitcher who is not overpowering but who has four legitimate major league pitches and will throw any of them at any time.

A hitter shouldn't be surprised if Romanick sneaks in a 3-2 change-up. What makes his pitches even more effective is that Romanick uses virtually the same overhand motion for all of them. He could help himself by being more assertive with his fastball. At times he will run it up to 88 MPH, but in general, it comes in at an average speed (around 85).

He can spot his fastball for strikes and get ahead in the count with it, then come in with a curveball, which will break down and away from a righthanded hitter, and come back with the slider that breaks across and down to them. He needs to run his fastball in on lefthanded hitters more to keep them more honest.

He does have a tendency to tire in the late innings. When that happens, Romanick gets wild in the strike zone. He pays the price by giving up home runs --he gave up a team-high 29 last year.

FIELDING:

Romanick is a good athlete with a

RON ROMANICK
RHP, No. 37
RR, 6'4", 195 lbs.
ML Svc: 2 years
Born: 11-6-60 in
 Burley, ID

1985 STATISTICS

W	L	ERA	G	GS	CG	SV	IP	H	R	ER	BB	SO
14	9	4.11	31	31	6	0	195	210	101	89	62	64

CAREER STATISTICS

W	L	ERA	G	GS	CG	SV	IP	H	R	ER	BB	SO
26	21	3.92	64	64	14	0	424.2	450	208	185	123	151

smooth motion. As a result, he is able to compensate for his not-so-sharp reflexes by being in a good position to field balls hit back at him.

He maintains his composure well and does not let baserunners bother him, even though his move to first can be best described as adequate. The move is something he needs to work on to improve his success.

OVERALL:

In Romanick, Kirk McCaskill and Mike Witt, the Angels have three of the top young righthanded pitchers in the AL. All three pitchers have durable arms and plenty of potential. Romanick needs to be a little more aggressive, which is something that should come from his successes over the past two seasons.

Killebrew: "The more he pitches, the better he will get. He is a smart young pitcher who has a strong arm and four good pitches--what more could you want?"

PITCHING:

So much ability, so little consistency, so many disappointments. The life and times of Luis Sanchez, the one-time Angels' hope as a stopper who has turned into more of an igniter of disaster.

The ability is there. This is a fellow who can come into a game and show the kind of stuff that overpowers hitters. He has an 88-90 MPH fastball with excellent movement down in the strike zone. It can be tough for the catcher to catch even when he knows what's coming, much less for a hitter to try to hit. Sanchez also has an awesome slider: it's hard and breaks late, giving the impression that it's a fastball before it takes off. It is a great pitch for him to run in on the hands of left-handers to keep them from leaning over the plate.

Sanchez has been fooling around with a forkball which, if he could refine it, would be an excellent off-speed pitch.

The problem with Sanchez is that he cannot harness all of his ability. He does not seem to have the kind of drive that a stopper needs to finish off a hitter; he lacks the killer instinct. It has put the brakes on his development. This is a pitcher with more career victories (28) than saves (27), despite the fact he has started only one game in his four major league seasons.

When he gets in trouble, he seems to retreat instead of going after hitters. When mistakes are made with him on the mound--whether they are fielding errors or umpires' calls that he questions--he falls apart. He starts to aim the ball and takes something off his pitches, that "something" being velocity and movement.

He doesn't come inside enough to keep hitters honest. And because he does not have that nail-'em-in-the-box attitude, his best role is in long relief. In long

LUIS SANCHEZ
RHP, No. 40
RR, 6'2", 215 lbs.
ML Svc: 5 years
Born: 8-24-53 in
Cariaco, VEN

1985 STATISTICS
W	L	ERA	G	GS	CG	SV	IP	H	R	ER	BB	SO
2	0	5.72	26	0	0	2	61.1	67	41	39	27	34

CAREER STATISTICS
W	L	ERA	G	GS	CG	SV	IP	H	R	ER	BB	SO
28	21	4.04	194	1	0	27	370	371	179	166	145	361

relief, he can keep the game within striking distance, place the peg and then hand over the hammer.

FIELDING:

Sanchez doesn't do the little things that a short-relief pitcher needs to do to help himself out of jams. His move to first base is average, at best. When a menacing runner is on base, he will throw over a lot, but he has a tendency to be wild with his throws. He fields his position fairly well, but once he catches the ball, the problems start again. He does not always throw to the right base, and he hurries his throws.

OVERALL:

The time has come for Sanchez to start taking command of his ability, or else he might find his time in the big leagues coming to an end. He has plenty of raw talent.

Killebrew: "He has a great arm, but seems to be a slow learner. Sanchez finds a way to beat himself in a tight situation. If he is going to make himself into a pitcher, the time is now."

HITTING:

Dick Schofield has been a big disappointment with the bat. As an amateur and in the minor leagues, he showed signs of being an exceptional offensive player: he would yank the fastball inside down the line, go up the middle with the off-speed pitch and drive the slider away to the opposite field. He was always right on the ball. In the major leagues, however, he has been completely overmatched.

How overmatched, you say? Well, last year's .219 average was considered a big improvement; it represented a 26-point increase from 1985.

Schofield is not going to be a home run hitter. He has to cut down on his stroke, be selective and make contact (70 strikeouts and only 35 walks) so he can get on base for other hitters to drive in. Right now, pitchers are just overpowering him in a predictable way—fastballs on the fists and breaking pitches away. His inability to connect in the big leagues puzzles scouts who remember him from the minors.

Schofield needs to relax at the plate and do the things that got him to the big leagues. It sounds trite, but it is true in his case.

One hitting skill which Schofield has maintained is his ability to bunt. He is excellent in sacrifice situations and is also capable of bunting for a base hit.

BASERUNNING:

He has excellent baserunning technique: he gets a good jump and knows when to steal a base because he reads the pitcher's move so well. Schofield slides hard and hustles for extra bases.

FIELDING:

With all of his trouble at the plate, Schofield showed a maturity in the field that earned the respect of the Angels' brass.

DICK SCHOFIELD
SS, No. 22
RR, 5'10", 176 lbs.
ML Svc: 3 years
Born: 11-21-62 in
    Springfield, IL

1985 STATISTICS											
AVG	G	AB	R	H	2B	3B	HR	RBI	BB	SO	SB
.219	147	438	50	96	19	3	8	41	35	70	11

CAREER STATISTICS											
AVG	G	AB	R	H	2B	3B	HR	RBI	BB	SO	SB
.206	308	892	93	184	31	6	15	66	74	157	16

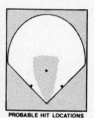

STRONG — VS. RHP   STRONG — VS. LHP   PROBABLE HIT LOCATIONS

He is as sure-handed as any shortstop in the American League. He has good initial reactions and plays hitters well. His range is average, which is plenty good on natural grass. What he lacks in arm strength, Schofield makes up for with a quick release and accuracy. He has the instinctive ability to go back on pop-ups well, including ranging into foul territory.

OVERALL:

Schofield will only get better once he settles down with the bat. He is young enough that it is reasonable to expect him to become more of an offensive force. His glove already is good enough to keep him in the big leagues.

Killebrew: "For now, his defense will carry him. If his bat comes around, he could become one of the top shortstops in the league."

PITCHING:

Jim Slaton is the Angels' Mr. Fixit. When the club has a problem with the pitching staff, Slaton gets the call. He is capable in both middle relief and spot-starting roles. In fact, he was one of the Angels' most consistent starters in late August before they picked up John Candelaria and Slaton went back to the bullpen.

There's nothing really special about the way Slaton goes about his job. He has a normal motion and just an average fastball, but he is able to spot his fastball very well.

Slaton has a short, quick curveball, which he must get over to be effective, and a quick-breaking slider that moves away from righthanded hitters. He also throws a straight change-up. When one of those pitches deserts him, Slaton is in trouble. He cannot get by on his fastball alone.

As well as keeping the ball down, he has to consistently come inside, off the plate, to keep hitters from sitting on the outside corner. If he gets the plate when he comes inside, he'll start to get hit because he doesn't have enough velocity to sneak the ball past hitters.

The key to Slaton is his willingness to pitch often and in any situation. He never claims to be tired, even though his career was once in jeopardy because of a small tear in the rotator cuff. He has a short, easy motion that limits the wear on his arm.

FIELDING:

As a fielder, Slaton does all the little things to help himself. He has a quick move to first base and will shorten his delivery with runners on base to

JIM SLATON
RHP, No. 47
RR, 6'0", 192 lbs.
ML Svc: 15 years
Born: 6-19-50 in
Long Beach, CA

1985 STATISTICS											
W	L	ERA	G	GS	CG	SV	IP	H	R	ER	BB	SO
6	10	4.37	29	24	1	1	148.1	162	82	72	63	60

CAREER STATISTICS											
W	L	ERA	G	GS	CG	SV	IP	H	R	ER	BB	SO
147	152	4.28	460	348	86	12	239.1	2642	1265	1138	964	1148

give the catcher some help. Slaton will throw over to first a lot and if a runner gets lax, he will pick him off.

He reacts quickly on balls hit up the middle, moving well to both his left and right. He does not get flustered in pressure situations and will go after the lead runner. He gets off the mound in a hurry when it's necessary to either cover first base or field a bunt.

OVERALL:

Slaton can be a bonus on a pitching staff. He has accepted his role and always gives his best effort. Over the last couple of years, however, he has created some problems for himself by nibbling too much and getting behind in the count.

Killebrew: "Since his arm injury, Slaton doesn't throw as hard, in my opinion, but he makes up for that with his pitch selection and his knowledge of hitters. He is a good competitor, but he might not have enough variation in his pitches."

PITCHING:

At the age of 41, Don Sutton knows all the tricks of pitching and winning. You don't hang around as long as he has without knowing how to make adjustments once time starts to erodes your skills.

Sutton doesn't throw as hard as he once did, but he changes speeds on all of his pitches and throws strikes. He may not be in the upper 80s anymore, but he can keep hitters off balance and he can get strikeouts (he holds the major league record of 20 years in a row with 100 or more strikeouts each season).

A big pitch for Sutton is his curve-ball. It has a tight rotation and an excellent break--it's the pitch he turns to in a time of need. He also has a bit of a slider, but only shows that to keep the hitters alert.

As important as any part of Sutton's repertoire is the mind games he plays with opposing hitters. He is suspected--and rightfully so--of scuffing the ball a lot, creating an abnormal change in the direction of his pitches. Any time he gets extra movement on a pitch, the head games have begun and the hitters start complaining.

With the loss of his natural stuff, Sutton can get into trouble in a hurry when he gets his pitches up or when he can't throw his curveball for strikes. His pitches become especially hittable, and the screws on Sutton tighten when he has to turn to his not-so-fast fastball.

Sutton has no difficulty coming inside to move hitters off the plate; he knows he has to establish the outside corner as his domain if he is going to be successful. Hitters get so anxious when Sutton comes in on them that they tend to jam themselves.

FIELDING:

Nobody works harder at keeping in top

DON SUTTON
RHP, No. 27
RR, 6'1", 190 lbs.
ML Svc: 20 years
Born: 4-2-45 in
    Clio, AL

1985 STATISTICS

W	L	ERA	G	GS	CG	SV	IP	H	R	ER	BB	SO
15	10	3.86	34	34	1	0	226	221	101	97	59	107

CAREER STATISTICS

W	L	ERA	G	GS	CG	SV	IP	H	R	ER	BB	SO
295	228	3.17	689	672	174	5	4795.2	4210	1866	1690	1223	3315

condition than Sutton and the effort is obvious in his movements on the field. He is fluid and quick. Not only does he field his position well, but he reacts well to situations and can get the lead runner on a force play.

Sutton has a decent move to first base. He has to work at keeping runners close because with all the breaking pitches he throws, if he lets them get too big of a lead, the catcher has no chance to try to throw them out.

OVERALL:

A goal-oriented individual, Sutton has the carrot dangling to keep him in the race for success: 300 wins. He enters this season just five victories short of the coveted level. It is just what a competitor like Sutton needs to push himself to be in top shape and to perform at his highest level.

Killebrew: "Sutton has pitched for 20 years in the big leagues and seems determined to notch 300 wins. He seems to be headed to the Hall of Fame. He might not be as sharp as he once was, but he still knows how to pitch and how to win."

PITCHING:

Mike Witt is the kind of pitcher a team builds a starting rotation around. He is big and strong and he is a winner. For the second year in a row, he led the Angels in victories and strikeouts and this time had the lowest ERA of any starter.

He throws two pitches that leave hitters at wit's end. There is a power-pitcher fastball, which runs well past 90 MPH and which he is able to maintain control of throughout the course of a game. And then there is a curveball that is earning the reputation of being the best in the American League (Reggie Jackson calls Witt's curve a Mercedes Benz).

With the kind of fastball Witt throws no righthanded hitter can hang in comfortably against a Witt curveball. The curveball begins by coming directly at the hitter and then breaks down hard and away from a righthanded hitter. It is a good pitch to lefthanders, too. Witt will start the pitch over the plate to them and then let it break in right on their hands. He also will come inside with his fastball, which is hard enough and has enough movement that it makes lefthanders just as uncomfortable as righthanders.

In the past few years, Witt has added a decent change-up to his pitching bag. This was the pitch he needed for keeping the big swingers off stride.

Witt gets himself in trouble when he gets wild. When he regroups quickly enough, he has the ability to pitch himself out of the jam by getting the big strikeouts. However, he does not regroup fast enough. His concentration tends to wander, which results in his pitches meandering either up in or out of the strike zone.

FIELDING:

A gangly type, Witt does not help

MIKE WITT
RHP, No. 39
RR, 6'7", 192 lbs.
ML Svc: 5 years
Born: 7-20-60 in
   Fullerton, CA

1985 STATISTICS

W	L	ERA	G	GS	CG	SV	IP	H	R	ER	BB	SO
15	9	3.56	35	35	6	0	250	228	115	99	98	180

CAREER STATISTICS

W	L	ERA	G	GS	CG	SV	IP	H	R	ER	BB	SO
53	49	3.71	167	135	29	5	959	927	445	395	351	613

himself out of problems with his movements around the mound. He has an adequate move to first base and normally has a long delivery to the plate. He does, on occasion, speed it up to catch runners off guard, but as a result winds up taking a little bit off his pitches, which can cause problems.

At 6'7", Witt has trouble getting balls hit back toward him on the ground, although he has put in plenty of overtime trying to improve.

OVERALL:

Witt has won 15 games in each of the last two years. Not too shabby, but nowhere near the type of results he is capable of.

Killebrew: "Witt has a good arm and an excellent curveball. To take full advantage of that, though, he has to have better command of his pitches for a longer period of time.

"He needs to become mentally sharp more often. He has the tendency to be extra sharp for a game here and there and then extra loose for weeks at a time."

PITCHING:

Geoff Zahn is one of those veterans who turn pitching into an art. He mixes pitches well, keeps hitters off stride and hits the spots with the precision of a surgeon. The problem last year was that he spent more time being tended to by doctors than he did operating on his own. He was sidelined in late April by tendinitis in his left shoulder and did not return until early August. Sixteen days later, Zahn's season came to a premature conclusion when the tendinitis acted up again.

Even when he is healthy, Zahn is not an overpowering pitcher, but his fastball will surprise some hitters with its velocity. It has become faster in recent seasons and is consistently major league average (85-86 MPH).

Zahn has excellent movement on the pitch and knows he has to pitch inside to righthanded hitters to get the job done. The ball has a sinking action, which helps him get ground ball outs.

Zahn also has both breaking pitches and uses them frequently. He will throw his curveball to righthanded hitters, trying to keep it away from them, and he will wear out the outside corner of the plate with his slider to lefthanders.

The big pitch, though, is his excellent change-up. He will throw it as much as 50% of the time and can do it successfully. It has almost a screwball action, breaking away from righthanded hitters.

Zahn needs to have all his pitches working to be successful. When he begins to get in trouble it is because he does not keep his pitches down. He does not have the velocity to get away with mistakes high in the strike zone. Nor does he have the ability to survive when pitching from behind in the count.

FIELDING:

Zahn is a student of the game who

GEOFF ZAHN
LHP, No. 38
LL, 6'1", 175 lbs.
ML Svc: 11 years
Born: 12-19-46 in
  Baltimore, MD

1985 STATISTICS

W	L	ERA	G	GS	CG	SV	IP	H	R	ER	BB	SO
2	2	4.38	7	7	1	0	37	44	19	18	14	14

CAREER STATISTICS

W	L	ERA	G	GS	CG	SV	IP	H	R	ER	BB	SO
111	109	3.74	304	270	79	1	1848.2	1978	889	769	526	705

does the little things that have helped him hang around for 11 major league seasons with below-average stuff. He has a quick move to first and a quick move to the plate that makes it tough for runners to get a good jump. He moves around the mound well and does not make mistakes fielding or throwing batted balls.

OVERALL:

At age 39 and with the nagging tendinitis problem of a year ago adding to arm problems earlier in his career, Zahn is a major question mark for the Angels. If he's healthy, he can help a team with his knowledge of pitching, but that is a big "if." With his arm problems, Zahn has to be a starter to help a team. He does not loosen up quickly enough or bounce back as soon as he would have to for him to be a reliever.

Killebrew: "You know that when this guy is on top of his game and when he is healthy he can put the ball through the eye of a needle. But he can't even put it in his pocket unless he's healthy. We're just going to have to see if his not-so-young body can recover."

CRAIG GERBER
INF, No. 2
LR, 6'0", 175 lbs.
ML Svc: 1 year
Born: 1-8-59 in
Chicago, IL

HITTING, BASERUNNING, FIELDING:

Late last season, Craig Gerber began to show enough with the bat that he earned some platoon time with Dick Schofield at shortstop. Gerber is a steady lefthanded hitter who goes up to the plate swinging and puts the ball in play (he had only two walks and three strikeouts in 97 plate appearances).

Gerber likes the ball out over the plate. Because of his lack of experience, pitchers would challenge him last year--as a result he saw a lot of fast-balls. This season, however, the seas will get rougher and he is going to have to show he can handle breaking pitches. He is a contact hitter who will hit the ball up the middle. He is also a capable bunter and will drag-bunt for a hit.

On the bases, Gerber shows the typical reactions of a young player afraid to make a mistake. He plays it safe instead of forcing the issue, especially in the area of stealing bases.

Gerber has a quick first step and a good arm. His arm is stronger than Schofield's and allows him to play deeper on artificial surfaces.

OVERALL:

Killebrew: "Gerber was impressive defensively last year. He knows what to do when the ball is hit in his direction. He can do a lot of little things at the plate and will improve further as he begins to feel more comfortable with his big league surroundings."

JERRY NARRON
C, No. 34
LR, 6'3", 195 lbs.
ML Svc: 6 years
Born: 1-15-56 in
Goldsboro, NC

HITTING, BASERUNNING, FIELDING:

Jerry Narron bats lefthanded--and he can catch. That's enough to keep him in the big leagues.

Basically a pull hitter, Narron goes up to the plate looking for a pitch to hit. He doesn't get enough hitting opportunities to be too selective. He has a long swing, and is vulnerable to fast-balls inside. Give him a low fastball, however, and Narron can put a charge in the ball. The long swing also makes it difficult for him to make adjustments to breaking pitches--especially from left-handers--against whom he does not bat very often (only 13 times in 1985).

He knows what to do on the bases and does as much as he can. He is a below-average runner, however, which limits his effectiveness.

As a catcher, Narron has had to overcome a rap from his younger days that he couldn't handle pitchers. As a young player with the Yankees, the word was that Narron always went to the fastball in clutch situations. With the Angels, the pitchers feel comfortable with the way he mixes pitches. He has a rather long throwing motion, but gets good velocity on his throws to second and is average in that area. He adjusts well to the pitches in the dirt.

OVERALL:

They call him Gabby because of his quiet nature. He is the ideal 25th man on a roster. He gives a team insurance as a catcher, first baseman and DH. He never says a discouraging word about a lack of playing time.

GEORGE HENDRICK
RF, No. 15
RR, 6'3", 195 lbs.
ML Svc: 15 years
Born: 10-18-49 in
Los Angeles, CA

HITTING, BASERUNNING, FIELDING:

George Hendrick was part of last year's late-season surprise trade which also sent Al Holland and John Candelaria to the Angels from the Pirates. The Angels surrendered two promising young players for three veterans whose contracts total $2 million per season.

Hendrick was a disappointment; he appeared in only 16 games for the Angels last year (the trade was made on August 2nd), batted 41 times for a .122 average. Before the trade, he had a .230 average in 256 at-bats for the Pirates. His hitting has been declining steadily since he hit .318 with the Cardinals in 1983. Previously known as a good clutch hitter and one of the game's best wrist hitters, Hendrick did not get many clutch opportunities while he was with the woeful Pirates last season and his bat was non-existent with the Angels.

He is a low fastball hitter who, when he is going well, can really take a good crack at the ball and land a good share of doubles.

On the bases, he is adequate, though he is slow out of the batter's box.

When Hendrick sets his mind to it, he still can be an above-average right fielder. His interest in hustling, however, seems to fluctuate.

OVERALL:

This season, Hendrick may shake off the complacency which set in while he was with the Pirates. He is playing close to home (he is a native of LA) and pursued an off-season workout program, which may indicate that he is ready to assume an everyday role in 1986.

AL HOLLAND
LHP, No. 19
RL, 5'11", 210 lbs.
ML Svc: 6 years
Born: 8-16-52 in
Roanoke, VA

PITCHING, FIELDING:

Along with John Candelaria and George Hendrick, Al Holland was traded to the California Angels from the Pirates on August 2nd last year. Holland began the 1985 season with the Phillies, who might have been more sympathetic to his loss of velocity off his fastball, shaky control and poor mechanics had he not reported overweight to spring training.

Holland is basically a one-pitch power pitcher, so when he is having trouble with his money pitch, that's about it; he has nothing to show if not the high, hard heat. He has a very aggressive, mucho macho approach to pitching.

Last season, he was falling into the bad habit of not picking up his target early enough; as a result, his location and velocity were off. He has to pick his head up early in his delivery to get proper synchronization.

The Angels were hoping that Holland would pair up nicely with Donnie Moore to give them a powerful lefty/righty bullpen combo. But Holland appeared in 15 games after the trade and was unable to rack up even one save. His ERA with the Angels was 1.48, he walked 10 batters and struck out 14 in 24.1 innings.

Holland is a big man, does not field well and concentrates on the hitter to the point where he forgets about the runners on base.

OVERALL:

Holland has always been one of the game's more colorful characters. If he can pitch this season the way he did in parts of 1984 and all of 1983, opponents could consider leaving the park after the seventh inning.

DARYL SCONIERS
1B, No. 6
LL, 6'2", 199 lbs.
ML Svc: 5 years
Born: 10-3-58 in
    San Bernardino, CA

HITTING, BASERUNNING, FIELDING:

Daryl Sconiers has had to wait so long for his chance in the big leagues that it is questionable whether he will ever have the opportunity to take a crack at a major league job. In the minors, he had a reputation for his quick wrists, which enabled him to drive the ball to any part of the field. His development was slowed last year by a combination of personal problems (he went through a chemical-dependency program) and injuries that limited his playing time to 98 at-bats.

Sconiers is a free-swinger who makes contact. He has a long swing that gets him jammed when power pitchers come inside on him.

Once a quick runner, Sconiers has been slowed by knee problems that leave him average, at best. His instincts on the bases are below average and he does not take advantage of opportunites to take the extra base. He forces plays on the bases when he simply has no chance of winning.

In the field, Sconiers isn't afraid of any ball hit in his direction; he will do whatever he can to knock it down. But he knocks too many down instead of fielding them smoothly. He also is slow in reacting to making throws either to first base or second base. His real future in the majors is as a DH.

OVERALL:

Killebrew: "He has a very live bat and can hit, but the inactivity and his personal problems may have taken a toll on him."

ROB WILFONG
2B, No. 9
LR, 6'1", 185 lbs.
ML Svc: 9 years
Born: 9-1-53 in
    Pasadena, CA

HITTING, BASERUNNING, FIELDING:

Rob Wilfong is the epitome of manager Gene Mauch's game of "little ball." Wilfong loves to bunt and is capable of putting the ball down at any time (in his limited role last year, he had eight sacrifices; with Minnesota in 1979, he had 22 bunt-hits). That's his only real threat with the bat, however. He never has been much of a threat to drive the ball.

As a part-time player, Wilfong becomes overly aggressive and swings at too many pitches. His best shot for a hit is a mediocre fastball up. Pitchers can knock the bat out of his hands. He is completely baffled by lefthanders, who bamboozle him with breaking pitches.

Wilfong's knowledge of the game and aggression on the bases makes him an above-average runner despite average speed. He gets a good lead and when he sees the opportunity, he will steal a base. He looks for the extra base running from first on a base hit and is not afraid of contact when he goes into a base.

"Steady" is the best way to describe Wilfong in the field. He doesn't have much range, but he catches what he gets to and makes the accurate throw. He turns the double play well, although his arm strength sometimes is a problem.

OVERALL:

Killebrew: "Wilfong is definitely a Gene Mauch-type of player. He is more aggressive against righthanded pitchers and doesn't make mistakes that cost a team a game."

CHICAGO WHITE SOX

HITTING:

When Harold Baines steps up to the plate at Comiskey Park, fans begin their rhythmic chant, "Har-old! Har-old! Har-old!" What these knowledgeable fans are doing is "Har-olding" the coming of a superstar. But when, oh when, will the rest of baseball finally realize it?

How many more years will Baines have to hit .309 and drive in 113 runs before he is recognized as one of the game's best hitters? Baines will become 27 years old shortly before the start of the 1986 season, yet he has already put in six full seasons in the majors. Over the last four seasons, his RBI totals have read: 105, 99, 94 and 113, respectively. Further, he has hit more than 20 home runs each year and raised his batting average consistently.

Baines' phlegmatic manner with the press may forever hide his light from fans outside Chicago, but every pitcher in the American League knows what he's up against.

Although he can pull the ball with enormous power, Baines has learned to think "left field." For the past several years, Baines has been following the hitting principles taught by the late Charlie Lau: stay back on the ball, drive the outside pitch to left field and become much more patient at the plate.

Baines is a low-ball hitter, although against lefties, he likes the ball up. Lefthanders used to tie him in knots with breaking stuff, but Baines is a very smart cookie. Lefthanders can't handcuff him any longer.

Pitchers will try to establish the inside part of the plate and then try to get him to chase breaking balls down and away. Righthanders will throw the fastball up. When Baines is hot, however, nothing gets him out. He is usually a slow starter and gets hot with the bat sometime in June.

BASERUNNING:

Baserunning is not a Baines strength.

HAROLD BAINES
RF, No. 3
LL, 6'2", 189 lbs.
ML Svc: 6 years
Born: 3-15-59 in Easton, MD

1985 STATISTICS

AVG	G	AB	R	H	2B	3B	HR	RBI	BB	SO	SB
.309	160	640	86	198	29	3	22	113	42	89	1

CAREER STATISTICS

AVG	G	AB	R	H	2B	3B	HR	RBI	BB	SO	SB
.285	847	3184	420	908	153	36	119	501	225	450	27

VS. RHP

VS. LHP

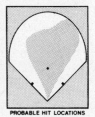

PROBABLE HIT LOCATIONS

He does not get a good lead. He has recorded only one stolen base in each of the past two seasons.

FIELDING:

At one time, it appeared as though Baines would be as sound a defensive right fielder as there is in the game. It doesn't look that way now. He has not quite mastered the knack of breaking back on fly balls.

OVERALL:

Baines is a quiet superstar who has not earned the public acclaim he deserves. He is one of the best in the game.

Killebrew: "Harold is the 'big play' man. He is the one who will beat you when the game is on the line. The best part about him is that I believe that he is going to get even better. He has not reached his peak just yet."

PITCHING:

Throughout Floyd Bannister's entire career, greatness, like a mirage, has loomed in the distance. But just before he gets there, it vanishes.

In nine seasons he has had just two winning records. He averages barely ten wins a year. Yet, many continue to consider him an outstanding pitching prospect. On the other hand, there are many hard-line baseball people who would have sent him back to the rock pile long ago.

He has been a very tempting guy to hang onto. He has a 90 MPH tailing fastball, which he throws from straight over-the-top with a delivery as smooth as cream from a pitcher. He has a biting slider, an exploding curve and a good straight change.

Each season, Bannister is near the head of the list in total strikeouts, testimony to the quality of his pitches. In general, he has good control. How does a guy like this post such an ugly 4.87 ERA?

The problem lies in his heart and in his ears. He won't pitch inside and he won't listen to advice. He continually falls short of expectations because he won't take the plate back from the hitter. No matter how many times he hears how great his stuff is, he has no confidence in his pitches.

Bannister gets much too fine with his pitches: it causes him to lose control and he finds himself looking at a home run smashed over the fence.

For three years, Carlton Fisk has tried in vain to convince Bannister that he does not need to use all of his pitches on a given night. Bannister will not listen and seems thick as a brick on the point.

FIELDING:

Bannister is an excellent fielder. He

FLOYD BANNISTER
LHP, No. 24
LL, 6'1", 193 lbs.
ML Svc: 9 years
Born: 6-10-55 in
  Pierre, SD

1985 STATISTICS

W	L	ERA	G	GS	CG	SV	IP	H	R	ER	BB	SO
10	14	4.87	34	34	4	0	210.2	211	121	114	100	198

CAREER STATISTICS

W	L	ERA	G	GS	CG	SV	IP	H	R	ER	BB	SO
91	103	4.08	272	257	43	0	1667.1	1609	827	755	632	313

has good body balance, which translates into excellent defensive skills. He is quick on bunts and covers first well.

He has a slow move to first and does not throw over very often. Occasionally, he likes to spin around for the pickoff at second base.

OVERALL:

For all of his latent ability, he is still more a thrower than a pitcher.

Until he challenges hitters with his best stuff, until he takes back the inside half of the plate, his career will continue to be more promise than fulfillment. Every hitter in the league knows that Bannister gives up a big part of the plate. If he ever decided to take it back--even in one game--headlines would roar.

Killebrew: "Floyd is a mystery man. He has great stuff, he really does. Everyone knows it but him. He should be taking the hitters on and challenging them instead of dancing around them the way he does. He needs to sharpen his sword and duel."

PITCHING:

Britt Burns has pitched better in other seasons than he did last year, but he has never been more successful. His 18 wins were a career high. If not for a slump in the last two weeks, he could very well have won 20 games.

He had just flat out run out of gas toward the end of the season. By then, he was also being hampered by a sore hip, which has plagued him since childhood. In fact, the pain was so severe that at age 26, when many pitchers are just coming into their own, Burns hinted that he might be forced to hang up his spikes. It would be very unfortunate for everyone except big league hitters.

The White Sox have been waiting for Burns to realize his promise. He was the American League Rookie Pitcher of the Year in 1980, when he went 15-13 for a miserable team. Since that time, however, his career has suffered one jolt after another. He lost his father in 1981, and a shoulder injury in 1982 prevented him from pitching in what could have been his best season. He was on the wrong end of the see-saw in 1983: while his teammates were romping to a division title, he was inconsistent.

He is basically a power pitcher who throws everything hard. Now and then, Burns will use a change-up. He challenges hitters inside and then throws the fastball up--the legendary high, hard one.

When he gets behind in the count, he start to nibble, and that is when he gets into trouble. He uses more off-speed pitches now when he is behind than he ever did before.

Burns pitches at an agonizingly slow pace and can be murderously frustrating for his fielders. He will suffer through spells of control problems that are sometimes brought on by his crawling rhythm.

BRITT BURNS
LHP, No. 40
RL, 6'5", 231 lbs.
ML Svc: 6 years
Born: 6-8-59 in
     Houston, TX

1985 STATISTICS

W	L	ERA	G	GS	CG	SV	IP	H	R	ER	BB	SO
18	11	3.96	36	34	8	0	227	206	105	100	79	172

CAREER STATISTICS

W	L	ERA	G	GS	CG	SV	IP	H	R	ER	BB	SO
70	60	3.65	193	161	39	3	1095.2	1045	499	445	362	734

FIELDING:

His congenital hip problem will always hamper him as a fielder. He is slow to react to balls hit up the middle. For a lefthander, he has a poor move to first. He gets over to first base well enough, but, overall, is a pitcher, not a fielder.

OVERALL:

Burns was once the true gem of the White Sox's collection of outstanding young pitchers. A little of the glitter seems to wear off each year. This season, he appears (once again) to be ready to reach his potential.

Killebrew: "Britt has become a bit tougher, a little meaner on the mound. He has embarked on a program of strenuous workouts and is constantly reading about physical fitness. His determination will help him.

"He works hard and could be a 20-game winner if he stays healthy and lucky. It was good to see him finally have his big year last season. He was overdue. Now let's see if he can have another."

HITTING:

They call him "Juice," but Julio Cruz has played the last two years as if he has been squeezed dry. His hitting, which has never been terrific, leveled off so dramatically that he was platooned for most of the season. Even swinging exclusively from the right side (always his preferred side), Cruz ended up hitting only .197.

After helping lead the White Sox to a division title in 1983, Cruz was rewarded with a big contract. An extremely sensitive player, he appears to be trying too hard to justify his salary.

From either side of the plate, Cruz swings from a closed stance. From the right side, his crouch is much more pronounced. Whatever power he has is from the right side. When he is batting left, the defense can play him shallow.

From any angle, Cruz likes fastballs. As a righthanded hitter, he is a high-ball hitter; lefthanded, he prefers the ball down. From the left side, a fastball up in the strike zone can handcuff him. Breaking pitches do the trick when he is batting righthanded.

BASERUNNING:

Cruz was a premier basestealer before joining the White Sox, but in the past two seasons Cruz has totalled just 22 stolen bases. One problem, of course, is that he can't steal first base. But even when he gets on, he is not getting the lead he once did.

FIELDING:

Cruz has great range, especially to his left. He regularly makes the spectacular play. There are occasions, however, when he loses his concentration on the routine plays. Lately, he also seems to be carrying his hitting problems with him onto the field. Nonetheless, one of the more exciting sights in baseball continues to be Cruz turning the double play. He leaps high into the air and

JULIO CRUZ
2B, No. 5
SR, 5'9", 180 lbs.
ML Svc: 8 years
Born: 12-2-54 in
Brooklyn, NY

1985 STATISTICS											
AVG	G	AB	R	H	2B	3B	HR	RBI	BB	SO	SB
.197	91	234	28	46	2	3	0	15	32	40	8

CAREER STATISTICS											
AVG	G	AB	R	H	2B	3B	HR	RBI	BB	SO	SB
.239	1075	3650	519	871	111	27	23	260	436	480	336

  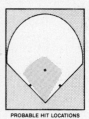

VS. RHP   VS. LHP   PROBABLE HIT LOCATIONS

tucks both of his feet under him in flashy acrobatic fashion. He can really get the ball away quickly and with style on the pivot.

OVERALL:

One bad season is one bad season. Two bad seasons, however, could mean the beginning of the end. At age 31, there should be a lot of baseball left for Cruz, but unless he returns to a level of respectability with the bat, he does not appear to have much of a future. Because his defensive skills are so superior, he does not have to hit a lot to play a lot. But he does have to hit a little.

Killebrew: "You hate to give up on a player who can cover the ground Cruz does and who has stolen 50 bases in one season. Last year was the first time he was platooned and it didn't work. With more playing time, he might just be able to come around and pick it up at the plate."

PITCHING:

Only two years after his 22-7 record led the American League in winning percentage, Richard Dotson's career faces an uncertain future. He had delicate shoulder surgery last season to relieve pressure on a blood vessel. It ended his year early.

Before his arm problems, Dotson was on his way to becoming one of the best pitchers in the league. Between the 1983 and 1984 All Star games, he posted a glittering 25-6 record with a 2.45 ERA. You know he can do it.

His downfall began with a groin pull in mid-season of 1984. His arm problems were already apparent in spring training of last year. He had only nine starts in 1985 before calling it off.

If all is well this year, expect this baby-faced pitcher to crowd hitters off the plate with an 88 MPH fastball. He has always been a mechanically sound and mentally tough pitcher. Coming off the injury, he will have to pay a lot of attention to his mechanics.

In the past, Dotson threw much harder than 88 MPH. He has learned to sacrifice velocity for more control. Control is still the key to his performance and is also his biggest problem.

He is basically a two-pitch pitcher: the fastball and a change-up. His change-up may be second only to that of the National League's Mario Soto in its effectiveness. That's high praise.

He has tried to develop a breaking ball. Dotson experimented with a curve and a slider before settling on his curveball. He had difficulty controlling it. When he is able to get the curve over, he is much more effective because his fastball appears quicker.

Dotson has also fooled around with today's popular pitch, the split-finger fastball. He wants to use it as a variation of his straight change.

RICH DOTSON
RHP, No. 34
RR, 6'0", 204 lbs.
ML Svc: 7 years
Born: 1-10-59 in
   Cincinnati, OH

1985 STATISTICS												
W	L	ERA	G	GS	CG	SV	IP	H	R	ER	BB	SO
3	4	4.47	9	9	0	0	52.1	53	30	26	17	33

CAREER STATISTICS												
W	L	ERA	G	GS	CG	SV	IP	H	R	ER	BB	SO
73	59	2.06	172	168	39	0	1998	1055	514	457	441	594

He might throw any of these pitches tight--Dotson has a reputation as a headhunter.

FIELDING:

Dotson has a slow delivery to the plate, but with a runner on first, he is able to compensate for that nick with a good move to first. It helps him to keep the runners close. He is a good athlete who fields his position well.

OVERALL:

The surgery he had is somewhat rare, making it difficult to give a prognosis. One thing is for certain. If Dotson comes back physically sound, he has the chance to become one of the best starters in the league.

Killebrew: "The White Sox were so high on Dotson that they let LaMarr Hoyt go. Rich's injury may have cost the Sox a chance at the division title in 1985.

"There is no question that he can pitch. He and the team will hold their breath until spring training. He is tough, gutsy type of pitcher whose mental toughness should help him."

HITTING:

Carlton Fisk became a muscleman last season. He pumped iron until he was blue in the face: the regimen paid enormous dividends.

Although he did not regain the consistency at the plate that had made him a .278 lifetime hitter going into the 1985 season, Fisk had a career high of 37 homers and 107 RBIs. Only a September slump kept him from leading the majors in homers.

Fisk was healthy once again. He had been forced to miss some 60 games during 1984 because of a severe abdominal pull, but was unencumbered last season. It was the weight-training program that seemed to be the obvious reason for his increased power.

Fisk uses a straight-up stance and is really a line drive hitter who now has the added advantage of showing power. He drives the outside pitch into right field.

Fisk is a low-ball hitter who can be pitched to with high and tight fastballs. He will drive the low fastball if it is over the plate. If a pitcher thinks about sending Fisk a breaking ball, he ought to keep it very low.

BASERUNNING:

Fisk is a deceptive runner. No one would expect a catcher, and a big man at that, to steal bases, yet Fisk stole 17 last season (another career high). While he is not fast, he is one of the most intelligent baserunners in the game. He very seldom makes a mistake on the basepaths and he will slide in hard at second to break up the double play.

FIELDING:

He is an excellent handler of pitchers. He is superb at blocking balls in the dirt. His arm is quick and strong, although it is not as good as it was when he was in his (catching) prime. He believes in pitching to his pitcher's

CARLTON FISK
C, No. 72
RR, 6'2", 215 lbs.
ML Svc: 15 years
Born: 12-26-47 in
   Bellows Falls, VT

1985 STATISTICS

AVG	G	AB	R	H	2B	3B	HR	RBI	BB	SO	SB
.238	153	543	85	129	23	1	37	107	52	81	17

CAREER STATISTICS

AVG	G	AB	R	H	2B	3B	HR	RBI	BB	SO	SB
.275	1702	6064	961	1666	305	42	257	914	597	914	113

  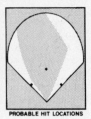

STRONG — VS. RHP   STRONG — VS. LHP   PROBABLE HIT LOCATIONS

strength rather than to the batter's weakness.

He is the ultimate take-charge type behind the plate and most pitchers seem to take to that approach.

OVERALL:

Fisk can't catch forever. While some have speculated that he might play a bit at third base, it is doubtful that he will have the range or quickness for that position. He might share a first base job or see time in left field. Fisk doesn't like any of the choices and likes the idea of playing in left field the least: it's too boring for him.

Killebrew: "He is still a smart, forceful handler of pitchers and a fine defensive receiver.

"Carlton picked a good time to have a career year but, then I knew he would. He has lasted longer than most catchers do and he is now going to get a good payoff. It is one which he deserves. The question for 1986 will be how he plays after getting all of that security."

HITTING:

The arrival of rookie sensation Ozzie Guillen has put the everyday career of Scott Fletcher on hold. Fletcher had been lifting his average and increasing his playing time each season prior to 1985, but that trend might be in reverse now. Still, Fletcher managed to make the best of his situation and was able to bring his average up to .256 by season's end.

He is a high fastball hitter and prefers to see a fastball on the outside part of the plate. Pitchers can get him out with breaking stuff if they can control their pitches in the strike zone.

For a player whose role is being clearly downscaled, Fletcher shows impressive patience at the plate. He waits for a fastball that he likes rather than chase breaking pitches thrown out of the strike zone.

Scott has a lot of valuable plate skills that give a manager many options. He is a contact hitter who is able to use all parts of the field. He is a good choice on the hit-and-run and has developed fine bunting skills. He is also reliable in clutch situations.

BASERUNNING:

Fletcher is an all-around aggressive ballplayer, though he has never been a big basestealer. He does take a decent lead and has adequate speed.

FIELDING:

He was essentially a shortstop until Ozzie Guillen arrived in Chicago. Ozzie appears to be so good that Fletcher can forget about shortstop for a while.

Fletcher's advantage is that he can play both second and third base. He does a good job at both of them and could be a valuable player because of his versatility.

He has good range, although he is slightly better to his left than he is to his right. He has a good arm and can turn the double play at second base.

SCOTT FLETCHER
SS, No. 1
RR, 5'11", 170 lbs.
ML Svc: 5 years
Born: 7-30-58 in
    Fort Walton, FL

1985 STATISTICS

AVG	G	AB	R	H	2B	3B	HR	RBI	BB	SO	SB
.256	119	301	38	77	8	1	2	31	35	47	5

CAREER STATISTICS

AVG	G	AB	R	H	2B	3B	HR	RBI	BB	SO	SB
.245	412	1089	136	267	41	9	8	99	116	124	20

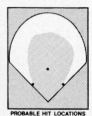

VS. RHP · VS. LHP · PROBABLE HIT LOCATIONS

OVERALL:

Fletcher does not have natural superstar ability. He is, however, a gritty, determined player who could probably hold down an everyday job for some other team. He can look to the Mets' Wally Backman as an example of a player who just worked and worked and worked with what talent he was given to earn a full-time job.

If Fletcher continues to play as a teammate of Guillen's, he will surely become a utility infielder. He was able to get the most of his playing time at second base last season and might get an opportunity there unless Julio Cruz returns to form.

Killebrew: "I like the way this kid attacks the game and I think he could be an everyday player. It is going to be tough for him to crack the White Sox lineup, however; it would really help Scott's chances if he could develop into a better hitter."

HITTING:

White Sox general manager Roland Hemond was fired at the conclusion of the season during which he traded Cy Young Award pitcher LaMarr Hoyt for (in part) Ozzie Guillen. Imagine what they might have done to Hemond if Guillen had not turned out to be the best White Sox shortstop since Luis Aparicio.

The White Sox had said all along that Guillen was the key to the trade. They maintained that judgment on the trade should be withheld for a few years until the 21-year-old shortstop had had the chance to get his feet wet. It didn't take that long for the jury to reach a verdict.

Guillen not only turned out to be every bit the shortstop the team thought that he was, but he hit much better than they ever expected.

He is that type of hitter most dreaded by pitchers: a free swinger who does not care what kind of ball he hits as long as it's a baseball. He likes the ball up and he likes the ball down, but he likes it much better if it's hard and straight--a fastball.

Guillen will sometimes swing out of control. Pitchers can make him look pretty bad with slow stuff. Guillen is a smart hitter and is able to make adjustments at the plate. It is unusual for such an inexperienced hitter to be able to adjust so well so early in his career.

Guillen can bunt for a hit and gets out of the batter's box quickly.

BASERUNNING:

Although he has excellent speed, Guillen's baserunning is one area which needs more work. Last season, he was able to steal only seven bases. Otherwise, he is a good, even daring, runner.

FIELDING:

Guillen is surely another in the line of outstanding Venezuelan shortstops who

OZZIE GUILLEN
SS, No. 13
LR, 5'11", 150 lbs.
ML Svc: 1 year
Born: 1-20-64 in
Oculare, VEN

1985 STATISTICS

AVG	G	AB	R	H	2B	3B	HR	RBI	BB	SO	SB
.273	150	491	71	134	21	9	1	33	12	36	7

CAREER STATISTICS

AVG	G	AB	R	H	2B	3B	HR	RBI	BB	SO	SB
.273	150	491	71	134	21	9	1	33	12	36	7

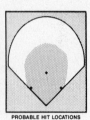

VS. RHP   VS. LHP   PROBABLE HIT LOCATIONS

have played for the White Sox. He now plays where Luis Aparicio and Chico Carrasquel once ruled. Not only does Guillen have great range, but he is a sure-handed shortstop.

His 13 errors were the lowest in the league and a club record as well. He can make even the hard plays look simple. He has a fine arm and turns the double play well. Guillen is already one of the best shortstops in the game.

OVERALL:

Guillen will never hit for power, but if he can produce as well at the plate as he did in his rookie year, he will be one of the better all-around players at his position for a long time.

Killebrew: "Guillen seems to have a lot of fun out there when he's playing. Who could blame him? He has so much to look forward to. The White Sox appear to have found their shortstop for the next ten years."

HITTING:

Plagued by a sore knee that required off-season surgery, Jerry Hairston saw his playing time diminish last season but his principle role on the White Sox remained the same. It is no small job. Hairston is establishing himself as one of the best pinch-hittters in the history of the game.

When manager Tony LaRussa first saw Hairston while on a scouting trip to Mexico in 1981, he envisioned Hairston as an outfield fill-in. At this point, however, Hairston doesn't see much time in the field.

Hairston comes off the bench ready to jump all over the ball, but he is a patient hitter who will take the first pitch if it is not where he wants it. He stalks his prey and waits.

He can switch-hit but is now asked to bat mainly from the left side of the plate. From the left, he has much more power than he does from the right side.

Hairston uses a short, compact swing. As a righthanded hitter he likes the ball high and will spray the ball to all fields. He is a more defensive hitter with two strikes on him when he is batting from the right side.

As a lefthanded hitter, Hairston has opened up his stance a little and will pull the ball. He prefers the ball down from the left side. Pitchers will oblige him but only with their breaking stuff. They throw him the fastball up and try to keep everything outside.

BASERUNNING:

Hairston can be too aggressive on the bases from time to time. Before his knee injury he had good speed but lacked confidence in his ability to steal a base. Overall, he is not a good baserunner.

FIELDING:

He does not see much action in the

JERRY HAIRSTON
PH/OF, No. 17
SR, 5'10", 190 lbs.
ML Svc: 10 years
Born: 2-16-52 in
   Birmingham, AL

1985 STATISTICS

AVG	G	AB	R	H	2B	3B	HR	RBI	BB	SO	SB
.243	95	140	9	34	8	0	2	20	29	18	0

CAREER STATISTICS

AVG	G	AB	R	H	2B	3B	HR	RBI	BB	SO	SB
.258	687	1343	170	347	68	6	20	159	231	189	9

STRONG

VS. RHP   PROBABLE HIT LOCATIONS

field. When he does, he has to play deep because he does not go back on the ball well. His arm is not strong, although he does get his throws away quickly.

OVERALL:

Successful pinch-hitters are a valuable commodity. Their fielding and baserunning are often weak, but those are not a source of concern. Hairston remains ready to hit. He is able to jump off the bench and can approach the plate confident that he will get a piece of the ball.

Killebrew: "Jerry gets the most out of his ability and is a tough out. He has the ability to rise to the occasion when the game is on the line. That's worth waiting for."

HITTING:

When a player hits .133 with no home runs and only four RBIs, there must be some reason that he is on a major league roster. In Marc Hill's case, the reason is simple: he is the ultimate team man.

By no stretch of the imagination is he a good hitter. By the same token, he is not as bad a hitter as he appeared to be last season. Hill's biggest problem was that Carlton Fisk was healthy: Hill was limited to just 75 at-bats.

Hill looks like a power hitter and does have the strength to drive the ball a long way. He rarely swings for the fences, however. Years ago, when he was with the San Francisco Giants, Hill learned that he would never challenge Babe Ruth. Hill tries to use the entire field and hits behind the runner well.

To his credit, Hill remains a patient hitter when he does get the chance to play. He uses a straight-up stance and is strictly a fastball hitter. He likes the fastball up. Pitchers throw hard sliders at him and will try to keep the fastball down. Hill will try to take the low pitch to right field or up the middle.

BASERUNNING:

Slow. Slow. Slow.

FIELDING:

Hill is an excellent catcher but as a teammate of Carlton Fisk, his only opportunity to strap on the tools had been when Fisk was injured. The White Sox staff loves to throw to Hill. He gets

MARC HILL
C, No. 7
RR, 6'3", 240 lbs.
ML Svc: 12 years
Born: 2-18-52 in
    Elsberry, MO

1985 STATISTICS

AVG	G	AB	R	H	2B	3B	HR	RBI	BB	SO	SB
.133	40	75	5	10	2	0	0	4	12	9	0

CAREER STATISTICS

AVG	G	AB	R	H	2B	3B	HR	RBI	BB	SO	SB
.224	715	1790	144	401	62	3	34	198	184	240	1

VS. RHP   VS. LHP   PROBABLE HIT LOCATIONS

the most from his pitchers. He takes charge of the game. He knows the hitters and moves well behind the plate. His arm is strong.

OVERALL:

Hill has just one job on the White Sox and he does it very well.

Killebrew: "Marc runs the game smoothly and seems to have earned the respect and confidence of the pitching staff. He is the ideal backup catcher. Hill has the temperament to accept his position on the club."

HITTING:

The first thing that the White Sox noticed several years ago about Tim Hulett was not his bat but his fine defense. Last season, he made them notice his bat as well.

Hulett hit a respectable .268 and showed some power with 19 doubles and 5 home runs. That should not have been very surprising, as Hulett had shown some improvement with the bat during his last few minor league seasons and had twice posted more than 20 homers.

Basically, he is a straightaway hitter but he takes a good rip at the fastball and will pull it. Nevertheless, it is best for pitchers to try to keep the fastball in on him and to throw the breaking ball away.

He likes to go after the first pitch, especially if he sees that it is a fastball. It is not a bad idea to start him off with breaking stuff and save the fastball for later. Hulett will chase the breaking pitch off the plate.

BASERUNNING:

Hulett has fair speed and runs hard. He is, however, only an occasional threat to steal. He does not get a good jump off first but is a hard and aggressive runner going into second on the double play.

FIELDING:

A natural second baseman, Hulett was forced to play third last year and did an acceptable job. His arm is strong enough to play the position and he has good hands. He moves better to his left than to his right.

As a minor league player, Hulett had a reputation as an excellent defensive second baseman. In the majors, however, he just hasn't had enough time to show all his stuff.

OVERALL:

Hulett was supposed to be a glove man

TIM HULETT
INF, No. 32
RR, 6'0", 183 lbs.
ML Svc: 1 year plus
Born: 1-12-60 in
  Springfield, IL

1985 STATISTICS

AVG	G	AB	R	H	2B	3B	HR	RBI	BB	SO	SB
.268	141	395	52	106	19	4	5	36	30	81	6

CAREER STATISTICS

AVG	G	AB	R	H	2B	3B	HR	RBI	BB	SO	SB
.263	155	407	53	107	19	4	5	36	82	85	7

STRONG — VS. RHP STRONG — VS. LHP PROBABLE HIT LOCATIONS

but it was his bat that kept him in the lineup last season. Good third basemen appear to be an endangered species in the majors and the White Sox continue their search for one. If they can come up with one, Hulett would then have to beat out Julio Cruz at second or settle for a utility role.

Killebrew: "Tim put up some decent numbers as a rookie but if he expects to play regularly at third base he still needs to improve his hitting. It seems to me that he has the ability to do it. If the White Sox do not make a trade, we could see Hulett become the regular third baseman. I think that he would be a good one.

"Defensively, his arm is good. He will need some time to get to know the hitters in the league. In the meanwhile, he really should work on what he can do at the plate."

PITCHING:

His former team, the Montreal Expos, had used him more as a setup man, but the White Sox expected Bob James to clean the table for them, and he did. The hard-throwing righthander led the team in ERA with 2.13 and set a team record with his 32 saves.

Last season, the White Sox might have lost a chance at the pennant in the three weeks he was on the disabled list with a knee problem. The knee continued to give him occasional trouble and when it did, it hurt his ability to control the curveball and lessened his overall effectiveness.

There is not too much subtlety about James' pitching. He goes right after the hitters, cranking up his 92 MPH fastball and saying, "Here it is." His fastball doesn't sink but has good movement. He also has an excellent curveball, which has a tight rotation. It further serves to keep the hitters off guard.

Basically, he sticks to the fastball-and-curve combination. He used to have problems controlling the curve, but did well with it last season when his knee was not acting up.

On the few occasions last year when James was ineffective, lack of control was the culprit. He got behind in the count and would then have to come in with the fastball. But even when the hitters know it's coming, his fastball has enough kick to it that they usually can't handle it.

James can be an intimidating pitcher, one who is not afraid to back a hitter off the plate. He is the type who can come in with men on base and escape by simply blowing the hitters away.

FIELDING:

James finishes his delivery squared

BOB JAMES
RHP, No. 43
RR, 6'4", 230 lbs.
ML Svc: 5 years
Born: 8-15-58 in
 Glendale, CA

1985 STATISTICS
W	L	ERA	G	GS	CG	SV	IP	H	R	ER	BB	SO
8	7	2.13	69	0	0	32	110	90	31	26	23	88

CAREER STATISTICS
W	L	ERA	G	GS	CG	SV	IP	H	R	ER	BB	SO
15	16	3.36	187	2	0	49	295	262	126	110	117	274

up, putting him in good position to field balls hit back at him. He covers first base well and in general is an adequate fielder. His move to first base is just so-so and runners will take advantage of him.

OVERALL:

The White Sox needed a stopper desperately and James was the answer to their prayers. Although he is generally inexperienced, he is already one of the premier short men in the AL.

He tends to have a little problem with his weight and, especially considering that he has had a knee problem, might well consider shedding some of his excess avoirdupois.

Killebrew: "James has one heckuva an arm. Now that he is able to throw his curveball over consistently, he is so much more effective in setting up his fastball. Coupled with his willingness to run a hitter off the plate, James has become an intimidating closer. If he can manage to keep his weight in check, he could be a top-shelf stopper for years."

HITTING:

The baseball strike of 1985 was over so quickly that most people have forgotten that there even was one. For Ron Kittle, however, the short-lived strike was the turning point of the season. After the one-day hiatus, Kittle came back a new man, determined to start a new season. Things had not been going well for him.

Until that time, the year had been a personal and professional disaster. He injured his shoulder banging into an outfield wall in April and he missed several games. When he returned to the lineup, the bruised shoulder greatly hampered his abilities.

At the time of the strike, Kittle was barely hitting .200 and had flashed few of his trademark titanic home runs. "I'm going to have fun the rest of the season," he declared on the night the strike ended. And he did. With just 379 at-bats, he ended the season with 26 home runs.

Kittle likes to extend his arms at the plate to drive the ball with power. He has enormous power, but pitchers have found that his glaring weakness is a propensity for swinging at breaking pitches in the dirt. He is essentially a low-ball hitter and will also chase a high fastball.

Pitchers can jam him with fastballs and then get him to go after slow stuff away. Kittle has been unable to get the hang of being selective at the plate. Many power hitters will swing at a lot of pitches out of the strike zone, but Kittle swings more than most.

BASERUNNING:

He is much faster than he appears to be and goes from first to third well. He will steal only an occasional base.

FIELDING:

It is difficult to be a good outfielder when you have trouble judging

RON KITTLE
LF, No. 42
RR, 6'4", 220 lbs.
ML Svc: 4 years
Born: 1-5-58 in
Gary, IN

1985 STATISTICS

AVG	G	AB	R	H	2B	3B	HR	RBI	BB	SO	SB
.230	116	379	51	87	12	0	26	58	31	92	1

CAREER STATISTICS

AVG	G	AB	R	H	2B	3B	HR	RBI	BB	SO	SB
.234	420	1394	197	326	48	3	94	239	122	391	12

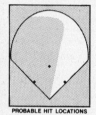

VS. RHP   VS. LHP   PROBABLE HIT LOCATIONS

fly balls. That's pretty much the case with Kittle in the field. He makes the routine play, but at the major league level, that's to be expected. He has difficulty making anything other than the routine play.

In previous seasons, he had a strong arm in his favor, but the shoulder injury he suffered during 1985 took that edge away. It really affected his ability to throw the ball.

OVERALL:

Kittle is more suited to be a designated hitter but is a better hitter when he plays in the field. His power potential is staggering.

Killebrew: "His inability to lay off bad pitches is more than a few seasons old. Offensively, he could be so much more consistent and better overall than he is. Kittle had a difficult season in 1985 but is the kind of guy who is able to overcome it and come back ready to play."

HITTING:

The law that seems to be in effect here is the law of diminishing returns. After two very good years for the White Sox, Rudy Law has put together back-to-back mediocre seasons. His .259 average in 1985 was a slight improvement over the previous year, but it is still not enough to guarantee him everyday employment.

Occasionally, Law will shock you with a home run. His home runs are almost exclusively pulled into the right field corner. Basically, however, Law is a slap hitter who relies on his speed to get on base.

He uses an open stance with his left foot almost on the plate. He likes the fastball up and away. Get it down and away, and Law will usually reward you with a nice fly ball to left. Or bust the slider in on his hands and you'll get a weak grounder.

He likes to hit on the ground to take advantage of his speed. He has little, if any, patience at the plate. He goes up swinging. As a result, he does not walk often. He is a leadoff-type of hitter, but should be able to eke out more walks than he does. He is an excellent bunter and is able to get out of the box quickly.

BASERUNNING:

Law was an excellent basestealer in the past but has slowed up over the last two seasons. He gets a good jump but will get picked off first base too often. He is not aggressive when sliding into second base on the double play. Even at his best, he makes the defense yawn.

FIELDING:

He is not a good overall outfielder. He has trouble going back on a ball and

RUDY LAW
CF, No. 23
LL, 6'2", 176 lbs.
ML Svc: 6 years
Born: 10-7-56 in
Waco, TX

1985 STATISTICS

AVG	G	AB	R	H	2B	3B	HR	RBI	BB	SO	SB
.259	125	390	62	101	21	6	4	35	27	40	29

CAREER STATISTICS

AVG	G	AB	R	H	2B	3B	HR	RBI	BB	SO	SB
.272	662	2114	337	576	75	32	17	162	155	188	214

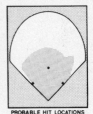

STRONG   STRONG

VS. RHP   VS. LHP   PROBABLE HIT LOCATIONS

is better when he is able to charge in. Law has a weak arm, which is why the White Sox try to play him in left field. His arm is weak, even for a left fielder.

OVERALL:

Law is at a critical point in his career. He needs to have a good spring this season or he could see himself on the bench—or even further.

Killebrew: "He has a lot of speed but you need a lot more than that to play this game. He must become more selective at the plate but it does not appear as if that will happen at this stage. His job is to get on base but he hasn't been doing that. Law is on a downward curve at an age when he should be at his peak."

HITTING:

What's in a name? Well, almost every-thing when it comes to Bryan Little. Little in name, little in stature--and it is his mastery of the little things that keeps him in the bigs.

It was almost as if the White Sox could not keep Little down. Every time they brought him up from the farm he did something to catch the team's eye.

This guy is an eye-popping expert at the bunt, a true modern master of the arcane art. He probably gets more bunt hits than anyone in baseball. In his one full year with Montreal, he had 24 bunt hits and was named best bunter in the majors by his peers--as a rookie.

Little is a switch-hitter and hit mostly from the left side for the White Sox. He stands close to the plate.

He seldom swings at the first pitch because he goes up to the plate looking for a walk whenever he can. He likes the fastball over the plate, although high fastballs will give him trouble. High, tight fastballs can also be rough for him, especially because he stands in so close at the plate.

BASERUNNING:

Everything points to Little being a basestealing threat. His quickness out of the box ought to translate to a quick jump. He has decent speed and gets a good enough lead. Yet he stole only one base for the White Sox and has never stolen more than four in a season. He does have good instincts on the base-paths and runs hard.

FIELDING:

A truly versatile player, Little was Montreal's starting shortstop at the beginning of 1983 but played more games at second base the following year. The White Sox used him mostly at second but Little can play all three infield posi-tions with sure-handed skill.

He moves his feet well and can go to

BRYAN LITTLE
INF, No. 47
SR, 5'10", 160 lbs.
ML Svc: 4 years
Born: 10-8-59 in
  Houston, TX

1985 STATISTICS

AVG	G	AB	R	H	2B	3B	HR	RBI	BB	SO	SB
.250	73	188	35	47	9	1	2	27	26	21	0

CAREER STATISTICS

AVG	G	AB	R	H	2B	3B	HR	RBI	BB	SO	SB
.251	293	846	120	212	35	5	3	75	114	68	8

STRONG — VS. RHP   STRONG — VS. LHP   PROBABLE HIT LOCATIONS

either side with equal facility. He throws well from both second base and shortstop, although his arm is probably more suited to second base. He turns the double play well.

OVERALL:

The White Sox probably got more than they bargained for when they obtained Little for pitcher Bert Roberge in what they considered a minor league trade. White Sox management did not expect him to make the club or to make as big a contribution as he did last season.

Killebrew: "A player who can play more than one infield position well and who can hit for a decent (.250) average has got a good shot to stay on a major league roster. You won't see his name in the headlines, but he'll be there.

"Little could be a regular player for some teams. 1986 could be a really good year for him as he has learned the AL a bit more now. He'll challenge for the job at second base."

PITCHING:

In Gene Nelson's young life, he has seldom known whether he is coming or going. In one sense then, 1985 was his most settled year to date: it was the first time he spent the entire season on a major league roster.

Just to be certain he didn't start to feel too comfortable, however, the White Sox had him on a shuttle between the starting staff and the bullpen all year long.

Nelson began the season as the setup man for closer Bob James. He was doing an excellent job in that role until Rich Dotson's injury and the trade of Tim Lollar which made it necessary to make Nelson into a starter. In the rotation, he was neither a miserable failure nor an unqualified success.

Nelson's fastball is not an overpowering type of pitch, but it comes in at 88 MPH and is not bad. When he throws the fastball down, the pitch sinks naturally. When he throws it up, it hops. Nelson's high leg kick helps him keep batters off stride. In relief, he goes almost exclusively with the fastball and the split-finger fastball (a pitch he taught himself in the minors).

When he is in a starting role, however, he has to use a greater variety of pitches. That's when the trouble begins. His breaking pitch is a spiked curve that is short and quick, but Nelson can not throw it consistently.

He has a fairly good change-up which he mixes in well with the fastball.

He appears to be more suited to a relief role. He is an aggressive pitcher who is not afraid to claim his share of the plate. He also tires quickly. Nelson does not generally have the stamina to go nine innings. In 1985 he completed just one of his 18 starts.

When he begins to tire, the first thing that goes is his control. Nelson

GENE NELSON
RHP, No. 30
RR, 6'0", 175 lbs.
ML Svc: 5 years
Born: 12-3-60 in
  Tampa, FL

1985 STATISTICS

W	L	ERA	G	GS	CG	SV	IP	H	R	ER	BB	SO
10	10	4.26	46	18	1	2	145.2	144	74	69	67	101

CAREER STATISTICS

W	L	ERA	G	GS	CG	SV	IP	H	R	ER	BB	SO
22	28	4.74	106	58	6	4	414	427	235	218	188	227

starts to get his pitches up in the strike zone and the batters tee off.

FIELDING:

Nelson has a snap move to first that is quick and very deceptive. It makes him effective at holding runners on. He falls off the mound toward first base after his delivery and is left in a poor position to field grounders hit back through the middle. He covers first well.

OVERALL:

Gene Nelson has been around the fringes of the big leagues for so long that it is easy to forget he is only 25 years old. He still has time to develop the stamina and the consistent delivery that would enable him to make it as a starting pitcher.

Killebrew: "Nelson has a durable arm and has already been able to show some ability as a setup man. Relief seems to be his best role at the moment. He will be better off when the White Sox define his role more clearly. He needs to show better control, particularly with his breaking pitch."

HITTING:

Reputations are easy to earn and almost impossible to shed, as Reid Nichols is beginning to learn. In five years in the majors, Nichols has never been a regular. When he came to the White Sox in a 1985 mid-season trade, it appeared that, at last, he would get a chance to play regularly. Sorry.

Yet, when he did get the opportunity, Nichols responded well. In 51 games for the White Sox he batted a very acceptable .297. Except for 1984, when he hit only .226 for the Red Sox, Nichols has always been in the .280 range.

Probably the biggest rap against him as a hitter--and the one that could preclude his ever playing on a day-to-day basis--is his lack of power. In more than 700 at-bats for the Red Sox, he had just 14 homers. While that might indicate a little bit of pop, it must be remembered he is a righthanded batter who was playing in Fenway Park. Ah, the old swing of the stats again a la Beantown.

Nichols has a level swing and likes the fastball high and on the outside part of the plate. He will drive the ball into the gaps. He has trouble with curves and sliders away and can be set up with the fastball inside.

He has an extremely quick bat and can get around on the inside pitch if he is anticipating it. He is patient at the plate, but may be wearing out his patience on the bench.

BASERUNNING:

Reid gets high marks in all phases of baserunning. He gets a good lead at first and will barrel into second to break up the double play. He's not afraid to go for the extra base and has the speed to back up his derring-do.

FIELDING:

He gets an extremely good jump and has excellent speed. Nichols is an above-average fielder. His arm is strong

REID NICHOLS
OF, No. 51
RR, 5'11", 172 lbs.
ML Svc: 5 years
Born: 8-5-58 in
    Ocala, FL

1985 STATISTICS

AVG	G	AB	R	H	2B	3B	HR	RBI	BB	SO	SB
.273	72	150	23	41	8	1	2	18	17	17	6

CAREER STATISTICS

AVG	G	AB	R	H	2B	3B	HR	RBI	BB	SO	SB
.271	389	877	125	238	51	5	16	93	74	113	20

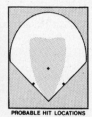

VS. RHP   VS. LHP   PROBABLE HIT LOCATIONS

and accurate and he throws to the proper base and hits the cutoff man. Believe it or not, there are a lot of major leaguers who don't execute these basics.

OVERALL:

Is somebody missing something here? Here is an outstanding defensive outfielder who is a good runner and who carries a lifetime average of .271 under adverse conditions. But he can't seem to win a starting job. His only deficiency is a lack of home run power. He is hardly the only one in the bigs with that "problem."

Killebrew: "Nichols doesn't beat himself or hurt his team in the field and seems to be a student of the game. He's never been put to the test every day and perhaps never will be. But the White Sox are not that set in center field. With this in mind, Nichols would do well to seize the opportunity to hustle and to hit like crazy in spring training: he might just find himself an everyday job."

HITTING:

Like a skyrocket on the Fourth of July, Luis Salazar burst brilliantly onto the major league scene in 1980, but the fireworks seem all but over now. He hit over .300 during his first full season (1981) but has not come anywhere near that mark since.

During the second half of 1985, he offered some evidence that he might be loading up for another explosion. Unfortunately, he had knee surgery at the end of the 1985 season and could be out of the lineup for much of 1986.

He is a free swinger with occasional power. It is his unpredictability that can make him dangerous. He swings at balls far out of the strike zone and then, in the next at-bat, can jump all over a pitcher's mistake.

He is a first-ball, fastball hitter who likes the pitch out over the plate. He has trouble handling breaking pitches and fastballs thrown inside. Pitchers try to keep him off balance, mixing in breaking balls and change-ups with high tight fastballs. Salazar has the ability to drive the outside pitch to right field.

Salazar does not bunt well, although he has good speed when he does get the ball down.

BASERUNNING:

He is fast and could steal a lot of bases if he got his hitting act together and earned more playing time. As it is, his baserunning skills have eroded. He gets only an average jump and is not an aggressive slider.

FIELDING:

Whether he is playing at third base or in the outfield, Salazar likes to show off his strong throwing arm and good range. At third base, he has a tendency to show off his arm strength a little too much and makes wild throws.

In the infield, Salazar goes to his

LUIS SALAZAR
INF, No. 31
RR, 5'9", 180 lbs.
ML Svc: 6 years
Born: 5-19-56 in
   Barcelona, VEN

1985 STATISTICS

AVG	G	AB	R	H	2B	3B	HR	RBI	BB	SO	SB
.245	122	327	39	80	18	2	10	45	12	60	14

CAREER STATISTICS

AVG	G	AB	R	H	2B	3B	HR	RBI	BB	SO	SB
.265	747	2129	231	564	79	24	39	232	83	355	103

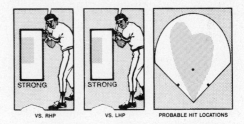

VS. RHP   VS. LHP   PROBABLE HIT LOCATIONS

left better than his right. At no position is he anything but ordinary.

OVERALL:

He has been a part-time player for the past two years, although he saw more action with the Sox in 1985 than he had the year before in San Diego.

His ability to play center field as well as third base makes him a valuable utility player. Offensively, however, he does not appear to be the type who can stay sharp coming off the bench.

Killebrew: "This was Salazar's first year in the American League and by the second half he was looking like a pretty good hitter. He would surely benefit from more playing time. Now that he has seen the pitching style of the AL, he might do better than he did for much of 1985. I don't think, however, that he will get more time in the field with the White Sox unless he can win the third base job during spring training."

PITCHING:

Tom Seaver wears his age.

Just ask him to turn around . . . it's number 41.

Other than that, you'd never know that Seaver is almost a middle-aged man. His 304 career wins puts him at number 15 on the all-time list. By the end of this season, Tom Terrific should crack the Top Ten.

No, he didn't regain his power; and yes, he still uses his head more than any other pitcher today. As a matter of fact, he uses his entire body when he pitches. His legs are the drive train of a tremendously effective pitching machine. His mechanics are so sound that he can probably pitch beyond the one year left on his contract.

You won't see his fastball cruising too much faster than 87 MPH, but it can still be his out pitch because he is able to spot it so well. He has a curve, a slider and a change-up: all of which he can get over for strikes.

Just as important, Seaver can keep his pitches tantalizingly off the plate whenever he wants to. He will still claim his share of the inside part of the plate.

FIELDING:

Because of his high leg kick, he is slow delivering the ball to the plate. His motion to first base is just average, though he will throw over there a lot. Despite keeping one eye on the runner, Seaver somehow manages to keep

TOM SEAVER
RHP, No. 41
RR, 6'1", 210 lbs.
ML Svc: 19 years
Born: 11-17-44 in
Fresno, CA

1985 STATISTICS

W	L	ERA	G	GS	CG	SV	IP	H	R	ER	BB	SO
16	11	3.17	35	33	6	0	238.2	223	103	84	69	134

CAREER STATISTICS

W	L	ERA	G	GS	CG	SV	IP	H	R	ER	BB	SO
304	192	2.82	628	619	232	0	4606	3791	1591	1442	1334	3537

both eyes focused on the man at the plate.

OVERALL:

Seaver has won 15 and 16 games respectively, in two seasons for the White Sox and there is no reason to believe he will not continue to be in double digits. He is no longer a great finisher (six complete games in 1985), but he continues to be one of the game's most dependable starters. He almost always give his team seven good innings.

Killebrew: "When Seaver retires, he will not pass Go, but will proceed directly to the Hall of Fame. The only question now is when. He has one year left on his contract, but might be persuaded to make it at least two if the White Sox trade him closer to his home in Connecticut."

GOOD CONTROL

PITCHING:

The White Sox came very close to cutting Dan Spillner from the team during spring training of 1985. By the end of the season, they were glad they hadn't. Once a premier closer for the Cleveland Indians, Spillner seemed to be at the end of the road. But when the 1985 season began, somewhere he took the right turn.

Despite an undistinguished record last year, he proved himself to be a versatile member of the White Sox staff. He made three emergency starts and pitched well. When Gene Nelson was called on to start, Spillner was asked to set the table and did that well, too. His 3.44 ERA was his best since 1982 when he went 12-10 with 21 saves for Cleveland.

At age 34, Spillner has had to make some adjustments to his pitching style. Although he still occasionally tickles the radar gun at 88 MPH with his fastball, he has become more of a control type of pitcher.

The fastball is still his primary out pitch, but Spillner has learned that he must be able to keep it down low in order to be effective. His slider has never been better than average and Spillner seldom uses it.

He has been able to come up with an overhand curveball that complements his fastball. Spillner also has a change-up which he will throw to power hitters.

At times, he begins to get wild with his pitches and his fastball rides up high in the saddle. When he is tiring, he loses velocity on the fastball as well.

Earlier in his career, Spillner posted two one-hitters. At this stage, however, he is clearly best suited to the bullpen.

DAN SPILLNER
RHP, No. 37
RR, 6'1", 190 lbs.
ML Svc: 12 years
Born: 11-27-57 in
Casper, WY

```
1985 STATISTICS
W   L  ERA  G   GS CG SV IP     H     R   ER  BB  SO
4   3  3.44 52  3  0  1  91.2   83    39  35  33  41
CAREER STATISTICS
W   L  ERA  G   GS CG SV IP     H     R   ER  BB  SO
75  89 4.21 556 123 19 50 1493.2 1585 786 699 605 878
```

FIELDING:

He has an adequate move to first and is enough of an old pro to be aware of the baserunner at all times. He throws to first well.

OVERALL:

Spillner still has a sound arm, and, bolstered by his success in 1985, should be able to stay around the league for a while longer.

Killebrew: "Spillner is like background music at the office: you'd notice if he was missing. He doesn't do anything flashy or particularly noteworthy. His value is now in his versatility--and he can still give a team six innings as a spot starter.

"He comes out of the bullpen ready to throw strikes. He has been around for a long time and works with a knowledge of pitching."

POWER POTENTIAL

HITTING:

Although he hit 24 homers and drove in 92 runs last season, Greg Walker may be miscast as a cleanup hitter. Most baseball experts look on Walker as a bona fide .300 hitter, yet he has failed to reach that level in his three full seasons in the majors.

He came close in 1984 when he batted .294, but, dropped to .258 in 1985 when he played in 163 games and batted fourth in the lineup. Part of his problem may have been that he is still learning to hit lefthanded pitching.

Walker admits that he sometimes tries too hard to hit home runs. It would appear that Walker has a lot of power in his stroke; he has hit 24 home runs during each of the last two seasons and could probably hit more if he stopped pressing.

Walker has a swing that is almost mechanically perfect and he looks good even when he's striking out.

He is basically a line drive hitter. He is a first-ball, fastball hitter, but does have patience at the plate. He can hit the low fastball, and if a pitcher makes a mistake by hanging a breaking ball, Walker will make the gaffe clear.

He has enough power to drive the ball into the left-center field alley. When he is going well, he sends the outside pitch into left-center.

Walker remembers pitchers' patterns and it is difficult for them to get him out the same way twice. As a result, pitchers try to keep him off balance by mixing up their stuff: fastballs inside, change-ups, and breaking pitches in no set pattern are the best bet against him. Breaking balls from lefthanders continue to give him trouble.

BASERUNNING:

Walker is not fast and is not a stolen base threat. He is just a heads-up baserunner.

FIELDING:

Walker made three errors on Opening

GREG WALKER
1B, No. 29
LR, 6'3", 198 lbs.
ML Svc: 4 years
Born: 10-6-59 in
Douglas, GA

1985 STATISTICS
AVG	G	AB	R	H	2B	3B	HR	RBI	BB	SO	SB
.258	163	601	77	155	38	4	24	92	44	100	5

CAREER STATISTICS
AVG	G	AB	R	H	2B	3B	HR	RBI	BB	SO	SB
.274	428	1367	174	375	85	10	60	229	109	226	15

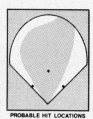

VS. RHP   VS. LHP   PROBABLE HIT LOCATIONS

Day when he was a rookie and he became gun-shy for a long time. But he has made himself into an adequate first baseman. He has worked hard at his fielding.

OVERALL:

Walker is one of the rising stars in the game. He has an even temperament, which helps him through his slumps. He shows increasing power with each season yet is capable of much, much more consistency.

Killebrew: "He should become a fixture at first base for years to come, and with more experience facing left-handed pitching, he should become a solid .300 hitter. He is a very dangerous hitter and has plenty of power to flash. At the plate, Greg is a tough out and does not show any glaring weaknesses. A player like him can keep his nose to the grindstone and only get better."

JUAN AGOSTO
LHP, No. 50
LL, 6'0", 187 lbs.
ML Svc: 3 years
Born: 2-23-58 in
    Rio Piedra, PR

PITCHING, FIELDING:

Juan Agosto is like a meal that looks great on the menu but turns out to be just a hamburger when it arrives. For the second year in a row, Agosto's statistics make him appear better than he is.

Although his 3.58 ERA is not bad, it does not indicate the number of inherited runners who scored. Ideally, Agosto would be a situation pitcher who comes into the game to pitch to a specific lefthander.

However, most of the success he has had has been in long relief. He will sometimes will look very good for two or three innings at a time. In short, he is better when he starts an inning than when he finishes one.

His basic pitches are a mediocre fastball and a sharp-breaking curve, which is his out pitch. He has control problems with it, however, and that is his basic deficiency. He cut down on his walks last year, but still gets behind too many hitters.

In the field, he is quick, and his delivery leaves him in good position. He has a dangerous snap throw to first base.

OVERALL:

Killebrew: "Agosto is still young and has a rubber arm. The best part about him is that he is a lefthander. Everyone wants a southpaw. Nonetheless, he must develop better control if he is going to have any kind of a future."

JOEL SKINNER
C, No. 22
RR, 6'4", 204 lbs.
ML Svc: 1 year plus
Born: 2-21-61 in
    La Jolla, CA

HITTING, BASERUNNING, FIELDING:

Joel Skinner may someday be the answer to a trivia question: Who was the first player ever selected in the free agent compensation pool? Yes, 'twas he. But the question that Skinner was waiting to have answered over the winter was: Would Carlton Fisk move on and give him the chance to be the regular catcher?

Skinner has been buried behind Fisk since being drafted from the Pirates in compensation for the loss of reliever Ed Farmer after the 1981 season. He has spent most of his time in the high minors since then.

The son of Atlanta Braves coach Bob Skinner, Joel made the most of his limited at-bats last year to post a .341 average. He is a high-ball hitter who likes to pull the ball to the left-center alley. He prefers the fastball out over the plate and is susceptible to breaking stuff and change-ups. He is a patient hitter and tries to get ahead in the count.

On the bases, he is slow and is no threat to steal. Behind the plate he seems adept at blocking balls in the dirt and throws well. It is too early to tell how he will handle a big league staff.

OVERALL:

Killebrew: "Only time will tell if Skinner has the tools to be a big league regular. If Fisk leaves, the time could be now."

DAVE WEHRMEISTER
RHP, No. 65
RR, 6'4", 195 lbs.
ML Svc: less than 1 year
Born: 11-9-52 in
    La Grange, IL

PITCHING, FIELDING:

With his record, you'd think that Dave Wehrmeister was a submarine pitcher. He made his big league debut ten years ago but keeps dropping out of sight for years at a time before resurfacing.

This time, however, he came up with guns blazing, and his 39 innings with the White Sox were his most by far in the majors since 1977.

He is a control pitcher who does not have overwhelming stuff but who knows how to spot his pitches. His fastball hits 88 MPH and runs. His next best pitch is a slider. He also throws a curveball and a change-up. He can get them all over the plate. The curve is not as good as it once was but seemed to be coming back toward the end of the season.

He is adequate defensively, but not very good at holding runners on first.

OVERALL:

Killebrew: "With his spotty record, Wehrmeister had to make an immediate impression when he was called up last year. He seems to have done just that. The key to his success was his strikeouts-to-walks ratio (32-10), which indicates pretty good control. As long as he puts the ball where he wants it, he can help a team in long relief."

CLEVELAND INDIANS

HITTING:

Quick, get Inspector Clouseau on the phone. There's a mystery in Cleveland and only he can help. Chris Bando's bat is missing--really missing.

No one knows why or how it happened, but Chris Bando pulled a no-show last season. He hit .139 with only 13 RBIs. He simply stopped hitting. At one point, he was 2-for-51; at another, he was 0-for-July.

All this from a player who seemed on the verge of moving into the upper echelons when the 1984 season ended. In only 220 at-bats, Bando hit .291 with 12 home runs and 41 RBIs. After that, nothing happened. Absolutely, positively, not a lick--nothing.

Bando took it well. Everyone was all over him. His brother, former major leaguer Sal, called with advice. Chris took hours of extra batting practice. Still, nothing.

Under less mysterious circumstances, Bando should be pitched down and away when he bats from the right side and be thrown off-speed stuff from the left side. But last year, the book on him was: just pitch him. Righthanded, Bando is a high-ball hitter and lefty he is a low-ball hitter . . . maybe.

BASERUNNING:

Bando runs hard--he just doesn't get to his destination quickly. He always hustles on the bases and will go hard into second to break up the double play. He wasn't on base much last year and may have to work on his baserunning skills especially hard this season--if he can work out his hitting problems first.

FIELDING:

Bando calls a good game. He blocks the plate well on "bang-bang" plays and is good at catching foul tips. He had a terrible year throwing out runners in 1985. Bando only threw out 14 of 56 basestealers, a 25% kill ratio. He was

CHRIS BANDO
C, No. 23
SR, 6'0, 195 lbs.
ML Svc: 4 years
Born: 2-4-56 in
  Cleveland, OH

1985 STATISTICS
AVG	G	AB	R	H	2B	3B	HR	RBI	BB	SO	SB
.139	73	173	11	24	4	1	0	13	22	21	0

CAREER STATISTICS
AVG	G	AB	R	H	2B	3B	HR	RBI	BB	SO	SB
.225	283	745	80	168	27	2	19	91	96	107	1

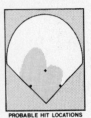

VS. RHP   VS. LHP   PROBABLE HIT LOCATIONS

hindered by a weak throwing shoulder and by a pitching staff that didn't work on holding runners on base.

OVERALL:

Bando started the season as the number one catcher in name only. He was bothered by a sore right shoulder and never got to play for a long period of time during which he could establish himself. About mid-season, he suffered a toe injury that sidelined him again.

The mystery might be solved somewhere other than in Cleveland. The Indians could be looking for a solution without him.

Robinson: "His health and confidence are important factors. Bando's shoulder hurt him most of last year and he really never got a chance to play his way out of his slump.

"He has to start living up to his 1984 season: I think that's his norm when healthy. He should hit .260 and hit between 12 and 20 home runs a year."

HITTING:

Tony Bernazard rose from the dead last year. After a winter of pumping iron in the Florida sunshine, Bernazard buried the memory of a disasterous 1984 season with his most productive year ever.

Bernazard set career highs in home runs, RBIs, doubles and walks last year. In the process, he salvaged a career that seemed to be sliding downhill.

Pitchers have success with Bernazard with fastballs in and up and hard breaking balls. He will murder a change-up and became a much more disciplined hitter last season. He drew 68 walks while striking out 72 times (1984: he struck out 70 times and walked 43).

When Bernazard came to spring training last year, the results of his weight training program were immediately visible: he needed a uniform twice as large as the one he wore in 1984.

The second baseman used his muscles the right way--hitting all his 11 home runs and knocking in 49 of his RBIs from the left side of the plate.

Bernazard is a good bunter, especially when it comes to moving the runner. Toward the end of the 1984 season, he was benched against lefthanded pitching; that was not the case last year as he played a career record 153 games.

BASERUNNING:

He always hustles down the first base line. Bernazard is a threat to steal, but is not the most intelligent baserunner. He stole 17 bases in 1985, but was thrown out nine times; for the most part, he tries to force something to happen in a close game by unwisely attempting to steal.

FIELDING:

As dramatic as Bernazard's comeback at the plate was in 1985, his revival on defense may have been greater. His range

TONY BERNAZARD
2B, No. 4
SR, 5'9", 160 lbs.
ML Svc: 6 years
Born: 8-24-56 in
Caguas, PR

1985 STATISTICS

AVG	G	AB	R	H	2B	3B	HR	RBI	BB	SO	SB
.274	153	500	73	137	26	3	11	59	68	72	17

CAREER STATISTICS

AVG	G	AB	R	H	2B	3B	HR	RBI	BB	SO	SB
.256	779	2619	362	672	123	24	44	269	316	446	96

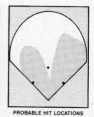

STRONG   STRONG

VS. RHP   VS. LHP   PROBABLE HIT LOCATIONS

improved dramatically both to his left and to his right.

Tony gives every ground ball his maximum effort and doesn't bail out when making the pivot on the DP, although he has been accused of that since breaking his leg in 1982.

His arm is average, but accurate.

OVERALL:

Bernazard kicked into high gear at the right time. Last year was his free agent season and he definitely increased his market value. Bernazard helped stabilize the play of Julio Franco at short and became one of the Indians' quiet leaders as he performed with injuries (thigh and hand) most of the year.

Robinson: "You saw the real Tony Bernazard in 1985 in the field and at the plate. He gets down on himself easily, so he has to keep his head together. He can reach his 1985 numbers again."

HITTING:

The Indians were lousy last year, but it wasn't Brett Butler's fault. The high-energy center fielder had the best overall year of his career, as he led the team in batting average, hits, runs scored, triples and stolen bases.

Butler set the Indians' offense in motion from the leadoff spot. He is a high-ball hitter who loves the fastball. He opens his stance slightly against lefthanders and likes to pull the ball to right field. The hard ground ball in the hole between first and second is his specialty.

Butler does not draw many walks for a leadoff hitter. That is largely because pitchers are taking their chances with him hitting the ball. That approach suits Butler's go get 'em attitude just fine.

He can be jammed by an inside pitch or by a breaking ball down.

Butler can bunt his way out of any slump. In 1984, he led the American League with 29 bunt singles. Last year, he had 20, including one bunt double. He is a nitpicking perfectionist and was disappointed with his bunting in 1985.

BASERUNNING:

Butler's stolen-base totals fell from 52 in 1984 to 47 in 1985--but sometimes less is better. He still gets picked off too often, but he was a smarter baserunner last season. He keeps a book on opposing pitchers, but perhaps he needs to study it just a bit more. The Indians love to run the double steal with him on base: Butler stole home twice on the front end of a double steal last year.

FIELDING:

Butler admitted that after reading THE SCOUTING REPORT:1984, he decided to play center field about 10 feet deeper last year. He had a Gold Glove season in 1985.

You name it, he did it. Playing deeper in the outfield enabled him to

BRETT BUTLER
CF, No. 2
LL, 5'10", 160 lbs.
ML Svc: 4 years
Born: 6-15-57 in
  Los Angeles, CA

1985 STATISTICS

AVG	G	AB	R	H	2B	3B	HR	RBI	BB	SO	SB
.311	152	591	106	184	28	14	5	50	63	42	47

CAREER STATISTICS

AVG	G	AB	R	H	2B	3B	HR	RBI	BB	SO	SB
.277	591	2108	350	584	78	39	13	147	247	212	168

  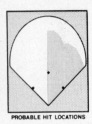

VS. RHP   VS. LHP   PROBABLE HIT LOCATIONS

get to the fence more quickly. He still has enough speed to catch almost anything hit in front of him. He has good range to both his left and his right. However, he tends to overlook the cutoff man.

Though small in stature, Butler can climb a wall with the best of them. He made just one error in 152 games to lead all AL outfielders in fielding percentage last year. His arm improved as the season went along and he finished second in the league in assists and double plays.

OVERALL:

Despite a terrible season for the Indians, Butler rose above the mire.

Robinson: "He does not have the power of a classic center fielder, but his wire-to-wire consistency has put him on the verge of becoming one of the best.

"I think he can repeat his 1985 performance. The team should be better and that will help him. You have to see him every day to really appreciate him."

PITCHING:

One of the biggest and worst moves the Indians made last year was rushing the surgery on Ernie Camacho's arm.

Without the benefit of a second opinion, Camacho underwent an operation to remove bone chips from his right elbow after the first week of the 1985 season. The feeling was: the sooner the surgery was done, the sooner Camacho would be back out of the bullpen dousing flames.

Camacho was unable to pitch for the entire season. The Indians got just 28 saves from six different pitchers last season; in 1984, Camacho had 23 all by himself. The loss of Camacho explains many of the Indians' 102 losses, their 14-29 record in one-run games and the fact that they were dead last in the AL in saves.

Camacho spent the rest of the season throwing on the sidelines, getting cortisone shots and complaining of pain. He could still throw over 90 MPH, which prompted the Indians to lick their collective chops and think he was ready. But Camacho's arm still hurt him and he couldn't pitch in a game.

It was strictly a major league soap opera with Camacho sitting in the corner of the locker room holding his elbow and the Indians grinding their teeth and wondering whether he was ever going to pitch again.

By mid-season, Camacho had turned his back on the Indians' team physicians and was being consulted by Dr. Arthur Pappas (the team doctor for the Boston Red Sox). By October, Camacho was emotionally drained from the ordeal.

Dr. Pappas performed surgery on Camacho's arm last fall. The saga will continue in April in Tucson.

When healthy, Camacho throws strictly heat. Indians' manager Pat Corrales

ERNIE CAMACHO
RHP, No. 13
RR, 6'1", 180 lbs.
ML Svc: 3 years
Born: 2-1-56 in
    Salinas, CA

1985 STATISTICS

W	L	ERA	G	GS	CG	SV	IP	H	R	ER	BB	SO
0	1	8.10	2	0	0	0	3.1	4	3	3	1	2

CAREER STATISTICS

W	L	ERA	G	GS	CG	SV	IP	H	R	ER	BB	SO
5	12	3.42	87	3	0	23	142.2	135	59	54	60	72

won't let him throw anything else. If Camacho tries to throw anything other than his 90 MPH fastball, Corrales runs to mound to yell at him. Sometimes, Corrales simply stands on the dugout steps and barks his displeasure.

FIELDING:

Camacho is an average to below-average fielder. Baserunners don't bother him. He gets off the mound quickly, and covers first consistently.

OVERALL:

Robinson: "Ernie was just coming into his own as a short reliever before the injury to his elbow. He had spent eight years in the minors and was never able to save more than four games in a season. He had a fantastic year in 1984, when he saved 23 games and looked as if he had the stuff to continue to win more each year. He is a tough son of a gun who has the temperament of a short man; he will need everything he's got to rebound in 1985."

HITTING:

Joe Carter's bat went AWOL for the first two months of the 1985 season. It fell into a hole somewhere and he could not find it until June. When he finally did, it took him almost another full month to correct the bad habits he had acquired due to a sprained left wrist. By that time, the season was halfway over. But Carter proved he was worth waiting for.

He finished the season strong, as he hit nine of his 15 home runs after the middle of August (including seven in September). He hit .282 in the last four months of the 1985 season.

Carter is a low-ball hitter who likes balls on the inside part of the plate that he can pull to left field. Carter will strike out a lot--74 times last year in 489 at-bats. Righthanded pitchers can jam him with fastballs, and lefties can get him out with breaking balls and change-ups.

The righthanded-hitting Carter has a hard time with any kind of curveball, though toward the end of last year, he showed signs of success with it. He is not the most selective of hitters and only drew 25 walks.

BASERUNNING:

The 6'3", 215-pound Carter shocked a lot of pitchers and catchers with his speed last season. A knee injury put his running game on hold in 1984, but last year he was ready to roll and stole 24 bases in 30 attempts. He stole home twice on the front end of double steals.

When he has a chance for an infield hit, he gets out of the box quickly and accelerates down the line. His one fault is breaking too early to steal second and getting nailed on the old 1-3-6 pickoff.

FIELDING:

While Carter struggled at the plate for the first two months, his defense

JOE CARTER
LF, No. 30
RR, 6'3", 215 lbs.
ML Svc: 2 years
Born: 3-7-60 in
Oklahoma City, OK

```
1985 STATISTICS
AVG  G   AB  R   H   2B 3B HR RBI BB SO SB
.262 143 489 64  128 27 0  15 59  25 74 24
CAREER STATISTICS
AVG  G   AB  R   H   2B 3B HR RBI BB SO SB
.260 232 784 102 204 34 2  28 101 36 143 27
```

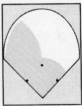

VS. RHP   VS. LHP   PROBABLE HIT LOCATIONS

benefited. He didn't let his poor hitting effect his fielding and he turned in a solid year.

He has a strong arm, charges the ball well and plays the fence with abandon. Carter has the leaping ability to keep the ball in the park, but sometimes has trouble with balls to his left. He was primarily a left fielder last year, but has also played in right field, as well as at first, second and third base. He could be the Indians' future first baseman.

OVERALL:

If Carter can start the 1986 season the way he ended 1985, the Indians' search for power may be over.

Robinson: "Last year, Joe put two important parts of his game together: defense and baserunning. It made a big difference to his overall game. He has a lot of ability.

"The Indians could really use what Carter can offer, but he has to remain healthy for a full season."

POWER POTENTIAL

HITTING:

It's a shame Carmen Castillo can't play the outfield. If he could, he would probably be a legitimate threat to hit 25 to 30 home runs a year. He has a pure home run swing and good power. There's just one problem: Castillo can't catch a fly ball.

Castillo is a low-ball hitter with a long whiplike swing. In only 184 at-bats last year, he hit 11 home runs.

Last season, Castillo appeared in 13 games with the Indians before being sent to Triple-A to work on cutting down his wild swing. Once retooled, he came back to Cleveland to share right field duties with George Vukovich.

Castillo faced an almost strict diet of lefthanded pitchers and hit all his home runs after his swing was somewhat corrected in the minors.

Sliders and off-speed breaking balls on the outside part of the plate give Castillo trouble. Righthanded pitchers can jam him because of his long swing, but he will make them pay if they get a fastball up in the strike zone.

He is a dead pull hitter, but has good overall power to all fields.

BASERUNNING:

Castillo gets out of the box quickly and is always a threat to beat out an infield hit. Surprisingly, he does not use his speed to steal bases or beat out bunts. One of the fastest Indians, he stole only three bases last year--his most ever in the big leagues.

He will take a good lead, but is seldom a threat to go. He is quick going from first to third and will go hard into second base.

FIELDING:

Castillo has never been a good outfielder, but last year he slipped badly. Every ball hit to him turned into an adventure. In close games, he was removed for defensive purposes as early as the

CARMEN CASTILLO
RF, No. 8
RR, 6'1", 185 lbs.
ML Svc: 3 years
Born: 6-6-58 in
    San Pedro de Macoris, DR

1985 STATISTICS

AVG	G	AB	R	H	2B	3B	HR	RBI	BB	SO	SB
.245	67	184	27	45	5	1	11	25	11	40	3

CAREER STATISTICS

AVG	G	AB	R	H	2B	3B	HR	RBI	BB	SO	SB
.245	224	551	83	135	20	4	24	75	42	95	5

STRONG

VS. RHP

STRONG

VS. LHP

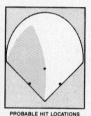

PROBABLE HIT LOCATIONS

seventh inning, despite his home run potential.

He has a strong arm, but seldom got a chance to show it off. Castillo had a sore shoulder in the beginning of the season and seemed hesitant to throw hard all year. Most of Castillo's problems occur when he has to come in on balls in front of him or move back on shots hit directly over his head. Most of his errors come when he charges ground balls, overruns them or kicks them away.

OVERALL:

Castillo's power potential remains intriguing.

Robinson: "His defensive play must improve if he is to attain the kind of power he indicates he has. I believe that it will happen and that this season he will surpass everything he has done in the majors to date.

"He wants a full-time job and is trying to shed the tag as a platoon player. He has a good chance to do that in 1986."

PITCHING:

Bryan Clark was one of 19 pitchers the Indians ran through their big league locker room last year. The fact that he finished the season with the Tribe was one of the biggest shocks of the year.

The Indians took a gamble when they signed Clark as a released player in mid-May 1985. They hoped that they had found a secret bargain and that he was finally ready to live up to his earlier promise. They were wrong.

Clark has a great arm. In the bullpen, catchers have trouble hanging on to his pitches because they move so much. But, once Clark gets out of the bullpen and onto the mound, his pitches begin to straighten out and start jumping off bats and knocking down walls.

He has good movement on his curveball and his slider and can be tough on lefthanded hitters. The fastball is his best pitch. In close games, however, he tightens up. Used mostly in middle relief, Clark was unable to get out the lefthanded hitters he was brought in to retire. A lack of control has always been his major problem. Clark puts runners on base, which forces him to give the hitter something across the plate. He gets burned.

In only 62 2/3 innings, he allowed 78 hits and walked 34 batters. A relief pitcher who puts 112 batters on base isn't fooling anybody and is just asking for trouble.

FIELDING:

Clark is an average fielder, although

BRYAN CLARK
LHP, No. 35
LL, 6'2", 185 lbs.
ML Svc: 5 years
Born: 7-12-56 in
Madera, CA

1985 STATISTICS

W	L	ERA	G	GS	CG	SV	IP	H	R	ER	BB	SO
3	4	6.36	31	3	0	2	62.2	78	47	44	34	24

CAREER STATISTICS

W	L	ERA	G	GS	CG	SV	IP	H	R	ER	BB	SO
18	23	4.24	158	37	4	4	477.2	500	260	225	241	243

he needs to be in a better position to field after his follow-through. He is easy to steal against despite the fact that he is a lefthander. He has a slow and deliberate windup, which allows runners the chance to get a good jump. He has an average move to first.

OVERALL:

Clark is the ninth or tenth man on the staff. That's what he was with the Indians and that says a lot in itself. He is best suited to long relief and spot-starting.

Robinson: "Teams always hate to turn their backs on a lefthander. You never know when it could all come together. Yet, several teams have already sent Clark packing. He has no consistency and throws everything at the same speed. An off-speed pitch might help."

PITCHING:

In baseball, a second chance is never too far away. Perhaps that's why the minors are full of players who are going to retire "in just one more year." Keith Creel is a good example. The Indians called him up from Triple-A last May. He was a flop. In 11 appearances, Creel went 0-5. When he was given the word that he was heading back to the minors, he thought about retiring before he got back on the bus. Then, like so many marginal players, he went back down. At Triple-A, Creel finished the season at 7-7, with a 3.70 ERA. He was home dove hunting in Duncanville, Texas, when the Indians recalled him late in the year to bail out their injured staff.

Creel did more than just bail the Indians out. He went 2-0 and gave up only four earned runs in 14 1/3 innings. They were Creel's first victories in the big leagues since 1983, when he pitched with Kansas City.

On a pitching staff the calibre of the Indians', a performance like that does not go unnoticed. In the last two weeks of a miserable season, Creel put himself in line for a starting job in 1986.

Creel is a control pitcher who made an important adjustment in his second tour of the minors. He switched grips on his fastball and--lo and behold--it started to sink.

The sinking action he was able to get on his fastball has made all the difference to him. Earlier in the season, all of his pitches were up in the strike zone and he was getting hammered. Creel has an average break on his curve and he can throw most of his pitches over for strikes on a consistent basis.

FIELDING:

Creel is a good fielder. He covers

KEITH CREEL
RHP, No. 21
RR, 6'2", 280 lbs.
ML Svc: 3 years
Born: 2-4-59 in
    Dallas, Tx

1985 STATISTICS

W	L	ERA	G	GS	CG	SV	IP	H	R	ER	BB	SO
2	5	4.79	15	8	0	0	62.0	73	35	33	23	31

CAREER STATISTICS

W	L	ERA	G	GS	CG	SV	IP	H	R	ER	BB	SO
5	14	5.64	49	24	1	0	193	232	129	121	83	75

first base well. Baserunners do not bother him and he doesn't throw to first very often. He is usually in a good position to field ground balls hit back to the mound.

OVERALL:

The 10 spots on the Indians' pitching staff for 1986 must be considered wide open. That means Creel has as good a chance as anybody.

Robinson: "The Indians used him as a reliever during his first stay with them last year, but he is better suited as a starter simply because he doesn't have one overpowering pitch. He will never have a better chance to make a major league club than he has this year.

"I think that he is, at best, a borderline big league pitcher. All of his pitches are average, though he was able to do some nice things with his sinker late in the year. But he will have to do better and keep the ball down all the time if he is going to make the grade."

PITCHING:

In the rubble of the Indians' 1985 season, Jamie Easterly was one of the few outposts of consistency and professionalism. Easterly did a little bit of everything last year. He began the season in long relief, was then moved to short relief and finished the season in the starting rotation. His best role, however, is in long relief.

No one would guess Easterly is a professional athlete unless they had to face him with a bat in their hands. He is on the chunky side at 5'10" and 180 pounds and is nicknamed "The Rat." He has had that nickname for so long, it doesn't even bother him anymore.

All the comedy ends when Easterly is on the mound. He's deceptively fast (between 87 and 88 MPH) and he has a nasty slider. Easterly had the lowest ERA (3.92) of any Indians' pitcher to work more than 90 innings last year.

Until the second-to-last game, he was on the verge of completing a perfect 4-0 record, but he lost in a starting assignment to Minnesota. It marked his first defeat since September 4, 1984.

Still, 1985 represented a milestone for Easterly. He passed the 20-victory mark for his career, as he ended the season with a 22-30 overall record. Sure, it took The Rat eight seasons to do it, but he said it was worth the wait.

Like most lefthanders, control has always been Easterly's downfall. Last year he was one of the few Cleveland pitchers to record more strikeouts than walks, but his concentration still tends to wander at times.

FIELDING:

He has a decent move to first and

JAMIE EASTERLY
LHP, No. 36
LL, 5'10", 180 lbs.
ML Svc: 8 years
Born: 2-17-53 in
Houston, TX

1985 STATISTICS

W	L	ERA	G	GS	CG	SV	IP	H	R	ER	BB	SO
4	1	3.92	50	7	0	0	98.2	96	52	43	53	58

CAREER STATISTICS

W	L	ERA	G	GS	CG	SV	IP	H	R	ER	BB	SO
22	30	4.47	291	36	0	14	560.1	604	320	278	290	319

does not get rattled when runners are on base. He is always in good position to field. Easterly gets off the mound quickly and has not made an error in six seasons. When he has to, he'll cover first.

OVERALL:

Easterly has helped the Indians tremendously since coming to Cleveland in a 1983 trade with Milwaukee. He is 11-4 with five saves for the Indians. He's never had a better spree in the big leagues.

The Rat doesn't have the stamina to start and he is not particularly fond of the role. He feels more comfortable in long relief and will spot-start when the team gets burdened with doubleheaders.

Robinson: "Jamie has a good live arm, but spotty control torments him. He has a fastball which is sneaky fast. He pitched well last year, but will always remain a pitcher who runs hot and cold."

HITTING:

Mike Fischlin changed his batting stance last season. Indians' hitting coach Bobby Bonds convinced him to abandon his Hunchback of Notre Dame style of hitting and adopt a more conventional upright stance. Just what kind of results the switch has made in Fischlin's hitting still can't be computed. He only batted 60 games last year and hit .200 in 73 games. It was the least playing time Fischlin has had since his first full season with the Indians in 1982.

Fischlin is a low-ball hitter who likes pitches on the inside part of the plate. He is not a power hitter and usually goes to center field. Pitchers can beat Fischlin with good fastballs down the middle and with breaking balls.

Patience is not a virtue for him. Given just 60 at-bats does not afford many hitters the chance to walk, and Mike didn't draw one all year.

Given a chance to play on a regular basis, Fischlin has proved himself to be a steady offensive player. When he sits for two or three weeks, his best offensive weapon is the sacrifice bunt. He excels at advancing runners and has good enough speed to beat out a bunt for a base hit.

BASERUNNING:

He is a good baserunner who always hustles. He doesn't have blazing speed, but usually gets a good jump. The team doesn't hesitate to use him as a pinch-runner.

FIELDING:

Mike makes his living with his glove. His defense has kept him in the majors for five years. Going into last season, he could play third, shortstop and second and even fill in at catcher. Last

MIKE FISCHLIN
2B, No. 22
RR, 6'1", 165 lbs.
ML Svc: 5 years
Born: 9-13-55 in
Sacramento, CA

1985 STATISTICS

AVG	G	AB	R	H	2B	3B	HR	RBI	BB	SO	SB
.200	73	60	12	12	4	1	0	2	5	7	0

CAREER STATISTICS

AVG	G	AB	R	H	2B	3B	HR	RBI	BB	SO	SB
.222	445	839	100	186	27	6	3	65	84	113	24

  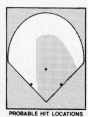

STRONG — VS. RHP   STRONG — VS. LHP   PROBABLE HIT LOCATIONS

year, Fischlin added first base to his skills, even though he played the position with an infielder's glove.

The major surprise last year was that Fischlin didn't end the season starting at second or shortstop. From 1982-1984, he always ended the season as a regular. Fischlin has a good arm and has provided the Indians with good defense off the bench: a vital role for a utilityman.

OVERALL:

Fischlin is the perfect utility man. He's aggressive defensively even though weeks can pass between his starts.

Robinson: "He works hard to try to stay sharp, but has to play more to really be a better hitter. He is usually ready when he gets called. His defensive versatility keeps him around."

HITTING:

All right, all right, so Julio Franco disappeared one night and missed a game in the Bronx just when he was leading the American League in hitting. Doesn't everybody?

Say what you will about the Indians' shortstop--but the man lives to hit. In 1985, he hit .288 and drove in 90 runs with the aid of only six home runs. That is the most RBIs by a Indian shortstop since Lou Boudreau had 106 in 1948.

Franco wraps the bat around his right ear as if it were a pretzel and consistently bangs the ball to right and center field. He's a first-ball, high-ball hitter who will crush high fastballs and low breaking balls. A pitcher should change speeds and keep everything down.

The Indians moved him to the number three spot in the batting order, a spot usually reserved for the best hitter on the ball club. He benefited from Brett Butler's ability as a leadoff hitter as well as from his own style of attack.

Franco could use some patience at the plate. He does not like to walk, and he hit into 16 double plays with runners in scoring position because he makes such hard contact. Franco is a good bunter when he goes for a hit. He's excellent at dragging the ball down the third base line. Oddly enough, he is not a good sacrifice bunter.

BASERUNNING:

Franco went on a vigorous weight-training program during the season and gained about 15 pounds. It's debatable whether it slowed him down or not. He did not steal a base until July because of hamstring problems, but then ripped off 12 steals in 13 attempts in just over a month, but stole only one after that.

He usually gets down the base line well and is aggressive when going from first to third, sometimes to the degree of taking unnecessary chances. He will go hard into second when he has to.

JULIO FRANCO
SS, No. 14
RR, 6'0", 160 lbs.
ML Svc: 3 years
Born: 8-23-61 in
   San Pedro de Macoris, DR

1985 STATISTICS

AVG	G	AB	R	H	2B	3B	HR	RBI	BB	SO	SB
.288	160	636	97	183	33	4	6	90	54	74	13

CAREER STATISTICS

AVG	G	AB	R	H	2B	3B	HR	RBI	BB	SO	SB
.282	485	1883	250	532	80	17	17	252	126	196	64

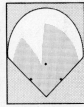

VS. RHP   VS. LHP   PROBABLE HIT LOCATIONS

FIELDING:

For the second straight year, Franco made more errors (36) than any player in the league. His errors come in bunches and usually early in the season. Last year, he made 22 of his errors by late June before settling down and playing a solid shortstop.

He has good range, especially to his left, but often boots the routine ball. He is good on foul balls down the left field line, but had some problems with soft pop-ups in short left field.

OVERALL:

The organization now seems sold on Franco at shortstop, but they're still trying to find a way to cut down on his errors early in the season.

Robinson: "He can do just about anything he wants to with the bat, and can be sensational in the field. All he lacks is concentration. If he can get himself 'into the game' more, he could really be special."

HITTING:

The signs were bad for Mel Hall even before the start of the 1985 season. When American League umpires passed the "Mel Hall" rule--no batting gloves would be allowed flapping out of back pockets at the plate--Hall should have known it was not his year.

On May 9, 1985, Hall was involved in a serious car accident and was disabled for the season with a variety of injuries, including a cracked collarbone and a fractured pelvis. The day before the accident, Hall had been named the Indians' everyday left fielder. The big question is how will Hall come back from the accident?

Hall is a low-ball, line drive hitter with good power to both center and right field. Like most National Leaguers who try to make the transition to the American League, Hall had trouble with the breaking ball in 1984, but he learned to adjust. He likes low fastballs on the inside part of the plate, but is susceptible to fastballs up and in as well as change-ups.

Hall was hitting .318 in 23 games when he was injured. He is an aggressive hitter with a wide-legged stance who was just getting a chance to play against lefthanded pitching when the accident occurred. Until then, he had only faced righthanded pitching.

BASERUNNING:

Weight training has given Hall the body of a fullback and he runs like one, too. He has a quick burst out of the box and runs the bases hard. While he is more than fast enough to steal, he seldom does. He will go hard into second on the double play and prefers the head-first slide.

FIELDING:

Hall surprised the Indians by how well he played left field when he came over from the Chicago Cubs in 1984 (he had played right for the Cubs). How-

MEL HALL
OF, No. 27
LL, 6'1", 185 lbs.
ML Svc: 3 years
Born: 9-16-60 in
Lyons, NY

1985 STATISTICS
AVG	G	AB	R	H	2B	3B	HR	RBI	BB	SO	SB
.318	23	66	7	21	6	0	0	12	8	12	0

CAREER STATISTICS
AVG	G	AB	R	H	2B	3B	HR	RBI	BB	SO	SB
.274	300	974	142	267	56	11	29	126	103	212	8

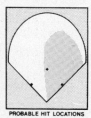

VS. RHP   VS. LHP   PROBABLE HIT LOCATIONS

ever, he might end up back in right field this season.

He has a strong arm and decent range and can make the difficult catch--especially while drifting backward. Hall is an all-out fielder. He will dive or go against the fence to catch a ball.

OVERALL:

So much depends on how Hall comes back from the accident. He lost 30 lbs. after the crash, but worked out with the Indians last September and by that time had regained all of the lost weight.

Hall went to the Florida Instructional League last winter for a refresher course. He will definitely have a chance to be an everyday player this season if he is healthy.

Robinson: "Write 1985 off and forget it. He suffered a real disappointment last season, but it looks like he is the type of player who loves to play baseball and can't wait to play again. His enthusiastic style might even be more exciting this year."

HITTING:

Mike Hargrove had almost convinced himself that he was destined to spend the 1985 season as a role player, and would rot away on the Indians' bench. But then Pat Tabler injured his knee and Jim Wilson broke his wrist. Suddenly, Hargrove was back at first base and playing every day for the last month of the season.

He took advantage of the situation and proved he could still hit. He hit .319 after the All-Star break and .348 in the last 34 games of the season.

Hargrove even picked up the pace of his notorious before-every-pitch ritual (digging a hole in the batter's box and then tugging at every piece of his uniform). He has always taken a lot of pitches and that's why he's one of the best hitters in the American League when he's ahead on the count. He's also the best two-strike hitter on the club because he knows the strike zone so well.

Hargrove is a low-fastball hitter. He will hit to straightaway center with little, if any, power. Pitchers have success with him when they get the fastball inside and low.

BASERUNNING:

Hargrove has never had any speed and at age 35, he is even slower. He goes one base at a time and can put a severe crimp in a rally by clogging the bases.

This is not news to him and he is a cautious runner. He takes few chances. He will slide hard into second base to break up the double play.

FIELDING:

After some rocky outings in previous years, Hargrove has become a decent defensive first baseman. He plays the line well, has an average arm and is adept at starting the 3-6-3 double play.

MIKE HARGROVE
1B, No. 21
LL, 6'0", 195 lbs.
ML Svc: 12 years
Born: 10-26-49 in
  Perryton, TX

1985 STATISTICS

AVG	G	AB	R	H	2B	3B	HR	RBI	BB	SO	SB
.285	107	284	31	81	14	1	1	27	39	29	1

CAREER STATISTICS

AVG	G	AB	R	H	2B	3B	HR	RBI	BB	SO	SB
.291	1666	5564	783	1614	266	28	80	686	965	551	26

VS. RHP   VS. LHP   PROBABLE HIT LOCATIONS

Error prone? How does six in one month sound? He has trouble with balls hit right at him, especially on artificial surfaces, where they pick up speed. He plays bunts and slow rollers well but he has no range.

OVERALL:

Hargrove became a free agent at the end of last season. First base is the most crowded corner in Cleveland. If he re-signs with the Indians, he'll go back to his role as a defensive replacement.

Robinson: "Mike will probably be able to hit until he's 40 years old, though I think that his lack of power has hurt his chances. He plays better as a regular, but doesn't have the defensive skills to do that and doesn't have the power to be a DH."

PITCHING:

Neal Heaton's performance over the last two years causes one to wonder if he will ever be as good as he appeared to be in his rookie year (1983) when he went 11-7. The numbers indicate the answer is no. Since 1984, the southpaw's record is 21-32. Look to the right for last year's stats and you'll see why the Indians wanted him to attend the Florida Instructional League over the winter (a tired arm he developed in late August nixed the trip).

Heaton tries to overpower hitters with a fastball that is only 86-89 MPH. That's risky business. His problems are compounded because his slider is often flat and his curveball is inconsistent.

For a long time, Heaton refused to accept the fact that his fastball was not good enough to strike out big league hitters all the time. He wouldn't change speeds or mix up his pitches. However, it appears the message may have begun to sink in a bit last year.

Heaton started the season well. In eight starts, he was 3-3 with a 2.44 ERA but got no run support. He was then 3-9 in his next 13 appearances (including six straight losses) and the season went down in a heap.

Heaton has always given up a lot of hits, but last year he outdid himself. He surrendered 244 hits in 207 2/3 innings. The year before he gave up 231 in 198 2/3 innings.

Little things upset him on the mound and he gets angry when he is taken out of games. He continues to have trouble getting the third out of an inning and he walks almost as many hitters as he strikes out.

FIELDING:

Heaton has a deliberate windup with a

NEAL HEATON
LHP, No. 44
LL, 6'1", 205 lbs.
ML Svc: 3 years
Born: 3-3-60 in
  Jamaica, NY

1985 STATISTICS
W	L	ERA	G	GS	CG	SV	IP	H	R	ER	BB	SO
9	17	4.90	36	33	5	0	207.2	244	119	113	80	82

CAREER STATISTICS
W	L	ERA	G	GS	CG	SV	IP	H	R	ER	BB	SO
32	41	4.83	121	87	13	7	586.2	664	347	315	215	246

high leg kick that gives runners a license to steal. He won't stop his hands momentarily during his windup, which would help to keep runners close.

Heaton's throw to first needs work, but he still led the Indians with two pickoffs. His fielding needs improvement, although he did cover first base better last year than he has in the past.

He falls off the mound to his left and misses hits through the middle. It cost him a couple of games last year.

OVERALL:

The Indians will wait for Heaton because they have no other choice. The solution to his problem may lie in his willingness to come to terms with the fallibility of his heater and to realize that he must use another tactic.

Robinson: "Neal has a good arm and very good stuff, but he doesn't keep the ball down. He doesn't seem to throw the right pitch at the right time. He should develop an off-speed pitch he can control with more consistency."

HITTING:

Brook Jacoby didn't say much for the Indians last year. All he did was hit 20 home runs in only his second big league season and more than double his RBI production, from 40 to 87.

Jacoby, a streaky hitter who led the Indians in strikeouts, adjusted to American League pitchers after a rookie year in which he hit only seven homers. He got jammed inside with fastballs, but when he started to look for that pitch, home runs flew off his bat.

Jacoby likes high fastballs from the middle of the plate out. He has power to all fields, but most of his home runs range from left to center field. He has a long swing and sliders on the inside of the plate give him trouble.

He became a much more aggressive, confident hitter last year. In the middle of his rookie year, he stopped trying to hit every ball out of the park and started to go to center and right field.

Jacoby is still a first-pitch hitter, although he tried to be more selective last year. He is prone to slumps during which he can look awful, and the strikeouts pile high and quickly, but the Indians think that could be tied to fatigue. Last year, he played in 161 of the Tribe's 162 games and the wear and tear surfaced more at the plate than in the field.

BASERUNNING:

When the team evaluated their players during the season last year, they concluded that Jacoby needed help running the bases. He has only fair speed and is no threat to steal, but the Indians want him to be better going from first to third. He'll go hard into second to break up the double play.

FIELDING:

Jacoby made 19 errors last season. He moves well to his left at third and

BROOK JACOBY
3B, No. 26
RR, 5'11", 175 lbs.
ML Svc: 2 years
Born: 11-23-59 in
   Philadelphia, PA

1985 STATISTICS

AVG	G	AB	R	H	2B	3B	HR	RBI	BB	SO	SB
.274	161	606	72	166	26	3	20	87	48	120	2

CAREER STATISTICS

AVG	G	AB	R	H	2B	3B	HR	RBI	BB	SO	SB
.267	302	1063	136	284	45	6	27	128	80	197	5

STRONG

VS. RHP

STRONG

VS. LHP

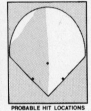

PROBABLE HIT LOCATIONS

charges bunts well. He has a deceptively strong arm and a quick delivery. His throws seem to float to first base and are easy to handle.

He does have problems going to his right. He is susceptible to doubles down the line and does not leave his feet well. He very rarely shies away from a hard-hit ball. He plays hard shots off his chest and calmly throws runners out.

OVERALL:

Despite his errors, Brook is a reliable, day-in-day-out ballplayer. He is the first one on the field for infield practice. Jacoby's hitting steadily improved compared to his rookie year.

Robinson: "Brook is turning out to be a better player than I originally thought. I wasn't the only one who was surprised, though--a lot of AL pitchers got caught off guard as well. He works hard on his defense, which is important for a young player to do. At the plate, he is going to get even better."

HITTING:

Otis Nixon has been a man bunting for his life. That is, until last year. He changed his image in 1985 and showed that he is capable of using the whole field and is not strictly a bunt-and-run type of guy. The switch-hitting Nixon even hit three home runs.

Corner infielders used to stand nose-to-nose with Nixon and dare him to bunt, but a more confident Otis simply slapped the ball past a lot of them last season. Gradually, he forced them to play him at a normal depth.

Nixon is a high-ball hitter whether he bats righthanded or lefthanded. A good inside fastball will overpower him and he will swing at curves low and away.

As his playing time increased last year, so did his patience at the plate. When he moved into the leadoff spot for a short span after the All-Star break, he started to walk more to reach base so he could kick-start the offense with his speed.

Nixon had seven bunt hits last year, but he bunted only out of necessity. It is no longer his only offensive weapon.

BASERUNNING:

One of Nixon's most prominent roles in 1985 was that of a pinch-runner late in a close game. As a pinch-runner, he scored 10 of his 34 runs. When he comes into a game as a pinch-runner, he is almost a sure bet to steal. He was 20 of 31 in stolen-base attempts and 11 of those steals resulted in runs.

He keeps a book of pitcher's moves, but relies mostly on flat-out speed to steal. He occasionally gets carried away with his speed and takes unnecessary chances, such as trying to steal third with less than two outs.

FIELDING:

Nixon's speed gives him great range in center field. He seems most comfortable in center and sometimes breaks back

OTIS NIXON
OF, No. 20
SR, 6'2", 180 lbs.
ML Svc: 2 years
Born: 1-9-59 in
Evergreen, NC

1985 STATISTICS											
AVG	G	AB	R	H	2B	3B	HR	RBI	BB	SO	SB
.235	104	162	34	38	4	0	3	9	8	27	20
CAREER STATISTICS											
AVG	G	AB	R	H	2B	3B	HR	RBI	BB	SO	SB
.202	166	267	52	54	4	0	3	10	17	43	34

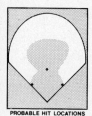

VS. RHP   VS. LHP   PROBABLE HIT LOCATIONS

on soft-hit balls when he plays left field.

He goes back on balls well, especially on line drives hit directly over his head. He has an average to below-average arm, and runners will challenge him by going from first to third and from third to home.

His ability to catch the ball is erratic; sometimes he will make a great catch and then just drop the ball. That might be the result of a lack of playing time.

OVERALL:

Nixon was a long shot to make the team out of spring training last year. He forced himself on the roster with his speed. He was aided by others' injuries, as well.

Robinson: "Otis took advantage of his opportunity last season by improving his defense and his abilities as a pinch-runner. He looked like a better hitter and was smart enough to add something other than bunting to his skills."

PITCHING:

Jerry Reed was one of the few nice surprises the Indians had last year in the pitching department. Though he was originally miscast as a starter when he was called up from Triple-A in July, the Indians made the right move at the right time when they shifted him to short relief later in the season.

A two-pitch pitcher, Reed found a home as the short man. The bullpen was not a new experience for him. Before coming to the Indians in the 1982 John Denny trade, Reed had spent five years pitching short relief with the Phillies.

Relying strictly on his fastball and slider, Reed saved eight games from August 12, and in his last 11 appearances he went 3-0 with four saves and had a 1.02 ERA. Reed was the only Tribe pitcher to break 90 MPH with any consistency.

Reed had success as a starter in the minors, but just didn't have enough pitches to start in the big leagues. Now he simply goes with his two best pitches and doesn't worry about the outcome.

Another key to Reed's emergence after eight years in the minors is his willingness to pitch inside. He had never been a pitcher to fight for his share of the plate, but when he did not make the club in spring training, he took the hint and started to move batters back.

His arm still seems sound. He has the ability to pitch on short notice, to strike out hitters efficiently and to protect a lead.

FIELDING:

Reed is an above-average fielder who works hard at this aspect of his craft.

JERRY REED
RHP, No. 35
RR, 6'1", 190 lbs.
ML Svc: 1 year plus
Born: 10-8-55 in
  Bryson City, NC

1985 STATISTICS

W	L	ERA	G	GS	CG	SV	IP	H	R	ER	BB	SO
3	5	4.11	33	5	0	8	72.1	67	41	33	19	37

CAREER STATISTICS

W	L	ERA	G	GS	CG	SV	IP	H	R	ER	BB	SO
5	7	4.78	57	6	0	8	122.1	126	76	65	40	64

He gets off the mound quickly, is good at fielding shots through the middle and covers first base well. He has a decent move to first base and runners don't seem to bother him when they reach base.

OVERALL:

It will be interesting to see where Reed fits in this season. He definitely opened some eyes last year when the team was crying out for a short reliever following the loss of Ernie Camacho and Tom Waddell because of injuries. If Camacho can come all the way back, Reed could serve as his set-up man. Or the Indians may keep him in short relief.

Robinson: "Jerry took advantage of a good opportunity last season and really helped his own cause. He knows how to pitch, but what is really going to help him is experience at the major league level. The Indians would be very lucky and very happy if he could repeat what he did in 1985, although I think he will do even better than that."

PITCHING:

Ramon Romero is a tall, skinny left-hander who is a bundle of nerves on the mound. The Indians bill him as the "winningest lefthanded pitcher from the Dominican Republic." Romero won that dubious billing because he has two wins in the big leagues--both of them coming last year. Cleveland coaches, scouts and front office people wracked their brains trying to think of another Dominican lefthander to win that many games, but came away empty. Hence, the title.

Now if they could only be as inventive in finding a way to calm down the excitable Romero when he's earning his money. If they could, Romero might turn into a decent pitcher.

For the last two or three years, the Indians has said Romero has the best arm in the organization; that is likely another overstatement. His problems are a lack of control and his anxiety on the mound. When Romero can get the ball over the plate, no one can hit him. He is especially tough on lefthanders because of his nasty slider, which breaks away from them, and his fastball, which moves all over the place. Sometimes, everything he throws moves everywhere but through the strike zone.

Toward the end of the season, he experimented with using a sidearm delivery against lefties and had some success with it. Ramon has a curveball with a big break, but mostly batters felt they were the ones getting a break when they faced Romero, who pitches strictly out of the stretch.

In 64 1/3 innings, Romero threw 13 home run balls, gave up 69 hits and threw 6 wild pitches. It may be that the high-strung Romero is simply overwhelmed by the big leagues after having spent eight years in the minors. On the mound,

RAMON ROMERO
LHP, No. 50
LL, 6'4", 170 lbs.
ML Svc: less than 1 year
Born: 1-8-59 in
    San Pedro de Macoris, DR

1985 STATISTICS

W	L	ERA	G	GS	CG	SV	IP	H	R	ER	BB	SO
2	3	6.58	19	10	0	0	64.1	69	48	47	38	38

CAREER STATISTICS

W	L	ERA	G	GS	CG	SV	IP	H	R	ER	BB	SO
2	3	6.30	20	10	0	0	67.1	69	48	47	38	41

he is as tight as a violin string. He sprints off the mound at the end of each inning.

FIELDING:

Romero has a good move to first. He was one of only three Indians' pitchers to pick a runner off first last year. He keeps the runners close and fields his position well.

OVERALL:

Romero is one of about eight or ten Indian pitchers who are similar in style and talent.

Robinson: "At first, the Indians believed Romero was too nervous to be an effective short man. Now they believe he's too nervous to start. Where does that leave him? He has a good arm and seems to be able to pitch anytime. He gets worked up on the mound, which is a sign of inexperience, but should settle down and become a good pitcher if he is given the opportunity to learn the style and the hitters of the American League."

PITCHING:

Has Vern Ruhle reached the end of the line? He made the Indians as a spring training invitee last year, but in the last two seasons his won-lost record is a dismal 3-19, including a 2-10 record in 1985.

Ruhle is a control pitcher who works fast and knows how to set up hitters. The major concern is that Ruhle's stuff simply isn't good enough to win consistently in the big leagues anymore.

Last year Ruhle began the season in the starting rotation. After seven games, he was 1-2 with a 2.79 ERA, but the Indians' offense didn't support him with many runs. Then he became injured. He suffered a pinched nerve in his neck and was out for 18 days. Just three starts after his return, he went back on the disabled list by bruising a floating rib in his side. Ruhle didn't pitch again until the middle of June.

Ruhle's control has to be perfect in order for him to be effective. When he returned from the DL for the second time last year, he left his control somewhere on a trainer's table and registered a 1-5 record in 10 starts. He was sent to the bullpen in August for the rest of the season.

Ruhle's best pitch is a slider. He also throws a fast curve and a change-up, and got into trouble when he relied too heavily on his fastball. He is not afraid to move a batter off the plate by throwing inside.

For a veteran pitcher, Ruhle made a lot of mistakes at critical moments last year. In 125 innings, he gave up 16 home runs. As usual, his strikeouts to walks ratio was good, but when he tired, he put the ball in the middle of the plate and line drives filled the air.

While in the bullpen, Ruhle worked mostly in middle relief and did a solid job. He was 0-3 with three saves and a 2.59 ERA in 42 2/3 innings of relief.

VERN RUHLE
RHP, No. 48
RR, 6'1", 195 lbs.
ML Svc: 12 years
Born: 1-5-51 in
Coleman, MI

1985 STATISTICS

W	L	ERA	G	GS	CG	SV	IP	H	R	ER	BB	SO
2	10	4.32	42	16	1	3	125	139	65	60	30	54

CAREER STATISTICS

W	L	ERA	G	GS	CG	SV	IP	H	R	ER	BB	SO
58	80	3.72	270	178	29	7	1248.1	1330	601	516	305	516

FIELDING:

Ruhle has a good move to first base, although sometimes he tends to throw over there too much. Runners seem to distract him, even ones without good speed. He is a decent fielder and gets off the mound quickly to cover first and to field balls hit back to him.

OVERALL:

Ruhle is past his peak and has been slipping for the last two years. He can still help a team in middle relief, but doesn't have the one overpowering pitch that would make him a short relief man. His inconsistency does not lend itself to a spot in the starting rotation.

Another consideration is his health: nagging injuries cost him a lot of time off duty.

Robinson: "His pitches are all average to below-average. He is a good pitcher when his control is on. When he is going well, he pitches effectively even when he is behind in the count. But without his control, he doesn't have much to work with."

PITCHING:

Don Schulze started off the 1985 season with a 3-0 record. By June 20, that 3-0 record had turned into a 3-7 record: after a string of three quick wins, he ran into a rope of seven losses in nine consecutive starts.

To save Schulze's psyche and preserve the confidence of a young pitcher they hold in high regard, the Indians sent Schulze down to Triple-A. He didn't resurface in the big leagues until late in the year, and when he did, he was not the same pitcher.

Schulze kept his composure on the mound and didn't lose his temper or concentration; most importantly, his sinking fastball was really sinking.

Schulze is nicknamed "The Rock." He is built like an offensive tackle. Two years ago, Angels' strongman Brian Downing hit him in the head with a line drive that would have staggered an elephant. Schulze only blinked.

For all his size, Schulze is not a strikeout pitcher. His out pitch is a sinking fastball that produces a lot of ground balls when he's on. He also throws a decent slider and will mix in a screwball for a change-up when he's behind on the count.

Earlier in his career, he pitched for the Chicago Cubs. They told him to forget about his curveball. The Indians, on the other hand, asked Schulze to start throwing it again last year, and he was able to throw it for strikes.

Schulze works quickly on the mound, but gets distracted by errors behind him. When he returned to the Indians last September, he seemed to be able to handle his fielders' mistakes with a calmer attitude.

Schulze throws between 84-88 MPH. On a good night, his fastball will average between 86-88 MPH. He's still trying to make the transition from being the power pitcher he was in the minors to more of

DON SCHULZE
RHP, No. 37
RR, 6'3", 225 lbs.
ML Svc: 2 years
Born: 9-27-62 in
    Roselle, IL

1985 STATISTICS
W	L	ERA	G	GS	CG	SV	IP	H	R	ER	BB	SO
4	10	6.01	19	18	1	0	94.1	128	75	63	19	37

CAREER STATISTICS
W	L	ERA	G	GS	CG	SV	IP	H	R	ER	BB	SO
7	17	5.66	43	36	3	0	197	260	143	124	54	86

a control pitcher in the big leagues.

At times, Schulze is his own worst enemy on the mound. He gets angry and tries to overthrow the ball. His poise is something else he is working on.

FIELDING:

Schulze tries to be a good fielder. Still, he's far from agile coming off the mound. He is usually in good position to field balls hit through the middle. His move to first is average and baserunners seem to rattle him. He needs work on his throws to second and third.

OVERALL:

He is only 23 years old and has just begun to show signs of maturing. If he is ready to start in the big leagues, the Indians will have a place for him.

Robinson: "Schulze still needs some polishing. He doesn't have anything that is overpowering, but his sinker is starting to show signs of being a consistent and effective pitch. He will need to have the support of a good defensive infield because of the amount of ground balls the sinker produces."

PITCHING:

Roy Smith had a great Triple-A season last year. The only time he ran into hard times was when the Indians promoted him to the big leagues. In the minors, he was 10-4, with a 2.39 ERA. In the majors, he was 1-4 with a 5.34 ERA.

When Smith didn't make the Indians' staff out of spring training, he became a frozen player at Triple-A. That meant the Indians couldn't promote him without exposing him to waivers. The Indians managed to get him through waivers in late June. It would have been much safer if they'd just left him in Triple-A.

In his second start, Seattle's Phil Bradley drilled Smith just above the right ear in a frightening accident. The ball bounced off Smith's head at least 20 feet in the air. After the accident, Smith was put on the disabled list. He spent his time throwing on the side trying to convince the Indians he was ready to pitch. They sent him to Triple-A for one start and then brought him back.

Smith won his first game back in a complete game over the New York Yankees on August 1. He didn't win again for the rest of the year. In nine appearances, he was 0-4. He missed the final three starts of the season with a weak right shoulder.

At one time, Smith threw hard. That was back when he was in the Philadelphia minor league system (1979-82). Now, he's strictly a control pitcher who throws in the mid-80s on a good day. Normally, most of his pitches are in the low 80s.

Smith's change-up, a slow overhand curve, can be devastating. He throws it at about 60-70 MPH and makes hitters look silly.

However, if Smith's control is not right on the money, he gets hit hard. He can strike out some batters even without his best control but most hitters can get the best of him.

ROY SMITH
RHP, No. 33
RR, 6'3", 200 lbs.
ML Svc: 2 years
Born: 9-6-61 in
    Mt. Vernon, NY

1985 STATISTICS

W	L	ERA	G	GS	CG	SV	IP	H	R	ER	BB	SO
1	4	5.34	12	11	1	0	62.1	84	40	37	17	28

CAREER STATISTICS

W	L	ERA	G	GS	CG	SV	IP	H	R	ER	BB	SO
6	9	4.92	34	25	1	0	148.2	175	89	81	57	83

Smith also continued to have trouble with the long ball. In 1984, he gave up 14 homers in 86 1/3 innings. Last year, he gave up eight.

He works quickly and is not afraid to move a batter off the plate.

FIELDING:

Smith is an average fielder. He isn't overly concerned about holding runners on base. On his follow-through, he falls off the mound in an awkward position that does not put him in good stead to field ground balls hit back toward the mound.

OVERALL:

If anything, he took a step backward last season. In 1984, he was tried in long relief and if he doesn't cut it as a starter, he could wind up back there.

Robinson: "Smith is one of eight or ten Cleveland pitchers who are of equal ability. His curveball is what keeps everyone looking at him. It comes in very slowly and with a big break that can fool just about any hitter. Obviously, he hasn't been able to get it over often enough to earn a big league job."

HITTING:

Pat Tabler loves to hit with runners on base. Last year, he hit .346 with runners in scoring position. He was 6-for-7 with the bases loaded. Tabler's season came to an end when he grounded out with the bases loaded against Milwaukee in late August and injured his left knee. Since joining the Indians, Tabler is hitting .669 (22-for-35, with 54 RBIs) with the bases loaded.

Tabler is a high-ball, fastball hitter. He likes the ball from the middle of the plate in and hits straightaway. He is an aggressive hitter, but one who is susceptible to inside fastballs and change-ups.

For a first baseman, Tabler does not have an overabundance of power. He hit only five home runs last year, but his RBI total probably would have been comparable to his 1984 total of 68 had he not missed the last month of the season.

BASERUNNING:

Tabler is not a burner out of the box, but he does a nice job going from first to third. He will go hard into second to break up the double play, but is definitely no threat to steal. He's an average baserunner, at best.

FIELDING:

Tabler works hard on his defense, but it is not something that comes naturally to him, as does hitting. He committed 14 errors in 117 games last year and his best position defensively is still probably third base, although he hardly saw any action there last year.

He has trouble on slow rollers down the line and hard shots right at him. His arm is average, but he is good at digging the ball out of the dirt on low throws.

PAT TABLER
1B, No. 10
RR, 6'2", 195 lbs.
ML Svc: 5 years
Born: 2-2-58 in
Hamilton, OH

1985 STATISTICS

AVG	G	AB	R	H	2B	3B	HR	RBI	BB	SO	SB
.275	117	404	47	111	18	3	5	59	27	55	0

CAREER STATISTICS

AVG	G	AB	R	H	2B	3B	HR	RBI	BB	SO	SB
.276	445	1493	189	412	69	14	23	204	149	226	5

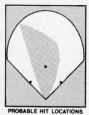

STRONG — VS. RHP · STRONG — VS. LHP · PROBABLE HIT LOCATIONS

OVERALL:

Tabler is an aggressive, heads-up player who makes a living with his bat. Usually a high-average hitter, his average dropped from .290 in 1984 to .275 last year, but he was plagued by his bad knee and related injuries (pulled hamstrings and lower back pain) for most of the season.

Robinson: "He is earning a well-deserved reputation as a notorious hitter with runners in scoring position. Pat has made a believer out of a lot of people, including me. You will see him perform in the same workmanlike way this season.

"There has been talk of his being traded to all sorts of teams. He has a higher market value than a lot of people realize."

PITCHING:

Rich Thompson was just another mediocre minor league pitcher when the Indians suddenly promoted him to the majors in late April 1985. Thompson was so shocked that when his Triple-A manager, Doc Edwards, called him into the office to tell him the good news, Thompson thought he was being sent to Double-A.

For a while, it looked as if the shock treatment might work. Pitching in relief, his three-quarters delivery and his sinking fastball kept hitters off balance early in the year.

One weekend in July, the Indians convinced Thompson to throw underhand a la Dan Quisenberry. His teammates began calling him "Frankenberry." For a while, even that experiment had some success, as Thompson registered three saves in six save opportunities.

Thompson's body rebelled against the new style, however. His knee hurt, his back hurt and so did his neck. His fastball began to come up in the strike zone and hitters literally wore him out.

Never completely sold on the underhand delivery, Thompson was able to throw only 80 MPH or less. When he started to get hit, he lost his temper and couldn't get out of jams. Mentally, Thompson was a mess because he believed he had better stuff using the three-quarters delivery.

Finally, Thompson scrapped the underhand delivery and tried a combination of the two styles near the end of the season. The results were disasterous; Rich was completely frustrated by the end of 1985.

When he threw overhand, Thompson challenged hitters. After he changed to a submarine delivery, he concentrated more on throwing strikes--something he did very badly--instead of pitching to a hitter's weakness.

Last season, Thompson was asked to do

RICH THOMPSON
RHP, No. 48
RR, 6'3", 215 lbs.
ML Svc: 1 year
Born: 11-1-56 in
New York, NY

1985 STATISTICS												
W	L	ERA	G	GS	CG	SV	IP	H	R	ER	BB	SO
3	8	6.30	57	0	0	5	80	95	63	56	48	30
CAREER STATISTICS												
W	L	ERA	G	GS	CG	SV	IP	H	R	ER	BB	SO
3	8	6.30	57	0	0	5	80	95	63	56	48	30

the impossible: experiment with a new pitch and a new delivery at the highest level of baseball competition.

FIELDING:

He has an average move to first, but needs a lot of work on his fielding. He must learn to eat the ball on high choppers and bunts rather than risk an error with a wild throw to first or second.

Thompson will get off the mound and cover first as necessary.

OVERALL:

The Indians believe Thompson's best bet for staying in the big leagues is to throw underhand, but left the final decision to him. The team needs someone who can come out of the bullpen, keep the ball low and force double plays.

Robinson: "His greatest strength is that he keeps the ball down with the submarine style. It does not appear to be a natural style for him, as it is for Dan Quisenberry. Thompson's going to have to think of something fast if he can't throw underhand."

HITTING:

Forget the first two months of the 1985 season for Andre Thornton. The DH was dazed and confused and still hurting from his spring training knee surgery.

Thornton came back ahead of schedule after injuring his knee, but he tried to do too much too soon. He was unable to get any drive from his legs; it wasn't until August that he could generate any kind of power at all.

With his knee better but still hurting, he hit 16 of his 22 home runs. He hit 19 homers and had 71 RBIs after the Fourth of July. He finished the season with a disappointing .236 average, but Thornton led the Indians in home runs and was second in RBIs with 88.

Thornton is a low-ball, pull hitter who has the ability to crush any inside pitch. Curves and breaking balls down and away give him trouble. The slider is also a tough pitch for him to hit.

Usually a patient hitter, he looked bad when he first returned to the line-up last year. He struck out frequently searching for his timing and for the first time in four years finished a season with more strikeouts than walks.

BASERUNNING:

He has never been fast, but has always taken pride in his baserunning skills. He knows when to go from first to second and likes to pull a surprise steal.

Last year's knee injury made him a liability on the bases, however. He was thrown out several times while trying to stretch singles into doubles. His knees hurt when he had to slide. He did steal home on the front end of a double steal, however. He will have to adjust his thinking on the bases in light of the condition of his knees for the rest of his career.

FIELDING:

Thornton didn't play a game at first

ANDRE THORNTON
DH/1B, No. 29
RR, 6'2", 205 lbs.
ML Svc: 12 years
Born: 8-13-49 in
Tuskegee, AL

1985 STATISTICS											
AVG	G	AB	R	H	2B	3B	HR	RBI	BB	SO	SB
.236	124	461	49	109	13	0	22	88	47	75	3

CAREER STATISTICS											
AVG	G	AB	R	H	2B	3B	HR	RBI	BB	SO	SB
.258	1409	4805	735	1240	228	22	236	824	801	759	43

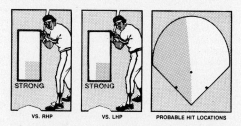

STRONG VS. RHP   STRONG VS. LHP   PROBABLE HIT LOCATIONS

base last year. Coming off knee surgery, the Indians didn't want to take a chance of further injury and used him strictly as a DH. He does not have great range at first base, but can get the job done in an emergency.

OVERALL:

During the second half of the season, he proved that his signing was not a mistake. Thornton finished fifth in the American League in RBIs-per-time-at-bat. He had one RBI every 5.23 at-bats, behind Don Mattingly, Eddie Murray, George Brett and Carlton Fisk.

Robinson: "Andre's injury was the most significant to any team in the league last year.

"He really came on in the second half of the season and was swinging at a lot more pitches with men on base. This year, I don't think he'll have the kind of year he had in 1984 when he hit 33 home runs, but I do think he'll continue to drive in runs and hit .270."

PITCHING:

Dave Von Ohlen is a lefthanded sinkerball pitcher. When he's on, he keeps the ball low and away from righthanded hitters and induces a lot of ground ball outs.

When Von Ohlen isn't on, the ground ball outs turn into rocket shots off the outfield fence. Von Ohlen made the club in spring training after they signed him to a Triple-A contract as a minor league free agent. All he did in Tucson was throw ground ball outs.

Then the regular season started and Von Ohlen disappeared. He tore muscles in his left forearm in mid-May and went on a 20-day rehabilitation program in the minors. Just before getting ready to rejoin the big league club, Von Ohlen twisted a knee getting out of the way of a line drive.

The injury resulted in more time on the disabled list and Von Ohlen didn't pitch with the Indians again until September 1--almost four months after his last appearance with them.

Of the 10 pitchers who ended the season with the Indians, Von Ohlen and Rich Thompson were the only two not to start at least one game. Dave worked strictly in long relief or to get out an occasional lefthanded hitter.

Von Ohlen was only one of two Cleveland pitchers to finish with a winning record. His sinking fastball is his best pitch, but he also throws a change-up when he's behind on the count.

Control problems plagued Von Ohlen when he returned last September. His knee was still tender and he couldn't bend down all the way to make his fastball sink. Since he isn't a strikeout pitcher, Von Ohlen was at a big disadvantage.

DAVE VON OHLEN
LHP, No. 70
LL, 6'2", 200 lbs.
ML Svc: 3 years
Born: 10-25-58 in
Flushing, NY

1985 STATISTICS

W	L	ERA	G	GS	CG	SV	IP	H	R	ER	BB	SO
3	2	2.91	26	0	0	0	43.1	47	20	14	20	12

CAREER STATISTICS

W	L	ERA	G	GS	CG	SV	IP	H	R	ER	BB	SO
7	4	3.14	99	0	0	3	146.2	157	60	51	53	52

FIELDING:

Von Ohlen is an average fielder. He will keep runners close at first simply because he's a lefthander. He pitched with a brace on his knee late in the season and that restricted his movements on the mound.

OVERALL:

Von Ohlen probably rates a second look simply because he didn't get to pitch that much last year. He could help the Indians in middle relief if his knee is sound and he is able to keep the ball down.

Robinson: "I think he's a ninth or tenth man on a staff. Lefties are hard to come by and that will help him. His best pitch is his sinking fastball, but everything else is average to below average."

HITTING:

George Vukovich's batting average dropped 60 points last year from a team leading .304 in 1984 to a weak .244. Vukovich thought he should have been the everyday right fielder in 1985, but when he couldn't break out of the platoon system with Carmen Castillo, both his performance and his attitude nosedived. He stopped talking to the media two weeks before the media knew it. It was that kind of year.

Vukovich is a high-ball hitter who likes to drive the ball to center or to pull it to right. He started the year trying to pull every pitch and that's what got him into trouble. He is at his best when he sprays the ball between the left-center field and right-center field alleys.

Having started his career in the National League, the lefthanded-hitting Vukovich is still a fastball hitter, but he had begun to adjust to off-speed pitches. The adjustment was not well-indicated last year, however. Pitchers get him out regularly by keeping the ball on the outside part of the plate. He is a sucker for an off-speed breaking pitch.

Vukovich is not a good bunter and does not show a great deal of concern for the lost art.

BASERUNNING:

He lumbers out of the box on most ground balls, but has good instincts once he reaches base. Vukovich goes from first to third with surprising speed even though he is not a threat to steal a base. He goes hard into second base to break up the double play and likes the headfirst slide.

FIELDING:

The Indians call Vukovich their best "fundamental" outfielder. That is not entirely the case, however. While he is an all-out defensive player, he lacks

GEORGE VUKOVICH
RF, No. 24
LR, 6'0", 198 lbs.
ML Svc: 6 years
Born: 6-24-56 in
Chicago, IL

1985 STATISTICS

AVG	G	AB	R	H	2B	3B	HR	RBI	BB	SO	SB
.244	149	434	43	106	22	0	8	45	30	75	2

CAREER STATISTICS

AVG	G	AB	R	H	2B	3B	HR	RBI	BB	SO	SB
.268	728	1602	164	430	76	10	27	203	127	229	9

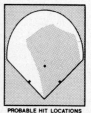

VS. RHP   VS. LHP   PROBABLE HIT LOCATIONS

speed and can look shaky on high flies that take a long time to come down. He breaks forward too quickly on line drives and has problems with balls hit directly at him.

He dives after balls and has no fear of fences. His range is decent and he has the most consistent arm on the team.

OVERALL:

Lots of things frustrated Vukovich last year: the Indians lost 102 games, he wasn't the everyday right fielder and he stopped hitting. Things aren't likely to improve if Mel Hall makes a complete recovery from last year's car accident. That will make the outfield picture much more crowded and cut down on Vukovich's playing time even further.

Robinson: "The younger Indians' players are more likely to play in 1986 than George. Because he needs to play every day to keep himself ready to hit, his numbers will probably take a turn for the worse."

PITCHING:

Tom Waddell was the most consistent pitcher on the Cleveland staff last year. While the Indians' pitchers registered the highest ERA in the history of the franchise, Waddell did everything for the Indians and did it well.

He started the year in short relief after Ernie Camacho went down with a bad elbow during the first week of the season. When his own elbow started aching, pitching in short relief became impossible for him. Waddell moved to middle relief and eventually to the starting rotation.

The Indians moved Waddell into starting rotation because his sore elbow made it impossible for him to pitch two days in a row out of the bullpen.

Waddell beat Ron Guidry and the New York Yankees in his first start, but he suffered from poor stamina as a starter.

He pitched extremely well no matter how he was used last year. He uses a deceptive three-quarters delivery that is tough for hitters to pick up. He has a sinking fastball that he throws between 84-87 MPH, but his slider is his best pitch. He also throws a knuckleball, though he will rarely use it.

Perhaps his best asset is that he throws strikes. He doesn't mess around or try to fool anybody. He just keeps the ball low, throws it over the plate and dares the hitter to make contact with it.

His bold approach is one of the reasons he gave up 20 home runs in 112 2/3 innings last year. Waddell's pitching arm hurt all season. Even in spring training, he knew that he would have to have his elbow operated on at the end of

TOM WADDELL
RHP, No. 54
RR, 6'1", 190 lbs.
ML Svc: 2 years
Born: 9-17-58 in
     Dundee, Scotland

1985 STATISTICS

W	L	ERA	G	GS	CG	SV	IP	H	R	ER	BB	SO
8	6	4.87	49	9	1	9	112.2	104	61	61	39	53

CAREER STATISTICS

W	L	ERA	G	GS	CG	SV	IP	H	R	ER	BB	SO
15	10	4.04	107	9	1	15	209.2	172	96	94	76	112

the season. He also pulled a leg muscle that affected his windup from July until he underwent surgery to remove bone spurs from his right tricep.

FIELDING:

Waddell handles balls hit in front of the mound well. He will cover first but does not bother himself excessively with runners on base.

OVERALL:

The Indians must decide what hole Tom will fill for them. His best role would probably be as a set-up man for Camacho, but he definitely opened some eyes by the way he pitched as a starter at the end of the year.

Robinson: "The Indians have to improve for him to get any better. He has good control and likes to work, though his ability to go any kind of distance is questionable."

PITCHING:

Curt Wardle was the only major league player the Indians received from the Minnesota Twins last year in the Bert Blyleven trade. He came to Cleveland as a reliever, but the Indians made him a starter. Wardle did something that a lot of other Indians' pitchers were unable to do in 1985: he actually won a few ballgames.

Only one season removed from Double-A ball, Wardle crawled his way through seven games after joining the Indians. He is a slow, deliberate worker. In fact, against Toronto last year, he was moving so slowly it seemed as if he had fallen into a coma on the mound.

Wardle is still learning how to pitch in the big leagues. He struck out 292 batters in 356 1/3 innings in the minors, but found the going much tougher in the majors.

A lack of control is Wardle's major problem, but he is the kind of pitcher who can lose it and find it all in the same inning.

His best pitch is a fastball. Wardle uses an off-speed curve as his change-up and he will also throw a slider on a high count pitch to get a strikeout. His slider is good.

The Indians still aren't sure where Wardle's future lies. Some in the front office believe he can start. Others do not feel he has enough pitches to be in the rotation and that the hitters will catch up with him after a short while.

However, it does appear that Curt's fastball is, at the very least, good enough for short relief and that his curveball could keep batters off balance for two or three innings.

Wardle came to the Indians with a touch of arthritis in his neck. As his neck responded to treatment and Wardle's stamina increased as a starter, he became more effective. Still, he gave up

CURT WARDLE
LHP, No. 36
LL, 6'5", 220 lbs.
ML Svc: 1 year
Born: 11-16-60 in
   Downey, CA

1985 STATISTICS
W	L	ERA	G	GS	CG	SV	IP	H	R	ER	BB	SO
8	9	6.18	50	12	0	1	115	127	83	79	62	84

CAREER STATISTICS
W	L	ERA	G	GS	CG	SV	IP	H	R	ER	BB	SO
8	9	6.18	50	12	0	1	115	127	83	79	62	84

127 hits in 115 innings--including 20 home runs.

FIELDING:

Baserunners don't seem to upset him. It's a good thing, too, because he walks a lot of batters. He is an average fielder and sometimes has trouble getting off the mound because of his large size. He does not throw to first base very often.

OVERALL:

He won seven games for the Indians last year, but was helped because the Cleveland bats were alive during those particular games. He is really an unknown quantity.

Robinson: "The Indians must decide how they want to use him. It appears that Wardle's move to the bullpen hinges on whether or not Ernie Camacho and Tom Waddell can come back from elbow surgery. He's a young pitcher who hasn't reached his peak yet. He suffers from two things common to rookie pitchers: inexperience and a lack of control. But he has a good fastball that looks as if it may help him."

HITTING:

Jerry Willard was in a deep freeze for the first five months of the 1985 season before deciding it was time to hit the baseball. Willard hit six of his seven home runs and drove in 16 of his 36 RBIs in September.

At the beginning of the season, Jerry disappeared behind catchers Chris Bando and Butch Benton. When he complained and said he wanted to play every day, the Indians granted his wish by sending him to Triple-A.

By the time Willard reappeared in Cleveland, he had decided to keep his mouth shut and play. When the season ended, Willard was the Tribe's number one backstop due mostly to his bat.

Willard is a dead pull hitter who can drive inside fastballs for home runs. Last year, though, he became a more aggressive hitter and stopped looking for the perfect pitch. The result was more singles up the middle.

Willard is a good hitter when he is ahead in the count. Still, pitchers can get him out by throwing breaking balls on the outside part of the plate.

His overall improvement included bunting. On a team that didn't bunt well, Willard showed the ability to advance runners with the sacrifice bunt.

BASERUNNING:

Like most catchers, Willard cannot run. To say he is slow is being kind. After being sent to Triple-A, though, Willard showed much more hustle going to first base. He will go hard into second to break up the double play.

FIELDING:

He did not become the Indians' number one catcher on the strength of his defensive abilities: almost every aspect of his catching needs improvement.

He gets out from behind the plate on bunts quickly and has a strong arm, but runners ran wild on him last year. He threw out only 26 of 94 basestealers in

JERRY WILLARD
C, No. 16
LR, 6'2", 195 lbs.
ML Svc: 2 years
Born: 3-14-60 in
  Oxnard, CA

1985 STATISTICS

AVG	G	AB	R	H	2B	3B	HR	RBI	BB	SO	SB
.270	104	300	39	81	13	0	7	36	28	59	0

CAREER STATISTICS

AVG	G	AB	R	H	2B	3B	HR	RBI	BB	SO	SB
.249	191	546	60	136	21	1	17	73	54	114	1

VS. RHP

VS. LHP

PROBABLE HIT LOCATIONS

1985. The pitching staff didn't help him because, in general, they do not hold runners on base, but even so Willard had trouble getting rid of the ball quickly.

Another area of concern is those "bang-bang" plays at the plate. Willard showed a disturbing tendency to drop the ball on tag plays at home. The threat of contact didn't scare him--he just has to learn how to protect the ball better. He is still shaky on foul pops, too.

OVERALL:

While it appears the offensive side of his game is about to surface, his defensive game needs loads of work. He must earn the respect of the pitching staff. He does not have a lock on the starting job this year.

Robinson: "With two years under his belt now, he should be a better offensive player in 1986; he has some ability with the bat. Defensively, there are a lot of things that need attention. His status will hinge on the work he does to correct that."

BENNY AYALA
DH/OF, No. 27
RR, 6'1", 195 lbs.
ML Svc: 8 years
Born: 2-7-51 in
    Yauco, PR

HITTING, BASERUNNING, FIELDING:

Benny Ayala is a professional hitter, which is why the Indians signed him at the beginning of the 1985 season. For a while, Ayala would start in left field, get two at-bats and then be replaced for defensive purposes in the fifth or sixth inning. The Indians told him to simply "back up all the way until you hit the left field fence with your back and stay there."

Ayala has made a living in the majors as a pinch-hitter, but he actually hit better for the Indians when he was in the lineup.

Ayala is a high-ball hitter who likes to pull the inside pitch.

He has below average speed and is no threat to steal.

OVERALL:

Ayala was eligible for free agency at the end of last year. At age 34, he is one of the oldest players on a club that is turning toward younger players.

Robinson: "His bat might keep him in the big leagues, though that depends on the makeup of team he is with. Benny is still an aggressive hitter."

JEFF BARKLEY
RHP, No. 49
SR, 6'3", 178 lbs.
ML Svc: 1 year
Born: 11-21-59 in
    Hickory, NC

PITCHING, FIELDING:

Jeff Barkley is a forkball pitcher whose best pitch forgot to fork last year. He pitched well in the minors, but found the going considerably tougher in his 21 games with the Indians.

When Barkley's forkball is on, he is an effective reliever; when it doesn't work, he gets his socks knocked off because he doesn't have another pitch to fall back on.

The Indians tried him in both middle relief and short relief. He was part of the Tribe's perpetual spring training pitching program, and the righthanded rookie just wasn't ready for the majors.

As a reliever, Barkley has at least three big problems: the first is that he has trouble pitching with men on base, the second is that he has trouble getting out the first batter he faces, and finally, he gives up too many home runs. Now, does this sound like a short reliever ready for the major leagues?

He has a good move to first base, but has to work on getting off the mound and fielding bunts down the first base line.

OVERALL:

Barkley still has a chance. He's only 25 years old and has one thing a reliever needs--a trick pitch. But he needs better control of it and he has to concentrate more when pitching in tight situations.

Robinson: "Inexperience is his major weakness. He has a good arm and can pitch anytime. He may get a shot this year."

RICK BEHENNA
RHP, No. 32
RR, 6'2", 170 lbs.
ML Svc: 3 years
Born: 3-6-60 in
   Miami, FL

PITCHING, FIELDING:

Rick Behenna underwent rotator cuff surgery in 1984 and has not been an effective pitcher since. He began the 1985 season on the disabled list in the minors. He was 3-1 in Triple-A in six starts before the Indians promoted him.

Behenna started four games for the big league club and went 0-2 before he was forced to return to the DL with a sore right shoulder. After the middle of July, his season was over.

Before the injury, Behenna was a power pitcher with a good live fastball and plenty of movement on his slider. He also had a good curveball.

In his four starts with the Indians, Behenna only had one good outing and did not have his old pop on the ball. He was hit hard.

He is a average fielder and gets off the mound quickly to field his position.

OVERALL:

If Behenna can ever get back to full strength, he could definitely help the Indians as a starter. This year is a key year for him, since it usually takes two years to recover from surgery.

Robinson: "He always had good movement on the ball, but no one will know if his stuff can return to its former promise because of the uncertainty of the type of injury he sustained."

DETROIT TIGERS

HITTING:

Tom Brookens won the third base job by default when rookie Chris Pittaro, who was handed the job in spring training 1985, proved inadequate. Brookens managed 47 extra-base hits (34 of those were doubles) in 485 at-bats, but drove in only 47 runs. That is not enough production from his position.

Brookens hits out of a crouch. He has a tough time handling inside fastballs—high or low. His home runs are generally the result of breaking pitches from the middle to the lower inside part of the plate.

Brookens is a much better hitter against lefthanded pitchers. Righthanders power him inside to set him up for big, sweeping breaking pitches away.

He gets to first base quickly for a righthanded hitter and could improve his average if he bunted more frequently for base hits, especially against righthanded pitchers. He does not protect the plate well with two strikes.

BASERUNNING:

No one on the club makes fewer baserunning mistakes or reads base hits better than Brookens. He is always likely to score from first on a double. He receives high grades for never missing a sign. Brookens stole 14 bases in 19 attempts and could steal more, but he has a slow slide into second base.

FIELDING:

At third base, Brookens is generally a solid fielder. His errors come in bunches, and most of them are on relatively easy chances.

He goes to his right well, but in going to his left, he usually dives instead of keeping on his feet. Brookens gets a good jump on topped balls and pop fouls. He does not bluff runners coming into third base on close plays. His arm

TOM BROOKENS
3B, No. 16
RR, 5'10", 170 lbs.
ML Svc: 7 years
Born: 8-10-53 in
    Chambersburg, PA

1985 STATISTICS
AVG	G	AB	R	H	2B	3B	HR	RBI	BB	SO	SB
.237	156	485	54	115	34	6	7	47	27	78	14

CAREER STATISTICS
AVG	G	AB	R	H	2B	3B	HR	RBI	BB	SO	SB
.244	829	2377	282	581	113	28	45	275	159	374	63

  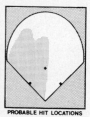

VS. RHP   VS. LHP   PROBABLE HIT LOCATIONS

is average in terms of strength; his accuracy, however, is erratic.

Brookens is best-suited as a utility player. In addition to third base, he can be used at shortstop and second. He has also played in the outfield and even caught five innings in an extra-inning game last season.

OVERALL:

He is a spunky player who is well-liked by his teammates. As an everyday player, however, he falls short.

Robinson: "I think that Tom is a valuable player to the Tigers. Last year, he was called upon to do something extra and he didn't let Sparky down in the field or on the bases. He is not spectacular at any spot in the field, but he can play three positions well and can be counted on to make the routine play. He could pay more attention to his throwing, however."

HITTING:

Life was beautiful for Marty Castillo in the 1984 World Series. He was inserted as the third baseman against left-handers and responded with three hits in nine at-bats, including the game-winning home run in Game Three.

At the time, it seemed that Castillo had seized his opportunity. But manager Sparky Anderson, the man who gave him that opportunity, also took it away; Castillo was relegated to the role of backup catcher to ironman Lance Parrish last season.

The results were disastrous. Castillo hit .119 and batted only 84 times last season. His career could be in jeopardy. Arguably, being backup to Parrish is not a career at all.

When he does get to the plate, Marty likes high fastballs over the fat part of the plate. Pitchers with the thought of throwing inside fastballs should also think about throwing them low and well off the plate. Castillo has a lot of trouble letting a high fastball off the outside corner from a lefthander go by without taking a stab at it.

He is vulnerable to breaking pitches from righthanded pitchers, especially when he's behind in the count. Lefthanders can jam him with low fastballs and hard sliders.

Castillo continually hurts himself by always trying to pull the ball, rather than shooting a pitch to right field once in a while. He will lay down an occasional bunt, but he doesn't have good enough speed to force third basemen to cheat.

BASERUNNING:

Castillo doesn't make a pitcher shake at the knees when he is on base. He will not steal and is not involved in the hit-and-run. His speed is below average.

FIELDING:

As a catcher, Castillo's throwing ac-

MARTY CASTILLO
C, No. 8
RR, 6'1", 205 lbs.
ML Svc: 5 years
Born: 1-16-57 in
Long Beach, CA

1985 STATISTICS											
AVG	G	AB	R	H	2B	3B	HR	RBI	BB	SO	SB
.119	57	84	4	10	2	0	2	5	2	19	0
CAREER STATISTICS											
AVG	G	AB	R	H	2B	3B	HR	RBI	BB	SO	SB
.190	201	352	31	67	11	2	8	32	19	78	3

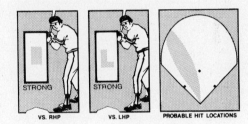

STRONG   STRONG   PROBABLE HIT LOCATIONS

VS. RHP   VS. LHP

curacy is erratic. He does not appear to be as comfortable catching as he does when playing third. But when he is playing third, he makes his manager antsy.

At third base, Castillo's range is average, at best. He has a strong and accurate arm, but does not charge bunts or topped balls very well.

OVERALL:

A woeful 1985 season casts a long, long shadow of doubt on his value to the Tigers. If his bat showed a little more life, he could make a living for a while as a backup catcher. He may be ready for a change of scenery.

Robinson: "Castillo was the forgotten man on the Tigers last year. He just did not play often enough to stay sharp. I must admit, that surprised me after his good performance in the World Series. Beyond that, however, he seems to be a borderline big league player."

HITTING:

The 1985 season was one of the most frustrating of Dave Collins' career. Generally a cinch to hit in the .280 range, Collins was struggling in the .240s in June when he began platooning in left field. In mid-July, he asked to be traded--and that pretty much finished him. Playing sparingly, he did little more than go through the motions for the rest of the season. He felt unwanted in Oakland and found it hard to play under those circumstances.

It's conceivable that the A's gave up on him too soon, because the switch-hitting Collins hasn't lost any of his basic skills. He is still a good low-ball hitter, with occasional power, from the left side of the plate, and a good high-ball hitter from the right side.

Collins is a hustler who explodes out of the batter's box. He can hit to the opposite field both ways. Because his job is to get on base, he seldom commits himself to the first pitch. He can also bunt his way on.

What Collins needs, apparently, is to be needed. When he lost his spirit, his batting average went down with him. He has a history of getting down on everything when things are not going right for him; it was not a surprise when he asked for a trade last season.

BASERUNNING:

When Collins broke into the majors, he was one of the fastest runners in either league. He's not the flat-out burner he once was, but he still runs well--and more importantly, he is a smart runner. The A's saw Collins as a replacement for departed leadoff man Rickey Henderson, because he has a far greater knowledge of pitchers' moves. Unfortunately, Collins was done in by the next category: defense.

DAVE COLLINS
LF, No. 11
SL, 5'10", 175 lbs.
ML Svc: 11 years
Born: 10-20-52 in
Rapid City, SD

1985 STATISTICS

AVG	G	AB	R	H	2B	3B	HR	RBI	BB	SO	SB
.251	112	379	52	95	16	4	4	29	29	37	29

CAREER STATISTICS

AVG	G	AB	R	H	2B	3B	HR	RBI	BB	SO	SB
.275	1244	4065	568	1118	153	48	31	317	378	545	342

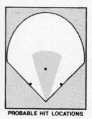

VS. RHP   VS. LHP   PROBABLE HIT LOCATIONS

FIELDING:

What might have hurt Collins most was his shaky play in left field. He has neither the soft hands nor the good judgment that makes a good outfielder, and his arm is only adequate.

That's why the A's turned to Dusty Baker, Steve Henderson, even Mike Heath in left field. They all out-performed Collins defensively. Strangely, for all his speed, Collins doesn't cover that much ground.

OVERALL:

Killebrew: "He could rebound for a good year, but I don't expect it. I believe he's going downhill."

HITTING:

The Tigers thought the curtain had dropped on the career of Darrell Evans in spring training of 1985. He wasn't getting around on fastballs. The club tried to unload him, but found no takers. Fortunately for the Tigers, everybody was wrong. Evans led the majors in home runs with 40, became the only player ever to hit as many as 40 home runs in both leagues and joined the elite circle of players who have hit 300 career homers. He managed all this after a slow start in 1985. He was hitting .167 until the middle of May and had only two home runs.

Evans adjusted by moving his hands back to quicken his swing and subsequently went on a tear. He definitely prefers low fastballs down the middle of the plate and in, but is a student of pitching and hit several home runs on off-speed pitches he guessed on.

Evans crowds the plate so he can flick outside pitches to right field. He has learned that home runs to right field in Detroit don't have to be monstrous, which is one reason his Tiger Stadium homers increased from six in 1984 to 21. None of his 40 homers were hit to the opposite field.

Evans has an exceptional knowledge of the strike zone and refuses to swing at a pitch unless its location and type are exactly what he is expecting. Evans will hit to the opposite field when he has two strikes on him and is behind in the count.

Pitchers will have their best success with him if they pitch him away. The better fastball pitchers can power him inside, but their pitches should be borderline high. Occasionally, Evans will chase a breaking pitch down and in from a righthander.

BASERUNNING:

Evans does not pose a threat to steal, but he also won't commit basic baserunning blunders.

DARRELL EVANS
1B, No. 41
LR, 6'2", 205 lbs.
ML Svc: 15 years
Born: 5-26-47 in
Pasadena, CA

1985 STATISTICS

AVG	G	AB	R	H	2B	3B	HR	RBI	BB	SO	SB
.248	151	505	81	125	17	0	40	94	85	85	0

CAREER STATISTICS

AVG	G	AB	R	H	2B	3B	HR	RBI	BB	SO	SB
.251	2135	7254	1097	1825	279	35	318	1067	1289	1086	88

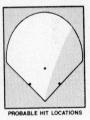

VS. RHP VS. LHP PROBABLE HIT LOCATIONS

FIELDING:

To compensate for his lack of range, Evans plays as deep at first base as anyone in the league. His pitchers have to be especially quick to cover first on ground balls hit to him. He knows game situations and is never out of position. His arm is accurate, but not strong.

OVERALL:

He could feast on fastballs as the number two hitter in the Tiger lineup. His lack of speed is not a factor because he usually lifts the ball into the air. He grounded into the same number of double plays (five) as Kirk Gibson.

Evans has adjusted to Tiger Stadium as well as the AL pitchers and the AL strike zone. He should enjoy spring training this time around.

Robinson: "I never lost my confidence in Darrell and honestly thought he would hit 30 homers back in 1984 (he hit 16). I guess I was a year late."

HITTING:

The Tigers challenged Kirk Gibson to duplicate his 1984 season when they refused to offer him a five-year contract worth $6 million.

He accepted the challenge, and won.

Gibson is very aggressive, highly competitive, and extremely confident. He stands even with home plate, crowds it slightly and has developed somewhat of a crouch. Like most sluggers, Gibson likes to extend his arms. He thrives on low fastballs and off-speed pitches from righthanded pitchers. He does not handle the high fastball well, although he has the strength to muscle some inside fastballs into the outfield for singles.

Certain lefthanders (Matt Young of Seattle, for instance) give him fits. His holes against lefthanders are fastballs up and in, and sliders and off-speed pitches low and off the outside portion of the plate.

Gibson will bunt against lefthanders in any situation. He is not cheated out of his swings as evidenced by his 137 strikeouts. He offset that figure, however, with career highs in doubles, home runs, stolen bases, RBIs, walks and runs scored.

BASERUNNING:

Gibson is electrifying on the bases. Singles become doubles and doubles become triples when he gets up a head of steam. He stole 30 bases in 34 attempts and could steal more, but Sparky understands the physical strain that would place on him.

Gibson is very tough at second when breaking up double plays.

FIELDING:

The many years Gibson has spent in spring training with Al Kaline are now paying off. Speed is Gibson's greatest asset in the outfield. His arm strength

KIRK GIBSON
RF, No. 23
LL, 6'3", 215 lbs.
ML Svc: 6 years
Born: 5-28-57 in
Pontiac, MI

1985 STATISTICS

AVG	G	AB	R	H	2B	3B	HR	RBI	BB	SO	SB
.287	154	581	96	167	37	5	29	97	71	137	30

CAREER STATISTICS

AVG	G	AB	R	H	2B	3B	HR	RBI	BB	SO	SB
.277	646	2282	349	632	104	30	98	334	241	489	106

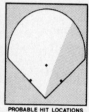

VS. RHP   VS. LHP   PROBABLE HIT LOCATIONS

has improved to a point of adequacy. He is fundamentally sound and hits the cutoff man and makes the relay.

Most of his errors result from overcharging singles.

OVERALL:

Gibson is the best blend of speed and power in the league. He has emerged as an offensive force with leadership qualities. He is one of the league's most feared game-breakers in late innings.

Gibson could become an impact player if he develops better discipline when facing lefthanded pitching.

Robinson: "Kirk has established himself as a star. He has worked very hard to overcome his weaknesses and is now playing with excitement and skill. His team has to have him healthy and ready."

HITTING:

There was ample concern for John Grubb's bat midway through the 1985 season. He wasn't pulling the ball, he was not hitting the ball with authority and he was approaching 37 years of age. His job was on the line.

Grubb must have had a terrific birthday party on August 16 last year because from there on, he raised his average from .182 to .245 and his home runs from one to five. The pop had returned to his tentative bat.

Grubb is a good bench player. He has the ability to reach base because he doesn't chase bad pitches. He has always been a disciplined hitter. He is a tough out because he usually doesn't pull off pitches and, apparently, he's still quick enough with his bat to reach the seats.

He likes the low fastball, which is a common trait of lefthanded hitters, and tries to spoil high heaters. He is vulnerable to tailing fastballs or breaking pitches low and away from righthanders.

Grubb never is used against lefthanded pitching unless the game is lopsided.

BASERUNNING:

It's one base at a time for Grubb. He has below average speed and makes the pivot easy for a second baseman turning the double play.

FIELDING:

While he is fundamentally sound, he doesn't cover much ground in the outfield. He is seldom called on to play

JOHN GRUBB
OF, No. 30
LR, 6'3", 180 lbs.
ML Svc: 14 years
Born: 8-4-48 in
  Richmond, VA

1985 STATISTICS
AVG	G	AB	R	H	2B	3B	HR	RBI	BB	SO	SB
.245	78	155	19	38	7	1	5	25	24	25	0

CAREER STATISTICS
AVG	G	AB	R	H	2B	3B	HR	RBI	BB	SO	SB
.268	1284	3830	512	1060	188	28	84	411	502	514	29

STRONG

VS. RHP

PROBABLE HIT LOCATIONS

in the field and probably will be used even less in that capacity as time goes by.

OVERALL:

Grubb serves the Tigers well as a pinch-hitter. His duties off the bench will be increasingly limited because he is injury-prone and is reaching an age where he could easily be replaced by a younger player.

Robinson: "John is a patient hitter and a part-time player who has been slowed by injuries. He has at least one good year left."

PITCHING:

The baseball world was this man's oyster in 1984. Willie Hernandez captured the dual awards of Most Valuable Player and Cy Young and earned a handsome multi-million dollar contract extension as a result of his incredible season two years ago. Hernandez saved 31 games last year as an encore. That's a tough number to criticize, but he did lose five leads of two or more runs in the final two innings within a span of 15 games in August.

His shortcoming was that he lacked pinpoint control of his fastball. He has the best screwball in the league, but it, too, suffered.

During his MVP season, Hernandez had a very simple pitching pattern: fastballs in at the knees and screwballs away. He caught a lot of righthanded hitters leaning outside for the screwball by coming back inside with the fastball.

Hernandez missed too frequently with his fastball in 1985. That negated the value of his screwball and forced him to use fastballs when he was pitching from behind. His home runs allowed jumped from six in 1984 to 13 last season.

His control is usually outstanding. Hernandez is a fast worker and uses an overhand delivery. He will come sidearm to lefthanded hitters when he has two strikes against them.

Fear is not part of his makeup. He goes right after hitters and he likes to be used often.

FIELDING:

Hernandez is an above average field-

WILLIE HERNANDEZ
LHP, No. 21
LL, 6'2", 185 lbs.
ML Svc: 9 years
Born: 11-14-54 in
   Aguada, PR

1985 STATISTICS												
W	L	ERA	G	GS	CG	SV	IP	H	R	ER	BB	SO
8	10	2.70	74	0	0	31	106.2	82	38	32	14	76
CAREER STATISTICS												
W	L	ERA	G	GS	CG	SV	IP	H	R	ER	BB	SO
51	45	3.54	520	11	0	90	807.1	726	324	318	276	323

er. He is prepared to field balls hit up the middle, but can be slow to cover first. He doesn't throw over to first often.

OVERALL:

Last season, Hernandez was bothered by a few nagging, but generally insignificant, injuries. The insignificance of some of them raised questions about his desire to pitch for a non-contending team.

Robinson: "Willie's strength is that he can pitch a lot and he has a great screwball. I think the hitters became more familiar with him last season and pretty much knew what to expect. But it really doesn't matter how many times most hitters see him, he will always be tough to hit."

HITTING:

Not many left fielders would have been given a second chance for regular duty after hitting only seven home runs and driving in 43 while stealing six bases. Anderson afforded Larry Herndon that opportunity because of his quiet nature and Herndon's desire to win. Unfortunately, Herndon fell short.

His days as a regular are over. Too many fastballs escape the slow bat of Larry, who once hit them with regularity. Herndon holds his hands high in a straight-up stance, but drops them too much before initiating his stride and swing. His power zone is restricted to pitches down the middle.

Righthanders power him inside and fool him frequently with breaking stuff away. Herndon is not a disciplined hitter facing righthanders, against whom he is hitting .231 over the past two years.

Lefthanders can bust him up and in and tail fastballs in on him effectively, but Herndon's .298 average against lefthanders in 1984-85 indicates much better discipline on his part.

BASERUNNING:

Knee problems have limited Herndon's effectiveness on the basepaths. He used to be good for 12-20 steals a season, but that is no longer the case. He has long strides but gets a slow start.

His headfirst slide slows him down at any base. Herdon will seldom slide into home plate.

FIELDING:

Herndon doesn't go after fly balls to the left-center field gap very well, though that's Lemon's territory anyway.

LARRY HERNDON
LF, No. 31
RR, 6'3", 200 lbs.
ML Svc: 10 years
Born: 11-3-53 in
   Sunflower, MS

1985 STATISTICS

AVG	G	AB	R	H	2B	3B	HR	RBI	BB	SO	SB
.244	137	442	45	108	12	7	12	37	33	79	2

CAREER STATISTICS

AVG	G	AB	R	H	2B	3B	HR	RBI	BB	SO	SB
.275	1266	4196	524	1152	155	73	86	446	280	681	89

VS. RHP   VS. LHP   PROBABLE HIT LOCATIONS

He gets to the line quickly to hold potential doubles to singles.

He shows good judgment in the field. His arm strength is average.

OVERALL:

Herndon can be a useful platoon outfielder on a grass field. He has several limitations, including bad knees, which may shorten his career. The Tigers would like to shop him around but not many teams want to pay a part-time player an annual salary of $700,000.

Robinson: "Larry has slowed down and is heading downhill. I don't think that he will play as much this year."

PITCHING:

Dave LaPoint suffered through his first losing season as a professional last year, but it was more a case of a poor supporting cast at San Francisco than his own poor pitching. This season, he should be a much tougher pitcher with the much tougher Tigers.

LaPoint is by no means a power pitcher. He uses a wicked change-up to make his average fastball and slider seem faster. His change-up ranked among the best in the National League; it deceives batters with its good movement (it often dips out of the strike zone at the last possible moment).

The change-up is his out pitch and he will throw it with confidence anytime. He walked more batters than usual last year, but most of his wildness occurred when he struggled down the stretch and was frustrated over his losses. But for the first half of the season, LaPoint's ERA was under 3.00, though the defeats kept mounting because he couldn't get any runs. He is a much better pitcher than his 1985 statistics suggest, as American League batters are apt to discover.

FIELDING:

LaPoint does not have a good move to first base for a lefty, but he is a decent fielder and not as sluggish as his plump physique would suggest.

OVERALL:

The Giants may have made a mistake in letting LaPoint get away, but it was not really his pitching performance that

DAVE LaPOINT
LHP, No. 40
LL, 6'3", 215 lbs.
ML Svc: 4 years
Born: 7-29-59 in
  Glens Falls, NY

1985 STATISTICS

W	L	ERA	G	GS	CG	SV	IP	H	R	ER	BB	SO
7	17	3.57	31	31	2	0	206.2	215	99	82	74	122

CAREER STATISTICS

W	L	ERA	G	GS	CG	SV	IP	H	R	ER	BB	SO
42	39	3.79	151	119	5	1	769.2	810	367	324	302	455

caused discontent in San Francisco. The Giants' management regarded LaPoint as out of shape and had no tolerance for LaPoint's beer-guzzling reputation.

Meanwhile, the Tigers (remembering Lolich) may feel a bit differently about LaPoint's large physique--if he wins. The Tigers have four starters who are better than LaPoint and LaPoint as the fifth man gives them an outstanding staff.

Campbell: "Dave's record was not very good last season, but still, he was one of the best competitors on the San Francisco staff last year--he comes right at the hitter with his best stuff. He is a bit of an illusionary pitcher-- his pitches look like strikes until they reach the plate.

"When his change-up is right, he can not be beat. LaPoint is tough--he's the kind I would want out there in a big game. The Tigers got themselves a good one here."

HITTING:

Chet Lemon suffered from a power shortage in the first four months of last season because he was a pitcher's best friend. Maybe he was anxious or tense, but he certainly was cooperative.

Lemon lost some of his aggressiveness by taking more pitches than usual. Then, he would get tired of waiting for inside pitches and would try to yank the outside pitch into the left field seats. Essentially, he struck himself out.

Lemon didn't hit his first home run until the end of May last year.

Righthanded pitchers give Lemon a heavy dose of fastballs down and in and off the plate. They also mix in a steady flow of pitches away to neutralize his power. Lefthanders come up and in with the fastball, down and in with the slider and tease him away with breaking pitches.

Lemon does not adjust well to off-speed pitches. He also has a tendency to "fly open," that is, rotate his hips, too quickly, which is a sign of a home run-conscious hitter.

BASERUNNING:

Lemon has been harnessed by the Tigers because, fundamentally, he is a weak baserunner. He does not get a good lead off first base and does not get a good jump on the pitch, especially for someone who gets a pretty good jump on batted balls in the outfield.

His tendency to dive headfirst into first base on close plays is a constant source of annoyance to the Tigers.

FIELDING:

In the outfield, Lemon slipped a bit in 1985. He didn't lose any steps and is still not afraid of padded walls, but his judgment on throws, especially to home plate, allowed many runners to move

CHET LEMON
CF, No. 34
RR, 6'0", 190 lbs.
ML Svc: 10 years
Born: 2-12-55 in
    Jackson, MS

1985 STATISTICS

AVG	G	AB	R	H	2B	3B	HR	RBI	BB	SO	SB
.265	145	517	69	137	28	4	18	68	45	93	0

CAREER STATISTICS

AVG	G	AB	R	H	2B	3B	HR	RBI	BB	SO	SB
.280	1340	4747	702	1328	281	45	154	613	990	692	51

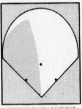

VS. RHP   VS. LHP   PROBABLE HIT LOCATIONS

up a base. He also missed his share of cutoff men.

Still, Lemon ranks among the top six center fielders in the league.

OVERALL:

Lemon may have attempted to exceed his abilities in 1985. He must revert to sound fundamental defense and recognize his offensive limitations in order to be able to play his best. The Tigers are expecting him to return to his 1984 form this year.

Robinson: "I think he got lulled into a false sense of security for a while. It was nearly impossible for Detroit to be in any kind of race without his bat. He is a key man for them in the lineup and on the field."

PITCHING:

The career of Aurelio Lopez is at a crossroads. The man affectionately known as "Señor Smoke" is 36-years-old. His smoke seems to have cleared.

Lopez was plagued by a lack of control and a proclivity for serving up home run pitches (15 in 86 innings) in 1985. He couldn't spot his 88-90 MPH fastball effectively and that was suicidal for this power pitcher. Lopez requires plenty of work to be effective. Sparky Anderson didn't use him nearly as frequently in 1985 as 1984 when Lopez was a tremendous support for teammate Willie Hernandez. The long periods of inactivity had a negative effect on the sensitive Lopez.

Lopez throws virtually every pitch in the book. He relies primarily on the fastball and slider, but has dabbled with a screwball and split-finger fastball. He will resort to the junk if he feels he can't spot his fastball. He deserts his fastball too quickly, however, and should give it more time to work.

His variety of pitches has carried him well in long relief, though Lopez himself thinks that he can be effective in short relief.

FIELDING:

Lopez covers first adequately, but it appears to be a chore. Opponents can bunt on him because he falls off the

AURELIO LOPEZ
RHP, No. 29
RR, 6'0", 225 lbs.
ML Svc: 8 years
Born: 10-5-48 in
Pueblo, MEX

1985 STATISTICS

W	L	ERA	G	GS	CG	SV	IP	H	R	ER	BB	SO
3	7	4.80	51	0	0	5	86.1	82	50	46	41	53

CAREER STATISTICS

W	L	ERA	G	GS	CG	SV	IP	H	R	ER	BB	SO
57	32	3.52	388	9	0	85	794	682	338	311	320	570

mound toward first base and he's not agile.

Lopez throws to first base often, but his slow delivery to home plate makes him a prime target for basestealers.

OVERALL:

Some team may be able to squeeze one decent year out of Lopez. He must feel a need to be wanted, however, or his confidence goes out the window.

Robinson: "Aurelio gave up a lot of home runs last season and pitched from behind more than ever before.

"His strengths are a great arm and the ability to pitch anytime. He's got to try to lose some weight, though."

ACE OF THE STAFF

PITCHING:

Jack Morris' strength is his stamina. There has been no righthander more durable than Morris in this decade. He has made 205 starting assignments and averaged 7.35 innings per start the past six years. He also has recorded more victories (102) than anyone in either league in this decade.

Morris is a power pitcher with a three-quarters delivery. He is a relatively fast worker with a competitive edge. His slider, once his best pitch, still ranks among the best. His split-finger fastball, which he began throwing with increased frequency at the end of the 1983 season, is a quality off-speed delivery. Morris has extreme confidence in the split-finger pitch and will throw it at anytime, but especially to power hitters.

He also throws a straight change-up. A fastball that reaches 88-92 MPH keys his other pitches. Morris must have control of his fastball to set up the split-finger pitch. He has command of all four pitches and isn't afraid to use any of them in a jam. Bad location with the fastball can spell trouble for him. He issued more walks (110) in 1985 than any previous season. His ERA did not fluctuate as much as it normally does throughout the season, reaching a high of 3.35 and finishing at 3.33.

Morris is not afraid to crowd hitters who attempt to take a portion of the plate away from him.

FIELDING:

Morris is a gifted athlete. He fields

JACK MORRIS
RHP, No. 47
RR, 6'3", 200 lbs.
ML Svc: 8 years
Born: 5-16-55 in
   St. Paul, MN

1985 STATISTICS

W	L	ERA	G	GS	CG	SV	IP	H	R	ER	BB	SO
16	11	3.33	35	35	13	0	257	212	102	95	110	191

CAREER STATISTICS

W	L	ERA	G	GS	CG	SV	IP	H	R	ER	BB	SO
123	86	3.62	267	245	95	0	1855.2	1769	807	747	672	1101

his position extremely well. His move to first base on pickoffs is quick, though he sometimes becomes lax holding runners close. He covers first base well.

He is tough to bunt against because he gets off the mound in a hurry.

OVERALL:

Morris has the pitches to dominate games. He can be counted on to take the ball whenever it's his turn. He used to be bothered by fielding lapses and/or cheap hits, but tempered his emotions to a great extent last season.

Robinson: "Jack is still one of the top pitchers in the league, even though his control was spotty at times last season. He's still overpowering, and if the team plays well he will win big."

PITCHING:

Randy O'Neal seems heir apparent to replace Aurelio Lopez as the primary righthanded pitcher in the bullpen.

O'Neal was once groomed as a starting pitcher, but was used exclusively in relief the final six weeks of the season. He was scored upon in only four of 16 appearances out of the bullpen.

He is a control pitcher with a three-quarters delivery. O'Neal has a good, sinking fastball that pushes 90 MPH. He is a good choice to get the call when the team needs an inning-ending DP.

He also throws a curve and a split-finger fastball. He must have an effective split-finger pitch to be successful. His control is good enough to allow him to crowd hitters, but he refrains from doing so. This probably stems from his lack of experience.

O'Neal is very hittable if his fastball isn't low in the strike zone.

FIELDING:

If you want to see how a good-fielding pitcher's delivery should end, take a look at Randy O'Neal. His position after his delivery is textbook-perfect.

He reacts well to bunts and beats hitters to first with time to spare.

OVERALL:

The adjustment from starting pitcher

RANDY O'NEAL
RHP, No. 49
RR, 6'2", 195 lbs.
ML Svc: 1 year plus
Born: 8-30-60 in
    Ashland, KY

1985 STATISTICS

W	L	ERA	G	GS	CG	SV	IP	H	R	ER	BB	SO
5	5	3.24	28	12	1	1	94.1	82	42	34	36	52

CAREER STATISTICS

W	L	ERA	G	GS	CG	SV	IP	H	R	ER	BB	SO
7	6	3.26	32	15	1	1	113	98	49	41	42	64

to reliever didn't seem to bother him. The frequency with which he can be used out of the bullpen remains to be seen. He pitched a total of one and two-thirds innings in making appearances on three consecutive days, but enjoyed at least one day of rest between his other 13 relief apperances.

Robinson: "I think O'Neal will get better. He just needs some more innings. He appears to be well-schooled in the fundamentals. His biggest problem is one that he has had no control over--a lack of experience."

LANCE PARRISH
C, No. 13
RR, 6'3", 220 lbs.
ML Svc: 8 years
Born: 6-15-56 in
  Clairton, PA

HITTING:

Lance Parrish has averaged 99 RBIs over the past four seasons, including 98 in each of the past two years. The line on this guy seems predictable: good power hitter but strikes out often, and so on, but wait one minute: there is something different here . . .

Last season, Parrish managed to hit his usual number of RBIs but without the usual number of strikeouts. He cut down from 120 in 1984 to 90 strikeouts last year. Not only did that help to raise his average from .237 to .273, but it also indicates that he is not chasing a lot of the pitches he used to go after.

Parrish had a reputation for chasing low, outside breaking pitches from righthanded pitchers. He can still plead guilty there, especially when faced with two strikes, but he has cut down on his penchant for them dramatically.

Parrish powders the belt-high fastball on the inside half of the plate. He will pull that pitch for home runs. He hits a lot of ground balls up the middle and through the hole on the left side. Several teams have developed a "Parrish Shift" designed to plug those holes. The shifts are something he might have to cope with more frequently this season.

Pitchers must keep fastballs up and in and change speeds often. Parrish has the power to drive an outside fastball for an opposite field home run.

BASERUNNING:

Parrish has typical catcher's speed: none. He does not get from the batter's box to first base quickly and grounds into more double plays than any other Tiger player. Parrish does not straight steal, but Anderson will hit-and-run with him on first base.

1985 STATISTICS											
AVG	G	AB	R	H	2B	3B	HR	RBI	BB	SO	SB
.273	140	549	64	150	27	1	28	98	41	90	2

CAREER STATISTICS											
AVG	G	AB	R	H	2B	3B	HR	RBI	BB	SO	SB
.263	1055	3946	524	1039	195	22	190	638	296	764	22

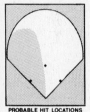

VS. RHP   VS. LHP   PROBABLE HIT LOCATIONS

FIELDING:

Parrish has the strongest throwing arm among American League catchers and has one of teh quickest releases. He breaks from the crouch quickly in pursuit of bunts and slow rollers. He will throw behind runners at first base.

In recent seasons, Parrish has become more assertive with his pitchers and has improved his ability to call games.

OVERALL:

Robinson: "All-Star catchers who average 99 RBIs and win Gold Gloves are hard to find. The Tigers are fortunate to have Lance.

"He is the best all-around catcher in the league. He does everything well behind the plate and has earned the full confidence of the pitching staff."

DETROIT TIGERS

PITCHING:

Dan Petry's 1985 season was only moderately successful in terms of the number of games he won. His 15 victories was his lowest total since 1982, but his numbers in two other categories indicate that he is continung to mature. Petry permitted 7.16 hits per nine innings, well below his career figure of 8.36 entering last season. He also walked 3.05 batters per nine innings, a significant reduction from his career figure (3.43).

Petry's future is bright. He enters this season seven victories shy of 100 at the relatively young age of 27.

The strapping righthander is a power pitcher who possesses one of the best sliders in the league. The break on his slider is sharp and quick, the perfect complement to his 87-90 MPH fastball.

Petry used to try to power his way out of jams but has learned to mix in straight changes and curves to keep hitters honest. He still relies to a great extent on his slider and fastball in tough situations, but not as often as in the past. He strives to get ahead in the count with his fastball and slider.

Petry must keep his pitches down to be effective. He surrendered 24 home runs in 1985, which, while it is still too many, is not bad for a pitcher whose home is Tiger Stadium.

His overhand delivery is mechanically sound. He is not afraid to run pitches in to move batters off the plate.

FIELDING:

Petry's landing position allows him to field his position well. He is square

DAN PETRY
RHP, No. 46
RR, 6'4", 200 lbs.
ML Svc: 7 years
Born: 11-13-58 in
Palo Alto, CA

1985 STATISTICS
W	L	ERA	G	GS	CG	SV	IP	H	R	ER	BB	SO
15	13	3.36	34	34	8	0	238.2	190	98	89	81	109

CAREER STATISTICS
W	L	ERA	G	GS	CG	SV	IP	H	R	ER	BB	SO
93	64	3.49	207	204	45	0	1388	1258	597	539	519	717

with the batter. Petry covers first base extremely well and is above average at pouncing on bunts. He never suffers from a lapse of concentration.

His pickoff motion is above average. He steps off the rubber and throws to first frequently.

OVERALL:

Petry's record could have been better last season. He started four of the six games in which the Tigers were shut out. Two of those four games were scoreless after nine innings. Petry very rarely allows himself to be rattled. He is a game competitor who should record a lot of victories for several years to come.

Robinson: "Dan has outstanding stuff and gives you everything he's got. He does have a tendency to give up a lot of home runs, but most of those are with the bases empty."

HITTING:

Questions were raised when the Tigers acquired Alex Sanchez from the San Francisco Giants on the final day of spring training last season. Sanchez had been voted the Most Valuable Player of the Pacific Coast League. He was blessed with some good tools. Why did the Giants trade him for minor league pitcher Roger Mason?

The answer soon became clear. Sanchez has not sharpened those tools. He is the epitome of the undisciplined hitter: he has yet to draw a walk in 195 trips to the plate.

He loves to swing at first pitches. He also jumps on thigh-high breaking pitches in the same zone. Sanchez is a pull hitter who has enough power to shoot balls to right-center field, but he doesn't. Breaking balls and off-speed pitches keep him off balance.

BASERUNNING:

Sanchez is prone to making mistakes. He exercises poor judgment in challenging left fielders when he is going from first to third on singles. His lead off first base doesn't draw many throws. He does not get a good jump. Sanchez aggressively hunts second basemen to break up double plays.

FIELDING:

Sanchez has a very strong arm, but demonstrates poor judgment and accuracy. He has difficulty hitting the cutoff man. His range is average.

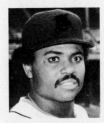

ALEX SANCHEZ
OF, No. 33
RR, 6'0", 185 lbs.
ML Svc: 1 year plus
Born: 2-26-59 in
  San Pedros de Macoris, DR

1985 STATISTICS

AVG	G	AB	R	H	2B	3B	HR	RBI	BB	SO	SB
.248	71	133	19	33	6	2	6	12	0	39	2

CAREER STATISTICS

AVG	G	AB	R	H	2B	3B	HR	RBI	BB	SO	SB
.241	99	195	27	47	7	3	8	20	0	57	4

VS. RHP   VS. LHP   PROBABLE HIT LOCATIONS

OVERALL:

Sanchez has skills, but is unable to apply those skills because of a poor grasp of fundamentals. He's running out of time.

Robinson: "Sanchez came to the big leagues with the reputation as an aggressive hitter with no position. The scouts were right. He will be hardpressed to remain in the major leagues."

BIG, BREAKING CURVEBALL

PITCHING:

Bill Scherrer is all arms and legs. He is a gangling lefthander who is spotted against lefthanded hitters. His 1985 season was a disappointment. Scherrer permitted 104 baserunners in 66 innings and allowed 15 of the final 27 runners he inherited to score. He can place much of the blame on Bill Buckner and Wade Boggs of the Boston Red Sox. Each lefthanded hitter collected four hits in five at-bats against Scherrer. The Tigers lost all four games Scherrer appeared in against Boston.

He relies heavily on a big, sweeping curveball. He can throw his curveball at two speeds. The curve is his best pitch and the one he uses in tough situations. His fastball is average and relatively slow (81-84 MPH); he does not have a slider.

His body language is detrimental. He often appears apathetic on the mound. This is a source of encouragement to the opposition, and a source of discouragement to his teammates.

Scherrer spent part of the winter at the Florida Instructional League trying to reduce his leg kick to have a better guard against basestealers.

FIELDING:

Scherrer is an average fielder. He

BILL SCHERRER
LHP, No. 17
LL, 6'4", 170 lbs.
ML Svc: 3 years
Born: 1-20-58 in
   Tonawanda, NY

1985 STATISTICS

W	L	ERA	G	GS	CG	SV	IP	H	R	ER	BB	SO
3	2	4.36	48	0	0	0	66	62	35	32	41	46

CAREER STATISTICS

W	L	ERA	G	GS	CG	SV	IP	H	R	ER	BB	SO
7	7	3.58	180	2	0	11	246.2	230	108	98	97	161

breaks off the mound well and generally reaches first base well ahead of the batter. He doesn't attempt to force the lead runner on bunt plays.

He is a fast worker, and does not worry too much about a runner on first.

OVERALL:

Robinson: "The jury is out on him. He must be effective against lefthanded batters to remain in the major leagues. He has not been effective in that role on a consistent basis."

HITTING:

Nelson Simmons is a physical specimen with tremendous upper body strength. The Tigers were skeptical of those muscles at one point and forced Simmons to swim laps daily to stretch him out.

Simmons is a switch-hitter with power from both sides. He likes the high fastball from the right side and the low fastball from the left side. His power is straightaway and to the alleys. One of his 10 home runs in 1985 cleared the center field fence in Tiger Stadium, 440 feet away.

Simmons keys on fastballs constantly. He is overly aggressive and often lunges at off-speed pitches, especially from the left side, as if he's afraid to fall behind in the count. He must learn discipline and be more selective at the plate to develop into a major offensive force.

BASERUNNING:

Simmons does not run well and cannot be considered an alert baserunner at this stage of his career. He does not distract pitchers and is not a threat to steal.

FIELDING:

Simmons has limited range in both left field and right field. He is slow to the line and into the alley and has shown poor judgment at times throwing to bases.

He needs a lot of work defensively.

NELSON SIMMONS
OF, No. 37
SR, 6'1", 195 lbs.
ML Svc: 1 year plus
Born: 6-27-63 in
Washington, DC

1985 STATISTICS

AVG	G	AB	R	H	2B	3B	HR	RBI	BB	SO	SB
.239	75	251	31	60	11	0	10	33	26	41	1

CAREER STATISTICS

AVG	G	AB	R	H	2B	3B	HR	RBI	BB	SO	SB
.260	84	281	35	73	13	0	10	36	28	46	2

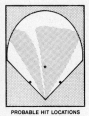

VS. RHP   VS. LHP   PROBABLE HIT LOCATIONS

OVERALL:

Simmons' bat has potential. He has home run power, but gives away too many at-bats because of his poor pitch selection. He may or may not fit into the Tigers' starting lineup this year, depending on how much Sparky Anderson wants to emphasize speed.

Robinson: "Simmons is beginning to exert himself. He came on strong the last part of the season and is on his way up the ladder. I think he should make his presence known as an everyday player this season."

PITCHING:

A funny thing happened to Frank Tanana after he was acquired by the Tigers from the Texas Rangers last June: he won as many games as Jack Morris (10) and more than any other Detroit pitcher.

Tanana was especially tough against the Eastern Division teams, compiling an 8-0 record and 2.37 ERA against the allegedly most powerful division in baseball. He was a splendid addition to the Tigers, considering the exchange was Double-A pitcher Duane James.

Tanana filled Detroit's need for a lefthanded starting pitcher. His success stems from his excellent control of a mixture of pitches. He throws a curve at two different speeds, a slider and an 80-82 MPH fastball. His low-velocity fastball is effective because of the precision of his off-speed pitches. He also throws a tailing fastball--it acts as a hybrid screwball.

The action on Tanana's pitches is very average and he does allow his share of base hits (9.21 per nine innings), but he is extremely knowledgeable and exceedingly shrewd on the mound.

Tanana's concentration level is high. He is fundamentally sound and an expert at exploiting weaknesses of hitters. He runs into problems when his control deserts him and he comes up in the strike zone with his pitches. Tanana is not afraid to buzz hitters inside.

He usually uses an overhand motion, but comes three-quarters to both left- and righthanded hitters on occasion.

FIELDING:

Tanana's move to first base is just

FRANK TANANA
LHP, No. 28
LL, 6'3", 195 lbs.
ML Svc: 13 years
Born: 7-3-53 in
     Detroit, MI

1985 STATISTICS
W	L	ERA	G	GS	CG	SV	IP	H	R	ER	BB	SO
12	14	4.27	33	33	4	0	215	220	112	102	57	159

CAREER STATISTICS
W	L	ERA	G	GS	CG	SV	IP	H	R	ER	BB	SO
147	144	3.34	376	361	120	0	2570	2400	1085	954	707	1806

average. He does throw there frequently, however. He is in a proper fielding position after delivering a pitch and gets off the mound quickly on bunts.

OVERALL:

Tanana is one slick pitching doctor. He has successfully completed the transformation from being a young pitcher with a blazing fastball to a veteran pitcher who has strike zones within the strike zone. He dissects hitters and keeps them off balance with an array of off-speed pitches and a fastball that, while it is not overpowering, can be very effective.

Robinson: "All of Frank's pitches are average to below average, but he knows how to pitch and has great control. He looks like he should be throwing harder, but he just can't. Nevertheless, he is making out alright."

PITCHING:

Walt Terrell made a smooth transition to the Tigers and the American League from the New York Mets and the National League. He can thank his sinking fastball for 15 victories.

Terrell pitched in the home run paradise of Tiger Stadium, yet he served up only nine home runs in 229 innings, which is one every 25.4 innings. Danny Jackson, of the Kansas City Royals, was the only AL pitcher to fare better.

The sinker is Terrell's best pitch and the one he leans on to skirt trouble. The long grass at Tiger Stadium gobbles up a lot of ground balls that are the product of that pitch.

Terrell throws his slider more often than any other pitch. He also has a palmball that he will throw when he is behind in the count. It keeps the hitters off balance.

He is a control pitcher who does not finish many games (five complete games in 34 starts). Terrell is a bulldog-type pitcher and very aggressive. He pitches inside regularly. Tough situations don't fluster him. He does not like to walk batters intentionally and his concentration is good.

Terrell finds himself in trouble when his sinker isn't working.

FIELDING:

Terrell appears slow, but he always manages to cover first base in time. He

WALT TERRELL
RHP, No. 35
LR, 6'2", 205 lbs.
ML Svc: 3 years
Born: 5-11-58 in
    Jeffersonville, IN

1985 STATISTICS
W	L	ERA	G	GS	CG	SV	IP	H	R	ER	BB	SO
15	10	3.85	34	34	5	0	229	221	107	98	95	130

CAREER STATISTICS
W	L	ERA	G	GS	CG	SV	IP	H	R	ER	BB	SO
34	33	3.65	91	90	12	0	598.2	598	275	243	274	311

is fairly quick off the mound to the third base line. His move to first is average.

OVERALL:

Terrell did as well as the Tigers could have expected. He missed only one starting assignment and used his sinker for maximum effectiveness in Detroit.

Robinson: "Being new to the league always helps a pitcher somewhat and he might have had that in his favor early. As a sinkerball pitcher, Walt is pitching in a good park. Hitters usually get the ball on the ground and balls don't sail through Detroit's infield grass too quickly.

"Walt appears to have a good attitude and is a solid workhorse."

HITTING:

Somewhere between capturing the World Series MVP honors in 1984 and spring training of 1985, Alan Trammell lost his concentration. His .258 average last season represents a 56-point plunge.

The primary reason for the nosedive was that Trammell, who built his reputation on being able to turn on inside fastballs, could not convince himself to lay off the high borderline fastball. His confidence wavered and he became a first-strike hitter, regardless of the type of pitch or its location in the strike zone. This often resulted in weak pop flies to the right side.

Sparky Anderson usually resorts to hit-and-run tactics for players mired in slumps. Trammell was not afforded many opportunities because the Tigers were playing catch-up much of last season.

If the Tigers can get a legitimate stolen base threat in the leadoff position, it would help Trammell to concentrate more. He can still turn on the inside fastball, and if he can keep himself focused at the plate, he should be able to drive the outside pitch with authority to right field.

BASERUNNING:

While he has only average speed, Trammell has superior judgment on the bases. He is always conscious of the outfield alignment and the strength of opposing outfielder's arms. He reads the ball off the bat very well, which frequently results in an extra base. He stole 14 bases in 19 attempts, and probably will be asked to run more in 1986.

FIELDING:

There is no question that arm surgery has reduced the strength of Trammell's throws. He no longer can make the play from the hole on a consistent basis. His range is slightly better to his left than right. He knows opposing hitters and positions himself accordingly. He

ALAN TRAMMELL
SS, No. 3
RR, 6'0", 175 lbs.
ML Svc: 8 years
Born: 2-21-58 in
   Garden Grove, CA

1985 STATISTICS

AVG	G	AB	R	H	2B	3B	HR	RBI	BB	SO	SB
.258	149	605	79	156	21	7	13	57	50	71	14

CAREER STATISTICS

AVG	G	AB	R	H	2B	3B	HR	RBI	BB	SO	SB
.281	1138	4057	595	1141	181	35	69	429	429	462	124

  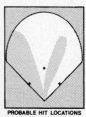

VS. RHP   VS. LHP   PROBABLE HIT LOCATIONS

has one of the best pair of hands in the league and is able to make all the routine plays regularly.

Trammell is steady and reliable in the field. His fielding chances should increase since the Tigers have added two lefthanded starting pitchers (Frank Tanana and Dave LaPoint) to their starting rotation.

OVERALL:

Trammell definitely lost some of his luster in 1985, and could be dropped to as low as ninth in the batting order this year. He will remain a fixture at shortstop, however, and is an intelligent player who should rebound.

Robinson: "I think he was at his peak in 1984. I never really believed that Trammell was a .314 hitter. I think he will settle in at .285-.290. Last season, his mechanics were out of synch for most of the year. He lunged for and chased more off-speed pitches out of the strike zone than he ever had before. It cost him."

HITTING:

Lou Whitaker added the dimension of power to his game in 1985. The lithe second baseman hit 21 home runs to break the club record for that position previously shared by Charlie Gehringer and Dick McAuliffe. The quest to replace Gehringer and McAuliffe in the Tiger record book took its toll on Whitaker's average, however. He finished at .279, his lowest average since 1981, and hit only .180 over the final six weeks after reaching his 19th home run.

Whitaker's power is generated by his bat speed. His wrists are quick. He stands just slightly bent at the knees and he keeps his weight on his back foot exceedingly well: this stamps him as one of the best off-speed hitters in the league.

He makes contact more frequently than any other Tiger player, which is the reason manager Sparky Anderson plans to move him to the third slot in the batting order this year. Whitaker has a good concept of the strike zone and will rarely chase a bad pitch.

The strength of his forearms and the quickness of his wrists make Whitaker a good fastball hitter. He turns well on fastballs down and in. Pitchers with above average fastballs who throw up and in can tie Whitaker up somewhat.

Lefthanded pitchers have best success powering him up and in with fastballs and low and away with sliders.

BASERUNNING:

Whitaker receives high grades going from first to third, or second to home, but does not like the straight steal. That is clearly reflected in his six stolen bases in 10 attempts for 1985. Anderson refrained from running him, which is another reason that Whitaker is better suited as the number three hitter than as the leadoff man.

FIELDING:

Whitaker's range is above average and

LOU WHITAKER
2B, No. 1
LR, 5'11", 160 lbs.
ML Svc: 8 years
Born: 5-12-57 in
New York, NY

1985 STATISTICS

AVG	G	AB	R	H	2B	3B	HR	RBI	BB	SO	SB
.279	152	609	102	170	29	8	21	73	80	56	6

CAREER STATISTICS

AVG	G	AB	R	H	2B	3B	HR	RBI	BB	SO	SB
.279	1139	4121	629	1163	175	43	73	449	513	505	82

VS. RHP

VS. LHP

PROBABLE HIT LOCATIONS

his arm is the strongest among American League second basemen. He will rob more people of hits going to his right than anyone at his position. His range to his left is more limited. He receives all relay throws from the outfield except on balls hit into the left field corner.

OVERALL:

Whitaker puts up better offensive numbers than any second baseman in the league. His production should be more significant if he winds up batting third in the lineup.

Robinson: "The fact that Lou has learned to pull the ball with power just impresses me more. I don't think that he will top his 1985 home run totals, but the addition of power is going to give pitchers something else to think about, and that is a big plus."

PITCHING:

Milt Wilcox looms as an early candidate for Comeback Player of the Year for 1986. He won one game last season after claiming 17 victories in 1984. Arthroscopic surgery on his pitching shoulder in early June ended his 1985 season prematurely. He can rebound: Wilcox is a wily veteran.

He has good control of four pitches: a fastball, a forkball, a curve and a change-up.

Wilcox uses the change-up effectively and will throw the pitch in any situation. His forkball breaks down and in to righthanded hitters and, because of the break, is a more effective pitch to lefthanded hitters.

The Wilcox fastball is straight but serviceable as long as he keeps it low in the strike zone. Wilcox establishes territorial rights; he is not afraid to move hitters off the plate.

He must have pinpoint control to be successful.

FIELDING:

Wilcox is a much better fielder than most people think. He reacts well to bunts and batted balls and wastes no time in getting to first base. He is decisive in going for the lead runner in a force situation.

He varies his pickoff moves to first base better than any Tiger pitcher by

MILT WILCOX
RHP, No. 39
RR, 6'2", 215 lbs.
ML Svc: 13 years
Born: 4-20-50 in
    Honolulu, HI

1985 STATISTICS

W	L	ERA	G	GS	CG	SV	IP	H	R	ER	BB	SO
1	3	4.85	8	8	0	0	39	51	24	21	14	20

CAREER STATISTICS

W	L	ERA	G	GS	CG	SV	IP	H	R	ER	BB	SO
119	105	4.04	382	273	73	5	1960	1917	975	879	742	1111

using a variety of head moves. He throws to first a lot.

OVERALL:

Wilcox bought a year of wear and tear on his arm by missing most of the 1985 season. He pitched in the Dominican Republic this past winter and should be ready to put together a good season this year.

Robinson: "He has had a lot of shoulder problems over the past few seasons and it's getting to the point where you wonder when it all is going to end. He's known as the 'Count of Cortisone.'

"It has to have been rough on him to be hurt so often. But, as in the past, we'll wait and see."

DAVE BERGMAN
1B/PH, No. 14
LL, 6'2", 180 lbs.
ML Svc: 10 years
Born: 6-6-53 in
   Evanston, IL

HITTING, BASERUNNING, FIELDING:

Dave Bergman would prefer that his 1985 statistics be excluded from his 1986 bubble gum card. Bergman's numbers include a .179 batting average, three home runs and seven RBIs. They were his worst numbers since 1980, when he batted only 78 times for the Houston Astros. In spring training, he sustained an elbow injury while swinging a bat. Bergman underwent arthroscopic surgery in June to remove bone chips from the elbow. He never recovered.

The low, inside fastball is the only pitch he drives with power. He chases high fastballs when he is behind in the count. He will flare pitches away to the opposite field, but does not have opposite field power. He lunges at off-speed pitches.

He rarely plays against lefthanders. Bergman doesn't constitute a threat to steal. He runs bases hard, slides awkwardly at times and is occasionally guilty of errors of aggression.

Bergman is very serviceable as a late-inning defensive replacement at first base. His range is good to both sides. His arm is above average and accurate.

OVERALL:

Robinson: "Dave is a good competitor with ordinary skills who accepts his part-time role without complaining."

DOUG FLYNN
2B, No. 23
RR, 5'11", 172 lbs.
ML Svc: 11 years
Born: 4-18-51 in
   Lexington, KY

HITTING, BASERUNNING, FIELDING:

Doug Flynn doesn't make a living with his bat. He is a first-ball, high fastball hitter without power. Flynn loves the inside pitch. Anything down and away will be successful against him. He has a difficult time handling breaking stuff away from righthanded pitchers.

Flynn gets a good jump out of the batter's box and is difficult to double up. He is smart and alert, but does not have the speed to merit much attention from the pitcher.

It is in the field where Flynn is at his best. His glove has kept him in the major leagues. He plays second base and shortstop and can also be used at third base, although his arm strength is inadequate there. His throws are accurate and his concentration level high. He anticipates game situations and reacts accordingly.

OVERALL:

Robinson: "Flynn is a very capable utility infielder, the kind every club needs. His keen knowledge of the game could land him a minor league managerial position."

KANSAS CITY ROYALS

HITTING:

Steve Balboni, the first baseman with blacksmith arms, is the prototypal power hitter. He swings hard and he swings freely. In 1985, he set a club record for home runs (36) and strikeouts (166, breaking his own record of 139).

Balboni likes the ball up and over the middle of the plate. Make a mistake with a breaking ball and he will drive it a long way. And he can do it in the clutch: 25 of his 36 home runs came when the score was close.

Pitchers can bust him with fastballs inside, but they have to make sure they are inside on the corner or off the plate. Then they can pitch him away and try to get him to chase off-speed stuff. When Balboni gets into one of his hot streaks, he hits a pitcher's every mistake. When he is in a slump, however, he doesn't hit anything. The only way for him to get out of a slump is to swing his way out of it.

Balboni is so strong that even when he gets his body moving too quickly through the strike zone, he is able to drive the ball because he is so good at keeping his hands back.

The day he is asked to bunt is the day you know the Royals are in trouble.

BASERUNNING:

Balboni is no threat to steal. Yet, for a man his size and with such a strong swing, Balboni can get going out of the box fast enough to catch lackadaisical infielders off guard.

FIELDING:

He is not the most agile first baseman in the league, but he is sure-handed. His range is only average; when he gets to the ball, he usually catches it. Royals infielders marvel at Balboni's ability to adjust on throws to first and to come up with balls in the dirt.

He will go through periods where he

STEVE BALBONI
1B, No. 45
RR, 6'3", 225 lbs.
ML Svc: 3 years
Born: 1-16-57 in
Brockton, MA

```
1985 STATISTICS
AVG   G    AB    R    H    2B  3B  HR  RBI  BB   SO   SB
.243 160   600   74  146   28   2  36   88   52  166   1
CAREER STATISTICS
AVG   G    AB    R    H    2B  3B  HR  RBI  BB   SO   SB
.238 355  1238  150  295   56   6  71  188  112  366   1
```

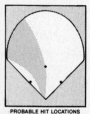

VS. RHP   VS. LHP   PROBABLE HIT LOCATIONS

has trouble making the throw to second base on a pickoff. He appears to be thinking too much about it instead of making a quick reactive throw.

OVERALL:

Balboni supplies much-needed power for the Royals, whose only other power threat is George Brett. If he can become a bit more selective while remaining an aggressive hitter, Balboni could move up from the bottom third of the order and become a solid fifth hitter. He doesn't show signs of ever hitting for the type of average a team wants from the number four man in the lineup.

Killebrew: "He is strong enough to hit the ball to any field and out of any park. If he can cut down on his strikeouts he will hit even more home runs. A big plus for Balboni is that he accepts the strikeouts as part of the game and does not let them keep him from going up to the plate swinging for the fences."

PITCHING:

In his two years with the Royals, Joe Beckwith's role has steadily diminished. He has gone from being the pitcher they hoped would fill a spot in the rotation, to the set-up man for Dan Quisenberry, to a middle reliever.

Beckwith seems most comfortable in the middle relief role, but he yearns for the job as the set-up man.

He has the ability to do that job, too. He throws an 87-88 MPH fastball which has good movement and he has excellent breaking pitches. He comes into the game and throws strikes. He can get out of a jam because of his ability to get a strikeout.

His problem last year was that he was too inconsistent. When he was good, he was very good. There were stretches of 15 1/3 scoreless innings in nine appearances; five earned runs and 17 strikeouts in 17 innings, and five earned runs in 29 innings to finish the season. But when he was bad . . . he was awful. He struggled through stretches of 12 earned runs in 15 innings and 20 earned runs in 17 2/3 innings.

When Beckwith goes bad it's no secret what is wrong: he is not getting his curveball over for strikes. As good as Beckwith's fastball may be, it is the breaking ball, especially the off-speed version, that keeps hitters tied up. When he doesn't have the curveball, he tries to force the fastball, which only adds to his problems. It straightens out and becomes easy prey for a waiting home-run hitter.

Beckwith's arm becomes tender after just a few throws; if he gets loosened up, he might as well pitch in the game because he usually can't come back for a day or two.

JOE BECKWITH
RHP, No. 27
LR, 6'2", 200 lbs.
ML Svc: 7 years
Born: 1-28-55 in
    Auburn, AL

1985 STATISTICS
W	L	ERA	G	GS	CG	SV	IP	H	R	ER	BB	SO
1	5	4.07	49	0	0	1	95	99	45	43	32	80

CAREER STATISTICS
W	L	ERA	G	GS	CG	SV	IP	H	R	ER	BB	SO
18	19	3.39	214	0	0	7	403.2	394	173	152	144	306

FIELDING:

Beckwith doesn't hurt himself with the glove, but then he doesn't help himself either. He has a decent pickoff move, but it is nothing special. He has a fast enough delivery to the plate to keep runners honest. He gets himself in position to field his position fairly quickly after he releases the ball.

OVERALL:

With the arrival of Steve Farr in mid-August last year, Beckwith's role diminished even more. His streakiness made it a gamble for the Royals to call on him in the middle innings with a lead to protect. He still, however, shows signs of the ability that made him so attractive to first the Dodgers and now the Royals, and who knows whom next.

Killebrew: "Joe might be best just coming in for those two or three innings to get the game to Quisenberry a few times a week. He throws hard enough that he should be able to hold the game because, in general, he throws strikes."

HITTING:

Buddy Biancalana became a cult hero during the World Series when he outhit and outplayed fellow shortstop Ozzie Smith of St. Louis. But as Biancalana said, "Ozzie has done it for quite a few years. I only did it for a couple of weeks." Biancalana's 1985 World Series performance notwithstanding, he needs to prove that he is an everyday player.

He is a free-swinger, which makes him susceptible to breaking pitches, especially away. He has to become more selective at the plate. Biancalana likes the fastball and he likes it high in the strike zone. He will chase the first pitch if it is close.

Biancalana hits for a better average righthanded than lefthanded (.269/.170 last year), but drives the ball better lefthanded. He was always a good bunter in the minor leagues, but he must learn to control his anxiety when he bunts in the majors. He completely missed the ball on three squeeze plays last season, including one in the 1985 AL playoffs.

BASERUNNING:

Biancalana is a good baserunner. He will take the extra base going from first to third or from second to home. In the minors, he was a threat to steal, but he has been too timid on the major league level. He doesn't take a big league lead. Not too many second basemen or shortstops are afraid of getting barrelled over by the 163-pound Biancalana on the double play.

FIELDING:

Biancalana's ticket to the majors is his good glove and his strong arm. He has quick reactions and good instincts. He can dive for a ball to his left and regain his balance quickly enough to make the throw.

He moves well into the hole and has a

BUDDY BIANCALANA
INF, No. 1
SR, 5'11", 160 lbs.
ML Svc: 2 years
Born: 2-2-60 in
    Larkspur, CA

1985 STATISTICS

AVG	G	AB	R	H	2B	3B	HR	RBI	BB	SO	SB
.188	81	138	21	26	5	1	1	6	17	34	1

CAREER STATISTICS

AVG	G	AB	R	H	2B	3B	HR	RBI	BB	SO	SB
.194	156	289	41	56	11	4	3	15	24	85	3

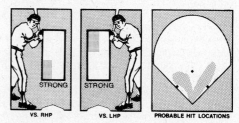

VS. RHP   VS. LHP   PROBABLE HIT LOCATIONS

strong enough arm to backhand the ball and still make a good throw. He hangs in well at second base on double plays, and again, his arm is strong enough to get off a late throw and still make the play.

OVERALL:

Biancalana has the type of enthusiasm that is contagious. The Royals won 23 of the 33 games Biancalana started after July 2, and he was their starting shortstop in all 14 post-season games.

Killebrew: "So far, Biancalana has shown he is a solid utility player who can fill in at short or second base or pinch-run. With his good defensive ability, if he could just hit .230 or .240, he could be an everyday player. However, he may not be durable enough to withstand the rigors of a 162-game season at shortstop."

PITCHING:

Buddy Black became the enigma of the Royals' starting rotation last year. He seemed to lose his aggressiveness after getting off to a 5-3 start. He went from being their number one starter to being the only member of the rotation with a losing record last season. But just when everyone was ready to write him off, Black came up with a strong finish, including a three-hitter against California, which moved the Royals into a tie for first in the AL West heading into the final four games of the regular season.

There were no arm problems: Black made every scheduled start last year, tying Charlie Leibrandt for the club lead with 33. Black can throw all four pitches for strikes, but the fastball is the pitch that sets up everything else. When he was going poorly last year, his fastball was just not there. Normally thrown in the upper 80s, it seemed to have lost some of its zip, though he did not lose his control of it.

He has good control of his change-up, his slider and curveball. He will throw anything he's got at any time in an effort to keep hitters off stride.

Black will pitch inside anytime--even against righthanders. When he comes in with his fastball, it makes the off-speed pitches more effective against anxious batters.

When Black is in trouble, as he was too often last season, he gets the ball up over the plate and hitters are all over the bases.

He is versatile. If the Royals were to come up with another starter, Black would be the ideal pitcher to move into the bullpen as a late-inning mate for Dan Quisenberry. Black can get loose in a hurry, can get strikeouts, and bounces back quickly.

BUD BLACK
LHP, No. 40
LL, 6'2", 180 lbs.
ML Svc: 4 years
Born: 6-30-57 in
  San Mateo, CA

1985 STATISTICS
W	L	ERA	G	GS	CG	SV	IP	H	R	ER	BB	SO
10	15	4.33	33	33	5	0	205.2	216	111	99	59	122

CAREER STATISTICS
W	L	ERA	G	GS	CG	SV	IP	H	R	ER	BB	SO
41	40	3.80	116	105	16	0	713.1	695	333	301	203	360

FIELDING:

Black never hurts himself when he has hold of the ball. He has an excellent pickoff move--so good, that in his first major league season, he was called for a club record seven balks before umpires accepted it as his natural move.

Black comes down in position to field the ball. He moves quickly off the mound and is good at making the force play on sacrifice attempts.

OVERALL:

Black could be the LaMarr Hoyt of 1986 if he re-establishes his fastball in spring training so that when the season begins, he has worked out all of the kinks.

Killebrew: "If Bud has his heater, everything else will fall into place. He must have command of it. He is one of those guys who seems to shine in the big games. Any time you have command of four pitches, you can make adjustments to get the job done."

HITTING:

By his--and just about everyone else's--estimation, George Brett had the best year of his career last year. He re-established himself as a major offensive force.

Brett uses all fields and can hit all types of pitches. Early in his career, he was an excellent fastball hitter who went to left field; but over the years, he has become almost as good at hitting breaking pitches and change-ups (he was thrown so many early on he had no choice but to learn how to hit them). He has also learned to pull the ball.

Brett keeps his weight on his back foot and glides through with a picture-perfect swing. He will swing at pitches that are not strikes if he feels he can drive them. In fact, when he hits home runs to left field, they usually come on pitches up and out of the strike zone.

Brett's strength is in adapting to situations. He takes what the pitcher gives him early in a game, but later on, he can turn on the same pitch and drive it to right field.

Brett hits left- and righthanders for equal average and power. When he is in a slump, he feels that facing a left-handed pitcher gets him going again because it forces him to go back to his fundamentals and stay on the ball longer. He has a tendency when he is going good to get lazy against righthanders.

BASERUNNING:

Once Brett hits a ball he is headed for second base--it is up to the defense to stop him. On double plays, the second baseman or shortstop is fair game to Brett's hard-sliding technique. He also showed in 1985 that when he is completely healthy, he can still steal a base if he wants to (nine out of 10).

FIELDING:

Of all the areas that benefitted from Brett's winter conditioning, his defense was the big winner. Last year he showed

GEORGE BRETT
3B, No. 5
LR, 6'0", 195 lbs.
ML Svc: 13 years
Born: 5-15-53 in
Glendale, WV

1985 STATISTICS

AVG	G	AB	R	H	2B	3B	HR	RBI	BB	SO	SB
.335	155	550	108	184	38	5	30	112	103	49	9

CAREER STATISTICS

AVG	G	AB	R	H	2B	3B	HR	RBI	BB	SO	SB
.316	1617	6234	1002	1967	400	108	193	977	615	443	140

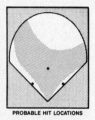

more agility and quickness than ever before. He was always better at moving to his left in the past, but he now has the quickness to make the play down the line.

Brett's arm strength was never a question, but the accuracy was. In the last two years, as he has become more confident of Steve Balboni's ability to adjust at first base, Brett has become more of a spontaneous, less hesitant thrower and his accuracy has improved.

OVERALL:

Brett dropped 25 pounds before the 1985 season, and the results were impressive. Best of all, he was injury-free.

Killebrew: "The numbers George can put on the board are unbelievable. The key to his season is staying healthy. He is a lifetime .300 hitter who shows power to go with his average. As well as ability, Brett has desire. He is an excellent competitor who knows how to play the game."

HITTING:

Prior to the 1985 season, the Royals felt so comfortable with Onix Concepcion at shortstop that they dealt away U. L. Washington so Concepcion would know the job was his. It was a nice thought. Onix never put together the type of season the Royals anticipated, and he wound up losing his job to Buddy Biancalana.

Concepcion is a high-ball hitter; in fact, his strength is actually the pitch up and out of the strike zone. He likes to swing from the bottom of the bat hoping to drive it somewhere. He makes good contact, but doesn't drive the ball much, and gets in trouble hitting the ball in the air. He does not even have warning-track power. Feed him fastballs up and pay the price. Bust him inside with hard pitches, and then use the breaking ball or change away and he will chase the pitches. Don't, however, get into a pattern and expect to consistently get him out. Concepcion can put down a sacrifice bunt, although he won't try to bunt for hits.

BASERUNNING:

Concepcion has the potential to steal bases in double figures. He measures his leads well and watches the pitcher's moves.

He doesn't make baserunning mistakes, but at times is too timid about taking extra bases. He is short but sturdy and will barrel into fielders to knock the ball loose.

FIELDING:

Concepcion's biggest asset is his arm. He has one of the quickest releases and strongest arms in the league. It allows him to play deep on artificial turf, but he does not always make the adjustments necessary to get to the ball quicker on the thicker turfs of natural grass.

ONIX CONCEPCION
SS, No. 2
RR, 5'6", 180 lbs.
ML Svc: 4 years
Born: 10-5-58 in
    Dorado, PR

1985 STATISTICS

AVG	G	AB	R	H	2B	3B	HR	RBI	BB	SO	SB
.204	131	314	32	64	5	1	2	20	16	29	4

CAREER STATISTICS

AVG	G	AB	R	H	2B	3B	HR	RBI	BB	SO	SB
.238	389	1040	108	248	34	7	3	80	47	93	25

STRONG   STRONG

VS. RHP   VS. LHP   PROBABLE HIT LOCATIONS

His range was a couple of steps less in 1985 than it used to be. Concepcion moves better to his left than to his right. He now seems too tentative when making throws.

OVERALL:

Concepcion has been bothered by nagging injuries throughout his career. To sharpen up, this year he played winter ball for the first time in his career.

Killebrew: "Onix is a quiet individual and, as a shortstop, needs to show a little more fire in the field. Perhaps he needs to feel pressure for a job. If so, he is getting plenty of it from Buddy Biancalana.

"If Concepcion could stay away from injuries it would help him to become more consistent with the bat. It looks like the injuires have slowed him down."

PITCHING:

Power, pure and simple.

Mark Gubicza's fastball is consistently in the low 90s and his slider comes close to the 90 MPH mark.

He is, however, his own worst enemy. He is a high-strung young man who does not merely want to strike out the hitters, he wants to bury them. He will be sailing along into the late innings of the game, and then get himself in trouble by overthrowing. He has not completed a regular-season game since the middle of 1984. He is, however, only 23 years old and should have plenty of time for complete games.

What Gubicza has that can't be taught is the live fastball and slider, and he throws them on the fists of hitters. When he doesn't overthrow his fastball, it sinks and is a heavy pitch. When he overthrows it, the pitch straightens out. Gubicza tried to add a split-finger fastball to use as an off-speed pitch last spring, but got so caught up in it that he almost lost his fastball.

Gubicza needs to get regular work. Too much idle time causes him to have control problems. When he was inserted into the starting rotation last season, he won five in a row and 13 of his final 19 decisions.

Because of his control problems, Mark is best-suited to be a starter. He does not warm up quickly. His only professional relief appearance was one that was planned in advance and provided him with the chance to take his time getting loose.

FIELDING:

Gubicza has a big motion, but he

MARK GUBICZA
RHP, No. 23
RR, 6'5", 210 lbs.
ML Svc: 2 years
Born: 8-14-62 in
  Philadelphia, PA

1985 STATISTICS

W	L	ERA	G	GS	CG	SV	IP	H	R	ER	BB	SO
14	10	4.06	29	28	0	0	177.1	160	88	80	77	99

CAREER STATISTICS

W	L	ERA	G	GS	CG	SV	IP	H	R	ER	BB	SO
24	24	4.06	58	57	4	0	366.1	332	178	165	152	210

keeps baserunners honest with a quick move to first base. He puts so much effort into his delivery that he oftens falls off the mound. He is a good athlete, though, and recovers well. It is not easy to bunt against him, a trait common to the Royals' staff.

OVERALL:

Of the Royals' five starters, Gubicza is the one with the most room for improvement. He is like a frisky puppy who just needs to get himself under control. The raw ability is there for him to be a quality power pitcher.

Killlebrew: "The development of Bret Saberhagen sometimes overshadows the job that Gubicza has been able to do at such a young age. He is going to be a tough pitcher once he learns from his experiences. He will keep a lot of hitters honest with that fastball of his."

PITCHING:

Danny Jackson came of age in the pennant stretch of 1985. He pitched the game against the California Angels that moved the Royals into first place for good, then shutout Toronto 2-0 in the fifth game of the playoffs, and beat the Cardinals in the fifth game of the World Series after giving up two runs in seven innings of a 3-1 loss in the opener. It was an important turnaround for Jackson, who had lost five of six decisions before the strong ending.

Better concentration helped Jackson to improve late in the season. His ritual of spending the day he was scheduled to start listening to rock music and thinking about his game plan undoubtedly contributed to his success.

He definitely has ability. His fastball has such good movement that he simply has to throw it over the plate. His hard slider is so good that it runs the radar gun up close to 90 MPH.

Once Jackson develops some type of an off-speed pitch, he will have no-hit potential. When he comes up with a pitch to keep the hitters off balance, he will become a super strikeout pitcher.

What Jackson can do now, however, is get himself out of jams. He can sink his fastball to get double play grounders. He doesn't get the ball up, as witnessed by the fact he gave up fewer home runs per innings pitched (seven in 208) than any starter in the major leagues.

Jackson gets himself in trouble by trying to be too fine. His ball moves so much that when he tries to hit spots, he misses the strike zone, which results in performances like the five consecutive walks he gave up against Baltimore on May 8; he got knocked out in the fourth inning after being spotted a 4-0 lead.

DANNY JACKSON
LHP, No. 25
RL, 6'0", 190 lbs.
ML Svc: 3 years
Born: 1-5-62 in
　San Antonio, TX

1985 STATISTICS												
W	L	ERA	G	GS	CG	SV	IP	H	R	ER	BB	SO
14	12	3.42	32	32	4	0	208	209	94	79	76	114
CAREER STATISTICS												
W	L	ERA	G	GS	CG	SV	IP	H	R	ER	BB	SO
17	19	3.74	51	46	5	0	303	319	147	126	117	163

FIELDING:

Only average with his move to first base, Jackson will throw over a lot to keep runners close. He does not have a particularly quick motion to the plate, and runners can get a little extra jump if they can pick up a key in his delivery. He is a decent fielder, but comes down so hard in his delivery that he is not always in control of his body.

Jackson occasionally gets rattled when going for a force play, but he can come back on the next play and make a great throw. He doesn't let his mistakes fluster him.

OVERALL:

Now that Jackson has a full season under his belt, the confidence of his strong late-season finish should carry him into the 1986 season.

Killebrew: "He is still young and will only get better. He already has the ability to dominate hitters. He might lead the league in broken bats with the way he comes inside with his hard stuff."

HITTING:

Lynn Jones is the most overlooked, but one of the most useful, players on the Royals. Known more for his defense than his offense, Jones is a capable player off the bench.

Like most backup players, his offensive numbers can vary from year to year (.301 in 1984 to .211 in 1985) because his role does not allow him enough regular work to get out of slumps.

Jones is not a power threat, but he does drive the ball into the alleys, and is an excellent contact man. Jones will be used in hit-and-run situations; he is also the best sacrifice bunter on the team.

He is an aggressive hitter coming off the bench. In late innings, he knows he is going to get fastballs and he goes up swinging. The fastball is his pitch. Get it up in the strike zone, and he will line it into the middle of the field. Defenses bunch him up the middle, knowing he does not pull the ball.

He has problems with breaking balls, especially from righthanded pitchers, which is why he was programmed into a part-time role when he first came to the big leagues with Detroit in 1979.

BASERUNNING:

Jones' average speed keeps him from being a basestealing threat. He has good instincts on the basepaths and can pick up the ball off the bat well. He knows enough to watch the coaches when the ball is behind him.

FIELDING:

Jones' ability to play any of the three outfield positions is what keeps him in the game. His main role is as a a late-inning replacement for Lonnie Smith in left field, but he is an above-average center fielder and an excellent right fielder. Jones breaks well on all

LYNN JONES
OF, No. 35
RR, 5'9", 170 lbs.
ML Svc: 8 years
Born: 1-1-53 in
Meadville, PA

1985 STATISTICS											
AVG	G	AB	R	H	2B	3B	HR	RBI	BB	SO	SB
.211	110	152	12	32	7	0	0	9	8	14	0
CAREER STATISTICS											
AVG	G	AB	R	H	2B	3B	HR	RBI	BB	SO	SB
.259	459	900	108	233	32	5	7	90	67	80	13

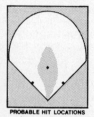

STRONG   STRONG   PROBABLE HIT LOCATIONS

VS. RHP   VS. LHP

balls and charges ground balls. He comes up with the ball quickly and is always ready to throw. He has a slightly above-average arm, but he makes it appear even stronger because of his quick release and accuracy. He never overthrows a cut-off man and never throws to the wrong base.

OVERALL:

Put into a backup role when he first came to the big leagues, Jones has come to accept it. He always has a smile on his face, never complains about a lack of opportuniy, and keeps himself mentally ready to take advantage of the opportunities he is afforded.

Killebrew: "Jones is a good defensive outfielder who is always ready to play. He understand what keeps him in the big leagues, which is being an extra man, and can help a team with both his ability and attitude."

PITCHING:

Willie Wilson put the artistry of Charlie Leibrandt in perspective when he said, "That's not Leibrandt, man . . . That's Rembrandt. The man can paint!"

A few years ago, Charlie Leibrandt was a struggling craftsman, but in the last year and a half he has drawn critical praise. There's nothing particularly impressive about Leibrandt except his results.

He is basically a two-pitch pitcher. He throws an average (at best) fastball, but sets it up well with a change-up that has the motion of a screwball. He also has a curve and slider, but they are only for show. Leibrandt will bust hitters inside with the fastball--and he has the guts to do it to righthanders as as well as lefties--and then go away with the change. He will throw either pitch at anytime.

Leibrandt's willingness to come inside is the biggest difference in him from his earlier days in Cincinnati. As a young pitcher, he was so intimidated by the likes of Johnny Bench that he wouldn't challenge Bench's refusal to call inside pitches from him.

Leibrandt's success comes not from throwing strikes, but from coming close enough to the strike zone to make hitters chase the ball. He never throws a pitch over the middle of the plate, and even when he is behind in the count, Leibrandt does not give in.

He can allow men on base but can escape the jam without serious damage by getting a rare, but big, strikeout, or by coming up with a double play grounder at precisely the right time.

In late innings, as he tires, he gets into trouble by pitching away too much. If he is tired and tries to come inside at that point in the game, he gets the pitch up too high in the strike zone. Righthanded hitters can tee off and drive the ball deep to left field.

CHARLIE LEIBRANDT
LHP, No. 37
RL, 6'3", 200 lbs.
ML Svc: 6 years
Born: 10-4-56 in
Chicago, IL

1985 STATISTICS

W	L	ERA	G	GS	CG	SV	IP	H	R	ER	BB	SO
17	9	2.69	33	33	8	0	237.2	223	86	71	68	108

CAREER STATISTICS

W	L	ERA	G	GS	CG	SV	IP	H	R	ER	BB	SO
44	33	3.67	138	98	14	2	697	741	317	284	225	267

FIELDING:

For a lefthander, Leibrandt is not good holding runners on. He has a good move to first base, but his motion has a bit of a kick in it, and he does not deliver the ball to the plate quickly. He lands balanced after he delivers the ball and is an average fielder.

OVERALL:

For a guy the Royals picked up to add experience to their Triple-A roster in the middle of the 1983 season, Leibrandt has emerged as one of their most valued and consistent pitchers. As well as ranking second to Bret Saberhagen in victories last year, he had the second lowest ERA in the AL, behind Toronto's Dave Stieb.

Killebrew: "Leibrandt fits into the Kansas City starting rotation nicely. He is a control pitcher sandwiched among power pitchers. Unlike a lot of pitchers who are not overpowering, he is not afraid to come inside, a necessity for a pitcher to suceed in the big leagues."

HITTING:

A classic example of not getting older but getting better, Hal McRae made major adjustments in his hitting approach last year and was a major part of the Royals' second half resurgence once he returned to the lineup on an everyday basis.

He is a good hitter who has a tendency to guess at pitches, but he can change his guess from pitch to pitch. He may be looking fastball in one situation, but has the ability to think along with the pitcher and switch to a change-up or a breaking ball as the count deepens. When he gets ahead in the count, he will open up his stance and look to drive a pitch. He tries to get an edge on a pitcher, by making the pitcher throw him the first strike. He makes contact on breaking pitches, but does his biggest damage on fastballs.

McRae thrives with men on base. He surprised quite a few people last year, including some of the Royals' management, with his ability to hit right-handers. Platooned for more than a season, he finally got a chance to face righthanders regularly beginning in late July. The result: he drove in 46 runs in his last 56 games. And while he had better power against lefties (eight home runs to six against righthanders), he hit for a better average against right-handers (.280 to .237).

In the right situations, infielders have to be alert. McRae is an excellent bunter.

BASERUNNING:

McRae still has the desire, but age has taken away his speed. He is no threat at all to steal bases, and he cannot stretch singles into doubles like he used to. Once the most feared man in the AL going into second base, he will still upend fielders--if he gets the chance.

FIELDING:

McRae has not played a game in the

HAL McRAE
DH, No. 11
RR, 5'11", 185 lbs.
ML Svc: 17 years
Born: 7-10-46 in
Avon Park, FL

1985 STATISTICS

AVG	G	AB	R	H	2B	3B	HR	RBI	BB	SO	SB
.259	112	320	41	83	19	0	14	70	44	45	0

CAREER STATISTICS

AVG	G	AB	R	H	2B	3B	HR	RBI	BB	SO	SB
.291	1954	6908	913	2011	467	66	183	1051	625	739	109

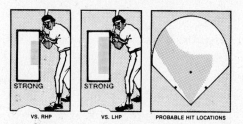

STRONG — VS. RHP   STRONG — VS. LHP   PROBABLE HIT LOCATIONS

field in the last three years, and only 17 in the last eight years.

OVERALL:

McRae is the emotional spirit of the Royals. He leads with his desire and attitude. The way he handled his part-time duty, without one complaint, was a lesson to his teammates about the importance of taking advantage of situations offered. He also gave the team a shove during the final month when he pushed himself despite a pulled muscle in his lower left side. It hurt enough that McRae didn't take batting practice, but it didn't keep him from coming up with big hits once the game started.

Killebrew: "Physically, McRae has slowed down some the past few years, but he does not show signs of slowing down with the bat. He remains an aggressive hitter and a tough out. If he stays healthy, he could probably DH on a regular basis for another couple of years."

HITTING:

Reduced to a platoon role in right field after the Royals traded for Lonnie Smith, Darryl Motley's overall offensive numbers were down drastically from 1984. He did continue to show power, however, and hit a career high of 17 home runs.

During his successful 1984 season, Motley drove the ball to the opposite field, but last year he got caught up trying to pull everything. As a result, his average dropped 62 points. When Motley gets his pitch--the fastball from the middle of the plate in--he has plenty of power. When pitchers throw him that pitch, it is usually a mistake; they work Motley away and let him try to pull the outside pitch. He generally winds up striking out or hitting ground balls to the shortstop. Despite part-time status, Motley led the Royals by grounding into 17 double plays.

He has to be more patient at the plate. Motley gets himself in a hole by chasing bad pitches, especially breaking balls out of the strike zone.

He is a decent bunter, but does not use the bunt to try to get base hits.

BASERUNNING:

Motley has slightly better than average speed, but has yet to make good use of it. He does not read pitchers well and he does not get a good jump. He is prone to being picked off. Motley will take the extra base, but he has to be more alert in picking up the third base coach when the ball is behind him.

FIELDING:

He is an above-average left fielder. He gets a good jump on the ball, pursues it hard, and has a strong arm for that position. With Smith in left field at this point, however, Motley has to play right field. He gets to the ball well enough, but his arm is average at best. He negates what edge his arm provides

DARRYL MOTLEY
OF, No. 24
RR, 5'9", 196 lbs.
ML Svc: 4 years
Born: 1-21-60 in
Muskogee, OK

1985 STATISTICS

AVG	G	AB	R	H	2B	3B	HR	RBI	BB	SO	SB
.222	123	383	45	85	20	1	17	49	18	57	6

CAREER STATISTICS

AVG	G	AB	R	H	2B	3B	HR	RBI	BB	SO	SB
.253	330	1098	133	278	49	9	37	138	53	153	19

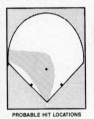
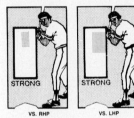

VS. RHP   VS. LHP   PROBABLE HIT LOCATIONS

him by not anticipating what runners will do and by taking several steps to wind up. In sacrifice fly situations, he almost always catches the ball on his glove side, requiring an extra step before he can unload the ball.

OVERALL:

Motley has made a dramatic comeback from a non-prospect two years ago to being a legitimate major league player. Credit that to his willingness to work on his shortcomings. What remains to be seen is if Motley can recapture his 1984 consistency or whether he will be no more than a platoon player. He has shown enough power to be secure as at least a fourth outfielder or platoon player.

Killebrew: "Motley is one of those guys who always gives 100%. He has good power to right-center, and needs to remember he can be as effective driving the ball that way as he is when trying to pull every pitch."

HITTING:

When Hal McRae got hot in the second half of the 1985 season, Jorge Orta's role was reduced to pinch-hitting and filling in late in the season when McRae was sidelined by a pulled muscle. Orta adapted well to limited usage and became the Royals' best pinch-hitter (8 for 28), including a stretch in September when he had four hits and a walk in six plate appearances. He combined with McRae to drive in 114 runs as the DH, which was the second highest total in the league.

A line drive hitter, Orta can take advantage of the quick artifical surface at Royals Stadium. He has a short, quick stroke and will jump on first-ball fastballs. Orta is at his best when he uses all fields, but he has a tendency to try to pull pitches. Pitchers have more success keeping the ball away from him, especially breaking balls which he will chase. But pitchers shouldn't make a mistake with the breaking ball. Orta can make them pay for their mistakes.

Orta has good bat control, and that includes being able to bunt (an important part of being a part-time player).

BASERUNNING:

Average, at best, as a runner, Orta is not aggressive on the bases. He is not a threat to steal and gets a poor jump on bunt attempts. He does not make many mistakes, but then he doesn't try to force the defense to make plays. He will surprise them, however, in getting down the line to first: he gets out of the box quickly and can catch an infielder off guard if he takes too much time making the throw to first. And middle infielders better not get lazy making double play pivots--Orta comes in hard to break them up.

FIELDING:

Orta's use is as a pinch-hitter and

JORGE ORTA
DH/OF, No. 3
LR, 5'10", 175 lbs.
ML Svc: 14 years
Born: 11-26-50 in
Mazatlan, MEX

1985 STATISTICS
AVG	G	AB	R	H	2B	3B	HR	RBI	BB	SO	SB
.267	110	300	32	80	21	1	4	45	22	28	2

CAREER STATISTICS
AVG	G	AB	R	H	2B	3B	HR	RBI	BB	SO	SB
.279	1628	5443	695	1517	249	61	119	695	474	674	119

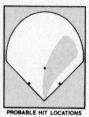

VS. RHP — STRONG   VS. LHP — STRONG   PROBABLE HIT LOCATIONS

as a DH. Originally a second baseman, he still takes infield practice at second but does so more out of fun than with expectations. He can fill in as an outfielder in a pinch. He looks more comfortable in right field.

His arm, however, is adequate at best for a left fielder. He does not move quickly on balls to his left or right, but catches what he gets to.

OVERALL:

Orta is a useful player who wants to play as much as possible, but does not complain or cause problems over his limited action.

Killebrew: "Orta can still hit, and when a team is in a need he will fill it in the field. You can't sell him short for his effort. He is getting older, but he takes care of himself and should be able to help the club off the bench."

HITTING:

There's nothing fancy about Greg Pryor as a hitter. He doesn't have a lot of power, but he is a solid man off the bench. The numbers don't always indicate that, but with the infrequent playing he receives, his slumps have a tendency to be accentuated; he doesn't get five or six games in a row to work things out. When Pryor had to fill-in during George Brett's lengthy 1984 knee surgery, he responded with a .263 average.

Pryor likes the fastball and has a quick enough bat to handle it. He will go with the pitch, aware that he is not a threat to drive it out of the park. Pryor does not chase many bad pitches, and can work a count until he gets something he likes. He will adjust when he gets a chance to play with some regularity, but coming off the bench so often he has a tendency to go after the first pitch, especially if it is a fastball.

Pryor has excellent bat control. He will hit-and-run when the opportunity is there, and does not swing and miss at pitches. Pryor is a solid man at laying down the sacrifice bunt.

BASERUNNING:

Speed is not an asset. Pryor has not stolen a base in the last three years. He tries to take the extra base and knows his limitations.

FIELDING:

Pryor keeps himself valuable by being one of the better-fielding third basemen in the AL. He is quick on the ball to his left, and using a big glove, scoops the chopper in front of him very well. He has a strong arm that lets him make the play deep at third and his throws are almost always right on target.

His second-best position is second

GREG PRYOR
3B, No. 4
RR, 6'0", 185 lbs.
ML Svc: 7 years
Born: 10-2-49 in
   Marietta, OH

1985 STATISTICS											
AVG	G	AB	R	H	2B	3B	HR	RBI	BB	SO	SB
.219	63	114	8	25	3	0	1	3	8	12	0

CAREER STATISTICS											
AVG	G	AB	R	H	2B	3B	HR	RBI	BB	SO	SB
.255	726	1771	197	452	81	9	14	139	101	171	10

VS. RHP   VS. LHP   PROBABLE HIT LOCATIONS

base, where his arm strength is an asset in turning double plays or going deep to field balls.

At shortstop, he is sure-handed but does not have the range necessary to be more than an emergency fill-in on an artifical surface. Most of his duty at shortstop comes on the road, on grass fields. He is a solid defensive fill-in at first base, but it is his fourth position. He can also provide relief in the outfield in an emergency.

OVERALL:

Killebrew: "Pryor is the perfect insurance for a club. He has the makeup to handle the uncertainity of a backup role and to be ready when he gets the opportunity to play. He knows what it takes to be a member of a winning team."

PITCHING:

Dan Quisenberry has reached the stage where being better than everybody else is no longer good enough. He led the AL in saves (37) for the fourth year in a row, had a 2.37 ERA and allowed only 22 of the 71 runners who were on base when he entered a game to score. All that did was make people wonder what went wrong.

Quisenberry did have a bigger problem than usual getting lefthanded hitters out (they hit .320 against him) last season. But he began coming inside to lefties late in the season and gave up only one hit to the last 16 he faced in the regular season.

Quisenberry's advantages are his submarine delivery and pinpoint control. His 16 walks last year were the most he had issued since 1980, when he walked 27 in his first full major league season. He also struck out a career high of 54.

His reputation is such that hitters frequently swing at his first pitch, not wanting to let Quisenberry get ahead in the count; however, he rarely throws them a first-pitch strike.

His fastball is not much, usually in the upper 70s and occasionally in the low 80s, although it has good sinking action and a lot of movement. His main pitch is a slider that breaks up and in on lefthanded batters and goes away to righthanded hitters. He also throws a change-up and a knuckleball, but they only get him in trouble.

His arm is remarkably resilient and never gets worn, despite what looks like a taxing style of delivery. He has admitted, however, that he gets mentally tired from the constant pressure of his role. This is indicated when he begins to force his pitches, which results in a loss of movement on his stuff.

He has to watch the hitters. In their efforts to try to get to his pitches before they break, hitters will move up in

DAN QUISENBERRY
RHP, No. 29
RR, 6'2", 180 lbs.
ML Svc: 6 years
Born: 2-7-54 in
  Santa Monica, CA

1985 STATISTICS

W	L	ERA	G	GS	CG	SV	IP	H	R	ER	BB	SO
8	9	2.37	84	0	0	37	129	142	41	34	16	54

CAREER STATISTICS

W	L	ERA	G	GS	CG	SV	IP	H	R	ER	BB	SO
44	35	2.48	444	0	0	217	764	737	237	211	100	259

the box, knowing Quisenberry does not throw too hard for them to react. When that happens, he has to pitch inside to move them back.

FIELDING:

As a late-inning reliever, he helps his own cause with his ability to field his position and hold runners. He has a quick jump move to first base and can throw over frequently without losing concentration on the hitter. Even though he doesn't throw too quickly to the plate, Quisenberry can get rid of the ball in a hurry when he is trying to throw out a baserunner. His follow-through leaves him in position to field balls hit back to him. He is quick off the mound and comes up with the bunt.

OVERALL:

Killebrew: "Dan is well-suited to short relief work: he can get loose in a hurry and he can pitch often. He does not let one day's failure carry over to the next game. His control carries him, and his delivery makes him very tough to have to hit against. I don't believe that he is faltering one bit."

ACE OF THE STAFF

PITCHING:

World Series MVP.
20-game winner.
American League Cy Young Award.

In his third year of pro ball and second in the majors, Bret Saberhagen established himself as one of the top pitchers in baseball.

Slender and frail-looking, Bret is a deceptive power pitcher. His motion is so short and smooth that he catches hitters off-guard with a fastball that picked up a couple of miles per hour last year (it is now in the upper 80s). His fastball should get even faster as he matures physically. As well as good velocity, Saberhagen has good movement on the pitch and can hit the corners with it.

His fastball and change-up are good enough that Saberhagen can win with just those two pitches. But he also has a curveball, and when he has command of it, he is dominating.

Saberhagen does not beat himself. He mixes his pitches well against the middle of the order, and he challenges the lesser hitters. He throws strikes. In 36 starts (including four post-season) he walked fewer than three batters 35 times. As a result, he works quickly and the defense responds behind him with strong support. "Catching him is like having a day off," catcher Jim Sundberg said. "He always hits his spot."

Saberhagen has enough confidence in his control that he will pitch inside to righthanded or lefthanded hitters.

His performance in the 1985 World Series clearly indicated that he is unfazed by pressure. It is not every pitcher who can force the team with the best record in baseball to disgrace themselves with an 11-0 loss in the seventh game of the World Series.

BRET SABERHAGEN
RHP, No. 31
RR, 6'1", 160 lbs.
ML Svc: 2 years
Born: 4-11-64 in
    Chicago Heights, IL

1985 STATISTICS
W	L	ERA	G	GS	CG	SV	IP	H	R	ER	BB	SO
20	6	2.87	32	32	10	0	235.1	211	79	75	38	158

CAREER STATISTICS
W	L	ERA	G	GS	CG	SV	IP	H	R	ER	BB	SO
30	17	3.11	70	50	12	1	393	349	150	136	74	231

FIELDING:

Overlooked by his statistical success is the fact that Saberhagen is among the, if not the, best-fielding pitchers in the league. He has a quick move to first base that forces baserunners to keep closer to the bag than they would like. His delivery is so smooth that he lands balanced and ready to field his position. He is quick off the mound and can make plays to his left and right. He also has quick instincts when a ball is hit to the right side of the infield and moves quickly to cover first base.

OVERALL:

It's hard to find fault with any part of Saberhagen's game. If he can maintain what he did in 1985, he will be one of the best ever. His motion is such that he will probably never have arm trouble.

Killebrew: "There is hardly anything bad to say about Bret. As a hitter, I wouldn't be thrilled at the thought that he is only going to get better. His curve is so good that a hitter simply doesn't have a prayer. He is the best righthander in the American League."

HITTING:

Pat Sheridan has become an enigma for the Royals. He shows every indication of being an exciting offensive player: he has a short, quick stroke, he can drive the ball in the alleys and pull the ball enough to hit 10 to 15 homers even in a pitcher's park like Royals Stadium. The problem, however, is that he is just too streaky.

He has a reputation as a fastball hitter, but actually looked more comfortable last year against off-speed pitchers. When he has an aggressive approach at the plate, Sheridan can really drive the ball; defenses cannot play him to pull. But when he is cold, he swings the bat as if he were in a daze. He takes poor swings and is especially vulnerable to breaking pitches away and out of the strike zone.

Sheridan has not proven he can hit lefthanded pitching well enough to be more than a platoon player.

He is a good bunter, and should use that tool more often when he is struggling. With his speed, he can force infielders to be more honest against him and open up some holes in the infield to drive the ball through.

BASERUNNING:

Sheridan has above-average speed, but is not aggressive enough on the bases to make use of it. He will, however, challenge an outfielder by attempting to stretch a single into a double. When he is on first, he tries to take the extra base on hits.

FIELDING:

Sheridan's speed is well suited to playing the outfield at Royals Stadium, where he can cut off balls in the gaps. He continues, however, to be too tentative when coming in on balls, perhaps remembering his early days when he was victimized by high hops off artificial

PAT SHERIDAN
RF, No. 15
LR, 6'3", 175 lbs.
ML Svc: 3 years
Born: 12-4-57 in
   Ann Arbor, MI

1985 STATISTICS

AVG	G	AB	R	H	2B	3B	HR	RBI	BB	SO	SB
.228	78	206	18	47	9	2	3	17	23	38	11

CAREER STATISTICS

AVG	G	AB	R	H	2B	3B	HR	RBI	BB	SO	SB
.267	328	1021	125	273	45	8	18	106	84	194	33

  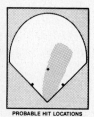

VS. RHP   VS. LHP   PROBABLE HIT LOCATIONS

turf. He goes back on the ball very well.

Sheridan has good arm strength and has worked on getting rid of the ball quickly to take advantage of it. He will have lapses of concentration and can get caught by surprise by baserunners because he has not anticipated the play.

His throws hit the target and he does not overthrow the cutoff man.

OVERALL:

Injuries and a continuing problem with lefthanded pitching have been a problem for Sheridan throughout his career.

Killebrew: "He has many of the offensive abilities to be an everyday player. It is possible that if he could get more playing time, he could put some good numbers together. At this point, it is difficult to give him an everyday role because of his streaky hitting and defensive lapses."

HITTING:

It took six weeks for Lonnie Smith to make the adjustment to the American League, but once he got comfortable, he made life miserable for Kansas City's opponents. By the end of the season, Smith fit in so well that he was moved from the number two spot in the order to leadoff, ahead of Willie Wilson. Smith hit .256 for the Royals, but ranked second on the team with a .326 on-base percentage.

Smith is a first-ball, fastball hitter, but had most of his trouble last year against power pitchers who pitched him tight. He is willing to take a walk, and can battle back after he is behind in the count.

Having hit second in the order quite a bit in recent years, Smith had been in the habit of trying to inside-out every pitch, but he finally got out of it in the middle of the season. He still went the other way on occasion, but was able to regain his ability to drive the inside pitch to left field.

Smith is an excellent hit-and-run man, and will bunt for a base hit.

BASERUNNING:

Smith was voted the most aggressive runner in the National League, and it didn't take long for the folks in the AL to see why. He goes hard on the bases, barrelling into fielders who are trying to make relay throws.

He has great baserunning instincts. He always seems to know where the ball is and does not hesitate taking the extra base if a poor throw is made or if a fielder does not come up cleanly with a base-hit. He teamed with Willie Wilson to give the Royals only the second tandem in the club's history to steal 40 or more bases each.

FIELDING:

Smith's bat carries him. He is erratic in the field, and has trouble just staying on his feet. He does not go back

LONNIE SMITH
LF, No. 21
RR, 5'9", 170 lbs.
ML Svc: 8 years
Born: 12-22-55 in
  Chicago, IL

1985 STATISTICS
AVG	G	AB	R	H	2B	3B	HR	RBI	BB	SO	SB
.257	120	448	77	115	23	4	6	41	41	69	40

CAREER STATISTICS
AVG	G	AB	R	H	2B	3B	HR	RBI	BB	SO	SB
.292	747	2544	476	744	139	28	33	238	265	360	261

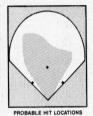

VS. RHP   VS. LHP   PROBABLE HIT LOCATIONS

well on balls, which forces him to have to play very deep in left field. This causes a lot of balls to fall in front of him, and he will make do-or-die efforts on them, though not always using good judgment.

Smith goes well to his left and right and gets an excellent jump. When he catches up to the ball, the excitement doesn't stop. His throwing is as erratic as his fielding. He gets rid of the ball in a hurry, and normally hits the cutoff man, but every once in a while he will try to throw out runners on his own. A big mistake. Smith's arm is below-average at best.

OVERALL:

Killebrew: "Because of the DH rule, the AL may be Smith's best bet. He is a good offensive player who can ignite an attack in a hurry with his aggressiveness on the bases.

"This should be a big year for him. He knows the league better now and should hit for a better average."

HITTING:

Satisifed just to make contact in his early years in the big leagues, Jim Sundberg has now learned to turn on the ball and drive it deep. While he is still not a power threat in the true sense, he can surprise opposing pitchers if they try to come inside with a fastball and don't get it far enough inside.

He drilled a career high of 10 home runs last year, and late in the season showed he could even hit the ball out of spacious Royals Stadium. Sundberg's final two regular season home runs, plus one in the playoffs, were hit at home.

Primarily a pull hitter in the past, Sundberg has learned to use the whole field which makes him more of a threat. His strength is up the middle. A good contact man, he is a likely candidate for the hit-and-run.

Pitchers work him with pitches away, either fastballs or breaking stuff. He won't chase bad pitches, though. He is a good bunter in sacrifice situations, but hitting low in the order, Sundberg is usually asked to hit-and-run instead.

BASERUNNING:

Sundberg has slightly above-average speed for a catcher, which means he won't steal many bases. He has never stolen more than three in a professional season, and has only one stolen base in the last three years.

He is, however, an excellent baserunner. He watches the ball in the outfield and knows when he can get that extra base. He pushes himself hard, and late in the season he began using a headfirst slide with success.

FIELDING:

Sundberg's strength is his defense. He is the only catcher to win six Gold Gloves. He was given a lot of credit for the fast development of the Royals' young pitching staff because of his ability to call a game and to settle

JIM SUNDBERG
C, No. 8
RR, 6'0", 195 lbs.
ML Svc: 12 years
Born: 5-18-51 in
  Galesburg, IL

1985 STATISTICS

AVG	G	AB	R	H	2B	3B	HR	RBI	BB	SO	SB
.245	115	367	38	90	12	4	10	35	33	67	0

CAREER STATISTICS

AVG	G	AB	R	H	2B	3B	HR	RBI	BB	SO	SB
.253	1623	5161	537	1304	220	43	71	537	585	820	19

  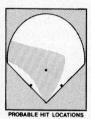

VS. RHP   VS. LHP   PROBABLE HIT LOCATIONS

down anxious pitchers.

Once the most feared thrower out of all the catchers in the league, Sundberg's arm strength has diminished in recent years. He has a long windup when getting rid of the ball, which enabled him to throw out only 26% of the runners that challenged him last season. He has good footwork, however, which, to some degree, compensates for his current throwing problems.

OVERALL:

Sundberg was just what the Royals needed for their young pitching staff-- a stabilizing veteran who can work young pitchers through tough situations.

Killebrew: "Sunny is durable. In 12 seasons, he has caught in 1,606 games, which is third highest among all active players and is only 312 games behind the all-time leader, Al Lopez.

"He is not flashy, but he is consistent in everything he does, from handling pitchers to his hitting."

HITTING:

John Wathan's playing time has steadily declined over the last two years, but with two years left on a four-year contract, he doesn't have to worry about a job. Wathan's 60 games in 1985 (41 of them were starts) was his lowest total since his rookie year (he played in 55 games in 1977).

Wathan is a contact hitter with little power. He likes the ball up and will use all fields, but he can go deep to any of them. He is the best hit-and-run man on the Royals and enjoys the task.

Wathan will try to force a pitcher to throw him strikes: he won't get into a hole by swinging at bad pitches. His ability to handle the bat also translates into good bunting skills.

BASERUNNING:

For a catcher, Wathan has well-above-average speed (he set a major league record for a catcher with 36 stolen bases in 1982). Even though he doesn't run often (1-for-2 on steal attempts in 1985), he gives pitchers something to think about. He is an aggressive runner and the Royals' best pinch-runner, although he hasn't been used that way much because Dick Howser doesn't want to get caught short of catchers if Sundberg has to leave the game.

FIELDING:

A major asset for Wathan is his versatility. He can play three positions: catcher, first base and outfield. Defensively, he is at his best at first base. He moves well around the bag and adjusts well to throws.

He does a capable job behind the plate. Sundberg worked hard with Wathan on his throwing mechanics. To strengthen his arm, Wathan also threw batting prac-

JOHN WATHAN
C, No. 12
RR, 6'2", 205 lbs.
ML Svc: 10 years
Born: 10-4-49 in
   Cedar Rapids, IA

1985 STATISTICS

AVG	G	AB	R	H	2B	3B	HR	RBI	BB	SO	SB
.234	60	145	11	34	8	1	1	9	17	16	1

CAREER STATISTICS

AVG	G	AB	R	H	2B	3B	HR	RBI	BB	SO	SB
.262	860	2505	305	656	90	25	21	261	199	267	105

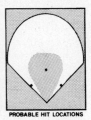

STRONG   STRONG

VS. RHP   VS. LHP   PROBABLE HIT LOCATIONS

tice several times a week. He credited both tactics with improving his throws to second base (he threw out 12 of 31 potential basestealers last year).

In the outfield, Wathan is steady but not spectacular. He gets a good jump on balls and knows what base to throw to. If the Royals go with three catchers in 1986, Wathan could see some more spot duty in the outfield.

OVERALL:

Killebrew: "John is a solid force on a club because he has a good attitude and can help a team in a number of ways. I don't know how much longer he plans on playing, but the fact that he has spent so much time trying to improve his physical skills tells you that he always wants to be ready to help the team."

HITTING:

With the changing of some of the Royals' guards over the last couple of years, Frank White decided it was time for him to pick up some of the power load. He did a good job of it.

After back-to-back 17 home run seasons in 1983 and 1984, White hit a career high of 22 home runs in 1985. His average suffered in exchange for the power. He also struck out a career high 86 times, and his .249 average was the lowest since he began playing regularly in 1975.

Once a hitter who sprayed the ball around, White has now become a dead pull hitter. He looks for the pitch up and in to yank down the left field line. He loves the fastball, especially up in the strike zone.

With his new concentration on power, White can be pitched to with breaking balls and change-ups.

While White isn't looking for average anymore, he does watch for third basemen who play too deep, and he will drop down a bunt for a base hit. He is also an excellent bunter in sacrifice situations and seems to enjoy that challenge as much as hitting home runs.

BASERUNNING:

White will catch pitchers off-guard. He doesn't run as often as he once did, but he can still pick up a stolen base on missed hit-and-run plays. He gets a good enough jump to take a base if a pitcher doesn't keep him close. He's from the Hal McRae School of Baserunning. He takes extra bases and goes into bases hard. If White is on the front end of a double play, the pivot man better get rid of the ball in a hurry.

FIELDING:

White remains a consistent second basemen. He may have lost a step or two, especially to his right, but he

FRANK WHITE
2B, No. 20
RR, 5'11", 175 lbs.
ML Svc: 13 years
Born: 9-4-50 in
  Greenville, MS

1985 STATISTICS

AVG	G	AB	R	H	2B	3B	HR	RBI	BB	SO	SB
.249	149	563	62	140	25	1	22	69	28	86	10

CAREER STATISTICS

AVG	G	AB	R	H	2B	3B	HR	RBI	BB	SO	SB
.258	1652	5534	667	1429	277	50	109	609	257	710	162

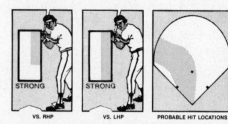

VS. RHP   VS. LHP   PROBABLE HIT LOCATIONS

fills the hole between himself and first in a hurry and his experience allows him to position himself well. He plays deep and has a strong arm which allows him to make plays other second basemen have to ignore.

White's arm is also an asset in turning the double play. He hangs in well at second base and adjusted to taking throws from three different shortstops last year without showing any drop in his ability.

OVERALL:

White is one of the elder Royals, second only to McRae in terms of seniority, and he has taken the leadership load on the field and off.

Killebrew: "Frank is getting a litle older, and he has used his experience to become more of a power hitter. He's made the big adjustments in the field to make up for any loss in range, which is minimal to begin with."

HITTING:

Willie Wilson keeps getting better. He has always hit for a higher average from the right (his natural) side, but last season, he emerged as a true threat to drive the ball from the left side.

There are two reasons for Wilson's lefthanded power rise: one is his experience, and the other is the strengthening of his right arm. As a result, he now pulls the bat through the strike zone harder lefthanded, and has gotten rid of the lightweight bat he used to use from the left side. He hit three home runs as a lefthanded batter last year--the first time he has hit a ball over a fence that way in his career. He also had 17 of his club-record 21 triples from the left side. Because of the added strength, pitchers can no longer bury him with fastballs inside when he bats from the left side.

Wilson is a fastball hitter. From the left side, he likes the ball down and in, and from the right side, he likes it up and over the plate. Pitchers have to work carefully against him now, mixing hard stuff with breaking balls.

Wilson still does not walk much and, despite his speed, he does not bunt. His increased power combined with these factors prompted his late-season move to the number two spot in the order.

BASERUNNING:

Wilson is a baseburner. He does not like to steal bases, but will give it a shot early in the game or in late-inning, game situations. He relies on his speed to get the job done. He is aggressive on the bases and is always looking for the extra base; there is nothing quite so exciting as his easy stride on a triple.

FIELDING:

Wilson is an ideal center fielder. He gets an excellent jump on balls to his left and right and also goes back on the ball very well. He is not afraid of

WILLIE WILSON
CF, No. 6
SR, 6'3", 175 lbs.
ML Svc: 10 years
Born: 7-9-55 in
    Montgomery, AL

1985 STATISTICS											
AVG	G	AB	R	H	2B	3B	HR	RBI	BB	SO	SB
.278	141	605	87	168	25	21	4	43	29	94	43

CAREER STATISTICS											
AVG	G	AB	R	H	2B	3B	HR	RBI	BB	SO	SB
.301	1111	4277	698	1287	156	90	21	313	218	564	436

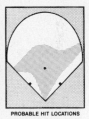

VS. RHP   VS. LHP   PROBABLE HIT LOCATIONS

fences and has the leaping ability to go above the top to make a catch.

He has a bit of a problem, however, on the ball in front of him: Wilson's initial instinct is to step back. He has an average arm, at best, but makes up for it with his speed. It allows him to cut off balls that would normally roll to the fence. He gets rid of the ball quickly and usually hits the cutoff man.

OVERALL:

Wilson is a changed man. And not just as a lefthanded hitter. He has learned to handle pressure situations better, and now deals with the media, teammates and fans with a consistency that has made him a welcomed member of the team.

Killebrew: "Wilson is the type of player who could help any team. He provides Kansas City with steady and reliable defense in center field and has now added the valuable asset of power to his hitting. In 1985, it appears he put his past problems behind him and is ready to play well everyday."

STEVE FARR
RHP, No. 34
RR, 5'11", 190 lbs
ML Svc: 1 year plus
Born: 12-12-56 in
Cheverly, MD

PITCHING, FIELDING:

In 1984, it was Charlie Leibrandt, a minor league reclamation project that helped a Royals' pitching resurgence. In 1985, it was Steve Farr. Out of baseball in April, he joined the Royals' minor league team system in May 1985, and by early August, he arrived prepared for the job of set-up man for Quisenberry.

Farr is a good competitor. He does not seem shaken by challenges. He can throw four pitches, all for strikes, and will throw any of them at any time. His fastball is average, but mixed with a decent change and slider and an outstanding curveball, it is plenty good enough.

He mixes his pitches well enough that he can get lefthanded hitters out almost as well as righthanded hitters. When he is in trouble, he is missing the corners and falling behind to hitters. He does not have the power pitches simply to challenge the hitters; he needs them to chase his pitches.

As a reliever, Farr has to work on his pickoff move to keep runners close. If they get too big a jump on him, they will steal bases. He has a very deliberate delivery to the plate: a slow leg kick, which is a cut-down replica of the one made famous by Bill Caudill of Toronto. He handles the ball hit back to him well and is not afraid to go for the lead runner.

OVERALL:

Farr is a rare find--he is a guy who actually prefers middle relief work to starting. He can get loose quickly and can pitch five days a week, making him a manager's dream for that role.

DANE IORG
OF/1B, No. 9
LR, 6'0", 180 lbs.
ML Svc: 9 years
Born: 5-11-50 in
Eureka, CA

HITTING, BASERUNNING, FIELDING:

Dane Iorg makes a living by coming off the bench swinging the bat. As a pinch-hitter deluxe, he knows pitchers are going to try to get ahead of him in a hurry by throwing fastballs. And that's the pitch he likes to hit.

Iorg has a good idea of the strike zone. While he doesn't have much power, he is a good contact hitter and responds to pressure situations (like the memorable bases-loaded, two-run, ninth-inning single in the Royals' 2-1 victory over St. Louis in the sixth game of the 1985 World Series).

He is strictly used against righthanded pitchers, and they have to be careful to mix up pitches against him because he is waiting for the fastball. In his role off the bench, he is not asked to bunt very often.

Iorg is not a threat to steal a base. If the game is on the line, he usually gives way to a pinch-runner.

Defensively, his main role is with the bat. Iorg is adequate in the outfield, though he does not have the speed to cover much ground. He can also fill in at first base with average ability, and if things are really tough, he can play third.

OVERALL:

Killebrew: "The more he pinch-hits, the better he gets. He knows how to get ready for the job and enjoys the pressure."

MIKE JONES
LHP, No. 17
LL, 6'5", 230 lbs.
ML Svc: 3 years
Born: 7-30-59 in
    Rochester, NY

PITCHING, FIELDING:

In his continuing comeback from a fractured neck suffered after the 1981 season, Mike Jones hit a snag in 1985. He made big strides in 1984, rekindling hopes that he could regain the form that made him a candidate for Rookie Pitcher of the Year in 1981 even though he only pitched for the Royals in the final half of that season.

But instead of improving what was his average 1984 fastball, he lost velocity on it. Jones has a decent curveball, but to be effective in a middle relief role, he has to get lefthanded hitters out. He had the tendency to come in against lefties in 1985 and immediately fall behind in the count.

His move is just average, and that's a problem because he has a big motion to the plate. He often comes down off balance and has to hurry to get in position to field.

OVERALL:

He needs to make a major improvement this year. No longer the power pitcher he was as a youth, Jones doesn't make excuses. He is the first to admit that he has a lack of discipline in training.

Killebrew: "It is hard to give up on a pitcher coming off an injury, even more so because he is a lefthander. It just takes time to get their arm strength built back up. The promising thing about Jones' injury is that he didn't hurt the arm, so it is just a matter of rebuilding strength."

JAMIE QUIRK
INF, No. 9
LR, 6'4", 200 lbs.
ML Svc: 9 years
Born: 10-22-54 in
    Whittier, CA

HITTING, BASERUNNING, FIELDING:

In the winter prior to the 1985 season, Jamie Quirk was begging for a minor league job. By the end of the year, he was part of the World Champion Royals and had proven he is a capable backup man off the bench.

A lefthanded hitter with some power, Quirk has learned to deal with spot appearances. He hit safely in 12 of the 19 games he played in last year for the Royals. He is a fastball hitter who likes the ball over the plate. His role limits his exposure to lefthanders. He is a capable bunter, but only for sacrifice attempts.

Quirk is not a threat on the bases. He plays hard but isn't fast enough to create problems.

Originally a third baseman when he came to the big leagues, Quirk established himself last year as a legitimate backup catcher. He got the chance to play regularly in the minors and surprised skeptics by throwing out 22 of 39 potential basestealers. He continued to show off his strong arm with the Royals, throwing out seven of 17 would-be basestealers. He has a quick release and his throws are accurate.

OVERALL:

Faced with what looked like the end of his baseball career, Quirk finally accepted being a part-time player. He now knows what he has to do to stay in the majors. A lefthanded hitter who can play three positions, he has value to the team.

MILWAUKEE BREWERS

HITTING:

Mark Brouhard is a big, husky out-fielder who has shown enough power potential for the Brewers to patiently await his emergence as a legitimate power-er hitter. Their patience is about to run out, however.

Although Brouhard has produced a one- or two-week display of strength almost every year to whet the appetites of team officials and Brewer fans, he has yet to put together a season that justifies all that hope. In past years, injuries have terminated his hot streaks. In 1985, his bat was the villain, and he spent the month of August in the minors.

Brouhard's problem is his limited hitting zone. If it is not belt-high, he won't hit it. That's it. Belt-high and right down the middle of the plate is the only pitch he likes. If the pitch is a little on the inside, his tendency to try to pull everything may produce a loud foul but little else.

While it's dangerous to throw him a fastball in his one power zone, a breaking ball away or a change-up will fool him. He is a poor bunter and is not likely to sacrifice.

BASERUNNING:

He will make a hard slide into second base to break up the double play, but the rest of his baserunning skills are poor. Brouhard drags out of the box, and although he as decent speed for a big man, he hasn't stolen a base since 1981.

FIELDING:

Brouhard has trouble judging fly balls and has trouble handling anything except when he has to come in on a ball. He has worked on his fielding and improved somewhat, but he makes a lot of sliding and diving catches on balls that should be routine.

MARK BROUHARD
RF, No. 29
RR, 6'1", 210 lbs.
ML Svc: 6 years
Born: 5-22-56 in
    Burbank, CA

1985 STATISTICS
AVG	G	AB	R	H	2B	3B	HR	RBI	BB	SO	SB
.259	37	108	11	28	7	2	1	13	5	26	0

CAREER STATISTICS
AVG	G	AB	R	H	2B	3B	HR	RBI	BB	SO	SB
.258	304	909	108	235	40	7	25	104	53	184	2

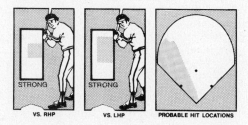

STRONG VS. RHP   STRONG VS. LHP   PROBABLE HIT LOCATIONS

His arm is only average--if that--and no one really knows where the ball is going to end up when he throws it. None of his defensive skills are impressive, although he is working hard to improve.

OVERALL:

Brouhard has to play to hit, but has never produced enough to earn a regular spot in the lineup. He has some power, but he also has a lot of weaknesses. His production has leveled off, and if he doesn't produce in 1986, it is doubtful that he ever will.

Robinson: "I think he is down to his last gasp. The Brewers lost confidence in him. He has that good, quick swing, but he still has so many holes. The ball has to be in one spot for him to hit it. All the pitcher has to do is keep it away from the middle of the plate."

PITCHING:

Ray Burris reached a couple of milestones during the 1985 season. He recorded his 1,000th strikeout in August and his 100th victory in his very next start. It took him two years longer to win 100 than it did to lose 100, so his 9-13 record is hardly surprising: it mirrors his lifetime record.

Things looked promising for him at the start of the 1985 season. Burris had a 2.84 ERA and a 4-5 record, which might have been better had he been given any kind of offensive support. After that, however, his season went downhill. His ERA over the rest of the year was a bloated 6.53 and he spent the last month in the bullpen. He gave up 25 home runs, 17 of which were after the All-Star break.

Basically, Burris uses a three-quarters delivery, though occasionally he will drop down and come in sidearm. He is a control pitcher whose best pitch is a quick slider, but he goes to his fastball, which is around 83 MPH, when he is behind in the count.

Burris also has an effective change-up and will throw it any time. He has good concentration and is very tricky at getting out of jams. He will use any of his pitches to get out of tough spots.

Burris likes to work fast, and hitters should step out to make him slow down. He is not a nine-inning pitcher, but he is a competitor and will give you seven strong innings.

More than anything else, the home runs he gave up hurt him last season.

Although he will move the ball in and out, Burris doesn't back hitters off the plate as much as he should. Knowing the ball will be near the strike zone enables hitters to be ready for a good one.

RAY BURRIS
RHP, No. 20
RR, 6'5", 210 lbs.
ML Svc: 13 years
Born: 8-22-50 in
Idabel, OK

```
1985 STATISTICS
W   L  ERA   G   GS  CG SV  IP     H    R    ER  BB  SO
9  13 4.81  29  28   6  0 170.1  182   95   91  53  81
CAREER STATISTICS
W    L  ERA   G   GS  CG SV  IP      H     R    ER  BB   SO
102 127 4.10 447 290  47  4 2082.1 2185 1058  949 720 1023
```

FIELDING:

His move to first is average, but Ray works hard to keep runners close. This doesn't keep him from concentrating on the plate, however. He gets off the mound quickly and his delivery leaves him in a good position: he is ready for the ball.

He is a good athlete and a fine defensive pitcher.

OVERALL:

Burris keeps himself in decent shape, but he appears to have dropped off after compiling a 13-10 record with a 3.15 ERA for Oakland in 1984. He will have to pitch better than he did last season. He will have to keep the ball in the park.

Robinson: "Although he is better suited as a starter, his role this season is expected to be in long relief. He knows how to pitch and has the all of the pitches, but he fell into the same pattern as the rest of the team and finished with a poor record.

"I think Burris is just an average pitcher on an average team."

HITTING:

Bobby Clark changed his stance in 1985, hoping to make better contact with the ball. Putting more weight on his back leg, he moved the bat flat behind his head. He made the change after he began the season in the minors, but it didn't help him that much when the Brewers recalled him last June. They shipped him back to the minors in August and then released him at the end of the Pacific Coast League season.

When he broke in with the California Angels, Clark was supposed to have a lot of potential. He sat around in California for three seasons before being traded to Milwaukee in 1984. After spending most of his first season as a Brewer on the trainer's table, his value plummeted.

A pull hitter, he likes the ball high and inside and will chase a first-ball fastball. He will hit a fastball up and in but will have trouble with breaking balls--curves or sliders--in on him.

He does not have a lot of patience as a hitter. Although he is supposed to be a power hitter, he can bunt very well.

BASERUNNING:

Clark has good speed and can get out of the box very quickly. He is a threat to steal and pitchers should keep an eye on him. He slides hard to break up the double play and rates as a very good baserunner.

FIELDING:

Defensively, Clark rates from good to very good. He has good range and moves quickly to his right and left. He has a strong arm, though not overwhelming. His throws are generally accurate.

BOBBY CLARK
OF, No. 25
RR, 6'0", 190 lbs.
ML Svc: 5 years
Born: 6-13-55 in
  Sacramento, CA

1985 STATISTICS

AVG	G	AB	R	H	2B	3B	HR	RBI	BB	SO	SB
.226	29	93	6	21	3	0	0	8	7	19	1

CAREER STATISTICS

AVG	G	AB	R	H	2B	3B	HR	RBI	BB	SO	SB
.234	396	967	97	231	34	7	19	100	55	199	4

STRONG

VS. RHP

STRONG

VS. LHP

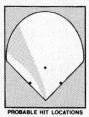

PROBABLE HIT LOCATIONS

OVERALL:

Despite his early promise, Clark is not an everyday player. His career has leveled off and time is running out. In order to play, he has to hit better and he has not been able to do that at the major league level.

Robinson: "I was surprised that he was sent to the minors last season, but I think it was the best thing for him. It made him work harder and he was able to play every day, something he has really never been able to do in the majors. Bobby has some tools, but not enough; he is just a borderline player."

PITCHING:

Jaime Cocanower has a rare problem--he can't throw the ball straight. Most pitchers would love to have a problem like that, but the Brewers spent the last half of the 1985 season teaching him to throw a fastball with little or no movement. Cocanower must develop a pitch that he can get over the plate when he absolutely has to throw a strike.

Lack of control has been Cocanower's major problem. He throws the ball over 90 MPH but walks almost twice as many batters as he strikes out. He led the team with 13 wild pitches in 24 games last year.

Cocanower throws a sinking fastball that doesn't produce many strikeouts, but hitters beat it into the ground when he gets it over the plate. He also throws a slider--again with spotty control.

Jaime came up with a good-breaking curveball last season. He doesn't mix in his change-up, but tries to spot it when he is ahead in the count. That, however, is not very often.

Cocanower will come inside to run hitters off the plate, but with his control problems, most hitters are already loose when they face him. He is big and strong enough to pitch a lot of innings. When he gets into trouble, he doesn't look to the bullpen--he wants to power his way out of it.

About the only thing he doesn't have is control.

FIELDING:

Cocanower lets runners on first base bother him, and he throws over a lot.

JAIME COCANOWER
RHP, No. 47
RR, 6'4", 190 lbs.
ML Svc: 2 years
Born: 2-14-57 in
   San Juan, PR

1985 STATISTICS

W	L	ERA	G	GS	CG	SV	IP	H	R	ER	BB	SO
6	8	4.33	24	15	3	0	116.1	122	72	56	73	44

CAREER STATISTICS

W	L	ERA	G	GS	CG	SV	IP	H	R	ER	BB	SO
16	24	3.92	62	45	5	0	321	331	179	140	163	117

He takes his defense seriously, but is not a good fielding pitcher. He is just average at getting to first base on anything hit to the right side.

OVERALL:

Cocanower has above-average stuff, but the Brewers no longer expect much from him because of his lack of control. Even though he was their best pitcher for the first half of the 1984 season, he began last season in the minors.

Manager George Bamberger likes control pitchers, which Cocanower obviously is not.

Robinson: "Jaime will be 29 years old this year, which is a little old for somebody to still be developing. All of his pitches are above average, but his lack of control just kills him.

"He got the chance last year and did not respond. It's almost too late for him to make any kind of mark."

HITTING:

Until 1984, Cecil Cooper had hit .300 or better each season since he joined the Brewers in 1977. He ranked as one of the better hitters in the game. In 1984, he hit only .275 with just 11 home runs and 67 RBIs. This was a big drop for someone who had been one of the AL's leading run-producers for years. Many people, including Cooper himself, began to doubt his ability.

Last year, Cooper erased a lot of those doubts. His stance remained the same: a crouched, open stance with his weight back. The results, however, were better: he finished with a .293 batting average (but he was hitting over .300 for most of the season) and drove in 99 runs.

His home run total was up a little from 1984; it is obvious, however, that he has lost some of his power.

Cooper has always used the whole park, but last season he went to left field a lot more than in the past. Don't let that fool you, though. He can still pull the ball when he gets his pitch.

Cooper is a dangerous hitter if he gets the pitch he likes, which is a low fastball on the inside of the plate. Pitchers shouldn't throw him any change-ups. If a pitcher has to throw him a low ball, it should be kept away from him.

He has problems with fastballs up and in, and it doesn't hurt to run him off the plate. Cooper takes his time getting settled in the batter's box. Although he can show patience as a hitter, he swings at the first pitch a lot and does not walk much.

An average bunter, Cooper rarely bunts in a sacrifice situation. He will occasionally try to bunt for a hit, especially if he is in a minor slump.

BASERUNNING:

He can get out of the box quickly but tends to jog to first base on routine plays, thereby not putting any pressure on the infielders. He has good speed and will steal occasionally. He slides hard

CECIL COOPER
1B, No. 15
LL, 6'2", 190 lbs.
ML Svc: 15 years
Born: 12-20-49 in
Brenham, TX

1985 STATISTICS

AVG	G	AB	R	H	2B	3B	HR	RBI	BB	SO	SB
.293	154	631	82	185	39	8	16	99	30	77	10

CAREER STATISTICS

AVG	G	AB	R	H	2B	3B	HR	RBI	BB	SO	SB
.303	1699	6557	941	1990	378	46	223	1014	390	773	87

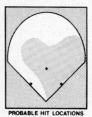

VS. RHP VS. LHP PROBABLE HIT LOCATIONS

to break up the double play.

He has always had good concentration on the bases. Cooper doesn't make many baserunning mistakes, though he appears to loaf at times. Looks can sometimes be deceiving, however. He has a long, easy stride and moves faster than it seems.

FIELDING:

Cooper still has quick reflexes and can move well to either his right or his left, but his fielding has slipped over the last few years. He is still excellent at digging throws out of the dirt and his long stretch can sometimes mean the difference in turning a fast DP.

OVERALL:

Robinson: "Cooper is still one of the best and has nothing to prove. His return to form after an off-season is not surprising. He makes things look easier than they are."

PITCHING:

If it weren't for bad luck, Danny Darwin would have had no luck at all in 1985. Despite a respectable 3.80 ERA, he finished with an 8-18 record, the most losses in the American League. His season included a 10-game losing streak, which tied a team record. It wasn't all his fault. The Brewers were shut out six times when he was pitching, and they scored a total of 20 runs for him while he was the losing pitcher.

Some of those losses were his fault, however. His lack of concentration hurt him, as did his league leading 34 home runs allowed. He also failed to hold big, early-game leads five times during the season.

Darwin doesn't throw as hard as he used to, but is still a power pitcher with a good fastball in the 86-89 MPH range. He also throws a big, sweeping slider that is a good pitch when it is working right.

The problems with the slider resulted in most of the home runs he gave up. He also throws an average curve, which he can get over for strikes. Darwin has a change-up that he doesn't mix in very effectively.

Darwin doesn't pitch his way into too many jams; most of his problems are the result of one bad pitch hit downtown.

He is an aggressive pitcher who will come in on the hitter. He likes to finish what he starts. He led the Brewers with 11 complete games last season.

FIELDING:

Darwin has a quick move to first. His delivery leaves him in good position to field the ball and he gets to first on

DANNY DARWIN
RHP, No. 18
RR, 6'3", 190 lbs.
ML Svc: 7 years
Born: 10-25-55 in
Bonham, TX

1985 STATISTICS
W	L	ERA	G	GS	CG	SV	IP	H	R	ER	BB	SO
8	18	3.80	39	29	11	2	217.2	212	112	92	65	125

CAREER STATISTICS
W	L	ERA	G	GS	CG	SV	IP	H	R	ER	BB	SO
61	68	3.62	256	119	32	18	1056.1	1005	490	425	356	669

balls hit to his left. Otherwise, he's an average fielder.

OVERALL:

Darwin has been used as both a starter and as a reliever in his career. The shuffle may have kept him from developing into a winning pitcher. He is probably better as a starter. He has the stuff to do well, but his lack of concentration has hurt him.

Robinson: "We keep waiting for Danny to emerge, and each year we hear that this is going to be his year. So far, not much has happened.

"He has good overall stuff but throws too many fat pitches to the wrong guy at the wrong time. Maybe he has got to study the hitters more and remember what they did to him the last time he faced them. He really needs to keep his head in the game from the first to the ninth inning."

PITCHING:

Rollie Fingers has saved more games than any reliever in history (341), but last season the only resemblance to the great relief pitcher of the past was his famous handlebar mustache. Fingers saved 17 games to lead the Brewers, but he had to struggle to do that. He also had a 1-6 record and fat 5.04 ERA, hardly the kind of numbers expected from the savior of the bullpen.

His knowledge of pitching has been as important as what he throws for most of his career. Last year, however, that wasn't enough. Fingers has lost a foot off his fastball, which is now in the 81-84 MPH range, and his control is shaky. In the past, he always had near-perfect control.

Throwing from a three-quarters delivery, Fingers mixes an assortment of fastballs, curves, sliders, screwballs and forkballs. He gets a good drop on his slider and an average break on his curve. He throws the forkball as his strikeout pitch--it's still a great one.

In the past, Rollie could get away with a fastball down the middle of the plate because hitters would be expecting a breaking ball. Last year, he didn't have the control that would allow him to nibble at the corners, and he often had to come over with the fastball just to get a strike. The hitters were waiting for it.

FIELDING:

Fingers has a good move to first and keeps the runners honest, but the hitter is the main person he has to worry about. He won't let the runner force him to lose concentration.

Physically, he is an average fielder,

ROLLIE FINGERS
RHP, No. 34
RR, 6'4", 200 lbs.
ML Svc: 17 years
Born: 8-25-46 in
    Steubenville, OH

1985 STATISTICS
W	L	ERA	G	GS	CG	SV	IP	H	R	ER	BB	SO
1	6	5.04	47	0	0	17	55.1	59	33	31	19	24

CAREER STATISTICS
W	L	ERA	G	GS	CG	SV	IP	H	R	ER	BB	SO
114	118	2.90	944	37	4	341	1701	1474	614	549	492	1299

but he is so fundamentally sound that it makes him an above-average fielder. He has been in too many difficult situations in his career to allow a fielding mistake to beat him.

OVERALL:

There were signs last year that it's over for Fingers, who is considered by some to be the best relief pitcher in history. Although he had a bad season, it was amazing that he was on the mound at all. He missed the entire 1983 season because of arm problems, then made a comeback in 1984 that was ended in July, when he needed back surgery. This comeback wasn't as successful, however.

Robinson: "Fingers is heading downhill. He is not throwing as hard, and for the first time in his career his control was just not there. He has to be letter-perfect with his control and he has to pitch more often to stay sharp. It is unlikely that either will occur this year."

HITTING:

Jim Gantner has been described as the heart of the Milwaukee Brewers. If so, the Brewers had heartburn last year. Gantner's batting average slipped as he struggled at the plate most of the season, and his fielding was erratic, especially early in the season. Still, he is a hard-nosed player who will do anything to help his team win a ballgame.

Gantner hits from a square stance and likes the ball high and inside. He is not a power hitter, but still tries to pull the ball too much. He would be better off using the whole field.

Although one of his goals for 1985 was to be more selective at the plate, it didn't work. Gantner also had more problems with lefthanded pitchers than in previous years. He becomes anxious with two strikes on him and will chase a fastball out of the strike zone.

He likes fastballs up in the strike zone, and pitchers should stay down and away with everything. Lefthanders who can throw hard sliders or big overhand curves outside will give him trouble. Righthanders can feed him low sliders and curves.

He is an average bunter and rarely bunts for a base hit; he is a fair bunter in sacrifice situations.

BASERUNNING:

Gantner also said he wanted to run more last year, but that did not happen. He doesn't run often and should be more aggressive on the basepaths. He will slide into second to break up the double play as hard as anyone and doesn't make many baserunning mistakes.

FIELDING:

Gantner has a strong arm and moves quickly to the ball. He goes to his left and right equally well. He is not very

JIM GANTNER
2B, No. 17
LR, 5'11", 175 lbs.
ML Svc: 8 years
Born: 1-5-54 in
Eden, WI

1985 STATISTICS

AVG	G	AB	R	H	2B	3B	HR	RBI	BB	SO	SB
.254	143	523	63	133	15	4	5	44	33	42	11

CAREER STATISTICS

AVG	G	AB	R	H	2B	3B	HR	RBI	BB	SO	SB
.276	981	3374	392	930	130	22	33	329	215	276	50

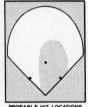

VS. RHP   VS. LHP   PROBABLE HIT LOCATIONS

smooth, but he does everything well. He gets the ball away quickly on the double play and is not afraid to hang tough when a baserunner slides in intent on knocking him into the next town. He is one of the best at turning the double play.

OVERALL:

Gantner's slow start last season hurt him and his play leveled off in all areas. Most of his problems were at the plate and he hit much lower than everyone expected.

Robinson: "I think that what you saw in 1985 will be his performance for the next couple of years. I don't think he is a .280-.290 hitter anymore.

"He just won't hit the ball the other way and utilize the whole field--it hurts him at the plate."

PITCHING:

Last year, with Rollie Fingers faltering, Brewers manager George Bamberger had to look for another short reliever in the middle of the season. He looked to Bob Gibson, who had pitched very well in long relief during the first half of the year. Gibson finished with 11 saves but was not nearly as effective as a short man as he had been in long relief.

One problem is his control. He has a tendency to walk the first hitter he faces and he gets into more trouble when he is used in short relief than when he comes into the middle of the game.

Gibson is a power pitcher. His delivery is between three-quarters and straight overhand. He throws an above-average fastball (85-89 MPH), but his slider and curveball are just average. He doesn't have an effective change-up.

He is a battler who will come in on a hitter and who doesn't give in when he gets into a bad situation--which is quite often. When he gets in trouble, look for his fastball.

FIELDING:

Gibson is only an average fielder. He has a quick move to first but doesn't throw over too often. He finishes his delivery in good position to handle balls hit back to the mound.

BOB GIBSON
RHP, No. 40
RR, 6'0", 195 lbs.
ML Svc: 2 years
Born: 6-19-57 in
Philadelphia, PA

1985 STATISTICS
W	L	ERA	G	GS	CG	SV	IP	H	R	ER	BB	SO
6	7	3.90	41	1	0	11	92.1	86	44	40	49	53

CAREER STATISTICS
W	L	ERA	G	GS	CG	SV	IP	H	R	ER	BB	SO
11	16	4.20	86	17	1	13	242	218	127	113	142	153

OVERALL:

Gibson has been used as a starter as well as in long and short relief, but he appears to be best suited to the bullpen. It is possible that he would be better as a long reliever.

Robinson: "Although he has a very good fastball, which will continue to get hitters out, his control problems will hurt him in a role as a short man. As a long reliever, I think that he is just a .500 pitcher. Gibson can't get enough pitches over the plate to be a big winner."

PITCHING:

One day early in the 1977 season, two scouts were overheard talking. One said, "That pitcher, Moose Haas? Oh yeah, he's got some potential."

One day late in the 1978 season, one scout said to the other, "That fellow Haas has some potential, huh?"

In 1979, same thing; 1980, ditto. And so on and so on.

Haas' "potential" is wearing thin on everyone. It's time to look at his numbers. They are not much. He has managed to win a total of 91 games.

His 1985 potential seemed to have been tapped early in the season, when Haas pitched a one-hitter in Yankee Stadium to improve his record to 7-3. He won only one game during the rest of the year, finishing with an 8-8 record and a 3.84 ERA.

In his first few seasons, Haas considered himself a power pitcher and was trying to throw the ball past everyone. Now he is a control pitcher who rarely issues a walk and mixes a good assortment of pitches. He throws an 84 MPH fastball and a sharp-breaking curve. He also has a good slider that he uses effectively. Haas' fastball sinks and hitters will chase it. He also has a split-finger fastball; he uses it a lot.

He changes speeds effectively and will throw a change-up when he is behind in the count. Haas always keeps his concentration and knows what he is doing on the mound. He is not a finisher and usually needs help from the bullpen.

When he begins to tire, he will get his pitches up around the belt. Until then, Haas will turn the ball over, keep it low and force hitters to go after it.

MOOSE HAAS
RHP, No. 30
RR, 6'0", 170 lbs.
ML Svc: 9 years
Born: 4-22-56 in
Baltimore, MD

1985 STATISTICS

W	L	ERA	G	GS	CG	SV	IP	H	R	ER	BB	SO
8	8	3.84	27	26	6	0	161.2	165	85	69	25	78

CAREER STATISTICS

W	L	ERA	G	GS	CG	SV	IP	H	R	ER	BB	SO
91	79	4.03	245	231	55	2	1542.1	1602	754	690	408	800

FIELDING:

As a pitcher, Haas is a very slow, deliberate worker. When a runner is on base, he will allow himself to be distracted and throw over there a lot. His move is just average. He has a classic three-quarters-to-overhand delivery that leaves him in good position to field the ball. As a fielder, he is above average.

OVERALL:

Robinson: "He has a wide variety of pitches. On some days, his pitches all look good and he mixes them up well. At other times, however, none of his stuff looks like it has much to it. He has never been able to put together a truly impressive season. Maybe he thinks too much on the mound; perhaps he doesn't think enough. Whatever the problem is, he is just an average pitcher."

PITCHING:

Comparisons between Teddy Higuera and Fernando Valenzuela are inevitable. Not only is the Brewer lefthander from Mexico, but his middle name is Valenzuela. To make the comparisons complete, Teddy also throws a screwball. Higuera won't make his fortune using the screwball in Milwaukee, however. Manager George Bamberger stopped him from throwing his screwball and curve just before mid-season last year.

Higuera began the season as a five-pitch pitcher. But after Bamberger played takeaway, Higuera used just three pitches: a change-up, a slider and a fastball.

The fastball, around 87-88 MPH, is his best pitch, but he also uses his slider and change-up well. He can throw any of them for strikes and will use his change-up when he is behind in the count. He throws from an overhand or three-quarters delivery and has a great motion that makes it difficult for the hitter to pick up the ball.

Higuera uses his good riding fastball, which he throws above the belt most of the time, as an out pitch. Although he was a rookie last season, he proved himself an aggressive pitcher. He challenges hitters with his fastball while working most hitters on the outside half of the plate.

He likes to finish his games and does not look over his shoulder for help when he is in trouble.

When he does start to struggle, which is rare, the first sign is his loss of control.

FIELDING:

Higuera has a good motion to first and keeps the runners honest. A man on

TED HIGUERA
LHP, No. 55
SL, 5'10", 178 lbs.
ML Svc: 1 year
Born: 11-9-58 in
  Los Mochis, MEX

1985 STATISTICS
W	L	ERA	G	GS	CG	SV	IP	H	R	ER	BB	SO
15	8	3.90	32	30	7	0	212.1	186	105	92	63	127

CAREER STATISTICS
W	L	ERA	G	GS	CG	SV	IP	H	R	ER	BB	SO
15	8	3.90	32	30	7	0	212.1	186	105	92	63	127

first doesn't rattle him. In fact, it's probably the opposite: the runners stay close to the bag when he is pitching. He finishes his delivery in good position to field the ball and gets to first on plays to the right side of the infield.

OVERALL:

Although he pitched a four-hit shutout against the Angels for his first victory, Higuera started slowly in 1985. He was the Brewers' fifth starter at the beginning of the season but their best pitcher by the middle of July.

Robinson: "He speaks little English and has trouble communicating at times, but his performance speaks louder than words. He gets the ball over the plate and has all the pitches.

"His record could be even better if the Brewers would start to help him out by scoring some runs. Ted is a good pitcher and is going to get better."

HITTING:

The Brewers spent most of the 1985 season looking for a power hitter. They may have found one in Paul Householder-- but by the time they noticed him, he had already spent most of the season sitting on the bench. He finished the season with 11 home runs, the fourth highest on the team. More impressive is the fact that he hit them in only 299 at-bats and hit eight in the final month.

Householder's potential has long been lauded by scouts, but he has never lived up to expectations. Brewer manager George Bamberger spent most of the winter of 1984-85 talking about Paul's potential, but didn't play him consistently until the end of the season, when Robin Yount was sidelined by shoulder surgery.

Lefthanded, Householder is a low-ball hitter. Righthanded, he is a high-ball hitter. He likes the inside half of the plate. From either side, he is more likely to hit a fastball. Either way, Paul has trouble with a hard breaking ball. A straight change is a bad pitch to throw to him whether he is hitting righthanded or lefthanded.

Although he has power from either side, he hits for a better average from the right side. Last season (his first year in the American League), he hit better in the second half, but that may have been because he played more often after the All-Star break.

He is a good bunter and has the speed to bunt for a base hit, although he usually does not attempt it.

BASERUNNING:

Although he has good speed, pitchers don't have to pay a lot of attention to him when he is on first base. He stole only one base, although he should have stolen a lot more. While he doesn't make any mistakes on the basepaths, he is only an average baserunner. There is a lot of potential there, but it is untapped.

PAUL HOUSEHOLDER
OF, No. 7
SR, 6'0", 185 lbs.
ML Svc: 5 years
Born: 9-4-58 in
    Columbus, OH

1985 STATISTICS

AVG	G	AB	R	H	2B	3B	HR	RBI	BB	SO	SB
.258	95	299	41	77	15	0	11	34	27	60	1

CAREER STATISTICS

AVG	G	AB	R	H	2B	3B	HR	RBI	BB	SO	SB
.239	610	1236	140	295	56	10	28	127	115	232	35

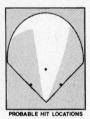

VS. RHP   VS. LHP   PROBABLE HIT LOCATIONS

FIELDING:

Householder has good range and a good arm, but cannot be rated as more than average in the outfield. He can handle anything coming in but has problems going back on a ball. Given the chance to play more, his fielding should improve.

OVERALL:

Householder was once considered one of the top prospects in baseball, but time is running out for him. He did a lot of bench-warming last season, which undoubtedly hurt him, but he played very well when he played regularly. Scouts have always said he had all the tools, but the jury is still out.

Robinson: "I believe that what you saw in 1985 is what you will see in 1986. I don't think that he can do it on an everyday basis. There are too many players in the Milwaukee system who can do at least what he does."

HITTING:

For all practical purposes, Dion James' 1985 season ended on the second day of spring training. Attempting a diving catch while shagging balls during batting practice, Dion dislocated his right shoulder and was on the disabled list for the first month of the season. Then he played just two weeks before he made another diving catch and dislocated his shoulder again. This time, he required surgery and was out until September, when he became available only as a pinch-hitter or pinch-runner.

Still, James has a lot of potential. He was the Brewers' Rookie of the Year in 1984, when he batted .295 and won a regular job in center field. He is not a power hitter, but he has hit for a high average everywhere he has played since signing a professional contract in 1980.

James uses a closed, straight-up stance and is generally a contact hitter with little power. He stands near the back of the box, making him seem vulnerable to outside pitches, but that is actually one of his strengths. He steps into the ball and slaps it to the opposite field.

James hits the low, outside pitch well. Pitchers can jam him with a slider or a fastball up and in, or change speeds on him. He is not particularly patient and could be a more selective hitter.

He is an excellent bunter and has the speed to bunt for a base hit.

BASERUNNING:

Although he stole 46 bases in the minors in his second season as a professional, James is still learning to harness his speed. He must be watched when he is on first base, but he is not a big threat to steal.

FIELDING:

James has good range and moves quickly to the ball, whether going to his right or to his left. He comes in on a ball better than he goes back on balls

DION JAMES
OF, No. 14
LL, 6'1", 175 lbs.
ML Svc: 2 years
Born: 11-9-62 in
    Philadelphia, PA

1985 STATISTICS

AVG	G	AB	R	H	2B	3B	HR	RBI	BB	SO	SB
.224	18	49	5	11	1	0	0	3	6	6	0

CAREER STATISTICS

AVG	G	AB	R	H	2B	3B	HR	RBI	BB	SO	SB
.278	157	456	58	127	20	5	1	34	40	49	11

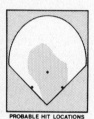

VS. RHP   VS. LHP   PROBABLE HIT LOCATIONS

hit over his head. He gets rid of the ball quickly but his arm is only average. His best position is probably center field, but Robin Yount will be playing there in 1986.

OVERALL:

Although he is a talented young player who has always hit for a high average, Dion's future with the Brewers is cloudy. With Yount moving to the outfield, James has been knocked out of his best defensive position and he doesn't hit with enough power to guarantee him a spot in right or left field.

Robinson: "He has a natural talent for putting the bat on the ball and could have a bright future--if he develops a little power as he matures.

"I have my doubts that he will get a chance to play much in 1986. He has to get 200 or 250 at-bats to help his club. If that is not going to happen, James should mature in the minors."

PITCHING:

Would the real Pete Ladd please stand up?

Is he the reliever who saved 25 games for the Brewers in 1983, when Rollie Fingers was out for the season with arm troubles? Or is he the reliever who, in 1985, saved only two games, had a 4.53 ERA and had to go back to the minors for a refresher course?

It's becoming pretty obvious that the 1985 version is the real Pete Ladd. It was his second straight disappointing season, following a 4-9, 5.24 ERA year with only three saves in 1984. Even in his big year (1983), he struggled early in the season and was shipped out to Vancouver for a month before returning to record 23 of those 25 saves.

Ladd is supposed to be a power pitcher. He throws 85-89 MPH from a three-quarters delivery, sometimes dropping down to throw sidearm. He throws his sinking fastball or his slider 99% of the time, occasionally mixing in a mediocre change-up (actually, it's a palmball).

Ladd's sinker hasn't sunk very well over the last two seasons, and he has lost some of the zip from his fastball. Even though he hides he ball well with a herky-jerky motion which keeps the hitters off stride, he still gets hit hard.

The sinker is his best pitch, but hitters have been whacking it over the last couple of years.

Ladd has been erratic in clutch situations, which is something that a short reliever cannot afford.

Occasionally, he will come inside,

PETE LADD
RHP, No. 27
RR, 6'3", 235 lbs.
ML Svc: 4 years
Born: 7-17-56 in
  Portland, ME

1985 STATISTICS

W	L	ERA	G	GS	CG	SV	IP	H	R	ER	BB	SO
0	0	4.53	29	0	0	2	45.2	58	26	23	10	22

CAREER STATISTICS

W	L	ERA	G	GS	CG	SV	IP	H	R	ER	BB	SO
9	17	4.25	153	1	0	33	216	206	114	102	78	156

but he generally sticks to working the outside of the plate.

FIELDING:

Ladd has just an average move to first. Runners tend to distract him and he can lose his concentration on the hitter.

OVERALL:

Ladd does not seem to have enough going for him. He has not been able to put together the kind of repertoire to be an effective reliever.

Killebrew: "Ladd has some tricky pitches, though they have not performed much magic for him lately. He doesn't seem to have command of his stuff and his pitches have been easy to hit. He should know how to pitch and to keep the hitters honest by now."

HITTING:

Rick Manning has a built-in radar system in the back of his head that lets him turn his back completely on fly ball and still know where to catch it. He could use that radar in his bat.

Manning would have been the perfect center fielder for the powerful 1982 Brewers, who flailed their way to the American League pennant. Since they have lost their power, however, he is a liability; they can't afford a good-field, no-hit center fielder.

Manning has little power and gets very few leg hits, despite his above-average speed. He stands deep in the box with a wide, closed stance. He likes the ball high and inside and often swings at the first pitch. He will hit the fastball up but not the breaking ball down and out. Pitchers can stay away from him and get him out with breaking balls down and away.

He tries to use the whole field, but still pulls a lot to the right side. He has little or no power. Despite his speed, he seldom bunts for a base hit. He doesn't strike out much and makes contact, but he hits a lot of ground balls to the right side of the infield.

For the first time in his career, he was platooned a lot during the last two years, facing mostly righthanders. His average dropped to .249 in 1984 and to .218 last season. Obviously, pitchers are keeping the ball down and away and not making too many mistakes.

BASERUNNING:

Manning has never stolen a lot of bases and has been running less and less since joining the Brewers. Pitchers cannot take him for granted, but they don't have to feel threatened, either.

He is a smart baserunner and will slide hard to break up the double play. He doesn't make too many mistakes, but he is not aggressive on the basepaths.

RICK MANNING
OF, No. 28
LR, 6'1", 180 lbs.
ML Svc: 11 years
Born: 9-2-54 in
   Niagara Falls, NY

1985 STATISTICS

AVG	G	AB	R	H	2B	3B	HR	RBI	BB	SO	SB
.218	79	216	19	47	9	1	2	18	14	19	1

CAREER STATISTICS

AVG	G	AB	R	H	2B	3B	HR	RBI	BB	SO	SB
.258	1369	4929	612	1271	175	39	48	418	442	578	159

  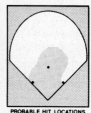

VS. RHP   VS. LHP   PROBABLE HIT LOCATIONS

FIELDING:

Manning plays a shallow center field, but can run down almost anything hit over his head. He goes equally well to his right or left and seldom dives for a ball. That's not because he is worried about getting his uniform dirty--it's because he doesn't have to. Manning easily gets to a lot of balls that other outfielders have to dive for. His arm is not strong, but it is accurate. He will hit the cutoff man consistently.

OVERALL:

On defense, Manning couldn't do anything better. On offense, he has been a big disappointment.

Robinson: "He will have to hit some to really help, and he hasn't done that since 1983, when he hit .278 with the Cleveland Indians. I think his best days with the bat are gone. There are just too many younger guys who can do the job that he is able to do."

PITCHING:

Bob McClure broke into the major leagues as a relief pitcher who wanted to be a starter. He was moved into the starting rotation for three seasons and had marginal success. He has been back in the bullpen for the last couple of years. He is used mainly in long relief, although he occasionally starts.

McClure has his best success when he sticks with his 85 MPH fastball, but he tends to rely too much on his big, breaking curve. He recently added a knuckleball and was throwing it almost 90% of the time for a while.

He has his greatest success, however, when he relies on his fastball, mixing it in with his curve to get lefthanders out. His change-up is not effective and he usually throws it only when he is ahead in the count.

BOB McCLURE
LHP, No. 10
SL, 5'11", 170 lbs.
ML Svc: 9 years
Born: 4-29-53 in
   Oakland, CA

1985 STATISTICS

W	L	ERA	G	GS	CG	SV	IP	H	R	ER	BB	SO
4	1	4.31	38	1	0	3	85.2	91	43	41	30	57

CAREER STATISTICS

W	L	ERA	G	GS	CG	SV	IP	H	R	ER	BB	SO
44	42	3.92	359	73	12	35	845	824	409	368	375	504

FIELDING:

McClure has the best pickoff move in baseball, and he is always among the league leaders in runners picked off first. He fools his share of umpires, too, and so he is always among the leaders in balks. Even if a runner is only a couple steps off the bag, McClure can pick him off. The move has gotten him out of a lot of trouble spots. He has quick reflexes and fields his position well.

OVERALL:

Despite his desire to be a starting pitcher, McClure's real niche is in the bullpen. He can be used effectively to get lefthanded hitters out, but his lack of concentration and his control problems have hurt him.

Robinson: "McClure always seems to be trying to come up with some new way to fool the hitters instead of just going after them with his good fastball. He doesn't like pitching out of the bullpen and, at times, he seems to be trying to prove he's not a reliever when he is on the mound.

"He has been a very average pitcher throughout his career. He is tough on lefthanded hitters, so that will keep him in the big leagues, but don't look for much improvement. He is as good now he's ever going to be."

EXCELLENT SPEED

HITTING:

Paul Molitor played in only 13 games in 1984 before needing the famous "Tommy John" ligament transplant surgery on his right elbow. As a result, no one knew what to expect from him last year.

What the Brewers got was a team leading .297 batting average in 140 games. "The Igniter" was as good as new.

Molitor bats from a slightly closed stance and will murder a high fastball in the middle of the plate. He is an aggressive hitter and will almost always swing at a first-ball fastball. Sliders will give him trouble. Pitchers should keep the ball down and feed him sliders away. He can be run off the plate once in a while.

He's not an especially patient hitter for a leadoff man, but can be selective. He hits righthanders as well as he does lefthanders. Although he is basically a singles and doubles hitter, Molitor can hit an occasional long ball.

Molitor is one of the best bunters in the league, and is always a threat to bunt for a base hit. First basemen and third basemen should always be ready for the bunt. He also will bunt in a sacrifice situation. Molitor can make a lot of things happen because of his hitting and his speed on the basepaths.

He is probably the most important hitter in the Brewers' lineup.

BASERUNNING:

Molitor has outstanding speed and great instincts on the basepaths. He is always a threat to steal and picks his spots well. He is rarely thrown out. He runs hard and constantly challenges the defense by taking the extra base. He always gambles and almost always wins.

PAUL MOLITOR
3B, No. 4
RR, 6'0", 175 lbs.
ML Svc: 8 years
Born: 8-22-56 in
St. Paul, MN

1985 STATISTICS

AVG	G	AB	R	H	2B	3B	HR	RBI	BB	SO	SB
.297	140	576	93	171	28	3	10	48	54	80	21

CAREER STATISTICS

AVG	G	AB	R	H	2B	3B	HR	RBI	BB	SO	SB
.292	905	3702	614	1080	176	39	70	335	324	434	211

  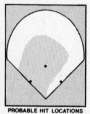

VS. RHP — STRONG VS. LHP — STRONG PROBABLE HIT LOCATIONS

FIELDING:

Molitor moves quickly and has good range but is only an average infielder. He goes to his left better than to his right. Most of his errors were throwing errors, which were probably a result of his elbow surgery. Before the surgery, his arm was average, but accurate.

OVERALL:

Molitor made a great comeback after missing most of the 1984 season. He is a very good player with a lot of ability.

Robinson: "There was a ton of questions concerning his abilities after his tricky surgery, but he bounced back and answered everything with his bat. With him in the lineup and feeling good, the Brewers have at least one less thing to worry about for 1986."

STRONG ARM

HITTING:

Last season, Charlie Moore ended up back where he started--behind the plate. After moving to the outfield and playing a key role in the Brewers' pennant-winning season in 1982, Moore's bat started to slip in 1984, and he lost his full-time job in right field.

He started the 1985 season as the backup catcher and ended up playing regularly when Bill Schroeder was sidelined by elbow problems. He performed well defensively, but his hitting didn't return to the levels he had reached earlier in his career. He hit well early in the season, but the rigors of catching every day wore him down by mid-season.

Moore hits from a slightly open, semicrouched stance and stands in the middle of the box. He is a straightaway hitter who likes the ball low and in the middle of the plate. He has trouble when he is pitched up, especially with high fastballs in on his hands. He frequently swings at the first pitch.

To get him out, pitchers should keep the fastball up and in and mix in breaking balls away. He feasts on low fastballs. Moore doesn't hit for power and is not a dangerous hitter with runners in scoring position. He is a very good bunter and will sacrifice and bunt for a base hit.

Basically a singles hitter, Moore fit in well with the power-hitting Brewers teams of a few seasons ago, but he does not add much offense to the punchless lineup of the last couple of years.

BASERUNNING:

Moore is not much of a threat to steal and pitchers don't have to be too concerned with him. Otherwise, he is a smart, aggressive baserunner who will gamble on the basepaths and go for the extra base.

FIELDING:

Moore moves quickly behind the plate,

CHARLIE MOORE
C/OF, No. 22
RR, 5'11", 180 lbs.
ML Svc: 12 years
Born: 6-21-53 in
Birmingham, AL

1985 STATISTICS

AVG	G	AB	R	H	2B	3B	HR	RBI	BB	SO	SB
.232	105	349	35	81	13	4	0	31	27	53	4

CAREER STATISTICS

AVG	G	AB	R	H	2B	3B	HR	RBI	BB	SO	SB
.262	1203	3691	417	968	165	39	32	362	312	420	46

STRONG

VS. RHP

STRONG

VS. LHP

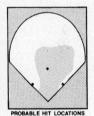

PROBABLE HIT LOCATIONS

but is an average defensive catcher at best. In the outfield, he can come in or go back and is not afraid of the fences. He has an excellent arm, both in the outfield and behind the plate.

His throwing as a catcher improved after he had spent time in the outfield.

OVERALL:

Moore's career is slipping fast as an everyday player. He played more than expected last season because of the injury to Bill Schroeder, but probably will be a backup catcher and outfielder again in 1986. He can be a valuable player in that role because he is a hard-nosed guy and seems to have accepted playing part-time.

Robinson: "Charlie is a good man to have around because of his versatility. He can do a lot of things, but if everyone on the team is healthy, he will not play much this season."

HITTING:

Ben Oglivie began the 1985 season as a platoon player, then returned to the everyday lineup in July and was the Brewers' most productive hitter for six weeks. Though his season ended prematurely, he finished with a .290 batting average.

Oglivie played in only a few games in the last six weeks of the season because of nerve damage to his right hand. The injury could have been caused by pitchers exploiting his weak spot. He uses a slightly closed, straight-up stance right on top of the plate, and sometimes fastballs inside can come a bit close to his fists. He has been nipped by a lot of pitches over the past few years.

Oglivie is a very aggressive hitter and tries to pull everything. He can be selective at the plate when he needs to be. When he swings, he swings as hard as anyone in baseball, intent on hitting the ball hard. Although he drove in 61 runs in just 341 at-bats, he hit only 10 home runs.

His age is catching up with him: he just doesn't have the power he did a few years ago, when he was one of the best home run hitters in the league.

He is a poor bunter and is rarely called on to sacrifice. Oglivie is still one of the most dangerous Brewer hitters with runners in scoring position.

BASERUNNING:

Oglivie has good speed, but is not a good baserunner. He does not run often and prefers not to slide. When he has to hit the dirt, he is a man of 1,000 slides, none of them orthodox and many of them executed at the last possible second.

FIELDING:

Oglivie is quick in the outfield and is good at cutting off balls hit down

BEN OGLIVIE
RF, No. 24
LL, 6'2", 170 lbs.
ML Svc: 14 years
Born: 2-11-49 in
Colon, PAN

1985 STATISTICS											
AVG	G	AB	R	H	2B	3B	HR	RBI	BB	SO	SB
.290	101	341	40	99	17	2	10	61	37	51	0

CAREER STATISTICS											
AVG	G	AB	R	H	2B	3B	HR	RBI	BB	SO	SB
.272	1651	5567	753	1517	257	32	230	847	530	819	86

VS. RHP

VS. LHP

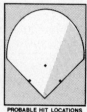

PROBABLE HIT LOCATIONS

the line, keeping them from going for extra bases. He has had a hard time living down his reputation as a bad outfielder. If he gets to it, he catches it, although he has problems with balls hit right at him.

His arm is average, and runners will run on him. He has occasional lapses and will throw to the wrong base.

OVERALL:

Oglivie's average was up after batting in the .262 range in the previous two seasons, but he has lost a lot of power and is past his peak. He is still an aggressive and dangerous hitter, especially with runners in scoring position, but he probably will be a platoon player this year.

Robinson: "I wouldn't be surprised if Ben's days in Milwaukee are numbered. He will play somewhere, though it is doubtful that he will be an everyday player."

HITTING:

When the season opened, the Brewers expected Robin Yount's shoulder to be ready for the throws from shortstop after just a couple of weeks. It was thought that Ernest Riles needed another year at Triple-A. Yount's shoulder did not improve, however, and the Brewers recalled Riles on May 14. He was more than ready.

Although his average dipped late in the year, he finished at .286 and was more than adequate in the field. His fine performance made possible a move that the Brewers had been considering for several years--Yount will be their center fielder when the 1986 season opens.

Riles hits from a low crouch, with an open stance similar to Cecil Cooper's and Rod Carew's. In fact, in his hitting he is a lot like both of them. Riles is a contact hitter and uses the whole park.

He is a low-ball hitter and likes fastballs down. He has trouble with fastballs inside or outside. Show him a hard breaking ball, then throw him a high fastball.

Riles will go for a first pitch if he likes it, but is a very selective hitter. He is an excellent hitter after two strikes. He also is a capable bunter.

He hasn't shown a lot of power, but he is still young and should get stronger as he matures. He has hit everywhere he has been and should continue to hit at the major league level.

BASERUNNING:

Riles has good speed out of the box, but is not one who gives pitchers a lot to worry about when he is on first base. However, he should be, and may become more of a baserunning threat. He is only an average baserunner and should be better.

FIELDING:

Even though he is still learning,

ERNEST RILES
INF, No. 58
LR, 6'1", 180 lbs.
ML Svc: 1 year
Born: 10-2-60 in
Whigham, GA

1985 STATISTICS

AVG	G	AB	R	H	2B	3B	HR	RBI	BB	SO	SB
.286	116	448	54	128	12	7	5	45	36	54	2

CAREER STATISTICS

AVG	G	AB	R	H	2B	3B	HR	RBI	BB	SO	SB
.286	116	448	54	128	12	7	5	45	36	54	2

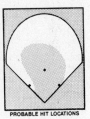

STRONG   STRONG

VS. RHP   VS. LHP   PROBABLE HIT LOCATIONS

Riles played better than most people thought he could. His range is a question mark, but he has made a lot of improvements in the last couple of years.

Riles is better going to his left than to his right and needs work at getting the ball away more quickly.

OVERALL:

Riles surprised a lot of people in 1985, coming from nowhere and making a strong bid for Rookie of the Year honors. He hits strikes and just doesn't make outs.

Robinson: "Riles is a big league hitter, no doubt about it. His swing is effortless and he has good bat speed. He is going to be here for a long time.

"It's always fun when a youngster comes, seemingly out of the blue, to impress everyone. Replacing Robin Yount could have made anyone nervous, and following an act like that is tough. To his credit, Ernest did a great job."

HITTING:

It was just another season for Ed Romero last year. The veteran utility player spent 1985 filling in wherever needed in the infield and occasionally in the outfield. Romero would like to play every day, but that is unlikely.

His "utility" label was stamped even more firmly last season when the Brewers called up Ernest Riles to take over at shortstop for Robin Yount.

Romero is no home run threat, but he is an aggressive hitter who makes good contact. He doesn't take many pitches and doesn't walk very often. He bats from a slightly closed stance, with his bat held high. As a result, he likes the high fastball over the middle of the plate. You can get him out by staying down with breaking balls. Although his .251 average was close to his lifetime mark, he is not an automatic out and can be tough with runners in scoring position.

Romero is a good bunter and can sacrifice but does not bunt for a base hit.

BASERUNNING:

Romero's speed is a little below average and he is not a threat to steal. Pitchers can't take him for granted, but they don't have to worry too much when he is on first base. He is a good baserunner who won't make many mistakes.

FIELDING:

He can perform well at second, short or third and moves quickly to the ball, going to his right and left equally well. He has a good arm, maybe a little above average, and throws quickly and accurately.

ED ROMERO
INF, No. 11
RR, 5'11", 150 lbs.
ML Svc: 5 years
Born: 12-9-57 in
    Santurce, PR

1985 STATISTICS

AVG	G	AB	R	H	2B	3B	HR	RBI	BB	SO	SB
.251	88	251	24	63	11	1	0	21	25	20	1

CAREER STATISTICS

AVG	G	AB	R	H	2B	3B	HR	RBI	BB	SO	SB
.257	411	1117	125	287	49	1	5	99	87	92	7

VS. RHP

VS. LHP

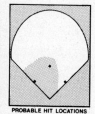

PROBABLE HIT LOCATIONS

Although Romero was originally a shortstop, he has adapted to the other side of the infield and turns the double play very well. He is a very good utility player who plays to his maximum and does not make mental lapses on defense.

OVERALL:

Robinson: "Romero's role is perfect for him. He is a good utility man but not an everyday player--certainly not with Molitor and Riles around. A team needs guys like Ed: he is dependable and keeps his head in the game."

HITTING:

When Bill Schroeder hit 14 home runs in just 61 games in 1984, Jim Sundberg got the message. Realizing that this new fellow Schroeder was one of the few legitimate power hitters the Brewers had, Sundberg figured that his playing time would be cut back and demanded a trade. Sundberg ended up wearing a championship ring in Kansas City and Schroeder was installed as the Brewers' number one catcher after just one full season in the major leagues.

Schroeder made the move look like a good one. He hit six of the team's first 12 home runs—but then spent most of the season on the disabled list because of elbow problems and hit only two more home runs the rest of the year. The elbow injury finally required surgery and his future as a catcher is questionable.

He bats from an extremely wide, closed stance and takes a big, healthy swing. He hits belt-high fastballs 400 feet but has trouble with breaking balls and strikes out a lot. Pitchers should stay away from him and throw him breaking balls. Righthanders and lefthanders can jam him with fastballs, which keeps him from extending his arms for that big swing.

BASERUNNING:

Schroeder is one of the slowest players in the league and is absolutely no threat to steal or take an extra base. He runs everything out—even if it takes him forever to get to the base—and he slides hard.

FIELDING:

He is average behind the plate, but he is still learning his trade. He is intelligent and calls a good game; his pitchers like to throw to him.

His throwing was poor last season, but that was probably because of his elbow problems. Ordinarily, his arm is

BILL SCHROEDER
C, No. 21
RR, 6'2", 200 lbs.
ML Svc: 3 years
Born: 9-7-58 in
Baltimore, MD

1985 STATISTICS
AVG	G	AB	R	H	2B	3B	HR	RBI	BB	SO	SB
.242	53	194	18	47	8	0	8	25	12	61	0

CAREER STATISTICS
AVG	G	AB	R	H	2B	3B	HR	RBI	BB	SO	SB
.239	137	477	54	114	16	1	25	57	23	138	0

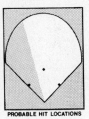

STRONG VS. RHP   STRONG VS. LHP   PROBABLE HIT LOCATIONS

considered better than average and he has a good, quick release.

OVERALL:

Because of his power, Schroeder still figures to be an everyday player, although his elbow problems have created some doubt about his ability to throw. Before he was injured, his numbers projected more than 30 home runs, but he was on the pace of more than 180 strikeouts.

Robinson: "This was Schroeder's first chance to play every day, but he was injured for most of the season. I expect him to bounce back and help the team offensively by hitting home runs and driving them in.

"He does not hit for average, but he would have helped the Brewers if he had been healthy. He is a tough, aggressive player who is just beginning to come into his own."

GOOD CLUTCH HITTER

HITTING:

Ted Simmons is no longer ranked among the best hitters in baseball, but he can still be dangerous. After slumping to .221 and driving in only 52 runs in 1984, Simmons bounced back with what had to be considered a very good year. He hit .273 and drove in 76 runs (second on the team) and was especially effective with runners in scoring position. His numbers were much better batting right-handed, hitting .307 with seven home runs and 30 RBIs in only 163 at-bats. In 365 at-bats lefthanded, he batted .258 with five homers and 46 RBIs.

Although Simmons normally bats from an upright stance, he will go into a crouch at times to work his way out of a slump. Righthanded, he is a high-ball hitter; lefthanded, he prefers it low. He likes it inside either way. He is still a dangerous hitter when he sees a fastball and not too many pitchers can fool him with a change-up.

Breaking balls on the outside half of the plate are the best bet against him. Pitchers should try to throw everything away because Simmons will pull the ball.

After his bad showing in 1984, Ted surprised a lot of people last year. He was basically the same hitter, although he did go to the opposite field more than he had in the past.

He is not likely to go for the first pitch, although there is no definite pattern. He is not a good bunter, but he will attempt to bunt for a hit if the third baseman is playing extremely deep. Because of his slow speed, however, he is not going to attempt that very often.

BASERUNNING:

Simmons always knows what is going on during a game and thinks of all the possibilities on a given play. On the basepaths, he calculates the risks of running before he goes. Because of his lack of speed, however, he is not an aggres-

TED SIMMONS
DH/C, No. 23
SR, 6'0", 200 lbs.
ML Svc: 16 years
Born: 8-9-49 in
    Highland Park, MI

1985 STATISTICS

AVG	G	AB	R	H	2B	3B	HR	RBI	BB	SO	SB
.273	143	528	60	144	28	2	12	76	57	32	1

CAREER STATISTICS

AVG	G	AB	R	H	2B	3B	HR	RBI	BB	SO	SB
.287	2229	8269	1034	2370	464	47	238	1323	807	648	19

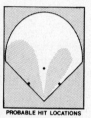

VS. RHP   VS. LHP   PROBABLE HIT LOCATIONS

sive baserunner and is not likely to try for the extra base on a routine play.

FIELDING:

Simmons is basically a DH now, although he will play an occasional game at first base or behind the plate. He is average to below-average behind the plate in all areas. He is an adequate first baseman with extremely limited range.

OVERALL:

Robinson: "He can still do the job, especially when he needs to drive in some runs. The DH rule has added a couple of years to his long and distinguished career. He will probably perform the same this season as he did in 1985--no more, no less. He is still a very aggressive hitter."

PITCHING:

In the beginning of the 1985 season, it looked as if Pete Vuckovich was going to be one of the big success stories of the year. After pitching in only three games over the previous two seasons because of shoulder problems that eventually required surgery, Pete Vuckovich surprised a lot of people just by making it back to the majors at all.

Early in the season, there were occasional returns to the kind of pitching performance that earned him the Cy Young Award in 1982, but there were a lot of bad outings, too. Directly following the All-Star break, Vuckovich seemed to have put everything together again. He won three of four starts, giving up just six earned runs in 26 1/3 innings. But then there was more bad news.

Vuckovich began to struggle, his shoulder started bothering him and he required additional surgery early last September. Once again, his career is in doubt.

Vuckovich is not a hard thrower, but he is a smart pitcher. He knows the hitters and he pitches to them as well as anybody can. He is a control pitcher whose herky-jerky motion and three-quarters delivery distracts the hitters. He throws a little bit of everything and throws all of his pitches at different speeds. His fastball is in the 83-85 MPH range. His slider is a big breaker and drops down sharply. He throws a curve that breaks over like a screwball. Vuckovich will use any of his pitches when he is behind in the count. He turns his change-up over; his fastball is his out pitch.

Vuckovich was one of baseball's great competitors when his shoulder was sound. He would challenge all hitters and glare at them from the mound. He was continually trying to nip the corners and loved to intimidate all comers. But be-

PETE VUCKOVICH
RHP, No. 50
RR, 6'4", 220 lbs.
ML Svc: 10 years
Born: 10-27-52 in
   Johnstown, PA

1985 STATISTICS
W	L	ERA	G	GS	CG	SV	IP	H	R	ER	BB	SO
6	10	5.51	22	22	1	0	112.2	134	74	69	48	55

CAREER STATISTICS
W	L	ERA	G	GS	CG	SV	IP	H	R	ER	BB	SO
91	65	3.68	280	180	38	10	1422	1421	647	581	534	870

cause of his continuing shoulder problems, he is not as much in control as he has been in the past and just doesn't throw well anymore.

FIELDING:

Vuckovich doesn't have a lot of range, but he handles anything he can. He gets over to first well and has a good move to first.

OVERALL:

Vuckovich's return to form might have helped give the Brewers much-needed stability to their starting rotation last year. Realistically, the Brewers will have to look elsewhere for a reliable starting pitcher.

Robinson: "There were very few guys who were as tough and as competitive as Pete before he began having so much physical trouble. If anyone can battle to come back, it's him, but the injury looks as if it might have gotten the better of him. His pitches are all just average now."

PITCHING:

Rick Waits was very successful as Rollie Fingers' setup man in 1984, but when Fingers was injured and missed the last two months of the 1985 season, the veteran lefthander wasn't as effective. He no longer had the great relief ace waiting to come in and bail him out.

Waits has been a reliever since 1983. A starter for most of his career, he has never really adjusted to his bullpen role.

The 1985 season showed that Waits is nearing the end of his career. He spent the first half of the season in the minors and did nothing to distinguish himself on the Brewers' weak pitching staff after he was recalled.

Waits is a control pitcher who throws three-quarters overhand to straight overhand. He has an average fastball and a sharp-breaking curve. He also throws a hard slider, though it does not break much. The slider, in fact, doesn't look much different from his fastball. He will mix in his change-up, which is below average, even when he is behind in the count. He will use his big, breaking curve or his fastball as an out pitch.

He doesn't come inside much, and hitters can take the plate away from him. When he gets into trouble, it can be attributed to either his lack of control or the fact that the hitters are just hitting him hard. He will use any of his pitches to get out of a jam, but by that time some other pitcher usually has gotten the call to try to restore order.

RICK WAITS
LHP, No. 36
LL, 6'3", 195 lbs.
ML Svc: 11 years
Born: 5-15-52 in
 Atlanta, GA

1985 STATISTICS
W	L	ERA	G	GS	CG	SV	IP	H	R	ER	BB	SO
3	2	6.51	24	0	0	1	47	67	37	34	20	24

CAREER STATISTICS
W	L	ERA	G	GS	CG	SV	IP	H	R	ER	BB	SO
79	92	4.25	317	190	47	8	1425.2	1514	741	674	568	659

FIELDING:

Although he is lefthanded, Waits has a move that is only adequate, and runners will run on him. He doesn't throw to first too often because he is so concerned with getting the hitter out.

OVERALL:

Waits can still come into the game to get a lefthanded hitter out. He has a rubber arm and can pitch any time and in any role. His versatility might keep him around for a couple more years, but he is definitely on the way down.

Robinson: "I think he is a number eight or nine pitcher on a staff. His his weaknesses are his lack of confidence, his lack of control and the fact that all of his pitches look too much alike."

HITTING:

It would be interesting to see what a healthy Robin Yount could do. Playing all last season with a shoulder so sore that it hurt just to raise his arm over his head, the former MVP still was one of the Brewers' offensive leaders.

Playing in pain is nothing new for him. His shoulder has bothered him for two seasons. It kept him from playing shortstop last year, but it did not stop him from hitting. The Brewers are hoping that the arthroscopic surgery last year has finally solved the problem.

Yount hits from a wide stance that is slightly closed. He stands deep in the box. He is a straightaway hitter and likes fastballs high and inside, but can handle high curves and sliders at the belt. A slow curve, down and away, is a good pitch to throw him. Lefthanders can throw fastballs up and in. For the most part, however, pitchers should try to keep everything on the outside half of the plate.

A slider is the best pitch for getting him out and it wouldn't hurt to run him off the plate once in a while.

Although not a pure power hitter, he is strong and will hit his share of home runs. When he is hitting well, his power is to right-center.

Yount is also a very good bunter and can bunt for a hit. Combined with Paul Molitor, the Brewers have one of the best one-two combinations in baseball-- when both players are healthy.

BASERUNNING:

Yount has very good speed and will steal in key situations. He plays hard all the time and runs out everything. He is a smart baserunner and will go for the extra base, forcing the defense to be constantly alert.

FIELDING:

After being one of the best short-stops in the game for years, Yount moved to the outfield last season because of

ROBIN YOUNT
OF, No. 19
RR, 6'0", 180 lbs.
ML Svc: 12 years
Born: 9-16-55 in
       Danville, IL

1985 STATISTICS

AVG	G	AB	R	H	2B	3B	HR	RBI	BB	SO	SB
.277	122	466	76	129	26	3	15	68	49	56	10

CAREER STATISTICS

AVG	G	AB	R	H	2B	3B	HR	RBI	BB	SO	SB
.285	1671	6515	961	1856	349	75	144	781	473	707	152

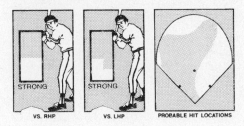

his shoulder problems. Although he could not throw well at all, Yount made a smooth transition to the outfield.

He has outstanding range and goes to his right and left equally well. He will be the Brewers' center fielder this season. If his shoulder is all right, he will also be one of the best.

OVERALL:

Despite playing all year with the injury, Yount still had a better-than-average major league season. He is not, however, your average player. If the surgery has cured his ailment, his numbers could be even better.

Robinson: "It appears that he has found a new home in center field. The injury slowed him down and his home run production has been cut in half. I don't see how Yount could hit 30 home runs again.

"He has always been a marvel to watch, and no matter where he plays, he always gives 100%."

BRIAN GILES
SS, No. 26
RR, 6'1", 162 lbs.
ML Svc: 3 years
Born: 4-27-60 in
    Manhattan, KS

HITTING, BASERUNNING, FIELDING:

Brian Giles is a defensive specialist but not much of a hitter. He spent the last half of the 1985 season in the minors after hitting just .172 with the Brewers. Giles' strength is a low ball from the inside to the middle of the plate. He stands fairly deep in the box and has trouble handling a breaking ball down and away. A fastball up will also get him out. He is a fair to good bunter but not a good hitter overall.

Giles has some running speed, and a pitcher has to keep an eye on him when he is on first. He is an average to good baserunner but doesn't come into second very hard to break up the double play.

Giles can play at either second base or short. He is an excellent second baseman and a very good to excellent shortstop. He has a strong, accurate arm and moves quickly, to either his right or his left. He has excellent hands and will rarely boot a routine play.

OVERALL:

Although he is still young, Giles appears to have already peaked and started slipping. He is not an everyday player.

Robinson: "I don't think that Giles will be in the major leagues in 1986. He cannot hit."

MINNESOTA TWINS

PITCHING:

For the first time in four seasons, Bert Blyleven went through an entire season without injury. He led the AL in shutouts, strikeouts, innings pitched and complete games and, in the process, went from the lowly Cleveland Indians to Minnesota for the final two months of the season.

There is a tendency to think of him as a curveball pitcher. While his curve is probably the best in baseball, it works especially well because he can also throw a 90 MPH sinking fastball, a change-up and an occasional slider.

His curveball is excellent because it has a big break and appears to drop as if it rolled off the edge of a table. In earlier days, there were times when he would telegraph it, but hitters can no longer read him. His curve is his out pitch; his change-up is saved for times when a hitter might be expecting a fastball. Of course, fastball situations for most pitchers can be curve situations for Blyleven.

The only problem that Blyleven has, and he recognizes it, is a tendency to rush himself. He is a fast worker but, past a certain point, that trait can mess up his rhythm. Blyleven has the experience and knowledge to dissect his game in the dugout and to remedy a problem that could nag another pitcher for much longer.

He is a fierce competitor and younger Twins pitchers said that some of his attitude rubbed off on them after he joined the team. Having a man of his stature around for advice, one of them said, is much more comfortable than hearing the same things from a coach or manager. He is the sort of go-between

BERT BLYLEVEN
RHP, No. 28
RR, 6'3", 205 lbs.
ML Svc: 16 years
Born: 4-6-51 in
    Zeist, HOLLAND

1985 STATISTICS

W	L	ERA	G	GS	CG	SV	IP	H	R	ER	BB	SO
17	16	3.16	37	37	24	0	293.2	264	121	103	75	206

CAREER STATISTICS

W	L	ERA	G	GS	CG	SV	IP	H	R	ER	BB	SO
212	183	3.01	505	499	200	0	3716.1	3343	1398	1244	1014	2875

player that has been lacking from the Minnesota roster since free agency began 10 years ago.

FIELDING:

Blyleven is proof that a pitcher can help himself by taking pride in defense. His motion leaves him in excellent position and he routinely snares hard one-hoppers and grounders that would otherwise go to center field. His move to first base is ordinary.

OVERALL:

Getting Blyleven signified that the Twins were making a commitment to winning. There appear to be several strong seasons left for the righthanded ace.

Killebrew: "Bert has won over 200 games while playing for some bad clubs. When he's healthy, he's durable and can go the distance. He doesn't have just one great pitch--he's got four. He's a fantastic influence on the entire club."

HITTING:

Until 1985, Tom Brunansky cultivated the image of a slow starter who more than compensated for his characteristic early-season slumps with very strong finishes. Last year was different. Brunansky got off to a steaming-hot start and earned a spot on the All-Star squad, but cooled off considerably after the break.

Brunansky knew what he was doing wrong--chasing poor pitches--but could not figure a way to keep from doing it. He was going after breaking balls outside the strike zone, which inevitably put him behind in the count.

High and inside fastballs also could render Brunansky ineffective. He showed the potential to be more than a home run-or-nothing type of slugger.

At his best, Brunansky will shorten his swing with two strikes against him and show the ability to go to right field. He can kill a pitch that he is expecting. Playing in the Metrodome does not help him much because he doesn't get many turf hits and the stadium's dimensions in left and left-center field rob him of home runs that a lefthanded pull hitter would get there.

Brunansky's profile always has been that of a power hitter with a mediocre average. By staying consistent for an entire season, there is evidence that he can combine his home runs with a .275 average and hold down the cleanup spot in the Twins order for years to come.

BASERUNNING:

Brunansky understands his limitations as a good runner who should be thinking more about fundamentals than flashiness. He seems to know when the extra base is there for the taking and seldom makes a dumb move. He moves fairly well to first and can make a second baseman cringe at the thought that Brunansky will be attempting to break up the double play.

FIELDING:

The company line is that Brunansky's

TOM BRUNANSKY
RF, No. 24
RR, 6'4", 211 lbs.
ML Svc: 4 years
Born: 8-20-60 in
  West Covina, CA

1985 STATISTICS

AVG	G	AB	R	H	2B	3B	HR	RBI	BB	SO	SB
.242	157	567	71	137	28	4	27	90	71	86	5

CAREER STATISTICS

AVG	G	AB	R	H	2B	3B	HR	RBI	BB	SO	SB
.246	601	2172	300	535	103	10	110	309	268	386	13

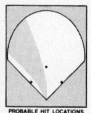

VS. RHP   VS. LHP   PROBABLE HIT LOCATIONS

arm is the equal of any of the American League elite (Boston's Dwight Evans and Toronto's Jesse Barfield). The truth is that his arm is a cut below both of them and that his arm is barely above average. Brunansky's arm gets help from the Metrodome's small right field. His release, however, is quick.

He suffers occasional lapses of concentration which cause him to bobble routine plays or to misread developing situations.

OVERALL:

Can Brunansky put together the magic season that would make the Twins happy and that they expected when they signed him to a six-year $6.1 million contract last April?

Killebrew: "Tom is expected to be the Twins' right fielder for many years and, despite some already solid statistics, still has room for improvement. He must hit for a better average and keep his home run totals up at the same time."

HITTING:

Next to Tom Brunansky, Randy Bush hit home runs more often than any other Twins player. His forte is an ability to hit fastballs and, on occasion, he can turn an inside fastball into a mammoth homer.

Bush has never been much of an average hitter and has a tendency to fall into long slumps. But despite his willingness to work (Bush doesn't slack off even when he isn't playing), he hasn't solved the mysteries of other pitches. He has been almost exclusively a platoon player and has never been able to do much with righthanders' breaking balls.

Because Bush crowds the plate, he gets hit by pitches more often than anyone on the team and doesn't ground into double plays. In 1983, he led the Twins in sacrifice flies (10) in only 311 at-bats. That was as many as Tom Brunansky and Kent Hrbek combined.

BASERUNNING:

Bush became more aggressive last season but will never be mistaken for one of the great runners of our generation. His baserunning is in keeping with his generally unspectacular profile.

FIELDING:

For his first 2 1/2 seasons with the Twins, it was only a formality that Bush was listed as an outfielder on the roster. He was really a DH who filled in a few times for Kent Hrbek at first base. Still, Bush could always be found shagging flies during batting practice and taking his turn in pre game infield drills. That paid off at mid-season when Bush went from being a platoon DH to a platoon left fielder.

It turns out that he has average

RANDY BUSH
DH/LF, No. 25
LL, 6'1", 186 lbs.
ML Svc: 4 years
Born: 10-5-58 in
    Dover, DE

1985 STATISTICS

AVG	G	AB	R	H	2B	3B	HR	RBI	BB	SO	SB
.239	97	234	26	56	13	3	10	35	24	30	3

CAREER STATISTICS

AVG	G	AB	R	H	2B	3B	HR	RBI	BB	SO	SB
.238	389	1037	128	247	60	8	36	147	97	169	4

  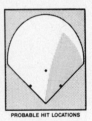

VS. RHP   VS. LHP   PROBABLE HIT LOCATIONS

ability in the field, nothing great but not bad. His range is adequate and his arm is average, at best. It helps to have speedy Kirby Puckett in center field.

OVERALL:

Bush outlasted Mike Stenhouse, who was dropped from the roster after last season. He has become a more valuable player because of his versatility. He seems to have a secure and evolving place in the majors.

Killebrew: "Randy could improve with more playing time. He plays hard, tries hard and gives a good effort. This season, he will probably platoon in left field and come off the bench as a left-handed pinch-hitter and DH."

PITCHING:

In his first season with the Twins (1984), John Butcher established himself as a successful starter because he threw one of the best change-ups in the majors. Last year, the junk pitches were being anticipated and Butcher was as disappointing as any member of the team. His consistency took a wrong turn.

Butcher's biggest weakness is pitches that are left up in the strike zone. Because his fastball is in the mid-80s, anything that isn't low is potentially dangerous. There is a double-whammy at work because good pitches turn into gap singles on the Metrodome turf. Butcher is resigned to giving up a lot of hits and has to keep them from coming in bunches--that includes too many homers.

His pitches are supposed to move away from righthanders. Butcher needs a lot of work to keep his arm from feeling too strong--if his arm is too strong, there is not enough movement on his pitches, and a lack of movement is one of the things that gets him into trouble.

Last season's performance removed him from being a definite member of the rotation. His future will depend on whether he can regain the precision that, at first, made the trade--Butcher & Mike Smithson from Texas for Gary Ward--seem so one-sided.

FIELDING:

Butcher falls off to the side of the

JOHN BUTCHER
RHP, No. 32
RR, 6'4", 190 lbs.
ML Svc: 6 years
Born: 3-8-57 in
  Glendale, CA

1985 STATISTICS

W	L	ERA	G	GS	CG	SV	IP	H	R	ER	BB	SO
11	14	4.98	34	33	8	0	207.2	239	125	115	43	92

CAREER STATISTICS

W	L	ERA	G	GS	CG	SV	IP	H	R	ER	BB	SO
35	61	4.05	135	95	21	6	713	763	351	321	192	318

mound at the end of his delivery. This contributes to a poor hits-to-innings-pitched ratio because he is not able to field many grounders up the middle.

He has an average move to first base but a quick delivery to the plate.

OVERALL:

Butcher went from being the most consistent of Twins starters to a jumbo question mark. This season should reveal whether he was merely a one-season flash or can adjust and recapture his previous success.

Killebrew: "John has one of the best change-ups around and will throw it any time. But he has to keep the ball down to be effective. When he hangs it, it's a breeze to hit."

PITCHING:

The best thing about banging your head against the wall is that it feels so good when you stop. That could be the story of Ron Davis' four seasons with the Twins. In 1985, after three years of ignoring the advice of others, Davis finally figured out that he must do more than throw fastball after fastball after fastball to be a high-quality reliever.

When he began to mix up his pitches, using a sneaky slider to keep hitters off balance, Davis became as efficient as anybody in a final-out situation. He went from the middle of May through late September without blowing a save opportunity, with each success reinforcing the reality that his fastball has lost enough zip that he can't use it alone.

David learned an important trick last season, too. He found that he is more effective when he takes some extra time between pitches, giving the batter time to think about the pitch that just flew by him--and whether he'll wear the next one. Davis has to be reminded not to throw the ball as soon as he gets it back from the catcher. He sometimes walks around the mound to reinforce that discipline.

Changing speeds off his fastball--which he can still throw at 92 MPH--has enabled him to strike out more than one batter per inning for the first time since he became a Twin. The fastball is still haunting enough that Davis can go an entire inning without even throwing one and still close the door with sliders alone.

Davis is wild enough to keep batters from digging in. He has dabbled in the bullpen with a split-finger fastball, which upon mastery could make him even more effective. What he discovered last season could inspire him to continue developing new weapons for coming years.

RON DAVIS
RHP, No. 39
RR, 6'4", 196 lbs.
ML Svc: 7 years
Born: 8-6-55 in
Houston, TX

```
1985 STATISTICS
W  L  ERA  G   GS CG SV IP    H   R   ER  BB  SO
2  6  3.48 57  0  0  25 64.2  55  28  25  35  72
CAREER STATISTICS
W  L  ERA  G   GS CG SV IP    H   R   ER  BB  SO
44 44 3.50 394 0  0  128 634.1 584 264 247 244 510
```

Now that he knows how valuable it is, Davis needs to take care of his pitching hand. He always has been susceptible to blisters and needs to follow prescribed therapy to keep that problem from sidelining him.

FIELDING:

Davis doesn't look to·be in good position in his follow-through, but he doesn't miss many balls. He is reckless in their pursuit. Most disturbing is his tendency to forget about baserunners, allowing them uncontested stolen bases. Davis has a mediocre move to first.

OVERALL:

Davis has established himself as the undisputed king of the Minnesota bullpen, one of the team's cornerstones, whose performance this season will determine the team's success or failure.

Killebrew: "Ron is finally learning how to pitch--using his breaking ball to make up for losing a little bit off the fastball. He is pitching with so much more confidence and will be the short man unless he pitches himself out of the job."

HITTING:

Dave Engle went from being an American League All-Star in 1984 to the far end of the Minnesota bench for the opening months of 1985, including an eleven month stretch during which he did not have a single RBI. Former manager Billy Gardner gave up on him for defensive reasons and Engle seemed to give up on himself, and has become too complacent of his non-player status.

A change of managers provided him with a sense of liberation and he was able to play more, filling a variety of roles.

Much of the time, he serves as as the designated hitter against lefthanded pitchers. Engle has not been able to decide whether he is a power hitter or an "average" hitter, perhaps hurting himself by not totally gearing for one or the other.

Engle crowds the plate and can be jammed with an inside fastball or fooled by sliders low and away. A pitcher who backs him away is the pitcher who will handle him. Because Engle plays with a variety of nagging pains, particularly in his shoulder, he has sometimes been limited at the plate. He went through a phase when he had a knack for hitting double play grounders.

BASERUNNING:

Engle is an average runner and his mistakes usually come from being too aggressive at the wrong time. He does not look good on the bases and doesn't get out of the batter's box well.

FIELDING:

Engle's arm became one of the great Minnesota soap operas. He developed a phobia about throwing the ball back to the pitcher in a style any harder than a simple lob. Former Twins manager Billy Gardner didn't want a catcher who threw

DAVE ENGLE
C, No. 20
RR, 6'3", 216 lbs.
ML Svc: 5 years
Born: 11-30-56 in
San Diego, CA

1985 STATISTICS

AVG	G	AB	R	H	2B	3B	HR	RBI	BB	SO	SB
.256	70	172	28	44	8	2	7	25	21	28	2

CAREER STATISTICS

AVG	G	AB	R	H	2B	3B	HR	RBI	BB	SO	SB
.268	439	1371	179	368	71	13	28	154	98	148	4

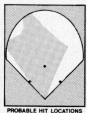

STRONG   STRONG   PROBABLE HIT LOCATIONS

VS. RHP   VS. LHP

like that; Ray Miller, the current manager, cured Engle's problem by saying that it wasn't a problem at all.

His throws to second are erratic. Engle enjoys the intellectual challenge of catching and is considered by Twins pitchers to have a good feel for handling pitchers and knowing the opponent.

OVERALL:

Engle appears to have missed his chance to be a full-time catcher for the Twins and, understanding that, can help the team most as a part-time catcher, part-time DH and part-time outfielder. Sitting on the bench for the first part of last season may have done his career irrepairable damage.

Killebrew: "Dave has to be honest with himself in what he wants to do. He has been hurt by his erratic performance in all phases of the game and needs to get into better shape."

PITCHING:

He looks like somebody's kid brother, but it seems that everything about the way Frank Eufemia pitches is kind of deceptive. Start off with a jerky motion that makes the ball difficult for a batter to pick up, especially for right-handers. That was the most distinguishing thing about Eufemia when he was called up last May and it helped get him off to a hot start.

Eufemia cannot blaze his fastball past a hitter and so he relies on a tight-breaking slider and his change-up (which he can usually keep low). He is working on a curve as a fourth pitch. He will throw the change-up regardless of the count and opposing hitters have returned to the dugout muttering about a pitch that looks hittable--but isn't.

While Eufemia can kill a batter's timing, he doesn't have much room for error. Pitches that are up in the strike zone are pitches that will be hit. His style is such that he works best in middle relief, where opponents see him once before he gives ways to someone else. Eufemia also serves the purpose of making Ron Davis, the Twins closer, appear that much faster.

FIELDING:

Eufemia is technically sound, ending his delivery squared toward home plate and ready to field anything hit toward him. He has a good move toward first that he continues to work on, but, at the same time, runners don't seem to distract him. His fielding skills make

FRANK EUFEMIA
RHP, No. 54
RR, 5'11", 180 lbs.
ML Svc: 1 year
Born: 12-23-59 in
Bronx, NY

1985 STATISTICS

W	L	ERA	G	GS	CG	SV	IP	H	R	ER	BB	SO
4	2	3.79	39	0	0	2	61.2	56	27	26	21	30

CAREER STATISTICS

W	L	ERA	G	GS	CG	SV	IP	H	R	ER	BB	SO
4	2	3.79	39	0	0	2	61.2	56	27	26	21	30

him an exception on a staff whose more established pitchers have a variety of problems.

OVERALL:

Whether Eufemia can add to his resources--mastering a curve would be the main thing--will go quite a way toward determining his major league future. Eufemia needs to be a battler and a thinker because, frankly, his physical tools are not the greatest.

Killebrew: "Frank makes the most of his ability in any situation. He is not a powerful pitcher, but he wants to take the ball all of the time and has the kind of determination about him that just might take him far. He is smart enough to know that he has to out-smart the hitters because he'll never be able to blow his fastball by anyone."

PITCHING:

The Twins are still trying to figure out Pete Filson, who can be stunningly good in one outing and then come back with a dreadful encore. His inconsistency has been a constant of his big league career. He has bounced from the starting rotation to middle relief without giving an indication as to where he would fit best.

Filson is one of those pitchers who pretty much calls his own game, shaking off signs from the catcher or amending them with "add-ons," pumping his glove across the front of his jersey to indicate the pitch he wants to throw.

There are people who say that his overthinking detracts from his performance because it puts more emphasis on which pitch will be thrown than on throwing it well.

Filson needs to be sharp because he isn't overpowering. He throws a slider that has a sharp downward break and a sinking fastball. His curveball is erratic and, on bad days, hangs up as if begging to be hit. Filson's overhand motion isn't particularly tough on left-handed hitters.

The unglamorous role of middle relief is probably best for Filson because he can be used for several innings on consecutive days--and rubber arms are hard to find. Starting, on the other hand, might give Filson too much to ponder and hinder his effectiveness.

FIELDING:

Filson doesn't have a strong move to

PETE FILSON
LHP, No. 23
SL, 6'2", 195 lbs.
ML Svc: 3 years
Born: 9-28-58 in
    Darby, PA

1985 STATISTICS
W	L	ERA	G	GS	CG	SV	IP	H	R	ER	BB	SO
4	5	3.67	40	6	1	2	95.2	93	42	39	30	42

CAREER STATISTICS
W	L	ERA	G	GS	CG	SV	IP	H	R	ER	BB	SO
14	13	3.95	126	24	1	4	316.2	303	144	139	121	160

first and keeps runners close by throwing over as often as anyone on the staff. That's something for him to work on. Otherwise, he fields his position fairly well.

OVERALL:

The Twins are waiting for Filson to blossom and are wondering what it will take for him to become consistent. Solid lefthanders are scarce and the Twins seem willing to stick with him in the hope that he'll pan out.

Killebrew: "It would help Pete to have a better idea of his limitations. He will throw every day and isn't afraid to work. His weakness is clear when he starts to outthink himself instead of just reacting."

HITTING:

In 1984, Gary Gaetti slipped from being a slugger who had hit 44 homers in his two previous seasons to being merely a batter who hit only 5. His average didn't rise enough to justify the power drop. Last season, he regained his home run form but continued to have a batting average and an RBI total lower than desired. For Gaetti, hitting is an exercise in perpetual adjustment.

His batting stance is subject to change on short notice, as nothing he does seems to work for an extended period of time. If something seems comfortable at the plate, Gaetti will try it.

A pitcher forced to rely on fastballs will have trouble with Gaetti, who is a pull hitter. His average picks up a bit on turf because more hard grounders become hard singles between third base and shortstop. He tries cutting down on his swing with two strikes but doesn't meet with much success. Breaking balls and change-ups are problems, especially when his heart is set for a fastball.

As long as the Twins don't expect too much from Gaetti, he will provide them with enough power to be a useful, everyday player. To expect him to hit .300 or drive in 100 runs is unrealistic.

BASERUNNING:

Gaetti's intelligent approach to baseball shows best in his baserunning. He has average speed but still stole 13 bases last season, second on the team behind Kirby Puckett.

He slides hard. Catchers and middle infielders must beware. Gary's one bad baserunning habit is looking at the ball while running toward first.

FIELDING:

Gaetti has good enough range going toward the foul line that he can cheat

GARY GAETTI
3B, No. 8
RR, 6'0", 193 lbs.
ML Svc: 4 years
Born: 8-19-58 in
   Centralia, IL

1985 STATISTICS
AVG	G	AB	R	H	2B	3B	HR	RBI	BB	SO	SB
.246	160	560	71	138	31	0	20	63	37	89	13

CAREER STATISTICS
AVG	G	AB	R	H	2B	3B	HR	RBI	BB	SO	SB
.246	633	2266	270	557	115	11	73	293	172	404	31

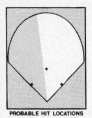

STRONG   STRONG   PROBABLE HIT LOCATIONS

VS. RHP   VS. LHP

in the other direction, playing an extra step toward shortstop to make up for a weakness in that direction. He also goes through streaks when his throws are wild on routine plays. But his defense was considered strong enough to be used as a late-inning replacement in several games in which he didn't start.

OVERALL:

Gaetti is out of place at the Metrodome because he can't get grass and mud stains on his uniform. Diving stops and headfirst slides are as much a part of his game as home runs and strikeouts.

Killebrew: "Gary is an all-out type of player who plays hard and is not afraid to make diving catches. He could help if he could hit for a higher average and still not sacrifice his power."

HITTING:

Greg Gagne has the proper skills to be a leadoff hitter and, had the Twins not been worried about putting too much pressure on him, might have been given a shot at that position last season. But after a strong start in 1985, Gagne went into a slump and was having enough problems making contact in the lower part of the batting order.

Gagne has the speed to be a contact hitter but established himself as a prospect with a combination of power hitting and shortstop play. But everyone will be better off once all images of another Cal Ripken are dropped. He needs to cut down on a swing that is too long and give himself more of a chance against curveballs and sliders.

Gagne can bunt for hits but doesn't do it enough. Most of his weaknesses appear curable and boil down to inexperience. His defensive potential is already known and his ability to handle the bat will go far toward deciding whether he becomes an everyday player.

BASERUNNING:

Gagne is one of the fastest Twins and was encouraged to work on his base-stealing technique. He forces pitchers to pay attention to him and is a good bet to go from first to third on a single--another reason to encourage him to put aside notions of power.

FIELDING:

Gagne has a very quick first step and is especially good at making plays behind second base. He turns double plays well and seems to know how much he can cheat on the pivot without get-

GREG GAGNE
3B/SS, No. 31
RR, 5'11", 185 lbs.
ML Svc: 1 year plus
Born: 11-12-61 in
   Fall River, MA

1985 STATISTICS

AVG	G	AB	R	H	2B	3B	HR	RBI	BB	SO	SB
.225	114	293	37	66	15	3	2	23	20	57	10

CAREER STATISTICS

AVG	G	AB	R	H	2B	3B	HR	RBI	BB	SO	SB
.215	126	321	39	69	16	3	2	26	20	63	10

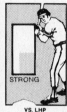

STRONG   STRONG
VS. RHP   VS. LHP   PROBABLE HIT LOCATIONS

ting called for it (a veteran's skill).

His main weakness is fielding balls hit at him or within a step or two, a sign that his confidence is not yet at the level it should be.

OVERALL:

If the Twins make his role clear and Gagne is willing to accept some limitations, he should have the inside track on being the everyday shortstop this year. His speed is a novelty on a team with a slow-footed profile.

Killebrew: "Gagne needs more consistency with the bat. He should be hitting for a better average to be considered an everyday player."

HITTING:

Mickey Hatcher has the tools of a contact hitter in the body of a lumbering slugger. His 1985 season was marked by trips to the disabled list for back and shoulder problems. Even in healthier years, Hatcher needed to cope with bumps and bruises owing to his not-so-graceful style of play.

Hatcher is an aggressive hitter who doesn't care if he doesn't appear fluid at the plate. Some of his biggest hits have come on pitches when he's appeared to be fooled, only to smack an outside pitch down the right field line or loop an inside one off his bat handle and between the outfielder. Hatcher rarely strikes out or walks.

He gives the appearance of someone who might suffer if he tried to figure out why he was successful instead of continuing to do whatever he does to get on base. Hatcher is at his best against high fastballs. Low pitches, especially breaking ones, are the best way to handle him.

Good bat control makes Hatcher a good hit-and-run candidate and he is a pretty good bunter. But his baserunning limitations keep him from the hits that speedier contact hitters get. One could say that a shortstop going into the hole or a second baseman diving behind the bag has a good chance to look spectacular with Hatcher chugging toward first. Of course, his batting style makes Hatcher an excellent turf hitter and one that must be played straightaway because his extra-base hits are likely to end up in either corner.

BASERUNNING:

Injuries have caught up with him on the bases. He hasn't stolen a base in two seasons and gets thrown at first on plays that one would expect most other players to beat out. None of this should be interpreted as a lack of effort. He is the type of runner who would try hard to break up a double play if he could get there in time.

MICKEY HATCHER
LF, No. 9
RR, 6'2", 199 lbs.
ML Svc: 7 years
Born: 3-15-55 in
   Cleveland, OH

1985 STATISTICS

AVG	G	AB	R	H	2B	3B	HR	RBI	BB	SO	SB
.282	116	444	46	125	28	0	3	49	16	23	0

CAREER STATISTICS

AVG	G	AB	R	H	2B	3B	HR	RBI	BB	SO	SB
.282	647	2226	229	627	120	13	25	238	99	156	6

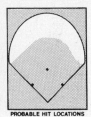

STRONG   STRONG

VS. RHP   VS. LHP   PROBABLE HIT LOCATIONS

FIELDING:

There are few dull moments with him in left field. He can create tension in the pursuit of a routine fly but turn a double into a spectacular out. Hatcher's flawed plays seem to come in bunches and don't happen for lack of effort.

Late-season shoulder problems last year make Hatcher's arm, once considered solid, very questionable for the future. His range has always been limited.

OVERALL:

Hatcher is a favorite of the Minnesota fans and returned the affection after the final game of last season by throwing his hat, glove and shoes into the left field stands.

Killebrew: "Mickey does some wild things on the bases . . . and he is a real crowd pleaser. Because his injuries have limited him elsewere, he will probably end up as DH soon."

HITTING:

After three charmed seasons, Kent Hrbek found out what it feels like to be in an extended slump. He did very little to help his team during the first half of the season and was far from the player who was MVP runner-up in 1984.

Previously, a pitcher needed to keep Hrbek off stride in order to get him out with any consistency. Home runs could come off either fastballs or breaking pitches. He was able to blend power with an average that was usually above .300. There was no slump that could not be cured in a few days. That's called natural talent.

Last season, Hrbek was unable to get around on inside fastballs and, like a struggling boxer, flailed more than he swung. He was expected to carry the team and publicly fought those expectations as well as his problems.

Toward the end of the season, when his team had dropped from contention, Hrbek returned to form. He became more selective at the plate and seldom looked overmatched. When that happens, Hrbek can pull most pitches while losing little power as he takes an outside pitch to left or left-center. He will bunt to third base if the infield is overshifted.

The one thing that Hrbek must learn to do is control his weight. He came to the majors as a 215-pounder but has checked into spring training weighing as much as 243 pounds. During the season, he has never shed as much weight as the Twins would like and, because of chronic shoulder and knee problems, that becomes a larger concern every year.

BASERUNNING:

The extra weight hurts, but Hrbek has the instincts of a solid runner. He could use an extra half-step, however, because topspin bouncers reach infielders more quickly on the Metrodome's artificial surface.

KENT HRBEK
1B, No. 14
LR, 6'4", 229 lbs.
ML Svc: 5 years
Born: 5-21-60 in
   Minneapolis, MN

1985 STATISTICS											
AVG	G	AB	R	H	2B	3B	HR	RBI	BB	SO	SB
.278	158	593	78	165	31	2	21	93	67	87	1
CAREER STATISTICS											
AVG	G	AB	R	H	2B	3B	HR	RBI	BB	SO	SB
.295	612	2266	320	668	129	14	88	383	248	334	9

  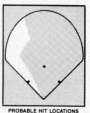

VS. RHP   VS. LHP   PROBABLE HIT LOCATIONS

FIELDING:

For some reason--even he doesn't know why--Hrbek has a natural ability to do a gymnastic-style spilt on a throw to first base. His defensive abilities save a lot of errors for his teammates.

He is quick to read and respond to situations and will dive, often successfully, for balls that should elude such a heavyweight. In bad times, Hrbek takes his slumps into the field and will miss an easy play when he has his poor hitting on his mind.

OVERALL:

Hrbek may have finally realized that being overweight is an open invitation to injury.

Killebrew: "If Hrbek keeps himself in shape, he could be a superstar. When he is swinging well, he is a very disciplined hitter. He is an excellent first baseman."

HITTING:

There was a time when Tim Laudner made home runs look very easy. The trouble is, that was 1981 and his 42 homers came in the minors.

He has never been able to establish himself as an everyday catcher, even though that job was his for the taking at the start of 1985.

His trouble has remained constant--an inability to make consistent contact. His stance has been tinkered with by coaches but some things have remained the same no matter how he stands.

Pitching Laudner high and away is the key to getting him out. Righthanders can fool him with sliders as well. He shows most of his power, and hits for a surprisingly high average, against lefties.

Laudner hurts himself with a lack of patience. He rarely seems to have the luxury of a 2-and-0 or 3-and-1 count, which are the times when many pitchers would have little choice but to throw the fastballs that Laudner so covets.

He doesn't bunt well and hits to right field only by accident. There are times when he seems to make improvement, but those conditions seem temporary. No one is expecting Laudner to become more than a low-average hitter with good power. There are enough flaws that his offense is considered one-dimensional. It has sent the Twins looking for alternatives behind the plate.

BASERUNNING:

Laudner isn't much to worry about on the bases; he doesn't get much chance for improvement because he doesn't get to run them very often.

FIELDING:

In earlier years, Laudner was an aw-

TIM LAUDNER
C, No. 15
RR, 6'3", 208 lbs.
ML Svc: 4 years
Born: 6-7-58 in
 Mason City, IA

1985 STATISTICS
AVG	G	AB	R	H	2B	3B	HR	RBI	BB	SO	SB
.238	72	164	16	39	5	0	7	19	12	45	0

CAREER STATISTICS
AVG	G	AB	R	H	2B	3B	HR	RBI	BB	SO	SB
.222	328	943	108	209	51	2	32	110	82	263	0

  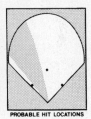

VS. RHP VS. LHP PROBABLE HIT LOCATIONS

ful defensive catcher--easy to run on and not very mobile behind the plate. He has worked hard to make himself adequate and can no longer be considered a chump. He still has a tendency to bounce throws into center field, however.

OVERALL:

The Twins are afraid to give up on Laudner, fearing he is just a step away from unleashing the kind of power he showed in the minors.

Killebrew: "He is not good enough defensively to allow the team to overlook his shortcomings at the plate. He might be close to being a good hitter if he got more playing time, but an every day role does not appear likely in Minnesota."

PITCHING:

Rick Lysander is a one-trick pony and when he can't perform the act of throwing a wicked sinker, there isn't much he can do to compensate.

His fastball is nothing to brag about and his slider tends to be flat and very hittable.

Lysander has struggled enough that he has spent parts of the last two seasons in the minors and has never figured in the Twins' plans as anything more than a set-up man during good times and a long reliever when starters suffer an early knockout.

The shame of that medocrity is that Lysander has the type of arm that can handle a lot of work. In 1983 (his rookie season), he appeared in 66 games and worked 125 innings. A sharp Lysander would be the pitcher of preference when a double play is needed because his tempting sinkers are often swatted into the ground.

There may be some frustration on his part because even his good pitches can get chopped for singles on the Metrodome turf when they would go for outs on a grass surface. He also has been second-guessed about his choice of pitches and his willingness to challenge opponents.

Lysander came along at a time when the Twins pitching staff was very thin. His future may be tenuous because club policy has shifted to where help, such as Bert Blyleven and Steve Howe (however ill-fated that decision was) will be acquired when the residents don't come through.

FIELDING:

Lysander tried fixing his form so

RICK LYSANDER
RHP, No. 19
RR, 6'2", 188 lbs.
ML Svc: 3 years
Born: 2-21-53 in
 Huntington Park, CA

1985 STATISTICS

W	L	ERA	G	GS	CG	SV	IP	H	R	ER	BB	SO
0	2	6.05	35	1	0	3	61	72	43	41	22	26

CAREER STATISTICS

W	L	ERA	G	GS	CG	SV	IP	H	R	ER	BB	SO
9	17	4.28	139	5	1	11	256.1	290	142	122	96	111

that he would finish up in good fielding position but decided that he couldn't pitch that way and still be effective. So, he continues to fall off the mound toward first base and fields grounders mostly by accident--a weakness that a sinkerball pitcher can hardly afford. His move to first is below average and Lysander throws over there mostly for effect.

OVERALL:

Lysander will have to prove himself during spring training in order to stay with the Twins because, at the end of last season, there were 10 pitchers who were held in higher regard.

Killebrew: "Rick has been trying to trick hitters instead of challenging them. That can't wash for long and it gets him into more trouble than he needs.

"He should let his ability take over instead of doubting himself."

KIRBY PUCKETT
CF, No. 34
RR, 5'8", 175 lbs.
ML Svc: 2 years
Born: 3-14-61 in
  Chicago, IL

HITTING:

Kirby Puckett has batted leadoff in every major league game that he has appeared in during his two-season career. There is suspicion that he could improve from being a solid to being an excellent offensive player if he were dropped to the number two spot in the batting order.

While some players must be coaxed to hit to the opposite field, Puckett does it so often that teams can stack their defense against him. A leadoff batter who reached first would force teams to open up that side of the infield, to Puckett's advantage.

He is a unique offensive player with interesting contradictions. Puckett has a small strike zone--but doesn't draw as many walks as one would expect. He has a muscular build--but only a handful of home runs. He is an excellent bunter--but has never been able to bunt toward first base.

Because of his speed, Puckett picks up more than a few hits because of the Metrodome turf and, because the park can be especially tough on visiting players, he can turn singles into doubles and doubles into triples. He strikes out too often for a contact hitter and, because of his opposite field hitting, he has been known to chase outside pitches that aren't a threat to the strike zone.

BASERUNNING:

At mid-season, Puckett was one of the Twins players who spent a weekend working with Hall of Famer Lou Brock on basestealing skills. It helped. Puckett stole 20 bases last season and could set a goal of doubling that total in 1986.

He is fast from first to third and doesn't need much of a defensive blunder in order to take an extra base. Of the Twins regulars, there is little doubt that he has been the fastest and the catalyst of an offense that otherwise has relied more on power.

FIELDING:

Puckett can make spectacular plays,

1985 STATISTICS											
AVG	G	AB	R	H	2B	3B	HR	RBI	BB	SO	SB
.288	161	691	80	199	29	13	4	74	41	87	21

CAREER STATISTICS											
AVG	G	AB	R	H	2B	3B	HR	RBI	BB	SO	SB
.292	289	1248	143	364	41	18	4	105	57	156	35

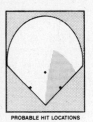

STRONG VS. RHP   STRONG VS. LHP   PROBABLE HIT LOCATIONS

especially going back. He reached over the Metrodome wall several times to rob opponents of home runs. He has allowed the Twins to use left fielders with limited range because he can patrol the power-alley gap.

Puckett has been first and second in the AL outfield assists the last two seasons. His arm is extremely accurate and very strong. Opponents, it seems, don't want to believe that a little guy can make long throws. But Puckett is among the best at getting into the right position to challenge a runner.

OVERALL:

Killebrew: "Kirby gives the Twins a sense of stability, both on offense and defense. He is an exciting player who makes things happen. He could become an even better ballplayer with more experience; soon he will steal more bases, hit for a better average and draw more walks."

HITTING:

Who is this guy? Where did he come from? How did he hit .300? Was it a fluke? Where does he go from here?

Nobody expected much from Mark Salas when he was drafted off the St. Louis Cardinals Triple-A roster in December 1984. After taking a brief look, the Cardinals gave up on him because they didn't think he had the right stuff to be a major league catcher.

It was something of a surprise when Salas made the Twins' Opening Day roster and an even bigger one when he hit well enough to become their platoon catcher against righthanded pitchers. His average never dropped as low as the .244 mark he logged with the Cardinals' minor league team just the season before.

Salas is the type of hitter whose style should keep him from falling into extended slumps. He has a compact swing and, while capable of hitting home runs, knows they will come along with the line singles to right and the gap doubles to right-center he hits with regularity.

He doesn't hit well with runners in scoring position; his frustration shows in a sudden impatience at the plate. He does not draw many walks, but is aware that these are two workable flaws. Overcoming them, as it is expected he will do with more experience, should turn him from a rookie novelty into a feared and consistent hitter.

BASERUNNING:

If Salas the catcher had chances to throw out Salas the baserunner, his defensive statistics would have been better. Still, if Salas can get to home plate, he's the type of player good to have on your team in the event of a collision.

FIELDING:

It took Salas 15 attempts before he threw out his first basestealer last year. He has worked hard on his defen-

MARK SALAS
C, No. 12
LR, 6'0", 180 lbs.
ML Svc: 1 year plus
Born: 3-8-61 in
    Montebello, CA

1985 STATISTICS

AVG	G	AB	R	H	2B	3B	HR	RBI	BB	SO	SB
.300	120	360	51	108	20	5	9	41	18	37	0

CAREER STATISTICS

AVG	G	AB	R	H	2B	3B	HR	RBI	BB	SO	SB
.289	134	380	52	110	21	5	9	42	18	40	0

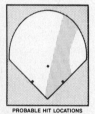

VS. RHP VS. LHP PROBABLE HIT LOCATIONS

sive shortcomings, spending extra time with bullpen coach Rick Stelmaszek and practicing on his own as well. He improved enough that he threw out Angels' speedster Gary Pettis at second twice in one game.

Still, Salas needs work on all sorts of mechanics--from better balance in throwing situations to better handling of pitches and pitchers. Others at his position could learn from the fearless way he handles himself on plays at the plate.

OVERALL:

Salas' rookie goal was to play in a handful of games and learn by watching. Instead, he got on-the-job-training and must now show that his success wasn't a fluke.

Killebrew: "Mark is a 'gamer.' He needs to keep working on his catching skills and not let complacency set in offensively or defensively. He was a nice surprise for the Twins and may have the chance to be the regular catcher."

PITCHING:

Ken Schrom carries several attributes of a quality pitcher: a good arm, determination, knowledge of his craft. He has become a conditioning fiend, a disciple of the strength and flexibility exercise program which has prolonged Steve Carlton's career. An early arrival at the ballpark could find Schrom in practice jersey and flowing headband, going through routines. While his diligence to physical fitness has helped him overcome the arm and back problems that might have hindered his career, it has not helped him throw strikes.

Schrom's success has always been based on being able to get ahead in the count. He is best when he can work the count to 0-and-1 or 1-and-2 because he can move the ball around the plate and keep batters guessing. Too often, however, especially after a few strong innings, that skill deserts him, and the defense seems to get a little too complacent while waiting for some action.

This has led to a related problem-- the home run ball. Schrom led the Twins by allowing 28 last season, also putting him among the league leaders, even though he pitched only 160 2/3 innings. Batters are able to wait for a situation where Schrom has to throw a strike and then take full advantage of it. His problems with his breaking pitches (he throws both a slider and a curve) allow them to wait for an average fastball. He does not keep batters off the plate by throwing inside.

Schrom does have a good change-up and, unlike some pitchers who possess that pitch, refrains from throwing it to excess. He shows it to the league's better hitters, which is his way of preventing them from digging in.

FIELDING:

Schrom is a slow worker with a delib-

KEN SCHROM
RHP, No. 18
RR, 6'2", 195 lbs.
ML Svc: 4 years
Born: 11-23-54 in
    Grangeville, ID

1985 STATISTICS
W	L	ERA	G	GS	CG	SV	IP	H	R	ER	BB	SO
9	12	4.99	29	26	6	0	160.2	164	95	89	59	74

CAREER STATISTICS
W	L	ERA	G	GS	CG	SV	IP	H	R	ER	BB	SO
31	31	4.43	110	75	15	1	540	561	291	266	214	224

erate delivery that works against him at holding runners. He throws over to first to compensate, slowing down a game's pace in concert with his falling behind in the count. And it's not as though he has Lance Parrish or Bob Boone behind the plate to compensate for that weakness. Otherwise, Schrom moves and fields his position well.

OVERALL:

If Schrom can work on his weaknesses without developing new ones, he will still offer the potential of being a winning pitcher.

Killebrew: "Ken has a sound arm and the capability to be a good pitcher but he pitches away from the batter too much. He is too slow a worker and works a lot of high counts. He's better when he's an 0-and-1 on a hitter.

"Ken doesn't have enough stuff to punch out a guy when he goes 3-and-2. He has the pitches but I don't know if it's a lack of concentration or too much concentration that effects his control."

HITTING:

The Chicago White Sox apparently were all too happy to return Roy Smalley to the place where his career once flourished--taking a couple of low-hope minor leaguers in return and agreeing to pay a hefty share of a contract that runs through 1989. Meanwhile, the Twins were hoping that he could rebound from his worst season in the majors and provide leadership for a young team.

The Twins opened the season by using the switch-hitting Smalley every day and he responded by showing some power from the left and hitting for average as a righthander.

Smalley has a keen sense of his own strike zone and uses it to his advantage. Unfortunately, his refusal to go after close pitches sometimes results in called strikes when an umpire doesn't share Smalley's view of the pitch.

When the Twins changed managers, Smalley's role in the offense was mostly that of DH against righthanded pitching. Ray Miller didn't have much confidence in his ability to hit lefties and Roy felt that his part-time status contributed to a slump toward the end of the season.

What Smalley does best is hit low fastballs. He can be made to look bad against off-speed pitches and is sometimes overpowered by high heat. Smalley is still a power hitter and is aided by the short right field wall at the Metrodome in the same way that the Yankee Stadium dimensions were to his benefit when he played there.

Because he keeps the ball in the air, he doesn't benefit from the idiosyncrasies of artificial turf.

BASERUNNING:

Smalley has become a conditioning buff and takes pride in the steps he's made to minimize the back problems that have plagued his career. Alas, conditioning hasn't done anything for his speed, which has never allowed him to

ROY SMALLEY
SS, No. 4
SR, 6'1", 182 lbs.
ML Svc: 11 years
Born: 10-25-52 in
   Los Angeles, CA

1985 STATISTICS

AVG	G	AB	R	H	2B	3B	HR	RBI	BB	SO	SB
.258	129	388	57	100	20	0	12	45	60	65	0

CAREER STATISTICS

AVG	G	AB	R	H	2B	3B	HR	RBI	BB	SO	SB
.257	1400	4889	654	1256	208	20	135	603	667	776	24

steal more than a few bases in any season or to run the bases with abandon.

FIELDING:

Although he opened last season as the regular shortstop, it became apparent that Smalley's ability to position himself could not make up for his lack of range. He played well at third base, where a strong arm is more important than covering ground. He can also play first base.

Smalley tries hard but doesn't always get the results both he and the Twins are looking for.

OVERALL:

Much to Smalley's disappointment, his career is approaching its twilight. He will likely find himself in the role of jock-of-several-trades in 1986.

If nothing else, Smalley would like a chance to bat righthanded on a regular basis to show what he can do.

Killebrew: "Roy looks like a left-handed hitting DH in 1986."

PITCHING:

Midway through last season, when he was losing games and getting hit hard, Mike Smithson realized that there was more to pitching than walking out to the mound every fifth day and seeing how long he could pitch. Smithson began throwing his change-up to righthanded batters, which was something he previously considered unnecessary. It turned out to be very necessary--and helped him have a winning season.

At 6'8", Smithson is an imposing presence on the mound. He could be an intimidating figure to face, but he does not use it to his advantage. His control is too good. When he had to rely on his fastball or slider, hitters knew almost exactly where the pitch would be and he became an easy mark.

One solution was to cut loose a bit more. Last season, Smithson didn't worry about control as much--he gave up 24 more walks than the year before and hit 15 batters, half of the staff total. He also allowed 10 fewer home runs and rallied to finish the season with a winning record.

By working inside to righthanders, Smithson opens up the outside half of the plate to finish them off. His slider does the trick on a good day. He has two different ways of throwing the pitch, one that looks more like a curve and the other that has a tighter break to it. All of his pitches are thrown from just below a three-quarters delivery.

Smithson has been fighting a battle against a lack of concentration throughout his career and is not hindered by the big innings as much as he used to be. He is a well-conditioned athlete and gives the appearance of getting stronger as the game goes on.

FIELDING:

Smithson has good hands, good funda-

MIKE SMITHSON
RHP, No. 48
LR, 6'8", 215 lbs.
ML Svc: 4 years
Born: 1-21-55 in
  Centerville, TN

1985 STATISTICS
W	L	ERA	G	GS	CG	SV	IP	H	R	ER	BB	SO
15	14	4.34	37	37	8	0	257	264	134	124	78	127

CAREER STATISTICS
W	L	ERA	G	GS	CG	SV	IP	H	R	ER	BB	SO
43	45	4.04	114	114	31	0	779	794	375	350	216	430

mentals and takes pride in getting off the mound to make a nifty play. But because of his height, he does have some trouble getting down for grounders, and the length of his delivery makes him a frequent target for basestealers.

He compensates by throwing to first a lot and that can sometimes have an impact on his concentration.

OVERALL:

Smithson is one of the tallest men in baseball and as a pitcher, he is constantly battling for the proper mechanics. Things go right for a few games and then sour just as quickly. If he ever figures out how to get his entire game under control, Smithson could become more than a barely-above-.500 pitcher.

Killebrew: "With a little luck, Mike could be a 20-game winner. He can't get carried away with nibbling at the corners. He is a tough competitor who throws hard and changes speeds. He can be overly critical of himself and should let go a bit."

HITTING:

Sometimes, baseball players talk of the need to do something called "staying within yourself." Well, Tim Teufel has been caught in a quandary: he can't decide whether to play inside or outside himself.

He tries to be a contact hitter, advancing runners and looking to the opposite field. But then again, he tries to provide more power than is normally expected from a second baseman. He does a little of both, but not enough of either one.

Teufel has an excellent eye for balls and strikes but too often appears helpless against a breaking pitch. His home runs are usually fly balls that clear the left-field fence in some stadiums but would be caught in others. His home runs are never towering--Teufel is not a power hitter and hurts himself when he feels an obligation to look for extra-base hits.

Teufel can do some things very well. He is another player who takes advantage of artificial turf and, in a disciplined mood, he can execute the hit-and-run and sacrifice himself to move a runner from second to third. He could be a leadoff type of hitter except for his lack of speed.

There has been much expected from Tim and now, after two season with Minnesota, he might be living up to part of his billing. He must quickly step back and evaluate his own talents to maximize his potential.

BASERUNNING:

Teufel has a good head for running the bases but doesn't have the physical gifts to match. He won't run himself into many unnecessary outs but his ability to take the extra base is limited.

FIELDING:

Teufel doesn't turn double plays well and there have been whispers that his

TIM TEUFEL
2B, No. 11
RR, 6'0", 175 lbs.
ML Svc: 3 years
Born: 7-7-58 in
  Greenwich, CT

1985 STATISTICS

AVG	G	AB	R	H	2B	3B	HR	RBI	BB	SO	SB
.260	138	434	58	113	24	3	10	50	48	70	4

CAREER STATISTICS

AVG	G	AB	R	H	2B	3B	HR	RBI	BB	SO	SB
.265	316	1080	145	286	61	7	27	117	126	151	5

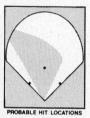

STRONG VS. RHP — STRONG VS. LHP — PROBABLE HIT LOCATIONS

main concern is not getting hurt. As a rookie, he established an obscure record for the fewest double plays by a second baseman playing at least 150 games. He didn't show much improvement last year.

His other problem is his lack of range. Teufel doesn't have a good first step and doesn't get to balls many second baseman would reach. The weakness became more obvious last September, when rookie Steve Lombardozzi was given a chance at Teufel's position and earned praise for his quickness. Teufel is more at home playing on grass than on turf.

OVERALL:

Killebrew: "Teufel has to take advantage of the things he does best and exploit them to the fullest. He must also work on his defensive shortcomings or else prepare himself for an uncertain future.

"One of the things that might help him is to try to use the whole field and not pull the ball so much."

PITCHING:

Frank Viola knows how close he came to winning 22 or 23 games last season, and he knows that there is only one person to blame for his shortcomings: Frank Viola.

His billing as one of the league's top lefthanders hasn't changed but he must now prove that he can tolerate a bad call or a bad defensive play without becoming unglued.

Unless he has learned his lesson, the pattern will remain the same. He loses his concentration and the opposition scores runs. He made a conscious effort to control his emotions and it began to pay off toward the end of the season.

Viola's arsenal is such that he can be overpowering. His fastball is usually clocked from 88-90 MPH and has good movement. He also throws a slider, a curve and a change-up, all of them with some degree of success. The fastball is his out pitch on a good day; his change-up serves that function when his fastball is off. He can use the slider to jam righthanded batters and the curve to throw them off stride.

His change-up fades away from righthanded batters, something he picked up from Johnny Podres, who was known for that pitch during his career with the Dodgers. Podres did a lot to help Viola in his transition from being a thrower to being more of a pitcher.

Viola won several games last season on days when he didn't have his best stuff, but he was able to adjust and pitch with his head instead of his arm. This knack of winning without his best pitches was not evident in earlier seasons and is a sign of pitching maturity.

When Viola is having problems, the source is usually a rushed delivery that keeps his pitches from staying low.

Viola is helped by pitching in the Metrodome because a team that loads its lineup with righthanded batters faces a

FRANK VIOLA
LHP, No. 16
LL, 6'4", 209 lbs.
ML Svc: 4 years
Born: 4-19-60 in
    Hempstead, NY

1985 STATISTICS												
W	L	ERA	G	GS	CG	SV	IP	H	R	ER	BB	SO
18	14	4.09	36	36	9	0	250.2	262	136	114	68	135

CAREER STATISTICS												
W	L	ERA	G	GS	CG	SV	IP	H	R	ER	BB	SO
47	51	4.34	128	127	26	0	844.1	881	455	407	271	495

much stiffer challenge hitting home runs to left and left-center in Minnesota. Ask Tom Brunansky about that.

FIELDING:

Viola has developed a quick move to first base that can freeze wary runners and pick off the unwary. He does the things that a pitcher should do to field his position but sometimes doesn't get down low enough for ground balls. He has no problems covering first.

OVERALL:

When Bert Blyleven joined the Twins, Viola no longer felt the pressure of being the staff ace. However, putting together the kind of season of which he is capable would turn him and Blyleven into one of baseball's premier lefty/righty combinations.

Killebrew: "Frank was the tough-luck pitcher of the staff last year and had a lot of balls booted behind him. In the past, it would have bothered him but he has learned from experience. He can be a big winner if he maintains his composure. This could be a tremendous year for him."

HITTING:

Utility infielders are usually known for their hot gloves and cold bats. But Ron Washington has always given the Twins a spray-hitting offensive threat coming off the bench--whether it be for a couple of at-bats or a couple of weeks. He has never been thrilled with the role but has not let that unhappiness affect his performance.

It took Washington 11 years to reach the majors and, because his future has been limited by age, the Twins have never given him the long look that younger prospects have gotten. They play, he sits. They slump, he plays-- for a spell, anyway.

While Washington will chase pitches outside the strike zone and is weak against breaking balls, he can also foul them off to wait for something that can be driven to the outfield. There seems to be a correlation between playing time and patience.

The best way to attack him is with pitches up and away. Most of his hits are from left-center to right-center and his more solid blows seem to go to the opposite field. He gets a fair number of topspin hits on artificial surfaces and can execute the hit-and-run.

BASERUNNING:

Washington has taken good care of himself and doesn't run like someone in his mid-30s. He gets out of the batter's box very well for a righthanded hitter and is not afraid to break up the double play. If the team continues its trend toward running more, it would provide Washington with another comfortable niche.

FIELDING:

A four-position player, Washington

RON WASHINGTON
SS, No. 38
RR, 5'11", 163 lbs.
ML Svc: 5 years
Born: 4-29-52 in
   New Orleans, LA

1985 STATISTICS											
AVG	G	AB	R	H	2B	3B	HR	RBI	BB	SO	SB
.274	69	135	24	37	6	4	1	14	8	15	5

CAREER STATISTICS											
AVG	G	AB	R	H	2B	3B	HR	RBI	BB	SO	SB
.267	413	1203	137	321	44	19	13	108	52	191	24

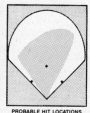

STRONG — VS. RHP   STRONG — VS. LHP   PROBABLE HIT LOCATIONS

probably does his best work at second base and will not embarrass himself at shortstop. He has a good aim and reasonably good range. When he makes errors, it's usually his hands that are at fault. Washington is also considered, for emergency purposes, as a reserve outfielder and catcher.

OVERALL:

Washington is among the most unappreciated of the Twins. He has always been ready to play anywhere he is asked. There will always be a market for a player like him.

Killebrew: "A pitcher must use all his pitches when Ron is at the plate because he is not an easy out by any means. He does a good job filling in."

DENNIS BURTT
RHP, No. 52
SR, 6'0", 187 lbs.
ML Svc: less than 1 year
Born: 11-29-57 in
   San Diego, CA

PITCHING, FIELDING:

Dennis Burtt has kicked around in the minors for 10 undistinguished seasons. But when he was called up for the final weeks of last season, he established himself as a candidate for the 1986 staff based on several strong outings. He pitched well both as a starter and in long relief and is the type of swing pitcher that the Twins could be looking for, someone who could fill those roles and not be considered a liability.

Burtt doesn't have any one pitch that's outstanding but mixes a complete arsenal that includes newly-improved breaking pitches. The Twins were impressed with the way that he listened to coaches and picked things up without having to be force-fed.

Otherwise, there are no traits that stick out. There's nothing strange about his delivery, he has an ordinary move to first and fields fairly well.

Burtt's success will be based on whether he can do all the little things that add up to success. After waiting so many years to get a chance, it does not seem likely that he will squander it by giving a less-than-total effort.

OVERALL:

The Twins looked at Burtt because there was dissatisfaction with several other pitchers. He made enough of that opportunity that he has a good chance to displace somebody and realize a dream deferred for so long that others would have given it up.

STEVE LOMBARDOZZI
2B, No. 49
RR, 6'0", 175 lbs.
ML Svc: less than 1 year
Born: 4-26-60 in
   Malden, MA

HITTING, BASERUNNING, FIELDING:

If Steve Lombardozzi hits for a good average, it will be considered a welcome surprise. He's one of those players who showed some power in the minors but will be expected to be a slap hitter in the majors, taking advantage of his speed and the artificial surface.

Lombardozzi has good speed and showed in 28 games in the majors that he can bunt and do other things to move runners ahead on the bases. He runs well but has never been much of a stolen base threat. If the Twins put more emphasis on that part of the game, however, he could emerge as another of their weapons.

His main contribution will come in the field. Lombardozzi is quick, and even though he is unaware of the proper positioning for each hitter, gets to balls that would seem destined for right field. He moves well in both directions and does a good job turning the DP (a definite Twins weakness over the last few seasons). His release is very quick.

Lombardozzi also can play third base and shortstop, skills that will come in handy if it's decided that he isn't yet ready to be a regular.

OVERALL:

It appeared that Lombardozzi established himself ahead of Tim Teufel as the front-runner to play second base this year. Whether he can live up to his September showing over a full season remains to be seen. He had a terrible spring training last year and can't afford to repeat that.

DAVE MEIER
OF, No. 7
RR, 6'0", 185 lbs.
ML Svc: 2 years
Born: 8-8-59 in
    Helena, MT

HITTING, BASERUNNING, FIELDING:

The Twins have expected more from Dave Meier than he has delivered and, at the same time, Meier has expected more of a chance than he's gotten. The resolution of that conflict might be a premature end to his career--and Meier may have to make use of his degree in economics from Stanford University.

Meier had only 104 at-bats last season and found himself the fifth outfielder on a team that used only four with any kind of regularity.

He is a line drive hitter whose timing appears to be off more often than not. He struggles at the plate. Barring an unexpected surge, Meier doesn't seem to have a much bigger place in his team's plans.

Meier is an average runner who appears to have more speed than he actually does. He tried to steal second base six times last year and was never successful.

Much of his playing time was as a late-inning defensive replacement for Mickey Hatcher or Randy Bush. Meier has a strong arm and good range and does especially well going back for balls. He does not look nearly as rusty in the field as he does at the plate.

OVERALL:

His .336 batting average at Toledo in 1983 hasn't translated into major league ability. Meier wants to believe he could make a bigger contribution but does not appear to be in line for the chance.

Killebrew: "Dave looks like an extra outfielder, a role player who can fill in as a left fielder."

NEW YORK YANKEES

Neil Allen regarded it as the break of his life when the St. Louis Cardinals shipped him to New York last July. The Cardinals had lost all faith in him and practically gave him away. Allen, for his part, compared his experience in St. Louis to doing time in the Missouri state penitentiary.

After enjoying success as the New York Mets' bullpen stopper (1980-82), Allen never really found his place in St. Louis. He was immediately under extreme pressure because the Cards gave up popular first baseman Keith Hernandez to get him. The heat got to Allen.

He started last season as the purported replacement for Bruce Sutter but failed miserably in that role. That was no surprise.

Allen has a limited repertoire, composed of a big, breaking curveball, an average slider, and an 87-90 MPH fastball that too often comes in straight and gets him in deep trouble. His curve can be outstanding--if he gets it over.

Allen claims that his lack of control was directly related to the Cardinals' loss of confidence in his ability, which in turn, caused him to lose confidence in himself. After the Yankees got him, he often threw much better in the bullpen than he did in games.

Allen has problems mixing in his change-up and needs to have that pitch working better this season. When he gets into jams (often they are of his own doing), he tries to power his way out. Sometimes that approach works. Sometimes it doesn't.

FIELDING:

Allen has an average move to first base. He is not distracted by baserunners, but he does pay them an unusual amount of attention. He finishes his delivery in good position to field the

NEIL ALLEN
RHP, No. 13
RR, 6'2", 190 lbs.
ML Svc: 7 years
Born: 1-24-58 in
      Kansas City, KS

1985 STATISTICS
W	L	ERA	G	GS	CG	SV	IP	H	R	ER	BB	SO
2	4	4.17	40	0	0	3	58.1	58	31	27	30	26

CAREER STATISTICS
W	L	ERA	G	GS	CG	SV	IP	H	R	ER	BB	SO
46	56	3.69	366	32	5	77	734.2	715	335	301	342	483

ball and wants the ball to be hit to him.

OVERALL:

Allen has been two different pitchers during his career: a stopper with the Mets, the last or next-to-last pitcher on the staff with St. Louis and the Yankees. His best work has been in relief, although the Yankees may try him as a starter.

Allen has been known as a pitcher whose psychological makeup is fragile. Lou Piniella may be the manager he has been looking for.

For Allen to be given a fighting chance, his role must be defined early, then he must be given a full opportunity to succeed or fail. If he is unsuccessful, he will have nobody to blame but himself.

Robinson: "His career has certainly leveled off. He is more of a thrower than a pitcher and you never know what he's going to do on a given day. Perhaps if he knows that he is wanted and he knows that his club is behind him, Neil will finally be able to fulfill his promise."

HITTING:

Time is catching up with Don Baylor. Last season, he hit a career-low .231, although he continued to be a dangerous hitter with men on base. He clouted 23 home runs and drove in 91 runs. His production was particularly impressive because for a chunk of the season he was platooned as designated hitter with lefthanded rookie slugger Dan Pasqua.

Baylor remains a pull hitter who feasts on fastballs and can yank out the low inside pitch. He generally bats in the cleanup spot and prides himself on driving in runs; over the past few seasons, he has lost quite a few homers to the vast dimensions of Yankee Stadium.

Baylor stands extremely close to the plate and holds the American League record for being hit by a pitch. He has taken one for the team 191 times and last season surpassed the AL mark held by Minnie Minoso.

BASERUNNING:

Baylor has suffered a noticeable loss of speed, but he compensates as best he can. He knows the strengths and weaknesses of each opposing outfielder's arm and will still take the extra base whenever possible. He has a burly build and is one of the hardest sliders in the game.

FIELDING:

Baylor is strictly a designated hitter. His arm never recovered from a serious injury he suffered playing football years ago. And he cannot cover enough ground to play the outfield--even if his arm was sound. He would be a liability even at first base.

DON BAYLOR
DH, No. 25
RR, 6'1", 210 lbs.
ML Svc: 14 years
Born: 6-28-49 in
   Austin, TX

1985 STATISTICS

AVG	G	AB	R	H	2B	3B	HR	RBI	BB	SO	SB
.231	142	477	70	110	24	1	23	91	52	90	0

CAREER STATISTICS

AVG	G	AB	R	H	2B	3B	HR	RBI	BB	SO	SB
.264	1912	6961	1048	1843	327	27	283	1085	664	855	277

  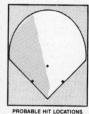

VS. RHP   VS. LHP   PROBABLE HIT LOCATIONS

OVERALL:

His skills are on the decline, but Baylor can still be a major offensive weapon in a lineup. He is a much better hitter against lefthanded pitching and may have to resign himself to platoon status. He is a tremendous leader in the clubhouse, a proven winner and a respected professional.

Robinson: "His average may be down, but Don is still doing the job he is supposed to do--hitting home runs and driving them in. Big RBI men like him are not easy to come by; his presence in the lineup can never be taken lightly."

PITCHING:

Rich Bordi performed quite well under difficult circumstances last season. He was used in short relief, in long relief and as a starter late in the season. He pitched well in the last two roles, although he was at his best in long relief, often completely shutting down the opposition while the Yankees worked their way back into the game.

Bordi has good control to go with a fastball in the 86-89 MPH range and an effective curve he throws often. He works the curve against lefthanded hitters and prefers to rely on a slider against righthanders. His sinkerball is another useful weapon, but he'll go to the slider and a hard forkball when he's in trouble.

Bordi did not do well last season when he entered in the late innings with the game on the line. One of his low points came when he failed to preserve a one-run lead in the 13th inning of a game in Oakland because he allowed a double to light-hitting Tony Phillips. The Yankees lost in 15. Then-manager Billy Martin blamed the damaging defeat on Bordi, who quickly became a forgotten man for a spell. Bordi showed his determination in his next outing, however. He started on an emergency basis and pitched extremely well, thus ingratiating himself again with Martin.

FIELDING:

Bordi is not always quick off the

RICH BORDI
RHP, No. 43
RR, 6'7", 220 lbs.
ML Svc: 3 years
Born: 4-18-59 in
    San Francisco, CA

1985 STATISTICS												
W	L	ERA	G	GS	CG	SV	IP	H	R	ER	BB	SO
6	8	3.21	51	3	0	2	98	95	41	35	29	64

CAREER STATISTICS												
W	L	ERA	G	GS	CG	SV	IP	H	R	ER	BB	SO
11	14	3.78	103	13	0	7	223.2	230	106	94	63	135

mound, but he doesn't hurt himself in the field. He tends to become preoccupied with baserunners who are a threat to steal and will throw over a lot.

OVERALL:

Bordi was an excellent acquisition for the Yankees. He had a very good year and can at least repeat that success if his role is made clear. He'll never be the staff ace, but he's the kind of pitcher you want on your club.

Robinson: "His biggest problem is that he has always been viewed as a borderline major league pitcher. He is still trying to shed that tag."

PITCHING:

Marty Bystrom would love to know what he could accomplish in one injury-free, pain-free season. But then, so would everyone else.

Bystrom's future as a major league pitcher is in question since major surgery was performed to repair the ulnar nerve in his right elbow in November 1984. His rehabilitation has progressed more quickly than the Yankees expected, and they placed him in the rotation at the end of July.

After being rocked in his first outing, Bystrom showed he still has some ability: he strung together three straight good performances. But then his arm became stiff and sore and, after some ineffective starts, the Yankees told him to take off the last few weeks of the season.

A healthy Bystrom would strengthen the Yankees' starting rotation. He has enough pitches to win: an 88-89 MPH fastball, an excellent curveball, an effective slider and a forkball. He will throw a breaking ball at any point in the count in any game situation, thereby making it difficult for hittters to figure out what his pattern is.

Bystrom was unhappy about being traded from Philadelphia to New York in June 1984 and said so. But he appreciates the patience the Yankees have shown with him (they gave the Phillies a good arm in Shane Rawley and are eager to justify that) and he knows time could be running out on his career.

FIELDING:

Bystrom is usually, though not always, in a good position to handle whatever comes his way. He has an average move to first base and needs to pay

MARTY BYSTROM
RHP, No. 50
RR, 6'5", 210 lbs.
ML Svc: 5 years
Born: 7-26-58 in
   Coral Gables, FL

1985 STATISTICS

W	L	ERA	G	GS	CG	SV	IP	H	R	ER	BB	SO
3	2	5.71	8	8	0	0	41	44	29	26	19	16

CAREER STATISTICS

W	L	ERA	G	GS	CG	SV	IP	H	R	ER	BB	SO
29	26	4.26	84	79	4	0	435.1	454	236	206	158	248

close attention to baserunners so he can throw the breaking ball with impunity. He is sometimes slow covering the bag on grounders to the right side.

OVERALL:

Bystrom has spent time on the disabled list every year since 1980, when he broke onto the National League scene in promising fashion, shutting out the Mets and winning five straight games to help the Philadelphia Phillies reach the World Series.

It's hard not to empathize with him. He has the ability to be one of the top winners on the ballclub. He knows it, and so does everyone in baseball.

If he is unable to pitch regularly this year, his career could end as one of unfulfilled promise.

Robinson: "What Marty needs more than anything is to get some innings in. He's got four pitches, and when they're working he can be really tough. He could definitely help the Yankees' rotation if he is healthy."

PITCHING:

Joe Cowley could blossom into a 20-game winner any time now. The key word here is "could." He has the ability-- but he does not have the maturity.

The Yankees signed Cowley out of the Atlanta organization as a minor league free agent in July 1984, and before long, began to wonder if he would ever reach his potential. Noting that Cowley spent eight aimless years in the Braves' minor leagues, many in the Yankees' front office feel he never will fulfill his promise: they shopped him heavily last winter.

Cowley is an inviting proposition because, despite a disregard for physical conditioning and a seemingly careless approach to the game, he is 21-8 in two seasons in New York.

He throws three-quarters and mixes an 87-89 MPH fastball with an excellent curveball and a big, dropping slider. He can use the curve as a strikeout pitch and has great confidence in it. He will come in with the curve in any situation.

When Cowley gets in trouble, it is often of his own doing. His lack of control, which is largely due to his lack of concentration, is his greatest weakness. It nearly caused the Yankees to return him to the minors in May.

Last season, Cowley incurred the wrath of owner George Steinbrenner by failing on two occasions. He was the losing pitcher when Tom Seaver gained his 300th victory at Yankee Stadium and he also suffered the defeat when Toronto eliminated the Yankees on the next-to-last day of the season.

Cowley's performance in the latter game was particularly disturbing because he reportedly ignored the scouting reports on certain batters. He was tagged for three home runs in 2 1/3 innings in

JOE COWLEY
RHP, No. 41
RR, 6'5", 210 lbs.
ML Svc: 3 years
Born: 8-15-58 in
Lexington, KY

1985 STATISTICS
W	L	ERA	G	GS	CG	SV	IP	H	R	ER	BB	SO
12	6	3.95	30	26	1	0	159.2	132	75	70	85	97

CAREER STATISTICS
W	L	ERA	G	GS	CG	SV	IP	H	R	ER	BB	SO
22	10	3.93	63	45	4	0	295.1	388	136	129	132	195

that game and yielded 29 homers on the season.

FIELDING:

Cowley has a good move to first. Runners can't take any liberties against him. Despite his lumbering appearance, he has surprising quickness off the mound and his sound delivery leaves him in perfect position to field.

OVERALL:

Although his winning percentage is an eye-opener, Cowley remains one of the game's most unpredictable pitchers. He managed only two victories after August 10th and failed to post a decision in seven straight starts during the stretch run. When the Yankees desperately needed him, he failed.

Robinson: "Cowley has not begun to realize his potential yet. He's just on the way up the ladder and is learning something every year. If a team is willing to deal with his casual approach and keeps giving him the ball every fourth or fifth day, he will do well."

PITCHING:

In 1984, the Yankees picked the Atlanta Braves' pockets almost clean. In January of that year, they signed Phil Niekro: in July, they signed Joe Cowley from Atlanta's minor league system; and in December, they pulled their last bump-and-roll, plucking Brian Fisher from their farm, leaving Rick Cerone to fend for himself.

In the minor leagues, Fisher was plagued by control problems and inconsistency. The Yankees, however, found a remarkably simple solution--they converted him into a reliever. Once Fisher had to throw strikes, he did. He thrived on pressure, posting 14 saves, and said he was able to relax more knowing he had made the majors. He formed a hard-to-match tandem with Dave Righetti.

Fisher, who comes three-quarters, is a two-pitch pitcher with an explosive fastball in the low-to-mid 90s and a hard, quick slider. The combination serves him much better in relief, where he rarely goes through the order more than once, than it did as a starter. The Yankees would like to see him develop another pitch--he has no off-speed stuff to speak of.

As it is, Fisher frequently overpowers batters. One of his most impressive developments last season was his ability to pitch well after a (rare) bad outing. Once he realized he could get out major league hitters, he stopped nibbling at the corners and started challenging everyone he faced. It wasn't much of a challenge for Fisher after that.

FIELDING:

Fisher rarely loses concentration on the batter by letting a baserunner dis-

BRIAN FISHER
RHP, No. 54
RR, 6'4", 210 lbs.
ML Svc: 1 year
Born: 3-18-62 in
    Honolulu, HI

1985 STATISTICS
W	L	ERA	G	GS	CG	SV	IP	H	R	ER	BB	SO
4	4	2.38	55	0	0	14	98.1	77	32	26	29	85

CAREER STATISTICS
W	L	ERA	G	GS	CG	SV	IP	H	R	ER	BB	SO
4	4	2.38	55	0	0	14	98.1	77	32	26	29	85

tract him. He doesn't throw to the base often, but makes up for it because the ball gets to the plate so quickly. His delivery leaves him in good position to field the ball and he is an aggressive fielder.

OVERALL:

The Yankees think Fisher can be another Goose Gossage for them. From all indications, that may, in fact, be the case (Fisher wears Goose's number, 54). Fisher was occasionally used in long relief last season, but is best as a short man. He is good enough to be given the role of stopper if the Yankees were to put Dave Righetti back into the rotation.

Robinson: "Brian is just learning how to pitch in the majors and has a great career to look forward to. Relieving brought out the best in him last season. He gets the ball over the plate consistently and goes right at the hitter with everything he's got."

HITTING:

As distinguished as his career has been, Ken Griffey's best days are over and his inconsistent play last year reflected that. His batting average the last two years, .273 and .274, is more than respectable. But together they represent his two lowest marks since he became a full-time player with the Cincinnati Reds in 1975.

Griffey has problems with both of his knees and requires careful handling to ensure he gets enough rest. There will be days when he is simply unable to perform to his high standards.

Griffey is intent on maintaining his lifetime .300 batting average and he is one of the most professional hitters around. There are times when he makes his craft look easy.

Griffey must be played straightaway. He is a low-ball hitter who is patient at the plate. Pitchers have their best success against him with the breaking ball. It's best to go high and away with the fastball.

Griffey can be jammed by fastballs, but if the pitch isn't in tight enough, Griffey will pull it out of the park. He is not noted for his power, but he can be dangerous, especially at home because Yankee Stadium's dimensions are well suited to his style of hitting.

BASERUNNING:

Griffey still moves fairly well on the bases, although he is not much of a threat to steal and he has definitely lost some zip. He is a smart baserunner and he is not afraid to slide hard when he has to.

FIELDING:

Griffey's play in left field last season was inconsistent. He made a few sensational catches, including a leaping grab over the wall in the left field corner at Yankee Stadium that preserved

KEN GRIFFEY
LF, No. 33
LL, 6'0", 200 lbs.
ML Svc: 13 years
Born: 4-10-50 in
Donora, PA

1985 STATISTICS

AVG	G	AB	R	H	2B	3B	HR	RBI	BB	SO	SB
.274	127	438	68	120	28	4	10	69	41	51	7

CAREER STATISTICS

AVG	G	AB	R	H	2B	3B	HR	RBI	BB	SO	SB
.300	1539	5636	914	1689	293	70	100	649	565	583	174

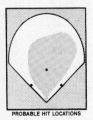

STRONG   STRONG

VS. RHP   VS. LHP   PROBABLE HIT LOCATIONS

a key victory over the Boston Red Sox in August. Griffey leaped high and was fully outstretched to make the grab. He fell, tumbled over backwards, and still held onto the ball. There were other times in the outfield, however, when he seemed slow and even absent-minded.

Griffey has an average arm. He can play first base in an emergency, but he prefers to leave the big first baseman's glove in the closet.

OVERALL:

Unhappy with his role in New York, Griffey asked the Yankees to trade him. His hefty contract and declining skills made a deal slow to come to pass, if indeed, it ever does.

Robinson: "Injuries are certainly taking their toll on Griffey; his playing time has been reduced because his production is down. His fragile knees make it unlikely that he will be able to play a full season in a full-time role."

PITCHING:

Last season, Ron Guidry proved just how special a pitcher he is by rebounding from the first losing record of his career to have a Cy Young-type season. Guidry led the American League in victories with a 22-6 record and would have added another Cy Young Award to the one he captured in 1978 if not for the brilliance of Kansas City's young sensation, Bret Saberhagen.

Nonetheless, Guidry is as proud of this latest accomplishment as he is of his probably-never-to-be-matched 25-3 record of 1978.

He realizes that the combination of his fastball (which is still formidable, in the 86-89 MPH range) and his big, dropping slider is no longer overpowering. And now he has adjusted, which was something he was unable to do in 1984.

Guidry has a very good change-up and is getting more comfortable with it all the time. He has learned to finesse his way and can scramble and win even when he is not at the top of his game.

He uses a three-quarters to overhand delivery and still describes himself as a power pitcher. It is an accurate label because, even though his Louisiana Lightning doesn't crackle any more, Guidry will still resort to the fastball in tight spots.

Last year, Guidry responded to the return of Billy Martin. The slightly built southpaw broke into the majors under Martin and responds well to the fiery former-former-former manager's complete confidence in him. Guidry's record is 84-25 under Martin, compared to 70-43 under other managers. It will be interesting to see how he reacts to rookie manager Lou Piniella.

FIELDING:

Guidry says he wouldn't trade his delivery for anyone else's, including

RON GUIDRY
LHP, No. 49
LL, 5'11", 157 lbs.
ML Svc: 11 years
Born: 8-28-50 in
   Lafayette, LA

1985 STATISTICS

W	L	ERA	G	GS	CG	SV	IP	H	R	ER	BB	SO
22	6	3.27	34	33	11	0	259	243	104	94	42	143

CAREER STATISTICS

W	L	ERA	G	GS	CG	SV	IP	H	R	ER	BB	SO
154	68	3.17	304	266	88	4	2027	1828	781	715	542	1510

Mets' sensation Dwight Gooden, because it has helped him become a Gold Glove winner. He is very quick and prides himself on his fielding. In fact, Guidry fulfilled a lifelong dream in 1983 by playing center field when the infamous Pine Tar Game with Kansas City was resumed.

He doesn't have a great move to first base, but he has an uncanny knack for sensing when to go over there. That earns him plenty of pickoffs.

OVERALL:

Guidry relishes the idea of being there when the team needs him--and they certainly could not have made their surprising pennant run last year without him. He may have difficulty providing an encore.

Robinson: "He has been able to adjust from being an overpowering pitcher to being one who can change speeds to get batters out. Not all power pitchers are able to do that. But age is creeping up on him. He worked 259 innings last season (his most since 1978), and his arm may show the strain this year."

HITTING:

Ron Hassey was an excellent acquisition for the Yankees--better than even they might have hoped. New York obtained him from the Chicago Cubs to back up regular catcher Butch Wynegar.

When Wynegar was struck by a foul ball in the on-deck circle in Baltimore in June and placed on the disabled list, Hassey responded well to the opportunity to catch full-time. By the time Wynegar recovered, Hassey had transformed a backup role into a platoon job.

Hassey is a low-ball pull hitter who will pounce on fastballs low and inside. He capitalized on Yankee Stadium's short right-field porch for a career-high 13 home runs last season.

If pitchers are going to show Hassey the fastball, they will fare best working him up and in, then going outside with the breaking ball. He makes most of his outs on breaking balls. Righthanders should go with the slider rather than the curveball against him.

Hassey has continued to work on his hitting and is open to suggestions. He now has a better understanding of what he wants to accomplish at the plate than ever before.

BASERUNNING:

Hassey has typical speed for a catcher, which is to say: none at all. He runs hard, but it takes him forever to get where he's going.

FIELDING:

Hassey is adequate defensively. Baserunners can't take liberties, but they can steal on him. He had all sorts of problems handling Phil Niekro's dancing

RON HASSEY
C, No. 12
LR, 6'2", 195 lbs.
ML Svc: 8 years
Born: 2-27-53 in
  Tucson, AZ

1985 STATISTICS
AVG	G	AB	R	H	2B	3B	HR	RBI	BB	SO	SB
.296	92	267	31	79	16	1	13	42	28	21	0

CAREER STATISTICS
AVG	G	AB	R	H	2B	3B	HR	RBI	BB	SO	SB
.275	680	1990	204	548	96	6	41	273	228	206	9

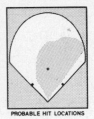

VS. RHP   VS. LHP   PROBABLE HIT LOCATIONS

knuckleball and took a beating during those games. His pitch selection is fine. He could play first base in an pinch, but not well.

OVERALL:

Hassey is not a full-time catcher, but his value is still high. He is willing to accept a lesser role if he has to and welcomes any opportunity that comes his way. He's a real pro.

Robinson: "The success Hassey enjoyed in 1985 has to help his confidence. He gave the Yankees a real boost when they needed it badly and forced everyone to view him in a new light."

RICKEY HENDERSON
CF, No. 24
RL, 5'10", 195 lbs.
ML Svc: 7 years
Born: 12-25-58 in
   Chicago, IL

HITTING:

Which Rickey Henderson will it be this year? The one who dominated the American League the first half of 1985 or the one who tailed off badly in the second half and seemed lackadaisical?

Attitude was an issue with Henderson before his trade to New York and it remains a legitimate concern. He was furious with the club when they docked him three days' pay for missing a double-header following the settlement of the players' strike, and he did not seem to play as hard after the fine was levied.

Still, the bottom line on Henderson's first season in pinstripes was outstanding. He scored 146 runs, batted .314, and established career highs in home runs (24) and RBIs (72). The latter is a tremendous total for a leadoff hitter and his power was a bit of a surprise.

He is a high-ball hitter who will take a rip at anything inside. He should be played straightaway. To have any chance against him, opposing pitchers must be able to throw the breaking ball for strikes, a difficult task because Henderson gets into his low crouch and moves about in the box, driving umpires to distraction. Pitchers must keep the fastball down and paint both sides of the plate with it. Henderson is improving every year as a hitter.

One of Henderson's few weaknesses is his poor bunting ability, which is surprising for a player with his speed. He hates the thought of bunting and shows little interest in it as another tool.

BASERUNNING:

No one does it better. You could look it up. Henderson has all the qualities essential to such larceny: he is fearless, loves playing cat-and-mouse with the pitcher and won't concede even half a step. He has tremendous acceleration—there may be some who are faster scoring from first, but no one kicks into gear as quickly as Henderson does.

With so much power in the Yankee lineup, there are times when it doesn't

1985 STATISTICS

AVG	G	AB	R	H	2B	3B	HR	RBI	BB	SO	SB
.314	143	547	146	172	28	5	24	72	99	65	80

CAREER STATISTICS

AVG	G	AB	R	H	2B	3B	HR	RBI	BB	SO	SB
.322	523	1866	446	601	83	23	41	223	372	270	329

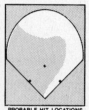

VS. RHP   VS. LHP   PROBABLE HIT LOCATIONS

make sense for Henderson to run; his 80 stolen bases last season will probably be his norm if everything else remains equal.

FIELDING:

Henderson made a good adjustment to center field last season. He covers lots of ground and his defense improved as the year progressed. He should be better this season. Last year, there were times when he was too tentative, usually when he was required to charge a sinking drive. He had some balls skip past him at crucial times and on several occasions he gambled unwisely.

OVERALL:

Robinson: "A motivated Henderson is one of the players who could lead the Yankees to a world championship. He will be watched closely to see how he performs for Lou Piniella. Rickey has all the talent in the world and is one of the game's most exciting players."

HITTING:

Here's how the 1985 season began for Don Mattingly: after missing the first part of spring training recovering from arthroscopic knee surgery, he stepped up to the plate in an exhibition game to face Montreal's Fred Breining. He looked over a ball from Breining, then hammered the following pitch out of the park. He doubled in his next at-bat before he was convinced to take the rest of the night off. That appearance set the tone for a sensational season that gained Mattingly the American League MVP award in only his second full big league season.

Mattingly is a high-ball hitter who can handle anything out over the plate. He goes to all fields well. He has no significant weaknesses as a hitter, although pitchers are better off trying to go after him with an off-speed pitch rather than the fastball.

Mattingly has already linked his name to Yankee legends. His 145 RBIs were the most by a Yankee since Joe DiMaggio's 155 in 1948. He was the first Yankee to lead the AL in RBIs since Roger Maris in 1961. He had 211 hits, making him the first Yankee to have consecutive 200-hit seasons since DiMaggio in 1936-37.

Mattingly's 35 home runs might be his most intriguing statistic, however. He was a 19th-round selection in the June 1979 free agent draft and never belted more than 10 home runs in a season as a minor leaguer, yet he has 58 home runs in his first two full major league seasons (compared to 37 in his five-year minor league career).

Mattingly credits his home run power to physical maturity and certain improvements in his weight shift at the plate: he doesn't readily discuss it, but Mattingly is concentrating on pulling the ball more and Yankee Stadium is a perfect place for him to do that.

BASERUNNING:

The only ingredient Mattingly lacks is speed, and if he could improve it, he would. But he compensates for it by be-

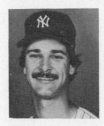

DON MATTINGLY
1B, No. 23
LL, 6'0", 175 lbs.
ML Svc: 3 years
Born: 4-20-61 in Evansville, IN

1985 STATISTICS

AVG	G	AB	R	H	2B	3B	HR	RBI	BB	SO	SB
.324	159	652	107	211	48	3	35	145	56	41	2

CAREER STATISTICS

AVG	G	AB	R	H	2B	3B	HR	RBI	BB	SO	SB
.323	410	1546	232	499	107	9	62	288	118	106	3

VS. RHP

VS. LHP

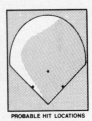

PROBABLE HIT LOCATIONS

ing alert to any opportunity.

FIELDING:

Mattingly's defense is overshadowed by his offense, but it shouldn't be. He topped AL first basemen in fielding percentage with a .995 mark. He is exceptional at turning the 3-6-3 double play, surpassed only by Keith Hernandez of the crosstown Mets. Mattingly is exceptional in his ability to track foul pops with his back to the plate.

OVERALL:

A batting champion in his first full season, an MVP in his second. What's next? Maybe the Triple Crown. It is early in his career and a lot can happen, but he seems to be a legend in the making.

Robinson: "He's eliminated any weaknesses he's had as a hitter. It's impossible to imagine him getting any better. Then again, he doesn't have to."

HITTING:

Bobby Meacham's first full big league season was somewhat disappointing considering the promise he showed when he broke in with the club in 1984.

The most negative aspect of the season was his hitting. He batted just .218, a precipitous 35-point drop from his rookie season, and seemed frequently overmatched at the plate.

Meacham is an anxious and impatient hitter who is not selective and, as a result, he constantly falls behind in the count. He is susceptible to breaking pitches and sees plenty of them. By mixing in the fastball away, pitchers can keep him off balance.

There is reason to think he can be a much better hitter, however, and that his .253 mark his rookie year was more indicative of his capabilities. A wrist injury hampered Meacham's swing for a significant portion of the season and because the Yankees lacked infield depth he never received sorely needed rest. A day off can work wonders, but Meacham never had the chance to sit back and reflect on what he was doing.

He showed that some hitting ability is there because he delivered in some clutch situations with men on base. He had only one home run, but finished with 47 RBIs.

BASERUNNING:

Meacham has excellent speed and is developing as a basestealing threat. But he is careless on the basepaths and is given to various blunders. His mistakes appear due to mental lapses, although he is a serious young man on and off the field. Last season, Meacham lost a wind-aided home run in Texas when he passed a teammate rounding first.

FIELDING:

Meacham improved considerably as a shortstop. He has excellent range and a strong arm. But he is careless sometimes

BOBBY MEACHAM
SS, No. 20
SR, 6'1", 180 lbs.
ML Svc: 2 years
Born: 8-25-60 in
Los Angeles, CA

1985 STATISTICS

AVG	G	AB	R	H	2B	3B	HR	RBI	BB	SO	SB
.218	156	481	70	105	16	2	1	47	54	102	25

CAREER STATISTICS

AVG	G	AB	R	H	2B	3B	HR	RBI	BB	SO	SB
.233	277	892	137	208	31	6	3	76	90	182	42

VS. RHP — STRONG VS. LHP — STRONG PROBABLE HIT LOCATIONS

on routine plays and committed 24 errors last season. Most were throwing errors. He would have had more if not for the work of Gold Glove first baseman Don Mattingly. But, with experience, Meacham can be an dependable shortstop.

OVERALL:

While there were negative aspects to Meacham's performance last year, he has done enough to maintain his position and keep alive hopes that he can develop into an above-average player. It is important for him to show improvement this season.

Robinson: "Meacham had a poor year at the plate last season, but I don't believe that he is that bad a hitter. He should settle in to hit .250 or better each year. He also needs to think about his fielding plays more--especially his throwing. If he took longer to set up, fewer throws would end up in the stands."

PITCHING:

The quality that distinguishes Joe Niekro from many other pitchers is his competitiveness under fire. In a big game, he's awfully tough to beat.

Niekro is a knuckleballer, but he does not rely on the darting, dancing pitch as much as his older and more famous brother, Phil. Because he has a more potent fastball, as well as a slider, Joe mastered the knuckleball later in life than Phil. Still, it proved to be his ticket to the majors and it is by far the weapon that serves him best.

Like any knuckleballer, Niekro will have control trouble. But even when he falls behind in the count, batters still have a problem: if he abandons the butterfly pitch, he can get outs with the fastball and slider.

FIELDING:

Niekro ranked as one of the best fielding pitchers in the National League and he rates as high in the junior circuit. He has aged gracefully and his reflexes are as sharp as ever.

He holds runners well and pays plenty of attention to them, knowing the knuckler can be a basestealer's delight and a catcher's nightmare.

OVERALL:

The Yankees showed their confidence in Niekro in big-game situations by mak-

JOE NIEKRO
RHP, No. 36
RR, 6'1", 195 lbs.
ML Svc: 20 years
Born: 11-7-44 in
  Martins Ferry, OH

1985 STATISTICS

W	L	ERA	G	GS	CG	SV	IP	H	R	ER	BB	SO
11	13	3.83	35	35	4	0	225.1	211	108	96	107	121

CAREER STATISTICS

W	L	ERA	G	GS	CG	SV	IP	H	R	ER	BB	SO
204	180	3.44	645	447	106	14	3300.1	3156	1422	1263	1126	1597

ing him a late-season acquisition. Unfortunately, he arrived too late to be a factor in their unsuccessful run for the pennant. They're counting on him this year for consistently strong performances. His pitching history shows he will deliver.

Robinson: "Joe had not had a losing season since 1976, and rarely misses a start. Each season, he pitches an extraordinary number of innings. The Yankees picked up a pitcher they can rely on, one who will always take the ball and who will win.

"He is 41 years old, yet he still should have several solid years left because the knuckleball does not put much of a strain on the arm."

PITCHING:

Phil Niekro can pitch forever--or maybe it just seems that way. He will be 47 years old on Opening Day this year, the oldest player in the major leagues, and he's still awfully hard to beat.

After being unceremoniously dumped by Atlanta, the team he served for more than twenty years, Niekro signed a two-year contract as a free agent with the Yanks in 1984. He has rewarded them by winning 32 games over the last two years.

The 300-game winner did it the way he has always done it--with a three-quarters delivery that he uses to toss knuckleball after floating knuckleball, the pitch his father taught him in the backyard as a boy. Batters still haven't caught up to it, though they are sometimes able to take advantage of his difficulty in controlling the pitch, a problem which has worsened in recent years and which caused him to be released by the Braves.

Batters now look over Niekro's first few pitches, hoping he will fall behind in the count and that they will be able to pounce on his slider (which is nothing special) or his fastball. Niekro likes to joke that they don't need a radar gun to clock his fastball. It is over the 55 MPH national speed limit--by just a bit.

Niekro proved his other pitches are at least respectable on the last day of the 1985 season. On the occasion of his 300th victory he threw only three knucklers--all to the last batter--in defeating Toronto. Not only did he reach the 300 plateau, he surpassed Satchel Paige as the oldest pitcher ever to throw a shutout.

A knuckleballer is by nature as unpredictable as his pitch. There are days when the floater is virtually unhittable and others when it barely moves at all. By now, Niekro has certainly learned to live with that--he is one of the game's

PHIL NIEKRO
RHP, No. 35
RR, 6'1", 193 lbs.
ML Svc: 21 years
Born: 4-1-39 in
Blaine, OH

1985 STATISTICS

W	L	ERA	G	GS	CG	SV	IP	H	R	ER	BB	SO
16	12	4.09	33	33	7	0	220	203	110	100	120	149

CAREER STATISTICS

W	L	ERA	G	GS	CG	SV	IP	H	R	ER	BB	SO
300	250	3.23	804	658	238	29	5054.2	4640	2112	1814	1648	3346

steadiest personalities--and so have the teams he's played for.

FIELDING:

Niekro, a winner of five Gold Gloves, has slipped in his fielding over the years, but his reflexes are still above average. He moves well when required to cover first and has a good, quick pick-off move that prevents runners from exploiting the knuckleball.

OVERALL:

Niekro's greatest asset is his fierce competitiveness. His desire to win is still evident even though he has reached the 300-win plateau. Niekro has never pitched in the World Series and he is driven by that goal. He has worn down physically each of the last two years, although he did not miss a turn last season.

Robinson: "If he gets the knuckleball over consistently and stays ahead of the batters, he can continue to win. But his age has to be a concern and I do think he has slipped a notch. Phil has been remarkably resilient for many, many years."

HITTING:

Mike Pagliarulo is coming along, but it is difficult to project when he will be ready to become an everyday player. He did well last year, which marked his first full major league season. He did not hit for average, but his power totals were impressive. This is a pattern Pagliarulo established in the minors and is reminiscent of former Yankee third baseman Graig Nettles.

Pagliarulo's development, however, must accelerate if he is to convince the Yankees that he is the answer at third base. Last season, there were times when he was overwhelmed by big league pitching. He has trouble handling the curveball and is vulnerable to a variety of breaking pitches. But if a pitcher sends him a fastball up and in, it is most likely gone. He is able to uncoil on the fastball low and inside. He is becoming a more selective, more patient hitter.

One of Pagliarulo's greatest problems is against southpaw pitching. In one game against Detroit last year, then-manager Billy Martin, completely frustrated because Pagliarulo had struck out twice against journeyman lefthander Mickey Mahler, ordered him to bat right-handed against Mahler in a critical situation. The puzzled Pagliarulo had not switch-hit since 1981. He struck out. (During the off-season, Pagliarulo was considering returning to switch-hitting to improve his chances of becoming a full-time player.)

BASERUNNING:

Pagliarulo's baserunning mistakes are those caused by overaggressiveness, but they are costly nonetheless. He has average speed and hasn't learned yet when to take the extra base and when to play it safe. There's an element of the fool-hardy gambler in him.

FIELDING:

Pagliarulo moves exceptionally well

MIKE PAGLIARULO
3B, No. 6
LR, 6'2", 195 lbs.
ML Svc: 2 years
Born: 3-15-60 in
Medford, MA

1985 STATISTICS

AVG	G	AB	R	H	2B	3B	HR	RBI	BB	SO	SB
.239	138	380	55	91	16	2	19	62	45	88	0

CAREER STATISTICS

AVG	G	AB	R	H	2B	3B	HR	RBI	BB	SO	SB
.239	205	581	79	139	31	5	26	96	60	134	0

  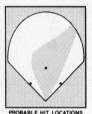

VS. RHP   VS. LHP   PROBABLE HIT LOCATIONS

to his left and right and already is among the finest third basemen in the league. Watching him everyday, you tend to get spoiled and overlook his range. He will make errors that have to be chalked up to inexperience.

He cost the Yankees a key game in Toronto by attempting an unassisted double play. He missed a lunging tag on the runner heading for third, then threw wildly to first, allowing the winning run to cross.

OVERALL:

Robinson: "Pagliarulo is on his way up. He is getting better every year and should be a regular before long. He has to stick with it and the organization has to stick with him. In time, his knowledge of the pitchers will increase and so will his confidence. He has a lot of talent."

HITTING:

Inside Dan Pasqua's 6'0", 205-pound frame are a lot of home runs begging to be set free. He is a strong pull hitter whose stroke is perfectly suited to Yankee Stadium.

In only his fourth season in professional baseball, Pasqua was named the International League's MVP. His sensational slugging forced the Yankees to bring him up the majors earlier than planned. Pasqua collected nine home runs and 25 RBIs in 60 games. There is a lot of potential here, to be sure, but he is however, far from being a polished major league hitter.

Pasqua is a typical home run hitter. He's extremely aggressive and streaky and strikes out often, a problem that has plagued him since the Yankees signed him as a third-round choice in the June 1982 free agent draft.

He loves to see fastballs. Throw it low and inside and it's a souvenir. It's best not to throw him any fastballs at all. The curveball is another story. Pasqua has great strength and anything off-speed will give him major problems. He is looking to crush every pitch. In his first Yankee start last season, he walloped two home runs into the upper deck in right field.

BASERUNNING:

Pasqua has average speed and doesn't take unnecessary chances. He plays hard all the time and isn't afraid to sacrifice his body when he has to.

FIELDING:

Pasqua is not noted for his fielding, but he is better than people think. What he loses in speed in the outfield he makes up for by getting a great jump on the ball. He has an average arm and rarely goes to the wrong base. He is more than adequate as an outfielder.

DAN PASQUA
OF, No. 21
LL, 6'0", 205 lbs.
ML Svc: 1 year
Born: 10-17-61 in
   Yonkers, NY

1985 STATISTICS
AVG	G	AB	R	H	2B	3B	HR	RBI	BB	SO	SB
.209	60	148	17	31	3	1	9	25	16	38	0

CAREER STATISTICS
AVG	G	AB	R	H	2B	3B	HR	RBI	BB	SO	SB
.209	60	148	17	31	3	1	9	25	16	38	0

VS. RHP

VS. LHP

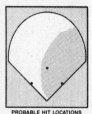
PROBABLE HIT LOCATIONS

OVERALL:

After last season, when other teams talked trade with the Yankees, Pasqua's name was always mentioned. The Yankees could do almost anything with him; they are notorious for either overlooking young talent or trading it away--which makes it impossible to project the club's plans for him.

Regardless, with his power, a team would do well to live with his strikeouts and give him the opportunity to see what he can do every day.

Robinson: "He surprised me by getting to the big leagues as quickly as he did. And then he performed better than anyone expected. He is a player on the rise who swings hard all the time and will pile up the strikeouts while he builds up his home run potential."

HITTING:

It is one of the surest things in baseball: Willie Randolph will have a good year. Not a great year, but a good one.

You can bank on him to hit right around .280. He never seems to change as a batter. Randolph's consistency is admirable because he avoids ruinous slumps.

Randolph must be played straightaway. What power he has is to right-center, but still, he will have a lot of trouble hitting the ball out of the park.

Randolph is a high-ball hitter who will make good contact on the high fastball. The way to set him up is with the slider and/or the low fastball. Then a pitcher can get him out with the slider; that's the pitch which gives him the most difficulty.

Randolph is a selective hitter and works a good number of walks. Because of that, the Yankees were planning to put him in the number two spot in the order behind speedster Rickey Henderson. But Randolph got off to a slow start last season and wound up in the bottom part of the order, a role which upset him. The Yankees might want to take another look at him in the number two slot.

BASERUNNING:

Randolph is a very good baserunner. He is a capable basestealer and must be treated as a threat. He is aggressive and opportunistic.

FIELDING:

There is only one field position over which no Big Apple argument has raged since 1975: second base. The keystone corner has belonged to Willie Randolph since the Yankees acquired him from Pittsburgh in 1975. He has been, in fact, the anchor of the infield since that time.

WILLIE RANDOLPH
2B, No. 30
RR, 5'11", 166 lbs.
ML Svc: 11 years
Born: 7-6-54 in
Holly Hill, SC

1985 STATISTICS

AVG	G	AB	R	H	2B	3B	HR	RBI	BB	SO	SB
.276	143	497	75	137	21	2	5	40	85	39	16

CAREER STATISTICS

AVG	G	AB	R	H	2B	3B	HR	RBI	BB	SO	SB
.274	1353	5019	821	1375	201	53	34	401	780	398	218

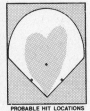

VS. RHP VS. LHP PROBABLE HIT LOCATIONS

He is one of the steadiest second basemen in the league. Randolph is reliable, consistent and steady. He has good, but not spectacular, range; he turns the double play well and hangs in as tough as anyone on the pivot. His throws are always accurate, his head is always in the game. Randolph simply does the job every time he steps onto the field.

OVERALL:

Randolph is a quiet leader who is proud of being a New York Yankee. His professionalism and devotion to a job done well should give cause for others more vocal in their assertion of "Yankee pride" to reassess its definition.

Robinson: "He just goes out there and gives it his best at the plate and in the field. To his everlasting credit, he has managed to stay out of the storm of the Yankee madness over the years."

PITCHING:

When Dennis Rasmussen broke into the big leagues with the Yankees two years ago, his future seemed bright. Now, however, his future is uncertain, at best.

Rasmussen spent much of last season back in the minors after an extremely disappointing start. The situation in New York deteriorated quickly for him when Billy Martin replaced Yogi Berra as manager just 16 games into the season.

Rasmussen was not Martin's kind of pitcher. His unwillingness to throw inside galled the manager, who felt that Rasmussen did not have the makeup to pitch at the major league level. Martin gave Rasmussen several quick hooks. The lefthander's confidence was badly damaged and his pitching went from bad to worse.

Rasmussen throws three-quarters. He does not throw hard at all for a man his size. His fastball is in the 84-88 MPH range. His change-up is not always effective, and that is a pitch he turns to when he slips behind in the count.

Rasmussen's most dependable tool is a big, slow-breaking curveball that he can throw for strikes and strikeouts. But he hasn't shown that his repertoire is large enough to win consistently. He might need another pitch.

FIELDING:

Although Rasmussen completes his delivery in an adequate position to field,

DENNIS RASMUSSEN
LHP, No. 45
LL, 6'7", 225 lbs.
ML Svc: 1 year plus
Born: 4-18-59 in
　　Los Angeles, CA

1985 STATISTICS

W	L	ERA	G	GS	CG	SV	IP	H	R	ER	BB	SO
3	5	3.98	22	16	2	0	101.2	97	56	45	42	63

CAREER STATISTICS

W	L	ERA	G	GS	CG	SV	IP	H	R	ER	BB	SO
12	11	4.21	50	41	3	0	263	234	140	123	110	186

he often does not appear ready for what might come his way. Baserunners are unable to capitalize on his big, breaking curve because he will throw over to first base often. He has one of the best pickoff moves on the club and regularly surprises runners.

OVERALL:

Rasmussen has a great deal to prove to an organization that twice traded for him but has since lost faith. This could be a pivotal season for Rasmussen.

Robinson: "He needs experience more than anything and may have to prove himself by filling several roles in order to stay in the big leagues."

PITCHING:

The melodrama surrounding the use of Dave Righetti has been one of the most interesting sagas at Yankee Stadium for two seasons. Central to the plot is the young man who was the American League's 1981 Rookie of the Year, a talented pitcher, who, if he had not already pitched his way into the hearts of Yankee fans, became a hero the day he threw a no-hitter against the Boston Red Sox on a steamy July 4th afternoon in 1983.

The following season, Goose Gossage flew the coop and the Yankees found themselves without a bullpen stopper. Meanwhile, backstage, Yankees' management decided to extend the talents of Righetti and give him a new role as the number one man in the bullpen. He responded by becoming one of the best short men in the game. He saved 31 of 40 opportunities, which put him fourth in the AL that season in saves and number three on the Yankee single-season list (behind Sparky Lyle, 35 in 1972 and the Goose, 33 in 1980). Righetti has saved 60 games in two years.

The problem is that the Yankees need starting pitching and that Righetti has the pitches to handle either job well. He comes overhand to three-quarters with an 89-92 MPH fastball that really explodes as it nears the plate. He has a sharp-breaking curveball and a good hard slider. He will have an occasional streak of wildness, which causes him to come in with a pitch that can hurt him. But most of the damage done against him is from bloop hits.

FIELDING:

Because Righetti pitches with such power, he often is in poor position to field. He relies instead on his great athletic ability and can make behind-the-back grabs and even some through his

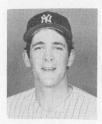

DAVE RIGHETTI
LHP, No. 19
LL, 6'3", 198 lbs.
ML Svc: 5 years
Born: 11-29-58 in
San Jose, CA

1985 STATISTICS

W	L	ERA	G	GS	CG	SV	IP	H	R	ER	BB	SO
12	7	2.78	74	0	0	29	107	96	36	33	45	92

CAREER STATISTICS

W	L	ERA	G	GS	CG	SV	IP	H	R	ER	BB	SO
50	36	3.09	220	76	13	61	725.1	609	281	249	305	616

legs. He is sometimes remiss in covering first base.

Righetti likes to surprise runners by going to first with a little snap throw.

OVERALL:

As last season began, Righetti seemed both mentally and physically settled into the bullpen. Enter stage right: Billy Martin.

The first time he turned to Righetti, Martin asked him for a very un-short-man-like four innings. Martin got his four as well as the victory, but the manager's requests for long appearances took its toll on Righetti, and the confused young pitcher plunged into a month-long slump in May.

With adequate rest, Righetti can be overpowering. He made 74 appearances and labored 107 innings in 1985, a workload that might be too heavy even for his powerful left arm.

Robinson: "Dave has been a great reliever but the back-and-forth speculation of returning to the rotation hurts him. I would prefer to see him start because that's where his heart is.

"But no matter how the team uses him, it's almost impossible to spot any weaknesses in his pitching."

PITCHING:

Some pitchers go through their entire major league careers without ever learning how to pitch. For a while, it appeared as though that would be the case with Bob Shirley, but not any longer. Since he first signed with the Yankees in 1982, Shirley has matured and his pitching has vastly improved.

Shirley used to work as if he was a strikeout pitcher, which was difficult considering the fact that his typical fastball is in the mid-80s. But now he relies on control and changing speeds. He has a good curveball and a short, snappy slider and he recently began to mix in his change-up at the most opportune times.

None of his pitches is outstanding, but he has come to understand how to use what he has.

Shirley can be invaluable to a pitching staff because he can fill any role (the Yankees can call on him as a short reliever, a long reliever and as a spot starter) and he has a tireless arm. His teammates joke that you can just wind up him up and send him out.

Shirley's ability to fill a variety of roles made it even more confusing when then-manager Billy Martin all but forgot about him last May. Remembering how poorly Shirley had pitched for him during Billy III, Martin called on him for only one inning in the entire month.

At the urging of his coaches, Martin finally gave Shirley a chance. Shirley was so impressive that suddenly Martin couldn't wind him up and send him out often enough.

Shirley has proved to be especially effective in spacious Yankee Stadium. Last season, he was 5-1 there with a 1.86 ERA.

BOB SHIRLEY
LHP, No. 29
RL, 6'1", 185 lbs.
ML Svc: 9 years
Born: 6-25-54 in
   Oklahoma City, OK

1985 STATISTICS

W	L	ERA	G	GS	CG	SV	IP	H	R	ER	BB	SO
5	5	2.64	48	8	2	2	109	103	34	32	26	55

CAREER STATISTICS

W	L	ERA	G	GS	CG	SV	IP	H	R	ER	BB	SO
66	90	3.64	380	155	16	15	1285	1278	597	520	481	713

FIELDING:

Shirley's delivery leaves him in a good position to field. He has an average move to first. Because of his confidence in his control, he is not afraid to pitch out.

OVERALL:

Shirley is one of the game's delightful characters. With turbulence all around, he remains carefree. He can be a positive, albeit sometimes unsettling, influence in the clubhouse.

Last season, pitching coach Jeff Torborg got a call in the bullpen ordering him to warm up Shirley. Torborg looked around frantically for a minute-- then realized that Shirley was already in the game. Laughing in the dugout, of course, was Shirley.

Robinson: "Bob stays ready all the time and has begun to get bigger and bigger strikeouts since he abandoned thoughts of power pitching in favor of changing speeds. He is going to win as long as he is able to pitch to locations."

PITCHING:

Ed Whitson is a power pitcher of average ability who was in the right place at the right time--sort of. He became available when there happened to be very few starting pitchers on the market; his five-year, $4.4 million contract put a tremendous burden on him and raised expectations that were never realistic.

Whitson never had a honeymoon with New York and never got near the altar with then-manager Billy Martin. Whitson dropped six of his first seven decisions and never really got on track. He was hit hard most of the year and Martin made matters worse with some rough handling of him.

Whitson is a fierce competitor and is a good enough pitcher to be of service in the right environment. He uses a three-quarters delivery to fire a quick, nasty slider and an 87-90 MPH fastball which is complemented by a palmball. (He developed the palmball in 1983 when he cut his finger while opening a soda can and did not want to miss a start.)

Still, he resorts to power when he is in trouble and never beats himself with wildness. But Whitson's inability to perform last season prompted hate mail to pour into Yankee Stadium, and the abuse he suffered at the hands of fans reminded one what a "Bronx cheer" could really mean.

The nightmare culminated in an ugly brawl between Martin and Whitson in a hotel in Baltimore. The late-September fight ended in a parking lot, with the pitcher slamming the manager to the pavement as police arrived. It left Martin with a broken right arm and cracked ribs. The Yankees, fearing fan backlash, suggested Whitson skip his

ED WHITSON
RHP, No. 38
RR, 6'3", 195 lbs.
ML Svc: 8 years
Born: 5-19-55 in
   Johnson City, TN

1985 STATISTICS

W	L	ERA	G	GS	CG	SV	IP	H	R	ER	BB	SO
10	8	4.88	30	30	2	0	158.2	201	100	86	43	89

CAREER STATISTICS

W	L	ERA	G	GS	CG	SV	IP	H	R	ER	BB	SO
63	64	3.77	273	173	16	8	1183	1196	557	495	417	656

last scheduled start at Yankee Stadium and he agreed.

FIELDING:

Whitson is an average fielder, although he is an aggressive one. He has a quick move to first and makes good use of it.

OVERALL:

It will be difficult for Whitson to put 1985 behind him. Aside from his troubles off the field, he was a confused pitcher. Sometimes he would think throwing the palmball more often was the answer to his problem, but other times he would feel that he should go with power. This season will be especially significant for him.

Robinson: "Until he developed the palmball, Whitson was just a journeyman pitcher. It is his key pitch and the one he should use in order to have a good chance at being a winning pitcher."

HITTING:

Dave Winfield is one of baseball's superstars. His enormous contract has never affected his play and he is an exceptional performer in every area.

Yet, for no apparent reason, he has never been adopted by New York fans the way Reggie Jackson was or even the way Don Mattingly is embraced now. And owner George Steinbrenner made matters worse last season by calling him "Mr. May" and saying he needed Jackson, "Mr. October," back in the Bronx. It was unjust treatment for a player who has driven in 100 or more runs four consecutive years.

Outfielders generally shade Winfield to left field, but he hits with power to all fields. And when he's on a tear, he can be nearly impossible to get out.

Winfield does everything aggressively, which can hurt him at the plate, where he is not as selective as he should be. Patience is not one of his virtues.

Pitchers constantly bust him inside with fastballs because if he gets his long arms outstretched, it's trouble. Once a pitcher has gone inside on him, he can get Winfield out with off-speed stuff pitched away.

Winfield can do whatever is required of him. In 1982, when the Yankees needed power, he responded with a career-high 37 home runs. In 1984, he went for average, dueling Mattingly for the AL batting championship through the last day of the season, and finished that year at .340.

BASERUNNING:

Once Winfield gets started, he chews up ground with tremendous strides. He is a sight to behold when he is in gear. He has a remarkable sense for the right time to take the extra base. Gambles that seem foolhardy when he takes off become great plays when the throw is off

DAVE WINFIELD
RF, No. 31
RR, 6'6", 220 lbs.
ML Svc: 13 years
Born: 1-3-51 in
St. Paul, MN

1985 STATISTICS

AVG	G	AB	R	H	2B	3B	HR	RBI	BB	SO	SB
.275	155	633	105	174	34	6	26	114	52	96	19

CAREER STATISTICS

AVG	G	AB	R	H	2B	3B	HR	RBI	BB	SO	SB
.288	1810	6722	1045	1935	322	66	281	1130	714	934	189

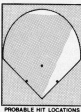

target or when he deftly slides around the tag. He can steal a base if needed.

FIELDING:

Winfield moves exceptionally well in every direction. Anything he can get to he will catch. He has a strong arm, but he goes to the wrong base too frequently. He likes to show off his arm.

OVERALL:

Winfield is a perennial All-Star who is not always appreciated. He will not live down his 1-for-22 disaster in the 1981 World Series against Los Angeles until he leads the club into another Series and sparkles there.

Robinson: "He is an outstanding player. No one plays harder and he has good instincts. He cannot play any better."

HITTING:

Butch Wynegar was struck in the head by a foul ball last June while kneeling in the on-deck circle in Baltimore. The injury forced him on the disabled list, and when he returned, he had lost his momentum and couldn't regain his stroke.

Wynegar's .223 batting average last season was his second lowest mark since he broke in with Minnesota in 1976. By the end of the season, he had lost his status as a regular and was platooned with Ron Hassey. He was a free agent this past winter, but teams seemed to be wary to sign Wynegar too quickly.

A switch-hitter, Wynegar is a high-ball hitter who likes the fastball on the inside part of the plate. When he is pitched a fastball, it should be low. Pitchers can send him plenty of breaking balls; Wynegar can be struck out by a curveball.

BASERUNNING:

On the bases, Wynegar is a typical lumbering catcher, or perhaps, he is even slower than most catchers. He runs the bases cautiously.

FIELDING:

Wynegar is a solid big league catcher and does everything well. He is an adept game caller, flags down a lot of potential wild pitches and throws out a good proportion of baserunners. He was most impressive in the way he handled knuckleballer Phil Niekro. Yankee pitching coach Jeff Torborg said he never saw

BUTCH WYNEGAR
C, No. 27
SR, 6'0", 192 lbs.
ML Svc: 10 years
Born: 3-14-56 in
York, PA

1985 STATISTICS

AVG	G	AB	R	H	2B	3B	HR	RBI	BB	SO	SB
.223	102	309	27	69	15	0	5	32	64	43	0

CAREER STATISTICS

AVG	G	AB	R	H	2B	3B	HR	RBI	BB	SO	SB
.258	1282	3989	467	1029	166	13	57	464	579	387	10

VS. RHP   VS. LHP   PROBABLE HIT LOCATIONS

anyone adjust to catching the knuckler so quickly or handle it so smoothly.

OVERALL:

Last season was extremely disappointing for Wynegar--especially since he was on the verge of free agency. His career has been marred by injury and illness. He needs a strong season to re-establish himself.

Robinson: "Butch is a pro and I do not think that he'll have too much trouble bouncing back this season. He is a steady catcher his team can rely on."

MIKE ARMSTRONG
RHP, No. 36
RR, 6'3", 205 lbs.
ML Svc: 6 years
Born: 3-7-54 in
    Glen Cove, NY

PITCHING, FIELDING:

Mike Armstrong is in the unenviable position of having to prove himself again as a major league pitcher. Last season was a nightmare for him. He was demoted to the minors when the Yankees broke camp, and he shuttled back and forth all season (he probably would not have pitched for the parent club at all if the Yankees hadn't been attempting to stir trade talks).

Armstrong approaches the plate at three-quarters and sometimes drops to a sidearm delivery with a hard-to-figure, herky-jerky motion. He is a power pitch-er with a sinking fastball and a hard slider. When he has to reach back, batters will see the sinking fastball. He also has a forkball and a very ordinary change-up.

Armstrong does not finish in good position to field the ball and prefers to let his infielders take over. He has an adequate pickoff move and makes good use of it.

OVERALL:

Armstrong's problems aren't entirely his fault. His career soured when he developed elbow problems that caused him to be disabled for almost two months in 1984. The Yankees have treated him shabbily since then and Billy Martin openly ridiculed him when he was manager.

Robinson: "His career has slipped considerably and he needs a change of scenery badly. He has done it before and he can be effective if he gets the opportunity to pitch."

DALE BERRA
3B, No. 2
RR, 6'0", 192 lbs.
ML Svc: 9 years
Born: 12-13-56 in
    Ridgewood, NJ

HITTING, BASERUNNING, FIELDING:

The acquisition of Dale Berra by the Yankees in December 1985 generated publicity for the club, but little else. His famous father was dumped as manager 16 games into the season and Dale was a forgotten reserve by the All-Star break.

Berra was an adequate run producer as the Pittsburgh Pirates' regular shortstop (1982-84), but he never adapted to the platoon system.

Berra looks for the high ball inside and tends to pull everything. He is a relatively easy out if pitchers keep everything low and throw him a steady stream of breaking balls.

Berra is one of the worst baserunners around and makes repeated mental errors. A low point of the season for him came when Chicago White Sox catcher Carlton Fisk tagged out shortstop Bobby Meacham on a play at the plate, then tagged Berra who was a couple of steps behind Meacham.

Berra is an erratic fielder. Although he feels third base is his best position and was pleased to move there with the Yankees, very few plays were routine for him. He had more than his share of boots and bobbles and erratic throws.

OVERALL:

At his best, Berra is a marginal major league ballplayer whose chief hope is expansion. At the least, Berra needs a change of scenery. His 1985 season was one he would likely choose to forget.

SCOTT BRADLEY
C/OF, No. 34
LR, 5'11", 185 lbs.
ML Svc: 1 year plus
Born: 3-22-60 in
    Essex Falls, NJ

HITTING, FIELDING, BASERUNNING:

The 1985 season was a lost one for Scott Bradley. He severely injured the little finger on his right hand and was placed on the disabled list on April 24. After a long recovery, he was sent to Columbus for further rehabilitation. He seemed to be forgotten there and didn't return to the Yankees until September.

Bradley didn't show it last year, but he is a formidable hitter. He has no power, but he can spray the ball to all fields. Although he rarely strikes out, he is vulnerable to off-speed stuff. It is best to get him out with the curve. He needs to play regularly to hit.

He is not a fast baserunner but remains alert on the basepaths.

Bradley is an outfielder, catcher, and even an infielder in emergencies. The lack of a set position and the fact he is average at best wherever he plays is holding him back.

OVERALL:

Bradley does not seem to fit into the Yankees' plans. He is an eager, aggressive player who will do anything asked of him to stay in the majors. He has the credentials--he was the International League's Most Valuable Player in 1984-- to get a good shot with some club.

HENRY COTTO
OF, No. 46
RR, 6'2", 178 lbs.
ML Svc: 1 year plus
Born: 1-5-61 in
    the Bronx, NY

HITTING, BASERUNNING, FIELDING:

A freak accident was part of a disappointing 1985 for Henry Cotto. He was cleaning his ears in the dugout in May and pierced an eardrum.

Cotto was forced onto the disabled list, then spent time in Triple-A, where he was not particularly impressive.

He is a dead pull hitter who has trouble with most everything except the belt-high fastball. He is vulnerable to the breaking ball outside--he will try to pull it--and he will chase balls out of the strike zone.

Cotto has blazing speed, but he did not show it off last year. With further development, he can be a player who makes things happen.

As an outfielder, Cotto gets excellent marks. He has a good, strong arm and can make difficult plays look routine because he covers ground so well.

OVERALL:

At this point, Cotto is a borderline major league player. He can help a team on a part-time basis. He needs to play to develop and it is doubtful he will get that opportunity in New York.

BILLY SAMPLE
OF, No. 11
RR, 5'9", 175 lbs.
ML Svc: 7 years
Born: 4-2-55 in
Roanoke, VA

HITTING, BASERUNNING, FIELDING:

Billy Sample appeared in only 59 games last season with the Yankees. He is an average player in all respects and it unlikely that he will ever develop into anything more than a part-time player.

He is a high-ball pull hitter who can turn on anything inside. Pitchers should keep the fastball low and away to him and go with a steady stream of curves.

Sample has good speed and could be a good stolen-base man. He would be effective as a pinch-runner.

As a fielder, he can look awkward--his style resembles that of a dog catching a frisbee. Even routine catches do not look routine for him and he exercises poor judgment in the field. He is better at coming in on a ball than going back.

OVERALL:

Sample can be a valuable reserve, but he is to be regarded strictly as a part-time player. As such, he can do a lot of things for a team.

ANDRE ROBERTSON
SS, No. 18
RR, 5'10", 162 lbs.
ML Svc: 4 years
Born: 10-2-57 in
Orange, TX

HITTING, FIELDING, BASERUNNING:

Andre Robertson, once a promising young player, hasn't been nearly the same since a tragic car accident in August 1983. A knee injury that required arthroscopic surgery last spring made matters worse.

Robertson hit much better than expected last year and displaced Dale Berra as the righthanded half of the Yankees' platoon at third base with Mike Pagliarulo. He made good contact consistently. He's not a power hitter, but he will drive some balls with surprising strength.

Robertson is a liability on the basepaths. He is slow and he does not always make good decisions. He really labors out there.

Robertson's range is too limited for him to play shortstop any more, even as a backup. He is uncomfortable at third and had more than his share of boots and bobbles. His arm is not what it was--his throws are erratic.

OVERALL:

Robertson may face a constant struggle to stay in the major leagues. There are plenty of players around who can do the things he can do. Sadly, this was not always the case with Robertson.

OAKLAND A'S

PITCHING:

Keith Atherton has been trying to wade his way through the big leagues with just one pitch: a fastball. It's a respectable fastball, clocked at around 88 MPH, but it is not a particularly overpowering one. That's why Atherton, who gave up 17 homers in 56 appearances last year, is fighting for his professional life.

The A's have worked with Atherton on developing a slider and change-up, but when it comes to a crisis--and Atherton saw a lot of them while bailing out the Oakland starters--he inevitably turns to the fastball.

He throws it overhand, occasionally three-quarters, and it can be very tough on righthanded hitters. But it has only average movement, which invites the hitters to step right in. Until Atherton develops command of the slider (instead of hanging it in the strike zone), he will continue to struggle.

Atherton seems firmly set in the role of middle reliever, the type who comes in for an inning or so to restore order or set up the stopper. He had a very effective rookie season in 1983, but the league seemed to catch up with him in 1984. Entering the 1986 season, opposing players are on intimate terms with him: he has become known as "Boom-Boom," for serving up so many home-run pitches.

There are times when he spots his fastball so effectively on the corners that hitters have trouble driving it. Those times come far too infrequently.

KEITH ATHERTON
RHP, No. 55
RR, 6'4", 200 lbs.
ML Svc: 3 years
Born: 2-19-59 in
  Matthews, VA

1985 STATISTICS												
W	L	ERA	G	GS	CG	SV	IP	H	R	ER	BB	SO
4	7	4.30	56	0	0	3	104.2	89	51	50	42	77
CAREER STATISTICS												
W	L	ERA	G	GS	CG	SV	IP	H	R	ER	BB	SO
13	18	3.93	142	0	0	9	277	252	124	121	103	175

FIELDING:

Atherton has only an average move to first base, but he has a quick delivery to the plate. He makes pickoff throws to first base only when he feels he has to; he'd prefer to go after the hitter.

A good athlete, he fields his position well and seldom hurts his cause.

OVERALL:

Killebrew: "The fastball is it with this guy. From what I've seen, it does not look as if he's going to get any better than he is right now. Starting is definitely out for him. He needs to come up with a couple of breaking pitches, maybe use the sidearm delivery a little more often. He can't get by with one pitch."

HITTING:

The forgotten man in San Francisco, Dusty Baker enjoyed a career revival in Oakland. By mid-July last year, he was a .300 hitter with 11 homers in a part-time role. The A's wisely decided to use him every day. Baker kept his average over .300 until mid-August, when a severely jammed thumb took away almost all of his power. He didn't have a single home run after the first week of August.

Baker, who refers to himself as "Dr. Scald," can still burn anyone's fastball. He is a first-ball, fastball hitter who likes the ball over the plate, and he inevitably tries to pull it. He has trouble with fastballs down and in, and while he's a good mistake hitter who tees off on the hanging curve, Baker is susceptible to the good breaking pitch away. Seldom, if ever, will he try to bunt.

A career National Leaguer, he adapted remarkably well to his new league. In only his second at-bat against Kansas City's relief ace, Dan Quisenberry, Baker hit a three-run, game-winning home run that gave the A's their best moment of the season. By the All-Star break, he had already homered in eight of the league's 14 parks, despite his part-time status. It appears his future will be as a DH.

BASERUNNING:

Baker is still a hustling baserunner, but he doesn't run nearly as well as he did in his glory years with the Dodgers. He is average in taking leads and sliding into second on the double play. He will steal a base only if it's given to him.

FIELDING:

Baker is not the defensive player he

DUSTY BAKER
OF, No. 12
RR, 6'2", 200 lbs.
ML Svc: 14 years
Born: 6-15-49 in
Riverside, CA

1985 STATISTICS

AVG	G	AB	R	H	2B	3B	HR	RBI	BB	SO	SB
.268	111	343	48	92	15	1	14	52	49	58	2

CAREER STATISTICS

AVG	G	AB	R	H	2B	3B	HR	RBI	BB	SO	SB
.280	1956	6875	939	1923	312	23	238	994	734	900	137

  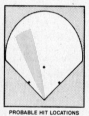

VS. RHP   VS. LHP   PROBABLE HIT LOCATIONS

once was. Earlier in his career, he was considered to be the best left fielder in baseball. He was given a long look in left field by the A's last season, but he became a defensive risk because of his limited range.

Still intact are his good hands and strong arm. Opposing baserunners tried to gamble on Baker's arm last year, and they often got nailed.

OVERALL:

Killebrew: "In his first year in the American League, he looked like a really tough hitter. Dusty knows how to swing the bat. I'd say that his overall game is leveling off, but if he can keep himself healthy, he will contribute offensively for several more seasons."

PITCHING:

By early August 1985, Tim Birtsas was a candidate for Rookie Pitcher of the Year. One of the prized prospects acquired in the Rickey Henderson trade with the Yankees, Birtsas was 9-2 with a 3.23 ERA. But then came two unfortunate developments: Birtsas developed a tired arm, and the league caught up with him. It is difficult to know what to project for him in 1986.

Physically, he is too heavy for a major league athlete. Birtsas is a slow, laborious worker who tends to run a three-ball count on every hitter. His best assets are his fastball, which arrives a little quicker (88 MPH) than it seems, and a curveball he uses at two different speeds. He also has a straight change-up that he masks well, but control is a constant problem for him. Although he has a knack for pitching out of jams, it's tough to make a living in the big leagues that way. When he is on, Birtsas uses his fastball to run in against lefthanders and tail away from righthanders. Although he throws over-the-top, he will come sidearm occasionally to give lefthanded power hitters something extra to think about.

Birtsas knows how to pitch, and he has a kind of gunslinger approach on the mound. Nothing seems to bother him, and he'll challenge anyone with his best stuff.

FIELDING:

For a big man, Birtsas has a respectable move to first base; he will throw over to keep runners honest. He's quick to cover first base, and he leaves him-

TIM BIRTSAS
LHP, No. 49
LL, 6'7", 225 lbs.
ML Svc: 1 year
Born: 9-5-60 in
 Pontiac, MI

1985 STATISTICS

W	L	ERA	G	GS	CG	SV	IP	H	R	ER	BB	SO
10	6	4.01	29	25	2	0	141.1	124	72	63	91	94

CAREER STATISTICS

W	L	ERA	G	GS	CG	SV	IP	H	R	ER	BB	SO
10	6	4.01	29	25	2	0	141.1	124	72	63	91	94

self in good position to field grounders in front of the mound. But he also is susceptible to stolen bases because of his laborious delivery.

OVERALL:

Concerned about Birtsas' weary arm in late summer, the A's have urged him to lose weight. They still have confidence in him as a starting pitcher.

Killebrew: "Birtsas is another Yankee farm product who was buried in the minors. I think he responded well to the chance he got with the A's. Lefthanded starters are at a premium now, and this guy has the stuff and know-how to be a good one.

"What Birtsas needs is better command of his curveball. He can't keep working behind the count or his defense will fall asleep. There's nothing wrong with his stuff. Hitters might come back to the dugout saying, 'He's got nothing,' but in the meantime they went 0-for-4."

HITTING:

Bruce Bochte needed just one year to come all the way back from his self-imposed retirement. After a disappointing 1984 season, when he struggled with his timing and hit .264, Bochte became one of the most consistent hitters in either league. He cleared .300 on the third day of the season, stayed there until late September. He ended the season at .295 only because he slumped in the last week.

There is no set way to pitch Bochte. He'll take the outside pitch to the opposite field, and he can pull the inside fastball--occasionally out of the park (his 14 homers in 1985 represented the second-highest total of his career). With his short, quick swing, he hits a lot of balls up the alleys. The key to pitching Bochte is to keep breaking balls down and inside. Lefthanders have had considerable success against him with sweeping breaking pitches to the outside corner, but Bochte seldom plays against lefties; he platooned at first base with Dusty Baker through most of the 1985 season.

Anytime Bochte bunts, it's a shock; he's one of the slowest runners in baseball. He's generally counted on as a run-producer.

BASERUNNING:

Bochte's fierce swing is great for hitting but costly to his baserunning. He whips the bat back toward the catcher on his follow-through which shifts his weight away from first base, taking him a moment or two to recover. He also has an awkward running style—even he admits that he looks goofy running the bases.

FIELDING:

Eleven years in the American League have paid off for Bochte. Last year, he

BRUCE BOCHTE
1B, No. 20
LL, 6'3", 200 lbs.
ML Svc: 11 years
Born: 11-12-50 in
      Pasadena, CA

1985 STATISTICS

AVG	G	AB	R	H	2B	3B	HR	RBI	BB	SO	SB
.295	137	424	48	125	17	1	14	60	49	58	3

CAREER STATISTICS

AVG	G	AB	R	H	2B	3B	HR	RBI	BB	SO	SB
.285	1413	4826	586	1374	237	20	94	615	588	594	40

  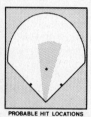

STRONG — VS. RHP | STRONG — VS. LHP | PROBABLE HIT LOCATIONS

played the best first base of his career, showing excellent knowledge of the hitters and a smooth style in picking up ground balls. His lack of range hurts him, especially on balls down the line. He's more than adequate picking up sharp grounders to his right, and he's adept at "leading" the pitcher on lob-throws to first.

OVERALL:

Killebrew: "Bochte has come back and done a good job for the A's. Bruce is at his peak right now.

"I don't believe he can play any better than he did last year, but you can expect another consistent year from him with a good batting average and some key home runs. Defensively, he is smart enough to play well without having exceptional natural skills."

PITCHING:

Chris Codiroli finally got his shot as a full-time Oakland starter in 1985, and the results were upsetting to him. He became known as a solid starter who showed good stuff for six or seven innings but who too often found a way to lose.

Codiroli uses a three-quarters delivery and will occasionally come sidearm to righthanded hitters. Once known as a painfully slow worker, Codiroli no longer wastes time dawdling around on the mound; he goes about his business at an average pace.

His fastball checks in around 87-88 MPH, but the slider is his out pitch. When it's on, Codiroli is extremely tough on righthanded hitters. He can also keep the slider down and in on lefthanders, making it almost impossible for them to drive the ball.

Codiroli has experimented with a straight change-up, mostly against the bigger and stronger hitters. His over-the-top curveball can also be effective, but it's not unusual to see Codiroli go strictly with his fastball/slider combo.

If Codiroli is struggling early in the game, there's a good chance he won't last long. That's when he's most likely to pitch himself into jams—often with a needless walk. Telltale signs of his ineffectiveness are fastballs up and his breaking pitches missing the mark.

Codiroli sees himself as a hard-luck pitcher, which is not the type of attitude coaches try to instill. Sometimes he will be the victim of tough breaks, but other times it is his own fault.

FIELDING:

The A's refer to the "Chris Codiroli

CHRIS CODIROLI
RHP, No. 23
RR, 6'1", 160 lbs.
ML Svc: 3 years
Born: 3-26-58 in
   Oxnard, CA

```
1985 STATISTICS
W   L  ERA  G   GS  CG SV IP     H    R   ER  BB  SO
14  14 4.46 37  37   4  0 226    228  125 112 78  111
CAREER STATISTICS
W   L  ERA  G   GS  CG SV IP     H    R   ER  BB  SO
33  32 4.06 105 85  12  2 537.2  563  315 280 188 245
```

school of fielding," and it's no compliment. Codiroli's delivery leaves him off to the left of the pitcher's mound, out of position to make defensive plays, and he probably took more grounders off the body than any pitcher in the league. Codiroli is also weak making a throw after fielding balls in front of him.

His fielding strength is his pickoff move; he's fairly adept at holding runners on.

OVERALL:

No 14-game winner can be taken lightly, especially on a mediocre team, but Codiroli needs to have more of a killer instinct.

Killebrew: "He has all the right ingredients to be a top-flight pitcher. He throws all four pitches well. I don't think that he is too far away from being a really effective pitcher . . . maybe he could use just a touch better command of his pitches."

HITTING:

Mike Davis arrived at spring training last season determined to make everyone forget about his dismal, .230 season the year before, and he did just that. By mid-May last season, he was hitting .325 with 12 homers, launching him toward his most productive season in the majors.

His fine performance last year was, in part, attributable to his everyday spot in the lineup. Davis has been considered a big talent for several years; it was not surprising that he was able to do so well when given the opportunity. The 1986 season affords him the chance to establish himself as a consistent player.

Davis became a much better hitter against lefthanders in 1985, although he still looks bad on breaking balls to the outside corner. Always known as a low-ball hitter, he has now learned to handle the high fastball as well. It is difficult to blow the ball by him. The key is to use breaking balls, either in or out, to keep him off balance.

Bolstered by the confidence the A's showed in him, Davis is a much more patient and selective hitter, a line drive artist whose home runs usually come by accident.

BASERUNNING:

His baserunning skills are the weakest part of his game. Davis runs well and knows how to slide, but he is too much of a gambler on the bases. And too often, he is an overanxious gambler. Aside from being caught stealing ten times in 34 attempts, he was thrown out many, many times trying to take an extra base.

The feeling is that if Davis could improve his hitting so dramatically, he could easily become a more intelligent baserunner. The talent is there.

FIELDING:

In 1984, Davis let his hitting prob-

MIKE DAVIS
RF, No. 16
LL, 6'3", 185 lbs.
ML Svc: 6 years
Born: 6-11-59 in
San Diego, CA

1985 STATISTICS

AVG	G	AB	R	H	2B	3B	HR	RBI	BB	SO	SB
.287	154	547	92	157	34	1	24	82	50	99	24

CAREER STATISTICS

AVG	G	AB	R	H	2B	3B	HR	RBI	BB	SO	SB
.267	407	1562	223	418	83	9	43	208	119	265	76

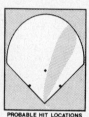

VS. RHP   VS. LHP   PROBABLE HIT LOCATIONS

lems affect him in the field. He showed occasional lapses of concentration and did not make plays he should have. He's still not the best right fielder he is capable of being--he committed eight errors and occasionally showed poor judgment--but he has all the tools: speed, soft hands and good jumping ability.

Davis' strong and accurate arm ranks up there with the best of league's right fielders (Jesse Barfield, Dave Winfield, Harold Baines and Dwight Evans).

OVERALL:

Killebrew: "Davis lived up to his potential last year and showed what kind of player he can be. Physically, he is at his peak. If he can have the same or an even better year this year than in 1985, he will really start to put some numbers on the board and become the kind of all-around player who can be counted on year after year."

HITTING:

Some instances of tardiness placed Barbaro Garbey in disfavor with the Tigers and cut into his at-bats in 1985. He's a part-time player who can't afford too many demerits.

Garbey proved to be a good support player two seasons ago, but pitchers caught up with him in 1985. Garbey is a low fastball hitter who does not have home run power, but insists on pulling every pitch anyway. He swings at a lot of first pitches. Pitchers served him a lot of high fastballs and changed speeds frequently.

He will chase pitches out of the strike zone when behind in the count, especially breaking pitches down and away from righthanders. Lefthanders power Garbey up and in and with hard sliders down and in.

Garbey is a free swinger with a limited power zone. He will not drop a bunt, but usually makes contact and is capable of executing the hit-and-run.

BASERUNNING:

Garbey is distinctly average on the bases. His lead off first doesn't draw many throws. His jump is average, his speed slightly better than average and his slide is average. He is capable of an occasional stolen base, but is not the kind of threat to force pitch-outs.

FIELDING:

Garbey's accuracy is erratic. He can sometimes come up with an outstanding play, but quite often has problems with routine plays. His demeanor in the field is aloof and his break off first base is

BARBARO GARBEY
OF, No. 27
RR, 5'10", 170 lbs.
ML Svc: 2 years
Born: 12-4-56 in
Santiago, CU

1985 STATISTICS
AVG	G	AB	R	H	2B	3B	HR	RBI	BB	SO	SB
.257	86	237	27	61	9	1	6	29	15	37	3

CAREER STATISTICS
AVG	G	AB	R	H	2B	3B	HR	RBI	BB	SO	SB
.274	196	564	72	155	26	2	11	81	32	72	9

STRONG   STRONG   PROBABLE HIT LOCATIONS

VS. RHP   VS. LHP

slow. When Garbey was with the Tigers, second baseman Lou Whitaker handled most pop-ups for him.

OVERALL:

Garbey's stock, along with his batting average (.287 to .257), has fallen. He's an average hitter without home run power, an average runner without stolen base speed, and an average defensive player without a keen awareness of game situations.

Robinson: "Garbey is strictly a part-time player on any team. He's not going to get any better."

HITTING:

If the A's fans had any doubts about Alfredo Griffin, Oakland's key player in the Bill Caudill trade, they were quickly erased. Griffin hit .270--his best since 1979, when he was the AL Rookie of the Year. He played in all 162 games for the third time in four seasons. And by the end of July, he had already established a personal high in RBIs (49).

Griffin came to Oakland with a reputation as a slashing, hacking, first-ball hitter. Right from the start, he made a bet with teammate Steve Henderson promising to pay $5 every time he swung at the first pitch. Not that Griffin is a model of patience (he actually walked 20 times), but he did begin to show a knack of waiting for his pitch and hitting the ball hard.

He is a straightaway/opposite field hitter who will surprise you with the home run two or three times a year. Pitchers should keep the fastball up, get ahead in the count, them finish him off with breaking balls. The pitch he hits most often is the fastball down. And teams are advised to not be fooled when Griffin squares around to bunt; if the infielders move in, he'll often try to chop it over their heads.

BASERUNNING:

Griffin stole 24 bases for Oakland and appeared capable of much more. He runs well and aggressively, and when he makes a mistake, it's usually because he is trying to hustle his way into an extra base. He takes a long lead, trying to distract the pitcher, and has no problem sliding hard into the double play pivot.

FIELDING:

The A's haven't had a respectable shortstop since Bert Campaneris in the 1970s, and Griffin was nothing short of a revelation. Although he made nine er-

ALFREDO GRIFFIN
SS, No. 3
SR, 5'11", 165 lbs.
ML Svc: 8 years
Born: 3-6-57 in
    Santo Domingo, DR

1985 STATISTICS

AVG	G	AB	R	H	2B	3B	HR	RBI	BB	SO	SB
.270	162	614	75	166	17	7	2	64	20	50	24

CAREER STATISTICS

AVG	G	AB	R	H	2B	3B	HR	RBI	BB	SO	SB
.253	1066	3814	427	964	136	57	15	285	159	336	102

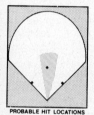

VS. RHP   VS. LHP   PROBABLE HIT LOCATIONS

rors, they were seldom the type that hurt the team.

Griffin has become known for his flashy style, spectacular plays and tremendous range--particularly to his left.

He gets rid of the ball quickly, has a strong arm, and makes all the plays.

OVERALL:

Killebrew: "Griffin was probably the MVP of the 1985 A's: a real steal, especially in light of Bill Caudill's sub-par year in Toronto.

"Alfredo is a lot of fun to watch at shortstop. He makes all of the routine plays but he likes to throw in a little pizzazz, too. He has given the A's tremendous respectability at an important position in the field. Offensively, he produced in excess of expectations. I don't think that his fine performance last year was the result of trying to prove himself; he's just an excellent all-around player."

HITTING:

Mike Heath has given up trying to be a dead pull, long ball hitter. He keeps his weight back, in Charlie Lau fashion, with an eye on the entire field. Heath is actually two types of hitters. When he is on a hot streak, he will remain patient, wait for his pitch, then drive the ball, whether it is up in the strike zone or down. Heath can go deep to the opposite field with the best of them.

Heath also has a lunging, one-handed follow-through that makes him look ridiculous when he doesn't make contact. He should realize that no good hitter, even the most unique in style, ever followed through the way he does.

Heath is also a notorious hothead and is too temperamental for his own good. When he is slumping, he gets overanxious. The slow breaking ball, down and away, gives him fits.

Very few catchers have Heath's offensive versatility. He is adept at hitting on the right side to move runners along, and he can bunt. At this point, he knows he is not going to be a .300 hitter. As long as he stays within his limitations, Heath can remain a dangerous weapon at the bottom of the order.

BASERUNNING:

Heath's baserunning became a sensitive issue around the Oakland clubhouse last year. Heath tends to "put on the dog" when he hits a routine grounder to the infield. In other words, he doesn't run it out. Heath says that he learned this from Thurman Munson when they both played for the Yankees, the idea being that catchers should save their legs whenever possible.

Not many managers will tolerate a lack of hustle of this sort. When Heath failed to run out a grounder against Detroit last year in effect, handing the Tigers a gift double play, A's manager Jackie Moore fined him $1000. Aside from that one little problem, Heath is a hustling, aggressive baserunner who will sacrifice his body for the team. When

MIKE HEATH
C, No. 2
RR, 5'11", 190 lbs.
ML Svc: 8 years
Born: 2-5-55 in
Tampa, FL

1985 STATISTICS

AVG	G	AB	R	H	2B	3B	HR	RBI	BB	SO	SB
.250	138	436	71	109	18	6	13	55	41	63	7

CAREER STATISTICS

AVG	G	AB	R	H	2B	3B	HR	RBI	BB	SO	SB
.162	758	3904	286	633	102	19	47	289	162	324	32

STRONG VS. RHP · STRONG VS. LHP · PROBABLE HIT LOCATIONS

he takes chances, he is usually right--and he will steal a base when necessary.

FIELDING:

When it comes to throwing, chasing down pop-ups or pouncing on balls in front of the plate, Heath ranks with the best. He has developed a reputation as a poor handler of pitchers, but he has not had much to work with in Oakland. Some of the pitching staff feel that Heath uses poor pitch selection to work the hitters--they don't agree with his approach. He seems to get the best out of them, though.

Heath also plays an adequate third base, left field and right field, making him a versatile guy to have around.

OVERALL:

Killebrew: "Heath is a solid defensive catcher who comes to play; I think he is one of the top five in the league. The only problem is his temper. He's got to get a better handle on it."

HITTING:

Steve Henderson, signed for a mere $100,000 as a free agent, turned into quite a bargain for Oakland. Content to come off the bench and get an occasional shot in left field, Henderson was a consistent .300 hitter who managed 31 RBIs in just 193 at-bats. Until September, when Oakland fell out of the race, he was hitting over .400 with runners in scoring position.

Henderson shows a remarkable knack for delivering key pinch-hits against even the toughest lefthanded pitchers. Henderson is a straightaway hitter who likes the ball away from him. He actually likes hitting the breaking pitch, which says something about his discipline and bat speed. Not that he's a particularly patient hitter; knowing he might only get one at-bat a game, he tends to go after anything he thinks he can handle.

A pitcher's best tactic is to throw him breaking pitches out of the strike zone and to stay ahead of him. The fastball should be in and hard. He can be teased by off-speed pitches down and away.

Henderson can bunt for a hit or to sacrifice, but he's seldom asked to do either. Although he had some decent years with the Mets earlier in his career, Henderson has become known as a player who is not as impressive playing everyday and who looks better coming off the bench. He is always ready to hit.

BASERUNNING:

At age 33, Henderson still runs fairly well. He's about average in all categories: getting a good jump, sliding hard into second and exercising good judgment. If he steals a base, though, it's a major upset. As a part-timer, he

STEVE HENDERSON
OF, No. 5
RR, 6'1", 188 lbs.
ML Svc: 7 years
Born: 11-18-52 in
    Houston, TX

1985 STATISTICS

AVG	G	AB	R	H	2B	3B	HR	RBI	BB	SO	SB
.301	85	193	25	58	8	3	3	31	18	34	0

CAREER STATISTICS

AVG	G	AB	R	H	2B	3B	HR	RBI	BB	SO	SB
.282	986	3298	439	931	152	49	65	411	367	639	78

VS. RHP VS. LHP PROBABLE HIT LOCATIONS

he can't afford to take his team out of a rally.

FIELDING:

Henderson is only an average outfielder--perhaps a bit below that--and his lack of playing time makes it unlikely he'll get better. He'll catch a ball if he can reach it, but his range is suspect. So is his arm, and runners feel they can take the extra base on him.

OVERALL:

Killebrew: "He'll probably have to fight for a job in spring training. He's not playing as much as he used to, and he has regressed in terms of his overall skills."

MOST IMPROVED

HITTING:

Donnie Hill was one of the biggest surprises in the American League last year. He suffered a humiliating spring training when he lost the second base job to Tony Phillips, then learned he'd been optioned to Triple-A ball. Hill got another shot at the majors when Phillips broke his foot near the close of camp. Hill took over and turned into a first-rate player, hitting for a .285 average with 48 RBIs.

How did a .247 lifetime hitter turn it around? The switch-hitting Hill said he had been trying to pull everything until A's hitting coach Billy Williams got him to wait on the ball and spray it around. Hill has become an opposite field hitter with a good eye.

The important thing for a pitcher to do is to get ahead of him in the count and then finish him off with a breaking ball. If pitchers fall behind, Hill has the discipline to either walk or get his pitch.

Like many switch-hitters, Hill is a low-ball hitter from the left side and a high-ball hitter from the right side. He is not much of a power threat, but he is an excellent bunter and adept on the hit-and-run play. He went on a 17-game hitting streak in August, raising his average to .298 and helping put Oakland in the thick of the pennant race. But on August 31, he suffered a broken bone in his right hand and was lost for the final month.

Interestingly, the A's went 3-13 from that point and fell from contention.

BASERUNNING:

Hill is a better-than-average baserunner with speed and good instincts. He has a problem, though: he seldom pays attention to pitcher's pickoff moves and rarely tries to steal. But he does play hard, and he'll slide aggressively into second base to break up the double play.

FIELDING:

Moving away from shortstop, where he

DON HILL
2B, No. 25
SR, 5'10", 160 lbs.
ML Svc: 3 years
Born: 11-12-60 in
   Pomona, CA

1985 STATISTICS

AVG	G	AB	R	H	2B	3B	HR	RBI	BB	SO	SB
.285	123	393	45	112	13	2	3	48	23	33	8

CAREER STATISTICS

AVG	G	AB	R	H	2B	3B	HR	RBI	BB	SO	SB
.267	249	725	86	194	26	2	7	79	31	56	10

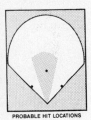

STRONG   STRONG

VS. RHP   VS. LHP   PROBABLE HIT LOCATIONS

opened the 1984 season, made all the difference for Hill last year. His rifle arm really stood out. He has what may be one of the strongest arms among AL second basemen. Playing second base effectively masked his lack of range, which was a problem for him as a shortstop.

Another interesting aspect of the switch to second was Hill's emergence as a reliable and always-in-the game type of player. Previously known as a spacey player whose concentration drifted in and out of the game, he became a steady guy on everything from turning the DP to running down pop-ups in short right field.

OVERALL:

Killebrew: "Hill still has to fight (with Phillips) for the second base job, but he is a much-improved player. He could probably be an everyday player on another team, if it comes to that."

PITCHING:

Jay Howell always wondered what it would be like to be a short reliever, the stopper who closes the door. He finally got his chance with he A's last year, and he responded with a 2.85 ERA, 29-save season that put him among the league's elite.

A fast worker with an overhand delivery, Howell doesn't try to fool anybody. He will throw either the fastball or the slider and they are both first-rate pitches. He's the first one to admit to not having an off-speed pitch--"because I don't need it." Howell also has that fearless, almost eccentric approach that characterizes the best short relievers. Give him the bases loaded with nobody out, and he's happy.

Howell is at his best working just one or two innings with his team ahead; he can be counted upon to do that two out of three nights. The A's occasionally lost sight of his role last year, using him in tie games, and the overwork took its toll. Howell developed shoulder tendinitis in August, and his ERA had jumped a full point by season's end. He was getting by mostly on guile and sheer willpower at the end.

When he is at his best, Howell will get ahead of the hitters with the fastball, then use the slider to finish them off. If a hitter crowds the plate, he had better turn up the bat speed a few notches.

Howell is a power pitcher, pure and simple, yet he seldom gives up the long ball. When he gets in trouble, wildness is usually the reason.

Howell has never forgiven himself for

JAY HOWELL
RHP, No. 50
RR, 6'3", 195 lbs.
ML Svc: 5 years
Born: 11-26-55 in
Miami, FL

1985 STATISTICS												
W	L	ERA	G	GS	CG	SV	IP	H	R	ER	BB	SO
9	8	2.85	63	0	0	29	98	98	32	31	31	68
CAREER STATISTICS												
W	L	ERA	G	GS	CG	SV	IP	H	R	ER	BB	SO
23	20	4.05	164	21	2	36	337	346	161	152	123	270

walking Jackie Gutierrez with the bases loaded to lose a game in Boston.

FIELDING:

Howell's move to first base is about average. He cheats a little as he comes set, not coming to a full stop before delivering, but he consistently gets away with it. For a big man, he's quick to cover first base and is generally an adequate fielder.

OVERALL:

Howell's late-season arm problems showed that he must be used judiciously to remain effective.

Killebrew: "Jay was asked to close the door—and he slammed it. He has not yet completely harnessed his control problems, but it actually seems to work to his advantage. He is just wild enough to keep hitters honest."

PITCHING:

The A's took a gamble on Tommy John, signing him as a free agent in late July with hopes he could restore order to a shaky rotation. Fortunately, the move only cost them $40,000, because John is now a creaky, injury-prone pitcher who went 1-6 after winning his first start.

In many respects, John is the same pitcher who has enjoyed so much success over the years. He is a fast worker who throws with a three-quarters delivery and keeps the ball down. Although his fastball is in the low 80s at best, he is very tough on lefthanded hitters with his variety of off-speed pitches.

He throws a slurve at two different speeds, and he has a very effective sinker that drops down below the knees. John can turn it over (a screwball effect), and righthanded hitters play right into his hands when they try to pull it.

But John needs that sinker to be effective, and when he can't get it down, he is in trouble. If hitters show enough patience to wait for the ball up, they can take John out of his game. One look at the scorebook gives you a pretty good idea of his effectiveness. If it shows a lot of ground ball outs through the first few innings, he's got his good stuff. If balls are being hit to the outfield, it's a good bet he won't be out there much longer.

FIELDING:

At age 42, John simply doesn't run that well any more, and he has a poor pickoff move to first base. He holds the

TOMMY JOHN
LHP, No. 25
RR, 6'3", 200 lbs.
ML Svc: 22 years
Born: 5-22-43 in
    Terre Haute, IN

1985 STATISTICS

W	L	ERA	G	GS	CG	SV	IP	H	R	ER	BB	SO
4	10	5.53	23	17	0	0	86.1	117	59	53	28	25

CAREER STATISTICS

W	L	ERA	G	GS	CG	SV	IP	H	R	ER	BB	SO
259	207	3.23	669	615	158	4	4209	4280	1754	1513	1129	2055

ball and doesn't throw over very often. Although his delivery leaves him in good position to field the ball, he is not a good fielder. Teams had success bunting against him last year, and they won't let up.

OVERALL:

Although John still fancies himself as a starting pitcher, his future might be in short relief--to get a couple of lefthanded hitters out.

Killebrew: "You wonder how much more Tommy can get squeeze out of himself. He is an experienced starter, and he knows how to pitch. When he has got everything working, he takes the hitters' timing away and makes them strike themselves out.

"He has managed to beat the odds so far, but you have to wonder how much longer he can roll the dice and win."

HITTING:

Dave Kingman put up some impressive power numbers for the A's last season-- 30 homers, 91 RBIs--but he wasn't nearly the offensive contributor he had been the year before.

His production has tailed off drastically with runners in scoring position and he no longer seems willing to cut down his swing with runners on base. Kingman is becoming disenchanted with the game of baseball in general, and even after belting his 400th career home run last year has said that 1986 might be his last season.

Kingman's approach to hitting hasn't changed a bit over the years. He still takes a wide, menacing-looking stance and is a guaranteed dead-pull hitter. Many teams put the shift on against him, aligning three infielders on the left side. He absolutely murders the inside fastball, high or low, and can send the hanging curve to Hawaii.

Understandably, pitchers try to keep fastballs away and frustrate him with breaking balls on the outside corner.

When he's hot, Kingman seems to hit everything and he can carry a team. When he's not, he gets down on himself and swings at anything. Late last season, when the A's had dropped out of the race, Kingman was content to take three half-hearted swings and sit back down.

At his best, he can still be a selective hitter, spreading out his stance a little more and cutting down on his swing for better contact. Not only does he bunt, but he occasionally becomes fascinated with the idea. Kingman was trying the surprise bunt (for a hit) almost once a game for a stretch last summer before the A's reminded him he's a power hitter.

BASERUNNING:

He looks gangly and awkward on the bases, but Kingman knows what he's doing. He was a very effective baserunner before suffering a knee injury midway

DAVE KINGMAN
DH, No. 10
RR, 6'6", 215 lbs.
ML Svc: 15 years
Born: 12-21-48 in Pendleton, OR

1985 STATISTICS

AVG	G	AB	R	H	2B	3B	HR	RBI	BB	SO	SB
.238	158	592	66	141	16	0	30	91	62	114	3

CAREER STATISTICS

AVG	G	AB	R	H	2B	3B	HR	RBI	BB	SO	SB
.238	1797	6116	831	1457	221	25	407	116	575	1690	82

  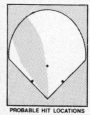

STRONG   STRONG

VS. RHP   VS. LHP   PROBABLE HIT LOCATIONS

through the 1984 season. He has been more conservative since then. He seldom makes a mistake, and he's a formidable obstacle for any second baseman trying to turn the double play.

FIELDING:

It was proven years ago that his defense is a disaster at any position. He is a born DH.

OVERALL:

Kingman seems to have lost some of his zest for the game, and he will no longer command the big salary of his power-hitting contemporaries. But he keeps himself in excellent shape and is always a good bet for a 30-homer season.

Killebrew: "Kingman is always ready to drive the ball out of the park. He is always looking for a pitch he can overpower. He may retire from baseball soon, but if Dave is still playing this year, there is little doubt that he will continue to hit his massive home runs."

PITCHING:

Bill Krueger broke into the major leagues in 1983 as a great-looking left-handed starter, but he tore a muscle in his forearm about halfway through the season. He has been a struggling, self-doubting pitcher ever since, barely able to make the best of his ability.

Krueger would appear to have it all: a classic overhand delivery, a better-than-average fastball, a big drop on his curveball, and a decent straight change-up. The curve is his out pitch, and when it's working, he can be very effective. He runs his fastball in on lefthanded hitters and tails it away from righties.

Too often, though, Krueger has trouble getting the curveball over. He does not challenge hitters like he did in the past, and he winds up trying to be too fine and falling behind in the count. When that happens, his fastball is not overpowering enough to save him.

Last season, Krueger's biggest problem was the same as in 1984: he worried too much for his own good. He has only been a pitcher for five years--he played first base until his junior year in college--and there are times he wears his insecurity on his sleeve. The A's found themselves wondering if he'd ever be the tough, aggressive pitcher they wanted to see.

FIELDING:

Krueger is an exceptional athlete who

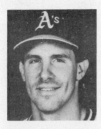

BILL KRUEGER
LHP, No. 32
LL, 6'5", 205 lbs.
ML Svc: 3 years
Born: 4-24-58 in
    McMinnville, OR

1985 STATISTICS

W	L	ERA	G	GS	CG	SV	IP	H	R	ER	BB	SO
9	10	4.52	32	23	2	0	151.1	165	95	76	69	56

CAREER STATISTICS

W	L	ERA	G	CS	CG	SV	IP	H	R	ER	BB	SO
26	26	4.35	75	63	5	0	403	425	244	195	207	175

handles his position well, with one exception: the pickoff move. The A's sent him to winter ball in December of 1984 to work on it. While he has improved the move a bit, he still has trouble holding runners on. To say the least, opposing teams are aware of this.

OVERALL:

Killebrew: "This is a young guy with a good arm and four good pitches. But he hasn't been the same since the injury. I don't think he's shaken it yet.

"He can be intimidated; he doesn't come at the hitters like he used to. He has to realize he's a control pitcher, not a power pitcher. Perhaps all he needs is experience and a few adjustments."

HITTING:

In 1985 Carney Lansford had an uncharacteristically poor season, struggling around the .250 range through much of the first half. He had just found his groove when he fractured his right wrist in late July. He tried to come back in late August, but played only five more games before being declared out for the season.

Lansford seemed to lose some of his patience at the plate last year, and that was at least partially responsible for his decline. A situation hitter, Lansford often found himself in the position of having to drive the ball--if not hit it out--on an Oakland club that was hungry for power. He's more of a line drive/singles hitter, and his ability to drive in runs proved disappointing. His average with runners in scoring position was in the low .200s all year.

His 1985 struggle aside, pitchers do not consider him a pushover. Lansford is a thinking-man's hitter who has the plate cornered. He can hit a good breaking ball with authority to the opposite field, and he constantly adjusts to the pitcher or situation in mid-at-bat. The key is to keep him off balance, change speeds, and stay away from set patterns.

Lansford is an aggressive, constantly hustling player who gets out of the batter's box quickly and is liable to hit the ball anywhere on the field. He had 13 homers at the All-Star break, showing a knack for driving the inside fastball out of the park.

A source of concern is his durability through the course of an entire season. He has become known as a brittle player who gets hurt often and takes a long time to recover. Last year was a perfect example.

BASERUNNING:

Lansford considers his baserunning as seriously as he does his hitting, and he

CARNEY LANSFORD
3B, No. 4
RR, 6'2", 185 lbs.
ML Svc: 8 years
Born: 2-7-57 in
San Jose, CA

1985 STATISTICS

AVG	G	AB	R	H	2B	3B	HR	RBI	BB	SO	SB
.277	98	401	51	111	18	2	13	46	18	27	2

CAREER STATISTICS

AVG	G	AB	R	H	2B	3B	HR	RBI	BB	SO	SB
.293	988	3887	554	1139	196	26	94	491	280	473	92

  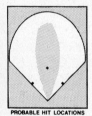

STRONG — VS. RHP   STRONG — VS. LHP   PROBABLE HIT LOCATIONS

takes the right base at the right time. He knows enough not to take himself seriously as a basestealer, too, and seldom tries it.

FIELDING:

Lansford has everything it takes to play third base: the quick first step, great reactions, a good arm, the willingness to dive, and the ability to make off-balance throws while charging the ball. Evidence: he had a streak of 47 consecutive errorless games last year.

OVERALL:

Killebrew: "Staying healthy has got to be his number one consideration. When he is not hampered physically, he is a good, proven hitter who fields his position and comes to play. Carney is a gamer; I wish there were more like him."

PITCHING:

The A's wished they could have taken Steve McCatty's competitive nature and attached it to some of their strong, young arms. Or vice versa. At this point in his career, McCatty is surviving mostly on heart.

He was a devastating power pitcher in 1981, the American League's ERA champ, but the days of live fastballs and un-hittable sliders are over. McCatty developed serious shoulder problems in 1982 and 1983, and, since his fastball checks in around 84 MPH, at best, the curveball is his best pitch now. When it is working for him, it moves down and in to lefties, down and away to righties.

McCatty still manages to get good movement on his pitches. His fastball often acts like a sinker, making it effective against all hitters, and he'll try a change-up every so often to keep the power hitters off balance.

His problem is that he has to consistently hit the corners. Check his hits-per-inning ratio, and you realize he was not often successful last year. If there is one thing McCatty hasn't lost, it's his competitiveness. He'll pitch inside to anybody, and he'll never back down from a challenge.

He works quickly from his overhand delivery, and he does not let the presence of baserunners bother him. His confidence is so strong, he often refuses to acknowledge a bad outing. He winds up rationalizing it, pitch by pitch, until it all makes sense.

STEVE McCATTY
RHP, No. 54
RR, 6'3", 210 lbs.
ML Svc: 8 years
Born: 3-20-54 in
Detroit, MI

1985 STATISTICS

W	L	ERA	G	GS	CG	SV	IP	H	R	ER	BB	SO
4	4	5.57	30	9	1	0	85.2	95	56	53	41	36

CAREER STATISTICS

W	L	ERA	G	GS	CG	SV	IP	H	R	ER	BB	SO
63	63	3.99	221	161	45	5	1189	1172	581	527	520	541

FIELDING:

Although he is a bit overweight, he is a good all-around athlete who helps himself with his fielding. McCatty has a good pickoff move, holds runners on, and makes all the plays around him.

OVERALL:

Killebrew: "Steve is pitching on guts. He is a great competitor. I hope his arm allows him to pitch a few more years, because he can help somebody. He looks as if he's capable of going out there for a few innings every other day or so. Sad to say, his days as a starter may be over."

HITTING:

Dwayne Murphy is still trying to find himself as a hitter. He came up to the majors as a line drive hitter and hit .274 in his first full season (1980). Batting second behind Rickey Henderson that season, Murphy showed a surprising amount of power (27 homers). Two years later, he slugged 33 homers and the A's thought they had found a first-rate run producer.

But Murphy slumped so badly last season that he did not have even a single hot streak. He was one of the A's biggest disappointments of the year.

Murphy's problem may be that he fell in love with the long ball. He takes a ferocious swing that has produced some tape-measure shots over the years. It appears that he is up at the plate to hit a 500-foot home run every time.

If that is so, it would really be a shame because Murphy has shown the ability to bunt. He's an expert at the drag-bunt single (to the right side), and the hit-and-run, and he can drive pitches to the opposite field.

Still, he's a dangerous hitter. A pitcher cannot make a mistake to him. Murphy has trouble with the breaking pitch and the change-up. Pitchers have to keep the fastball up and in if they are thinking of challenging him.

Murphy never allows himself to get cheated at the plate. The best thing that could happen to him would be to have a balanced lineup around him. With two or three power hitters to lend a hand, he could stop worrying about the long ball and start using the entire field again.

BASERUNNING:

Murphy has constant problems with his feet; he is susceptible to various minor injuries--it has taken away his running game. He will steal the occasional base, but he seldom takes chances at the risk of further injury. But he is a 100% type of player and will willingly take out the second baseman on the double play.

DWAYNE MURPHY
CF, No. 21
LR, 6'1", 185 lbs.
ML Svc: 8 years
Born: 3-18-55 in
  Merced, CA

1985 STATISTICS

AVG	G	AB	R	H	2B	3B	HR	RBI	BB	SO	SB
.233	152	523	77	122	21	3	20	59	84	123	4

CAREER STATISTICS

AVG	G	AB	R	H	2B	3B	HR	RBI	BB	SO	SB
.247	1033	3499	525	865	111	8	136	489	580	742	92

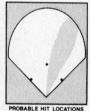

VS. RHP   VS. LHP   PROBABLE HIT LOCATIONS

FIELDING:

Few players can play center better than Dwayne Murphy. He has become more accomplished in center field each season. He has won five consecutive Gold Gloves. Although he doesn't have the flat-out speed of Gary Pettis, for example, Murphy is a master at playing shallow, running down drives in the alleys and making graceful catches against the fences. His arm is not as strong as it once was, but Murphy makes up for it by charging the ball hard and getting rid of it quickly.

OVERALL:

Killebrew: "Even when he's slumping, Murphy is the type you can't afford to take out of the lineup. He is outstanding in the field. Last season, he took on too much responsibility at the plate and it hurt him. I don't think he has lost his touch, however."

PITCHING:

Steve Ontiveros (not to be confused with the former infielder of the same name) made a dramatic entrance into the big leagues last year. Called up from Triple-A in June, he kept his ERA under 1.00 through 27 appearances. His hits-per-inning ratio was one of the best in either league. And he gave up only four home runs all year, firmly establishing himself as a middle reliever to be reckoned with.

A former number one draft choice whose career had been set back by injuries, Ontiveros was transformed from a starter to a reliever in the minors. He worked as Jay Howell's set-up man last year, but appears to be capable of handling the number one short relief role if necessary.

Ontiveros uses an overhand delivery, though he will occasionally go to three-quarters, and basically throws just two pitches: the fastball and the hard slider. He has very good movement on the fastball, which enables him to keep it away from lefthanded hitters, and he throws it around 87-88 MPH. His slider breaks sharply away from righthanded hitters. Opposing teams figured that he would be in trouble if he could not keep his pitches on the corners--that seldom happened.

Ontiveros is a fast worker who likes to challenge the hitters and stay ahead in the count. There's no wasted effort with this man, and he's most effective when he mixes in the sinking fastball. His slider is so good that he tends to fall in love with it sometimes. On the few occasions when he looked vulnerable, it was because his pitches flattened out.

STEVE ONTIVEROS
RHP, No. 61
RR, 6'0", 180 lbs.
ML Svc: 1 year
Born: 3-5-61 in
Tularosa, NM

1985 STATISTICS

W	L	ERA	G	GS	CG	SV	IP	H	R	ER	BB	SO
1	3	1.93	39	0	0	8	74.2	45	17	16	15	36

CAREER STATISTICS

W	L	ERA	G	GS	CG	SV	IP	H	R	ER	BB	SO
1	3	1.93	39	0	0	8	74.2	45	17	16	15	36

FIELDING:

It was tough to judge Ontiveros' reaction to baserunners, because there were so few of them. For every one crisis, he would have about ten tension-free innings. Steve is a good athlete with a fluid delivery and a sound follow-through. He seems to have little trouble holding runners on.

OVERALL:

Ontiveros has had serious arm trouble in the past, and it is a sensitive issue with him. Relief pitching seems to be his strong suit--only one or two innings at a time, if possible.

Killebrew: "He was very effective out of the bullpen. If he's going to start, he needs to come up with another pitch; something with a different speed.

"But at this point, he should remain in the bullpen. He has two great pitches and hitters are having a lot of trouble with both. Steve has the ability to come in and finish a hitter off quickly."

HITTING:

Tony Phillips will be starting from scratch after spending most of the 1985 season on the disabled list. He broke his left foot during a workout in January 1985, then rebroke it in spring training after winning the A's second base job outright. He managed to hit a solid .280, playing mostly third base, after returning to the club in late August.

Phillips is a switch-hitter who has abandoned the exaggerated-crouch stance he used at the beginning of his career. He practices the weight-back theory when batting lefthanded. He is a better, more patient hitter from this side. He will hit low pitches with authority, and so pitchers try to work him away with fastballs and breaking pitches. From the right side of the plate, he is more of a straight-up hitter and is vulnerable to the low pitch.

He likes the fastball down the middle, and he'll take curveballs to the opposite field if they are high in the strike zone. The key is to get ahead of him, from either side, because he still strikes out too often for his own good.

Phillips will never be a consistent power threat, but he has added body strength. He hit 12 doubles in just 161 at-bats last year, consistently driving balls up the alleys from both sides of the plate.

BASERUNNING:

In 1985, Phillips played a full month without stealing a base, undoubtedly because he feared reinjuring himself. With his confidence intact, Phillips is a quick baserunner but not necessarily a daring one. If he were to take a few more chances, he would be a valuable part of any team's running game. He gets only an average lead off first base and

TONY PHILLIPS
2B, No. 18
SR, 5'10", 160 lbs.
ML Svc: 3 years
Born:11-9-59 in
Atlanta, GA

1985 STATISTICS

AVG	G	AB	R	H	2B	3B	HR	RBI	BB	SO	SB
.280	42	161	23	45	12	2	4	17	13	34	3

CAREER STATISTICS

AVG	G	AB	R	H	2B	3B	HR	RBI	BB	SO	SB
.257	384	1105	150	284	50	10	12	97	115	215	31

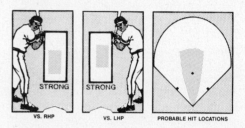

VS. RHP — STRONG | VS. LHP — STRONG | PROBABLE HIT LOCATIONS

is not aggressive trying to take out the second baseman on double plays.

FIELDING:

Phillips broke in as a shortstop, but his average throwing arm and lack of confidence hurt him. He is far more suited to second base, where his quickness is more noticeable and his throwing doesn't need to be spectacular. Phillips filled in admirably at third base when Carney Lansford was injured, but his future is at second base.

OVERALL:

Killebrew: "Phillips' broken foot made him a forgotten man in 1985, but he is an exceptional athlete who deserves a full-time shot at second base. This may be his year to get it."

PITCHING:

Jose Rijo was supposed to be the next great Yankee pitcher. He was so impressive two years ago that the Yankees made him a starter as an 18-year-old rookie. But Rijo didn't live up to the comparisons with crosstown star Dwight Gooden, and it was a tremendous blow to his confidence. The Yanks demoted him to the minor leagues midway through the 1984 season, then sent him to Oakland in the Rickey Henderson trade.

The A's played it cautiously with Rijo, but when they finally called him up in mid-August, he opened some eyes. His 94 MPH fastball and hard slider ranked him with the hardest throwers in the American League, and he struck out batters with cool regularity.

Rijo throws overhand, works at about an average pace, and throws almost exclusively hard stuff. The curveball is his off-speed pitch, but he'll abandon it when he has trouble getting it over. If there's any problem with Rijo's live fastball, it's that it comes in much too straight. Still, he's capable of striking out even the league's best hitters with it. Many of his opponents, including the Tigers' Lance Parrish, said that Rijo was the hardest thrower they saw all year.

Rijo's problems can invariably be traced to the walks he issues. He has never had pinpoint control, and when he walks himself into jams, he has trouble concentrating. Instead of mixing breaking pitches in with the fastball, he'll try to blow the ball past everyone. Even for such a hard-thrower, that does not always work in the majors.

In the early innings, few hitters dare crowd the plate against him. Later on, around the seventh or eighth, Rijo

JOSE RIJO
RHP, No. 38
RR, 6'2", 180 lbs.
ML Svc: 1 year plus
Born: 5-13-65 in
    San Cristobal, DR

1985 STATISTICS

W	L	ERA	G	GS	CG	SV	IP	H	R	ER	BB	SO
6	4	3.53	12	9	0	0	63.2	57	26	25	28	65

CAREER STATISTICS

W	L	ERA	G	GS	CG	SV	IP	H	R	ER	BB	SO
8	12	4.14	36	14	0	0	126	131	66	58	61	112

tends to lose his velocity. That's when it's time to call for help.

FIELDING:

Rijo has a powerful but smooth delivery that leaves him in good fielding position. He's an average fielder who can afford to bobble a ball once because of his rocket arm. His pickoff move is only average, and he needs work in holding runners on. Even Dwight Gooden has come to accept the fact that runners get on base.

OVERALL:

Rijo has the raw talent to become a superstar in the major leagues. His confidence has already been torn down once; the A's don't want that to happen again.

Killebrew: "It's amazing what you can find at tag sales. The Yankees unwrapped Jose Rijo, but when he disappointed them, they couldn't get rid of him fast enough. If he continues to throw his heat past the hitters, he'll be a great pitcher."

HITTING:

The A's, dissatisfied with the temperamental Mike Heath behind the plate, gave Mickey Tettleton every chance to be the team's number one catcher last year. He handled the job well defensively, but there remains serious doubt whether he can hit big league pitching.

He is a switch-hitter with a quick, fluid-looking swing, and he can drive the ball with authority from the left side. But this scouting report must indicate "no real pop," because Tettleton seldom makes long-ball contact.

He can handle the fastball down, but he has trouble with hard stuff away and any type of breaking ball. Pitchers can bust him inside, then go away. As an overanxious hitter trying to prove himself, Tettleton has been having trouble with off-speed pitches. The more experienced pitchers in the league can get him to strike himself out.

He is an unproven hitting commodity who is trying to get his feet wet in the big leagues. He is just an average bunter but can move a runner along. He gets out of the batter's box quickly.

BASERUNNING:

Tettleton is an average baserunner with below-average speed, which is not unusual for a catcher. But he's quick for a big man, and as a former football player, he can do some damage breaking up the double play or trying to jar the ball loose. The team likes his hustle and alertness.

FIELDING:

Tettleton came to the big leagues with a reputation as a moody catcher who couldn't work well with pitchers. A couple of seasons in the big leagues took care of that, because Tettleton is now rated a strong presence behind the plate. Veteran Don Sutton praised his

MICKEY TETTLETON
C, No. 6
SR, 6'2", 200 lbs.
ML Svc: 2 years
Born: 9-16-60 in
    Oklahoma City, OK

1985 STATISTICS											
AVG	G	AB	R	H	2B	3B	HR	RBI	BB	SO	SB
.251	78	211	23	53	12	0	3	15	28	59	2
CAREER STATISTICS											
AVG	G	AB	R	H	2B	3B	HR	RBI	BB	SO	SB
.254	111	287	33	73	14	1	4	20	39	80	2

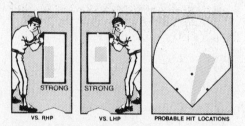

VS. RHP   VS. LHP   PROBABLE HIT LOCATIONS

"quiet confidence," and as the season went on, more and more of the staff preferred working with him.

Tettleton has good range and agility for a big man. He has a strong arm and gets rid of the ball quickly, although he showed a tendency toward high throws last year, giving opponents a stolen base they often didn't deserve.

The feeling is that he'll be a good catcher in time.

OVERALL:

Killebrew: "More playing time will definitely help this guy. He handles himself well behind the plate, and he has the tools to improve as a hitter."

"Good catchers are hard to come by. Tettleton is in a good position in Oakland; they are looking for someone like him. He'll move along more quickly as he improves his hitting."

PITCHING:

The Oakland A's were so excited about Curt Young last year, they wouldn't have been surprised to see him win 18 games. Now, they're wondering if he has any future in the big leagues.

They figured something was wrong when Young gave up seven home runs in his first two starts. As it turned out, he had shoulder tendinitis, a condition that kept him out until July. But even when he returned, Young had terrible long ball problems and seemed eminently hittable.

Young has a better-than-average fastball, around 87 MPH, but he's known as a control pitcher. He throws overhand and has a curveball that breaks effectively down and in to righthanded hitters and away from lefthanders. His slider is actually more of a cut fastball that he runs inside to righthanders. He'll try to keep power hitters off balance with a change-up, but he's been burned in the past with that pitch; it needs work.

In 1984, his impressive rookie year, Young's out pitch was the curve. Last year, he had trouble spotting the curve, and the fastball wasn't good enough to bail him out. He also walked 22 batters in 46 innings, meaning another one of his strong points--good control--had turned into a weakness.

At this point, there is considerable doubt whether Young is a starter (he was 0-4 in that role) or a reliever. If he no longer has the stamina to pitch nine innings, he might best be used as a short-relief man to get lefthanded hitters out.

CURT YOUNG
LHP, No. 29
RL, 6'1", 175 lbs.
ML Svc: 2 years
Born: 4-16-60 in
   Saginaw, MI

1985 STATISTICS

W	L	ERA	G	GS	CG	SV	IP	H	R	ER	BB	SO
0	4	7.24	19	7	0	0	46	57	38	37	22	19

CAREER STATISTICS

W	L	ERA	G	GS	CG	SV	IP	H	R	ER	BB	SO
9	9	5.61	47	26	2	0	163.2	192	108	102	58	65

FIELDING:

Young has a respectable move to first base, and with the advantage of being a lefthander, he holds runners on pretty well. He is an adequate fielder who never seems to create unnecessary problems for himself.

OVERALL:

This will be a critical year for him. His stock fell so drastically in 1985.

Killebrew: "Something happened to him; he gave up so many home runs, you have to wonder what it did to his confidence. But I look for him to rebound, to regain the command of his pitches.

"I think he has enough poise that he will start the 1986 season in a competitive spirit, ready to show that he deserves a spot in the starting rotation."

JOSE CANSECO
OF, No. 33
RR, 6'3", 195 lbs.
ML Svc: less than 1 year
Born: 7-2-64 in
    Havana, Cuba

HITTING, BASERUNNING, FIELDING:

Jose Canseco joined the A's last September as one of the most talked-about minor leaguers in years. He was considered the best nonpitching prospect in the country. After hitting .302 with five homers in his brief trial for the A's, Canseco is projected as a full-time player in 1986.

His wide-open stance is as exaggerated as anyone's in baseball, but when the pitch arrives, Canseco brings his left foot back to a conventional position. He takes a vicious cut that produces a lot of strikeouts, but he has tremendous power to all fields. In his first visit to Chicago, he became one of the few players ever to put a ball on the roof at Comiskey Park.

Like any other rookie, Canseco will have to work on curveballs on the outside corner; he was very vulnerable to that pitch last season. Canseco runs well for a big man, and he has an excellent throwing arm from the outfield. He looked a little shaky defensively, showing bad judgment on balls he could have handled, but that might have been due to first-year jitters.

OVERALL:

Everyone is excited about seeing him play every day in the big leagues. He was so dominant in the minor leagues, he left nothing else to prove. The A's will have plenty of room for him, either as an outfielder or DH.

RICK LANGFORD
RHP, No. 22
RR, 6'0", 185 lbs.
ML Svc: 10 years
Born: 3-20-52 in
    Farmville, VA

PITCHING, FIELDING:

Rick Langford has a solid reputation as a smart pitcher and a hard-nosed competitor, but he needs more than a reputation now. He's been battling back from arm problems for three years, with very mixed results.

Langford remains the over-the-top, fast-working pitcher who had so much success for Oakland in the early 1980s. But his fastball is in the low 80s now, and he no longer has the hard, consistent slider that he could move to either corner. If he isn't razor-sharp every time, he gets burned.

The A's, in their reluctance to have Langford's confidence broken, gave him only three starts last year.

Defensively, Langford is one of the best. He has a variety of pickoff moves to first base, fields his position expertly, and has command of everything going on around him.

OVERALL:

Killebrew: "His arm problems may end his career, which is a shame for someone who knows the game this well. We'll see if he can regain some of the velocity of his pitches, or at least get full command of them again. His future has been in question for quite a few years now; to their credit, both he and the club are still trying."

STEVE MURA
RHP, No. 38
RR, 6'2", 188 lbs.
ML Svc: 5 years
Born: 2-12-55 in
New Orleans, LA

PITCHING, FIELDING:

Called up as an emergency measure by the A's last June, Steve Mura became a reliable middle reliever and stuck with the club the rest of the season. He allowed just 41 hits in 48 innings.

He throws over the top, works quickly and has an 86-87 MPH fastball.

Mura rarely throws a slider; when he is on, he's a very effective pitcher. He uses the fastball and the straight over-hand curve that arrives down around the knees. The curve is his best pitch; when he's throwing strikes with it, he can be tough. If he's wild (he averaged nearly five walks per nine innings), he doesn't have the commanding stuff to get away with it.

Defensively, Mura is better than average. He's been around pro ball for several years, and the presence of baserunners doesn't bother him. If he has a problem, it is that his follow-through leaves him off to the left of the mound, which is not an ideal position to field ground balls.

OVERALL:

Killebrew: "The A's gave Mura a break after a long spell in the minor leagues, and he responded to it. He showed his capability as a long reliever who is particularly tough on righthanders."

ROB PICCIOLO
INF, No. 8
RR, 6'2", 180 lbs.
ML Svc: 9 years
Born: 2-4-53 in
Santa Monica, CA

HITTING, BASERUNNING, FIELDING:

Rob Picciolo has given up any notions of being an everyday infielder in the big leagues, but he's become a valuable man off the bench. He was hitting .300 into September before a late-season slide brought him down to .275.

Picciolo is a straightaway hitter with little power (and less patience, as evidenced by just eight walks over the last four years). Since he does not play often, pitchers usually go right after him with fastballs inside and breaking balls away.

He is a fair bunter and a better-than-average baserunner who plays hard when he gets the chance. Picciolo has established himself as a respected back-up infielder at shortstop and second base. He has a strong, accurate arm and turns the double play well from either position. When asked to play third base last year (in place of injured Carney Lansford), Picciolo felt uncomfortable and admitted he couldn't handle it.

OVERALL:

Killebrew: "Rob has made a living as the backup for some of the game's better infielders--Robin Yount and Alfredo Griffin, to name two. If that's all you need from him, he's the right man."

SEATTLE MARINERS

PITCHING:

It looks as though injuries will prevent Jim Beattie from ever reaching his considerable potential. Tendinitis in his right shoulder has plagued him since the 1980 season and persisted into last year. He underwent surgery on his right shoulder at the end of 1984; he was disabled twice in 1985 and then underwent arthroscopic surgery again on August 30 last year. He pitched a career low of 18 games last season and his future is in question.

When he is healthy, Beattie is one of the dominant pitchers in the AL. He is a power pitcher with a hard overhand curveball and an excellent slider. When Beattie pitches well, he works quickly and throws strikes. He doesn't give hitters the chance to adjust.

It is easy to tell when Beattie is in trouble: he walks around the mound, shakes off his catcher's signs and tries to guide the ball. He will also fall behind in the count.

Beattie's fastball is a 90 MPH pitch. It has excellent movement and its sinking action helps him get ground balls. What makes his slider so effective is that there is little loss of velocity. He will run the fastball in on right-handed hitters and use the slider to move lefthanded hitters off the plate.

FIELDING:

Beattie uses a slow, winding motion which turns his body toward second base and features a big leg kick before his delivery. Even when he is pitching from the stretch, he has a slow move toward the plate. He has made a conscious effort to improve with runners on base; now he can occasionally hasten his delivery, shorten his stride and keep the runner on first off balance. He will throw over frequently and can be sur-

JIM BEATTIE
RHP, No. 45
RR, 6'6", 225 lbs.
ML Svc: 7 years
Born: 7-4-54 in
  Hampton, VA

1985 STATISTICS
W	L	ERA	G	GS	CG	SV	IP	H	R	ER	BB	SO
5	6	7.29	18	15	1	0	70.1	93	61	57	33	45

CAREER STATISTICS
W	L	ERA	G	GS	CG	SV	IP	H	R	ER	BB	SO
55	82	3.61	186	172	42	1	1215.1	1105	534	488	430	658

prisingly quick for a man of his size.

Sometimes though, he will push off the mound so hard that he is not balanced after he releases the ball.

OVERALL:

Beattie's career is in jeopardy--he has been plagued with arm problems since he first signed with the Yankees out of Dartmouth College (1975), but the latest ailment could be the final blow. When he is healthy, he is the type of pitcher who fits perfectly into the role of the number three starter because he can keep a team in a game and consistently pitch into the later innings. It is, however, hard to count on him in that spot because it is a given that at some point in the season, he will be sidelined by an injury.

Killebrew: "It's a shame to see a guy with so much talent unable to put together a full season.

"When Beattie is healthy, he has one of the best sliders in the AL and he has the fastball of a power pitcher. The key to his success is throwing strikes and staying ahead in the count."

KARL BEST
RHP, No. 39
RR, 6'4", 210 lbs.
ML Svc: 1 year plus
Born: 3-6-59 in
Aberdeen, WA

PITCHING:

Just when it looked as if Karl Best was the answer to the Mariners' short reliever quandary, he was knocked out by a shoulder injury. That was the bad news. The good news is that his right shoulder was repaired by mid-August.

Best is a two-pitch pitcher, but those two pitches are the kind which make him well-suited for short relief work. His best pitch is a fastball that he can throw over 90 MPH. He complements his heater with a hard slider which breaks down and in to lefthanded hitters and down and away to righthanders.

He was on a roll last year when he was sidelined by the shoulder injury. He did not allow a run in his last six appearances (12 innings and 11 Ks) and earned a save in each of the four times he came in with a lead to protect.

Best has the kind of mental makeup which makes him a good short reliever. He is not afraid to bust any hitter inside. His aggressiveness makes it very dangerous for hitters to get too comfortable in the batter's box. He comes into the game ready, willing and able to challenge any and all comers. He takes to the mound looking for strikeouts.

Most importantly, he throws strikes-- just check his ratios: 25 hits in 32 1/3 innings and 32 strikeouts and only six walks.

FIELDING:

Short relievers cannot afford to give up stolen bases. Best has a solid pick-off move and relinquishes nothing to any runner on base. He is able to maintain his focus on the hitter while keeping the baserunners close.

He is a good athlete, which helps him field his position well. He has a short delivery out of the stretch and

1985 STATISTICS												
W	L	ERA	G	GS	CG	SV	IP	H	R	ER	BB	SO
2	1	1.95	15	0	0	4	32.1	25	9	7	6	32
CAREER STATISTICS												
W	L	ERA	G	GS	CG	SV	IP	H	R	ER	BB	SO
3	3	3.54	24	0	0	4	43.2	46	20	17	11	41

lands in good position to field balls hit back up the middle.

OVERALL:

What problems Karl had in the minor leagues stemmed from his lack of an off-speed pitch. As a starter, he had to pace himself, and in doing so, he lost the effectiveness of his hard stuff. As a short reliever, he doesn't have to worry about that now. All he is asked to do is strike out a few hitters; he doesn't have to save himself, nor does he have time to think his way into problems.

Keep an eye on the medical reports this year. If Best is healthy, he will help the Mariners recover in the bullpen. Best is a young pitcher with lots of ability, but he must be healthy.

Killebrew: "Best's strength is his ability to throw hard. He is definitely a power pitcher with one of the better sliders in the big leagues. We'll just have to see how he comes back this spring. He has to come back with his peak speed on his fastball."

MOST IMPROVED

PHIL BRADLEY
OF, No. 29
RR, 6'0", 178 lbs.
ML Svc: 2 years
Born: 3-11-59 in
    Bloomington, IN

HITTING:

Talk about magic! Mariner hitting instructor Deron Johnson did some kind of a hocus-pocus trick on Phil Bradley last spring. Johnson took a fellow who in four professional seasons and 1,445 at-bats had hit only three home runs (none in his 389 major league at-bats) and turned him into a true power threat.

Check the numbers: Bradley set a team record with 67 extra-base hits, including 26 home runs and had a .498 slugging percentage. And, on five separate occasions last year, Bradley came to the plate as the potential final Mariner at-bat and hit a home run to win the game.

Bradley still stands on top of the plate. But what he doesn't do anymore is choke up. He has lowered his hands on the barrel of the bat which allows him to get the bat into a hitting position more quickly. He now snaps the head of the bat through the strike zone instead of guiding it just to make contact.

Pitchers still have their best success throwing fastballs up and in; he will chase the high fastball. He can also be fooled by change-ups.

Bradley can--if asked to--bunt for either a base hit or as a sacrifice. He helps himself by showing the bunt now and then, giving the infielders the notion that he just may do it.

Bradley was able to raise his power output significantly last year--and hit .300 in the process.

BASERUNNING:

Bradley is an instinctively good baserunner. He reads pitchers well and has above-average speed. In his two major league seasons, he has stolen 46 bases. He gets a good lead and uses his above-average speed and his intelligence to his best advantage.

FIELDING:

Bradley looks as though he was born to play center field, but in fact he

1985 STATISTICS

AVG	G	AB	R	H	2B	3B	HR	RBI	BB	SO	SB
.300	159	641	100	192	33	8	26	88	55	129	22

CAREER STATISTICS

AVG	G	AB	R	H	2B	3B	HR	RBI	BB	SO	SB
.298	306	1030	157	307	47	12	26	117	97	195	46

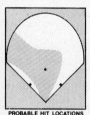

VS. RHP   VS. LHP   PROBABLE HIT LOCATIONS

doesn't like the position. He prefers left field and as long as he shows the kind of power he did last year, he will stay where he is. He has good instincts for plays in the outfield; he goes back well on the ball and he closes the gaps.

Bradley has worked hard on improving his arm and now has an adequate one. He makes up for what he still lacks in arm strength by anticipating the ball and by hitting the cutoff man.

OVERALL:

Bradley left everyone very impressed last year with his display of power, his run production and his ability to hit in the clutch.

Killebrew: "Before the jury returns a verdict on his power, he is going to have to do it for more than just one season to prove that 1985 was not just an exception to the rule. He is still short on experience, but I believe he has room to grow into his new-found abilities."

HITTING:

Ivan Calderon is a natural hitter. He has a short, quick, powerful stroke. He is capable of driving the ball to all fields. His biggest problems over the last two years have been injuries. He broke a bone in his left wrist in 1984 and it continued to bother him and forced him to spend the final two months of the 1985 season on the disabled list.

When Calderon does play, he plays very well. He is a productive hitter, and hit .286, with 8 home runs and 28 RBIs in just 210 at-bats.

He is a first-pitch, fastball hitter. Pitchers have to pound him inside with hard stuff and make sure they keep it inside. Calderon will chase the fastball up and can be set up for the off-speed breaking pitch away (45 strikeouts, 210 at-bats). If pitchers get the ball out over the plate at all, he will make them pay for the mistake: 28 of his 60 hits were for extra bases.

He responds to pressure situations well (16 for 48 with runners in scoring position), but tends to get lazy if a game gets out of hand. He can bunt, but doesn't get the sign to do so often: he can create too much offense too quickly to take the bat out of his hands, especially in the tiny confines of the Kingdome.

BASERUNNING:

Ivan is not showing all of his cards. He is a basestealing threat who has run only when the spirit has moved him. He has the potential of stealing 30 bases but lacks motivation on the basepaths. Likewise, he is capable of more extra bases than he registers and could break up more double plays if he wanted to.

FIELDING:

Calderon is capable of playing any outfield position. He is best suited to left field, but with Phil Bradley in that spot, Calderon gets most of his

IVAN CALDERON
LF, No. 13
RR, 6'1", 205 lbs.
ML Svc: 1 year plus
Born: 3-19-62 in
Fajaro, PR

1985 STATISTICS

AVG	G	AB	R	H	2B	3B	HR	RBI	BB	SO	SB
.286	67	210	37	60	16	4	8	28	19	45	4

CAREER STATISTICS

AVG	G	AB	R	H	2B	3B	HR	RBI	BB	SO	SB
.278	77	234	393	65	17	4	9	29	21	50	5

  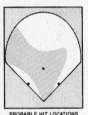

STRONG   STRONG

VS. RHP   VS. LHP   PROBABLE HIT LOCATIONS

playing time as either the DH or right fielder. He has an above-average arm and a quick release, but he gets lazy, and runners will take the extra base when Calderon misses the cutoff man or throws to the wrong base.

OVERALL:

With Calderon, it appears that attitude is everything. He has to be pushed to reach his capabilities. If he ever learns to motivate himself, he could be a dominant offensive player and a solid defensive player.

The lack of motivation is really immaturity--he should have grown up by now. The Mariners even have to motivate him to keep his weight down; he will get heavy the minute no one is looking.

Killebrew: "He definitely has the power to exploit the Kingdome's conditions. Defensively, he is too weak at this point to play every day, but as a hitter, he can do anything he wants to."

HITTING:

Scouts watched Darnell Coles in the minor leagues and saw a quick bat and a nice short swing. They looked at his .299 composite minor league average and his numerous extra-base hits.

They brought him to spring training: same thing, nice work, looking good.

But when the season began, it looked as though Coles thought he was out in the field to catch some sun and up at the plate just for a little exercise.

Coles knows he can hit. He is a fastball hitter and likes the pitch off the plate and up in the strike zone. He knows he can drive the ball into the alley. And Coles is just as willing to go to right-center field as to left-center field.

Pitchers run the ball in on his hands hard and use breaking pitches, especially away, which he will chase. Coles should be able to lay off these pitches as he gains more experience and learns how to concentrate. Coles' willingness to concentrate, however, is the problem.

He could improve his game by bunting. He has the ability to bunt, but what Coles seems to be concentrating on is looking good, not on what would be best for the team.

BASERUNNING:

Coles is a guy the Mariners talk about in terms of 20-20 potential (home runs and stolen bases). He has the speed to get the job done, but does not seem to have the motivation to push himself to take advantage of or to create opportunities. For a player with his speed, Coles does not challenge the outfielders enough and doesn't seem fond of contact on the bases.

FIELDING:

Finding a position for Coles has been a problem. Signed as a shortstop, he has the hands and arm and range to play the position, but gets lazy and makes too many errors. Given his bat potential,

DARNELL COLES
3B, No. 19
RR, 6'1", 185 lbs.
ML Svc: 1 year plus
Born: 6-22-62 in
San Bernardino, CA

1985 STATISTICS

AVG	G	AB	R	H	2B	3B	HR	RBI	BB	SO	SB
.237	27	59	8	14	4	0	1	5	9	17	0

CAREER STATISTICS

AVG	G	AB	R	H	2B	3B	HR	RBI	BB	SO	SB
.214	102	294	32	63	14	1	2	17	33	55	2

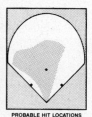

VS. RHP   VS. LHP   PROBABLE HIT LOCATIONS

the Mariners decided to try him at third base, where he was adequate. But with the development of Jim Presley, Coles has played in the outfield as well.

He could be a smooth center fielder or left fielder. He has the good speed and instincts that enable him to cover the ground and an exceptionally strong arm. But he must concentrate on little things and realize that natural ability will carry him only so far.

OVERALL:

His biggest enemy has been himself. He acts as if he expects opportunities to be handed to him. His gig is not going over very well.

Killebrew: "The Mariners are trying to find a spot for him, but he sometimes makes it difficult. He has been used as a utility type of player, but has the ability to earn a regular spot. His future is pretty much up to him to make or to break."

HITTING:

As with all of the followers of the Charlie Lau theory of hitting, Al Cowens is an aggressive hitter. He does not need to see a strike--rather, Cowens wants "to see the ball and drive it."

He stands deep in the box and off the plate. If a pitcher has a plan to pitch him inside, it had better be way inside; he stands far from the plate and can't be jammed. Cowens' position in the batter's box is the result of having his jaw broken by a tight pitch in 1978.

Cowens keeps his weight on his back foot and tries to drive the ball into the alleys. When he is swinging well, he will not pull balls foul. Pitchers have to mix up their offerings to him. When he is in a slump, Cowens will chase the slider away.

He enjoys hitting in the Kingdome, where he hit .284, compared with .249 on the road. Cowens is a good clutch hitter; he raised his average by more than 40 points (.265 to .308) with runners in scoring position last year and he can bunt for a hit or to move the runners along.

Cowens provides a steadying influence on the young Mariner team. He is a veteran who has been through championship races. Though he can no longer do all of the things he did when he was younger, he still knows how to go about his job and has shown younger Mariners how to work their way through down periods.

BASERUNNING:

Once a premier thief, Cowens doesn't run much any more. He didn't even try to steal a base once last year. He knows what he can and cannot do. He will take the extra base and force the outfielder to come up with the ball in a hurry. He is not afraid of contact on the bases when it comes to breaking up the double play.

FIELDING:

Cowens is no longer one of the best

AL COWENS
RF, No. 16
RR, 6'2", 205 lbs.
ML Svc: 12 years
Born: 10-21-51 in
    Los Angeles, CA

1985 STATISTICS

AVG	G	AB	R	H	2B	3B	HR	RBI	BB	SO	SB
.265	122	452	59	120	32	5	14	69	30	56	0

CAREER STATISTICS

AVG	G	AB	R	H	2B	3B	HR	RBI	BB	SO	SB
.271	1556	5452	699	1479	272	68	108	711	386	641	119

  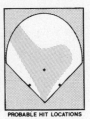

STRONG — VS. RHP   STRONG — VS. LHP   PROBABLE HIT LOCATIONS

outfielders in the business. His arm does not have the strength of its youth, but it continues to hit its mark with accuracy. He gets rid of the ball quickly but he cannot throw it as far as he once did. He goes back on the ball well and is not afraid of fences. He plays a respectable right field.

OVERALL:

Cowens seems to have found a home in Seattle. While he has never come close to matching his sparkling 1977 season, when he was the runner-up in the MVP balloting, Cowens has been a consistent part of the Mariners' offense since he joined the club in 1982.

Killebrew: "The Mariners are a young, developing club and a ballplayer like Cowens can make a big difference by his presence alone. He does more than provide influence, however; he continues to be a good hitter and play good defense."

HITTING:

After a quick start to his big league career in 1984, Alvin Davis struggled in the opening weeks of 1985. But by hitting .310 after the All-Star break, he finished strong and hit for a .287 average overall, although his RBI total did drop from 116 to 78. That is what happens once a hitter establishes himself as a definite threat and pitchers start to work around him instead of challenging him.

And Davis is a threat. Basically a pull hitter, he has already shown the ability to make adjustments with two strikes against him. He will go with the pitch--and he will get his hits. He has never hit below .284 in pro ball.

Davis also has shown the ability to adjust to different types of pitchers. He is a fastball hitter and prefers the ball down, but can handle off-speed stuff from breaking-ball pitchers as well. He will also thwart the pitcher if he spots a trend developing.

He has an excellent idea of the strike zone. He knows what to go after and what to lay off. Davis has walked his way on base 187 times in two seasons.

He can bunt, but doesn't get the call: he's a middle-of-the-lineup hitter. He's the guy who produces runs--he doesn't set them up for others.

BASERUNNING:

Davis has below-average speed, but he is a smart player. If he catches the opposition ignoring him, he will take off. Davis doesn't try too often for the extra base, but then with the small outfield in the Kingdome, outfielders can cut off the balls more quickly there than in most parks.

FIELDING:

As a first baseman, he is nothing

ALVIN DAVIS
1B, No. 21
LR, 6'1", 190 lbs.
ML Svc: 2 years
Born: 9-9-60 in
   Riverside, CA

1985 STATISTICS

AVG	G	AB	R	H	2B	3B	HR	RBI	BB	SO	SB
.287	155	578	78	166	33	1	18	78	90	71	1

CAREER STATISTICS

AVG	G	AB	R	H	2B	3B	HR	RBI	BB	SO	SB
.286	307	1145	158	327	67	4	45	194	187	149	6

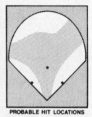

VS. RHP   VS. LHP   PROBABLE HIT LOCATIONS

special. He has soft hands, and adjusts his feet for off-target throws. His range is limited, but he makes the routine plays. His arm is adequate. He can make the throw to second, which is all it really takes to play first.

OVERALL:

In two years, Davis has established himself as a legitimate major league player. He has a good attitude that is infectious. He pushes himself to succeed and reaps the rewards.

Killebrew: "Davis is a complete offensive player. He can hit for average and hit home runs and is not afraid to take a walk. With the development of Jim Presley and the resurgence of Gorman Thomas, Davis had some of the pressure to carry the Mariners removed from him. He should become a better hitter in the next couple of years."

HITTING:

Someday, Dave Henderson is going to put all of the pieces of his game together and have a great season. He has the distinction of being the Mariners' original first-round draft pick (1977), but has not distinguished himself since with anything except inconsistency and flying bats.

Some things are looking up for him, but some things are looking down. He finished the season with a career-worst .241 average, but he also had a career high of 28 doubles. He continues to show flashes of power: he hit 14 home runs last season.

Henderson gets himself in trouble by trying to pull every pitch he is thrown. When he does get into a good groove, he will drive the ball to right-center, but he does not do that consistently.

Pitchers throw him inside fastballs and then get him to chase off-speed breaking pitches away--including ones that bounce in the dirt. His penchant for chasing breaking balls in the dirt is responsible for his career average of one strikeout for every 5.2 at-bats.

Henderson can get so fooled on a pitch that he has become famous for losing his grip on the bat and letting it fly--sometimes beyond the infielders.

BASERUNNING:

Before knee problems inhibited his running and before chronic hamstring pulls forced him to slow down, Henderson was a good baserunner. As far as pure speed, Henderson still has the stuff, but his legs are not healthy enough to help him. He also does not read pitchers well enough to be a threat on the bases.

He enjoys taking out the second baseman or the shortstop on the double play pivot, but he has been known to run out of control advancing on a base hit.

FIELDING:

Henderson is a true center fielder.

DAVE HENDERSON
CF, No. 42
RR, 6'2", 212 lbs.
ML Svc: 5 years
Born: 7-21-58 in
  Dos Palos, CA

1985 STATISTICS

AVG	G	AB	R	H	2B	3B	HR	RBI	BB	SO	SB
.241	139	502	70	121	28	2	14	68	48	104	6

CAREER STATISTICS

AVG	G	AB	R	H	2B	3B	HR	RBI	BB	SO	SB
.253	551	1786	226	452	95	8	65	227	147	344	24

  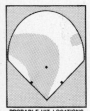

VS. RHP   VS. LHP   PROBABLE HIT LOCATIONS

He plays shallow and backpedals well. Some balls will get over his head, but by playing in he more than makes up for those few hits by taking some singles away.

He moves well to both his left and his right, but he can get caught trying to cut off balls sailing by him.

Henderson has one of the stronger arms among American League center fielders. It is good enough that he could even play right field. Good arm or not, however, he has a tendency to forget to hit the cutoff man.

OVERALL:

Killebrew: "Henderson is not a young player any more and it is time that he became more consistent. He has the kind of power that should enable him to hit more home runs than he has so far. Certainly, the first step would be to lay off the outside breaking pitch. The second step would be to let the high fastball out of the strike zone go by."

HITTING:

Bob Kearney has not shown much power, yet he goes up to the plate hacking, and he acts as if he can hit home runs. His numbers indicate otherwise: he has hit 21 home runs in 1,105 major league at-bats. His power-thinking approach at the plate causes slumps (like the 0 for 33 skid early last season) that can leave him struggling from Opening Day until the end of the year.

He stands so far off the plate that he cannot cover the outside portion. Pitchers will jam him with fastballs and can then throw him almost anything outside to send him back to the dugout. The one pitch Kearney can handle is the high fastball pitched over the inner part of the plate.

One would think that a catcher, whose thoughts should be on the nuances of positioning and adjustments, would have tried to make some himself, but he hasn't done anything to help himself to date.

Kearney is a skilled bunter and the Mariners let him use it on a squeeze play. He will do whatever it takes to get his bat on the ball in that situation.

BASERUNNING:

Kearney is a threat on the bases--not as a basestealer, mind you--just a plain old threat. He loves to make contact with whoever is covering a bag. He will try to force the extra base, but doesn't really have the speed to be a good baserunner.

FIELDING:

It makes Kearney bristle to hear such talk, but the fact remains: he does not call a good game and the Mariner pitchers complain about throwing to him. The Seattle staff is composed of young, strong arms, yet Kearney gets carried away with off-speed breaking pitches, which negates their best weapon.

BOB KEARNEY
C, No. 11
RR, 6'0", 185 lbs.
ML Svc: 3 years
Born: 10-3-56 in
   San Antonio, TX

1985 STATISTICS

AVG	G	AB	R	H	2B	3B	HR	RBI	BB	SO	SB
.243	108	305	24	74	14	1	6	27	11	59	1

CAREER STATISTICS

AVG	G	AB	R	H	2B	3B	HR	RBI	BB	SO	SB
.234	374	1105	103	259	52	2	21	107	54	191	9

STRONG   VS. RHP   STRONG   VS. LHP   PROBABLE HIT LOCATIONS

Defensively, however, Kearney is among the best. He had a 40% kill ratio against potential basestealers last season. The key for him is his quick release and good carry on the ball. He gets the ball to second base quickly enough to compensate for any of his inaccuracies. He led all American League catchers in fielding, committing only three errors in 582 chances.

OVERALL:

Kearney was the key player two years ago in the trade which sent reliever Bill Caudill to Oakland. He hasn't come close to filling the Mariners needs. The Mariners are shopping, a trip which, to some extent, was launched because the team was disturbed over Kearney's refusal to respond to constructive advice.

Killebrew: "Because of the way he calls a game, Kearney is not an everyday catcher. He has a great throw and is difficult to steal against; his arm will keep him around as a backup."

PITCHING:

After a tremendous rookie season in 1984, Mark Langston came crashing to the ground last year. Though part of his disasterous performance can be traced to an injury to his left elbow which put him on the disabled list for six weeks, the real problem is deeper than that.

During the 1984 season, everything seemed to go his way and he got away with inconsistent control (118 walks) because he also got lots of big strike-outs (204). Last year, however, the control problems that were overlooked in 1984 came back to haunt him. He averaged 6.5 walks per nine innings and had fewer strikeouts (72) than walks (91).

The raw ability is there. Langston is a lefty with a fastball consistently in the upper 80 MPH range. He has a good overhand curve that he keeps in on left-handed hitters and works away from righthanders.

When Langston is in a groove, he changes speeds off the breaking ball. He can use his slider as a reverse to his curveball, which can completely baffle hitters and prevents them from guessing what is coming. His change-up is good enough, though still marginal and, if he doesn't overuse it, can make his hard stuff look better.

So, with all this stuff, how can he go through stretches the way he did last year, when he lost six games in a row and then finished the season by losing five in a row?

In 1984, it was almost as if he was trying harder: he kept himself mentally sharp for his games. It appears that the ease with which he earned a 17-10 record that year caused him to sit back and re-lax too quickly. He needs to maintain his concentration and to realize that every game is a challenge he must pre-pare for. He has to be the aggressor and should learn to shake off catcher Bob Kearney, who does not call pitches well.

MARK LANGSTON
LHP, No. 12
RL, 6'2", 180 lbs.
ML Svc: 2 years
Born: 8-20-60 in
   San Diego, CA

1985 STATISTICS												
W	L	ERA	G	GS	CG	SV	IP	H	R	ER	BB	SO
7	14	5.47	24	24	2	0	126.2	122	85	77	91	72
CAREER STATISTICS												
W	L	ERA	G	GS	CG	SV	IP	H	R	ER	BB	SO
24	24	4.15	59	67	7	0	351.2	310	184	162	209	276

FIELDING:

Langston has an average move to first base, but being lefthanded helps compen-sate for a less-than-good throw. He also knows he has to keep runners close, even more so because the Mariners' catchers are not much help.

He is an excellent fielder and a good athlete. He moves around the mound well and reacts quickly to balls hit back to him. If he stays around a few years, he could be a Gold Glove candidate.

OVERALL:

Look for Langston to bounce back this year. He is a quick learner and got a harsh lesson in 1985.

Killebrew: "Langston is a young guy who should get better with experience. He has all of the pitches it takes to win, and if his arm is healthy, Mark should do well this season. He has to remember to challenge hitters all the time and to throw quality strikes. His control problem could be a sign that he has to bear down a little bit more."

PITCHING:

The wait is over.

The number one draft pick in the June 1981 draft has finally blossomed into a first-rate major league pitcher.

Mike Moore was able to rebound from a dismal 7-17 season in 1984 to pitch his way to an impressive 17-10 record last year. After returning from the disabled list in June, Moore came on strong. He completed 11 of his 22 starts and won 13 of 19 decisions.

Moore always had the arm strength to pitch well, but he lacked consistency. He throws a 93 MPH fastball and can maintain full velocity for a full nine innings. He always had that ability, but in the past he was never around long enough to prove it.

One of the factors that helped make the difference is that Moore is now able to throw his other pitches for strikes. His breaking pitch has the break of a curveball, but the quick action of a slider. He runs it in on the hands of righthanded hitters and uses his fastball to come in tight to lefthanders.

The turnaround pitch, however, was the change-up. In the past, he showed hints of a good change-up, but until 1985, he didn't have enough confidence to throw it in a game situation. He now uses it very well and can keep almost any hitter off stride.

FIELDING:

Moore has a deliberate motion to the plate. He has to keep runners especially close to prevent them from taking advantage of his motion. He has developed a good pickoff move which does just that. He gets the ball to first quickly and throws over often to remind the runner

MIKE MOORE
RHP, No. 25
RR, 6'4", 205 lbs.
ML Svc: 4 years
Born: 11-26-59 in
Eakly, OK

1985 STATISTICS												
W	L	ERA	G	GS	CG	SV	IP	H	R	ER	BB	SO
17	10	3.46	35	34	14	0	247	230	100	95	70	155

CAREER STATISTICS												
W	L	ERA	G	GS	CG	SV	IP	H	R	ER	BB	SO
37	49	4.49	119	115	24	0	731.1	755	393	365	294	494

that he's watching.

As with many big pitchers, Moore is off balance in his follow-through. But he is a good athlete and recovers quickly enough so that it does not hinder his fielding ability.

OVERALL:

Moore has just scratched the surface of his potential. He has the chance to become a dominating pitcher for several years.

Killebrew: "Mike is an excellent competitor and does not back down from anyone. Since he developed a breaking ball and gained some confidence in his change-up, he has the ability to get the big strikeout.

"Last year, he became one of the best pitchers in the American League. He can get a little wild occasionally, but he has the type of arm which enables him to regain his control and get out of a tight spot."

EDWIN NUNEZ
RHP, No. 30
RR, 6'5", 235 lbs.
ML Svc: 2 years
Born: 5-27-63 in
  Humacao, PR

PITCHING:

For Edwin Nunez, the transformation from starter to reliever was completed in 1985. In his second full season out of the bullpen (and his first full year in the big leagues) Nunez was one of the few consistencies on a Mariner pitching staff that was torn apart by injuries.

Nunez has the type of pitches which would make him an effective starting pitcher, but, mentally, he seems better suited to short relief. He needs to come into a situation which does not allow him to relax. He needs to pitch "tense."

Nunez has the perfect short-reliever fastball. It consistently lights up the radar guns at 90 MPH or even faster. He has good movement on it and can keep the ball down. He enjoys running it in on the hands of both lefthanded and right-handed hitters. He loves to break bats.

Nunez is especially intimidating to righthanded hitters. He is a big, strong man and varies his delivery point from almost over-the-top to sidearm and he releases the ball at several points in between.

Nunez has more than just a good fast-ball. He also throws a hard slider, a good curveball and (although he doesn't throw it very often) a good change-up. He throws the change-up with the same basic motion as his fastball.

When he was used in the rotation, Nunez tended to nibble at the corners and tried to make the hitters chase his pitch. He does not have that luxury as a short reliever and seems to be a bet-ter pitcher for it.

Late in the season, Nunez appeared to lose something off his fastball. The remedy will be to develop the kind of durablity that should come with experi-ence as a short reliever as well as from his own physical maturity. His 70 ap-pearances last year were his career high and the most on the Seattle staff.

1985 STATISTICS

W	L	ERA	G	GS	CG	SV	IP	H	R	ER	BB	SO
7	3	3.09	70	0	0	16	90.1	79	36	31	34	58

CAREER STATISTICS

W	L	ERA	G	GS	CG	SV	IP	H	R	ER	BB	SO
10	11	3.55	129	10	0	23	230.1	173	101	91	93	177

FIELDING:

For a big man, Nunez is more agile than many might suppose. He has an ex-cellent pickoff move with a quick step and a hard throw to first base. He loves to play games with the runners and gets as much a thrill from a pickoff as he does from a strikeout.

His motion has a tendency to leave him off balance after he delivers the pitch, and it prevents him from fielding his position as well as he should.

OVERALL:

Signed as a 16-year-old out of Puerto Rico in 1979, Nunez finally put things together in 1985. With his competitive-ness and ability, he should be around for a long time in whatever role the Mariners ask him to fill.

Killebrew: "Nunez really has the mak-ings of a good short reliever. He comes into the game and throws hard and he throws strikes. Even though he has been around the big leagues off and on since 1982, Nunez is still young and should improve with more experience."

HITTING:

A switch-hitter, Spike Owen makes good contact and needs to in order to take full advantage of his ability. He struck out only 27 times last year. He is a natural righthanded hitter, but has worked hard to improve his lefthanded hitting prowess; last season, he hit five of his six home runs from the left side and had an overall .261 average as a lefthanded hitter while stroking .250 from the right side.

Owen's strength is the fastball up, but he still has a tendency to chase the pitch too far up and out of the strike zone. Pitchers try to keep the ball down on him, and if a pitcher has a better-than-average fastball, he can overpower Owen inside.

Part of Owen's offensive game is the bunt--he does what he has to do to get on base.

He hitting style is well suited to the Kingdome, not because of the stadium's dimensions but because of its artificial surface (last season, Owen hit .274 at home and .238 on the road).

BASERUNNING:

Be alerted. Owen is ready to run when he gets on base. He has above-average speed and is a good student of pitchers' moves. He will take off on a pitcher's motion. If he guesses incorrectly, Owen doesn't slow down going into second base and will beat the throw if the first baseman isn't alert. Although he is not a big man, Owen is not afraid of contact.

FIELDING:

When it came to the Mariners' turn to select in the first round of the June 1982 draft, they wanted a shortstop right away who wouldn't embarrass them on the major league level. They found one in Owen, who caught the Mariners' interest because he had played on ersatz grass at the University of Texas.

SPIKE OWEN
SS, No. 7
SR, 5'10", 160 lbs.
ML Svc: 3 years
Born: 4-19-61 in
Cleburne, TX

1985 STATISTICS

AVG	G	AB	R	H	2B	3B	HR	RBI	BB	SO	SB
.259	118	352	41	91	10	6	6	37	34	27	11

CAREER STATISTICS

AVG	G	AB	R	H	2B	3B	HR	RBI	BB	SO	SB
.237	350	1188	144	281	39	17	11	101	104	134	36

  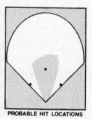

VS. RHP   VS. LHP   PROBABLE HIT LOCATIONS

Owen is not flashy, but he is steady. He moves well to his left and has an accurate arm, although it is not as strong as a team would want from an artificial turf shortstop. Last year, Owens finished third in fielding among AL shortstops with at least 100 games, committing 14 errors in 571 total chances.

OVERALL:

As far as ideal shortstops go, Owen is not going to meet many of the criteria-- but he grows on you. He plays hard and does the little things to help a team. He is not a shortstop a team builds around, like an Alan Trammell or Ozzie Smith, but he is the type of player who can play on a championship team.

Killebrew: "Owen has been honest with himself and doesn't try to do things that are out of his reach. He is a enthusiastic player who keeps his head in the game and makes up for his shortcomings with hustle and intensity."

HITTING:

Jack Perconte would be a nice number nine hitter in a lineup: he doesn't have much power, he doesn't drive in many runs and he doesn't walk as much as a team wants from a leadoff man. But the Mariners did not have much of a selection of hitters last season, so Perconte hit in the number one spot in the order.

Prior to May 17, 1985, Perconte held a dubious major league record: the longest streak by a non-pitcher without a home run (990 at-bats). By the end of the season, Perconte had crushed another into the seats. When he is not powering the ball, Perconte is a slap hitter; he chokes up on the bat and tries to make contact. He doesn't step to the plate with thoughts of pulling the ball.

Perconte can handle the fastball, especially over the plate, but not if it is too high in the strike zone; he likes to hit the low fastball by just dropping the bat head to the ball. Most of his hits go to the opposite field.

Pitchers get him out by keeping their fastballs inside and tight. Perconte is not strong enough to fight the ball off. But he does know how to keep himself out of a prolonged slump. He can bunt his way on base and is good enough with the bat that he is not afraid to bunt even if the infielders are playing in.

BASERUNNING:

One of Perconte's biggest assets is his baserunning ability. He finished the season with a streak of 27 consecutive stolen bases and already ranks third on the Mariners' all-time list with 60 stolen bases in two seasons.

He gets a good lead and watches key moves a pitcher makes in his delivery. Perconte is always aggressive on the bases. He is not a big man, but he goes into the bases hard and does whatever little things he can to help his team.

FIELDING:

As a second baseman, Perconte's over-

JACK PERCONTE
2B, No. 14
LR, 5'10", 160 lbs.
ML Svc: 3 years
Born: 8-31-54 in
 Joliet, IL

1985 STATISTICS

AVG	G	AB	R	H	2B	3B	HR	RBI	BB	SO	SB
.264	125	485	60	128	17	7	2	23	50	36	31

CAREER STATISTICS

AVG	G	AB	R	H	2B	3B	HR	RBI	BB	SO	SB
.273	409	1368	185	373	46	15	2	72	131	113	76

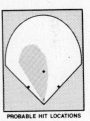

VS. RHP   VS. LHP   PROBABLE HIT LOCATIONS

all fielding is, at best, average. He goes to his left fairly well, but he is one of the worst second basemen in the American League at turning the double play. Seattle manager Chuck Cottier, himself a former infielder, has worked with Perconte to improve his double play skills. To date, no appreciable improvement has been observed.

OVERALL:

Perconte is a manager's player. From a scouting standpoint, there is not much to get excited about. But Perconte seems to win the favor of whatever manager he plays for because he is a hard worker who wants to win and never gives up.

Killebrew: "Perconte doesn't do anything well except battle for survival. He is a hard-nosed player who gets the most out of what ability he has."

HITTING:

Ken Phelps doesn't like it much, but at least he's still got a job. For the last two years, he has been a pinch-hitter and occasional DH while also filling in at first base.

Phelps is a power threat who, over the past two seasons, has averaged one home run for every 12.3 at-bats. With infrequent usage, it is not surprising that he also has averaged one strikeout for every 3.8 plate appearances.

He is a selective hitter in an aggressor's role. He often takes a called strike if it doesn't look like a pitch he can drive. He also draws too many walks for a power hitter (1 walk per 4.8 at-bats in 1984-85).

Clearly, something or someone is confused. He is a power hitter who has trouble with power pitchers. He lives off breaking balls and off-speed stuff because he waits well on the ball and follows the break. He creams a mistake.

In the minor leagues, Phelps turned his career around by learning to hit to the opposite field. The dimensions and the conditions of the Kingdome have served him well.

BASERUNNING:

Phelps is so slow, George Burns could finish his cigar before he gets to first base.

FIELDING:

Defensively, Phelps' only hope is at first base--and even then, only on a limited basis. He doesn't have much range, though he does a decent job on throws in the dirt. He has soft hands and needs them because he uses one of

KEN PHELPS
DH, No. 44
LL, 6'1", 204 lbs.
ML Svc: 4 years
Born: 8-6-54 in
Seattle, WA

1985 STATISTICS

AVG	G	AB	R	H	2B	3B	HR	RBI	BB	SO	SB
.207	61	116	18	24	3	0	9	24	24	33	2

CAREER STATISTICS

AVG	G	AB	R	H	2B	3B	HR	RBI	BB	SO	SB
.228	246	567	81	129	16	2	40	152	99	149	5

VS. RHP VS. LHP PROBABLE HIT LOCATIONS

the smallest gloves of any first baseman in the big leagues.

OVERALL:

At this point, Phelps needs to accept his role. He can contribute to his team as a pinch-hitter as well as if he were playing more often. He has the opportunity to stick around for a while if he comes to terms with that reality.

Killebrew: "Phelps can give a team a big lift as a pinch-hitter or designated hitter. Pitchers have to watch what they throw him and continually vary their pattern to him. He is a home run threat every time he steps up to the plate."

HITTING:

Jim Presley is the prototype of a third baseman. The only season in the last five that he didn't hit 20 or more home runs was 1983 when in Double-A where he had 14. (He played in a ballpark with a high fence in left field that is 350 feet down the line from home plate.)

Last season, he proved he could carry that power into the big leagues. In his first full season with the Mariners, Presley ranked second on the team with 28 home runs and third with 84 RBIs.

Presley has a long sweeping swing, but he may find that he needs to shorten it up to get a quicker stroke this season--pitchers will make adjustments to him this year. He hits for power in streaks, but one thing that he always is is aggressive. He steps up to the plate swinging and knows that he will stay in the big leagues for one reason: run production.

Presley has the ability to fight off the fastball inside and make a pitcher pay if the pitch isn't inside enough. Righthanded pitchers were especially tough on him with hard breaking balls and change-ups. He hit only .246 against them while punching lefthanders at a .358 clip.

BASERUNNING:

Presley is a below-average runner, but is aggressive. If he sees the opportunity, he might try for it. In general, though, a stolen base is a gift from a napping defensive player. He will try to take the extra base when possible and has no qualms about barreling into second base to break up the double play.

FIELDING:

Presley's bat will carry him. The Mariners were surprised that he turned out to be even an average third baseman last year. He doesn't really have much

JIM PRESLEY
3B, No. 17
RR, 6'1", 185 lbs.
ML Svc: 2 years
Born: 10-23-61 in
   Pensacola, FL

```
1985 STATISTICS
AVG  G   AB  R  H    2B 3B HR RBI BB  SO  SB
.275 155 570 71 157  33 1  28 84  44  100 2
CAREER STATISTICS
AVG  G   AB  R  H    2B 3B HR RBI BB  SO  SB
.261 225 821 98 214  45 2  38 120 50  163 3
```

  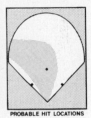

STRONG   STRONG
VS. RHP   VS. LHP   PROBABLE HIT LOCATIONS

lateral movement, but he has a quick initial reaction and winds up making a lot of diving plays.

His arm is strong enough that he can make the play behind third base.

OVERALL:

After eight years of searching, the Mariners finally found the answer to their third-base problems: Jim Presley. Now that he has proved himself to be a tough hitter, it will be interesting to see, as the swords sharpen, who will outsmart the other--the hitter or the pitcher.

Killebrew: "Presley is still learning the ropes. He's not much on defense, but his offense is good enough to carry him. He had an exceptional year and looks as if he is only going to become a better player. His play at third base should get better in time."

HITTING:

Domingo Ramos is a pure contact hitter. He chokes up on the bat, crouches at the plate and gets a good look at the pitch. He is an aggressive hitter and goes up to the plate ready to swing; if the first pitch is a fastball, he's got it.

Because of his part-time duty, Ramos has numbers that can be deceiving: sitting on the bench for long periods between at-bats can lead to elongated slumps which take a quick cut at a batting average.

Ramos uses all the fields, though most of his hits are in the hole between first and second base. Ramos is content to get base hits and never tries to show any power.

Pitchers have to go right at him, pounding him with inside fastballs and then pitching him away with breaking balls. The key is to get ahead in the count and stay there. A smart pitcher can lead Ramos to chase pitches out of the strike zone. He doesn't like to walk.

He is a good bunter, but the infielders know this and they know that he cannot power it past them. As a result, he often finds the infielders shortening up on him in an effort to take the bunt away.

BASERUNNING:

Ramos doesn't try to steal very often. Most of what goes down in the scorebook as stolen base attempts for Ramos are, in reality, missed hit-and-runs.

He is not an aggressive baserunner and is often content with taking one base at a time.

FIELDING:

Ramos can play all four infield positions as well as serve as a backup catcher. However, his best defensive po-

DOMINGO RAMOS
INF, No. 3
RR, 5'10", 154 lbs.
ML Svc: 4 years
Born: 3-29-58 in
  Santiago, DR

1985 STATISTICS

AVG	G	AB	R	H	2B	3B	HR	RBI	BB	SO	SB
.196	75	168	19	22	6	0	1	15	17	23	0

CAREER STATISTICS

AVG	G	AB	R	H	2B	3B	HR	RBI	BB	SO	SB
.219	195	402	42	88	14	0	3	28	32	49	5

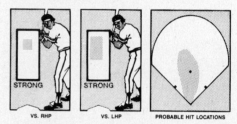

STRONG   STRONG   PROBABLE HIT LOCATIONS

VS. RHP   VS. LHP

sition is third base. He has a strong arm and can make the play down the line. His reactions are quick enough to react well on shots to both his left and his right.

He remains well balanced when he charges screaming shots and has to throw from an awkward position. Ramos does not have the range of a shortstop--especially for artificial turf parks but he is sure-handed nonetheless. The more opportunity he has to play at second base, the better he might become. His arm is strong for the double play and his lack of range is less of a factor there.

OVERALL:

Killebrew: "Ramos seems to win his job each spring. He is versatile, plays hard and has a good attitude. He is a utility player who does a lot of things well, but not well enough to have an everyday spot in the lineup."

HITTING:

What Harold Reynolds needs is a real chance. So far, he hasn't had it. He earned it in mid-season last year, but there was so much screaming and yelling about Jack Perconte being demoted to make room for Reynolds that the pressure was too much for Reynolds to relax.

His minor league numbers indicate potential. He has a .302 minor league average, including .363 in 52 games at Triple-A last year. He is a switch-hitter who will fit into a lineup as a leadoff man or possibly as the number nine hitter.

Reynolds is a pesky hitter. He will keep pecking at the ball, fouling it off until he gets a pitch he likes. He will go after the ball low from the left side and up from the right side. Batting lefthanded, he is quick enough to handle the inside pitch and to inside-out it to right field.

He is not afraid to take a walk, and knows that his future will depend on his getting on base and scoring runs, not driving them in.

Like most younger players, Reynolds is a victim of breaking-ball pitchers, but he has the type of self-discipline that should enable him to adjust.

Bunting is a big part of Reynolds' game. He can lay down a bunt hit from both sides of the plate, and has the speed to beat the throw to first. He is an excellent sacrifice bunter who can push the ball past charging infielders.

BASERUNNING:

A key to Reynolds' future will be his ability on the bases. He creates havoc. He has the ability to steal 60-70 bases every year. Right now, he gets by mainly on speed, but he keeps track of the pitchers' moves; and the more he plays in the big leagues, the more aggressive he can be expected to become.

FIELDING:

Reynolds has the defensive potential

HAROLD REYNOLDS
INF, No. 24
SR, 5'11", 165 lbs.
ML Svc: 1 year plus
Born: 11-26-60 in
 Eugene, OR

1985 STATISTICS											
AVG	G	AB	R	H	2B	3B	HR	RBI	BB	SO	SB
.173	95	173	26	30	7	2	0	7	19	14	3

CAREER STATISTICS											
AVG	G	AB	R	H	2B	3B	HR	RBI	BB	SO	SB
.185	124	242	37	45	17	3	0	8	21	24	4

VS. RHP   VS. LHP   PROBABLE HIT LOCATIONS

to be a star. He is quick to both his left and right and has the good reactions that give him even more range than his superb speed alone. His arm is average for a second baseman, but he is quick at turning the double play, getting the ball out of his glove in one movement and not being intimidated by oncoming runners.

OVERALL:

Players like Reynolds are what give the Mariners a bright future. He has all the tools a team looks for from a middle infielder as well as an attitude which will allow him to get the most out of his ability. He needs to know that he will be to learn on the job.

Killebrew: "Reynolds has the potential to win the second base job away from Jack Perconte. He is a hustling player, like Perconte, but Harold has more physical ability."

HITTING:

Don Scott was once billed as the hope for the future of the Texas Rangers, yet he found himself traded to the Mariners in a minor league trade last spring. Scott has proven that he can hit in the minors, but he still has a long way to go at the major league level--he sports a .220 career average over parts of three seasons.

Scott is having trouble discerning the major league strike zone. He strikes out too often and doesn't walk enough. A switch-hitter, he seems to be a better hitter righthanded, but if he is going to be platooned as a catcher, he is going to have to survive from the left side.

He likes the inside pitch when he is hitting lefthanded and looks for the pitch away from the right side. From either side, he is a better low-ball hitter. As with most younger players, Scott can be set up by pitchers who pound him inside and then go away with breaking pitches.

He can bunt to move a runner over, but he is no threat to try to get a hit by bunting.

BASERUNNING:

Even by catchers' standards, Scott is slow. He will stay in the big leagues because he can hit lefthanded pitching and because he can catch; his footspeed will have nothing to do with his success or failure in the major leagues.

FIELDING:

Scott always gives his best effort, but sometimes that's just not enough. He tries to adjust to pitches in the dirt and can block low ones, but he also misses a lot because he gets crossed up on his signs. However, the Mariner pitchers like the way he calls a game.

When he was in the minors, he had the reputation of having a strong and accurate arm, but he has not been able to

DONNIE SCOTT
C, No. 12
SR, 5'11", 185 lbs.
ML Svc: 2 years
Born: 8-16-61 in
   Dunedin, FL

1985 STATISTICS

AVG	G	AB	R	H	2B	3B	HR	RBI	BB	SO	SB
.222	80	185	18	41	13	0	4	23	15	41	1

CAREER STATISTICS

AVG	G	AB	R	H	2B	3B	HR	RBI	BB	SO	SB
.219	163	424	34	93	22	0	7	43	35	85	1

  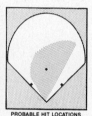

VS. RHP   VS. LHP   PROBABLE HIT LOCATIONS

cultivate similar respect in the big leagues. He gets up too quickly and rushes his throws, which leads to inaccuracy. He should settle down and do better with his throws as he earns more playing time, however.

OVERALL:

Scott has some of the intangibles teams look for in a young catcher: he enjoys the position and wants to learn. Scott has to keep pushing himself to improve, however. He is not ready for a job as an everyday catcher, even as a backup, except perhaps, on a team in dire needing of catching help (like the Mariners).

Killebrew: "Scott is young and guys who can catch are at a premium these days. Because he is a switch-hitter, he will get an even closer look. If he can bring his hitting around a bit and improve, he could become a real asset."

PITCHING:

Bill Swift was rushed to the majors last year when various injuries put seven Mariner pitchers on the DL. He became yet another young pitcher the Mariners have hustled through their organization: it was his first professional season.

Swift does have four major league pitches. His fastball is consistently in the 86-88 MPH range and he can keep it low in the strike zone. His ability to keep the fastball down indicates big league talent. However, the fastball is not good enough for him to get by on it alone. He has the makings of the other pitches that could highlight the heater.

His curveball has a tight rotation and breaks quickly just above the plate. His slider also breaks late and dips sharply down and away from righthanded hitters. So far, however, he has not shown the willingness to throw it to lefthanded hitters.

Swift has confidence in his change-up. He will throw it whether he is ahead or behind in the count. He keeps it away from lefthanded hitters and uses it to set up his other pitches. Swift has to learn to pitch inside to lefthanded hitters before he will reach his potential.

Swift had trouble getting his breaking pitches over after the first time through a lineup. It forces him to rely on his fastball, and again, it is not yet good enough to use for a strikeout.

FIELDING:

Swift is an excellent athlete. He has a quick move to first base and does not seem distracted by runners on base. He gets rid of the ball quickly to home

BILLY SWIFT
RHP, No. 58
RR, 6'0", 170 lbs.
ML Svc: 1 year
Born: 10-27-61 in
S. Portland, ME

1985 STATISTICS

W	L	ERA	G	GS	CG	SV	IP	H	R	ER	BB	SO
6	10	4.77	23	21	0	0	120.2	131	71	64	48	55

CAREER STATISTICS

W	L	ERA	G	GS	CG	SV	IP	H	R	ER	BB	SO
6	10	4.77	23	21	0	0	120.2	131	71	64	48	55

plate, which gives the catcher a better chance at throwing out runners. Swift gets himself in a good fielding position quickly and does not seem flustered once he fields a ball hit up the middle. He is quick to cover first base on balls hit to the right side of the infield.

OVERALL:

Swift's development seems to be just a matter more experience. At times he appears intimidated by major league hitters, but has he gains experience, he should develop the confidence to overcome that timidity.

Killebrew: "Swift was very impressive last year in light of his professional inexperience. Being forced to learn so much about pitching at the major league level is not an easy task. He seemed to have caught on to a lot quite quickly, though. He looks like the type of young pitcher who will be better in his second season."

HITTING:

The reports of Gorman Thomas' demise were premature. After undergoing rotator cuff surgery on his right shoulder in June of 1984, Thomas came back in a big way for the Mariners last season. He set a club record with 32 home runs, which was his highest total since he tied for the American League lead with 39 homers in 1982. Thomas got stronger as the season progressed last year and hit 18 of his home runs and drove in 52 of his 87 runs in the second half.

His swing seems to have a bit more of a loop in it since his shoulder surgery, but it hasn't affected his overall approach. Thomas is a free-swinger and a guess hitter who will murder a pitch if he has guessed it correctly.

Thomas doesn't waste any time at the plate and will swing at the first pitch that meets his approval. He is not embarrassed to swing and miss.

When he is going well, he can be more selective; it is when his bat is hot that he seems more able to draw a walk. On the whole, however, he is not in the big leagues to get on base via the base on balls.

The best way to go after Thomas is with curveballs and sliders--but they had better curve and they had better slide. A pitcher who hangs a pitch to him will spend the next 30 seconds or so waiting for Thomas to trot around the bases.

Thomas will sit on a breaking ball if a pitcher is unwilling to throw him a fastball.

BASERUNNING:

There was a time when Thomas had above-average speed, but not anymore. He is not much of a threat to steal a base. He is, however, a threat to endanger the life of an infielder who gets in his way on the double play. Thomas runs at one speed: full speed.

FIELDING:

Though the shoulder surgery limited

GORMAN THOMAS
DH/OF, No. 20
RR, 6'2", 215 lbs.
ML Svc: 11 years
Born: 12-12-50 in
Charleston, SC

1985 STATISTICS

AVG	G	AB	R	H	2B	3B	HR	RBI	BB	SO	SB
.215	135	484	76	104	16	1	32	87	84	126	3

CAREER STATISTICS

AVG	G	AB	R	H	2B	3B	HR	RBI	BB	SO	SB
.227	1334	4362	636	992	204	12	252	746	639	1234	47

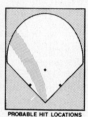

VS. RHP   VS. LHP   PROBABLE HIT LOCATIONS

him to DH'ing last year, Thomas is intent on proving he can play the outfield again. However, the Mariners have some strong, young outfielders and probably won't put him there.

During his days in Milwaukee, Thomas was a workingman's center fielder. He never looked pretty, but he more than covered enough ground and never worried about running into fences. He also had an above-average arm, but even before the rotator cuff tear, his range had fallen off enough that left field was his best spot.

OVERALL:

Thomas pushes himself to the limit. Not many players would have had the drive to come back from the injury that sidelined him--especially with a guaranteed contract.

Killebrew: "Gorman is playing in a home run park that looks even smaller every time he hits a home run. He can continue to help the Mariners as a DH."

PITCHING:

On a pitching staff marked by disasterous performances, one of the few bright spots was the emergence of Roy Thomas as a consistent long reliever. After starting the year in the minors (for the 14th time in 15 pro seasons), Thomas won all seven of his decisions, tying a Mariner record for consecutive victories.

Thomas has a variety of pitches. His fastball will range from the lower 80s to 90 MPH. When he is throwing well, he gets good movement and a sinking action on the pitch. Thomas will also use an off-speed pitch, especially to lefthanders. He tries to keep the ball down and away from them, enticing them to attempt to pull the ball but ending up with ground outs.

Thomas' big pitch is a slurve. When he can get it over for a strike, it is extremely difficult on righthanded hitters. The pitch starts its flight heading directly for the hitter, but quickly breaks into the strike zone. Righthanded hitters also have trouble reading his funky motion. Thomas is all arms as he prepares to deliver the ball, and it is difficult to tell how, when, and from what point he will release the ball.

What gets Thomas in trouble is his control. He seems unable to throw good strikes when he gets behind in the count. His slurve flattens out and his fastball stays up in the strike zone; both pitches become very hittable.

FIELDING:

His whirlybird windup, combined with a below-average move to first base, makes Thomas an easy mark for the stolen base. He has to improve in that area if

ROY THOMAS
RHP, No. 49
RR, 6'6", 200 lbs.
ML Svc: 5 years
Born: 6-22-53 in
   Quantico, VA

1985 STATISTICS												
W	L	ERA	G	GS	CG	SV	IP	H	R	ER	BB	SO
7	0	3.36	40	0	0	1	93.2	66	37	35	48	70
CAREER STATISTICS												
W	L	ERA	G	GS	CG	SV	IP	H	R	ER	BB	SO
10	2	4.02	61	1	0	2	143.1	118	70	64	85	112

he has any hope of ever moving into a more integral part of a pitching staff than long relief.

His delivery leaves him off balance and he falls from the mound toward first base. This causes problems, especially when he should be covering the third base line--and can't.

OVERALL:

It's hard to imagine Thomas improving or changing any aspect of his game at this point. This year marks his 16th season in professional ball, yet he has spent only one full season in the majors (1983).

Killebrew: "Given the fact that Thomas has been around as long as he has, you would think that he would have refined his game enough to have better command of his pitches.

"He is competitive and performed well enough in an unglamorous role with an average team last year, but if he was going to make a mark in the major leagues, he would have done so already."

NEEDS ANOTHER PITCH

PITCHING:

Ed Vande Berg is a role pitcher. Bring him in from the bullpen to get a lefthanded hitter. That's it.

Two seasons ago, the Mariners tried to make him into a starting pitcher. The move served only to rattle his already-shaky confidence. Given the job of facing a lefthanded hitter, Vande Berg is fine. Last year marked the third time in four seasons that he had more appearances than innings pitched.

Vande Berg is sneaky fast. He has an easy motion, but the ball comes toward the plate in the upper 80 MPH range. He also throws a good slider which breaks away from lefthanded hitters and sets them up for his sweeping curveball.

His curveball is very good and breaks across the plate. Vande Berg gives a little flick of his glove just before he releases the pitch. That is enough to break the concentration of lefthanded hitters.

What Vande Berg needs, if he is going to develop into more than just a one-or-two-batter pitcher, is a pitch that can be effective to righthanders. He is too tentative to righties: he won't snap off his curve and he leaves it hanging over the plate. His fastball is good enough that all he really needs to do is keep it down in the strike zone, but he tries to be too fine with it.

FIELDING:

Vande Berg has a good move to first base. He comes close to a balk with his front foot, but umpires have accepted it as his natural move. He makes strong throws to first and usually keeps the

ED VANDE BERG
LHP, No. 32
RL, 6'2", 180 lbs.
ML Svc: 4 years
Born: 10-26-58 in
   Redlands, CA

1985 STATISTICS
W	L	ERA	G	GS	CG	SV	IP	H	R	ER	BB	SO
2	1	3.72	76	0	0	3	67.2	71	30	28	31	34

CAREER STATISTICS
W	L	ERA	G	GS	CG	SV	IP	H	R	ER	BB	SO
21	21	3.75	272	17	2	20	338.1	349	159	141	135	214

ball down, enabling the first baseman to make a quick tag.

He reacts well to bunts and balls hit back up the middle. He is quick off the mound and gets to first base in a hurry on balls hit to the right side.

OVERALL:

Vande Berg does well in his limited role. He has the type of arm that allows him to get loose in a hurry and to pitch often. His 76 appearances ranked second in the AL last year. He set a record for a rookie when he led the league with 78 appearances in 1982.

Killebrew: "He could get more mileage if he developed another pitch and could face righthanded hitters. But for a team that can afford it and likes having a guy who can be relied on to get out that lefthanded hitter, he's your man."

PITCHING:

The report on Frank Wills remains the same today as it did when Kansas City made him a first-round draft choice in June 1980: strong arm, but erratic.

Wills throws hard. His fastball is consistently in the 90 MPH range; the problem with it, however, is that it does not have good movement and tends to stay up high in the strike zone. His fastball has the potential to become his most lethal weapon, but Wills has to learn to keep the ball down.

Wills gets a decent rotation on his curveball; he throws it down and in to lefthanded hitters and keeps it away from righthanders. Righthanded hitters tend to lean over the plate waiting for his breaking stuff; Wills should bust his fastball inside on them more often to reclaim his half of the plate. He also needs to come up with another type of off-speed pitch to make his fastball more effective.

His slider is more like a cut fastball. He gets himself in trouble by falling behind in the count and then takes some velocity off his pitches in trying to guide them into the strike zone. His fastball loses some of its zip when he works out of the stretch position, and he doesn't know how to pitch his way out of jams when he doesn't have everything working properly.

In the minors, he was able to overpower hitters, but in the major leagues, hitters adjust more quickly to pitchers like Wills who try to throw harder than they really can.

Unless Wills is able to become more consistent, his future in the majors will be as a spot-starter and long reliever. At this point, he is not the type of pitcher a team can rely on to pitch effectively every time out. Last season, he won four of his first five starts--not because he pitched well, but

FRANK WILLS
RHP, No. 19
RR, 6'2", 200 lbs.
ML Svc: 1 year plus
Born: 10-26-58 in
New Orleans, LA

1985 STATISTICS
W	L	ERA	G	GS	CG	SV	IP	H	R	ER	BB	SO
5	11	6.00	24	18	1	1	123	122	85	82	68	67

CAREER STATISTICS
W	L	ERA	G	GS	CG	SV	IP	H	R	ER	BB	SO
7	12	5.59	30	22	1	1	157.2	157	102	98	83	90

because the Mariners gave him good run support. Then he lost his next eight decisions. Following this was an eight-inning stretch during which he allowed only one hit. As a finale, Wills got knocked out in his last two starts.

FIELDING:

Wills is a very ordinary fielder. He has an average move to first base and has a tendency to forget about runners--especially the runner on second base. He is deliberate in his move to the plate, which gives runners an extra step in their attempts to steal. He doesn't move around well on the mound and tends to be late covering first base.

OVERALL:

Wills is getting to that age when potential must become reality.

Killebrew: "Frank has to get on some kind of roll soon. He needs to maintain better control and to develop an off-speed pitch if he hopes to remain in the majors. He can throw hard, but he hasn't been able to pitch consistently enough for any prolonged period."

PITCHING:

Matt Young remains a puzzle. He throws a fastball that is consistently in the 88-90 MPH range, yet he has had a losing record in each of his three major league seasons.

Young's fastball can sometimes get even faster than 90 MPH and it has good movement to it. When he is going well, the fastball stays down. That, of course is the problem--he has not been able to go well long enough. He gets the heater up--and it heads downtown. He led the Mariners by allowing 23 home runs last year.

Young's bread-and-butter pitch is a slider that he runs in hard on the fists of righthanded hitters. He has the makings of a good curveball, but has not shown the consistency which would allow him to bring it out when he's in a jam.

His change-up suffers from the same malady: inconsistiosis. He will try to throw it to the hitters in middle of the lineup, but even against the lesser hitters in the order, he gets beat. His change simply is too flat.

Young shows traces of being willing to pitch inside, and when he does, he seems to win. But he has trouble maintaining that concentration and will go for an extended vacation on the outside part of the plate. Many pitchers, afraid of having hitters pull their pitches out of the windless Kingdome, pitch away, but Young has been in Seattle long enough and can no longer use the Dome as an excuse. He nibbles too much, falls behind in the count too much and takes too much off his pitches in his attempt to throw strikes. His stuff is too good for him to be walking more than three batters per nine innings.

FIELDING:

Even though he is lefthanded, Young has a predictably slow move to first base. He also has a leg kick in his de-

MATT YOUNG
LHP, No. 40
LL, 6'3", 205 lbs.
ML Svc: 3 years
Born: 8-9-58 in
  Pasadena, CA

1985 STATISTICS
W	L	ERA	G	GS	CG	SV	IP	H	R	ER	BB	SO
12	19	4.91	37	35	5	1	218.1	242	135	119	76	136

CAREER STATISTICS
W	L	ERA	G	GS	CG	SV	IP	H	R	ER	BB	SO
29	42	4.45	92	89	11	1	535.1	561	302	265	212	339

livery to the plate which allows hitters to get a couple of extra steps when he goes home. Young finishes his motion in a good enough position to field balls hit back up the middle, but he has trouble throwing the ball once he has caught it. He tries to guide the ball to the bag when he throws it in an attempt to compensate for the natural movement of his throws.

OVERALL:

So far, Young has only teased his manager with occasional glimpses of winning form. He was "lucky" enough to be the only member of the original 1985 Seattle rotation not be on the disabled list at some point last year. He might take heart in knowing that the 19 losses he suffered last year will probably be the most he'll ever accumulate in a single season.

Killebrew: "Matt has a good enough arm and seems to be able to keep his head in the game well enough that he should have already become a top lefthander. He must come up with some type of consistent off-speed pitch to make his fastball and slider more effective."

BARRY BONNELL
LF, No. 9
RR, 6'3", 208 lbs.
ML Svc: 9 years
Born: 10-27-53 in
Milford, OH

HITTING, BASERUNNING, FIELDING:

As he has grown older, Barry Bonnell has refined his approach to hitting. He is not a power hitter and no longer tries to pull the ball. He will go with the pitch and has enough sock in his bat to drive the ball into the alleys.

With his main role last year being that of pinch-hitter and DH, Bonnell now has to be more aggressive. He takes too many pitches and gets himself behind in the count too often (19 strikeouts and only six walks in 111 at-bats).

He is still primarily a fastball hitter and will go after the first pitch. He has to realize that in the American League, with the small parks, pitchers mix up their pitches more than in the National League. Bonnell still has to make that adjustment.

He is a smart player; he uses his average speed to his best advantage. He can steal a base, but doesn't run often. He knows when to get the extra base and does the little things that create plays on the bases.

Bonnell is a solid extra outfielder. He can play any of the three positions and has an average arm with above-average accuracy. He hits the cutoff man and throws to the right base. He also can fill in during an emergency at third base, but only as a stop-gap measure.

OVERALL:

Killebrew: "Bonnell is at the point in his career where he will have to make the team each spring and then work hard during the season to keep the job."

ROBERT LONG
RHP, No. 42
RR, 6'3", 185 lbs.
ML Svc: less than 1 year
Born: 11-11-54 in
Jasper, TN

PITCHING, FIELDING:

Robert Long is a trick pitcher. He has a submarine delivery that gives him a bit of an edge because of the rarity of the delivery style. He is especially tough on righthanded hitters. He has an average major league fastball (85 MPH), but the key is that he is able to throw it for strikes. His motion causes the ball to sink, which forces the hitters to hit a lot of ground balls.

Long has a slider/curveball combination which also benefits from his delivery. Long has not yet shown that he can throw the slider or curve for strikes. He is not tricky enough or overpowering enough with his fastball to pitch behind in the count.

For a reliever, Long's move to first base is adequate, nothing more. He needs to speed up his delivery a little to give his catcher the chance to throw out runners. He does seem to come down in good position to field balls hit back up the middle.

OVERALL:

A journeyman pitcher at best, Long has kicked around the minor leagues long enough to accept that role. It could keep him with the Mariners for another year or two.

Killebrew: "Long's delivery makes him special, but he hasn't shown enough so far to insure himself a major league job. He really only throws two pitches and neither of them is unique."

BRIAN SNYDER
LHP, No. 22
LL, 6'3", 185 lbs.
ML Svc: 1 year
Born: 2-20-58 in
    Flemington, NJ

PITCHING, FIELDING:

Brian Snyder was about to march into oblivion until a rash of injuries tore the Mariner pitching staff apart last year. However, given a chance in the big leagues, Snyder didn't do much with it. He has a slightly better than average fastball and an overhand curveball which has a big break. It goes down and in to righthanded hitters and down and away to lefthanders.

Snyder has difficulty with his control. He issues a walk for almost every strikeout he registers.

He seems best suited as a middle reliever, though he may have the potential to become a starter. To even think of entering the rotation, however, he will have to be more consistent with both his fastball and his curveball and develop a change-up that he has the confidence to throw. Snyder is also going to have to realize that he must throw inside to righthanded hitters to keep them honest.

Snyder does a decent job holding runners on base, but he seems to take something off his pitches when he works from the stretch position. Otherwise, he is an adequate fielder.

OVERALL:

Killebrew: "He didn't show enough last year to make anyone take notice. He looks as if he has a decent arm and his curveball is somewhat impressive, though he is not a candidate for much major league action at this point."

DAVE VALLE
C, No. 41
RR, 6'2", 200 lbs.
ML Svc: 1 year plus
Born: 10-30-60 in
    Bayside, NY

HITTING, BASERUNNING, FIELDING:

Dave Valle has finally begun to show some offensive potential at the Triple-A level over the last two years. The Mariners are getting optimistic. Now, if he can just stay healthy enough to carry it over to the big leagues . . .

Valle is a strong hitter with a looping swing, but is quick enough to handle fastballs from the middle of the plate out. Pitchers challenge him inside and then get him to chase breaking pitches away. They have to stay ahead of him because if they fall behind and try to come at him with nothing but fastballs, Valle can take them deep.

Baserunning is only a sidelight for Valle. He is no threat to steal a base, but he is still big and strong enough to create problems if the relay man is slow to get rid of the ball on the double play.

Valle's glovework should get him a chance to stay around the big leagues for a few years. He moves well behind the plate, enjoys calling a game and can bring a pitcher through a tough day. Valle has a strong arm, is accurate with his throws and has a quick release.

OVERALL:

He has not had more than 318 at-bats in a season (at any level) since 1980, when he had 430. Various arm and leg problems have retarded his development.

Killebrew: "With the mess the Mariners have at the catching position, Valle will get the opportunity to show his worth."

TEXAS RANGERS

HITTING:

Glenn Brummer gave the Rangers a lot more than they bargained for in 1985. He was signed to a minor league contract before last season, mostly because the organization was thin on catching. He was not expected to be called up to the majors.

That changed when Luis Pujols went on the disabled list in April, but the team sort of yawned and were not expecting much out of Brummer. They were not even planning on using him.

Pujols never got healthy and regular catcher Don Slaught pulled a hamstring: the stage was set. Enter Glenn Brummer. The season ended 100 at-bats later for him and he turned in a nice performance.

Brummer doesn't get cheated at the plate. Perhaps in part because he knew that he had something to prove, Brummer began to swing harder at the ball. He also shortened up his swing, and the adjustments worked. Although he still did not provide much power, his production far exceeded all expectations.

In the past, he hit into right field a great deal, but last season, he began trying to pull the ball more. The worst thing a pitcher can do is throw him a mediocre fastball on the first pitch. He will jump on it--especially if it's up and in.

Conversely, he has a lot of trouble with breaking balls low and away. He still has a long swing and can't get to low pitches with authority.

BASERUNNING:

Brummer is a slow runner but creates excitement when he gets on base. If anything, he is overly aggressive and several times was thrown out or almost tagged out after over-sliding or rounding a base too far. He is not a threat to steal, although he will try it from time to time.

GLENN BRUMMER
C, No. 11
RR, 6'0", 200 lbs.
ML Svc: 5 years
Born: 11-23-54 in
   Olney, IL

1985 STATISTICS

AVG	G	AB	R	H	2B	3B	HR	RBI	BB	SO	SB
.278	49	108	7	30	4	0	0	5	11	22	1

CAREER STATISTICS

AVG	G	AB	R	H	2B	3B	HR	RBI	BB	SO	SB
.250	178	347	23	87	16	0	1	27	25	54	4

STRONG

VS. RHP

STRONG

VS. LHP

PROBABLE HIT LOCATIONS

FIELDING:

Brummer is adequate behind the plate, especially considering his limited playing time. He has experience but, because he hasn't played that much the past few years, his tools are a little rusty. The pitchers seem to enjoy throwing to him, though. In one stretch the Rangers won seven of eight games that he started.

OVERALL:

Brummer is strictly a backup catcher who accepts that role. Offensively, he's not bad for as few games as he appeared in.

Killebrew: "His most outstanding characteristic is that he plays the game like a Marine hitting the beach. He has tremendous desire and makes the most of limited talents. He is helping to firm up the back-up end of the Rangers' catching situation."

PITCHING:

There is an old scouting prejudice against small righthanded pitchers. Glen Cook is a trying to become an exception to that rule.

He showed flashes of promise when he was brought up at mid-season, although he still must progress to make it to the big leagues for good.

Cook has an average fastball which complements a good overhand curve. His curveball breaks straight down. He also gets a good drop on his slider. The slider breaks down and away from right-handed hitters.

He can also mix in an excellent change-up. He changes speeds well but his breaking stuff is the key. He gets into trouble when he can't get those breaking pitches in for strikes. When that happens and he begins to lose his ability to place his fastball, Cook is getting tired.

He has good concentration and is able to pitch himself out of some trouble spots, but not often enough as of yet.

He also needs to pitch inside more often than he does.

FIELDING:

Cook has only an average move to first and he rushes his delivery with

GLEN COOK
RHP, No. 33
RR, 5'11", 180 lbs.
ML Svc: 1 year
Born: 9-8-59 in
    Buffalo, NY

1985 STATISTICS

W	L	ERA	G	GS	CG	SV	IP	H	R	ER	BB	SO
2	3	9.45	9	7	0	0	40	53	42	42	18	19

CAREER STATISTICS

W	L	ERA	G	GS	CG	SV	IP	H	R	ER	BB	SO
2	3	9.45	9	7	0	0	40	53	42	42	18	19

runners on base. He fields his position well.

OVERALL:

Cook hasn't reached his potential. He has a good arm but a lot to learn. He is being handled well in Texas.

Killebrew: "More than anything, he needs a chance to start. He must learn the league and the hitters. He is a great worker, a good student and a good competitor. His biggest weakness is that he depends on his breaking pitches and off-speed stuff too much."

HITTING:

Last season, most teams in baseball agreed that Toby Harrah was washed up. The Rangers took a chance, in part because they were desperate for a leadoff hitter, but even more important was that general manager Tom Grieve believed in his old teammate and roommate.

When the season started, Harrah concentrated on getting on base and ended the season with over 100 walks. Later in the year, the Rangers needed more run production, so Harrah began hitting home runs.

He also moved to a new position, second base, making the transition without letting it affect his offense.

All in all, it was the kind of season that had the Rangers, who have so often been on the short end of deals, taking quiet bows and pushing Harrah for Comeback Player of the Year.

Harrah is a savvy, veteran hitter who once said that he would have a job "as long as long as there are stupid pitchers in the league."

He tries to make the pitcher throw him the pitch he is looking for, a fastball inside and up in the strike zone. That is his home run pitch.

Harrah handles the bat well and can execute the hit-and-run. He has a deep, open stance that is more upright now than it used to be.

Because he has a good eye and is a patient hitter, he is at his best when he gets ahead in the count and can put a charge in a cripple pitch if it's in his zone.

Pitchers can sometimes overpower him with a fastball or fool him on a slider away. As a general rule of thumb, all pitches should be kept down but should also be mixed up.

Harrah is really a smart hitter: he can go to right on an outside pitch, he will bunt and is willing to take a walk.

BASERUNNING:

Harrah still has some quickness. He

TOBY HARRAH
2B/3B, No. 11
RR, 6'0", 180 lbs.
ML Svc: 15 years
Born: 10-26-48 in
Sissonville, WV

1985 STATISTICS

AVG	G	AB	R	H	2B	3B	HR	RBI	BB	SO	SB
.270	126	396	65	107	18	1	9	44	113	60	11

CAREER STATISTICS

AVG	G	AB	R	H	2B	3B	HR	RBI	BB	SO	SB
.265	2060	7113	1079	1891	289	38	188	877	1109	815	236

STRONG — VS. RHP   STRONG — VS. LHP   PROBABLE HIT LOCATIONS

does not take a long lead, which can lead a pitcher to believe that he does not have to pay attention to Harrah on the bases. He stole bases in double figures last season with a success rate approaching 80%.

FIELDING:

He moves better to his left than his right. Although he lacks great range, Harrah was sure-handed on grounders he got to, making only six errors all year and turning in the highest fielding percentage among American League second baseman. He also adapted to the double play pivot well, getting rid of the ball quickly. He still has a strong arm.

OVERALL:

Killebrew: "One of the most pleasant surprises for the Rangers was the way that Harrah fielded his position. Though he spent most of his career and third base and shortstop, Toby adjusted to second base quickly and played it well."

BIG, BREAKING CURVEBALL

PITCHING:

Greg Harris has two chances to make it in the big leagues: one is as a left-handed pitcher and the other is as a righthanded pitcher. He is ambidextrous and would love to try to pitch both ways in an actual game. He often throws batting practice as a lefty. But let's stick to the righthanded facts.

Harris turned out to be one of the few bright spots in another dismal Rangers season. He was among the leaders for American League relievers in strike-outs, innings pitched, appearances and saves. He notched career highs in each category. His double-digit saves total was especially impressive, as he pitched in long relief for most of the year.

Harris is a fast worker with a nice, fluid delivery. He relies on control and an exceptional curveball. He rarely has difficulty getting the curveball over for strikes.

The curve is easily his best pitch. He actually throws two varieties of it. One is thrown from the over the top and breaks straight down; the other breaks across the plate at an angle similar to that of a slider. Harris will throw either one in any situation regardless of the count.

Harris also throws an 85 MPH fastball and will throw a sinker to lefthanded hitters.

Now and then, Harris will throw a change-up. He is more likely to throw the change-up when he is ahead in the count. Generally, he can throw any of his pitches for a strike, although he is a bit hesitant to use his fastball.

When things begin to unravel, Harris hangs that beautiful curve. A hanging curve is a pitcher's nightmare.

FIELDING:

His move to first base might be the

GREG HARRIS
RHP, No. 42
SR, 6'0", 168 lbs.
ML Svc: 4 years
Born: 11-2-55 in
  Lynwood, CA

1985 STATISTICS

W	L	ERA	G	GS	CG	SV	IP	H	R	ER	BB	SO
5	4	2.47	58	0	0	11	113	74	35	31	43	111

CAREER STATISTICS

W	L	ERA	G	GS	CG	SV	IP	H	R	ER	BB	SO
12	17	3.61	143	25	1	15	328.2	275	148	132	135	277

fastest by a righthander in the American League. He is not concerned with runners on base.

He gets over to first quickly to cover and is usually in a good position to field the ball.

OVERALL:

He seems to be just now coming into his own and may be getting better at age 30. Harris has proved that he can be a great long reliever. He likes to throw often and, unlike most long men, says that he likes the job.

Killebrew: "The key for Greg is going to be careful and continued development. The Rangers ought to stick with him and keep his confidence level high. He is a good competitor and a hard worker.

"He has shown the kind of abilities that might make him a good choice for the starting rotation. It's good for a staff to have a guy like Harris who is well-suited to long relief and can be used to spot-start as well. If he has a beautiful curveball, the team is luckier still."

PITCHING:

When Bobby Valentine was trying to decide whether or not to accept an offer to manage the Rangers last May, the first Texas player he talked to was Burt Hooton. Hooton was in manager Doug Rader's doghouse at the time and offered Valentine two pieces of advice. The first was to take the job; the second was to give him the ball and let him start. Valentine did both. Hooton became the Rangers' most effective starter in June.

Hooton tapered off after that and wound up back in long relief. He could often be found in the recess of the Rangers' clubhouse, watching videotapes of himself pitching in the 1977 World Series, trying to recapture the magic.

Hooton no longer has great stuff. He is a savvy pitcher who throws an 82 MPH fastball from a straight overhand delivery. As would be expected of an old pro, he hides the ball well.

His best known pitch is the knuckle/curveball. He throws two kinds: one breaks straight down, while the other breaks away from a lefthanded hitter.

He has no slider and no sinker but throws an excellent change-up off the fastball motion. He has no qualms about pitching inside.

At this point in his career, Hooton must be picture-perfect in his mechanics for him to pitch effectively. He still has good concentration on the mound, but his inconsistent delivery can get him into jams.

A clue as to when he is tiring or if it is a day when he simply doesn't have his best stuff is when the other team starts hitting his curve.

FIELDING:

Hooton has a below-average move to

BURT HOOTON
RHP, No. 46
RR, 6'1", 210 lbs.
ML Svc: 14 years
Born: 2-2-50 in
 Greenville, TX

1985 STATISTICS

W	L	ERA	G	GS	CG	SV	IP	H	R	ER	BB	SO
5	8	5.23	29	20	2	0	124	149	78	72	40	62

CAREER STATISTICS

W	L	ERA	G	GS	CG	SV	IP	H	R	ER	BB	SO
151	136	3.38	480	377	86	7	2651.2	2497	1112	996	799	1491

first but doesn't let runners on base distract him. He is in good fielding position after he releases his pitches. He is a fundamentally sound fielder and has average speed covering first.

OVERALL:

Hooton's future is a question mark. He has one more year and then a buy-out clause on the free agent contract he signed. He is a great competitor but his confidence has been knocked down by a lack of consistent success over the past few seasons.

Killebrew: "His best chance to help the team would probably be in the starting rotation. He should be put there right in spring training and told that the job is his. The Rangers are in the midst of a rebuilding phase, however, and may decide to go with youth.

"No matter what, he needs to work on his mechanics. He is going to have to be more consistent and get the kinks out. At his age, that may not be very easy to do."

PITCHING:

WINNING SEASON

1 cup knuckleball
1 below-average fastball (76 MPH)
14 years, experience

Add savvy, gritty nature.
Stir well.

* * *

While the Rangers were made into mincemeat, Charlie Hough was making mousse. He was their only consistent starter.

He has always been bedeviled by slow starts in April and May. Noticing the fast start that fellow knuckleballer Phil Niekro of the New York Yankees got off to in 1984, Hough prepared differently for last season. During spring training last year, he pitched mostly in "B" games and threw his knuckler almost exclusively. It worked: Hough pitched brilliantly at the start of the season.

Hough has a slow fastball, no curveball and a cut fastball that stands as his slider. What allows him to be successful is, of course, his knuckleball. While he will show his other pitches to set up the knuckler, or even try to get a batter to swing at a fastball outside the strike zone, Hough lives and dies with the knuckleball. What makes it even more effective is that he can change speeds with it.

He is at his best in big games or in the late innings with the result on the line. He is a good competitor with great concentration.

Hough is not the kind of pitcher who gets himself into jams; it is so easy to see if the knuckler is working that he will get the hook before things go awry.

FIELDING:

When he first arrived in the American

CHARLIE HOUGH
RHP, No. 49
RR, 6'2", 190 lbs.
ML Svc: 16 years
Born: 1-5-48 in
　　 Honolulu, HI

1985 STATISTICS

W	L	ERA	G	GS	CG	SV	IP	H	R	ER	BB	SO
14	16	3.31	34	34	14	0	250.1	198	102	92	83	141

CAREER STATISTICS

W	L	ERA	G	GS	CG	SV	IP	H	R	ER	BB	SO
114	105	3.51	576	160	58	61	1938.1	1650	848	757	829	1237

League, Hough watched several other pitchers pick a couple of runners off first. Incredulous that a move which he considered a balk was being allowed by the umpires, Hough decided to use it as well. He does. And it works. And it's a borderline balk every time.

With no runners on base, he pitches slowly. With runners on, however, he speeds things up. Sometimes, it works to his disadvantage. Hough is a good fielder overall, but can be slow to cover first base.

OVERALL:

Hough is the ace of the Texas staff. He is a leader both on the field and in the clubhouse.

Killebrew: "Even though knuckleball pitchers have a history of success at advanced ages, Hough may be beginning to level off. He keeps to his physical-conditioning program rigorously and that should work in his favor. He is a great competitor able to throw a tough pitch. He knows how to do a lot of things that help to keep him in the game."

HITTING:

Bobby Jones doesn't know what he would do if he weren't a baseball player. His days in Vietnam caused the loss of most of the hearing in one ear and he does not think that his employment prospects are promising. He made the 1985 Rangers because the team released Mickey Rivers in a surprise move.

All the Rangers wanted Jones to do was to supply some pinch-hit power from the left side. He did not do too much of that early in the season, but he picked up the pace with two key homers later on. It may have enhanced his chances of remaining a ballplayer in 1986.

Jones is pretty much a one-pitch hitter. He looks for fastballs, preferably down and from the middle of the plate in. He will jump on the first pitch if it is a fastball, especially if he is up at the plate as a pinch-hitter.

A pitcher who pays attention to Jones' scouting report would start him out with an off-speed pitch--away. If there is a fast runner on first and Jones is at the plate, a pitcher could throw a fastball if he must but would have to keep it out of the strike zone.

Jones prefers pitches down in the strike zone that he can hit to the opposite field. Pitchers should keep the ball away from him and make him try to pull the pitch. Most of the time, Jones will ground out to the right side on an off-speed pitch low and away. That is something handy to keep in mind when a double play is needed.

BASERUNNING:

Jones does not have outstanding speed but he makes the most of what he has on the basepaths. As an experienced veteran, he doesn't make many blunders.

FIELDING:

As an outfielder, Jones is able to come in well on fly balls. He has just

BOBBY JONES
OF/1B, No. 6
LL, 6'3", 215 lbs.
ML Svc: 4 years
Born: 10-11-49 in
Elkton, MD

1985 STATISTICS

AVG	G	AB	R	H	2B	3B	HR	RBI	BB	SO	SB
.224	83	134	14	30	2	0	5	23	11	30	1

CAREER STATISTICS

AVG	G	AB	R	H	2B	3B	HR	RBI	BB	SO	SB
.225	301	582	64	131	17	0	20	83	48	102	5

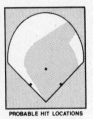

VS. RHP   VS. LHP   PROBABLE HIT LOCATIONS

average range but has a strong, accurate arm. He knows enough to aim for the cut-off man.

Jones's best position, however, may be first base. Unfortunately for him, the Rangers are happy with the play of Pete O'Brien at that spot.

OVERALL:

Jones will probably be a ballplayer for at least another year. He may not be with the Rangers, however, since they have some decisions to make about their rebuilding program. Jones is a good man to have coming off the bench. He becomes attractive to teams looking for an inexpensive ($100,000) role player.

Killebrew: "He is strictly a pinch-hitter who can also fill in as designated hitter against selected starters. Not Not everyone can be a star or an everyday player. Jones is neither, but his is still not a bad job."

PITCHING:

First, the Rangers wanted Mike Mason in the bullpen. No, no, no, the rotation. No, the pen. No, try the rotation. It was difficult for Mason to figure out how to pitch last season.

Mason has a pretty good fastball (84-85 MPH) but has to use his other pitches in order to be effective. He throws his curveball with a nice, easy delivery. But the break he gets on it is inconsistent. Sometimes it breaks sharply but he frequently hangs it, too. More than a fair share of the 20 home runs he gave up last season were off the hanging curveball.

Mason also has a cut fastball, which breaks in on a righthanded hitter. He can also turn the ball over and get a sinking action on the pitch. When he does that, batters just swing through it.

He can turn over his already-excellent change-up so that it behaves like a screwball. He loves that pitch and will throw it at any time.

Mason does not have a single out pitch; rather, he relies on good control to be effective. When everything is working well for him, he is able to get all of his pitches in the location he wants. He likes to use the change-up in tight situations.

At times, he tries to work the outside part of the plate too much and will allow the hitter to get too much of the inside part of the plate. He tries to outsmart hitters when he is tired or does not have his best stuff. At least, he thinks that he is outsmarting them.

His good control can also be his downfall. Sometimes, Mason will pitch "backwards." He will get too fine and fall behind in the count. When he is behind, then he has to come in with strikes. Add that to his hanging curves and you get his home-runs-surrendered totals.

MIKE MASON
LHP, No. 16
LL, 6'2", 205 lbs.
ML Svc: 2 years
Born: 11-21-58 in
Faribault, MN

1985 STATISTICS

W	L	ERA	G	GS	CG	SV	IP	H	R	ER	BB	SO
8	15	4.83	38	30	1	0	179	212	113	96	73	92

CAREER STATISTICS

W	L	ERA	G	GS	CG	SV	IP	H	R	ER	BB	SO
18	32	4.31	83	58	5	0	397	402	211	190	139	222

There are occasions when the opposition can get to Mason after just five innings. When he is in the rotation, he seems to breathe a sigh of relief at that point and loses his concentration.

FIELDING:

Mason is a good-fielding pitcher. He covers first quickly and his delivery leaves him in a good position to move. If he has a problem, it comes after the runners reach base. He has a poor move to first and can be slow in releasing the ball to the plate. He appears to be easily distracted.

OVERALL:

At age 27, Mason is nowhere near his potential. He is still learning and growing. The Rangers are hoping to keep him as a starter this season.

Killebrew: "In order to improve, Mike needs better concentration and to work on getting--and staying--ahead of the hitters. His biggest weakness is his poor location. He must become more aggressive and work on his breaking stuff. He appears to be a 'student' of pitching and should heed some basic lessons."

ODDIBE McDOWELL
OF, No. 0
LL, 5'9", 160 lbs.
ML Svc: 1 year
Born: 8-25-62 in
    Hollywood, FL

HITTING:

Oddibe McDowell did not open the 1985 season on Rangers' roster. Texas officials were worried that the blustery ways of then-manager Doug Rader would upset McDowell, but once Bobby Valentine became the manager, McDowell was quickly promoted. He had a season that earned him Rookie of the Year mention. There is logic there somewhere.

McDowell is so good and so versatile that the Rangers could not decide where to play him. They considered batting him as the leadoff man and at the number two spot in the order--the former because he has so much speed and the ability to get on base; the latter because he has such good bat control. As it ended, McDowell prefers leadoff and seems to produce better when hitting first.

McDowell is a first-ball, fastball hitter. He is always looking for fastballs over the plate. Pitchers have their best success against him when they are able to keep him off balance; at this point in his career he will sometimes lunge at bad pitches. McDowell is having some trouble getting used to big league lefthanders. He can be fooled by good curves or off-speed pitches.

It looks as though he has the talent that will make him a tough out. Pitchers will really have to work to get him. For such a young player, McDowell has an amazingly sure strike zone set for himself. He knows exactly where his own "box" is. Even in batting practice, he refuses to swing at pitches he does not believe are strikes.

McDowell is also an excellent bunter and frequently tries to bunt for a hit.

BASERUNNING:

McDowell gets out of the box quickly and has good acceleration. Even though he was a rookie last year, he had the green light to steal when he thought he could get a jump. He is always conscious of looking for the stolen base. He takes a good, long lead at first and should

1985 STATISTICS

AVG	G	AB	R	H	2B	3B	HR	RBI	BB	SO	SB
.239	111	406	63	97	14	5	18	42	36	85	25

CAREER STATISTICS

AVG	G	AB	R	H	2B	3B	HR	RBI	BB	SO	SB
.239	111	406	63	97	14	5	18	42	36	85	25

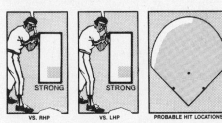

VS. RHP   VS. LHP   PROBABLE HIT LOCATIONS

get even better as he learns pitchers' moves. He plays hard and will break up the double play.

FIELDING:

McDowell is a natural center fielder and covers a lot of ground. He has good range coming in, going back and moving to his left or right. He is not afraid to leave his feet to dive for a ball.

He has shown that he has a good arm but he takes some time getting rid of the ball. Improving his release is one of the few things that McDowell needs to work on.

OVERALL:

There is a new "Big O"--in baseball!
Killebrew: "The Rangers' veterans breathed a sigh of relief when McDowell arrived. They knew they needed him and they knew he should be with them. He was the best thing that happened to Texas last season. He is the type you hang on to and build a club around."

PITCHING:

Under his uniform, Dickie Noles often wears a T-shirt which touts his favorite tourist hotspot in Ohio: the Cincinnati City Jail. That's a reminder to Noles of the early part of his career, when control was a problem. Not control of his pitches--control of himself.

Noles has turned his life around. He talks happily and at length about how he got it all together. Now, he is trying to turn around his baseball career.

By mid-season of 1985, he had been sent to the bullpen. This year, he will have to try to make his mark as a reliever.

Noles has a quick arm with a sneaky fastball. He works quickly, with an overhand delivery. He also uses the overhand delivery for his curveball. His curve has a short, quick-breaking motion but he has problems throwing it consistently for strikes.

A lack of consistency is also the problem with his change-up. It is a good pitch but he simply cannot rely on getting it over when he needs to. He uses breaking stuff for his out pitch.

His most effective pitch is his slider. It is hard and quick and breaks late. This is the pitch that he can use very well. When he is getting it over, hitters swing right over it.

A pitcher with Noles' kind of problems finds himself in trouble often. He gets behind in the count and will have poor location. At times when he is pitching poorly, he begins to lose his concentration as well. Put that together with poor pitching and you get the hook.

When he is pitching well, he is a stiff competitor who is not afraid to move a hitter off the plate.

DICKIE NOLES
RHP, No. 36
RR, 6'2", 190 lbs.
ML Svc: 6 years
Born: 11-19-56 in
Charlotte, NC

1985 STATISTICS

W	L	ERA	G	GS	CG	SV	IP	H	R	ER	BB	SO
4	8	5.06	28	13	0	1	110.1	129	67	62	33	59

CAREER STATISTICS

W	L	ERA	G	GS	CG	SV	IP	H	R	ER	BB	SO
29	46	4.52	197	93	3	7	735	779	414	369	280	389

FIELDING:

Noles has developed a quick move to first, but because his delivery to the plate is so slow, most runners are able to get a big jump even with a short lead.

His follow-through leaves him in a good position to make fielding plays and he is quick to cover first on balls hit to the right side of the infield.

OVERALL:

While he appears to have successfully changed his personal life for the better, he still needs some magic on the mound.

Killebrew: "If Dickie could find the strike zone more often than he does, he might turn in a good season. He is a good competitor who is able to pitch often. He has a lot of tools that might make him a good long reliever, but he needs to be able to keep his composure when the game gets tight."

HITTING:

When Peter O'Brien is in a slump, he can't sleep. Staring at the ceiling in the middle of the night usually helps him figure out the problem. Once he finds a solution, he gives the pitchers nightmares while he sleeps like a baby.

O'Brien signed a long-term contract early last season, then got off to the worst start of his career. Into May, his average was far below .200. Because of his slump, he couldn't sleep and because he didn't care for late-night TV, Pete would take his bat back to his hotel room with him when the Rangers were on the road.

One night, while studying his stance in the mirror, he noticed a mechanical flaw in his swing. In the next game, he began hitting the ball hard, a trend that continued for almost the rest of the season.

O'Brien has one of the most textbook swings in baseball when it's right. He will look for pitches low and outside and has enough power to drive balls into the gaps. He used to be strictly an opposite field hitter, but last year, he began to turn on pitches and pull the ball more often.

He has developed into a tough hitter. He has quick hands and is difficult to fool. Pitchers must really work to get him out, mixing up their pitches and trying to get their breaking stuff over. He's still something of a streak hitter but has great confidence in himself and doesn't get down when the hits are not there.

Although he will hit for a high average, O'Brien also has some power and led the Rangers in both home runs and runs batted in.

BASERUNNING:

He is a poor basestealer; O'Brien was thrown out trying to steal three times more often than he was successful in 1985. He makes up for a lack of pure speed by being an aggressive runner who

PETER O'BRIEN
1B, No. 9
LL, 6'1", 198 lbs.
ML Svc: 3 years
Born: 2-9-58 in
Santa Monica, CA

1985 STATISTICS

AVG	G	AB	R	H	2B	3B	HR	RBI	BB	SO	SB
.267	159	573	69	153	34	3	22	92	69	53	5

CAREER STATISTICS

AVG	G	AB	R	H	2B	3B	HR	RBI	BB	SO	SB
.262	475	1684	192	442	88	11	52	238	186	173	14

  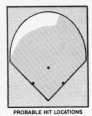

VS. RHP   VS. LHP   PROBABLE HIT LOCATIONS

plays and slides hard. He must learn to pick his spots better, however.

FIELDING:

O'Brien could win a Gold Glove someday. He covers a lot of ground around first base, and is adept at scooping a low throw out of the dirt. He is also one of the best in the league at starting a double play, then getting back to first in time to take the return throw.

OVERALL:

O'Brien continues to improve at the plate because he is an intelligent hitter and does things like carry his bat around. He is a much more disciplined and dangerous hitter now than when he first came into the majors.

Killebrew: "Pete is one of the bright spots on the Rangers. He looks like a solid player. He is still improving. The Rangers might be able to look for even more home runs and runs batted in from him in 1986. He needs some help around him, though."

HITTING:

Hindsight is 20/20. Larry Parrish considered having arthroscopic knee surgery following the 1984 season but decided against it. By mid-season 1985, he had no choice. The surgery interrupted what was an already-poor season for him. He was inconsistent all last year.

What made it especially obvious that he was struggling was that he was missing his pitch: a fastball out over the plate.

When Parrish is in a groove, he will crush the juicy fastball. Even if the pitch is a little inside, he will drive it to right field. If the pitch is on the outside part of the plate, he can take it to right-center.

Parrish steps up to the plate looking for the fastball but he can be jammed. A pitcher can get away with throwing it to him if the ball is kept on the inside corner or even just off the plate inside. He will also have trouble with good breaking stuff and good off-speed pitches. The best way to work him is to change speeds and move the ball around a lot, trying to keep him off balance.

Because he has a big swing, Parrish can look foolish on one pitch and then hit the next one a long way. He will often swing because he has guessed that the pitch will be a breaking ball---if he is right, kiss it goodbye.

He doesn't like to walk and wants to swing. He gets angry at pitchers who nibble at the corners.

Parrish did make one noticeable change last season: he seemed to be going with the pitch more often and was hitting to right and right-center more than he had in recent years.

BASERUNNING:

Parrish is not a bad runner for a big man. His knees bother him when he runs; he tries to be as aggressive as he can.

FIELDING:

Parrish does an adequate job in right

LARRY PARRISH
RF, No. 15
RR, 6'3", 215 lbs.
ML Svc: 12 years
Born: 11-10-53 in
   Winter Haven, FL

1985 STATISTICS

AVG	G	AB	R	H	2B	3B	HR	RBI	BB	SO	SB
.249	94	346	44	86	11	1	17	51	33	77	0

CAREER STATISTICS

AVG	G	AB	R	H	2B	3B	HR	RBI	BB	SO	SB
.265	1490	5365	672	1424	303	30	182	746	400	980	24

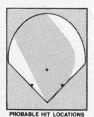

STRONG   STRONG
VS. RHP   VS. LHP   PROBABLE HIT LOCATIONS

field. His range is fair and he is able to catch most of the balls that he can get to. He throws well and has an accurate arm but has trouble getting rid of the ball quickly.

After Buddy Bell was traded to the Reds last season, there was speculation that Parrish might be moved back to third base (a position he had played in the minors). At this point, his knees are not good enough to enable him to make the quick starts and stops that it takes to play the infield.

OVERALL:

Killebrew: "Parrish is still a power threat every time he comes to the plate. He has hit some towering blasts. It seems that his injuries confused him last season and he was grasping at straws trying to end his slump. If he comes back relaxed and is able to put all of his 1985 troubles into the background, he should be able to regain his power."

PITCHING:

Before the 1985 season began, the Rangers went into the free agent market intent on signing Dave Rozema. Once they got him, however, they really didn't know what to do with him. He opened the season as a starter but then was sent to the bullpen. Even Bobby Valentine was uncertain of his role.

Rozema bounced back and forth between the starting rotation and the bullpen until he finally had arthroscopic surgery on his knee last July. Rozema's knee trouble was likely the cause of his inconsistency last year.

Rozema is a control pitcher with a sneaky 83 MPH fastball. He works quickly and has a fast delivery.

He does not have a sharp-breaking curve. Instead, Rozema comes over-the-top and spins a good, slow curveball. He gets a lot of break on his slider. The slider moves down and away from a right-handed hitter.

Rozema is basically a sinker-slider pitcher. He has an excellent sinker which drops out of the strike zone. Hitters chase it a lot. He also has an excellent straight change that can really fool the hitter.

He has developed a sinking forkball that looks as though it could become a very good pitch for him.

When Rozema is going well, he works quickly and throws a lot of strikes with all of his pitches. He makes the hitters swing, which helps keep his defense alert.

Because he doesn't have an overpowering fastball, Rozema must keep the ball down in order to be effective. When he becomes tired, his pitches inch up too high in the strike zone. He can get hit pretty hard when that happens.

Rozema is a smart pitcher who will use the entire plate to his advantage.

DAVE ROZEMA
RHP, No. 30
RR, 6'4", 200 lbs.
ML Svc: 9 years
Born: 8-5-56 in
  Grand Rapids, MI

1985 STATISTICS

W	L	ERA	G	GS	CG	SV	IP	H	R	ER	BB	SO
3	7	4.19	34	4	0	7	88	100	45	41	22	42

CAREER STATISTICS

W	L	ERA	G	GS	CG	SV	IP	H	R	ER	BB	SO
60	53	3.44	242	132	36	17	1095.1	1106	481	419	255	443

FIELDING:

Rozema does not concern himself with runners on base and uses the same quick move to first whether there are runners on base or not. He is generally a good fielder although he is slow to cover first base. Place the blame on the knee.

OVERALL:

The Detroit Tigers let Rozema become a free agent at least partly because manager Sparky Anderson did not like Rozema's free-spirited ways. He reported to spring training with the Rangers saying that he had turned over a new leaf and further showed that he was serious by getting married. It is not possible to judge how his pitching was affected by all of this; it did not heal Rozema's injury.

Killebrew: "Right now, Rozema is probably as good as he is going to get. He appears to be losing some velocity and has had periods of arm trouble. His best role at this point would probably be that of spot starter and long reliever. His biggest trick, however, will be to stay healthy."

PITCHING:

Scouts have always been impressed with Jeff Russell because he has a good, live arm. His managers have been less impressed, however, because he has had trouble winning games.

The Rangers chalked up Russell's poor season to bad luck. Late in the season, manager Bobby Valentine announced that he had discovered a few mechanical flaws in Russell's delivery. Valentine hopes that might solve Russell's problems.

Russell has a 90 MPH fastball but delivers it straight up with very little deception. He tries to simply throw it past hitters. His curve has a slow break and his slider looks more like a slurve (slider-curve). It gets a quick break from a righthanded hitter.

He lacks a soft touch on his change-up. He forces it across the plate when he throws it (which is infrequently). Russell's erratic control gets him into jams and he has trouble pitching out of them. He gets anxious in tight spots and it affects his body control as well. As a result, he has have trouble coordinating strikes.

FIELDING:

He does not pitch well from the stretch. He has a poor move to first.

JEFF RUSSELL
RHP, No. 46
RR, 6'4", 200 lbs.
ML Svc: 2 years
Born: 9-2-61 in
Cincinnati, OH

1985 STATISTICS

W	L	ERA	G	GS	CG	SV	IP	H	R	ER	BB	SO
3	6	7.55	13	13	0	0	62	85	55	52	27	44

CAREER STATISTICS

W	L	ERA	G	GS	CG	SV	IP	H	R	ER	BB	SO
13	29	4.64	56	53	6	0	312	329	182	161	114	185

He will try for any ball hit in front of the plate but is just average covering first.

OVERALL:

Russell is nowhere near his potential. He needs better control, better concentration, better mechanics. And it wouldn't hurt if he lost a few pounds.

Killebrew: "He is still young and has a good arm. He will go right at the hitters, but is often unsure where his pitches are going."

PITCHING:

Before the 1984 season, Dave Schmidt filed for salary arbitration. He settled shortly before the hearing and was awarded $117,000 per year. Schmidt was told by then-general manager Joe Klein that the team resented having to pay him that kind of money. Before last season, Dave went to arbitration again. This time he won and his salary almost tripled. Some members of the front office shook their heads and muttered that that was what was wrong with salary arbitration.

But the fact is that Schmidt had quietly been one of the Rangers' most effective pitchers over the past two seasons. If he keeps it up, Schmidt might even come to be regarded as a bargain.

Schmidt's biggest asset is the sinking action he gets on his pitches. It makes him the ideal type of pitcher to come into games with runners on base when the team needs a double play.

What makes him less than ideal, however, is the history of elbow problems that has caused the team to be reluctant to pitch him two days in a row. That certainly limits his effectiveness as a short reliever.

Schmidt throws an 85 MPH fastball but relies on control and keeping the ball down to be effective. His slider breaks down sharply and away from righthanded hitters--it's his out pitch to a righty.

He can get the hitters to chase his sinker and will throw it when he needs a ground ball. Some hitters claim that his sinker is not really a sinker at all but is actually a spitball.

The most effective pitch in his repertoire is his change-up. He throws it like a palmball and will nail the hitter with it regardless of the count. Schmidt has the ability to remain focused on the job at hand. He likes to pitch in big games. He considers the entire plate to

DAVE SCHMIDT
RHP, No. 24
RR, 6'1", 185 lbs.
ML Svc: 4 years
Born: 4-22-57 in
   Niles, MI

1985 STATISTICS

W	L	ERA	G	GS	CG	SV	IP	H	R	ER	BB	SO
7	6	3.15	51	4	1	5	85.2	81	36	30	22	46

CAREER STATISTICS

W	L	ERA	G	GS	CG	SV	IP	H	R	ER	BB	SO
20	22	3.14	172	13	1	26	344	341	142	120	92	203

be his own and will pitch inside to keep the hitter loose in the box. He is intensely competitive.

FIELDING:

One of his best attributes is his ability to remain cool under pressure. Schmidt has sound fielding fundamentals on the mound: a quick pickoff move, the the ability to keep runners close, a good position following his delivery and quickness in covering first.

OVERALL:

It takes steady nerves to be a major league short reliever. It also takes a lot of guts to personalize your license plates as, "TUF 2 HIT."

Killebrew: "Schmidt is not exactly a hard-luck pitcher; he has never pitched for a winning team. A change of scenery might make him really come into his own, although he seemed to pitch better under Bobby Valentine last season.

"He has immense confidence in himself and might develop as a spot starter in the right circumstances."

BIG, BREAKING CURVEBALL

PITCHING:

Bob Sebra's 1985 season didn't get off to a great start. Invited to spring training as a non-roster player, he sprained his ankle badly doing calisthenics the day after he reported and spent most of the time with his foot in a cast.

It was only after he recovered and went to the minors that he began showing the Rangers something. Enough, in fact, that he was called up for a couple of starts in June, when injuries depleted the rotation.

Sebra has a live arm and an excellent curve. His curveball has a big break and tails off at the end of its journey. He also throws a cut fastball that rides away from a righthanded hitter. Occasionally, Sebra will throw a change-up, but his curve is his out pitch.

His inexperience leads one to a conclusion that he lacks command of his pitches. His concentration wavers. As the game goes on, he tends to fall behind hitters and has trouble getting his curve over.

FIELDING:

Like many young pitchers, Sebra lets runners on base distract him and rushes his delivery to the plate. He has a good move to first and is a good fielder. He

BOB SEBRA
RHP, No. 55
RR, 6'2", 195 lbs.
ML Svc: less than 1 year
Born: 12-11-61 in
   Ridgewood, NJ

```
1985 STATISTICS
W  L  ERA  G  GS CG SV IP    H   R   ER  BB  SO
0  2  7.52 7  4  0  0  20.1 26  17  17  14  13
CAREER STATISTICS
W  L  ERA  G  GS CG SV IP    H   R   ER  BB  SO
0  2  7.52 7  4  0  0  20.1 26  17  17  14  13
```

is not as mobile as he should be off the mound.

OVERALL:

Sebra has a lot to learn. He is coming along well.

Killebrew: "He should be used as a starter because what he needs more than anything else is to pitch. He is a good competitor with an excellent curve. He needs to be able to throw it over for strikes more often."

HITTING:

When the Rangers traded for Don Slaught, they admitted they had made a mistake. The mistake was trading Jim Sundberg for Ned Yost. When Yost didn't pan out, it seemed that Yost was all Rangers fans wanted to talk about.

The highest compliment that was paid to Slaught was that nobody talked much about the Rangers' catching in 1985 except for two long stretches when Slaught was disabled with a pulled hamstring.

Slaught stablized what had been a major weakness for the Rangers, but now must prove that he can stay healthy.

Slaught doesn't have much power, but he is a pretty good contact hitter. He will spray the ball around and occasionally get a line drive into the gaps for extra bases.

The more experience he gets, the better he is able to understand his limitations and play within them.

He will jump on a fastball up and away, but he can be overpowered. Hard stuff in can handcuff him and he will chase good breaking stuff away. However, Slaught is excellent at hitting an average fastball or a change-up--and a lot of pitchers have them.

He is an excellent bunter who will try to put one down even with two strikes on him. He is also a good hit-and-run man because he has good bat control and will usually make contact.

BASERUNNING:

While Slaught has only average speed, that's pretty good for a catcher. He is not a threat to steal but is a heads-up runner who will take an extra base if the outfielder doesn't pay attention. He is not afraid to break up a double play.

FIELDING:

Behind the plate, Slaught is fair and needs some improvement. In the minors, he was considered a top-notch catcher, but the major league level is a whole other ballgame.

DON SLAUGHT
C, No. 18
RR, 6'1", 190 lbs.
ML Svc: 3 years
Born: 9-11-58 in
    Long Beach, CA

1985 STATISTICS
AVG	G	AB	R	H	2B	3B	HR	RBI	BB	SO	SB
.280	102	343	34	96	17	4	8	35	20	41	5

CAREER STATISTICS
AVG	G	AB	R	H	2B	3B	HR	RBI	BB	SO	SB
.281	352	1143	117	322	63	12	15	113	60	135	8

  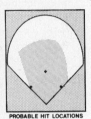

VS. RHP   VS. LHP   PROBABLE HIT LOCATIONS

He has become a better catcher with increased playing time, but suffers from a lack of consistency. He is a comfortable receiver to throw to and calls a pretty good game. One rap against him is that he isn't able to improvise during a game, noticing adjustments that batters might make from one at-bat to another.

He improved markedly on throwing runners out in 1985, but still needs to smooth out some rough edges.

OVERALL:

Slaught should continue to improve. As a catcher who can hit for average, he has value. He comes to play, but needs to work on his defensive skills.

Killebrew: "Don came into a bad situation for the Rangers, but a good one for a catcher to try to make a name for himself. There was such disappointment over the Yost-for-Sundberg trade that Slaught really did not have to do much to make everyone happy. Defensively, he must work hard to pay attention to the hitters."

HITTING:

Early last season, the Rangers tried to shop Wayne Tolleson around. There was talk, but no takers. It was one of the few breaks the Rangers got all year.

The Rangers developed a three-man shortstop/second base rotation with Toby Harrah, Curtis Wilkerson and Tolleson. It worked out well for Wayne; 1985 was his finest year in the majors. Tolleson had played well in stretches before but always seemed to follow the hot streaks with an ice cold one.

Manager Bobby Valentine realized that Tolleson's slumps might be because he got tired; Tolleson was rested frequently and responded by batting well over .300.

A switch-hitter, Tolleson looks for high pitches when batting righthanded and for low balls from the left side. He takes a harder swing righthanded than left but likes the ball out over the plate from either side. He is a patient hitter who will try to work a pitcher until he gets the pitch he wants. He is usually looking for a fastball on the outside half of the plate.

Tolleson can be jammed or made to swing and miss at good breaking pitches. He tries to hit line drives or hit the ball on the ground, hoping he can beat the throw or that the ball will find a hole. Pitchers can be successful if they can make him hit the ball in the air.

The first and third basemen must also be alert when Tolleson comes to bat because he can bunt for a base hit.

Although Tolleson still has a streaky tendency, the manner in which he was used was probably as responsible as anything for keeping him from having prolonged slumps and allowing him to finish the season with the good numbers that he had.

BASERUNNING:

Tolleson runs well and is a definite threat to steal a base, achieving a 2-to-1 success ratio this season. Pitchers

WAYNE TOLLESON
2B/SS, No. 3
SR, 5'9", 160 lbs.
ML Svc: 4 years
Born: 11-22-55 in
  Spartanburg, SC

1985 STATISTICS

AVG	G	AB	R	H	2B	3B	HR	RBI	BB	SO	SB
.313	123	323	45	101	9	5	1	18	21	46	21

CAREER STATISTICS

AVG	G	AB	R	H	2B	3B	HR	RBI	BB	SO	SB
.250	427	1225	156	307	52	9	4	50	94	180	79

  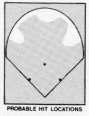

VS. RHP   VS. LHP   PROBABLE HIT LOCATIONS

must work to keep him from getting a good jump off first.

For a small player, he is also very aggressive. He is not afraid to mix it up and will slide in hard to break up a double play.

FIELDING:

Tolleson is a versatile infielder. He played mostly at shortstop and at second base last season, but he can also play third base and does an adequate job at each position. His throws are accurate.

OVERALL:

Even though Tolleson had a good year, he is still considered a utility-type player. He has not proved that he can play and be productive playing every day over the course of a full season.

Killebrew: "His versatility, determination and aggressiveness give him value to a ballclub. He is a good extra man and role player. Wayne is very capable with the bat and can make all the plays in the field."

HITTING:

Even now that Gary Ward is one of the highest paid players on the team, he is still one of the first to arrive at the ballpark and one of the last to leave. While some players in the league sleep in the trainer's room during batting practice, Ward spends more than his share of time in the batting cage.

Ward is a power hitter, but unlike most big sluggers, he does not have a lot of holes in his swing. He likes the ball out over the plate but can also inside-out an inside pitch to right field or can turn on pitches and drive the ball into the alleys.

He is a patient hitter who isn't prone to swinging at the first pitch. He prefers to hit fastballs but also does an excellent job of guessing on a breaking pitch and then driving it.

He is not an easy hitter to fool. Occasionally, he can get crossed up by pitchers who change speed a lot with change-ups and sliders. The best way a pitcher can hope to beat Ward is to mix up pitches to get him off balance.

Even that act won't work consistently because Ward is simply an outstanding hitter. He is tough to pitch to because he is always making adjustments at the plate. He is always looking for a way to beat defenses. He can lay down a sacrifice bunt if he has to.

BASERUNNING:

Ward is a good runner who has decent speed and is smart on the basepaths. He slides hard and comes to play every day. He takes a good lead off first; pitchers must be aware of him when he's on base. He has a good success rate in stolen-base attempts.

FIELDING:

In left field, Ward goes well both ways and, if necessary, will climb the

GARY WARD
LF, No. 32
RR, 6'2", 202 lbs.
ML Svc: 5 years
Born: 12-6-53 in
   Los Angeles, CA

1985 STATISTICS

AVG	G	AB	R	H	2B	3B	HR	RBI	BB	SO	SB
.287	154	593	77	170	28	7	15	70	39	97	26

CAREER STATISTICS

AVG	G	AB	R	H	2B	3B	HR	RBI	BB	SO	SB
.281	726	2738	390	770	129	34	87	368	209	452	59

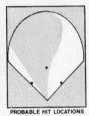

STRONG   STRONG
VS. RHP   VS. LHP   PROBABLE HIT LOCATIONS

wall to make a play. He occasionally has problems with fly balls hit right at him, which may have something to do with the way the lights at Arlington Stadium shine in left and right fields. Ward has a good strong arm and throws well. He knows where to play the hitters.

OVERALL:

Ward did a good job for the Rangers in 1985, and not just on the field. He is a team leader.

Killebrew: "He keeps himself in good shape and is not an injury-prone player. He is a big factor for Texas if they are ever going to challenge in a divisional race. He has been a streaky hitter in the past, ice cold and then red, red hot, but last year he was a more consistent hitter. He appeared more disciplined at the plate and a tougher out than ever."

PITCHING:

When Chris Welsh joined the Rangers last May, he made a list of all the things that are better in the majors than in the minors. It was a long list. Although he remained with the team and their big league luxuries all season, his so-so statistics might be on the list of reasons for his getting sent back to the bush leagues.

Welsh has a distinctive delivery. His arm is extended to almost full length and the ball, not well hidden from the batter, appears almost to be flung from a three-quarters angle. This all-arms-and-legs delivery keeps batters off stride.

Welsh has only a fair fastball (82-83 MPH) but he gets a big break on his curveball. He can throw his curveball over for strikes. It breaks down and away to lefthanded hitters.

He throws a cut fastball which serves as his slider, and a sinker he can make the hitters chase. Welsh is able to change speeds on his sinker. He is able to change speeds on all his pitches; accordingly, he does not have a straight change. He uses control and varying velocities to fool the hitters. There is no one pitch that he will throw as his bankable out pitch.

When Welsh begins to give up consecutive hard-hit balls, you know that he is in trouble. He is not usually able to regain his stuff.

Overall, each of his pitches comes up a bit short.

FIELDING:

Although he has had most of his success as a starter, Welsh has some skills

CHRIS WELSH
LHP, No. 41
LL, 6'2", 185 lbs.
ML Svc: 4 years
Born: 4-14-55 in
Wilmington, DE

1985 STATISTICS

W	L	ERA	G	GS	CG	SV	IP	H	R	ER	BB	SO
2	5	4.13	25	6	0	0	76.1	101	40	35	25	31

CAREER STATISTICS

W	L	ERA	G	GS	CG	SV	IP	H	R	ER	BB	SO
16	12	4.33	98	51	7	7	398.2	428	218	192	149	152

that help him in relief. He has, for example, a very deceptive pickoff move to first base and holds runners on well without letting it affect his delivery to the plate.

As a fielder, he is very sound fundamentally. He consistently covers first on balls hit to the right side of the infield and maintains good control of his body at all times.

OVERALL:

Welsh would probably be best used as a starter or a long reliever. He has a strong desire to pitch and believes in himself.

Killebrew: "Welsh has to be nearly perfect with all of his pitches almost all of the time if he is going to have a good day. That just can't be the case all season long. He might be able to establish his rhythm more consistently if he were able to pitch on a constant schedule. It is questionable, however, that he will get that opportunity."

HITTING:

Curtis Wilkerson did all that could have been expected of him offensively as a rookie in 1984, but the Rangers could not leave well enough alone. In spring training last year, they suggested that he drop his bat back, almost horizontal to the ground, to get more power. It did not work. Not only was this new bat angle unable to locate any power, but Wilkerson was barely able to locate any hits at all. He became too tentative and lost confidence, especially when he began to be benched occasionally.

It was already too late in the season when he finally decided to get back to his old stance with his bat upright. He began to hit the ball again, salvaging what he could, and wound up with decent numbers.

A switch-hitter, Wilkerson looks for pitches up when batting righthanded but prefers low pitches from the left side. In both cases, he wants the ball out over the plate.

He can be jammed and has some problems with breaking pitches. The pitchers who are successful against him generally are those who can get their breaking pitches over and don't fall behind in the count. They are the ones who don't have to throw a fastball.

Wilkerson swings a little harder from the right side than he does from the left. He hits for a better average from the right side as well. Batting lefty, he tends to let his bat drop and is more of a defensive hitter.

He can bunt for a hit and, once he got his stance straightened out, was an improved hitter in 1986. He made better contact and didn't strike out as often as he had in the past.

BASERUNNING:

Wilkerson is a good baserunner with decent speed, but needs to become more aware of the fact that runners can steal bases in this game. He gets a good lead off first and makes a pitcher pay atten-

CURT WILKERSON
SS/2B, No. 19
SR, 5'9", 158 lbs.
ML Svc: 2 years
Born: 4-26-61 in
Petersburg, VA

1985 STATISTICS
AVG	G	AB	R	H	2B	3B	HR	RBI	BB	SO	SB
.244	129	360	35	88	11	6	0	22	22	63	14

CAREER STATISTICS
AVG	G	AB	R	H	2B	3B	HR	RBI	BB	SO	SB
.243	298	879	89	214	23	7	1	49	46	140	29

VS. RHP   VS. LHP   PROBABLE HIT LOCATIONS

tion to him. He runs hard and cut down on baserunning mistakes in 1985.

FIELDING:

Wilkerson does an adequate job at both second base and shortstop and turns the double play well. His range is good, although he goes to his left better than to his right. His arm strength is adequate and his throws are usually accurate. Wilkerson has more trouble making the routine or "easy" play than he does on the ones he has to pay attention to.

OVERALL:

With more experience, Wilkerson will probably improve his batting average. If he does, he will end up scoring more runs and be a valuable asset.

Killebrew: "There are a lot of basic principles of hitting which should be followed, not the least of which is finding a stance that is comfortable for you. He has potential with the bat and glove, but is having a rocky start."

HITTING:

In 1983, Wright had an outstanding season. He was the Rangers' Player of the Year and appeared to be only one step away from superstardom. Now, after two poor seasons, he is one step away from being traded or sent back to the minors.

1984's problem could be attributed to a variety of injuries. The letdown of 1985 is not so easy to explain. He spent much of last year trying to find his stroke. He had lost some of his swinging mechanics when he tried to compensate for the previous season's injuries. His confidence was at a low point last season: the team wasn't feeling too much better.

When he is going well, Wright prefers the ball down when he is batting left-handed, and likes it up from the right side of the plate. From either side, he prefers it out over the plate, where he can extend his arms. Defenses should play Wright as a straightaway hitter.

He will swing at the first pitch if it is a fastball. He has trouble with really good fastballs but does a pretty good job of hitting slower fastballs (84 MPH). For some reason, his bat speed seems to have slowed down from a couple of years ago, which may explain why he has so much trouble with hard stuff. Good breaking pitches also give Wright a rough time.

BASERUNNING:

Wright gets out of the batter's box quickly, runs well and slides hard. He will take a long lead off first and will force the pitcher to pay attention to him. Yet, despite his above-average speed, he does not attempt many stolen bases. When he does try, he doesn't succeed very often. He needs to pay attention to the pitchers' moves, but since he has been having so much trouble at the plate, he probably figures, "One thing at time."

GEORGE WRIGHT
CF, No. 26
SR, 5'11", 180 lbs.
ML Svc: 4 years
Born: 12-12-58 in
    Oklahoma City, OK

1985 STATISTICS

AVG	G	AB	R	H	2B	3B	HR	RBI	BB	SO	SB
.190	109	363	21	69	13	0	2	18	25	49	4

CAREER STATISTICS

AVG	G	AB	R	H	2B	3B	HR	RBI	BB	SO	SB
.249	522	1937	209	484	80	15	40	196	111	264	15

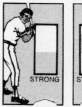
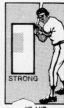
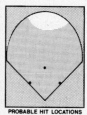

STRONG — VS. RHP   STRONG — VS. LHP   PROBABLE HIT LOCATIONS

FIELDING:

Wright's natural position is center field, but with Oddibe McDowell around, it appears unlikely that Wright will see much time there. He is a good outfielder and can play hitters very shallow because he is able to go back on balls so well. In the past, Wright has shown that he has a good arm, but that was not the case last season.

OVERALL:

Killebrew: "Some players are able to come back from injuries more quickly than others; some never regain their form.

"A fresh start on a new team may or may not be what Wright needs to get it going again. It takes a lot of determination to come back up to snuff at the major league level; many players are not used to working hard to get back what they've lost."

TOMMY DUNBAR
OF, No. 13
LL, 6'2", 190 lbs.
ML Svc: 1 year plus
Born: 11-24-59 in
Graniteville, SC

HITTING, BASERUNNING, FIELDING:

Part of Tommy Dunbar's problem in his quest for a regular major league job is that he has a long, looping swing and needs to play every day to keep it in synch. Last season, he sat on the bench for several days in a row over several stretches. When he is playing well, he goes to the plate looking to swing.

Dunbar likes the fastball up in the strike zone. He is a disciplined hitter and will take a walk if the pitcher will not throw strikes.

A pitcher who works the ball inside and outside on him while changing speeds should have success. Dunbar can be set up by inside fastballs which are followed by breaking stuff low and outside the strike zone. He has a little power but is not a home run threat.

Dunbar has average speed, but hasn't learned to efficiently use what he has. He runs hard and will break up the double play but is not going to distract a pitcher when he's on base.

Defense is the weakest part of his game. There is no such thing as a routine fly ball for him. His arm and range are only average.

OVERALL:

Killebrew: "Dunbar is pretty much a one-dimensional player. At age 26, he is reaching the point in his career where he must find his niche soon. The Rangers might decide to platoon him as designated hitter or they might try to move him to a team that could better utilize his skill."

DUANE WALKER
OF, No. 26
LL, 6'0", 185 lbs.
ML Svc: 4 years
Born: 3-13-57 in
Pasadena, TX

HITTING, BASERUNNING, FIELDING:

Duane Walker did not show the Rangers what they were hoping to see last year. He will have to produce fast if he wants to make the team in 1986.

Walker will hit a low, inside fastball. He has trouble with breaking balls and fastballs outside. He is willing to take a strike on the first pitch.

He looks as if he should be a tough out but pitchers have been able to keep him off balance and get him out over the last couple of years.

Walker is a fast, smart runner. He gets a good lead at first, has good acceleration and slides hard.

In the field, he is able to cover quite a bit of ground and appears to have sure hands. He throws well, has good speed and generally looks like a pretty good oufielder.

OVERALL:

Killebrew: "Walker seems to have the potential to be an everyday player somewhere. He has not been in the American League long enough for anyone to guess whether his poor start last year was the result of his having to adjust to a new league or a problem that he'll have a hard time solving."

TORONTO BLUE JAYS

PITCHING:

Jim Acker was supposed to be used in long relief again last season, but he blossomed as a stopper during the first half of the year. Whereas in two previous seasons Acker had only two saves, he was 5-2 with nine saves at the All-Star break.

During the second half of the season, he began to have trouble getting the first batter out. Relief pitchers have to get the first batter out. Once Tom Henke arrived in the Blue Jays bullpen, Acker was used infrequently. He worked 22 innings after the All-Star break.

Acker is a power pitcher. He uses a three-quarters delivery and has four above-average pitches. He throws his sinking fastball in the 88-90 MPH range. He throws a knuckle curve, a slider and has worked with teammate Doyle Alexander to improve his change-up.

Acker likes to throw the change-up when he is ahead in the count. He tries to power his way out of jams with the fastball or slider. His control is spotty, especially when he has not pitched for a while. That hurts him.

He is not afraid to pitch inside.

FIELDING:

Acker's delivery leaves him in a good position to field balls, whether they are comebackers or bunts. He is quick to cover first base. He is, however, careless with his throws.

JIM ACKER
RHP, No. 31
RR, 6'2", 210 lbs.
ML Svc: 3 years
Born: 9-24-58 in
    Freer, TX

1985 STATISTICS
W	L	ERA	G	GS	CG	SV	IP	H	R	ER	BB	SO
7	2	3.23	61	0	0	10	86.1	86	35	31	43	42

CAREER STATISTICS
W	L	ERA	G	GS	CG	SV	IP	H	R	ER	BB	SO
15	8	3.97	131	8	0	12	256	268	126	113	106	119

Runners don't distract him. He has a good move to first, although he doesn't throw over often.

OVERALL:

Acker did a good job of keeping the ball down in the first half of the year. Hitters do not like to hit against him unless he is getting the ball up in the strike zone--then they like it a lot.

Robinson: "He has a great, hard sinker that comes in at around 90 MPH. When a pitcher can do that, he's really got something. The trick, however, is to keep the ball down low. If he can learn to come out of the bullpen quickly and keep it down consistently, the defense should be able to do the rest."

PITCHING:

Doyle Alexander is the American League master of the change-up. He will throw overhand or three-quarters and will even drop down and come sidearm occasionally. He can change speeds on his fastball, curve and slider. Though he doesn't use it often, he does have a knuckleball and likes to show it now and then just to keep the hitters thinking. To confuse them further, Alexander has a variety of release points. Batters have a very rough time reading him.

Alexander uses his change-up to set up his 82-86 MPH fastball. He spots his fastball well. He will throw it in and out and up and down. He works the outside part of the plate with his slider and change-up.

Because Alexander has such excellent control, the fact that he gives up about a hit an inning doesn't hurt him. Early last year he was hurt by home runs but was at his best in the second half, when he gave up just nine home runs in 133 innings pitched. He had an 11-3 record at home, which is pretty amazing considering that Exhibition Stadium is a hitter's park.

He knows the strengths and weaknesses of all the hitters in the league, and he will get hitters out with all of his pitches.

No pitcher can get ahead of a hitter faster than Alexander. He will throw his change at any time, and he is always working on a new wrinkle. It is his variety and interest in changing that keeps him effective at the age of 35.

FIELDING:

His move to first is good and he will throw over as much as is necessary. He

DOYLE ALEXANDER
RHP, No. 33
RR, 6'3", 200 lbs.
ML Svc: 15 years
Born: 9-4-50 in
Cordova, AL

1985 STATISTICS

W	L	ERA	G	GS	CG	SV	IP	H	R	ER	BB	SO
17	10	3.45	36	36	6	0	260.2	268	105	100	67	142

CAREER STATISTICS

W	L	ERA	G	GS	CG	SV	IP	H	R	ER	BB	SO
149	125	3.67	433	336	120	3	2480	2464	1114	1012	766	1060

is always in excellent positon to field the ball. He covers first well and always throws to the proper base. The last thing he wants to beat him is his own fielding.

OVERALL:

He has won 17 games in back-to-back seasons, making him the top winner on the Blue Jays' staff. He is a tough competitor who is at his best in the big game: he pitched a complete game to wrestle the American League East division title from the Yankees on the second-to-last day of the season.

Robinson: "He knows how to pitch and mixes all of his pitches well. I think that he can continue to win for quite some time. The amazing thing is that he is winning on basically average stuff. He has a great change-up, but after that, he really doesn't have anything that is exceptional. He just has an uncanny sense of what to throw and when to throw it."

STRONG ARM

HITTING:

Jesse Barfield finally got the opportunity to play every day last year. Not only did he do all the things expected of him, but he was the Blue Jays' standout performer in the second half of the season.

Barfield likes the low-and-inside fastball. He is primarily a pull hitter, although he will go with the pitch at times and take it out of the park. He stands deep in the box, with a slightly closed stance, feet spread. Last season, Barfield moved closer to the plate to get better coverage and dropped his hands lower.

Righthanded pitchers throw him breaking balls low and away, and lefties throw him up and in with the fastball. He hit .304 against lefties and .280 against righthanders.

Barfield is becoming a more selective hitter, and although he still strikes out a lot (143 times), he improved his ability to draw a walk last season. He made the pitchers throw better pitches.

He does not like to bunt and prefers to wait for a pitch he can drive. He had a 16-game hitting streak in May and led the team with a dozen game-winning RBIs. He set a team record with 70 extra-base hits and was third in the league in slugging percentage.

BASERUNNING:

Barfield became the first Blue Jay to qualify for the 20/20 club in steals and home runs. He gets out of the box quickly and is always looking for the extra base.

Through experience, he has learned to get a better lead off first. He runs hard and will try to break up the double play.

FIELDING:

Barfield is an excellent fielder. He has good range both to his left and

JESSE BARFIELD
RF, No. 29
RR, 6'1", 200 lbs.
ML Svc: 4 years
Born: 10-29-59 in
    Joliet, IL

1985 STATISTICS

AVG	G	AB	R	H	2B	3B	HR	RBI	BB	SO	SB
.289	155	539	94	156	34	9	27	84	66	143	22

CAREER STATISTICS

AVG	G	AB	R	H	2B	3B	HR	RBI	BB	SO	SB
.267	557	1736	264	464	77	17	88	268	169	432	37

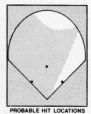

VS. RHP   VS. LHP   PROBABLE HIT LOCATIONS

right. He comes in and goes back on the ball equally well. He positions himself well to make throws and has a strong and accurate arm. He led the league with 21 outfield assists and had just four errors all season. He plays textbook defense in the outfield.

OVERALL:

Barfield needed to prove that he could hit righthanded pitching. His strong second half, especially his increased selectivity at the plate, bodes well for him.

Robinson: "He has really improved everywhere. He has always been a good outfielder and his determination to become a better hitter paid off. He was platooned in the past, but as long as he maintains his ability against righthanders, those days are behind him. Jesse continues to learn and to pick up new skills each season. That's always good to see."

HITTING:

A very strong and aggressive hitter, George Bell led the Blue Jays in home runs and runs batted in despite a late-season slump last year.

Bell is a durable, everyday type of player and missed only the final game of the 1985 season. He played with a sore knee at the beginning of the year as well as with a sore shoulder at the end. He has played baseball every day, in both winter and summer, for two full seasons.

Bell is a pull hitter and likes the high fastball. He will also go out and get the low fastball--unless it is very low. He has a tendency to go after the first pitch, especially if he sees that it's a fastball.

Bell has a better average and hits for more power against righthanders (he hit most of his home runs vs. RHP). Mike Boddicker of the Orioles is about the only pitcher who gives Bell fits. He is 0 for 16 against the Baltimore starter. Boddicker throws him off-speed stuff and breaking balls away and Bell goes nuts.

He is neither a patient nor selective hitter and he doesn't bunt. In fact, Bell has never had a sacrifice bunt in his major league career.

He put on an awesome display of power in Chicago in late August, hitting two roof shots and another into the center field bleachers in successive games. After that, however, he got carried away with the long ball and hit only one home during the final two months.

BASERUNNING:

He gets out of the box quickly and runs hard. Last season, he had a career high of 22 steals (in 30 attempts). He tends to ignore stop signs going from first to third or from second to home.

FIELDING:

With the departure of Dave Collins, Bell was no longer forced to flip-flop

GEORGE BELL
LF, No. 11
RR, 6'1", 190 lbs.
ML Svc: 4 years
Born: 10-21-59 in
San Pedro de Macoris, DR

1985 STATISTICS

AVG	G	AB	R	H	2B	3B	HR	RBI	BB	SO	SB
.275	157	607	87	167	28	6	28	95	43	90	22

CAREER STATISTICS

AVG	G	AB	R	H	2B	3B	HR	RBI	BB	SO	SB
.276	415	1488	196	412	74	15	61	211	76	220	36

VS. RHP — STRONG   VS. LHP — STRONG   PROBABLE HIT LOCATIONS

between left and right field last year. Having the stability of a set position helped his defensive play.

He is better coming in than going back on a ball, and still has some difficulty with balls near the wall, as if he is wary of the fence. He has good range both right and left. His arm is strong and accurate and surprised more than one runner last season.

OVERALL:

Bell has a short fuse, and it sometimes hurts his concentration. He suffered a broken jaw in the minors and he bristles after pitches near his head (he was suspended for three-days when he charged the mound after being hit by a Bruce Kison pitch).

Robinson: "He will be only 26 years old this year and continues to learn. He afforded himself the luxury of passing up winter ball this time, and it won't hurt him a bit. He should be better in 1986."

PITCHING:

Since their inception, the Blue Jays have never had a quality reliever. Their 1984 priority was to shore up the bullpen. They imported Bill Caudill and he broke their hearts.

Caudill was a major disappointment to the point that then-manager Bobby Cox did not use him in the American League Championship Series against the Kansas City Royals. By that time, Caudill had already lost his job as top bullpen banana to Tom Henke. Caudill, who had totalled 88 saves over the three previous seasons, managed just 14 saves in 1985. In doing so, he broke a Blue Jay record, but it wouldn't have taken much to do that.

His season was marked by blown leads and failed save opportunites. It appears that a major problem was the loss of velocity from his 90 MPH fastball. In the past, it had been his bread-and-butter pitch.

Used infrequently, Caudill's control suffered and his fastball slowed down--it was clocked at 85-88 MPH. He is a power pitcher who didn't have much power last year.

Caudill throws a curveball, but it is not a good one. He also uses a cut fastball as a slider. He can throw it well. Out of 20 pitches, 19 will be either fastballs or cut fastballs. Now and then, he will throw a change-up, but it is not very effective.

His out pitch is his fastball, but he's having trouble finding those extra miles. He still challenges hitters, but but with a lesser degree of success.

Caudill got himself into trouble and was unable to get out of it. He got hit hard and often.

He keeps his pitches on the outside part of the plate. Hitters can look away and get it every time.

BILL CAUDILL
RHP, No. 36
RR, 6'1", 210 lbs.
ML Svc: 7 years
Born: 7-13-56 in
Santa Monica, CA

1985 STATISTICS

W	L	ERA	G	GS	CG	SV	IP	H	R	ER	BB	SO
4	6	2.99	67	0	0	14	69.1	53	26	23	35	48

CAREER STATISTICS

W	L	ERA	G	GS	CG	SV	IP	H	R	ER	BB	SO
33	48	3.46	399	24	0	103	623	541	264	240	270	582

FIELDING:

Caudill was having trouble holding runners on base because of his high leg kick. He worked during spring training to improve it. Later, he felt that the new leg kick had caused him to alter his delivery and had something to do with his troubles.

He is a bit slow in coming to the plate and runners will take advantage of him. His move to first is good.

OVERALL:

Robinson: "Bill can still pitch every day but is not the dominant force he had been before. When the Jays first got him, it was a great psychological boost not only for the bullpen, but for the entire team. Now, they don't know what to think.

"He is going to continue to work on the mechanics of his delivery. The problem may or may not be there. He was very erratic last season, and his fastball was not consistent at all. Much of his past success has been because he was so confident in himself. It is one of his strengths. He's got to remain on top of himself and the game this year."

PTICHING:

Jim Clancy was one of the Blue Jays' original players from the expansion draft of 1976. He has never been able to reach the lofty heights that were predicted for him.

Last season, Jim was initially hampered by an appendectomy during spring training. He missed the month of April and he was on the disabled list again because of tendinitis in his shoulder. The problems set him back just when he seemed ready to reach his potential.

Clancy is a power pitcher. He is working to develop a change-up. His fastball is in the 88-91 MPH range. He throws a slider as well as a curveball. He improved his control last season with just about all of his pitches, though he still has difficulty getting the slider in and breaking well consistently.

Because he was having trouble with the slider, Clancy was forced to rely on the fastball more often as an out pitch last season. He is able to throw the fastball to get himself out of the tight spots he creates when his pitches creep up too high. He throws the fastball up and in to righthanded batters to get them off the plate. Clancy will throw his change-up when he is behind in the count.

FIELDING:

Clancy has worked hard to become an average fielder. He now does a much better job on balls hit back at him. In the past, anything hit up the middle was surely a hit, but now he is able to get down for a few of them. He has also im-

JIM CLANCY
RHP, No. 18
RR, 6'4", 220 lbs.
ML Svc: 9 years
Born: 12-18-55 in
   Chicago, IL

1985 STATISTICS
W	L	ERA	G	GS	CG	SV	IP	H	R	ER	BB	SO
9	6	3.78	23	23	1	0	128.2	117	54	54	37	66

CAREER STATISTICS
W	L	ERA	G	GS	CG	SV	IP	H	R	ER	BB	SO
88	102	4.16	245	243	58	0	1549	1542	795	716	624	813

proved his move to first, but still does not throw over much.

His follow-through limits his ability to field balls hit to either side of him. Sometimes he appears immobile.

OVERALL:

Clancy could be on the verge of becoming a great pitcher this time. By the end of last season, he was starting to put it all together and won seven of his last eight decisions.

Robinson: "I'm not the only one who has been waiting for Jim to have a big year. Watching him last season has made me think that 1986 could be his year if he can stay healthy.

"More than anything else, he needs to have good control, and it seemed to be getting better last year. Clancy throws hard, has very good stuff and all of the pitches that a guy could want."

HITTING:

Tony Fernandez likes the high pitch whether he is batting from the left or the right side of the plate. He is basically a straightaway hitter, though he will pull more often when he is batting lefthanded. He stands square to the plate, with his knees slightly bent, with his bat held high. Batting left, he spreads his hands on the bat handle just a bit more than he does righty.

While Fernandez likes to go after the first pitch, he is one of the few Latin players who gets more walks (43 in 1985) than strikeouts (41). Yet, he must learn to be a more patient hitter: he is not selective enough at this point.

He hits equally well from both sides of the plate, but has most of his power batting lefthanded.

Fernandez hits the fastball up and on the inside of the plate. Breaking balls give him more trouble than the fastball. He gets into the most fits with pitchers who stay away from him and throw a lot of breaking balls.

Now and then, when he is batting lefthanded, Fernandez will try to push the ball past the pitcher toward the shortstop; he is usually able to beat it out for a hit.

He hits well with runners in scoring postion and is an excellent bunter.

BASERUNNING:

Whether batting left- or righthanded, Fernandez gets out of the box quickly. He is a good runner and stole 13 bases last season in 19 attempts. He will do better with more experience—he has good baserunning instincts.

He takes a good, long lead off the base and really forces the pitcher to keep an eye on him. He slides hard into second on the double play.

FIELDING:

Fernandez is a master of the flip-throw and seems able to throw off either

TONY FERNANDEZ
SS, No. 1
SR, 6'2", 165 lbs.
ML Svc: 3 years
Born: 8-6-62 in
  San Pedro de Macoris, DR

1985 STATISTICS

AVG	G	AB	R	H	2B	3B	HR	RBI	BB	SO	SB
.289	161	564	71	163	31	10	2	51	43	41	13

CAREER STATISTICS

AVG	G	AB	R	H	2B	3B	HR	RBI	BB	SO	SB
.282	264	831	105	235	37	14	5	72	62	58	18

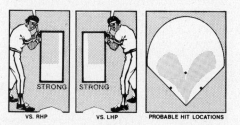

VS. RHP   VS. LHP   PROBABLE HIT LOCATIONS

foot. Even when he is off balance, he is able to get something on the throw. He made a way-too-high number of errors last season (30), but will be able to cut down this season. Most of his errors were careless: he would make a great defensive move, but then throw the ball away.

He has outstanding range and moves quickly to the ball. His range in either direction might be the best in the league. He is outstanding at coming in on slow rollers as well as going back for pop-ups.

Fernandez has something that very few young infielders have--tremendous instincts and anticipation.

OVERALL:

Robinson: "Last season, Fernandez had the kind of year that everyone in the Toronto organization always thought he could have. He is a fast learner, and as he gets stronger physically, he will hit with more power. Defensively, I think we are all in for some treats."

PITCHING:

The Blue Jays have shown the patience to build their club with the help of good scouting. The Jays were on Tom Filer's doorstep on the very first day he was eligible to sign as a six-year minor league free agent. The team found him a job in winter ball, where he led the Dominican League with an 8-3 record and a 1.75 ERA. He pitched five shutouts in 11 starts.

Filer made a big impression on the team in spring training last year, but the Jays had their pockets full of starters and sent him to the minors. He was called up when Luis Leal began to have problems. He quickly posted a 7-0 record in nine starts. But as he pitched more often, questions were raised about his future.

His biggest problem is his tender elbow. Filer does not seem able to pitch more than six or seven innings. He can only give you five good ones before his elbow stiffens up--it is a problem which took him out of most games last year. He hopes that rest over the winter will be the cure.

He is a control pitcher with a three-quarters delivery. He throws his fastball at around 87-88 MPH. His stuff is average, but he has good control and can throw strikes.

Filer gets a good break on his curveball and can get it over the plate when he is behind in the count. His slider is average. His fastball is his out pitch. Filer has a tendency to get his pitches up when he tires and does not like to pitch inside very much.

TOM FILER
RHP, No. 49
RR, 6'1", 198 lbs.
ML Svc: 1 year
Born: 12-1-56 in
Philadelphia, PA

1985 STATISTICS

W	L	ERA	G	GS	CG	SV	IP	H	R	ER	BB	SO
7	0	3.88	11	9	0	0	48.2	38	21	21	18	24

CAREER STATISTICS

W	L	ERA	G	GS	CG	SV	IP	H	R	ER	BB	SO
8	2	4.65	19	17	0	0	89.1	88	46	46	36	39

FIELDING:

Filer has just an average move to first base and will throw over often. His delivery leaves him in good position to field the ball and he is ready to do it. He is a heads-up fielder.

OVERALL:

Filer finally got an opportunity to pitch in the major leagues and was able to make a key contribution to the Jays' division title.

Robinson: "He will have to fight for a job this year. All of his stuff is average or even below average. The biggest thing he seems to have going for him is that he knows how to pitch and did well last year with pitches that didn't look tough to hit. His best bet could be long relief since he has a good supporting cast around him."

HITTING:

Damaso Garcia hates to walk to first base. In 600 at-bats, he had only 15 bases-on-balls. In the few times that he walked, it appeared as if he stepped to the plate determined not to swing until he had two strikes.

He is a man of a thousand stances, but usually has his feet close together with his toes pointing in. He is notorious for going after the first pitch and loves it when that pitch is a fastball. If he is pitched outside, he will hit the ball hard to right field and right-center. Garcia is an excellent bunter and gets a fair share of leg hits that way.

Garcia has trouble with the breaking ball away. Some pitchers try to run him off the plate, but they should be careful because he hit a career high of eight home runs last year.

He is a high-ball hitter who lashes the ball straightaway. Garcia does not fit the usual mold of a leadoff hitter, but it is his most productive spot in the lineup. He hit .320 with runners in scoring position and drove in a career high of 65 runs in 1985. He also had 11 game-winning RBIs, which was one shy of the team lead.

BASERUNNING:

Garcia strides into the pitch and hits to the opposite field frequently, so it is a good thing that he gets a fast start out of the box. He takes a big lead off first and draws a lot of throws from the pitcher.

He is one of the best in the league at stealing third and taking a walking lead. He has a string of 22 consecutive successful steals of third over the past four seasons. He runs hard, and will try to break up the double play. He is always looking to take the extra base. He had 23 of his 28 stolen bases in the first half, before he was hampered by a sore left leg.

DAMASO GARCIA
2B, No. 7
RR, 6'0", 175 lbs.
ML Svc: 8 years
Born: 2-7-57 in
Moca, DR

1985 STATISTICS

AVG	G	AB	R	H	2B	3B	HR	RBI	BB	SO	SB
.282	146	600	70	169	25	4	8	65	15	41	28

CAREER STATISTICS

AVG	G	AB	R	H	2B	3B	HR	RBI	BB	SO	SB
.287	809	3227	404	927	151	26	26	255	102	260	187

  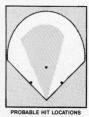

VS. RHP   VS. LHP   PROBABLE HIT LOCATIONS

FIELDING:

Garcia is excellent at charging the slow roller and making the barehand pickup and quick throw. He has great range on pop-ups to shallow center and down the right field line.

He throws well and turns the double play with the best of them. Because of his agility, he is seldom taken out. When Rickey Henderson nailed him with a block last September, it was the first time in six years that Garcia has been hit while making the DP.

OVERALL:

Robinson: "Damaso is at his peak right now and is doing well both offensively and defensively.

"I think that he can hit a pitcher's best pitch better than anyone on the team. He knows what he is supposed to do when he goes up to the plate and what he likes to see."

TORONTO BLUE JAYS

PITCHING:

The Texas Rangers' bullpen was even less effective than the Blue Jays' was in 1984, so it was a big surprise when the Jays plucked Tom Henke from the compensation pool. But the Blue Jays had taken a good look at him: he averaged better than a strikeout per inning in Triple-A and their scouting reports on him were impressive.

Henke pitched well in spring training of 1985, but with the addition of Bill Caudill, the Jays thought their bullpen was solid and sent Henke back to Triple-A. In Syracuse, Henke had an incredible season. He was scored on in only two of his 39 appearances and gave up 13 hits in 58 innings.

It wasn't until almost the end of last July before the Jays brought him up. When they did, they threw him right into the fire. The only thing that burned was the ball in the catcher's glove. He ended the season with 13 saves, one less than Bill Caudill, who was with the team all year.

Henke is a 6'5" power pitcher with a fastball in the 92-94 MPH range. And if that is not enough, he also throws a nasty slider and a split-finger fastball. He uses his slider very effectively. Henke uses the split-finger fastball as his change-up and throws it often enough to keep the hitters off balance.

His out pitch is his fastball. He will drop down and come sidearm occasionally to righthanded hitters when he gets two strikes on them. That's usually all it takes--game's over.

Now and then, he will have control problems with his fastball and will get the pitch too high in the strike zone. But that doesn't happen very often: Henke seems to have gotten his act together in his last stint in the minors.

Hitters don't try to crowd the plate on him.

TOM HENKE
RHP, No. 50
RR, 6'5", 215 lbs.
ML Svc: 1 year plus
Born: 12-21-57 in
 Kansas City, MO

1985 STATISTICS

W	L	ERA	G	GS	CG	SV	IP	H	R	ER	BB	SO
3	3	2.03	28	0	0	13	40	29	12	9	8	42

CAREER STATISTICS

W	L	ERA	G	GS	CG	SV	IP	H	R	ER	BB	SO
6	4	3.33	69	0	0	16	100	95	41	37	40	93

FIELDING:

Henke has an average move to first but does not have to throw over often. His catcher gets a good jump on any potential basestealer because Henke gets his fastball to the plate so quickly. He appears to be an alert fielder and will field what he can get to.

OVERALL:

Initially, Henke made the mistake of trying to be too fine and pitch to spots. With his fastball, he doesn't have to do that and can simply overpower hitters.

Robinson: "The Blue Jays shortened his delivery last season. He now has more control of his body and that helped his breaking pitches.

"I don't know how he could pitch any better than he did last season. He did a great job and burned the ball by everyone. His control might get the best of him once in a while, but just keep putting him in games--he'll be terrific!"

HITTING:

Garth Iorg raised his average by 83 points last season, lifting it from a disappointing .227 in 1984 to a team-leading .313 last year. He also found some power: he hit seven home runs--one more than in 541 previous career games.

Iorg is a low-ball hitter. He likes the ball inside and is able to hit to all fields. Like many Blue Jays hitters, Iorg likes to go after the first pitch. If that first pitch is thrown outside, Iorg will go to right field.

He uses an unusual stance: square to the plate, deep in the batter's box, with all his weight back on his right foot.

He likes to see the fastball, but can also handle a slider. Pitchers can curve him and throw a lot of breaking balls. In the past, he was considered a high-ball hitter but now he can lay off pitches that are too high in the strike zone.

He was a bit more selective at the plate in 1985, but needs to improve even more in this area. If he were to show some discretion, he would get more good pitches to hit.

He is the second-best pinch-hitter on the team (after Mullinks) and is a good bunter.

BASERUNNING:

He gets out of the box quickly, although once he gets on is not much of a threat to steal. He runs hard and will attempt the break up of the DP.

FIELDING:

Although he has gained fame as a platoon third baseman with Rance Mulliniks, Iorg has also spelled Damaso Garcia at second base. He does not have the range to do that too often, however.

GARTH IORG
3B, No. 16
RR, 5'11", 175 lbs.
ML Svc: 7 years
Born: 10-12-54 in
    Arcata, CA

1985 STATISTICS

AVG	G	AB	R	H	2B	3B	HR	RBI	BB	SO	SB
.313	131	288	33	90	22	1	7	37	21	26	2

CAREER STATISTICS

AVG	G	AB	R	H	2B	3B	HR	RBI	BB	SO	SB
.266	672	1813	186	483	95	15	13	164	73	199	17

VS. RHP   VS. LHP   PROBABLE HIT LOCATIONS

Iorg is better at moving to his left than his right. He gets rid of the ball quickly and his throws are adquate.

OVERALL:

Robinson: "He and Rance Mulliniks are almost mirror images of each other. In all phases of the game, Iorg did better than almost everyone had expected. He and Mulliniks are fortunate to have found each other. Without the benefit of the platoon situation they are in, I don't think that either one would be playing as regularly as they have. Some players need to play everyday in order to be effective, while others perform best in tandem with another. Iorg is the latter and it suits him just fine."

PITCHING:

It's hard to believe that the Blue Jays had gone 614 games without a victory from a lefthanded starting pitcher until Jimmy Key beat the Angels on May 1, 1985. He went on to set team records for wins (14) and ERA (3.00) for a lefty starter. Although he is best-suited for a starting role, he spent his entire rookie season in the bullpen. Being in the starting rotation gives Key a better opportunity to make use of all of his pitches.

Key is not an overpowering pitcher. He has an average major league fastball (85-88 MPH) and so he relies more on his breaking pitches to get along. Key's curveball is a big, slow one. His slider gets a good drop, and he uses it well. He will mix in all of his pitches with a change-up which he will throw anytime in the count.

His out pitch is his fastball. It is a sneaky one and he cuts it a lot. But he still uses his breaking pitches to support the fastball.

For such a young pitcher, Key has a great deal of poise on the mound. He is unflappable and likes to pitch the big, pressure games. He does well in them. The first time the Jays met the defending world champion Detroit Tigers last season, he threw a no-hitter for eight innings and went 10 shutout innings.

FIELDING:

Runners can go after Key's first throw to first. He has an average move and will not throw over often. He does not think about the runners all of the time.

JIMMY KEY
LHP, No. 22
RL, 6'1", 185 lbs.
ML Svc: 2 years
Born: 4-22-61 in
   Huntsville, AL

1985 STATISTICS

W	L	ERA	G	GS	CG	SV	IP	H	R	ER	BB	SO
14	6	3.00	35	32	3	0	212.2	188	77	71	50	85

CAREER STATISTICS

W	L	ERA	G	GS	CG	SV	IP	H	R	ER	BB	SO
18	11	3.38	98	32	3	0	274.2	258	114	103	82	129

Jimmy is an outstanding athlete and an excellent fielder, both on hard-hit balls back at him and on bunts. Key gets over to cover first quickly.

OVERALL:

The Jays picked a good lefty to get them on track. What stands out the most about Key is the way he approaches the game. He gears himself up and has an excellent makeup; he did not look like a first-year starter in 1985. He doesn't get down on himself and keeps his head in the game at all times. He was good from beginning to end. He is the type of pitcher who could win 18 or 20 games.

Robinson: "Jimmy throws strikes and mixes his pitches well. I wasn't able to discern any real weakness in him last season. He doesn't have overpowering stuff, but he is able to use good control to move the ball around in the strike zone. He challenges the hitter to find his pitch."

PITCHING:

Dennis Lamp was a major disappointment in 1984 when the Blue Jays signed him as a free agent. They tried and failed to make him a stopper. Placed back in the more familiar role of long relief in 1985, Lamp turned in an outstanding season. He was undefeated in 11 decisions last year.

Lamp is a power pitcher. He throws a fastball that sinks and a slider that sinks, too. He had great success using a cross-seams grip on his fastball. The grip was new for him last year.

His fastball is in the 86-88 MPH range and his slider has a good drop. He uses the slider to its maximum effectiveness. Hitters will chase his sinkerball. Occasionally, when he is ahead in the count, Lamp will come in with a change-up.

Lamps's sinking fastball is his out pitch: generally, all a hitter can do is make a ground ball out.

Lamp stays pretty much on the outside and lower part of the strike zone. He will power himself out of jams and can get the strikeout when he needs it.

In order for Lamp to be effective, he must be used often. Regular work is important for him to maintain his control. When he gets into trouble, it is because he is getting the ball up in the strike zone. Because Lamp does not pitch inside much, hitters can crowd the plate and look for the ball down and away.

FIELDING:

Lamp has a good move to first and will throw over a lot, although he does not let baserunners distract him. He always seems prepared to go for the double play on balls hit back at him.

DENNIS LAMP
RHP, No. 53
RR, 6'3", 215 lbs.
ML Svc: 9 years
Born: 9-23-52 in
  Los Angeles, CA

1985 STATISTICS

W	L	ERA	G	GS	CG	SV	IP	H	R	ER	BB	SO
11	0	3.32	53	1	0	2	105.2	96	42	39	27	68

CAREER STATISTICS

W	L	ERA	G	GS	CG	SV	IP	H	R	ER	BB	SO
72	70	3.83	356	155	21	31	1280.2	1371	620	546	388	560

OVERALL:

It was Lamp's versatility that enabled the Blue Jays to stick with him. He can start as well as pitch in long or short relief. His best role, however, is clearly long relief.

Lamp uses a form of self-hypnosis to help him with his concentration. All he needed was to regain his confidence; he seems to have done that.

Robinson: "Lamp got plenty of help last season from the bullpen, but he did a great job of keeping the game under control until he could turn it over to the short men. He did his job with precision. Most pitchers don't like the job of long relief--you don't get the start and you're not in it in the ninth inning. Lamp seems to thrive on it, however.

"Dennis can pitch often and comes out throwing strikes. His control improved tremendously last season. His weakness, though, is that he is basicaly a two-pitch pitcher. Both of his pitches are almost the same speed, which means that if his sinker or control are off, he can get hurt."

PITCHING:

When the Blue Jays dealt with the San Francisco Giants for Gary Lavelle, it marked the first time the Jays ever had a quality lefthanded reliever. Unfortunately, Lavelle was bothered by a tender elbow all season. He even went to Dr. Frank Jobe for an examination on the eve of the American League playoffs. Both Lavelle and the Blue Jays hope that a winter of rest has been the cure.

When he is right, Lavelle is a power pitcher. He uses a three-quarters delivery, but will drop down and come sidearm occasionally. He is a fast worker on the mound. He throws his fastball at around 85-89 MPH. His fastball is just a bit better than average. Lavelle has a good slider, which can be very effective against lefthanded hitters.

When he is ahead in the count, he will throw a change-up from time to time. Otherwise, he sticks to the fastball and slider. His fastball is his out pitch and he will challenge the hitters with it. Lavelle keeps his cool when he is in trouble; sometimes he can't buy a strike, other times he is in over his head because he tries to be too fine with his pitches.

FIELDING:

Lavelle has an average move to first base. Because of his big leg kick, he is slow in coming to the plate and runners are able to get a good jump. He covers first quickly.

GARY LAVELLE
LHP, No. 46
RL, 6'1", 200 lbs.
ML Svc: 11 years
Born: 1-3-49 in
   Scranton, PA

1985 STATISTICS

W	L	ERA	G	GS	CG	SV	IP	H	R	ER	BB	SO
5	7	3.10	69	0	0	8	72.2	54	30	25	36	50

CAREER STATISTICS

W	L	ERA	G	GS	CG	SV	IP	H	R	ER	BB	SO
78	74	2.83	716	3	0	135	1053	964	389	332	418	746

OVERALL:

Lavelle seldom pitched without some kind of twitch in his arm last season. There were times when he had to sit down after he began to warm up because his elbow was so stiff. The elbow problem began in spring training when he was throwing too many breaking balls too early in the season in the hopes of making a good impression.

Robinson: "For the last several seasons, Gary has blown hot and cold. This year was no exception, though he did have the injury to point to. He keeps the ball in the park, but that won't be for long if he is not able to maintain his control. He did not do a bad job last season, but he could have done better. Things should look up this year."

HITTING:

Buck Martinez had a month-long dry spell early in the 1985 season. He was just beginning to pick up his average when he was on the wrong end of a spectacular collision at home plate last July. He sustained a dislocated ankle and a fractured leg in the play, yet Martinez still made a double putout at the plate.

He made a great effort to try to get ready for post-season play on the outside chance he could do it, but was still limping when the Blue Jays entered the ALCS.

Martinez is a low-ball hitter. He likes the ball on the inside half of the plate. He hits mostly to left-center, although he can occasionally pull the ball sharply. He tends to hit a lot of warning track fly balls.

Martinez hits the fastball no matter where it is: up, away, or right over the plate. Pitchers can get him out by keeping the ball away from him and from the belt down. They can also send him a breaking ball, down, and change speeds on him. He can be selective at times.

He is a poor bunter who cannot sacrifice that way, but he is excellent at getting a runner home from third with less than two outs by lofting a sacrifice fly.

BASERUNNING:

Martinez has no speed and is no threat to steal, but he is smart enough not to make mistakes on the basepaths. He slides hard into second.

FIELDING:

Martinez shares the catching chores with lefthanded hitting Ernie Whitt. It is a combination that has worked out well in the past, but may be in its last season. The leg injury and his increas-

BUCK MARTINEZ
C, No. 13
RR, 5'11", 200 lbs.
ML Svc: 16 years
Born: 11-7-48 in
Redding, CA

1985 STATISTICS

AVG	G	AB	R	H	2B	3B	HR	RBI	BB	SO	SB
.162	42	99	11	16	3	0	4	14	10	12	0

CAREER STATISTICS

AVG	G	AB	R	H	2B	3B	HR	RBI	BB	SO	SB
.228	968	2583	232	589	120	10	56	309	210	394	5

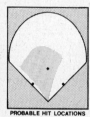

STRONG VS. RHP   STRONG VS. LHP   PROBABLE HIT LOCATIONS

ing age will make it difficult for Buck to return to top form.

He is not a great catcher, but has done well in the platoon role. If he played every day, he would tire easily and all phases of his game would suffer.

He calls a good game and is outstanding at blocking the plate. His throws are generally accurate. Last season, he threw out 10 of 26 attempted basestealers. He is good on foul pop-ups.

OVERALL:

Robinson: "He has always been a gutsy catcher, but his leg injury may force him to think about continuing. He will be 37 years old this season. His injury is a tough one for a catcher to overcome because of all of the up-and-down movement the position requires.

"I have my doubts that Buck will be able to make it back."

HITTING:

At a glance, it appears that Lloyd Moseby slipped, for the second year in a row, from his .315 peak in 1983. But the fact is: his second-half comeback last year is a sign of his growing maturity as a ballplayer.

Moseby is a high-ball hitter and likes it on the inside of the plate. He hits to all fields, although he did not hit to left as much last season as in previous years; pitchers were working him high and tight in 1985. It wasn't until late in the season that he altered his stance and backed off the plate to defense himself. Batting coach Cito Gaston worked with him to get him to look for a pitch he could drive every time; Moseby hit a dozen homers after the All-Star break.

Moseby stands deep in the box, square to the plate, with his legs spread wide. He dropped his hands slightly last year to chest-high. If the pitch is a fastball, he likes is about belt-high. However, he has a tendency to chase fastballs out of the strike zone after two strikes. He also has trouble with low breaking balls.

Moseby has learned to become a more patient hitter. He doesn't go after the first pitch all that much, and led the team last year with a career high of 76 walks.

He's an excellent bunter. He can drop one down toward third base and beat it out. He hits for about the same average against righthanders as lefthanders, although he strikes out more frequently against lefties. He hit seven of his 18 home runs off lefthanders. His average climbed after he moved from third to second in the batting order last year.

BASERUNNING:

Moseby likes to run. He is fast in getting out of the box. He takes a good lead and forces the pitcher to throw over. He likes to use the headfirst slide and is able to get up quickly to be ready to take an extra base on a poor

LLOYD MOSEBY
CF, No. 15
LR, 6'3", 200 lbs.
ML Svc: 6 years
Born: 11-5-59 in Portland, AR

1985 STATISTICS											
AVG	G	AB	R	H	2B	3B	HR	RBI	BB	SO	SB
.259	152	584	92	151	30	7	18	71	76	91	37
CAREER STATISTICS											
AVG	G	AB	R	H	2B	3B	HR	RBI	BB	SO	SB
.232	822	2969	424	779	149	41	81	385	287	575	129

  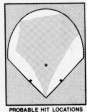

VS. RHP   VS. LHP   PROBABLE HIT LOCATIONS

throw. He goes from first to third on anything and will slide hard to break up the double play.

FIELDING:

He covers a lot of ground and is the Blue Jays' take-charge guy in the outfield. He cuts off balls in the alleys well and is equally good whether coming in or going back on a ball. He has a good arm and releases the ball quickly. Each year, he becomes a better defensive player.

OVERALL:

He did not hit as well as was expected, but Moseby still has the capability of becoming a star in all areas.

Robinson: "I don't think he has quite reached his peak. I believe he is going to explode and have a great year soon.

"Lloyd should be hitting more home runs; there is no reason for a hitter of Moseby's ability to struggle like he did in the first half."

HITTING:

One of the most underrated hitters in the league, Rance Mulliniks is a fast-ball hitter who always has a good idea of what he wants to do at the plate.

Mulliniks will hit the ball where it is pitched. He will pull inside pitches to right field and slap outside pitches to left. Sometimes, he is so anxious to get down to it, he will jump on the first pitch. Mulliniks is one of the best 2-0 or 3-1 fastball hitters in the league.

He has trouble with the curveball and off-speed pitches. Pitchers should keep everything down on him. Righthanded pitchers can throw the curveball down-- he usually swings right over them.

While he will occasionally be too impatient at the plate, he also has the ability to wait for his pitch when he has to. He was the Jays' best pinch-hitter (9-for-19 with 6 walks) and had a team leading .378 average with runners in scoring position.

During most of last season, Mulliniks hit high in the order, in the number two or three spot, and had a career high of 56 RBIs.

BASERUNNING:

Mulliniks starts off well; he gets a good jump out of the box, but has no speed to capitalize on his first dash. He is not able to leg out a hit. He is a smart baserunner, but he doesn't steal or take chances. He slides hard into second and is always in the game.

FIELDING:

Mulliniks and Garth Iorg platoon at third base for the Blue Jays and between them both, they get the job done well.

Mulliniks has worked hard and has

RANCE MULLINIKS
3B, No. 5
LR, 6'0", 170 lbs.
ML Svc: 8 years
Born: 1-15-56 in
Tulare, CA

1985 STATISTICS

AVG	G	AB	R	H	2B	3B	HR	RBI	BB	SO	SB
.295	129	366	55	108	26	1	10	56	55	54	2

CAREER STATISTICS

AVG	G	AB	R	H	2B	3B	HR	RBI	BB	SO	SB
.270	705	1940	245	524	128	12	32	228	224	279	10

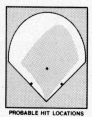

VS. RHP   VS. LHP   PROBABLE HIT LOCATIONS

learned to come in on the bunt and the slow roller. He is quick and moves well to both his left and right. He has a shortstop's arm and his throws are generally accurate. He has made himself into a fine fielder.

OVERALL:

Mulliniks is an aggressive hitter. Both at the plate and in the field, he is better than a lot of people think.

Robinson: "I like him more every time I see him play. I would not change a thing with him. Rance has definitely reached his peak--he cannot play any better than he is right now. He and Iorg make an ideal platoon combination and both seem comfortable sharing the job."

ACE OF THE STAFF

PITCHING:

Dave Stieb is one of the premier pitchers in the American League. Yet he continues to be his own worst enemy.

He has difficulty maintaining consistency over the course of an entire season. Although he led the league in earned run average (2.48) last year, that figure can really be looked at in two parts. He had a 1.87 ERA with a 9-5 record before the All-Star break, but was 3.22 in the second half while he lost eight of 13 decisions (he might have had more wins, but there were several occasions when the bullpen was simply unable to hold onto big leads).

During the latter half of the season, he complained of a sore elbow, but he didn't miss a turn. He continued to throw his fastball in the 90s, but the soreness might have taken its toll on his otherwise-nasty slider. He couldn't get it to break the way he wanted and he was unable to use it as his out pitch. To compensate, he threw a curveball.

He throws two fastballs: one that sinks and another that rides. He is very active on the mound and likes to work quickly. He goes right after the hitters and will challenge them with his best pitch. He pitches inside a lot to lefthanded hitters and is as effective as anyone in the league at moving them back.

His inconsistent control in the second half of the season was a problem based, in part, on his mechanics. He was unable to maintain a consistent release point on his throw.

FIELDING:

Stieb is the Blue Jays' best-fielding pitcher. He has a good move to first base and will throw over a lot to hold the runners. Stieb is a good athlete and is always in a position to field the ball. He is one of the best in the game

DAVE STIEB
RHP, No. 37
RR, 6'1", 195 lbs.
ML Svc: 7 years
Born: 7-22-57 in
    Santa Ana, CA

```
1985 STATISTICS
W   L  ERA   G   GS  CG SV IP      H    R   ER  BB  SO
14  13 2.48  36  36  8  0  265     206  89  73  96  167
CAREER STATISTICS
W   L  ERA   G   GS  CG SV IP      H    R   ER  BB  SO
95  80 3.16 222 220 84  0  1654.1 1434 645 582 544 942
```

at fielding sharp smashes back to the mound. He is quick to pounce on bunts and always covers first base.

Prior to 1985, Stieb had never made a fielding error: all of his errors came on errant pickoff throws. Last season was the first time he ever mishandled fielding plays. Still, he is far above average as a fielder.

OVERALL:

Stieb's problem may be that he does not give himself enough room for error. He is a perfectionist and gets furious when things go awry.

He has all the pitches it takes to be the best but has to learn to handle himself. He pumps himself up to get the big hitters in the lineup, but gets beat by hitters lower in the order.

Robinson: "I'm beginning to think we are looking for too much from him. Sometimes he looks unhittable, but there are other times when he looks like a shadow of himself. He had great numbers last year, but to me it was not a true Stieb year. He should be the best pitcher on this team. He has got to come to terms with his own abilities."

HITTING:

Back in 1983, it seemed as though Willie Upshaw was ready to join the corps of major league big boys such as Eddie Murray and Cecil Cooper. That year, Upshaw hit 27 home runs and had 104 RBIs. Since then, however, his numbers have tailed off.

Upshaw is a powerful, lefthanded pull hitter with a quick bat. At the plate, he is always poised and ready to swing. He will go for the first pitch, especially if it is his favorite pitch, the low fastball. Upshaw can also handle the hard slider.

His weaknesses are the high, inside fastball and low breaking balls. Last season, Upshaw did not get many good pitches to hit and became a little frustrated, a factor which led to his impatience at the plate.

Upshaw has had good success against southpaws, hitting almost half of his 1985 RBIs and five of his 15 homers against them. Early in the season, when he was facing lefties more regularly, Upshaw tried to pull the ball too often (his natural stroke sends the pitch to the opposite field vs. LHP).

Although he does not attempt it frequently, Upshaw is a good bunter.

BASERUNNING:

He is very quick out of the batter's box, runs well and can beat out an occasional grounder. Upshaw runs aggressively and will try to break up the double play. He does not try to steal very often, but will if he is ignored. He has good instincts on the bases.

FIELDING:

Upshaw is one player who has benefitted from the installation of the new artificial surface at Exhibition Stadium in Toronto. The old carpet was badly worn and regularly caused some balls to skip instead of bouncing. The skipping led to more than one "error."

WILLIE UPSHAW
1B, No. 26
LL, 6'0", 185 lbs.
ML Svc: 7 years
Born: 4-27-57 in
Blanco, TX

1985 STATISTICS

AVG	G	AB	R	H	2B	3B	HR	RBI	BB	SO	SB
.275	148	501	79	138	31	5	15	65	48	71	8

CAREER STATISTICS

AVG	G	AB	R	H	2B	3B	HR	RBI	BB	SO	SB
.271	910	2625	385	713	127	32	88	360	254	529	43

  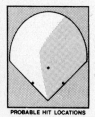

VS. RHP — STRONG VS. LHP — STRONG PROBABLE HIT LOCATIONS

He is a very good fielder and has worked hard to improve himself; he has good range and he can go to his right well and makes the force play. He covers a lot of ground when scavenging pop-ups down the right field line. Upshaw is also adept at digging balls out of the dirt. Frankly, he really can't play the field any better than he does right now.

OVERALL:

The Blue Jays were expecting more power from him this year. His 1984 power loss was blamed on his sore right wrist in the second half of that season. But there were no excuses in 1985.

Robinson: "He is a hard worker who will most likely make a diligent attempt to regain his power this season. But he must adjust to the steady diet of breaking pitches he sees.

"I think that his 1983 season was as good as he can do and he is not going to get any better. This year, I believe that we will see a repeat of his play of 1985: nothing tremendous, just steady."

HITTING:

Ernie Whitt finally got the opportunity to play every day in the final five weeks of the 1985 season. It was poor timing, however. He had a sore right shoulder at the time, which was the result of trying to break up a double play. Whitt played despite the injury, but his average tumbled.

He hit a career high 19 home runs last season, primarily because he opened his stance a little and spread his feet more than he had been doing. Surprisingly, Whitt hit 12 of his 19 home runs away from Exhibition Stadium, which is considered to be a hitter's park.

Whitt is a high-ball hitter and likes to pull the inside pitch. He generally plays against righthanded pitchers. They can get him out with breaking balls and change-ups thrown down and in or down and away.

Whitt is one of the best bunters on the team and will surprise the opposition occasionally by bunting for a hit.

He posted career highs in several offensive categories mostly because he played more often after regular catcher Buck Martinez was injured.

BASERUNNING:

Whitt is a below-average baserunner and is slow to leave the batter's box. He slides hard on the double play (which is how he injured his shoulder last year). He knows when he can take advantage of a nonchalant defense by going to third from first base.

FIELDING:

Two-thirds of all the runners who attempted to steal on Whitt were successful. While he is an excellent handler of pitchers and calls a good game, he has trouble with some catching fundamentals. He hurries his throws, which usually leads to inaccuracy. He is good on foul pop-ups and pounces on bunts.

ERNIE WHITT
C, No. 12
LR, 6'2", 200 lbs.
ML Svc: 8 years
Born: 6-13-52 in
Detroit, MI

1985 STATISTICS

AVG	G	AB	R	H	2B	3B	HR	RBI	BB	SO	SB
.245	139	412	55	101	21	2	19	64	47	59	3

CAREER STATISTICS

AVG	G	AB	R	H	2B	3B	HR	RBI	BB	SO	SB
.243	704	1908	218	465	88	9	70	146	213	273	13

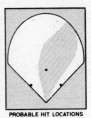

VS. RHP   VS. LHP   PROBABLE HIT LOCATIONS

Whitt shows good judgment in moving out to get a throw from the outfield: he stays back and lets the ball come to him.

It would help him if the Blue Jays staff, in general, kept runners close.

OVERALL:

Robinson: "Like Iorg and Mulliniks, Whitt and Buck Martinez have benefitted from the presence of each other. They have worked out well sharing catching duties. Martinez has a difficult injury that he may not recover from completely. Whitt would not be able to take over the everyday detail, however. He is able to perform as well as he has because he has been platooned. You are seeing him at his best.

"Whitt would not be as effective offensively or defensively as the regular catcher. He needs a righthanded hitting complement."

LUIS LEAL
RHP, No. 48
RR, 6'3", 220 lbs.
ML Svc: 6 years
Born: 3-21-57 in
    Barquisimeto, VEN

PITCHING, FIELDING:

Luis Leal's trouble began late in the 1984 season when he won only one game after August 1. He never got things back together all last year either. He had only one good outing in 14 starts and was demoted to Syracuse at mid-season.

Leal's fastball is far from sizzling at 85-88 MPH. He throws an overhand curve, but his best pitch is his hard slider. He can throw the overhand curve to righthanded hitters and keeps the slider low and away to both left- and righthanded hitters.

Leal has a lot of difficulty controlling any of his pitches. When things are going badly, he tries too hard to get the ball over for a strike and winds up sending everything right down the heart of the plate where he gets hit for the gopher ball.

He loses his concentration on the mound quickly.

In the field, Leal is just average. He can keep runners close, but sometimes he concentrates so hard on making his pitch that he forgets that there are runners on base. He also has a tendency to forget that he is supposed to cover first.

OVERALL:

Leal needs to work harder. He has enough pitches to be a good starter, but is having trouble applying himself.

Robinson: "He really ought to slim down. He doesn't seem to want to put up with the kind of sacrifices it takes to be a big league starting pitcher. There are plenty of Jays who have got a lot more going for them."

RON MUSSELMAN
RHP, No. 30
RR, 6'2", 185 lbs.
ML Svc: 2 years
Born: 11-11-54 in
    Wilmington, NC

PITCHING, FIELDING:

It is extremely difficult to pitch effectively as the tenth man on a 10-man pitching staff, but Ron Musselman was 3-0 for the Jays in 1985. He even started four games, but was used only occasionally and worked only 52 innings before he was demoted at the end of August. The Blue Jays needed to make room for another lefthander.

Musselman is a control pitcher who can also use power to be effective. His fastball is in the 85-88 MPH range. He also has a slider which he uses well.

But it is the forkball, which he uses as a change-up, that has really helped him. Unfortunately, he was more effective with the forkball early in the season, when he got enough work to control it. He showed it a lot, but after periods of inactivity, Musselman began to have difficulty throwing it for strikes.

When he is unable to control his forkball, his fastball becomes his out pitch.

Musselman is undistinguished as a fielder. His move to first is average. He is not very quick on balls hit back at him and is only fair in covering first base.

OVERALL:

Robinson: "He is just a borderline major league pitcher. Ron could get more work if he is able to control his forkball consistently. Otherwise, he is nothing special."

CLIFF JOHNSON
DH, No. 00
RR, 6'4", 225 lbs.
ML Svc: 12 years
Born: 7-22-47 in
   San Antonio, TX

HITTING, BASERUNNING, FIELDING:

Cliff Johnson left the Blue Jay flock to sign with the Texas Rangers as a free agent in December 1984, but when the pennant race really got hot late last season, the Jays wanted him back. And Johnson accepted the invitation to depart the last place Rangers to come to the aid of his former teammates in Toronto.

He platooned with Al Oliver against lefthanded pitchers in the stretch drive and proved to be one of the Jays' most productive hitters. He had 42 RBIs and hit .424 with runners in scoring position.

Johnson loves the challenge of facing a good hard fastball; his power is against the fastball down and in. Oddly enough, Johnson hit 11 of his 13 home runs last season against righthanded hitters. No pitcher should make a mistake to Johnson. He has one job and that is to hit the ball as often and as hard as he can.

He is an aggressive all-out player whether he is stalking a pitcher or chasing his next base. He will knock down anything in his way to get an extra base.

Last season, the Jays used him a bit at first base, a position he had not played for a full year. He would rather hit. Period.

OVERALL:

Johnson is big, dangerous hitter. He has been such for a long time. He loves to hit and as long as he's having a good time and someone will give him a job, Johnson will probably remain in the majors as a DH.

AL OLIVER
DH/1B, No. 0
LL, 6'1", 185 lbs.
ML Svc: 17 years
Born: 10-14-46 in
   Portsmouth, OH

HITTING, BASERUNNING, FIELDING:

In the last three seasons, Al Oliver has played for five different teams. Last year, he was traded from the Phils to the Dodgers and then to the Blue Jays. His first three months of the 1985 season were spent in Los Angeles; his career seemed to be at a dead end. Seemingly revitalized after his early July trade to the Blue Jays, Oliver got his old swing back in Toronto.

Playing mostly as the lefthanded DH, he quickly hit 5 home runs and had driven in 23 runs by season's end.

In the past, Oliver could be counted on to hit .300 just about every year; his .252 average in 1985 was his career low.

He has always been an excellent breaking ball hitter and though he prefers low pitches can hit any pitch in any location if it feels right to him.

Defensively, he is a liability; he has no range and no arm.

OVERALL:

A great career looks as though it is winding down. Oliver believes that he can still be an everyday player; the Blue Jays, however, think otherwise. Over the winter, Oliver considered his options.

1985 National League Leaders

BATTING AVERAGE:
Willie McGee, St. Louis, .353
Pedro Guerrero, Los Angeles, .320
Tim Raines, Montreal, .320

HOME RUNS:
Dale Murphy, Atlanta, 37
Dave Parker, Cincinnati, 34

HITS:
Willie McGee, St. Louis, 216
Dave Parker, Cincinnati, 198

DOUBLES:
Dave Parker, Cincinnati, 42
Glenn Wilson, Philadelphia, 39

TRIPLES:
Willie McGee, St. Louis, 18
Tim Raines, Montreal, 13
Juan Samuel, Philadelphia, 13

RUNS:
Dale Murphy, Atlanta, 118
Tim Raines, Montreal, 115

RUNS BATTED IN:
Dave Parker, Cincinnati, 125
Dale Murphy, Atlanta, 111

GAME-WINNING RBI:
Keith Hernandez, New York, 24
Gary Carter, New York, 18

WALKS:
Dale Murphy, Atlanta, 90
Carmelo Martinez, San Diego, 87
Mike Schmidt, Philadelphia, 87

STOLEN BASES:
Vince Coleman, St. Louis, 110
Tim Raines, Montreal, 70

WON-LOST:
Dwight Gooden, New York, 24-4
John Tudor, St. Louis, 21-8

ERA:
Dwight Gooden, New York, 1.53
John Tudor, St. Louis, 1.93

GAMES:
Tim Burke, Montreal, 78
Mark Davis, San Francisco, 77

COMPLETE GAMES:
Dwight Gooden, New York, 16
John Tudor, St. Louis, 14
Fernando Valenzuela, Los Angeles, 14

INNINGS PITCHED:
Dwight Gooden, New York, 276.2
John Tudor, St. Louis, 275

STRIKEOUTS:
Dwight Gooden, New York, 268
Mario Soto, Cincinnati, 214

SHUTOUTS:
John Tudor, St. Louis, 10
Dwight Gooden, New York, 8

SAVES:
Jeff Reardon, Montreal, 41
Lee Smith, Chicago, 33

THE NATIONAL LEAGUE

ATLANTA BRAVES

PITCHING:

Once again, Len Barker had a horrible season because of arm injuries. After off-season elbow surgery, Barker was hopeful of bouncing back strong last year, but by mid-season it was clear that it would be at least another year before that might happen--if, indeed, he ever does.

The injuries have cost Barker both velocity and fluidity and forced him to try to make the conversion from power pitcher to something approaching a finesse pitcher. The Braves hope his arm comes around to the point that he can pitch in his old style. Otherwise, they may have to release him.

Barker is strictly a starter. He uses an unorthodox, high leg kick. At his best, he throws an overpowering fastball, a deadly curveball, a slider and a change-up. But at his worst, the fastball loses velocity, the curve is easily telegraphed and hitters can knock him around. He also battles control problems in the bad times.

The Braves sent Barker to the Florida Instructional League after last season and, since he has three years remaining on a lucrative contract, they are not giving up on him. But if he does not show encouraging physical signs this spring, then they may move in that direction.

FIELDING, HITTING, BASERUNNING:

The high leg kick does not leave him in a good defensive position, but he generally recovers well enough to play batted balls. He has an average move to first base, but sometimes seems oblivious to baserunners.

As far as hitting and baserunning, he does both jobs as most NL pitchers do: poorly.

LEN BARKER
RHP, No. 39
RR, 6'4", 230 lbs.
ML Svc: 9 years
Born: 7-7-55 in
    Fort Knox, KY

1985 STATISTICS

W	L	ERA	G	GS	CG	SV	IP	H	R	ER	BB	SO
2	9	6.35	20	18	0	0	73.2	84	55	52	37	47

CAREER STATISTICS

W	L	ERA	G	GS	CG	SV	IP	H	R	ER	BB	SO
72	75	4.32	237	183	35	5	1278.1	1235	668	613	496	953

OVERALL:

A status report on Barker could better be given by a doctor than a pitching coach. His future hinges entirely on whether he regains strength and comfort in his injury-ravaged right arm. The bottom line is this: a healthy Barker could boost the Braves' starting rotation, but an unhealthy Barker is a liability to a staff already burdened with too many liabilities.

Campbell: "Unless there is a miracle cure somewhere, his better days are behind him. Since he is signed to a long-term contract, it wouldn't hurt the Braves to take him to spring training and see if his arm is better. But if it isn't, the Braves may just have to write off the contract.

"You hate to see a guy with that much ability succumb to injury, but pitchers will have arm problems. And when they become chronic, as it appears Barker's have become, it's time to move on."

PITCHING:

Steve Bedrosian made the move from reliever to starter in 1985, though the switch may not be permanent. Since Bruce Sutter became available as the Braves' number one shortman and Bedrosian had a three-year track record of late-season arm problems and decreasing effectiveness, the move was well-timed. However, things did not go as smoothly as was originally hoped.

Bedrosian pitched well enough, but the Atlanta offense did not give him much to work with. He was not awesome as a starter, either. It is not clear what his best role is. There are still a lot of scouts around the game who think that if Bedrosian is taught an off-speed pitch, he can become devastating as a relief pitcher. The Braves probably won't decide until the end of spring training how to use him.

He is, in any case, the hardest thrower on the Atlanta pitching staff; he throws from a three-quarters motion and does nothing tricky. His fastball consistently clocks around 91-92 MPH and sometimes gets faster. That tends to be early in the season; his fastball seems to lose velocity later in the year.

Bedrosian also has a hard slider that he throws with almost the same velocity as a fastball. He still does not have a top-quality change-of-pace pitch; he could desperately use a straight change or a slow curve.

Another problem for Bedrosian is his control. He puts too many hitters on base and has to pitch with runners on base too often.

FIELDING, HITTING, BASERUNNING:

He fields his position adequately. He is an excitable person who will occa-

STEVE BEDROSIAN
RHP, No. 32
RR, 6'3", 195 lbs.
ML Svc: 4 years
Born: 12-6-57 in
Methuen, MA

1985 STATISTICS

W	L	ERA	G	GS	CG	SV	IP	H	R	ER	BB	SO
7	15	3.83	37	37	0	0	206.2	198	101	88	111	134

CAREER STATISTICS

W	L	ERA	G	GS	CG	SV	IP	H	R	ER	BB	SO
34	39	2.77	226	46	0	41	672	480	227	207	267	461

sionally botch a play in the field. His move to first base is adequate. However, he gets the ball to the plate quickly and gives his catcher a competitive chance at throwing out runners.

Bedrosian is a futile hitter, to the point that his baserunning skills are moot. Bedrosian hacks away at the plate and only rarely connects.

OVERALL:

The Braves had such a poor season in 1985 that few of their players retained much marketability. Bedrosian, however, remains highly regarded. The consensus among baseball people is that his greater value is as a reliever. One of the key questions for the Braves this year will be to determine Bedrosian's role.

Campbell: "If he could develop an off-speed pitch, he could be one of the most effective pitchers in the National League. On a staff which had trouble staying healthy, Bedrosian and Rick Mahler were the workhorse starters last year. He is a pretty good competitor."

HITTING:

Since hitting .298 in 1983, Bruce Benedict has slumped considerably with the bat and the two-year-long hitting slump has cost him his status as the Braves' regular catcher. There is no easy explanation; his stance has not changed and he still tries to hit the ball to left field. But the results have surely deteriorated.

Benedict, who stands rather far off the plate, can do some damage with off-speed pitches over the inside part of the plate. But a pitcher can get him out by mixing up the pitches or by overpowering him.

He is a patient hitter, but takes too many called strikes. He is a streak hitter and will be hot and then very cold. But his hot streaks have not been frequent enough in the past two years to get his average out of the low .200s. He is not a good bunter.

BASERUNNING:

Speed? Benedict has none. He is a smart baseball player, so he rarely makes a mistake on the bases. But he runs extremely slowly, clogs up the bases and is vulnerable to double plays. His lack of speed allows pitchers virtually to forget about him when he is on first base. Will he slide hard to break up a double play? Probably, if he's there in time.

FIELDING:

Benedict's defensive skills have deteriorated along with his hitting. Early in his career, Benedict was as proficient as any catcher in the league at throwing out opposing baserunners. But no more.

Last year, he threw out only 20% of the runners that challenged him. His

BRUCE BENEDICT
C, No. 20
RR, 6'1", 185 lbs.
ML Svc: 7 years
Born: 8-18-55 in
    Birmingham, AL

1985 STATISTICS

AVG	G	AB	R	H	2B	3B	HR	RBI	BB	SO	SB
.202	70	208	12	42	6	0	0	20	22	12	0

CAREER STATISTICS

AVG	G	AB	R	H	2B	3B	HR	RBI	BB	SO	SB
.250	725	2227	176	558	77	5	16	217	254	182	11

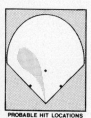

VS. RHP   VS. LHP   PROBABLE HIT LOCATIONS

mechanics and footwork become confused with irregular playing time, which led to all sorts of problems.

He does not block the plate well. His biggest asset as a defensive player is the way he handles the knuckleball, but the Braves have not had a knuckleballer since releasing Phil Niekro at the end of the 1983 season.

OVERALL:

Benedict has had two straight poor seasons on both offense and defense; yet, the Braves signed him to a new three-year contract. So, barring a trade, he'll get another shot at winning the catching job in spring training.

Campbell: "At best, Bruce is a backup catcher. He has not shown any skills at the plate or behind the plate to prove otherwise in the last two years."

PITCHING:

Once upon a time, Rick Camp was one of the very best relief pitchers in the game. That was back in 1980 and 1981, when his sinkerball made him virtually unbeatable. Since then, however, Camp has slipped into mediocrity. He has become just another body on a poor pitching staff. He pitches in long-to-middle relief and rarely gets an opportunity to truly distinguish himself.

Chuck Tanner's positive approach might suit Camp well and help him find what he has lost--his sinker. A few years ago, his sinker dipped so sharply that hitters would expect it to come in around the thigh, would swing at it and then find it was below the knees. At this point, it stays up in the strike zone. Even when he gets it down, hitters seem able to lay off it.

It is, however, an unpredictable pitch: one never knows when it'll come or go. And Camp can always hope it'll come back to him.

Camp throws overhand to three-quarters. His fastball is in the mid-80 MPH range. He also has a curveball, a slider and a change-up. He challenges hitters with all of them and won't back down.

FIELDING, HITTING, BASERUNNING:

Camp is an adequate fielder with a slighty better than average move to first base. He can handle himself defensively.

Camp's lack of skill as a hitter has always been a joke among teammates. So imagine their shock when he homered in the 17th inning in a game against the Mets last July 4. That home run not-

RICK CAMP
RHP, No. 37
RR, 6'1", 198 lbs.
ML Svc: 8 years
Born: 6-10-53 in
   Trion, GA

1985 STATISTICS
W	L	ERA	G	GS	CG	SV	IP	H	R	ER	BB	SO
4	6	3.95	66	2	0	3	127.2	130	72	56	61	49

CAREER STATISTICS
W	L	ERA	G	GS	CG	SV	IP	H	R	ER	BB	SO
56	49	3.37	414	65	5	57	941.2	970	420	353	336	407

withstanding, Camp remains a dismal hitter, a living endorsement of the designated hitter rule. He has below-average speed.

OVERALL:

Camp is at a crossroads in Atlanta. After several years in a peculiar limbo, he needs to re-establish a role for himself on the staff.

Campbell: "Like most of the Braves pitchers, he had too may walks and not enough strikeouts per innings pitched. When teams play the Braves, their batting coaches emphasize to the hitters that they must make sure the ball is up. Part of the success of Atlanta's pitching staff depends on the sinker and whether the ball falls out of strike zone. Rick is just not the type of pitcher who can pitch up--he does not have enough velocity. To me, Camp just seems to be another guy the hitters certainly don't fear as they once did."

HITTING:

Rick Cerone's hitting has declined in recent seasons. He had one outstanding, 80-RBI season with the Yankees, but has been an undistinctive hitter since then. The Braves thought he might be revived by the sight of cozy Atlanta-Fulton County Stadium and become a home run and RBI producer. It has not worked out that way.

He is a straightaway hitter, often going to center or right-center with the ball. He has only occasional power. He is not prone to striking out, however, and generally makes contact.

Cerone prefers the ball up and out over the plate so that he can fully extend his arms. To get him out, pitchers should keep the ball down and in. He can be overpowered at times, but the best way to pitch him is to mix the pitches. He is an average bunter.

BASERUNNING:

Like his catching counterpart, Bruce Benedict, Cerone has no speed. He clogs up the bases and is vulnerable to double plays. He is, however, a tough player who'll do his best to break up a double play or jar a ball loose. He runs the bases aggressively.

FIELDING:

Cerone is an aggressive, assertive catcher who will take control of a game. Pitchers like this. They also like the way he calls pitches.

As far as throwing out opposing baserunners, Cerone is better than Benedict, though neither of them is very good. Cerone throws out 30% of those who run on him, which is about the league average.

He reacts well to bunts and other fielding situations, and usually seems in command.

RICK CERONE
C, No. 5
RR, 5'11", 185 lbs.
ML Svc: 9 years
Born: 5-19-54 in
Newark, NJ

1985 STATISTICS

AVG	G	AB	R	H	2B	3B	HR	RBI	BB	SO	SB
.216	96	282	15	61	9	0	3	25	29	25	0

CAREER STATISTICS

AVG	G	AB	R	H	2B	3B	HR	RBI	BB	SO	SB
.225	790	2700	244	609	112	12	39	286	183	262	3

  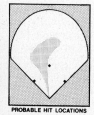

VS. RHP   VS. LHP   PROBABLE HIT LOCATIONS

OVERALL:

The Braves traded bright pitching prospect Brian Fisher to the Yankees for Cerone at the 1984 winter meetings. They regretted the move almost immediately. While Fisher established himself as a mainstay in the Yankees' bullpen, Cerone did not establish himself at all in Atlanta. It is not clear what his role will be in 1986. Ideally, Braves' management would like to obtain a top-flight catcher, but they are going to have trouble doing so with little trade-bait.

Campbell: "Rick was supposed to stabilize the catcher's job for the Braves, but his weak hitting has forced him into a platoon role. As an offensive player, he had never matched his one good year with the Yankees (1980)."

"He is a good defensive catcher and calls a good game, though none of his skills are extraordinary."

HITTING:

Chris Chambliss began to decline as an offensive threat in 1984 and continued the dip last season. He was reduced to the role of pinch-hitting and bench-warming and he did not do well.

Chambliss had always been tough on righthanded pitching and particularly weak against lefthanded pitching. In his prime, he could hit both power pitching and off-speed pitching, and he could hit pitches all over the plate. He would go the other way with outside pitches and pull inside pitches. So, with his combination of experience and power, he would seem to have the tools to be a dangerous pinch-hitter against right-handed pitchers in clutch situations.

That is, if his bat speed has not slowed irreversibly. The 1986 season will tell the story on that point. It sure looked slow last season.

BASERUNNING:

Chambliss never was blessed with anything more than average speed, and he has struggled to keep off some extra pounds over the last couple of seasons. In his new role, Chambliss can expect to be lifted for a pinch-runner when he gets on base.

FIELDING:

Once a fine defensive first baseman, Chambliss does not figure to get much time in at first any longer.

OVERALL:

The Braves seem convinced that Chris is no longer an everyday player, although Chambliss himself still clings to

CHRIS CHAMBLISS
1B, No. 10
LR, 6'1", 221 lbs.
ML Svc: 15 years
Born: 12-26-48 in Dayton, OH

1985 STATISTICS

AVG	G	AB	R	H	2B	3B	HR	RBI	BB	SO	SB
.235	101	170	16	40	7	0	3	21	18	22	0

CAREER STATISTICS

AVG	G	AB	R	H	2B	3B	HR	RBI	BB	SO	SB
.278	2077	7448	899	2071	384	42	183	958	617	901	57

VS. RHP — STRONG   VS. LHP — STRONG   PROBABLE HIT LOCATIONS

the belief that he can play and produce regularly. In any case, he will have to accept pinch-hitting in this, the final year of his contract. Chuck Tanner thinks Chambliss could be a major asset to the team in this role.

Campbell: "It may be the end of the line for Chris. When the Braves moved Horner to first, it was the first clue. Chambliss is a veteran who knows game situations, so he should be a better pinch-hitter than he showed last year unless his bat really has slowed down. Sometimes, pinch-hitters will have one bad year followed by a great one, and if he is to continue his baseball career beyond 1986, Chambliss is going to have to have a good year off the bench."

PITCHING:

A lot of scouts like Jeff Dedmon's potential as a short reliever. Countless times over the past three years, other teams have asked about his availability when the Braves talk trade. The Braves have resisted.

He has the tools of a top-notch reliever: a sinking fastball (85-86 MPH) with good movement, a knucklecurve which is an effective out pitch and confidence in himself. The fastball/knucklecurve combination serves him well. His fastball is a heavy pitch and moves in on righthanded batters. He is not a power pitcher, although on a given night, his fastball has surprising velocity. He has a good record at retiring the first batter he faces--a crucial late-inning skill.

He keeps the ball down, which forces a lot of ground balls, and allows very few home runs.

There is, however, one mark against Dedmon as a big league reliever: his control. So far, it has not been good. He walks far too many batters and a lack of control gets him into trouble.

FIELDING, HITTING, BASERUNNING:

Dedmon fields his position like the athlete that he is. He reacts well, moves quickly and has good instincts. He is rarely befuddled by a play.

He holds runners on base well and has improved in this area over the past season. He has the ability to focus on the baserunner and the batter at the same time.

Dedmon does not get up to bat much.

JEFF DEDMON
RHP, No. 49
LR, 6'2", 200 lbs.
ML Svc: 2 years
Born: 3-4-60 in
   Torrance, CA

1985 STATISTICS

W	L	ERA	G	GS	CG	SV	IP	H	R	ER	BB	SO
6	3	4.08	60	0	0	0	86	84	52	39	49	41

CAREER STATISTICS

W	L	ERA	G	GS	CG	SV	IP	H	R	ER	BB	SO
10	6	4.15	119	0	0	4	171	180	97	79	84	95

When he has been at the plate, he is a fish out of water.

OVERALL:

The time is nearing when Dedmon will have to make his mark as a big league pitcher. Either he will have to separate himself from the endless pack of "good prospects" and become an established big leaguer with credentials, or he will slip the other way and be labeled as a journeyman or worse: marginal. A lot of baseball people still expect Dedmon to move forward, rather than backward.

Campbell: "On a staff that otherwise was beleaguered in 1985, I think he is a pretty good prospect. If Bruce Sutter continues to falter, Jeff Dedmon looks like the guy who can perhaps best slam the door.

"Based on what the Braves have on their ballclub, maybe they will have to take a look at Dedmon as their stopper."

PITCHING:

Terry Forster has become known as much for his waistline as his left arm. New manager Chuck Tanner insists Forster will lose weight before the 1986 season "or I'll kill him." Tanner believes that Forster once again can be a key contributor in the bullpen if he trims down.

He has been slowed by elbow and shoulder injuries the past three years, but the Braves feel most of the injuries have resulted directly or indirecty from the excess weight. Last season, Forster almost always had some type of nagging injury.

But he still has the pitching tools to be an effective reliever, and he benefits from the scarcity of good left-handed relief pitchers in the game. He has a good fastball (88-89 MPH) that tails into lefthanded hitters, a sharp slider and a good-enough change-up. But more significant than his pitches is his competitiveness. Even at 40 pounds overweight, there is no better competitor in the league.

He is a short reliever at heart, although the combination of excess weight and injuries have reduced his role over the past few seasons to pitching sparingly against lefthanded hitters. He is most effective against lefthanders, but he also can get out righthanded hitters. He is caught in a vicious circle: while he is more effective when he pitches frequently, he recently has been too fat and too injury-prone to pitch often. Still, he had the lowest ERA on the Braves' staff in 1985.

FIELDING, HITTING, BASERUNNING:

Forster has lost a split-second of whatever quickness and fluidity he possessed, making his encounters with batted balls more uncertain. His move to

TERRY FORSTER
LHP, No. 51
LL, 6'4", 270 lbs.
ML Svc: 15 years
Born: 1-14-52 in
Sioux Falls, SD

1985 STATISTICS

W	L	ERA	G	GS	CG	SV	IP	H	R	ER	BB	SO
2	3	2.28	46	0	0	1	59.1	49	22	15	28	37

CAREER STATISTICS

W	L	ERA	G	GS	CG	SV	IP	H	R	ER	BB	SO
50	64	3.22	573	39	5	122	1064.1	987	436	381	440	763

first base is only slightly better than non-existent, and his delivery to the plate invites basestealing. When he lifts his leg, runners can take off. This is a big liability for a late-inning reliever.

Forster remains a tough out at the plate, and he approaches hitting with fierce competitiveness.

OVERALL:

If he were a righthander, Forster would have a harder time finding a team willing to tolerate his recent weight gains and injuries. But the Braves desperately need all the lefthanded relief pitching they can find.

Campbell: "A pitcher in his 30s should take care of his body and Terry obviously hasn't done that. I don't think you can count on him as your number one short reliever, and I don't think, based on the last couple of seasons, that his arm can hold up over the long haul. However, he could well serve a championship calibre team which can afford to pay a big salary to someone who'll occasionally face a lefthanded hitter."

PITCHING:

As with Bruce Sutter, as with Rick Camp, as with Len Barker, as with so many pitchers on their staff, the Braves would love to see Gene Garber revert to his form of the past. In 1982, he saved 30 games as the Braves won the National League West. But he has not had such success since then.

His role has slipped from short reliever to middle reliever and his contributions have slipped from vital to marginal.

Garber pitches with an unorthodox, back-to-the-plate delivery unlike any other pitcher in the league. His repertoire includes a sinking fastball, a slow curve, a sweeping slider and a change-up. When he's pitching at his best, the sinker darts below the strike zone as the batter commits to it and his change-up is virtually unhittable. At other times, the sinker stays up around the thighs and gets belted around and the change-up is less devastating. With Garber, location is everything.

He gives you everything he's got. Even when his stuff is not at its best, he remains a determined professional who tries to out-think the hitter. He has consistently good control in the sense that he doesn't walk many hitters, but in Garber's case, it is not enough to throw strikes. He must throw them around the knees and the corners of the plate.

FIELDING, HITTING, BASERUNNING:

Garber's delivery is an invitation for opposing baserunners to roam--and they do. He tries to compensate by throwing frequently to first base, a routine that sometimes causes his fielders to doze. He is an intelligent player who knows what to do with batted balls. He plays bunts well.

GENE GARBER
RHP, No. 26
RR, 5'10", 172 lbs.
ML Svc: 13 years
Born: 11-13-47 in
Lancaster, PA

1985 STATISTICS

W	L	ERA	G	GS	CG	SV	IP	H	R	ER	BB	SO
6	6	3.61	59	0	0	1	97.1	98	41	39	25	66

CAREER STATISTICS

W	L	ERA	G	GS	CG	SV	IP	H	R	ER	BB	SO
83	94	3.33	782	9	4	170	1315.1	1259	572	487	383	813

In his prime years, Garber was a short reliever who rarely batted. Now, he is a middle reliever who generally gets lifted for a pinch-hitter when it is his turn to hit. Garber will take his swings at the plate in a determined manner, but that's about it. He likes to run, but does not have good speed.

OVERALL:

Garber is another Atlanta pitcher who needs to re-establish territory quickly. It has been three years since his 30-save season and the memory has blurred in Atlanta. Still, at times, he shows flashes of that form.

Campbell: "His main asset may be that he can come in and pitch to particular young hitters who haven't seen him a lot and really mess them up.

"If the hitter can make Garber throw strikes, he can be hit hard. He is an illusionary-type pitcher. He makes the ball look like it's going to be in the strike zone and then it dips out--sometimes.

"Garber's best position is middle relief; unfortunately, the Braves have too many pitchers who are best in middle relief."

HITTING:

Terry Harper won the Braves' left field job by hitting for average, home runs and RBIs. He did it with the same cool, classic swing that made him a success in the minors and that prompted New York Mets batting coach Bill Robinson to say that Harper's swing ranks among the five purest swings in the league.

A key to Harper's improvement in 1985 was that he became more selective and more adept at waiting for his pitch.

He likes the ball out over the plate and, ideally, a little above the belt. He is a good fastball hitter who became less overmatched by quality off-speed pitchers. Still, to get him out, the best bet is to keep the ball down and change speeds consistently.

Harper hits the ball to all fields, although last season he drove it principally to center and left-center field.

BASERUNNING:

Harper has good speed--not basestealing speed but the type of speed that allows him to move from first to third on singles and to score from second base on sharply hit singles.

He probably could become a stronger basestealer by studying pitchers and getting better jumps. He is an intelligent, alert player who rarely makes a mistake on the bases.

FIELDING:

As left fielders go, Harper is an outstanding defensive player. He is adept at both coming in and going back on balls, although he is probably a little better at going back. He has average range for a center fielder, and better than average range for a left fielder. He has a strong, accurate arm.

OVERALL:

It seemed somewhat unjust that, after

TERRY HARPER
LF, No. 19
RR, 6'1", 202 lbs.
ML Svc: 6 years
Born: 8-19-55 in
    Douglasville, GA

1985 STATISTICS

AVG	G	AB	R	H	2B	3B	HR	RBI	BB	SO	SB
.264	138	492	58	130	15	2	17	72	44	76	9

CAREER STATISTICS

AVG	G	AB	R	H	2B	3B	HR	RBI	BB	SO	SB
.253	367	1072	109	271	37	5	24	133	99	190	33

VS. RHP   VS. LHP   PROBABLE HIT LOCATIONS

finally producing in the big leagues, Harper was asked to return to the bench in September so that the Braves could take a look at rookie Milt Thompson in left field. The Braves desperately need a leadoff hitter, and they wanted to see if Thompson could fill the role. The results were inconclusive.

So Harper is once again in limbo. This time, the question is not whether he will start the coming season in the majors or the minors, but whether he'll start it in the Braves' starting lineup or on their bench. It's an improvement, anyway.

Campbell: "He was a pleasant surprise for the Braves in 1985. In fact, their biggest breaks were the comeback of Bob Horner, the continued fine play of Dale Murphy and the arrival of Harper. Terry is approaching the crossroads of his career, but I think he hit enough to assure himself a spot in the major leagues for the next two years."

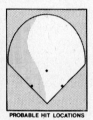

PATIENT HITTER

HITTING:

Bob Horner is one of the most difficult hitters to pitch to in the National League. He has bounced back from ultra-complicated wrist surgery beyond all expectations to re-establish himself as a top-flight hitter. Despite the surgery, Horner made no amendments in his successful stance or quick, compact swing.

Horner is essentially a pull hitter, although he will occasionally go to right field with power. Most of his home runs, though, are to left field.

He hits pitcher's mistakes with as much consistency as anyone in the game; it is virtually impossible to hang a breaking ball to him without paying the price. The best way to pitch him is to bust him inside with hard stuff (which he will often take) and then go down and away with a breaking ball. But if he gets a breaking ball up or a fastball out over the plate, forget it. Horner doesn't leave the pitcher much room for error.

Because of his short swing, Horner has the ability to wait well on the pitch. He also is a classic streak hitter, going two or three times a year where he is virtually unstoppable.

BASERUNNING:

Horner is a one-base-at-a-time type of runner. He has below-average speed and shows no confidence on the bases. Earlier in his career, Horner was extremely aggressive at breaking up double plays. However, after many injuries, he now takes more care and seems to go in hard at second base only if it is a crucial game situation. Given his injury history and his value to the team, that is wise.

FIELDING:

In a largely unexpected move, Horner was shifted from third base to first base last season. As a third baseman, Horner had good hands and an accurate

BOB HORNER
1B, No. 11
RR, 6'1", 215 lbs.
ML Svc: 8 years
Born: 8-6-57 in
   Junction City, KS

1985 STATISTICS

AVG	G	AB	R	H	2B	3B	HR	RBI	BB	SO	SB
.267	130	483	61	129	25	3	27	89	50	57	1

CAREER STATISTICS

AVG	G	AB	R	H	2B	3B	HR	RBI	BB	SO	SB
.279	819	3054	475	853	138	7	188	565	285	417	13

STRONG   STRONG   PROBABLE HIT LOCATIONS

VS. RHP   VS. LHP

arm to go with extremely limited range. The move to first base seemed to benefit him offensively, perhaps lessening his worries about defensive shortcomings, and he also fielded the position well.

As at third base, Horner has limited range at first. But he is the type of fielder who will put himself in front of the ball and at least knock it down.

OVERALL:

Going into last season, Horner had some serious concerns that perhaps his wrist injury could end his career. The radical surgery was such a success that Horner's future looks brighter than ever. He still missed some games last year with an occasionally stiff wrist and a hamstring pull, failing once again to play a full, injury-free season.

Campbell: "Horner is one of the most feared hitters in the game. There aren't too many players you can count on for 30 home runs and 100 RBIs a year, but Bob is one of them. If he can just find a way to avoid injuries . . . "

HITTING:

Glenn Hubbard has regressed as a hitter over the last two years. At one time, he was a good RBI man, a good hit-and-run man, a dangerous hitter with surprising power for the number seven spot in the batting order. But he has not done much with the bat lately.

He has not changed his stance or anything else visibly. He is the type of hitter who should hit line drives and ground balls, but he hasn't been doing that enough. He has fallen into a tendency of popping the ball up much too often. He is an ordinary bunter.

Pitchers have found that an effective way of dealing with Hubbard is to pound him inside with hard stuff and then move the ball out over the plate or outside while keeping it down. Hubbard is essentially a high-ball hitter, but he has been hitting a lot of harmless fly balls with these pitches the past two seasons.

Hubbard is a straightaway hitter. Defensive players should not play him to pull the ball.

BASERUNNING:

Hubbard has average to slightly below-average speed and is not a stolen base threat. He is vulnerable to hitting into double plays. He is a tough, determined player who will consistently go in hard at second base, doing his best to break up a play. Despite his size, or lack thereof, he does not back off a collision at the plate, either.

FIELDING:

Fielding is Hubbard's forte. It has been his ticket to a continued starting spot in the big leagues. He is not a graceful defensive player, but he makes all the plays.

He does not have outstanding range, but he compensates for that by playing hitters expertly. He has the knowledge and the foresight to get a two-step jump

GLENN HUBBARD
2B, No. 17
RR, 5'8", 169 lbs.
ML Svc: 7 years
Born: 9-25-57 in
　Hahn AFB, GER

1985 STATISTICS

AVG	G	AB	R	H	2B	3B	HR	RBI	BB	SO	SB
.232	142	439	51	102	21	0	5	39	56	54	4

CAREER STATISTICS

AVG	G	AB	R	H	2B	3B	HR	RBI	BB	SO	SB
.244	912	3165	387	772	147	17	55	329	344	439	29

on a lot of plays by positioning himself perfectly for the situation. He considers the hitter at the plate, the pitcher on the mound and the pitch being called.

Hubbard is one of the best at turning the double play. He handles quickly both the toss to the shortstop and the relay to first base. He also has extremely sure hands, rarely booting a play that is within his reach. He is a very steady, dependable fielder.

OVERALL:

The Braves always have contended that Hubbard earns his keep with his glove, that his offensive contribution is incidental. Hubbard has made them prove that contention the last two years.

Campbell: "The Braves would like to get more offense from Hubbard in 1986, and if they don't, they might be tempted to look elsewhere for a second baseman, especially if the lineup as a whole is not more productive than they were last season. His biggest asset is easily his defensive capabilities."

HITTING:

After sterling minor league stats, Brad Komminsk arrived in Atlanta amid high expectations. The Braves expected him to claim a position in the outfield and take his place alongside Dale Murphy and Bob Horner in the middle of the batting order. It has not worked out that way.

Komminsk has been consistently over-matched by big league pitchers, and his swing has deteriorated into disarray. He now has a very mechanical swing that, in many cases, seems to give him no chance to hit the ball.

He has an upright stance and bends a little at the knees. He seems to swing in the same plane almost all of the time, and if the ball is there, he'll hit it. His stance and swing need a major overhaul.

Pitchers have found a lot of ways to pitch to him. The fastball can be kept inside to set him up for the breaking ball. Pitchers should not throw him fastballs out over the plate or straight changes in the strike zone; he waits well on these pitches.

BASERUNNING:

He hasn't gotten on base enough to make any type of mark as a baserunner. But he has good natural speed and appears to have good baseball instincts, so he should have the potential to be a good baserunner, perhaps capable of stealing 20 or so bases a year.

FIELDING:

Scouts have differing opinions on Komminsk as a defensive player, ranging from "average with a weak arm" to "above average with a strong arm." Most likely, if he ever solves his offensive problems and settles into an outfield position, he would play very well defensively.

He has the natural tools: good speed,

BRAD KOMMINSK
LF, No. 36
RR, 6'2", 205 lbs.
ML Svc: 2 years
Born: 4-4-61 in
  Lima, OH

1985 STATISTICS

AVG	G	AB	R	H	2B	3B	HR	RBI	BB	SO	SB
.227	106	300	52	68	12	3	4	21	38	71	10

CAREER STATISTICS

AVG	G	AB	R	H	2B	3B	HR	RBI	BB	SO	SB
.215	215	637	91	137	24	3	12	61	72	155	28

  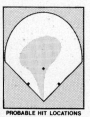

STRONG — VS. RHP   STRONG — VS. LHP   PROBABLE HIT LOCATIONS

good instincts and a powerful arm. He needs to find a position, left field or right field, and master it by learning the hitters. But first, he must hit.

OVERALL:

The Braves confidence in his potential is eroding. He has gone from the category of "can't miss prospect" to "how long can we wait for him to come around?"

Campbell: "I don't know how the Braves are going to get him out of his troubles at the plate. They have to find somebody who can break his swing down completely and start from scratch. His swing looks almost robot-like. I'm sure the problems he's had with the bat have left the Braves in an absolute quandary as to what to do with him. He has just not shown the consistency that would allow him to be a regular."

ACE OF THE STAFF

RICK MAHLER
RHP, No. 42
RR, 6'1", 202 lbs.
ML Svc: 5 years
Born: 8-5-53 in
Austin, TX

PITCHING:

Two years ago, the Braves coaching staff put Rick Mahler on the block and whispered that he could be a bargain. Owner Ted Turner intervened and pulled him off the market, wisely noting that the team was short of healthy arms. For two seasons in a row, Mahler has been the Braves' most dependable pitcher, the mainstay of their starting rotation. Last year, he was on a 20-win pace when a late-season injury to his finger sidelined him.

He is the consummate craftsman on the mound. Not blessed with overpowering velocity, Mahler has made himself a good pitcher with a repertoire that includes a sinking fastball (83 MPH on the average), a slider, a straight change-up and a slow curveball. He also dabbles with a knuckleball, but it is not a big part of his repertoire. The slow curve is his best pitch, the one which on a given day can make hitters appear helpless.

Mahler has extraordinary control and relishes in out-thinking a hitter, setting him up and putting him away. When he's at his best, Rick is a delight to watch. With Mahler, pitching is as much mental as physical, as much psychological as tangible. He can get into a groove where he appears to be pitching above his normal level.

One of his greatest strengths is that he is dependable; Mahler will always take his turn and give the team seven or more good innings. One of his greatest weaknesses is that, like most off-speed pitchers, he can be hurt severely when he makes a mistake.

FIELDING, HITTING, BASERUNNING:

Mahler is a sound, dependable fielder. He anticipates situations and reacts well. He is an expert handler of

1985 STATISTICS

W	L	ERA	G	GS	CG	SV	IP	H	R	ER	BB	SO
17	15	3.48	39	39	6	0	266.2	272	116	103	79	107

CAREER STATISTICS

W	L	ERA	G	GS	CG	SV	IP	H	R	ER	BB	SO
47	41	3.56	177	115	21	2	846.1	849	373	335	266	392

bunts. His move to first base is good, although his high leg kick can be an invitation to run. He gives baserunners a lot of attention.

As a hitter, he is one of the best-hitting pitchers in the National League. He has spent a lot of time in the batting cage and his hitting has kept him in a lot of games. He is not gifted with great speed, but he knows how to run the bases.

OVERALL:

Suffice it to say that every staff could use a Rick Mahler. He throws strikes and loves to take the ball. And when he is pitching, he wins.

Campbell: "He is a tough competitor, a battler who has learned how to pitch. You get the absolute maximum out of Rick Mahler. Anytime he goes out to start, the Braves have to feel they have a good chance of winning if they can get runs home. He's not the type of guy who can go the distance very often, but I think a lot of people in baseball would take Mahler in a minute if the Braves thought about trading him again. He is a pro."

PITCHING:

Three years ago, Craig McMurtry was the outstanding rookie pitcher in the National League and his future appeared glistening. Since then, he has bounced back and forth between the major leagues and the minor leagues. His future appears very much up in the air.

Why the decline? He is another mystery on the Braves' pitching staff. He has had no serious physical problems, but he has simply not been able to make the pitches he made as a rookie. Last year, he allowed too many hits per innings pitched, walked too many hitters and constantly pitched in trouble. In both 1984 and 1985, he appeared to have some kind of psychological barrier in the early innings, especially the first inning, and often was knocked out before he could get into the flow of the game.

As a rookie, McMurtry distinguished himself with a good, sinking fastball, a sharp slider, a good-enough change-up, excellent control and location and remarkable composure. Now, he has almost none of them.

His pitches stay up in the strike zone, which indicates a loss of location. What McMurtry needs is to regain the confidence and composure that he had as a rookie. That's not easy when one is getting belted badly.

To pitch effectively, McMurtry must have good location, must mix his pitches well and move them around well, must have movement on his fastball and must get into the flow of a game.

FIELDING, HITTING, BASERUNNING:

He has had hard times against hitters the last couple of years, but McMurtry

CRAIG McMURTRY
RHP, No. 29
RR, 6'5", 195 lbs.
ML Svc: 3 years
Born: 11-5-59 in
Temple, TX

1985 STATISTICS
W	L	ERA	G	GS	CG	SV	IP	H	R	ER	BB	SO
0	3	6.60	17	6	0	1	45	56	36	33	27	28

CAREER STATISTICS
W	L	ERA	G	GS	CG	SV	IP	H	R	ER	BB	SO
24	29	3.93	90	71	6	1	453	444	222	198	217	232

has become increasingly tough on baserunners. His move to first base now ranks among the two or three best in the league for righthanded pitchers. Tall, lanky and athletic, McMurtry also fields his position well.

He is nothing special as a hitter or baserunner.

OVERALL:

There does not seem to be any tangible reason why McMurtry has been unable to pitch as well as he did a few seasons ago. He will go to spring training as one of the Braves' many candidates for the starting rotation. If he does not do well quickly, he will most likely be in the minors.

Campbell: "He does not have the sheer velocity to pitch in the big leagues without good location. If he can get into a ballgame, he's OK. But the best thing he has going for him now is his move to first base."

HITTING:

Dale Murphy's consistency and excellence continue. His stance, his swing and the results remain the same. He is one of the very best hitters in the game.

As always, he is a streak hitter who simply cannot be pitched effectively when he's hot. In these periods, he'll hit anything. The best strategy when he is hot is to keep the ball out of the strike zone and hope he will chase it.

In other, more mortal periods, there are ways to pitch to Murphy. When he is not in a good groove, he will chase high fastballs and bad breaking balls and can be set up for low-and-away breaking balls with hard stuff inside. The most minimal pitching-mistake might turn into a home run to right field and the start of another Murphy streak.

About 60% of Murphy's homers are to right field, with the others split between center field and left field. Most of his home runs come on pitches out over the plate, pitches on which he can fully extend his arms. But he will hit other pitches to all fields, making him an exceedingly difficult hitter to pitch against. He hits for average, for home runs, for doubles, for RBIs. He is a pure hitter.

BASERUNNING:

Murphy is a very good, intelligent baserunner who has better-than-average speed and long, graceful strides. His stolen base total, which peaked at 30 in 1983, fell off dramatically in 1985, but that was mostly because then-manager Eddie Haas played a conservative game that rarely included the stolen base. Look for Murphy to steal more bases in 1986 under manager Chuck Tanner. Murphy rarely makes a mistake on the bases and is a master at taking the extra base when the opportunity presents itself.

DALE MURPHY
CF, No. 3
RR, 6'5", 215 lbs.
ML Svc: 8 years
Born: 3-12-56 in
Portland, OR

1985 STATISTICS

AVG	G	AB	R	H	2B	3B	HR	RBI	BB	SO	SB
.300	162	616	118	185	32	2	37	111	90	141	10

CAREER STATISTICS

AVG	G	AB	R	H	2B	3B	HR	RBI	BB	SO	SB
.278	1200	4403	724	1225	185	25	237	739	542	953	122

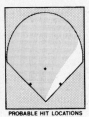

VS. RHP   VS. LHP   PROBABLE HIT LOCATIONS

FIELDING:

Murphy has developed into an outstanding center fielder, a perennial Gold Glover. He knows how to play the hitters, gets a good jump on the ball, displays confidence coming in or going back, sets up well and throws strongly and accurately. He is the consummate center fielder.

OVERALL:

In this age of specialization and one-dimensional ballplayers, Murphy is a complete player. He plays every day; he hits; he runs; he fields; he does it all. And he has emerged, additionally, as a mature and articulate team leader.

Campbell: "He certainly is one of the most valuable pieces of property in major league baseball. No matter how poorly the team does, Dale is always there, producing runs, driving them in and robbing the opposition."

HITTING:

On a team short of lefthanded hitters, Ken Oberkfell provides the Braves with a bat from that side of the plate.

He likes the ball up and out over the plate. He is a line drive type hitter who will get most of his hits to center, left-center and right-center. The best defensive strategy is to bunch the middle and take away the lines.

The best way to pitch to Oberkfell is to follow hard stuff inside with breaking pitches low and away. He will hit pitches that stray out over the plate.

The Braves need Oberkfell to provide the stereotypical contribution of third basemen--that is, home runs and RBIs. He is not a productive clutch hitter, but he will punch some singles and doubles and get on base a lot. The Braves might utilize him for hit-and-run plays if they ever find a speedy leadoff batter to hit in front of him. He is also an adequate bunter.

BASERUNNING:

Oberkfell has only average speed and is not a baserunning threat. He seems to fight a battle against putting on excess weight, which presumably slows him down a little on the bases. He is an intelligent player who doesn't make foolish or careless mistakes on the basepaths.

FIELDING:

In his big league career, Oberkfell has played both second base and third base. As a third baseman, Oberkfell is adequate, not outstanding.

Last year, his defensive play might have been hampered by knee and elbow injuries. He has average range, good hands and a very average arm. He plays the bunt well.

He will make the routine play, rarely bobbles it or makes a wild throw to first base, but he does not make a lot of extraordinary plays.

KEN OBERKFELL
3B, No. 24
LR, 6'1", 210 lbs.
ML Svc: 8 years
Born: 5-4-56 in
    Highland, IL

1985 STATISTICS

AVG	G	AB	R	H	2B	3B	HR	RBI	BB	SO	SB
.272	134	412	30	112	19	4	3	35	51	38	1

CAREER STATISTICS

AVG	G	AB	R	H	2B	3B	HR	RBI	BB	SO	SB
.270	908	3092	346	834	145	33	15	255	331	213	47

VS. RHP　　　VS. LHP　　　PROBABLE HIT LOCATIONS

OVERALL:

The Braves acquired Oberkfell early in 1984, when they lost Horner for the season and desperately needed a replacement at third base. With Horner back at third, Oberkfell opened last season as a utility infielder but wound up back at third when Horner moved to first base.

Now, with Horner permanently at first and no third-base prospect in the organization, Oberkfell seems set at third base for a while. But the Braves will have to decide whether they can get by with a third baseman who doesn't drive in runs. If they decide they can't, they might attempt a trade and make Oberkfell a utilityman or give him a shot to supplant Glenn Hubbard at second base.

Campbell: "I think Oberkfell is a decent major league player whose best attribute is the bat, although he is not what I consider a good RBI man. Nor is he a real plus at third base."

PITCHING:

Pascual Perez's past success was built on these elements: an active, sinking fastball, a good slider, a decent change-up, an intense, highly charged nature on the mound and a willingness to pitch hitters inside. Last year, he showed none of them.

He was told to abandon his theatrics on the mound. Then, without being told, Perez decided to abandon his fastball and his propensity for pitching inside as well. Perez tried to become an off-speed pitcher who threw the ball out over the plate. The results were disastrous.

Perez later said he had a sore shoulder which caused him to change his methods. But soon after making that claim, he said the shoulder was fine. He was twice on the disabled list, and by late in the season, the Braves honestly didn't know whether his shoulder posed a serious problem or not.

The low point of Perez's season came when he jumped the team soon after the All-Star break. No one knew where he was for two days. When he surfaced, he said that he needed a break from the pressure.

In short, it was a wasted year. Late in the season, he began to throw a decent fastball, but it was not clear if he'd be able to transform himself completely back to the successful Perez of the past.

His future? Well, one imagines that Perez will go back to the mound mannerisms that he thinks benefit him--hot-dog stuff--and the Braves hope he'll go back to being a power pitcher. If so, there's always a chance he'll re-establish himself in the team's starting rotation. There's also a chance he won't.

FIELDING, HITTING, BASERUNNING:

Perez is a good athlete and he fields his position well. He keeps his mind on opposing basserunners and has a pretty

PASCUAL PEREZ
RHP, No. 27
RR, 6'2", 163 lbs.
ML Svc: 4 years
Born: 5-17-57 in
Haina, DR

1985 STATISTICS

W	L	ERA	G	GS	CG	SV	IP	H	R	ER	BB	SO
1	13	6.14	22	22	0	0	95.1	115	72	65	57	57

CAREER STATISTICS

W	L	ERA	G	GS	CG	SV	IP	H	R	ER	BB	SO
36	41	3.92	120	111	13	0	699.2	728	347	305	212	428

good move to first base. His move to the plate gives catchers a fighting chance to throw out runners, too.

Perez seems to enjoy himself at the plate, but he isn't much of a hitter. Throw the ball up and over the plate, and he might do some damage with it. But overall, he's a typical hitting pitcher. He runs pretty well.

OVERALL:

It appears that Perez has a lot of problems. His eccentricities and antics have gone beyond the point of amusement and entertainment. There might be the chance that the Braves will give him one more opportunity, but there is also ample reason to forget all about him.

Campbell: "To me, he is a very mixed up young man. He doesn't have to hit batters in the back of the neck, but he does have to pitch inside to win. I don't see him as a value to a ballclub in any way, shape or form unless the arm heals, and even then, it's going to take a very understanding organization to put up with his foolish tactics. It would be tough to unload him; I don't think many teams want him."

HITTING:

Gerald Perry arrived at spring training last year with a running start on winning the Braves' first base job, but his poor hitting forced him to spend most of the season on the bench. Perry did not perform well as a pinch-hitter, either. He has been overmatched by big league pitching.

Perry is a straightaway hitter who stands in the middle of the batter's box and likes the ball high; this is unusual for a young, lefthanded batter. The best way to pitch against him is with savvy: set him up, move the ball around, keep it down. He is not an patient hitter.

His muscular build and minor league numbers suggest he has power, but he has not shown much of that at the big league level. He hits a lot of harmless fly balls.

With Horner entrenched at first base, Perry probably will be reduced to a pinch-hitting role in 1986 if he remains with the Braves.

BASERUNNING:

Perry has good natural speed and stole bases in the minor leagues. When the Braves were fondly awaiting his arrival, they saw him as a 20-homer, 20-stolen-base player. But no one talks of his baserunning ability right now. Until he learns to hit big league pitching, baserunning is not a problem.

FIELDING:

Perry is not a good fielder. The decision to rush Bob Horner over to first from third base was, in part, because Perry looked so bad at first. With considerable work, Perry could be an adequate defensive first baseman, although his height is a slight liability.

GERALD PERRY
INF, No. 28
LR, 5'11", 180 lbs.
ML Svc: 3 years
Born: 10-30-60 in
 Savannah, GA

1985 STATISTICS

AVG	G	AB	R	H	2B	3B	HR	RBI	BB	SO	SB
.214	110	238	22	51	5	0	3	13	23	28	9

CAREER STATISTICS

AVG	G	AB	R	H	2B	3B	HR	RBI	BB	SO	SB
.251	259	624	79	157	19	2	11	66	89	70	24

STRONG   STRONG   PROBABLE HIT LOCATIONS

VS. RHP   VS. LHP

OVERALL:

Two years ago, the Braves' bright hopes for the future hinged largely on their high expectations for Perry and Brad Komminsk. Other teams constantly wanted to talk about trades for both of them, but the Braves would not listen. Now, Perry has lost much of his marketability as well as his place in Atlanta's plans. He will have to re-establish himself almost from scratch.

Campbell: "My suggestion would be: if he has an option left, send him to the minors and say, 'Gerald, this is your last chance.' And see if he really wants to play. If he does, if he works at it and makes it back, then use him as a pinch-hitter, maybe increasing his value in a trade to another team. Besides, the Braves need pinch-hitters."

HITTING:

Each year, Rafael Ramirez is very productive before the All-Star break and virtually non-productive afterward. Last season, he hit .150 over the last six weeks of the season.

When he's in a groove, Ramirez is a good line drive hitter with some power to the gaps. He will hit a few home runs, drive in runs and produce in the clutch. Otherwise, he does little more than hit ground balls to the infielders and routine fly balls to the outfielders. He led the Braves in 1985 at grounding into double plays.

Ramirez is a free-swinging hitter. He likes the pitch out and over the plate. He can hit both fastballs and off-speed pitches if he gets an opportunity to fully extend his arms. He is most vulnerable on pitches that jam him (hard stuff) or pitches that encourage him to reach (low-and-away breaking balls, for example).

When Ramirez first reached the big leagues, he did not look like much of a hitter. But then for a couple of years he showed great promise and fancied himself as the next Dave Concepcion. But now, after two erratic seasons, it is hard to know what to make of Ramirez as an offensive force.

BASERUNNING:

Ramirez has average speed. He is not a good basestealer at all. His ratio last year was three caught-stealings for every stolen base.

FIELDING:

His fielding is just as erratic as his hitting. After averaging around 30 errors per season, Ramirez started last season as if he were a new person on defense. But just as the Braves began to get excited about his impeccable defensive play, Ramirez went into another error-prone rut.

RAFAEL RAMIREZ
SS, No. 16
RR, 6'0", 185 lbs.
ML Svc: 5 years
Born: 2-18-59 in
    San Pedro de Macoris, DR

1985 STATISTICS
AVG	G	AB	R	H	2B	3B	HR	RBI	BB	SO	SB
.248	138	568	54	141	25	4	5	58	20	63	2

CAREER STATISTICS
AVG	G	AB	R	H	2B	3B	HR	RBI	BB	SO	SB
.266	737	2862	308	763	106	20	28	247	144	310	68

STRONG VS. RHP   STRONG VS. LHP   PROBABLE HIT LOCATIONS

He has good range, both to his left and right, and some of his errors come on plays other shortstops would never touch. He has a strong arm, and he is a master at turning the double play.

Ramirez and Glenn Hubbard, along with a pitching staff that has put a lot of runners on first base, have contributed to the Braves leading the league in double plays for four straight years (1981-84). His liabilities as a fielder are that he doesn't concentrate on the routine plays and sometimes throws away balls he should keep in his glove.

OVERALL:

It doesn't look right now like he is going to blossom into anything but an average player.

Campbell: "In spite of some fine-looking defensive plays he throws in from time to time, I would consider him an average major league shortstop on a weak ballclub."

PITCHING:

Zane Smith figures prominently as the pitching-poor Braves look to the future. While the Braves have a poor history of producing quality young arms that show more than promise, Zane Smith might make the breakthrough. Bobby Cox and Chuck Tanner were impressed with Kansas City's success with their mostly young pitching staff last year and will give Zane Smith every consideration. If Smith has a good spring this year, he could become the number two starter.

Smith throws hard, sporting a fastball that reaches close to 90 MPH, an overhand curveball and an occasional straight change. He throws three-quarters to overhand and has good competitive instincts. He appears to have an understanding of how to set hitters up and how to put them away. He has good poise on the mound.

His weakness has been his control; he was part of the staff that led the league in walks. Still, he gives indications that he can get a hold of himself and keep his heater in check. If he does, he could develop into a good strikeout pitcher.

FIELDING, HITTING, BASERUNNING:

Smith has an average move to first base, one which will probably improve with seasoning. His 90 MPH fastball gives his catcher a bit of an edge against basestealers. He plays the bunt well and keeps his cool even in non-routine plays around the mound.

As a hitter, he looks disoriented, if not alien. He works at his bunting and will move the runners along now and

ZANE SMITH
LHP, No. 34
LL, 6'2", 195 lbs.
ML Svc: 1 year
Born: 12-18-60 in
    Madison, WI

1985 STATISTICS

W	L	ERA	G	GS	CG	SV	IP	H	R	ER	BB	SO
9	10	3.80	42	18	2	23	88.1	91	46	44	29	52

CAREER STATISTICS

W	L	ERA	G	GS	CG	SV	IP	H	R	ER	BB	SO
10	10	4.07	45	21	2	23	108.1	107	53	49	42	68

then. Smith runs as well as most pitchers, for whatever that is worth.

OVERALL:

The Braves have a serious pitching situation and Smith is one of their hopes for clearing it up. They hope that he matures into a solid, dependable, winning major league pitcher. And if he is to do so, 1986 should be the season.

Campbell: "I think that Zane Smith, along with Steve Bedrosian, Rick Mahler and maybe Jeff Dedmon, are the pitchers Atlanta should definitely not let go. (They don't have a chance of trading Bruce Sutter with his enormous contract.) Zane looks like the kind of pitcher you hang onto.

"He has a great fastball and looks like he knows what he is doing on the mound. His ability to work the hitters is impressive."

PITCHING:

Bruce Sutter holds a contract that pays him an astounding salary. He has made the split-finger fastball famous. He may have serious arm problems. He may make Ted Turner jump off a bridge.

Sutter lives and dies by the action of his split-fingered pitch. When all is well, he is its master. In order for him to pitch effectively, his arm must be sound, free of aches, pains and tenderness. When his arm is hurting, as Sutter admitted it was last season, the split-finger fastball becomes a different pitch, tantalizing and sweet for the hitter.

While it is still not clear whether Sutter's 1985 problems were physical or simply the kind of off-year typical of short relievers from time to time, it was obvious that the split-finger was was not the same. When the pitch is working, it starts at the batter's thigh then instantly drops below the knee. The hitter hasn't got a chance and he ends up flailing away at a pitch no longer in the strike zone.

Last season, Sutter was unable to get the break to start low enough. Instead of beginning its break at the thigh, it started coming in around the belt and ended up around the thigh. He managed to save a respectable number of games, but he did it in a very unconvincing, very un-Sutter-like way. His ERA was the highest it had ever been and his ratio of saves to opportunities his lowest to date.

The other elements of his repertoire are marginal, including a fastball that rarely exceeds the mid-80s in velocity. He has good control, does not walk hitters in clutch situations and does not back away from any late-inning challenge. He has the psychological makeup of the consummate short reliever.

FIELDING, HITTING, BASERUNNING:

The key to Sutter's success through

BRUCE SUTTER
RHP, No. 40
RR, 6'2", 190 lbs.
ML Svc: 10 years
Born: 1-8-53 in
     Lancaster, PA

1985 STATISTICS

W	L	ERA	G	GS	CG	SV	IP	H	R	ER	BB	SO
7	7	4.48	58	0	0	23	88.1	91	46	44	29	52

CAREER STATISTICS

W	L	ERA	G	GS	CG	SV	IP	H	R	ER	BB	SO
65	67	2.71	607	0	0	283	977	813	335	295	289	823

the years has simply been keeping hitters off base. But he has an adequate move to first base--useful in the good old days for holding on inherited baserunners. He fields his position adequately and always appears in command.

As a short reliever, Sutter rarely bats. And when he does, his team almost inevitably has a lead. Then the attention is riveted on Sutter the holder, not Sutter the hitter. He has average speed and average mechanics at the plate.

OVERALL:

Campbell: "Whether his poor 1985 performance means the end of the road, no one knows. This year is clearly important for him--that's for darn sure.

"The success of the Braves, however, does not revolve solely around Sutter. In order to get what you pay for with him, the team has got to give him something to save. Even if he were effective last season, it would not have mattered much because the Braves were so miserable. Still, he will be under a microscope this spring."

HITTING:

The Braves traded Brett Butler to Cleveland in 1983, just as he appeared to be the answer to their leadoff woes. The team has endured the past two disappointing seasons without a qualified number one hitter. This brings us to Milt Thompson. He is the Braves' latest hope to fill the role. In brief, inconclusive trials, he has shown the ability to get on base--and he can make things happen once he gets there.

Thompson is a straightaway hitter who the Braves see as a line drive or hit-the-ball-on-the-ground-and-run threat. He has had limited exposure to big league pitching and at times appears overwhelmed by both the overpowering and the overly-crafty pitchers in the NL. But for the most part, he looks like the type of hitter who can adapt and be productive.

He has shown a pretty good eye in the minor leagues and will need to further refine his pitch selection to be an effective leadoff hitter. The Braves want him to draw more walks than he now does.

BASERUNNING:

Thompson does not have the blazing speed of, say, a Vince Coleman or a Willie McGee. But he does have speed comparable to Brett Butler and so, if he gets on base enough, he could steal 40 to 50 bases a year in the big leagues. This would be a big improvement for a Braves team that mostly plodded along last season.

In addition to his natural speed, Thompson appears to have good instincts on the bases. He studies pitchers, gets a decent jump for an inexperienced player and slides tough. The Braves will work with him in spring training on further refining his baserunning skills and continue his education on opposing pitchers' moves to first base. But the bottom line is that the Braves know Thompson will steal a lot of bases if he gets on first base often enough.

MILT THOMPSON
OF, No. 30
LR, 5'11", 160 lbs.
ML Svc: 1 year plus
Born: 1-5-59 in
  Washington, D.C

1985 STATISTICS

AVG	G	AB	R	H	2B	3B	HR	RBI	BB	SO	SB
.302	73	182	17	55	7	2	0	6	7	36	9

CAREER STATISTICS

AVG	G	AB	R	H	2B	3B	HR	RBI	BB	SO	SB
.302	98	281	33	85	8	2	2	10	18	47	23

STRONG — VS. RHP   STRONG — VS. LHP   PROBABLE HIT LOCATIONS

FIELDING:

It is not Thompson's defense that has made him a top prospect, but it looks as if he can be an adequate left fielder. He has an average arm, and his speed should allow him to compensate for any number of mistakes in the field. He gets a pretty good jump on the ball, goes back on the ball better than he comes in for it, but needs to learn to position himself better and become more assertive in the outfield.

OVERALL:

If Thompson looks good in spring training, he could supplant Terry Harper as the starting left fielder. If he has a tough time against southpaw pitching, he might platoon in left field.

Campbell: "He is a pretty good-looking player--his speed is tantalizing, but he will have to hit somewhere in the .300-.310 range to be really valuable to the Braves' offense. He still has a lot to learn about big league hitting."

HITTING:

The best of Claudell Washington is very good. He is a lefthanded batter with power and speed, an experienced hitter who knows the pitchers and goes to the plate with confidence.

But over the past few seasons with the Braves, Washington has been an erratic hitter who has had a lot of difficulty producing with runners on base. Because of this, the Braves decided in August not to re-sign him for 1986. But team owner Ted Turner reversed that decision in September and signed Claudell to a one-year contract for this season.

No one doubts that Washington still has the skills to put together a fine offensive season. He can hit for a .280-.300 average, has great power to the alleys and should hit 15 or so home runs. He hits the ball to all fields, making him a very difficult batter to defense. He likes the ball out over the plate.

The best way to pitch to Washington is with curveballs down and fastballs in. He is a streak hitter who, unfortunately, often follows his productive streaks with slumps in which he is a virtual non-entity as a hitter. Claudell thinks of himself as a leadoff man in the order, but the Braves prefer him to hit in the number three spot.

BASERUNNING:

Washington still has exceptional speed and there is no reason why he cannot steal a lot of bases. He is very capable of going from first to third on a single or taking the extra base or scoring on medium-depth fly balls. He is an asset as a baserunner, especially on such a speed-poor team as the Braves.

FIELDING:

Washington is inconsistent in the outfield, sometimes making a dazzling, leaping catch at the fence and sometimes watching passively as a fly ball

CLAUDELL WASHINGTON
RF, No. 15
LL, 6'0", 195 lbs.
ML Svc: 11 years
Born: 8-31-54 in
    Los Angeles, CA

1985 STATISTICS

AVG	G	AB	R	H	2B	3B	HR	RBI	BB	SO	SB
.276	122	398	62	110	14	6	15	43	40	66	14

CAREER STATISTICS

AVG	G	AB	R	H	2B	3B	HR	RBI	BB	SO	SB
.279	1435	5216	726	1455	259	61	119	635	425	917	260

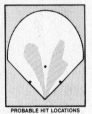

STRONG — VS. RHP   STRONG — VS. LHP   PROBABLE HIT LOCATIONS

drops in front of him. Washington once had a very strong arm, but it has grown weaker over the last couple of seasons. He prefers to play in right field, but his arm is more suited for left field.

He is the type of player who seems to be at his best when motivated by a pennant race. And it may be too ambitious of the Braves for them to expect to be involved in a pennant race in the immediate future.

OVERALL:

Chuck Tanner, who managed Washington at Oakland, vows that the player will have the best season of his career in 1986. Time will tell.

Campbell: "The Braves certainly could use a productive lefthanded hitter and an experienced basestealer. They are going to give Washington another shot at consistency and maybe he will do better under Chuck Tanner's guidance.

"Washington has the potential to help the Braves but he has been much too erratic over the past few years."

PAUL RUNGE
INF, No. 12
RR, 6'0", 175 lbs.
ML Svc: 1 year plus
Born: 5-21-58 in
Kingston, NY

HITTING, BASERUNNING, FIELDING:

Paul Runge and Paul Zuvella were the DP combo at the Braves' Triple-A farm club for three years before arriving together in Atlanta in 1985. They are now in the position of having to fight for the same job.

At the plate, Runge is a line drive, singles hitter who might be able to develop into a productive player off the bench. As a rookie last year, he was vulnerable to wicked breaking balls and hard sliders and had the most success against fastballs out over the plate and straight changes over the plate.

Runge has only average speed and is not a basestealing threat.

His primary position is second base, although there is little chance of him beating out Glenn Hubbard for the starting job there. Runge also can play third base well and can play shortstop adequately. He has average range, good hands and an accurate arm.

If he remains in the big leagues for a few years, it will be because of his ability to play several positions well. He does not become rattled and can make all the routine plays with consistency.

OVERALL:

Campbell: "My opinion is that a team can afford to carry one utility infielder who is a good glove man at three positions--but not two players. A bench should have one good defensive backup catcher, one good defensive utility infielder and one good defensive reserve outfielder. But beyond that, you need four bats on the bench."

PAUL ZUVELLA
INF, No. 18
RR, 6'0", 175 lbs.
ML Svc: 1 year plus
Born: 10-31-58 in
San Mateo, CA

HITTING, FIELDING, BASERUNNING:

Paul Zuvella is a young Brave who was greatly hyped by the club in his minor league days (in the minors, he looked like a solid .280 hitter). But like many of their other prospects, he has yet to justify the hype.

As a hitter, Zuvella appears to be a punch-and-judy singles hitter who can be overwhelmed by both the hard-throwing and the savvy big league pitchers. He likes the ball thigh-high and out over the plate.

As a fielder, he appears to have good hands and instincts to go with only average range and an average throwing arm. Shortstop is his best and most familiar position, but he also can play second base and third base.

As a baserunner, he has slightly better-than-average speed but is not a basestealing threat.

OVERALL:

Just a year ago, the Braves were seriously wondering if they should make Zuvella their starting shortstop or use him to satisfy one of the many requests they had received for trades. He had a great spring training last year, but was shuttled back and forth to the minors all year long: 1985 became a wasted year for him.

Campbell: "It would be unfair and hasty to write him off or to forget his fine minor league accomplishments on the basis of such a confusing season. Paul looks as if he could be a utility infielder who can play three positions."

CHICAGO CUBS

HITTING:

While Thad Bosley insists he is an everyday player, his niche with the Cubs was probably settled forever last season. As a pinch-hitter and late-inning fill-in and he proved to be remarkably good. He had 20 hits and 10 RBIs in 60 pinch at-bats. His pinch-hits led the National League and set a Cubs record. At age 29, it now seems he has accepted the role, especially after his success last year.

Lithe and strong, Bosley became a tough major league out last year. Having accepted the job as pinch-hitter, he now prepares for it. He loves fastballs and will pull them most of the time. He does not mind swinging at the first pitch, which is the sign of a good pinch-hitter, but he also has patience at the plate. He rarely bats against lefthanders but seems to be able to handle any pitch from a righthander.

Bosley showed more power last year than ever before--even in the minors--and is maturing as a hitter. His flaws show up when he is forced to play for more than three or four days at a time, although he hit in 23 of the last 30 games he started. His forte has become pinch-hitting.

BASERUNNING:

A veteran of the minor leagues, Bosley has good speed, though he has not played enough to become a good baserunner. He can make some blunders on the basepaths.

FIELDING:

Bosley is not an everyday player because he is not a good fielder. Although he has better-than-average speed, he has

THAD BOSLEY
OF, No. 20
LL, 6'3", 175 lbs.
ML Svc: 6 years
Born: 9-17-56 in
Oceanside, CA

1985 STATISTICS

AVG	G	AB	R	H	2B	3B	HR	RBI	BB	SO	SB
.328	108	180	25	59	6	3	7	27	10	29	5

CAREER STATISTICS

AVG	G	AB	R	H	2B	3B	HR	RBI	BB	SO	SB
.311	206	350	54	109	12	6	11	53	33	63	11

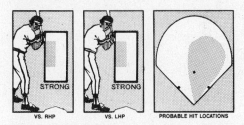

no range, which is surprising. He has trouble going back for balls. He has a fair arm, one that is better suited for left field than right field. If he plays anywhere, it must be in the outfield.

OVERALL:

Bosley has matured into a good role player but is still young enough that he can pinch-run and play the field without hurting the team. He wants to play every day, but probably never will with the Cubs.

Snider: "He replaced Richie Hebner as the Cubs' top pinch-hitter last season. He's a real quiet guy who seems to be ready to hit whenever he gets the call. Bosley did a great job last year and could have a nice career going."

PITCHING:

What happened to the Cubs starting pitching staff had a direct effect on Warren Brusstar's season. The longer his teammates were on the disabled list, the higher Brusstar's ERA climbed. He found himself in action almost every day as the young replacement starters ran into early-inning problems.

Through mid-May, Brusstar had made eight appearances and had compiled a 0.93 earned run average. He finished the season with 51 appearances, a 6.05 ERA and four saves. Through June, opponents hit only .252 against him, but were .313 the rest of the season.

Not all of Brusstar's troubles should be blamed on overwork, however. He says he likes to have his arm tired so that he won't overthrow the ball. But he let 13 inherited runners score and he allowed more hits than innings pitched.

He will be pitching as a 34 year old this season and the question should be raised whether he has seen his better days. If his ball no longer sinks, he can't be effective and last season the ball definitely had its days when it wouldn't stay down. He has a workable change-up, but it isn't much good when the sinker isn't working. He was worse at Wrigley Field, where opponents hit .319, than on the road, where opponents hit .265.

When Brusstar is on top of his game, he can be as good as any middle reliever in the game. When his game is down, he might as well not pitch. Last year, he was down more than up and his ERA was three points higher than usual because of it.

FIELDING, HITTING, BASERUNNING:

Brusstar's sinker means he gets a

WARREN BRUSSTAR
RHP, No. 41
RR, 6'3", 200 lbs.
ML Svc: 7 years
Born: 2-2-52 in
    Oakland, CA

1985 STATISTICS

W	L	ERA	G	GS	CG	SV	IP	H	R	ER	BB	SO
4	3	6.05	51	0	0	4	74.1	87	55	50	36	34

CAREER STATISTICS

W	L	ERA	G	GS	CG	SV	IP	H	R	ER	BB	SO
28	16	3.54	340	0	0	47	480.1	476	203	189	181	273

lot of ground balls but he has learned through the years to be a good fielder. He is very good at covering first base. He also has a good move to first base and a quick delivery to the plate.

Brusstar batted only seven times last year but did have a hit and a walk. For his little time on the basepaths, he is not a bad baserunner.

OVERALL:

Like several other Cubs veterans, Brusstar should find this to be a key season. His performance in 1986 should determine whether he is still an effective pitcher. Physically, Brusstar still keeps himself in good shape and he likes to pitch in pressure situations.

Snider: "You like to have guys like him in the bullpen--you know what they can do. But the problem is, you are never sure what he can do anymore. He's not afraid, he's a battler, but he will have to work exceptionally hard this year."

HITTING:

Is time finally catching up with Ron Cey? After his disappointing season last year, it certainly looks that way. His 63 RBIs were a career low (except for the strike-shortened 1981 season) and he struck out over 100 times for only the third time in his career. His .232 batting average was his lowest ever; his 22 home runs were his lowest output in 11 years.

Cey is still a fastball hitter. His short, quick swing is not as quick as it used to be. Despite his power, he had only eight game-winning hits and two sacrifice flies. He continued to have trouble reaching outside pitches and swung at too many balls over his head. He may have lost his fastball reflexes.

Known as a pull hitter in his glory years, Cey will have to start to go to right field more now than he ever has before; if he is going to remain in the lineup at age 37, he is going to have to produce more RBIs--and going to right field might prolong his career as a full-timer.

Cey continues his constant bickering with umpires on strike calls, which can make each at-bat seem eternal and costs him strikes. He is going to have to learn to hit low in the order.

BASERUNNING:

Never known for his speed, Cey has slowed down even more; he was thrown out at home several times last year while trying to score from second base on a single. He hardly fits in with the Cubs' new style of running.

His batting average has suffered all these years by his inability to beat out infield grounders.

FIELDING:

Cey had an unheard of total of 21 errors at third base last year (his most since 1974). He has never been known for his range; even so, his reflexes are not what they used to be. He had trouble

RON CEY
3B, No. 10
RR, 5'9", 185 lbs.
ML Svc: 13 years
Born: 2-15-48 in
Tacoma, WA

1985 STATISTICS											
AVG	G	AB	R	H	2B	3B	HR	RBI	BB	SO	SB
.232	145	500	64	116	18	2	22	63	58	106	1

CAREER STATISTICS											
AVG	G	AB	R	H	2B	3B	HR	RBI	BB	SO	SB
.261	1931	6802	923	1775	301	21	299	1092	946	1137	24

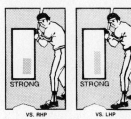
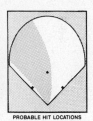

STRONG — VS. RHP   STRONG — VS. LHP   PROBABLE HIT LOCATIONS

handling ground balls hit directly at him, though he is still good at fielding bunts.

Cey has an adequate arm for throws to first base. Because he is a veteran, he has good instincts when he fields the ball.

OVERALL:

Cey must realize that he has to change his style or his days as an everyday player will be over. His role might be diminished to spot starting and pinch-hitting if the Cubs are able to locate another third baseman.

Snider: "He's got to realize that if his batting averge is down, his only hope is to drive in a bunch of runs. Defensively, he is not as good as he once was.

"This is decision time for Ron and he has got to get in good shape. He still has that little lift in his swing, which makes it a perfect stroke for Wrigley Field."

HITTING:

If there was one Cub asked to shoulder more than his load last year, it was Jody Davis. Not only did he try to pick up the team's slumping offense, but he was asked to be the catcher and the confidante to a young pitching staff not yet ready for prime time. Davis suffered at the plate and rarely took a day off even though the team was out of the pennant race early in the year.

Hospitalized during June for stomach bleeding, Davis never did seem to gain back his strength. But because the Cubs did not feel they had an adequate replacement for him behind the plate, he worked more innings than he should have. He missed 12 games due to sickness or injury and still caught in 142 games last year. The Cubs need a better backup catcher to give him more days of rest.

Davis continues to be a pull hitter and improved in his ability to go to right field in certain situations. He is a fastball hitter and needs improvement on reaching for breaking balls but he has learned to lay off bad pitches. Davis has a long, Wrigley Field uppercut swing and is capable of producing big power numbers if he isn't tired. Maybe a few games playing first base would help.

BASERUNNING:

Davis is slow and is not a good baserunner. He can't go from first to third or from second to home on a short base hit. Even taking into account his below-average speed on the bases, Davis could still be more aggressive on the bases.

FIELDING:

Davis' biggest improvement last year was his ability to throw out would-be basestealers. His arm is good, not great, and throwing out runners has always been the weakest part of his defense. Last season, Davis worked on getting rid of the ball more quickly, made some adjustments and became more precise in throwing out basestealers at

JODY DAVIS
C, No. 7
RR, 6'3", 210 lbs.
ML Svc: 5 years
Born: 11-12-56 in
   Gainesville, GA

1985 STATISTICS

AVG	G	AB	R	H	2B	3B	HR	RBI	BB	SO	SB
.232	142	482	47	112	30	0	17	58	48	83	1

CAREER STATISTICS

AVG	G	AB	R	H	2B	3B	HR	RBI	BB	SO	SB
.255	629	2113	213	539	110	7	76	309	185	395	6

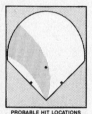

STRONG   STRONG

VS. RHP   VS. LHP   PROBABLE HIT LOCATIONS

second base.

Because the Cubs pitching staff was torn apart by all kinds of injuries last season, Davis was forced to work with a very young and inexperienced pitching staff. As a result, he had to take charge more than he had with the veterans and improved his overall style in calling a game. He still has a tendency to get lazy behind the plate, which results in a lot of passed balls.

OVERALL:

There are still questions concerning Davis' continuing stomach problems and the Cubs feel that he hasn't yet reached his potential either on offense or defense.

Snider: "Jody has improved a great deal but would develop more quickly and be a better hitter if he could have a few days off. If he were well rested, he could really put up some outstanding numbers. He was dragging his bat to the plate by the end of last season."

HITTING:

Like so many Cubs, it is unfair to judge Bob Dernier from his 1985 statistics. Early season foot surgery slowed him down for the entire season. He was out for more than a month because of the surgery and didn't play at full speed for the rest of the summer. In fact, he stole only one base and drove in only two runs in August. In contrast, he hit .255 and stole 12 bases in May.

Last season, his hitting was hindered by his foot injury. He struck out more often than he walked, not good for a leadoff hitter. He choked up on the bat more than he had in the past.

The long grass at Wrigley Field can hurt him. Dernier's hitting is more suited to artificial turf; he likes to chop at the ball and is more of a contact hitter. He had 20 doubles last season, but only three triples. His average would have been adequate if he was on his running game yet it is lower than the Cubs would like. He has a tendency to become overanxious as the plate and does not always swing at prime-cut pitches. He has the potential to hit in the .270s.

Dernier's greatest offensive weakness is not being able to bunt. With his kind of speed as well as batting in the leadoff spot, bunting would be an effective means of getting on base. Bunting would also open up more of the field to him by making the first and third base lines accessible.

BASERUNNING:

The injury slowed him on the bases, but Dernier still managed to steal 31 bases while being caught only 8 times (he stole 60 bases in 1984 when he was healthy). He can steal at least 60 bases each season if he is healthy.

Dernier's speed (he can score from first on a double) helps Ryne Sandberg see better pitches. Dernier has no problems taking the extra base.

FIELDING:

Dernier has learned to play the wind

BOB DERNIER
CF, No. 22
RR, 6'0", 160 lbs.
ML Svc: 4 years
Born: 1-5-57 in
　　　Kansas City, MO

1985 STATISTICS

AVG	G	AB	R	H	2B	3B	HR	RBI	BB	SO	SB
.254	121	469	63	119	20	3	1	21	40	44	31

CAREER STATISTICS

AVG	G	AB	R	H	2B	3B	HR	RBI	BB	SO	SB
.260	528	1607	259	418	66	10	9	90	158	199	158

STRONG　　　STRONG

VS. RHP　　VS. LHP　　PROBABLE HIT LOCATIONS

and the sun in Wrigley Field. Over the past two years, he has been asked to do more than his share in center field because he does not play alongside outfielders who have good range (Matthews & Moreland). But he wants any ball he can get to.

Dernier did start to get a little sloppy late in the season when the Cubs were out of the race. Otherwise, he is quickly becoming as good as any center fielder in the league, although his arm is only average.

OVERALL:

The Cubs count on Dernier to get them going, but his foot must be healthy if he is to kickstart his offense.

Snider: "He covers center field like a blanket. I would like to see him bunt more and not swing at the first pitch as much as he does. You can't put the take sign on your leadoff hitter, but he has to have a better eye and not chase so many bad pitches."

HITTING:

If the Cubs have hope for Shawon Dunston, it is because of his natural athletic ability. He was rushed to the major leagues last spring after being the nation's number one draft choice in 1982. He wasn't ready to handle the pressure--or the pitching.

He must learn to find the same stance at the plate all the time. Early in the year, he was swinging late at almost every pitch, including curveballs. Since he has learned to hit the fastball, he will now have to learn to handle the curveball the second time around.

Dunston must overcome a tendency to be overanxious at the plate. He swings at almost any pitch when he is ahead in the count.

He has decent power, but tries to hit every ball in the air. He has to accept the fact that he is more of a line drive hitter and that his speed will stretch his hits into extra bases.

Early in the season Dunston took his poor fielding with him to the plate which bought him a ticket back to Triple-A. When he came back to the Cubs in September, he showed signs that he was not all hype. After hitting just .194 in the first five weeks of the season, he made good enough contact with the ball to register a .330 average in September. He ended the season with 17 multi-hit games in 69 starts and seemed to be on the way to correcting some of his flaws.

BASERUNNING:

At this point, Dunston gets too anxious to prove himself on the basepaths at times and tends to make careless baserunning mistakes. Once he irons out his problems at the plate, his base-stealing potential should become more evident. He has great speed and should someday be a burner on the bases.

FIELDING:

As a fielder, Dunston's best asset is his rifle arm. He has one of the best

SHAWON DUNSTON
SS, No. 24
RR, 6'1", 175 lbs.
ML Svc: 1 year
Born: 3-21-63 in
   Brooklyn, NY

1985 STATISTICS

AVG	G	AB	R	H	2B	3B	HR	RBI	BB	SO	SB
.260	74	250	40	65	12	4	4	18	19	42	11

CAREER STATISTICS

AVG	G	AB	R	H	2B	3B	HR	RBI	BB	SO	SB
.260	74	250	40	65	12	4	4	18	19	42	11

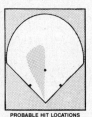

VS. RHP   VS. LHP   PROBABLE HIT LOCATIONS

shortstop arms in the game. His greatest weakness is that he has not yet learned whether to charge a ball or stay back on it. He does not go well to his left, but is good when going to his right.

He makes too many fundamental fielding mistakes, but is getting better (especially on the double play) with the help of Ryne Sandberg.

OVERALL:

The pressures of replacing veteran Larry Bowa were too much for Dunston to handle early in the season. He still has a long way to go both offensively and defensively. He must overcome the pressure of others' expectations.

Snider: "He has yet to show me the real Shawon Dunston--I have been seeing a kid out there who is not himself. Although it might take two years, I know that we are going to see him become a good ballplayer. He will do better as soon as he overcomes his anxieties and learns to relax."

HITTING:

Proving again he is a Wrigley Field hitter, Leon Durham belted 15 of his 21 home runs there and hit .331 at home as opposed to .239 on the road. Not only does he appear more relaxed in its cozy confines, but his power is well suited to the winds blowing out in Chicago.

Durham is basically a fastball hitter but has trouble with a good breaking ball, either from a righthanded or lefthanded pitcher. He has good power to the alleys and is not considered a pull hitter, which is something the Cubs would actually like to see him do more of.

Durham was not as productive as the Cubs would have liked for the first half of the season, but he found his swing in September. In July, when the Cubs were still in the race, Durham hit .276 but had only nine RBIs and three homers.

His biggest failure has been lack of a timely hit. He had only 75 RBIs and only six game-winners, three of them in the last three weeks of the season. Despite batting in the fifth spot in the order for much of the season, Durham had only one sacrifice fly. The Cubs would like to see him cut down on his swing in certain situations. He struck out 99 times last year.

BASERUNNING:

Durham has good speed, but if he is ever to be a running threat, he must cut down on his weight. He tends to be conservative on the bases, though he can score from first on a double. He steals many bases but gets caught nearly as often as not. In the past, he has been slowed by back and leg problems, but he played most of 1985 injury-free.

FIELDING:

In his second year at first base, Durham improved in some areas, but he is still just average. He is getting better

LEON DURHAM
OF, No. 10
LL, 6'2", 210 lbs.
ML Svc: 6 years
Born: 7-31-57 in
Cincinnati, OH

```
1985 STATISTICS
AVG   G   AB    R    H   2B  3B  HR  RBI  BB  SO  SB
.282 153  542   58  153  32   2  21   75  64  99   7
CAREER STATISTICS
AVG   G   AB    R    H   2B  3B  HR  RBI  BB   SO  SB
.284 721 2522  370  717 142  31  96  393 310  453  96
```

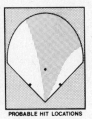

STRONG   STRONG   PROBABLE HIT LOCATIONS
VS. RHP   VS. LHP

at handling the short-hop throw from his infielders.

He doesn't go well to his right (with Ryne Sandberg at second base, he really doesn't have to) and does not play bunts well.

OVERALL:

Even though he is 28 years old, the word "potential" is continually affixed to Durham's name. He had one outstanding season (1982) but has not produced much since. This should be a key season for Durham's career. He needs to remain injury-free and to maintain a slim er physique.

Snider: "He's a bear-down-type of guy who tries to do everything he can to win ballgames. He seems to be slipping over the past few years, possibly because he tries too hard with runners in scoring position."

PITCHING:

As underrated as any pitcher in the league, Dennis Eckersley didn't have a chance to prove his full worth last season because of shoulder problems. He did manage 25 starts, but five of them were with severe pain. Still, his earned run average was only 3.08.

Because of his three-quarters delivery, Eckersley is very tough on right-handed hitters, who hit less than .200 against him last year. He is not short on nerve or desire and loves to pitch. He kept his place among the top five pitchers in baseball in his walks-to-innings pitched ratio. He walked only 15 batters unintentionally last year and struck out 117.

Eckersley's fastball is above average and he has learned to ride it or sink it. His slider and change-up are average and are used to set up his fastball, but he isn't afraid to throw them on any count. His weakness is the home run pitch, but it rarely hurt him last year because he walked so few batters. He must keep the ball down to be effective.

Eckersley rested his shoulder in mid-season and proved he was back in form late in the year by winning three of his final four games. If not for the injury, Eckersley might have been a 20-game winner. From April 16 through May 1, he pitched four complete games and became the first Cub pitcher since 1977 to hurl back-to-back shutouts, one of them 10 innings. By the end of June, he had a 2.95 ERA.

FIELDING, HITTING, BASERUNNING:

A good athlete, Eckersley is nonetheless an average fielder. Balls down the third base line cause him trouble

DENNIS ECKERSLEY
RHP, No. 43
RR, 6'2", 190 lbs.
ML Svc: 11 years
Born: 10-3-54 in
Oakland, CA

1985 STATISTICS

W	L	ERA	G	GS	CG	SV	IP	H	R	ER	BB	SO
11	7	3.08	25	25	6	0	169.1	145	61	58	19	117

CAREER STATISTICS

W	L	ERA	G	GS	CG	SV	IP	H	R	ER	BB	SO
141	113	3.55	334	318	97	3	2229	2104	951	880	568	1457

because of his delivery. His move to first base is improving but his big move to the plate allows runners to get a good jump. He improved on both his fielding and his move last year.

As a hitter, he laughs at himself, although he hit his first career homer last year. He led Cub pitchers with seven walks. His baserunning ability is below average just because he spent much of his career in the American League.

OVERALL:

Eckersley's statistics over the last two seasons make him the Cubs' best pitcher, which is a well-kept secret. He seems to take the game more seriously now than when he was younger. Once considered a flake, he has worked harder than ever in the last two off-seasons.

Snider: "I like him because he has become such a great competitor. He knows how to do all the things that win ballgames. He can go out to the mound with just mediocre stuff and still win."

PITCHING:

Is Ray Fontenot a starter or is Ray Fontenot a reliever? Or is he neither? The Yankees were never sure and neither are the Cubs after his first season in Chicago. But if the rest of the pitching staff is healthy, Fontenot probably will be limited to bullpen duty.

There are those who say Fontenot does not throw hard enough and have enough good pitches to keep him in the majors. He certainly isn't overpowering with his fastball and gets in big trouble when it straightens out and gets up into the middle of the strike zone. He uses the sinkerball as his best pitch but needs to use his above-average change-up more.

His biggest problem is improving his so-so slider to go with the sinker. He has a tendency to try to overthrow to compensate for his lack of speed. That only straightens the ball out more.

Fontenot had several starts last year where he was effective for four or five innings, then suddenly lost everything. He started 23 times and relieved 15 but wasn't terribly effective at either. He allowed a team-high 23 homers, which seemed to come in streaks. In fact, he gave up first-ever career homers to Montreal's Sal Butera and pitcher Bryn Smith--on back-to-back pitches! The number of home runs he allowed gave him a terrible tendency to allow big innings and he continued his problem of letting home runs bother him too much mentally.

Fontenot has a three-quarters motion that can be tough on lefthanders, who hit .181 and just one home run against him.

FIELDING, HITTING, BASERUNNING:

Fontenot is a better-than-average

RAY FONTENOT
LHP, No. 31
LL, 6'0", 175 lbs.
ML Svc: 3 years
Born: 8-8-57 in
    Lake Charles, LA

1985 STATISTICS

W	L	ERA	G	GS	CG	SV	IP	H	R	ER	BB	SO
6	10	4.36	38	23	0	0	154.2	177	86	75	45	70

CAREER STATISTICS

W	L	ERA	G	GS	CG	SV	IP	H	R	ER	BB	SO
22	21	3.83	88	62	3	0	420.2	467	671	179	128	182

fielder who gets off the mound quickly, although he has had trouble in the past covering first base. His move to first may be the best on the Cubs staff and he needs it because his lack of a good fastball gives the advantage to the runner.

A poor hitter, Fontenot is also not a very good bunter. It was hard to tell, in his first National League season, whether he was a good baserunner, since he reached base only twice.

OVERALL:

Perhaps Fontenot was asked to take on too much of the load when the entire Cubs starting rotation was on the disabled list. He may have tried too hard when asked to take over the number one starting duties. He will get his chance this year to come out of the bullpen without the game being on the line.

Snider: "He's not an intimidating pitcher--everything he throws is very hittable. I think he might be helped by coming up with a trick pitch."

PITCHING:

If pitchers have nightmares, it comes from the type of season through which George Frazier suffered last year. He finished with a 7-8 record, 6.39 ERA, a bruised ego and off-season knee surgery. He had troubles with both knees through the last five weeks of the season.

Frazier's last appearance in late September was what his season was all about: 4 runs, 4 hits and 1 walk in only 1 1/3 innings. In his appearance before that, he walked 6 and gave up 3 runs in 1 2/3 innings. The walks were more of a problem than the hits; he gave up 52 in 76 innings. It was the second highest total on the staff. He also threw four wild pitches.

All of Frazier's pitches can be above average, including a moving fastball. He also throws a split-finger pitch and has admitted to throwing a spitball. But he has a tendency to nibble on the corners and that gets him into trouble.

Frazier's knees and a tired arm may have had something to do with his control problems. Although he appeared as a middle reliever in only 51 games, most of them came in the middle and late months when the Cubs staff was decimated by injuries. And that doesn't count the times he threw in the bullpen without getting into a game. Frazier seemed to wear out in September, compiling an ERA in double figures.

When he is healthy and on his game, Frazier can be valuable by going three or four innings and giving Lee Smith a rest. He finished 17 games last year but had only two saves.

FIELDING, HITTING, BASERUNNING:

Frazier is one of the best fielders

GEORGE FRAZIER
RHP, No. 39
RR, 6'5", 205 lbs.
ML Svc: 8 years
Born: 10-13-54 in
  Oklahoma City, OK

1985 STATISTICS

W	L	ERA	G	GS	CG	SV	IP	H	R	ER	BB	SO
7	8	6.39	51	0	0	2	76	88	57	54	52	46

CAREER STATISTICS

W	L	ERA	G	GS	CG	SV	IP	H	R	ER	BB	SO
27	33	4.12	311	0	0	21	515	490	251	236	212	325

among Cubs pitchers. He gets to bunts and seems to know where to throw it. For a righthander, he has an above-average move to first base, helped by his quick delivery.

As a reliever, he doesn't bat much, which is a good thing. He had no hits last year, no sacrifice bunts and no walks. He struck out four of the six times he batted. No one really knows how good a baserunner he is.

OVERALL:

A good athlete, Frazier is a better pitcher than he showed last year. He seems suited to middle relief if he can overcome his control problems. His knees should be healthy and it could help him if the rest of the staff were healthy so he wouldn't have to be used so often.

Snider: "I don't think you can judge him from last year. I would like to see him become more of a pitcher than a thrower. He's knows the game well."

HITTING:

If enthusiasm meant anything, Billy Hatcher would have been a major leaguer a long time ago. But the chunky young outfielder didn't get his chance until last year and then he didn't show enough physical skills to match his attitude. Hatcher made the typical rookie mistakes caused by anxiety.

Rookiness aside, however, there are questions concerning his ability to hit major league pitching. He was fooled by almost every pitcher, getting over-matched by the fastball and fooled by the curveball. Hatcher was better as a fill-in player when he first arrived on the major league scene. The more he batted while subbing for injured players, the more his weaknesses showed.

With very little power, Hatcher will have to learn to hit for average in the majors. He has never hit more than 10 home runs at any level and he has hit over .300 for only one season. With short arms, he has trouble reaching an outside pitch. He must learn to have more patience at the plate.

BASERUNNING:

Hatcher has great speed and stole more than 50 bases in each of his three minor league seasons. At the big league level, however, he is too tentative on the bases. His timidity is not related to his status as a rookie, however, but rather to a broken wrist he suffered in the minors. Fear of reinjuring it prevents him from taking too big a lead, which makes it impossible to steal bases.

As long as he is not trying to steal he is a good baserunner, somewhat over-anxious at times, but he turns on his exceptional speed going from first to third and from second to home. He has yet to learn major league pitchers and major league arms in the outfield. With good coaching, Hatcher could turn into a good baserunner.

BILLY HATCHER
OF, No. 22
RR, 5'9", 175 lbs.
ML Svc: less than 1 year
Born: 10-4-60 in
 Williams, AZ

1985 STATISTICS

AVG	G	AB	R	H	2B	3B	HR	RBI	BB	SO	SB
.245	53	163	24	40	12	1	2	10	8	12	2

CAREER STATISTICS

AVG	G	AB	R	H	2B	3B	HR	RBI	BB	SO	SB
.245	53	163	24	40	12	1	2	10	8	12	2

VS. RHP   VS. LHP   PROBABLE HIT LOCATIONS

FIELDING:

Hatcher does not bring his speed with him into the outfield and is only a fair defensive player. He gets a poor jump on the ball. Originally tried in center field for the injured Bob Dernier, Billy was inadequate, but proved to be a much better left fielder. He does not have the range to play center field, at least at this time. His arm is only average.

OVERALL:

At age 25, Hatcher still has time to develop and the Cubs should be patient with him.

Snider: "His energy could overcome his physical shortcomings. He is over-matched by the major league fastball and has to slow down at the plate and watch the pitches closely. He has potential, however, it is as yet just that."

HITTING:

At age 38, Richie Hebner may be near the end of his career. His .217 average was his worst ever and he finished the season on a down note, losing his status as the Cubs' number one lefty pinch-hitter to Thad Bosley. His last pinch-hit was a home run in the middle of August: after that, he was 0-for-22.

The question is whether Hebner can still hit the fastball. He had trouble with power pitchers last year and seemed to be rusty. Still dangerous on low pitches, he can golf them out of the park at Wrigley Field. He can look bad on one pitch and poke the next pitch over the wall.

He rarely faces righthanders; his role has been reduced strictly to pinch-hitting, though now he may not even have that job.

The pop in Hebner's bat may be going slowly. He hit only three homers and two doubles last year. But he continued to show an uncanny ability to stay away from the double play ball, grounding into only two last year. What power he has left is exclusively to right field with some punch to center field and right-center field.

BASERUNNING:

Hebner's experience makes him a good runner for his age. He will rarely make a major mistake on the basepaths, but his speed is completely gone. He is at the stage now where he has trouble scoring from second base on a single.

FIELDING:

Hebner insists he can still play third base and first base, but the Cubs have shown little confidence in him. It does appear he is not as good as he once was; he committed four errors last year, mostly on ground balls hit right at him

RICHIE HEBNER
INF, No. 18
LR, 6'1", 195 lbs.
ML Svc: 17 years
Born: 11-26-47 in
    Boston, MA

1985 STATISTICS

AVG	G	AB	R	H	2B	3B	HR	RBI	BB	SO	SB
.217	83	120	10	26	2	0	3	22	7	15	0

CAREER STATISTICS

AVG	G	AB	R	H	2B	3B	HR	RBI	BB	SO	SB
.276	1908	6144	865	1694	270	57	213	990	687	741	38

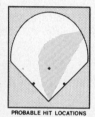

STRONG   STRONG

VS. RHP   VS. LHP   PROBABLE HIT LOCATIONS

at third base. Hebner is much better as a fill-in first baseman, although he has trouble with the short-hop throw to him and has limited range. He rarely plays the outfield. A shoulder injury two years ago has left him with a very mediocre arm.

OVERALL:

This is an important year for Hebner, who still has a great zest for the game. One of his greatest assets is his free-and-easy nature and his ability to get along with almost anybody. He adds a touch of class to the bench, but his playing days may be numbered.

Snider: "He has a relaxed attitude and knows his role by now. His strength lies in his experience and his willingness to give it all he's got. He can be pitched to, but pitchers must be careful with him. He can still hurt them."

HITTING:

If there is hope for the older set, it is molded into the body of Davey Lopes. At age 39, Lopes has learned that he is not an everyday ballplayer and seems to thrive in the role of fill-in. He can hit anywhere in the order and can hit for power and run production.

When Lopes is hot, there seems to be few pitches he can't hit. He is still a high fastball hitter and, even at his age, pulls mostly to left field. His weakness is a good breaking pitch. He played in 99 games for the Cubs and hit .284 with 11 homers and 44 RBIs, his highest totals since 1983 when he was with Oakland. He also walked 46 times and struck out only 37.

Lopes has a swing which is well suited for Wrigley Field, where he has extra-base power. He is good at putting the ball in play, although he is not great at moving runners over a base. He is also an asset as a pinch-hitter on days he is not playing in a regular spot. He had four hits, including a homer, and five RBIs in 22 pinch-appearances, with his value off the bench increased because he can stay in the game and get more than one at-bat.

BASERUNNING:

This is where Lopes excels. He is the only player in major league history to steal more than 30 bases after his 39th birthday. He seems to be able to steal any time off any pitcher, even though he no longer plays every day.

He stole 47 for the Cubs and was caught only four times. He was 11 for 12 in steals of third and had 11 multi-steal games, making him one of the most valuable extra men in baseball.

He knows when he can take the extra base, gets a good jump and has enough speed to score from first on a double.

FIELDING:

What makes Lopes even more valuable is his versatility. Last year he filled

DAVEY LOPES
OF/INF, No. 12
RR, 5'9", 170 lbs.
ML Svc: 13 years
Born: 5-3-46 in
  E. Providence, RI

1985 STATISTICS												
AVG	G	AB	R	H	2B	3B	HR	RBI	BB	SO	SB
.284	99	275	52	78	11	0	11	44	46	37	47

CAREER STATISTICS												
AVG	G	AB	R	H	2B	3B	HR	RBI	BB	SO	SB
.263	1699	6056	970	1591	220	47	147	573	777	819	530

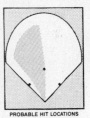

STRONG VS. RHP   STRONG VS. LHP   PROBABLE HIT LOCATIONS

in for Ryne Sandberg at second base and for Gary Matthews in left field and Bob Dernier in center field.

He is slightly better than average in the outfield and still has a good arm. His range in the infield is also just better than average but he makes few errors and rarely throws to the wrong base.

OVERALL:

Lopes keeps his compact body in good shape, but with his age, he is becoming more prone to injuries. Last year, he was slowed several time by a variety of leg injuries and by eye infections caused by contact lenses; he can't be used for extended periods of time.

Snider: "I like Lopes. He still knows how to play the game. He's good to have around, still has some pop in his bat and is almost guaranteed to steal a base. At this point, he has probably stolen a base off every pitcher in the league."

HITTING:

If there is a question mark for the Cubs this season, it is whether Gary Matthews is over the hill at age 35. He missed 48 games last year and was on the disabled list twice because of leg ailments. It affected him in every phase of his game, but most especially at the plate, where he hit a career low .235 and was a major disappointment.

Matthews had more trouble than ever before handling the fastball last year. Still, the Cubs had enough confidence in him to re-sign him as a free agent. He led the league in walks and was tied for the on-base percentage lead in 1984, but lost his number three spot in the batting order to Ryne Sandberg last year. And for good reason: he had only 40 RBIs and his on-base percentage was .362. He also struck out 64 times in 298 at-bats.

Matthews still shows his sporadic power. His hits usually come in bunches and are usually line drives. He has better-than-average power to center field. Because he's having trouble getting around on a fastball, he may have to learn to hit the ball to the opposite field more often rather than pulling the ball. He may also have to accept the fact that he will be batting sixth or seventh in the order, as he did for the final month of last year.

BASERUNNING:

Always a daring baserunner, Matthews' leg problems have slowed him down considerably. His ability to stretch a single into a double is gone. But he remains an aggressive baserunner and is still one of the best at breaking up the double play. He has put on some weight in the past few seasons, and probably won't regain his past baserunning form unless he loses the excess baggage.

FIELDING:

Matthews' sore knee and legs didn't

GARY MATTHEWS
OF, No. 34
RR, 6'3", 190 lbs.
ML Svc: 13 years
Born: 7-5-50 in
    San Fernando, CA

1985 STATISTICS

AVG	G	AB	R	H	2B	3B	HR	RBI	BB	SO	SB
.235	97	298	45	70	12	0	13	40	59	64	2

CAREER STATISTICS

AVG	G	AB	R	H	2B	3B	HR	RBI	BB	SO	SB
.283	1821	6618	1021	1876	299	50	210	909	869	1033	1984

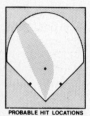

STRONG VS. RHP   STRONG VS. LHP   PROBABLE HIT LOCATIONS

help his long-held reputation for below-average fielding. He cannot run down fly balls or get into the corner or left-center to cut off a ball. Even when he is healthy, Matthews is a risk as a left fielder, having the most trouble on balls hit right to him. He has only an average arm and is even more of a liability in the field if he is not hitting enough to cover for his weak defense.

OVERALL:

Matthews' gung-ho enthusiasm won't help unless he can play every day and get on base. The Cubs have placed a lot of faith in him.

Snider: "I've always been a Matthews booster, although sometimes I don't like what I see. His outfield play appears to have slipped and he is not getting to a lot of balls he should. He will have to come back this season and have a great year with the bat."

HITTING:

An example of what hard work and determination can do, Keith Moreland has made himself into a consistently good hitter. Once considered a hothead and free-swinger who could be fooled by any good pitcher, Moreland has calmed down and picked up his statistics.

Asked to bat cleanup last season, he responded. Ironically, his home run total of 14 was his lowest as a Cub, but he compensated with a career high of 106 RBIs. His .374 on-base percentage was the best among the Cubs' regulars. He is better suited to bat fifth or sixth, but he may be a good enough hitter now to adjust to any spot.

Pitchers discovered last year that he has very few weak spots. He struck out a career low of 58 times and worked the count to a base-on-balls 68 times. He can hit most any type of pitch, though he does seem to have trouble with the high fastball.

Earlier in his career, Moreland was pretty much a pull hitter, but he now sprays the ball to all parts of the field. He has extra-base power to all fields.

Last season, he was the most consistent Cub and was the best at driving in runners with two outs. He produced five game-winning hits in the seventh and eighth innings, and had six game-tying hits in the seventh through ninth innings.

BASERUNNING:

Many of the 12 bases Moreland stole last year were actually the result of missed hit-and-runs. He is still not a threat to steal. He does not have good speed, though he has learned to run the bases intelligently, which has made him appear to be faster than he is.

He is aggressive at breaking up double plays and knows his limitations in taking the extra base.

FIELDING:

Right field at Wrigley may be the

KEITH MORELAND
RF, No. 6
RR, 6'0", 200 lbs.
ML Svc: 7 years
Born: 5-2-54 in
Dallas, TX

1985 STATISTICS

AVG	G	AB	R	H	2B	3B	HR	RBI	BB	SO	SB
.307	161	587	74	180	30	3	14	106	68	58	12

CAREER STATISTICS

AVG	G	AB	R	H	2B	3B	HR	RBI	BB	SO	SB
.289	731	2496	291	721	112	13	71	398	242	305	17

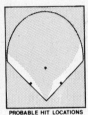

VS. RHP   VS. LHP   PROBABLE HIT LOCATIONS

toughest outfield position in the business. The wind is always blowing, and then, of course, there is the sun.

Still, Moreland has made himself into a more-than-adequate fielder. His arm is good, but he has trouble cutting balls off because of his lack of speed. Among the areas he has improved in are: throwing to the right base and hitting the cutoff man, both of which were weak spots in the past.

OVERALL:

Moreland has turned himself from just another player into one of the more respected hitters and fielders in the NL. He and Ryne Sandberg have become the two most consistent Cubs players who never take days off.

Snider: "Keith used to be an easy out--but no more. He has become a very tough hitter to strike out and has learned how to hit. He has disciplined himself to become a better all-around ballplayer."

PITCHING:

For the second year in a row, Dick Ruthven had to wonder what he had done wrong. Two summers ago, it was shoulder surgery for a blocked artery. Last summer, it was a line drive off his left big toe--his season ended August 9 when Keith Hernandez's shot up the middle was stopped by Ruthven's toe. It ended with a disappointing and inconclusive 4-7 record and 4.53 earned run average.

The question now is whether, at age 34, Ruthven can overcome the last two seasons, when he appeared in only 53 games, and most of them ineffectively.

He no longer appears to be a nine-inning pitcher; he hasn't had a complete game since 1983. And he never has been much of a strikeout pitcher; he had only 26 in 87 1/3 innings last year. Used again as the fifth starter, which means starting the year in the bullpen, he may lose that status this year and find himself in the bullpen full-time.

His fastball is about average, but he has a good change-up to go with it. He also throws a slurve, which is not a bad breaking pitch at times. Ruthven has to rely on keeping his pitches down at the knees or he is hurt by home runs. His best outing last year was on August 20 against the Giants, when he had a no-hitter for 4 2/3 innings. He made only one more start (10 hits and 5 runs in 5 innings against the Dodgers) before his toe was broken.

Always a hard worker in the off-season, Ruthven's future lies in his rehabilitation. The shoulder operation took some pop off his fastball and left his arm weaker than before. How much the time missed from the broken toe will mean won't be known until this season.

The Cubs are hoping a new no-windup motion will make him more effective.

DICK RUTHVEN
RHP, No. 44
RR, 6'3", 190 lbs.
ML Svc: 12 years
Born: 3-27-51 in
    Sacramento, CA

1985 STATISTICS

W	L	ERA	G	GS	CG	SV	IP	H	R	ER	BB	SO
4	7	4.53	20	15	0	0	87.1	103	49	44	37	26

CAREER STATISTICS

W	L	ERA	G	GS	CG	SV	IP	H	R	ER	BB	SO
123	127	4.14	349	332	71	1	2097.1	2143	1066	964	761	1142

FIELDING, HITTING, BASERUNNING:

Ruthven is a good enough athlete to be a good fielder and covers first base very well. Always having had a problem with holding runners on first base, he improved on that last season.

He is annually among the leading hitters on his team and had five hits and six sacrifice bunts last year.

OVERALL:

This is a pivotal year for Ruthven particularly if the rest of the Cubs starters are healthy. If he comes back strong, he could still have the chance to be the fifth starter, even though he doesn't have the stuff he once did.

Snider: "He really has to keep the ball down. He's a good battler but he beats himself a lot because of his poor control. Ruthven will never be a winning pitcher if he continues to give away first base."

HITTING:

Despite a slow start, Ryne Sandberg nearly repeated his tremendous offensive statistics of 1984, when he was the NL's Most Valuable Player. Last year he hit only .192 in April but finished at .305 with 26 homers and 83 RBIs. His best months were July at .355 and September at .347. How good is Sandberg offensively? He became only the third player in baseball history to have 25 or more homers and 50 or more stolen bases in one season. Cesar Cedeno and Joe Morgan each did it twice.

Sandberg has a strange and unique hitch in his swing: he shifts his weight to his back foot just before he swings. It leaves him off balance when he swings and misses, but the hitch doesn't affect his hitting otherwise.

His power is almost completely to left field, but he hits well all the way into right-center. Last year, he stopped swinging at so many bad pitches, but he struck out nearly 100 times in trying for extra-base hits.

Primarily a fastball hitter, if he has a weakness at the plate, it is the breaking ball down and away. He has improved each year at situational hitting, going for a single with runners in scoring position and for extra-bases with a man on first.

Sandberg is a good bunter but rarely uses it for a base hit. When he matures and uses all his skills, there will be few better offensively.

BASERUNNING:

Sandberg is an instinctively good runner. He is tall and lean and deceptively fast. He stole 32 bases in 1984, and brought his totals up to 54 last year. His potential may be 60 steals, although his amount of homers and doubles will cut down on that number.

He rarely makes a mistake; still, he is very conservative on the basepaths. He needs to get more aggressive at taking extra bases and at stealing on any count.

RYNE SANDBERG
2B, No. 23
RR, 6'2", 185 lbs.
ML Svc: 4 years
Born: 9-18-59 in
   Spokane, WA

1985 STATISTICS

AVG	G	AB	R	H	2B	3B	HR	RBI	BB	SO	SB
.305	153	609	113	186	31	6	26	83	57	97	54

CAREER STATISTICS

AVG	G	AB	R	H	2B	3B	HR	RBI	BB	SO	SB
.287	636	2519	200	724	125	34	60	269	196	368	155

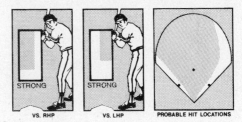

FIELDING:

What makes Sandberg so good is his consistency. He is already a Gold Glover. If he has a defensive weakness, it is an average arm for a second baseman. His range is not great, but with his speed, it is well above average. He has learned how to become very good at the double play but will have to break in new shortstop Shawon Dunston.

OVERALL:

When scouts look at a hitter, they want to see him hit, hit with power, run and throw. Owners look for players who are durable; managers look for players who play well and don't complain. Fans just want to see good baseball. Ryne Sandberg pleases the entire crowd.

Snider: "An ideal guy. You just put his name in the lineup and don't worry about managing him. I love to watch him play. If there is something he can't do, someone should tell us about it."

PITCHING:

Once again, Scott Sanderson had one of the league's best ERAs. But once again, it was for only part of a season. The lanky righthander is arguably among the best pitchers in the game--when he is healthy. And that has become a big "when" because Sanderson has started only 18, 24 and 19 games over the last three seasons.

Several injuries sidelined him last season, but the one which ended his season was a stretched knee ligament caused by pushing off the mound. Sanderson also suffered a sore elbow and has a chronically bad back.

So the question remains whether Scott Sanderson can pitch an entire season. The Cubs aren't sure, signing him to a new contract which is guaranteed for only one year if he can't take his regular turns.

When Sanderson does take his turn, he turns in a good performance. His earned run average with the Cubs the last two years has been 3.14 and 3.12, despite pitching with his miseries. Opponents hit only .205 against him with runners in scoring position.

His effectiveness comes from above-average fastballs and curveballs. He also throws a slider and change-up, both of them average, though the change-up needs improvement. He uses his wicked curve as an out pitch much of the time. Sanderson gets in trouble only when he starts getting the ball up, which is the reason for his high home run ratio.

FIELDING, HITTING, BASERUNNING:

Sanderson is an average fielder but has trouble getting off the mound to field bunts because of his size and back problems. He bothers opponents and

SCOTT SANDERSON
RHP, No. 21
RR, 6'5", 198 lbs.
ML Svc: 7 years
Born: 7-22-56 in
Dearborn, MI

1985 STATISTICS

W	L	ERA	G	GS	CG	SV	IP	H	R	ER	BB	SO
5	6	3.12	19	19	2	0	121	100	49	42	27	80

CAREER STATISTICS

W	L	ERA	G	GS	CG	SV	IP	H	R	ER	BB	SO
69	58	3.29	192	179	29	2	1143	1078	466	418	291	759

teammates by taking so much time with runners on base, holding the ball in his stretch for up to 20 seconds. Runners can steal off him because of his long motion to the plate. Although he has improved, Sanderson remains one of the most deliberate workers in the league.

Although he never has been much of a hitter, Sanderson prides himself on his bunting. He isn't great at it, but he was second on the Cubs in sacrifice bunts last year.

A less-than-average baserunner, he looks lost when he does reach base, which isn't very often.

OVERALL:

At age 29, it is time to wonder if Sanderson really has a body which is injury-prone or whether he has just run into bad luck.

Snider: "He seems like a guy who may have to build up his body a bit more for more strength. He goes through times when he gets tired too easily. However, he has a good idea what he wants to do on the mound."

LEE SMITH
RHP, No. 46
RR, 6'6", 220 lbs.
ML Svc: 5 years
Born: 12-4-57 in
    Jamestown, LA

PITCHING:

While most of the Cubs pitchers were nursing injuries last year, Lee Smith was trying to play doctor. But even he couldn't heal a broken season, despite saving 33 of 42 opportunities and having a hand in more than half of the club's victories. The best news is that Smith continued what he started two years before, keeping up his reputation as being in the upper echelon of short relievers.

Smith will never be accused of having finesse. He throws over 90 MPH and has been clocked at close to 100 MPH. Obviously, his fastball is his out pitch, although sometimes he has a tendency to overthrow it. His slider has improved, but he still has trouble getting it over the plate consistently.

If he needs to work on a pitch, it is a change-up. Even a mediocre change-up could keep him in games when his fastball is wild. He also needs to pitch inside to batters more to keep them from digging in.

The rap against Smith has been his streakiness. He lost four games last year and had a 3.04 ERA. But he did strike out more than one batter per inning and struck out the side nine times. Singles hitters continue to give him problems, especially when his fastball gets up in the strike zone. Lefthanders also gave him problems. They hit .291 against him, while righthanders hit only .202. Opponents hit .185 with runners in scoring position when they faced him last year.

FIELDING, HITTING, BASERUNNING:

With healthy knees, Smith is not a bad fielder but his bulk makes him slow in getting off the mound. He is not particularly good at ground balls hit back

1985 STATISTICS												
W	L	ERA	G	GS	CG	SV	IP	H	R	ER	BB	SO
7	4	3.04	65	0	0	33	97.2	87	35	33	32	112

CAREER STATISTICS												
W	L	ERA	G	GS	CG	SV	IP	H	R	ER	BB	SO
27	32	2.85	330	6	0	113	507.2	438	178	161	190	455

to him and he lumbers after bunts. His fastball holds runners on base but his pickoff move is mediocre.

He has never claimed to be a hitter and rarely bats, getting to the plate only six times last season. His inexperience makes him an awful baserunner.

OVERALL:

There is no reason Smith shouldn't continue to be among the best relievers if he keeps his weight down and develops a change-up. If the starters are healthy, he won't have to be used as many times this season as in the past, which is good news for his knees.

Smith has proved to be a proud person and has begun to take the game seriously. He dropped some weight a year ago so his sore knees would take less of a pounding. He must continue on his diet and leg exercises.

Snider: "He's still not a pitcher-- he's a thrower all the way. But he sure has something to throw. He just stands out there, fires the ball and dares anyone to hit it. Smith is top shelf."

PITCHING:

If Lary Sorensen wants to stay in the major leagues, this year could be his last chance. Sorensen hasn't had an ERA below 4.00 since the strike season of 1981 and he wasn't helped by last year's 3-7 record and 4.26 ERA with the Cubs.

A sometimes-starter but mostly a reliever, Sorensen's future appears to be in the bullpen if he wants a spot on the Cubs' staff. Not only are the starting spots filled (if the staff is healthy), but Sorensen was a failure as a starter last year. He started three games and had a 9.00 ERA. As a reliever, he had a 3.38 ERA. But the Cubs didn't have much faith in him; he finished 18 games but was not trusted enough to get a save.

Like the rest of the Cubs' healthy staff last year, Sorensen was hurt by overuse. If he found any hope for the future, it was in September. He made 11 appearances, covering 18 2/3 innings, and compiled a 0.48 ERA. Opponents hit only .206 against him in that stretch. He also had a 2.25 ERA in June, which means that he was terrible the rest of the season.

Sorensen's major problem when he gets into trouble is that his sinker doesn't go down. It is his best pitch and his out pitch. His fastball is very average, as are his curveball and slider. He has been throwing a knuckleball for the last few years but without great success. He may have to rely on it more now.

Last year's statistics tell the story of Sorensen's career. He allowed more hits than innings pitched, struck out only 34 batters and led the Cub in hit batters with four. But Sorensen walked very few and allowed very few home runs. Righthanders hit only .233 against him but lefthanders hit .339. His most im-

LARY SORENSEN
RHP, No. 42
RR, 6'2", 200 lbs.
ML Svc: 8 years
Born: 10-4-55 in
Detroit, MI

1985 STATISTICS
W	L	ERA	G	GS	CG	SV	IP	H	R	ER	BB	SO
3	7	4.26	45	3	0	0	82.1	86	44	39	24	34

CAREER STATISTICS
W	L	ERA	G	GS	CG	SV	IP	H	R	ER	BB	SO
190	99	4.12	311	230	69	3	1671.2	1880	849	766	387	539

pressive statistics as a reliever were that only five inherited runners scored and he got seven double play ground balls.

FIELDING, HITTING, BASERUNNING:

Sorensen is a good athlete and, so, a good fielder. He has the ability to field bunts and to cover first base. He also has a good move to first base and a fairly quick delivery to home plate.

He is not a good hitter with no hits in six at-bats, but he did get down four sacrifice bunts.

OVERALL:

Sorensen has gained weight the last two seasons and must drop some of it. Last year proved he could still be a long reliever given the right situation, but he will be challenged this year.

Snider: "Sorensen has to prove he is still a major league pitcher. He seems to have good control but he has to get his sinker over consistently."

PITCHING:

Now that he has the Cy Young jinx out of the way, perhaps Rick Sutcliffe can resume his pitching career. Last year was a triple disaster for him, with time spent on the disabled list for three related ailments. First, it was a hamstring pull from running the bases, then the ailment was a groin pull caused by coming back too soon and then he had shoulder problems which were caused by a compensation in his motion related to the first two injuries.

It was all but a lost season for the big redhead, who salvaged part of it by making two semi-successful starts before the season ended. Neither was of Cy Young quality nor very long, but they did prove he was on his way to rehabilitation.

If he is healthy, Sutcliffe should take his place again at the head of the Cubs' pitching class. And he does have class--both on and off the mound. He has become one of the game's best pitchers and it helps that he knows it. Even last season, when his shoulder and his legs kept him from being at his best, Sutcliffe got hitters out. The transition from a thrower to a pitcher has been completed.

Control is what has changed Sutcliffe into a super pitcher since his trade to the Cubs. He does it all without a world-class fastball, but one that is good enough to slip past hitters. His curveball, slider and change-up keep hitters off stride, as does his herky-jerky motion, where he seems to hold the ball at his side until the last moment.

He can throw any of his pitches for strikes any time he wants. If he has an out pitch, it is his slider, which hitters see even on a full count.

FIELDING, HITTING, BASERUNNING:

Still one of the best fielders in the

RICK SUTCLIFFE
RHP, No. 43
LR, 6'6", 215 lbs.
ML Svc: 8 years
Born: 6-21-56 in
    Independence, MO

1985 STATISTICS

W	L	ERA	G	GS	CG	SV	IP	H	R	ER	BB	SO
8	8	3.18	20	20	6	0	130	119	51	46	44	102

CAREER STATISTICS

W	L	ERA	G	GS	CG	SV	IP	H	R	ER	BB	SO
77	49	3.62	208	149	35	6	1145	1051	517	460	457	754

league, Sutcliffe takes pride in his defense. He looks slow, but is very quick for his size. His pickoff move is not bad, but runners can steal off him because of his slow delivery to the plate.

Sutcliffe also has pride in his hitting. He led all Cubs pitchers with a .233 average last year. He is a good enough hitter to be used occasionally as a pinch-hitter and has enough power to reach Wrigley Field's bleachers (he is a lefthanded swinger). He is average, at best, at running the bases.

OVERALL:

At age 29, Sutcliffe may have discovered that he had better work harder during the off-season. A pitcher's legs are the first to go and maybe they were trying to tell him something last year.

Snider: "Rick is a pure kind of pitcher. For this season, it is just a matter of the doctor saying OK. If he goes through the whole season with a Cub team that is healthy, he has a very good chance of winning 20 games. I am sure that he will be able to pitch well right away and will have lost little because of his injuries."

PITCHING:

When his career is over, Steve Trout may best be remembered for a game he didn't pitch in 1985. It was Sunday, September 8, in Wrigley Field and Trout was scheduled to pitch against the Cincinnati Reds. But he had fallen off his bicycle at home the night before and didn't start. Pete Rose, originally not scheduled to start against the lefthanded Trout, started against righty Reggie Patterson and got two hits to tie Ty Cobb's all-time hit record.

It was a strange year for Trout, who has had a strange career of ups-and-downs. He recovered quickly from the bicycle accident scrape wounds, but it took him longer to overcome the serious elbow problems which limited his starts to 24 games.

When he was healthy, he proved again that he can be a dominating pitcher. He finished the season on a positive note, throwing a complete game victory in late September. It was his first victory since July 9.

Trout almost exclusively throws a sinkerball, which is a hard pitch on the elbow. He has developed a good change-up, but needs more work on his weak slider. His style is suited to the long grass infield at Wrigley Field, which slows up ground balls (opponents grounded into 18 double plays against him on grass, but only four on artificial surfaces last year).

Trout is not a strikeout pitcher, fanning only 44 batters in 140 2/3 innings. He still goes through wild spells when he aims the ball instead of throwing it.

FIELDING, HITTING, BASERUNNING:

Unlike his early years when he was considered a flighty fielder, Trout has

STEVE TROUT
LHP, No. 34
LL, 6'4", 189 lbs.
ML Svc: 7 years
Born: 7-30-57 in
  Detroit, MI

1985 STATISTICS

W	L	ERA	G	GS	CG	SV	IP	H	R	ER	BB	SO
9	7	3.39	24	24	3	0	140.2	142	57	53	63	44

CAREER STATISTICS

W	L	ERA	G	GS	CG	SV	IP	H	R	ER	BB	SO
69	68	3.83	205	165	29	4	1132	1229	560	482	388	497

cut down on his fielding mistakes. In the past, he would make wild throws to first base after fielding ground balls or bunts. In general, his fielding has improved. For a lefthander, he doesn't have an outstanding move to first base and it does not help that he has a slow motion to the plate.

As a hitter and baserunner, he might as well forget it. He is becoming better at bunts, however, leading the Cubs with nine sacrifices last year.

OVERALL:

Trout has matured mentally and also has gained weight after going through several diets in past years. He is now strong and he is learning how to pitch. If he maintains his control, he can be even more effective.

Snider: "He's one of those guys who has to keep the ball down. I think he got to thinking too much last year because of the injury and it hurt him. He has to be sound to be effective because he is not yet able to get batters out without his best stuff."

JAY BALLER
RHP, No. 43
RR, 6'6", 215 lbs.
ML SVC: less than 1 year
Born: 10-6-60 in
Stayton, OR

PITCHING, FIELDING,
HITTING, BASERUNNING:

What Jay Baller did when he got back to the major leagues with the Cubs was forget about the past. His record in the minors was dotted with tales of wildness and the statistics to back it up.

Throughout his career, the massive righthander had walked more than one batter every two innings. But once he got a second chance with the Cubs, he walked only 17 in 52 innings.

It earned him a job as a setup man for short reliever Lee Smith. It was a job held in 1984 by an older clone of Baller's, Tim Stoddard. Baller couldn't even get his ERA under 4.50 in his last four minor league stops but finished last year with a 3.46 ERA. During September, he had a scoreless string of 20 2/3 innings.

Baller's fastball isn't overwhelming but he changes speeds on it well and mixes it up with a good curveball and a quick slider.

He's a fast worker and holds runners on base well. Despite his size, Baller fields his position fairly well. He does not seem to bemuch of a hitter.

OVERALL:

Baller hadn't been in the majors since 1982, when he had a stint with the Phillies. He is big and strong and, at age 25, has found good pitches.

Snider: "He may have matured and have found the right job with the Cubs. He is big enough if he maintains his good control."

STEVE LAKE
C, No. 16
RR, 6'1", 190 lbs.
ML Svc: 3 years
Born: 3-14-57 in
Inglewood, CA

HITTING, BASERUNNING, FIELDING:

Even Steve Lake makes jokes about his hitting. He once quipped that it was a shame that bats came without instructions. If Lake could hit, he could start for many major league teams. If he played more, however, he might hit more. He got only 119 chances to hit last year and ended up with a .151 average. He shows a weakness for good fastballs but has a real soft spot for curveballs.

Lake is experienced and knows how to play the game. He had four sacrifice bunts last year but he also struck out 21 times while walking on only 3 occasions.

Not a good baserunner, Lake has catcher's speed. His lack of playing time makes him only a so-so man on the basepaths.

But as a defensive catcher, he has few peers. He is as good as anyone in either league at throwing out baserunners, mostly because of his quick release and shotgun arm. He is a more-than-capable handler of pitchers.

OVERALL:

Lake is a capable defensive player and could hit more if he were used more often. He would do well to find himself another team, as the Cubs have made it clear that they have no intentions of letting Jody Davis take a breather.

Snider: "Each year that he doesn't play enough, all of his skills go backwards. It's a shame. He's a good guy to have around and seems to be able to keep his good attitude despite his awkward role."

RON MERIDITH
LHP, No. 38
LL, 6'0", 175 lbs.
ML Svc: less than 1 year
Born: 11-26-58 in
     Birmingham, AL

**PITCHING, FIELDING,
   HITTING, BASERUNNING:**

At age 27, Ron Meridith may have found himself as a pitcher. With the Cubs' Triple-A farm club at Iowa, he went through 11 appearances covering 16 2/3 inings without a run. The smallish lefthander got to the major leagues and continued his good relief pitching. Despite two horrendous outings, he figures in the future for the Cubs.

His fastball is only average but his curveball can get him by when it is on. Because of those two bad nights his ERA with the Cubs ended up at 4.47.

Meridith showed a tendency to have wild streaks and is not a strikeout pitcher. He is at his best against left-handers, who have trouble handling his curveball.

Meridith fields his position well and is decent at holding runners on base. He is a lefthander, which helps his chances of sticking in the major leagues. He has some potential with the bat, but won't get much of a chance to prove it since he is a short reliever.

OVERALL:

Meridith showed an ability to throw strikes and get outs most of the time. Like most young pitchers, he needs to get more consistent with his pitches and with finding the strike zone.

Snider: "He's a little short in stuff but has a good curveball to lefthanded hitters. He seems to want to pitch."

CHRIS SPEIER
SS, No. 28
RR, 6'1", 180 lbs.
ML Svc: 14 years
Born: 6-28-50 in
     Alameda, CA

HITTING, FIELDING, BASERUNNING:

Given a vote of confidence with a new contract, Chris Speier has proved to be the extra veteran infielder every team would like to have. He showed flashes of timely hitting, defense and good speed. But he didn't show enough of any of them at age 35 to be considered an everyday player. What Speier did show was a surprising amount of power, with four homers and 24 RBIs. He has six game-winning hits even though he batted only 218 times.

Speier is a more than capable hitter for an extra man and has become a good pinch-hitter. Last year he was 5-for-12 with five RBIs and whacked a game-winning homer as a pinch-hitter.

He is no longer the baserunner that he was, but his experience makes him more than capable. He has no stolen-base speed.

Versatile as an infielder, Speier can play third, second or short, any of them adequately. He is prone to making errors.

OVERALL:

Speier won't be tagged an over-the-hill infielder if he can match his statistics of last year. He also is a good man to have on the bench, since he realizes that his role is now as a reserve.

Snider: "He has an accurate throwing arm. He won't hurt you defensively and he could help a little on offense."

BRIAN DAYETT
OF, No. 24
RR, 5'10", 185 lbs.
ML Svc: 2 years
Born: 1-22-57 in
   New London, CT

HITTING, BASERUNNING, FIELDING:

No one on the Cubs is quite sure yet what Brian Dayett can do, since he spent almost all of 1985 on the disabled list. He is 29 years old and has not had much time at the major league level.

When he was with the Yankees' Triple-A club, he had good power (35 homers) and used it well to drive in runs (108). He can smash a fastball, though he appears to have trouble with off-speed and breaking pitches. His power is to left field. He played in only 22 games with the Cubs last year before undergoing ankle surgery, but he did have four hits in 14 pinch at-bats, including a grand slam home run.

Dayett's baserunning will not be helped by his surgery. He is a very average baserunner, he does not have stolen-base speed and is inexperienced at big league baserunning.

Used mostly as an outfielder, Dayett could be switched to third base, but does not show great promise at either position. He does, however, have a good arm.

OVERALL:

The Cubs are not counting on Dayett, but feel that they should give him a chance to duplicate his minor league numbers.

Snider: "Brian is a kid with a good attitude and shows some power. He has been around for a long time and is a bit old to be just getting his chance. But if he can hit 30 home runs and do a decent job defensively, he won't be the first good player the Yankees let get away."

GARY WOODS
OF, No. 25
RR, 6'2", 190 lbs.
ML Svc: 6 years
Born: 7-20-53 in
   Santa Barbara, CA

HITTING, BASERUNNING, FIELDING:

If the National League had more lefthanded pitchers, Gary Woods might be a regular. He makes his living as a pinch-hitter and spot starter against lefties, especially Philadelphia's Steve Carlton (over the past four years, Woods is .452 against Carlton). Woods' trouble is that righthanders throw him curveballs and he just can't hit 'em.

He makes himself valuable because he still has good speed and baserunning savvy. He can be a threat to steal when he gets a hit, but is not capable of stealing any time he wants.

As an outfielder, Woods is a more than capable late-inning replacement. He rarely misjudges a fly ball, gets a good jump on it and has the speed to catch up with balls in the corner or alleys.

Woods can play any outfield position and can fill in as a catcher in an emergency. His arm is very good to exceptional.

OVERALL:

Snider: "Woods would be a good player on any club. He is best used mostly as a late-inning defensive replacement, but he is also an exceptional pinch-hitter against lefthanded pitchers."

CINCINNATI REDS

HITTING:

After years of coveting Buddy Bell, the Reds finally acquired him at mid-season last year. In doing so, they have solidified a position which has long been an organizational sore spot.

However, Bell never really got it going offensively and completed the year with a horrible .229 batting average. Obviously, NL pitchers had their way with him after he had spent his entire career in the American League. Many argue that his offensive numbers last year are understandable: the old stand-by of getting to know the new pitchers.

There are holes, however, which are evident. Bell has trouble with the fast-ball up and in--real trouble. He opens up his swing. He often fell quickly behind in the count.

Bell was better when he was facing a breaking ball pitcher. He proved himself a good breaking ball hitter, although even then he was not making good, consistent, authoritative contact.

When Bell does hit, he is a straight-away hitter with power to the alleys. Defenses are better off bunching the middle on him and giving him the lines. He doesn't pull much and doesn't punch the ball.

With all his shortcomings in 1985--reason enough to raise doubts about his ability--Bell was excellent in hit-and-run situations. He hit better when he was lower in the order, an indication that he was pressing when placed in the cleanup spot.

BASERUNNING:

Bell's speed is average, at best. He makes up for it by being aggressive, but he can take it a bit too far. He runs into outs in ill-timed attempts at extra bases.

Bell is not a threat to steal a base, but he will surprise an infield with his ability to beat out a bunt for a base hit.

FIELDING:

The Gold Gloves are part of the past,

BUDDY BELL
3B, No. 25
RR, 6'2", 185 lbs.
ML Svc: 14 years
Born: 8-27-51 in
Pittsburgh, PA

1985 STATISTICS

AVG	G	AB	R	H	2B	3B	HR	RBI	BB	SO	SB
.229	151	560	61	128	28	5	10	68	67	48	3

CAREER STATISTICS

AVG	G	AB	R	H	2B	3B	HR	RBI	BB	SO	SB
.282	1978	7500	957	2115	363	50	157	918	659	666	46

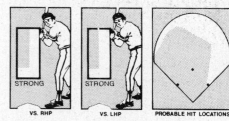

VS. RHP   VS. LHP   PROBABLE HIT LOCATIONS

but Bell remains one of the most impressive third basemen in the game. He is quick, has excellent mobility, a strong arm and a top-notch pair of hands. More than that, he seems totally at home at the position and ready for every possible situation.

Nothing seems to be beyond his reach. He exhibits far better range to his left than to his right, but he still cuts off more balls down the line than most third basemen around.

OVERALL:

Campbell: "This is a key year for Bell. His hitting was a major disappointment. The original intention of shoring up third base with a consistent hitter may be short-lived.

"The Reds need someone who can help them over the next several seasons and Bell may have already had his best years."

HITTING:

Dann Bilardello's hitting, or lack thereof, will probably put in him the role of backup catcher for the remainder of his career. He is a scrappy and devoted player, but he simply does not get to first base often enough to merit a regular spot in the lineup.

When Bilardello is hitting, he is a low-ball hitter, though even that is touch-and-go. His pitch has to be down and right over the middle of the plate. If it's inside or away, he's in trouble. Breaking balls away will fool him most of the time and he cannot handle the high, hard fastball at all.

Part of his problem is that he is always looking to pull the ball, but he generally hits it up the middle. He does not have much power and defenses will bunch him up the middle and not play very deep. If he does manage to burn them by pulling the ball down the line or by taking it to the warning track, it must be viewed as a fluke.

Like Gary Redus, Bilardello is a player in need of a change of scenery. He is convinced that he can play--and play well--for another team. His disenchantment may be partly responsible for his diminishing performance with the Reds.

BASERUNNING:

Bilardello is slow. He is no threat to steal and won't leg out an infield hit. He drags out of the batter's box and does not move well from first to third.

FIELDING:

Bilardello has a strong, accurate arm and one of the quickest releases in the National League. Some observers feel that his release is in the class of Gary Carter and Tony Pena; some say that Bilardello's release time is the quick-

DANN BILARDELLO
C, No. 11
RR, 6'0", 190 lbs.
ML Svc: 3 years
Born: 5-26-59 in
 Santa Cruz, CA

1985 STATISTICS

AVG	G	AB	R	H	2B	3B	HR	RBI	BB	SO	SB
.167	42	102	6	17	0	0	1	9	4	15	0

CAREER STATISTICS

AVG	G	AB	R	H	2B	3B	HR	RBI	BB	SO	SB
.216	219	582	49	126	25	0	12	57	38	98	2

  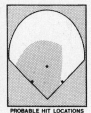

VS. RHP   VS. LHP   PROBABLE HIT LOCATIONS

est of all.

However, he has difficulty working with his pitching staff and his ability to call a game frequently comes into question. If he could learn to use his pitchers' strengths to their best advantage and coax them to their maximum effort, Bilardello might have a chance as a full-time catcher. At this point, however, he earns merely average marks.

OVERALL:

Bilardello is not ready to accept a backup position. He is looking for the opportunity to be the number one catcher on a club that believes he's their man.

Campbell: "Defensively, Dann is adequate and not much more. His hitting is not going to compensate for any of his defensive liabilities. I do not think that Dann will be more than a backup catcher."

PITCHING:

Tom Browning did only one thing wrong last season--he started his major league career the same year that Vince Coleman started his . . . if not for Coleman, Browning probably would have been the National League Rookie of the Year.

A 20-game winner, the Reds' first since 1970, Browning has an impressive array of pitches and almost unbelievable in-game composure. He didn't look like a rookie and he didn't pitch like one, either. He never rattled and seldom yielded the upperhand to the hitter.

His repertoire is built around two screwballs: a quick one that breaks sharply and another, which he uses as a change-up, that fades away and out of the strike zone. Add to this a fastball and slider, and the ability and confidence to throw all of his pitches for strikes, and you have Tom Browning.

He is not an overpowering pitcher. He may occasionally throw a fastball in the 90 MPH range, but his forte is placement and variation. Browning works a hitter "backwards," that is, exactly the opposite way a hitter might expect. When behind in the count, Browning goes to a breaking pitch. When ahead, he works the fastball or one of his breaking pitches. Hitters have to guess what's coming; if they set up for a breaking pitch, he has enough on the fastball to push it past them.

Browning's one evident weakness was a tendency to wear down in the sixth and seventh innings, when his breaking stuff often lost its bite and his fastball would start to climb in the strike zone.

Because Browning never gives in to the hitters, challenging them means that he tends to give up a lot of home runs at this point.

TOM BROWNING
LHP, No. 32
LL, 6'1", 190 lbs.
ML Svc: 1 year plus
Born: 4-28-60 in
  Casper, WY

1985 STATISTICS
W	L	ERA	G	GS	CG	SV	IP	H	R	ER	BB	SO
20	9	3.55	38	38	6	0	261.1	242	111	103	73	155

CAREER STATISTICS
W	L	ERA	G	GS	CG	SV	IP	H	R	ER	BB	SO
21	9	3.38	42	42	6	0	284.2	269	114	107	78	169

FIELDING, HITTING, BASERUNNING:

Browning may be just as good a fielder as he is a pitcher. He throws himself into this part of the game just as he does into his pitching. It is not uncommon to see him dive off the mound to make a catch. His move, however, is just average.

He will hit and show some power and can bunt for a hit. He is not afraid to try to break up a double play at second base.

OVERALL:

There is little not to like about Browning. He is a throwback type of player who plays hard all of the time.

Campbell: "Browning is an excellent competitor. He goes right after the hitters and shows an awful lot of savvy for a kid his age. I think that he's the closest thing to being another Fernando Valenzuela in the National League. He has the same types of pitches and the same type of superb ability."

HITTING:

The good days are definitely gone. Though Dave Concepcion had a 17-game hitting streak last year (the longest of his career), he was spotty too often at the plate. He was undependable in the clutch, where he once excelled, and he was unreliable with men in scoring position, where he originally made his reputation.

Most of Concepcion's offensive problems stem from the fact that he can no longer get around on the high fastball and is terribly fooled by breaking stuff away. Occasionally, he will take the high fastball to right field but he has a tendency to pull off the ball and consequently doesn't have much success. He needs to shorten up on his swing, narrow his strike zone and recognize that he is no longer 25 years old.

In one respect, however, Concepcion acts as if he's 22. When he starts going badly, he really goes down, allowing the slump to rule him not only at the plate but in the field. Last season, in one particularly bad stretch, Concepcion seriously considered retiring. He can still contribute, and does at times, but he is also a player who can really hurt his club because of his inability to bounce back in the bad times.

Concepcion can bunt for hits. In hit-and-run situations, he will put the bat on the ball. In that respect, his fundamentals are still sound.

BASERUNNING:

When the mood strikes him, Concepcion can still get out of the box quickly, beat out an infield hit, steal a base or score from first on a double. But the mood isn't always with him; sometimes Concepcion runs the bases as if he is tired. With a game on the line, he still gives his all.

FIELDING:

Concepcion's range has decreased significantly. His arm has lost a lot of

DAVE CONCEPCION
SS, No. 13
RR, 6'1", 190 lbs.
ML Svc: 16 years
Born: 6-17-48 in
Aragua, VEN

1985 STATISTICS

AVG	G	AB	R	H	2B	3B	HR	RBI	BB	SO	SB
.252	155	560	59	141	19	2	7	48	50	67	16

CAREER STATISTICS

AVG	G	AB	R	H	2B	3B	HR	RBI	BB	SO	SB
.267	2210	7936	908	2117	352	46	97	879	664	1096	301

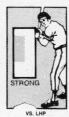
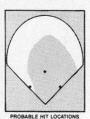

STRONG VS. RHP   STRONG VS. LHP   PROBABLE HIT LOCATIONS

its pop and he doesn't always make up for his losses with good positioning. But there are frequently times when his former brilliance at shortstop returns. He still gets up about as high as anyone around for line drives and still uses his patented one-hop, Astroturf throw to first when pushed deep in the hole at third. The presence of Bell at third and Oester at second helps a lot.

OVERALL:

Pete Rose argues that with a renewed concentration on his work habits and recognition of his limitations, Dave can still be productive. This is a make or break year for him as an everyday shortstop. The Reds are looking closely at minor league prospect Kurt Stillwell.

Campbell: "I think if Pete Rose has one major project this year, it's Dave Concepcion. Davey can do just about anything he wants to in this game; the trouble, however, is making him want to play well everyday."

HITTING:

Much of Eric Davis's problems last year were the result of listening to banquet circuit puff and praise all winter long. By the time he arrived at spring training, he believed he was Willie Mays. He is not.

He is a powerful hitter with amazingly fast, strong hands but was swinging for the stars while believing he was one himself in the early part of 1985. He was overswinging the bat to such an extent that he nearly hurt himself on more than one occasion.

For all his gifts--which begin with power to all fields--Davis would not tame his stroke. When he rejected direction from the club's hitting instructor, he was quickly sent packing and found himself carrying a sub-.200 average onto a minor league bus.

Reprieved in September, Davis returned to the Reds a changed and humbled player. He was less vulnerable to high, hard stuff and showed signs of improvement in adjusting with the count and shortening his swing when necessary. He also displayed a willingness to work on his swing and to listen to his coaches.

Early in the year, Davis needed a sweet fastball out over the plate to display his breathtaking power, but in September he would go with the pitch and line balls out of the park to the opposite field. He was also content with a base hit to right and didn't always bite on the fastball up and in. He still has trouble with slow breaking balls, but is showing improvement in that area as well. However, the best course for opposing pitchers remains working him up and in and also with breaking stuff away.

BASERUNNING:

Exceedingly fast. If he can get on, he can steal. He has Vince Coleman-like ability in this area, except that Davis cannot get on base as often as the Cardinals' sensation. Davis has the raw speed that can turn a mistake into an

ERIC DAVIS
OF, No. 44
RR, 6'2", 170 lbs.
ML Svc: 2 years
Born: 5-29-62 in
Los Angeles, CA

```
1985 STATISTICS
AVG  G   AB   R   H  2B 3B HR RBI BB SO SB
.246 56 122 26 30  3  3  8  18  7 39 16
CAREER STATISTICS
AVG  G   AB   R   H  2B 3B HR RBI BB SO SB
.233 113 296 59 69 13  4  18  48 31 87 26
```

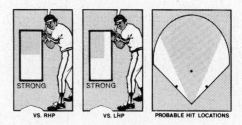

extra base. His speed can freeze his opponents into wide-eyed hesitation.

FIELDING:

Blessed with a tremendous arm and speed, Davis can be dazzling in the outfield. He gets a good read on the ball and those he does not judge well he simply runs down. He shows no weaknesses in going to his right, left or back on a ball. He does, however, show off his arm and will overthrow the cutoff man.

OVERALL:

Davis needs discipline in every aspect of his game outside of baserunning. He needs to prove that he wants to stick with what is best for the team.

Campbell: "Eric is a tremendously gifted athlete with extraordinary power and speed. He makes amazing catches in center field. He has so much potential but he must develop a more suitable approach at the plate."

HITTING:

Bo Diaz has a stance for every occasion, every pitcher, different pitches, day games, night games and doubleheaders. A bit of an exaggeration, perhaps, but Diaz is a classic free-swinger who changes his stance at the plate as whimsy dictates.

Regardless of the stance used or the changes he may make during an at-bat, Diaz likes the ball up in the strike zone, especially the fastball, and has problems with breaking balls away.

A pull hitter by nature, Diaz has trouble with anything thrown down and away. He'll whale at it, but seldom with productive results. He will hit the mistake pitch.

Diaz doesn't walk much, but he can bunt and generally makes some sort of contact. However, he's not the type of hitter who should be called on for a hit-and-run play.

Many believe he is not the hitter he was in 1980. There is some indication that his faults at the plate last season were the result of his limited playing time in 1984, when he was sidelined by injuries, and his infrequent appearances with the Phillies early in 1985.

BASERUNNING:

Diaz is among the slowest of the slow runners in baseball. Can't get out of the box. Can't steal a base. Can't score from second on a base hit. Knee injuries have really taken a tremendous toll on his baserunning.

FIELDING:

After several unsuccessful experiments with various catchers (the position has been a Reds weak spot since John Bench retired), Diaz seemed to be the type of catcher the team felt would perform well both defensively and offensively.

He gave the Reds just what they were

BO DIAZ
C, No. 6
RR, 5'11", 200 lbs.
ML Svc: 8 years
Born: 3-23-53 in
 Cua, VEN

1985 STATISTICS

AVG	G	AB	R	H	2B	3B	HR	RBI	BB	SO	SB
.245	77	237	21	58	13	1	5	31	21	25	0

CAREER STATISTICS

AVG	G	AB	R	H	2B	3B	HR	RBI	BB	SO	SB
.256	584	1857	196	475	99	4	51	271	126	256	7

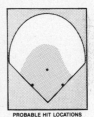

VS. RHP   VS. LHP   PROBABLE HIT LOCATIONS

looking for. He has a strong, accurate arm, and after he arrived, the Reds gave up fewer stolen bases. He also proved himself as a handler of pitchers. The staff ERA dropped by nearly a point after Diaz took over the everyday job.

OVERALL:

The Reds will be happy if Diaz can maintain his defensive skills and bat .260 this year. However, they would like him to improve his run production and hit with more consistency in the clutch. Some observers believe that won't happen and that Diaz is another whose best years are gone.

Campbell: "Diaz is facing a key year. Maybe it was just that he had a lot of rust on him and he needed some time to get his sea legs. Maybe not. But to me, he doesn't look like the same hitter he was in his prime years, 1982-83. He has to improve at the plate to show that he is not just another Reds Band-Aid."

HITTING:

Last season can be noted as the year Nick Esasky gave notice of his arrival. In only 125 at-bats, he hammered 21 home runs and knocked in 66 runs. Esasky's improvement was based on two changes. First, he shortened his batting stroke, and consequently, made better contact. The second change--moving from third base to left field--gave him an opportunity to play every day and to refine his stroke. Not only did he get more at-bats, but he seemed to be more relaxed in the outfield.

Esasky still needs work on his swing. From time to time, he tends to revert to a big, uncontrolled cut at pitches up and out of the strike zone. That's his primary weakness--hard stuff up. He chases breaking balls away, particularly when he is behind in the count. At times, he forgets himself completely and chases really bad pitches down, up, in, away--anything but strikes.

A powerful pull hitter with extremely strong hands, Esasky likes the fastball, and he likes it between the belt and the letters. That's the pitch he will burn and hit to all fields. A year ago he would have tried to pull it; he now goes with the pitch to drive it to the alley in right-center.

The key element in Esasky's production is concentration. He oscillates between being a thoughtless free-swinger in one at-bat and a disciplined, dangerous power hitter in the next.

Red's hitting instructor Billy DeMars has been responsible for Esasky's emergence as a competent hitter. When Esasky is at the plate, watch DeMars in the third base coach's box. DeMars continually urges Esasky to stay alive and shorten his stroke. Even when a play is not on, Esasky will step out of the box and look at DeMars for instruction.

BASERUNNING:

Esasky is faster than he looks. He gets out of the box well and will beat out a chop-hit in the infield. He is not

NICK ESASKY
3B, No. 12
RR, 6'3", 200 lbs.
ML Svc: 3 years
Born: 2-24-60 in
    Hialeah, FL

1985 STATISTICS

AVG	G	AB	R	H	2B	3B	HR	RBI	BB	SO	SB
.262	125	413	61	108	21	0	21	66	41	102	3

CAREER STATISTICS

AVG	G	AB	R	H	2B	3B	HR	RBI	BB	SO	SB
.241	323	1037	132	250	41	10	43	157	120	304	10

  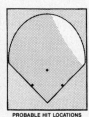

STRONG STRONG

VS. RHP   VS. LHP   PROBABLE HIT LOCATIONS

a threat to steal, however. He sometimes fades out of a play and makes mistakes.

FIELDING:

Right now, Esasky is probably a below-average fielder, but he is still learning a new position. He doesn't exhibit great range. He is better at coming in on balls and going to the line than he is going into the alley. Like Dave Parker, however, he benefits from the greyhounds in center field. His arm is good, better-than-average, but he hesitates at times deciding exactly where to throw.

OVERALL:

Campbell: "Nick has improved. He has cut his strikeouts down from one in every three at-bats to one in every four. But the verdict is still out on him as a hitter. He has enormous power, but he has yet to prove himself with the type of consistency that puts fear in the heart of a pitcher."

PITCHING:

John Franco was one of the true finds of the 1985 season. Working as the setup man for reliever Ted Power, Franco reeled off a string of 11 consecutive victories without a loss and kept the Reds in just about every game he appeared in.

Though slight of stature, Franco is a power pitcher who relies on a fastball, a slider and an especially nasty little change-up which has the appearance of a screwball.

More often than not, the change-up is Franco's out pitch. He sets up lefthanded hitters with the fastball and slider away and then throws the change-up in on the fists. With its 90-plus MPH velocity and good location, his fastball is a weapon in its own right. Against righthanded hitters, Franco runs the fastball in, mixes in the slider and throws the change-up down and away.

He is equally confounding to left- and righthanded hitters. The fastball/change-up combination makes it difficult for hitters to draw a bead on Franco. He has enough velocity on the fastball that hitters cannot wait for the change-up.

When Franco is on, hitters will go down in a rapid succession of ground ball outs and routine pop flies.

He's tough to hit and tougher to scare. Brooklyn-born, Franco takes a street-wise savvy and determination to the game. That often gets him by when he doesn't have his best stuff.

FIELDING, HITTING, BASERUNNING:

Franco has an excellent move to first base; it's probably the best move on the

JOHN FRANCO
LHP, No. 31
LL, 5'10", 175 lbs.
ML Svc: 2 years
Born: 9-17-60 in
Brooklyn, NY

1985 STATISTICS
W	L	ERA	G	GS	CG	SV	IP	H	R	ER	BB	SO
12	3	2.18	67	0	0	12	99	83	27	24	40	61

CAREER STATISTICS
W	L	ERA	G	GS	CG	SV	IP	H	R	ER	BB	SO
18	5	2.37	121	0	0	16	178.1	157	55	47	76	116

staff. He fields his position well and has a keen sense of the game--he will seldom be caught hesitating or throwing to the wrong base.

He can bunt and will put the bat on the ball. He's quick and alert on the bases.

OVERALL:

Franco made great strides during the 1985 season. He showed stamina he didn't seem to have the year before and was able to pitch the entire season whenever he was needed. His off-season conditioning and Nautilus program enabled him to be a stronger pitcher throughout the year.

Campbell: "A tough little competitor. All in all, Franco was one of the big pitching pluses for the Reds. He was an excellent setup man for Ted Power and in this day and age, the setup man and the stopper are two of the most important people on a baseball team."

CINCINNATI REDS

PITCHING:

Tom Hume took a large step last season toward reclaiming a career that appeared to be on its last legs. His sinkerball was back, the velocity on his fastball improved and he showed a curveball that may have become his best pitch.

Such were Hume's overall improvements--not the least of those a rise in confidence--that player-manager Pete Rose had no reluctance in using Hume in save situations though his primary role was as a set-up man and middle reliever.

Hume, who works with a classic overhand motion, can throw all three pitches for strikes but thrives on the sinker and curve. He'll mix in a change and a slider here and there, but they are not out pitches. Hume showed no reluctance in challenging hitters with the fastball, as he did in 1984, which only made his curveball more effective.

Like most sinkerball pitchers, Hume is subject to "bad break" hits--ground balls that get through the holes and broken bat bloopers over the infield. When he isn't on his game, he gets the ball up and those bloopers and seeing-eye hits turn into line drives. He is a pitcher who can't hide his bad days.

Possibly most important in all his improvements is his change in self-confidence. There were times in the past two years when Hume admitted he had lost the belief that he would throw strikes and get hitters out. He seems to have whipped that attitude which threatened to abbreviate his career.

FIELDING, HITTING, BASERUNNING:

A shortstop as a high school player, Hume is a reliable fielder who keeps his

TOM HUME
RHP, No. 47
RR, 6'1", 185 lbs.
ML Svc: 9 years
Born: 3-29-53 in
    Cincinnati, OH

1985 STATISTICS

W	L	ERA	G	GS	CG	SV	IP	H	R	ER	BB	SO
3	5	3.26	56	0	0	3	80	65	33	29	35	50

CAREER STATISTICS

W	L	ERA	G	GS	CG	SV	IP	H	R	ER	BB	SO
51	66	3.82	446	48	5	88	908	928	430	386	307	452

head in the game. His move is average, but he manages to keep runners fairly honest.

He will put the bat on the ball and is a reliable bunter in sacrifice situations. Though not fleet-footed, he can be counted on as a baserunner.

OVERALL:

Hume still hasn't regained the stuff that made him one of the game's premier relievers--and he may not. However, he has made key improvements, not the least of those adjusting to the role of middle reliever and setup man.

Campbell: " I said last year 1985 would be a make or break year for Tom Hume. I think he showed enough to warrant another shot in '86. It was nice to see him come back. He's a quality individual, a hard worker. He finally got his arm nearly back to what it was, though his stuff is still not what it used to be.

"Hume is not a pitcher who will beat himself."

HITTING:

If every pitcher in baseball was a righthander, Wayne Krenchicki would be a perennial .300-plus hitter. He thrives on righthanded pitching and gets killed by lefthanders. His inability to hit southpaw pitching prevents him from being an everyday player.

Strictly a spot player and pinch-hitter since the Reds acquired Buddy Bell to play third base, Krenchicki is a pull hitter who will occasionally hit with power. He could help himself, however, by going with the pitch more often.

Primarily a first-ball, fastball hitter, Krenchicki likes the ball belt-high and inside. Unlike many other hitters, however, he can hurt you on a fastball down and in. He'll go get it and line it to right field or to the alley in right-center.

Krenchicki has a big swing and sometimes commits himself early. Consequently, he can be fooled on slow breaking balls. He also has trouble with fastballs away because he tries to pull the pitch.

The deeper a pitcher can work him in the count, the better; Krenchicki does not adjust well, and in the long run, this may hurt him as a pinch-hitter. In any case, the best course against him is a steady diet of breaking balls.

At this stage in his career, he is a player who needs playing time to be at his best. Whether or not he makes it as a pinch-hitter will probably depend on how many at-bats he receives between assignments as a pinch-hitter.

BASERUNNING:

Krenchicki is not fast, but he is not dumb. He can steal a base and perform effectively in a hit-and-run situation. But on a team with so much speed off the bench, Krenchicki is usually dropped for a pinch-runner late in a tight game.

FIELDING:

Krenchicki can be downright flashy

WAYNE KRENCHICKI
INF, No. 15
LR, 6'1", 180 lbs.
ML Svc: 7 years
Born: 9-17-54 in
Trenton, NJ

1985 STATISTICS											
AVG	G	AB	R	H	2B	3B	HR	RBI	BB	SO	SB
.272	90	173	16	47	9	0	4	25	28	20	0
CAREER STATISTICS											
AVG	G	AB	R	H	2B	3B	HR	RBI	BB	SO	SB
.273	449	842	86	230	38	3	13	101	84	109	5

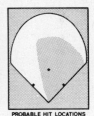

VS. RHP VS. LHP PROBABLE HIT LOCATIONS

at third base. A product of the Orioles organization, he throws in a manner reminiscent of Brooks Robinson. He has the same dramatic overhand motion and puts some juice on the ball. His range is average and is better to his right than to his left.

A third baseman by trade, Krenchicki can also fill in at second and short. He excels at covering bunts down the third base line.

OVERALL:

Krenchicki is a gamer and a hard worker in the process of adapting to the role of pinch-hitter. He is a good back-up who is aware of his limitations.

Campbell: "Wayne is the type of hitter who doesn't scare in the clutch and always gives you his best. His best role is as a pinch-hitter.

"Do not throw this guy first-ball, fastballs anywhere near the middle of the plate!"

GOOD CONTROL

PITCHING:

Andy McGaffigan is finally getting some respect. Previously viewed by most as a middle reliever of modest skills, he developed a change-up last season. It has made a big difference.

Prior to the change-up, McGaffigan was, well, not mediocre, but undistinguished. He is now a quality starting pitcher with strikeout artist potential.

He blends the change-up, whose development was suggested in these pages last year, with a fastball that crests at 87-88 MPH. His change-up does what it is supposed to do very effectively: it falls off to about 75 MPH and drops out of the strike zone. It's not uncommon for McGaffigan to register seven or eight strikeouts with this fastball/change-up routine in five innings.

His change-up, similar in disguise to Mario Soto's best, is thrown with good arm-speed. As it approaches the plate, it drops down and in to a righthanded hitter, and goes down and away to a lefty.

His fastball is sound, has good movement and is generally well placed. Andy will mix in a breaking pitch now and then, but neither his slider nor his curve is very good. He lacks confidence in both.

McGaffigan's goal is to set up the change-up. He has a good mental approach to the game, doesn't weaken when things go wrong and isn't afraid to turn back to the change-up even if it is hit hard.

McGaffigan is not yet a dominating pitcher. It may be that he will have to refine one of his breaking pitches to complement the fastball/change-up combo.

FIELDING, HITTING, BASERUNNING:

McGaffigan is an agile athlete whose

ANDY McGAFFIGAN
RHP, No. 37
RR, 6'3", 195 lbs.
ML Svc: 3 years
Born: 10-25-56 in
W. Palm Beach, FL

1985 STATISTICS

W	L	ERA	G	GS	CG	SV	IP	H	R	ER	BB	SO
3	3	3.72	15	15	2	0	94.1	88	40	39	30	83

CAREER STATISTICS

W	L	ERA	G	GS	CG	SV	IP	H	R	ER	BB	SO
10	18	3.80	94	37	2	3	312.2	289	139	132	96	239

daily routine includes a round of Hacky-sack. He is a good fielder and although his move to first is just average, he does keep baserunners honest. As with Soto, McGaffigan's change-up gives base-stealers an advantage.

He can bunt, but he is not a hitter. On the bases, he is smart and quick.

OVERALL:

Formerly a middle reliever and spot-starter, McGaffigan now earns his pay as a starter. He had a tough time getting wins in 1985, but he kept the Reds in many games in the last half.

Campbell: "Here is a guy who proved that an extra pitch can turn a career around. McGaffigan is now on his way to creating a reputation as a quality performer. The key is the change-up. While it has not made him the number one man in the rotation, he has shown that he is a good fourth or fifth starter."

HITTING:

Eddie Milner is 20 points short of being an excellent leadoff man. A .250 spray hitter, he bunts well, can hit to all fields and has a reasonably good idea of the strike zone.

Used primarily against righthanded pitching, Milner likes the ball up and is a fair breaking ball hitter.

He has a tendency to jump at the fastball up an in, but he generally misses it; pitchers work on that weakness. The best way to deal with Milner, however, is to work the ball in and out, up and down with hard stuff. Move the ball around and he has trouble. Milner works the count deep on most occasions but he will swing on a mistake pitch and has definite extra-base power to the gaps in left- and right-center.

Milner is not afraid to give himself up and do what is most beneficial to his club. He prides himself not on numbers but on overall contributions--not the least of them being his defensive play.

Milner is not an easy out, but he's not a lightweight either.

BASERUNNING:

Milner is one of the quickest runners around. He can turn bunts and chop hits in the infield into base hits. He will steal bases, but he doesn't always get a good read on a pitcher or a good jump. He is often in the position of having to make up for a mistake in judgment on a stolen base by turning on his speed.

FIELDING:

Fielding is Milner's forte. His defensive ability in center field might be surpassed in the National League only by the Cardinals' Willie McGee.

Besides having excellent speed, Eddie

EDDIE MILNER
OF, No. 20
LL, 5'11", 170 lbs.
ML Svc: 6 years
Born: 5-21-55 in
Columbus, OH

1985 STATISTICS

AVG	G	AB	R	H	2B	3B	HR	RBI	BB	SO	SB
.254	145	453	82	115	19	7	3	33	61	31	35

CAREER STATISTICS

AVG	G	AB	R	H	2B	3B	HR	RBI	BB	SO	SB
.303	535	1706	265	434	74	22	23	127	222	182	115

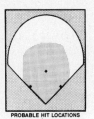

gets a tremendous jump on the ball and is seldom fooled. He leaps well and makes up for the limitations of both the left and right fielders. He has a strong (not excellent) arm and is accurate with his throws. He doesn't miss his cutoff men and stays in the game.

OVERALL:

Milner is an adequate leadoff man whose defensive abilities make up for his offensive limitations.

Campbell: "The only thing wrong with Milner is that he will probably never hit .280 or .290 consistently and draw the 100 walks or so you would like to see out of a leadoff man. Defensively, however, he is an excellent center fielder."

HITTING:

Ron Oester finally put together a full, productive season. He has broken his pattern of producing for only half a season and played consistently throughout the entire 1985 season.

Oester's 1985 performance was the result of changes he made at the plate under the guidance of Reds' hitting instructor Billy DeMars. Instead of trying to pull every pitch no matter where it was, Ron has worked to become a solid contact man who now hits the ball to all fields and with authority from both sides of the plate.

Oester has developed the ability to hit the ball where it is pitched and is content with base hits. He no longer envisions himself as a run producer and power hitter.

He has shortened and flattened his swing and now hits the down and away pitch to the opposite field. A pitcher's best bet is to work him up and in with hard stuff and down with breaking balls. Oester still likes any pitch that allows him to extend his arms and pull the ball --often with extra-base results.

As a switch-hitter, he used to be a much better hitter lefthanded, but he is now equally effective as a righthanded hitter. Yet another improvement is his increased selectivity. He has become more aware of the strike zone and is a much more patient hitter these days.

BASERUNNING:

Oester is a faster, longer, leaner version of Pete Rose. He runs the bases with the same sort of headfirst enthusiasm but not always with the same wisdom. Oester is a gambler, but picks his spots --particularly when stealing. He has better-than-average speed, but his judgment is poor. He can botch a rally with an inexplicable baserunning mistake.

FIELDING:

Oester may be the best second baseman in the league. He has a better arm than

RON OESTER
2B, No. 16
SR, 6'2", 190 lbs.
ML Svc: 6 years
Born: 5-5-56 in
   Cincinnati, OH

1985 STATISTICS
AVG	G	AB	R	H	2B	3B	HR	RBI	BB	SO	SB
.295	152	526	59	155	26	3	1	34	51	65	5

CAREER STATISTICS
AVG	G	AB	R	H	2B	3B	HR	RBI	BB	SO	SB
.267	827	2845	325	760	126	24	31	240	244	446	27

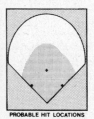

VS. RHP   VS. LHP   PROBABLE HIT LOCATIONS

anyone else at the position. His range is average, though it is better to his left than his right. He makes up for any range shortage by anticipating and reacting well. No one around makes the double play pivot as well or with as much grit. He will take his knocks and still make an accurate throw.

He can also play shortstop--a weak spot for the Reds--but he is such a good second baseman that it would hurt the team too much to move him.

OVERALL:

Oester is beginning to come into his own as a hitter. His power numbers were sacrificed for getting on base and hitting for average.

Campbell: "I believe that Ron is the best defensive second baseman in the NL. He is a much-improved hitter and helped the Reds climb from fifth place to second last year. In my opinion, he is one of the most underrated players in the National League."

HITTING:

Dave Parker played with a vengeance in 1985, determined to prove one thing: that he was far from finished. Parker achieved that goal, ending the year as the league leader in both RBIs and doubles, and second in the league in home runs and hits. He was just a whisper away from being named the National League's MVP.

There is only one way to pitch to Parker: inside with hard stuff; give him little else. With a peculiar, almost awkward-looking stance (he waves his bat high above his head), he sprays breaking balls pitched away to left field, often for extra bases. If pitchers work him low, they will find him an awesome low-ball hitter.

Nevertheless, Parker's favorite pitch is the fastball up and right over the plate. He pulls it fiercely, hitting line drives that often soar out of the park.

Parker displays a rare ability for a capable power hitter--he does not look at each at-bat as a home run opportunity. He assesses each situation separately: the count, the pitcher, the options and the best way to help his team.

From a spectator's standpoint, he is a joy to watch. But from the mound, he is a big, bad nightmare.

BASERUNNING:

Parker is aggressive on the bases and has relatively good speed--once he gets started. He will attempt to steal (he was 5 for 18 in 1985) but does not get a good jump. He used to have better-than-average speed, but now doesn't seem to understand that those days are gone.

Few go after the pivot man on a double play ball with as much fervor as Parker--it doesn't matter if it's the first or ninth inning, April or August.

FIELDING:

Parker used to have a cannon for an arm; it is no longer what it once was,

DAVE PARKER
RF, No. 39
LR, 6'5", 230 lbs.
ML Svc: 13 years
Born: 6-9-51 in
   Jackson, MS

1985 STATISTICS
AVG	G	AB	R	H	2B	3B	HR	RBI	BB	SO	SB
.312	160	635	88	198	42	4	34	125	52	80	5

CAREER STATISTICS
AVG	G	AB	R	H	2B	3B	HR	RBI	BB	SO	SB
.304	1617	6090	889	1850	366	66	216	977	439	946	139

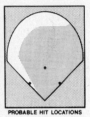

VS. RHP   VS. LHP   PROBABLE HIT LOCATIONS

but it remains better than average. He still enjoys challenging baserunners and most pay him due respect, holding up on anything Parker plays waist-high and in front of his body. He covers right field well, but is blessed by having speedsters like Eddie Milner and Eric Davis in center field to help with the alley.

Hard-hit balls that sail toward his ankles or knees give him a lot of trouble; it is a flaw which has plagued him during his entire career. Heads-up baserunners take advantage of him.

OVERALL:

Dave Parker has re-established himself among the best in the game. How long he can continue playing 160 games a year is another question.

Campbell: "Dave had an MVP season. Obviously, baseball was fun again for him and 1985 was a year of vindication. What we saw was vintage Dave Parker. He was certainly the reason the Reds made such a strong move in the Western Division last year."

PITCHING:

For the second straight year, an injury stalled Frank Pastore just as it appeared he was about to regain his position as a quality major league pitcher. Generally regarded as a pitcher with excellent stuff, he was disabled at midseason and underwent surgery on his right elbow.

When healthy, Pastore is a fastball pitcher with a newly developed curveball/sinker, a pitch with such a good break that some have suspected it of being a spitter. That suspicion, when combined with a change-up and precise location, can make Pastore a formidable opponent on his good days.

Before his surgery last season, he was pitching as if he were finally on the verge of taking over a permanent spot in the Reds' starting rotation. Not only did his control problems appear to be behind him, but it also seemed he had shelved the mental games which, in the past, belabored his efforts.

However, as good as Pastore looked on his best days, there were others, though fewer in number, when he looked no better than mediocre--and maybe worse--prompting the conclusion once again that Pastore was through.

When he pitches badly, his fastball is flat and what location he has favors the hitter. It can look as though he is throwing batting practice instead of pitching a game.

Early in the season, Pastore experimented with an abbreviated, no-kick style of delivery. He abandoned it just before he went on the disabled list in July, returning to a more traditional, over-the-top delivery.

Pastore, once a cornerstone in the Reds' pitching plans, is probably destined to do middle relief and mop-up work until he proves he can once more be a consistent, reliable starter. The surgery might help him get there.

FRANK PASTORE
RHP, No. 35
RR, 6'3", 215 lbs.
ML Svc: 7 years
Born: 8-21-57 in
Alhambra, CA

1985 STATISTICS

W	L	ERA	G	GS	CG	SV	IP	H	R	ER	BB	SO
2	1	3.83	17	6	1	0	54	60	23	23	16	29

CAREER STATISTICS

W	L	ERA	G	GS	CG	SV	IP	H	R	ER	BB	SO
45	57	4.30	187	138	22	4	937	975	479	448	277	523

FIELDING, HITTING, BASERUNNING:

Pastore is a good fielder, though not flashy. Regardless of his difficulties on the mound, he is reliable in the field. He's a tad slow in getting off the mound for bunts and to cover first, but generally gets the job done. His move, even when using his traditional windup, is one of the quickest in the league.

Not much of a hitter, Pastore will get the bunt down to move a runner over.

OVERALL:

For the past two years, some observers have been poised to throw a blanket over Pastore and write him off as finished. It is entirely possible that his elbow problems were the primary cause for his ineffectiveness on the mound. The last bit of his career may well depend on how he responds to surgery.

Campbell: "Unless there is a miracle in the arm, or unless he comes up with the split-finger pitch or something of that nature, I think his career is basically over."

HITTING:

One of the great clutch RBI men ever to play the game, Tony Perez continues to produce the big hit, whether as a pinch-hitter or a platoon player.

Never mind that he will be 44 years old this season. If Perez has lost anything to age, it is a consistent display of power, though he still goes deep, particularly if a pitcher gets the ball up in his sweet spot.

Perez remains a smart hitter. Reduced bat speed has been replaced by concentrating on hitting to all fields while going with the pitch, the count and the situation.

Perez is extremely difficult to pitch to for three reasons. One, he has an excellent awareness of the strike zone and, two, he has good bat control. This becomes a complicated matter for opposing pitchers because, lastly, Perez is also an excellent bad-ball hitter. A pitcher who works him carefully is often victimized when he tries to waste a pitch.

Reduced bat speed does lead to one vulnerability: power pitchers can get Perez out by working him up and in with fastballs and down and away with breaking pitches. This is particularly true for the stronger righthanded pitchers.

Perez's greatest strides in the past two years have been made as a pinch-hitter. Like Rusty Staub and a few others in the game, he is one who anticipates his situation--late innings with the game on the line--readies himself and, more often than not, produces. The delight in watching Perez in this situation is the way he alters his swing to fit the need.

BASERUNNING:

Perez was once called the "Cuban Comet" because of his speed. But time has taken away his flash. Perez is slow. He plays it safe and gets by on smarts. He won't take his team out of a rally and is still heads-up enough that

TONY PEREZ
1B, No. 24
RR, 6'2", 210 lbs.
ML Svc: 22 years
Born: 5-14-42 in
    Camaguey, CU

1985 STATISTICS
AVG	G	AB	R	H	2B	3B	HR	RBI	BB	SO	SB
.238	72	183	25	60	8	0	6	33	22	22	0

CAREER STATISTICS
AVG	G	AB	R	H	2B	3B	HR	RBI	BB	SO	SB
.280	2700	4578	1258	2681	493	78	377	1623	900	1842	49

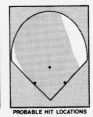

STRONG — VS. RHP   STRONG — VS. LHP   PROBABLE HIT LOCATIONS

the Reds will put on the hit-and-run with him at first. Late in a game, though, he will usually be replaced by a pinch-runner.

FIELDING:

Perez still has good hands and quick reactions, but his lateral movement is restricted and his footwork is slow. This shows up particularly in a 3-6-3 double play attempt. Basically, Perez handles the balls hit at him but not much more.

OVERALL:

Few will come through at the plate with the consistency of Perez. He is strictly a role player now, platooning with Pete Rose at first base against lefthanded pitchers and pinch-hitting.

Campbell: "Perez continues to contribute. The situation with Tony and Pete platooning at first is ideal. Perez cannot play more than 60 or 70 games a year, but he is still a great clutch hitter who knows his limitations."

PITCHING:

Under the tutelage of former Reds' pitching coach Jim Kaat and player-manager Pete Rose, Ted Power brings a no-nonsense, strength-to-strength attitude to the game. Whether he succeeds or fails, Power sticks with his hard stuff, which is consistently in the 90-plus MPH range. His fastball has exceptional movement; hitters will often swing wildly over it. On occasion, he will mix in a change-up, but that pitch is a gift for the hitter.

Like most short relievers, Power is best when he is working frequently. After too many days off, he will overthrow the ball and his control suffers. When he is off, he is off in the worst possible place--up in the strike zone.

Short relievers must be able to come into the game quickly and be ready to retire the first batter he faces. On this point, Power has been inconsistent; he often makes a tight game tighter before he is able to powerpunch his way out of it. When the first couple of hitters sense this, the diamond can be his deathtrap.

It's possible that he has not yet developed an efficient warmup routine or that he is unable to bear down quickly enough to maintain his control. Whatever the case, Power must be able to come in and shut the door more reliably.

FIELDING, HITTING, BASERUNNING:

He is an adequate fielder with an average move to first base. For a guy his size, Power is quicker and more agile than might be expected.

TED POWER
RHP, NO. 48
RR, 6'4", 225 lbs.
ML Svc: 4 years
Born: 1-31-55 in
Guthrie, OK

1985 STATISTICS

W	L	ERA	G	GS	CG	SV	IP	H	R	ER	BB	SO
8	6	2.70	64	0	0	27	80	65	27	24	45	42

CAREER STATISTICS

W	L	ERA	G	GS	CG	SV	IP	H	R	ER	BB	SO
24	23	3.73	208	12	1	40	347.1	332	159	144	170	202

He is not much of a hitter at all and is questionable when called upon to lay down a sacrifice bunt. He won't stun anyone with his footspeed on the bases and generally plays it safe.

OVERALL:

Power is coming off his finest professional season, one which many believe will be the foundation for an illustrious career. If he conquers those early control problems, he could be a perennial contender for Fireman of the Year.

Campbell: "Power is a reliever who seemed to come into his own last year. He is not the type of guy who scares or minds the tough situations. It does seem, however, that he lets his some of the bad outings get to him and affect his next appearance.

"He has a great fastball and the potential to be one of the league's best short relievers."

PITCHING:

Tall and lanky in stature, slow and deliberate in motion, Joe Price works the corners with a slider, change-up and curveball, and then brings in a fastball with surprising velocity.

At his best, Price hits the corners and has good velocity on the fastball. Hitters are continually off-balance and behind in the count. With the count in the batter's favor, Price is forced to come into the strike zone; then he can run into trouble. Without benefit of surprise and guile, his stuff is not overpowering.

Price has confidence in all of his pitches, but he uses the fastball to set up his breaking pitches. He was hampered last season because an arm injury (which subsequently led to surgery) limited the use of his breaking ball. Price uses any of his breaking stuff as an out pitch; without them at his beck and call, he is ineffective.

A thinking man's pitcher, Price approaches each outing as a problem and each hitter as a necessary step toward the correct solution. Preferring a spot in the rotation, he was somewhat affected by his role as a setup man and would sometimes let his disappointment affect his performance on the mound. He needs both his wits and his best stuff to win. If either are not in place, he will have problems; generally, they manifest early as walks.

When Price is on top of his game, hitters will be off-stride and ahead of the breaking pitches. He is doing well when hitters can only manage weak fly balls, routine ground outs and a scarcity of walks. If it is not his day, hitters will be on him from the start.

FIELDING, HITTING, BASERUNNING:

Price's move to first is nearly as

JOE PRICE
LHP, No. 49
RL, 6'4", 215 lbs.
ML Svc: 6 years
Born: 11-29-56 in
Inglewood, CA

1985 STATISTICS

W	L	ERA	G	GS	CG	SV	IP	H	R	ER	BB	SO
2	2	3.90	26	8	0	1	64.2	59	35	28	23	52

CAREER STATISTICS

W	L	ERA	G	GS	CG	SV	IP	H	R	ER	BB	SO
35	29	3.37	201	73	10	2	618	563	262	236	217	420

deliberate as his motion. He will keep runners close, but will not pick off many baserunners. He is adequate as a fielder, but he is not a hitter. He is not a good bet to get down the necessary bunt. On the bases, he is slow and unaggressive yet alert.

OVERALL:

Price is something of an enigma. He either has it all or he has nothing. The latter was more the case last season. Part of that problem could have been bouncing back from shoulder ailments in 1984 and the elbow problem that led to surgery late last season. His rehabilitation from surgery will be the story for Price this year. Projections are that he will be fit and in top form.

Campbell: "Price has shown that when he is right he can be an effective pitcher. He sets up the hitters well and uses his fastball as the element of surprise. His future, however, is going to depend on his health."

EXCELLENT SPEED

HITTING:

Gary Redus is a player of abundant but undisciplined talent. This shows up nowhere as much as it does in his hitting. Redus has a huge, home run swing and chases a lot of bad pitches, particularly anything up. He is also vulnerable to breaking balls down.

He doesn't adjust with the count, doesn't make consistent contact and is unable to take advantage of his incredible speed, which could lead to infield hits. He is in love with the home run and consequently leads the league in fly ball outs. Refining his strike zone and shortening his swing would do Redus a world of good.

He can bunt, but he doesn't like to and obviously can't be relied on in hit-and-run situations.

At this stage in his career--and he's approaching 30--Redus is a streak hitter who, for short periods of time, can be brilliant. But the streak always runs out, ebbing in a collection of pop flies and strikeouts.

Redus allows his slumps to get to him. He broods over his sluggish hitting and causes himself more grief by letting his pique affect the rest of his play.

BASERUNNING:

Redus has tremendous speed and base-stealing abilities. He reads pitchers well and is always a threat to take a base. He accelerates from first to third as quickly as anyone in the league, including the Cardinals' Vince Coleman.

The only thing that holds Redus back from taking more bases is his on-base percentage.

FIELDING:

With his speed, Redus has great range but he doesn't react well to the ball. More often than not, the absence of a good jump forces him to chase the ball down. Fortunately for him, he has the

GARY REDUS
OF, No. 2
RR, 6'1", 180 lbs.
ML Svc: 4 years
Born: 11-1-56 in
 Limestone County, AL

1985 STATISTICS

AVG	G	AB	R	H	2B	3B	HR	RBI	BB	SO	SB
.252	101	246	51	62	14	4	6	28	44	52	48

CAREER STATISTICS

AVG	G	AB	R	H	2B	3B	HR	RBI	BB	SO	SB
.282	369	1176	222	292	58	18	31	108	172	255	146

STRONG

VS. RHP

STRONG

VS. LHP

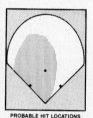

PROBABLE HIT LOCATIONS

speed to do so. He is best when coming in on the ball, but has trouble going back and, particularly, back to the corner in left field. He can play center, but he is only average there. With an average arm, he is best-suited for left.

OVERALL:

Redus is a player who needs to find himself in order to realize his potential. The consensus throughout the National League is the same. Redus needs a change of scenery.

Campbell: "Gary's biggest problem is getting to first. He has brilliant base-stealing abilities, but everyone knows there is one base you cannot steal . . .

"Someone needs to convince Redus that, in his case, a .280-.290 average and no home runs is better than a .235 average and maybe nine or 10 home runs. If he can be convinced of that, he might be a real sleeper."

PITCHING:

Reds officials remain high on this young righthander, projecting him as a front-line starter. For now, however, Ron Robinson is a toiler who is most effective in middle relief.

Robinson has slightly better-than-average pace on his fastball. In the minor leagues, he made his reputation with an effective curveball, but he now appears inconsistent with that pitch as well as with his change-up. Because he can't rely on his breaking pitches, Ron has a predictable tendency to go to his fastball when he is in trouble. What broke in the minors isn't breaking in the big leagues; he is going to have to work on his off-speed stuff this year.

What Robinson can do is put the ball where he wants it. On his best days, he keeps his pitches low in the strike zone and just off the plate. His success is dependent on his precision. When he slips, he can get in trouble very quickly.

While lacking in some refinements, Robinson compensates for them with his determination and workmanlike approach to the game. Few on the Reds pitching staff take the job as seriously or failures more to heart than Robinson. He is going to need more to reach the level expected of him by the Reds.

FIELDING, HITTING, BASERUNNING:

Robinson has good, quick hands and

RON ROBINSON
RHP, No. 33
RR, 6'4", 215 lbs.
ML Svc: 2 years
Born: 3-24-62 in
  Woodlake, CA

1985 STATISTICS

W	L	ERA	G	GS	CG	SV	IP	H	R	ER	BB	SO
7	7	3.99	33	12	0	1	108.1	107	53	48	32	76

CAREER STATISTICS

W	L	ERA	G	GS	CG	SV	IP	H	R	ER	BB	SO
8	9	3.64	45	17	1	1	148	142	71	60	45	100

fields his position well. He is a heady defensive player and stays in the game. His move is average: baserunners can get a good jump on him.

He takes his hitting and baserunning seriously. He will get the bunt down and he plays it safe and smart on the bases.

OVERALL:

Robinson may yet realize his potential, but there is work to do. While he works out his kinks, he will be slotted in middle relief.

Campbell: "Neither his breaking ball nor his change-up is consistent. He doesn't have any kind of fastball to speak of and so he has to learn a couple of off-speed pitches to become more effective."

HITTING:

Pete Rose continues to amaze opposing pitchers. He remains a good fastball hitter, a good breaking ball hitter and a hitter blessed with an incredible eye for the strike zone.

There is no safe way to pitch to Rose. He protects the plate and doesn't give an inch. Because of his reputation as a good breaking ball hitter, he gets more than his share of fastballs--a fact that is to his liking. Most pitchers try to blow the fastball by Rose, up and in, and then try to nip him with off-speed pitches away.

Rose doesn't have the same hitting skills he had 10 years ago, but he has adjusted and doesn't take a chance on anything he does not consider a true strike. He is not about to give away the strike zone.

His batting stance--the deep crouch and small strike zone--makes him difficult to pitch to. He has deepened the crouch and squeezed his strike zone even more from the left side of the plate. What he wants is a fastball out over the plate. He will flair a fastball to left field or drive it up the middle when batting lefthanded, while he will pull a hanging breaking ball.

Batting righthanded, he probably has more power and pulls more pitches. From the right side, he is less apt to punch the pitch down and away to the opposite field for a base hit.

The only area that is beginning to show Rose's age is his ability to get around on the high, hard fastball. He does not get on it as quickly as he once did; he used to foul them off to stay alive in the count. Now, more often than not, he will miss it, then tighten down further in the crouch to make another strike more difficult. His goal is to get on base.

BASERUNNING:

Rose is not fast, but he knows which outfielders have or haven't got a good arm and calculates the chances for their

PETE ROSE
1B, No. 14
SR, 5'11", 200 lbs.
ML Svc: 23 years
Born: 4-14-41 in
   Cincinnati, OH

1985 STATISTICS

AVG	G	AB	R	H	2B	3B	HR	RBI	BB	SO	SB
.264	119	405	60	107	12	2	2	46	86	35	8

CAREER STATISTICS

AVG	G	AB	R	H	2B	3B	HR	RBI	BB	SO	SB
.304	3490	13816	2150	4204	738	133	160	1289	1536	1112	195

error. He always tries to force the play. He continues to slide headfirst.

FIELDING:

Rose plays an aggressive first base and shows surprising quickness and mobility. His arm is weak, as it has been for years, but he'll make up for it--in some cases--by getting rid of the ball quickly. He is not good coming in on bunts, and shallow pop flies in foul territory are a problem. Rose lets second baseman Ron Oester take what he can.

OVERALL:

One more year? Two more years? Ten? Campbell: "Pete won't swing at anything that isn't a strike. His only goal is to get on base for Parker and those other guns.

"In the long-range plan, he and Perez are not the Reds' answer at first base. But unless there is some phenom on the horizon, that's the way it will be this year."

PITCHING:

For Mario Soto, 1985 was a year to forget. He lost the zip from his fastball, the movement off his change-up, and, worst of all, his resilience. Confronted with little else but hard times, injury and futile efforts, Soto found last year's frustrations overwhelming.

The elements of his style remained: the dominant fastball and unpredictable change-up each delivered from an identical motion. But his over-reliance on the change-up, first exhibited in 1984, resurfaced in 1985. Even when behind in the count, the hitters were able to wait for the change and found it a suddenly hittable pitch.

Often criticized in 1984 as one who had to find a third pitch, Soto turned to a slider. After some success with it (it is the least effective pitch in his repertoire), he ran into trouble again by using it too frequently.

FIELDING, HITTING, BASERUNNING:

Soto is a good all-around athlete. He fields his position well and gets off the mound quickly for bunts and to cover first. His move is average and his motion is time-consuming. Runners can get a good jump on him.

A free-swinger at heart, Soto is a better hitter than he is a bunter and will occasionally come through with an extra-base hit. He's quick on the bases and generally alert.

MARIO SOTO
RHP, No. 36
RR, 6'0", 190 lbs.
ML Svc: 9 years
Born: 7-12-56 in
    Bani, DR

1985 STATISTICS

W	L	ERA	G	GS	CG	SV	IP	H	R	ER	BB	SO
12	15	3.58	36	36	9	0	256.2	196	109	102	104	214

CAREER STATISTICS

W	L	ERA	G	GS	CG	SV	IP	H	R	ER	BB	SO
89	73	3.28	258	185	68	4	1506.1	1160	604	549	571	1337

OVERALL:

An off year? Perhaps. Time will tell, but among the sobering thoughts Soto took into his winter was the knowledge that a more characteristic season on his part might have given the Reds a divisional title.

Campbell: "Mario is still a quality pitcher but he lets too much bother him. If all is not just perfect, he can be very temperamental. When that happens, he loses his concentration on the job at hand. He lets his fielders' errors distract him and he continues to give up too many home runs.

"If he can resolve his tendency to lose his focus, he'll be much better off. Obviously, he is a key to the Reds' future."

PITCHING:

Unfortunately, there is no award given to the hardest worker in baseball. If there were, John Stuper would surely be a candidate for the honor. He subjects himself to physical rigors that test the imagination--2,000 sit-ups per week, for example. Unfortunately, no amount of sit-ups or push-ups can give him the kind of pitches he needs.

Without the blessing of superior stuff, Stuper survives, occasionally, on good location. He has the standard mix of pitches: fastball, curveball, slider, and straight change. None of them are overly impressive.

A dedicated and straight-on pitcher, Stuper must have his control to be successful. However, he often tends to fall behind in the count. Even more troubling than that is his penchant for giving up a lot of two-out hits and walks.

There is also some indication that he loses his concentration on the mound, but the fact is that he does not have enough on his pitches to get out of trouble and that he treads too far into the strike zone.

Stuper tends to get down on himself and occasionally gets annoyed with errors, miscues or botched plays by his teammates. He is affected by his own lack of confidence and allows himself to be shaken too easily.

Intense on and off the field, a crash course in relaxation may be in Stuper's best interest. He no sooner takes the mound than it appears he is preparing himself for the worst possible outcome. His funk worsens if everything doesn't go right.

FIELDING, HITTING, BASERUNNING:

His move is average, but, like everything else, he works at it. Stuper is an aggressive fielder and baserunner, but

JOHN STUPER
RHP, No. 42
RR, 6'2", 200 lbs.
ML Svc: 4 years
Born: 5-9-57 in
Butler, PA

1985 STATISTICS

W	L	ERA	G	GS	CG	SV	IP	H	R	ER	BB	SO
8	5	4.55	33	13	1	0	99	116	60	50	37	38

CAREER STATISTICS

W	L	ERA	G	GS	CG	SV	IP	H	R	ER	BB	SO
32	28	3.96	111	76	9	1	495	528	249	218	183	191

he is a horrible hitter. He gives meaning to the phrase "sure out."

He will get the bunt down, but he does not warm to the task.

OVERALL:

At this point in his career, Stuper is a journeyman pitcher best-suited for middle relief or mop-up work. He was cut loose by the Cardinals in 1984 because they had lost confidence in his ability to get outs in critical situations. That is a problem which plagues him and it seems to be the result of his lack of self-assuredness as much as anything else. He appears to be caught in the terrible circle of needing success to boost his confidence and needing confidence to gain success.

Campbell: "A pitcher like Stuper, who doesn't have any one pitch that is particularly good, has to have his control more than anything else. Control is a fickle element in pitching, but you have to do everything you can to help it along--that means keeping your wits at all times. John has not been able to do that consistently."

PITCHING:

Jay Tibbs, a smooth, savvy and productive performer, had the world by the tail heading into the 1985 season. But, as it often does, the world turned, and this young righthander found himself taking a precipitous fall from the number two spot in the rotation.

Tibbs was terribly spotty early last year. After an inning or two of good work, the bottom would completely fall out. His fastball, normally an effective weapon in the 86-88 MPH range, would become stick-straight and his sharp slider would become dull and fat. His curveball grew round and his change-up would also become fair game. Tibbs was battered to the extent that he became a study in frustration.

His demotion to the minors during the season was almost a relief to him. After a relatively short stay at Triple-A, Tibbs returned to the Reds and to more characteristic form. Though he made some mechanical alterations to his classic straight, overhand style of delivery, mental adjustments were also evident. Tibbs began to pitch more within himself and stopped trying to overpower hitters with stuff he just didn't have.

His forte is his ability to make hitters hit his pitches. When he is right, he spots his pitches well and constantly changes speeds to keep hitters off-balance. When he strays from this formula, he is in trouble.

FIELDING, HITTING, BASERUNNING:

Tibbs is a good fielder with good hands and quickness. His move is aver-

JAY TIBBS
RHP, No. 28
RR, 6'1", 180 lbs.
ML Svc: 1 year plus
Born: 1-4-62 in
   Birmingham, AL

1985 STATISTICS
W	L	ERA	G	GS	CG	SV	IP	H	R	ER	BB	SO
10	16	3.92	35	34	5	0	218	216	111	95	83	98

CAREER STATISTICS
W	L	ERA	G	GS	CG	SV	IP	H	R	ER	BB	SO
16	18	3.59	49	48	8	0	318.2	303	145	127	116	138

age. He doesn't help his catcher much, but neither does he hurt him.

Jay may be the worst bunter on the Reds team and he doesn't really hit. On the bases, he is fundamentally sound and has the speed to take an extra base. In a tight situation, he can be used as a pinch-runner.

OVERALL:

This is a key season for Tibbs. While Pete Rose insists that Tibbs will bounce back, questions remain.

Campbell: "Tibbs is one of those guys who must learn to get the big strikeout. That quality is what separates the winners from the losers.

"His stuff appears to be good enough to make him a consistent pitcher, particularly on a club like the Reds, which will score some runs for him. He has to get mentally tougher when his game is on the line."

DAVE VAN GORDER
C, No. 23
RR, 6'2", 205 lbs.
ML Svc: 3 years
Born: 3-27-57 in
    Los Angeles, CA

HITTING, BASERUNNING, FIELDING

Dave Van Gorder is the catcher the Reds keep putting away and continually retrieve because of his defensive ability. He is not in the big leagues because of his hitting.

Van Gorder is a spray hitter. He'll make contact, won't strike out much and will drive in some runs. His limited power is to left-center. He can go with the pitch and hit it to right field.

He likes the fastball up. Pitchers will work him up and in with hard stuff and down and away with breaking balls. He'll hit their mistakes and doesn't waste his at-bats. He is generally selective and knows the strike zone.

He is fundamentally sound, can bunt and is reliable in the hit-and-run. A singles hitter in the past, last season Van Gorder proved that he can come up with an occasional extra-base hit.

His baserunning is marked by the same gamer quality present in other areas of his play. He is intelligent and is not subject to mistakes.

A good handler of pitchers, Van Gorder sorts through a pitcher's game early and can make quick adjustments. He has improved greatly in this area. His arm is average in strength and is generally accurate.

OVERALL:

Campbell: "Dave is a backup player and late-inning defensive replacement. He has improved significantly as a hitter, but is still a .230 man."

MAX VENABLE
OF, No. 49
LR, 5'10", 185 lbs.
ML Svc: 7 years
Born: 6-6-57 in
    Phoenix, AZ

HITTING, BASERUNNING, FIELDING:

There is a widespread argument in baseball that younger players usually don't make good pinch-hitters--and then there is Max Venable, who knocks a sizeable hole in that argument.

Last season, Venable was 13-for-35 (.371) as a pinch-hitter: by far, the best performance in that area by a Reds player. He continually seemed to come up with the big hit. Venable is a fastball hitter who likes the ball up and over the plate. As long as it's a fastball, Venable can adjust whether the pitch is inside or away. He will take the inside fastball down the right field line and the outside fastball down the line into left field. He has trouble with slow, breaking pitches--he gets way out in front of them. A good change-up will get rid of him fast.

Venable makes contact with the ball, is a good man on the hit-and-run, is not a good bunter and will draw many walks.

He has better-than-average speed and will steal some bases. He is a smart baserunner and is quick when going from first to third. He is often used as a pinch-runner.

Venable has average range and an average arm. He can get the ball to the plate when he absolutely has to, but in general, his throws are not always accurate.

OVERALL:

He is not an everyday player, but unlike many ballplayers with similar talents, Venable has accepted his role on the club as his only ticket to remaining in the major leagues.

HOUSTON ASTROS

HITTING:

It happened again! Alan Ashby is a man whose career has been marred time after time by injuries, and last year one of his fingers was smashed so badly that a pin was required to help it heal. He missed most of the second half.

It's a shame, too, because Ashby was enjoying a good year offensively prior to the injury. Indeed, lost in the considerable praise accorded young catcher Mark Bailey in Houston is the fact that Ashby has had two straight productive seasons when healthy.

Until the injury, the combination of Ashby and Bailey was giving Houston more offense than some more highly regarded catchers in the league.

A switch-hitter, Ashby is primarily a straightaway hitter from both sides, but is more likely to pull down the line when he is batting lefthanded. He'll go to right-center batting righty. He has decent power from both sides of the plate.

He prefers the ball high, especially batting righthanded. A pitcher's best approach is to change speeds and keep the ball down. He should not stick to a set pattern because Ashby is a smart hitter who will adjust.

Ashby is a patient hitter who is willing to take a walk. He's not tense in pressure situations.

BASERUNNING:

By catchers' standards, Ashby is a good runner. He is not a basestealing threat but he will not hurt his team. Toe injuries have slowed him at times. He is usually cautious on the bases.

FIELDING:

Because of his experience, Ashby knows the National League hitters well and has been an asset to numerous Astro pitchers.

ALAN ASHBY
C, No. 14
SR, 6'2", 195 lbs.
ML Svc: 13 years
Born: 7-8-51 in
Long Beach, CA

1985 STATISTICS

AVG	G	AB	R	H	2B	3B	HR	RBI	BB	SO	SB
.280	65	189	20	53	8	0	8	25	24	27	0

CAREER STATISTICS

AVG	G	AB	R	H	2B	3B	HR	RBI	BB	SO	SB
.240	1030	3134	297	754	141	12	62	379	346	469	6

  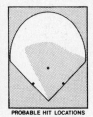

VS. RHP   VS. LHP   PROBABLE HIT LOCATIONS

Ashby's arm isn't the league's best, but it's far from the worst. Houston catchers have seldom been aided by the pitching staff in holding runners, so figures showing a high stolen base ratio for opponents don't necessarily reflect any Ashby deficiencies.

OVERALL:

With Mark Bailey already starting and several promising catchers in the farm system, it wouldn't be surprising to see Ashby traded. And it wouldn't be surprising if other teams show interest.

Campbell: "It's like a broken record, but Ashby's injuries are perplexing. No one keeps himself in better condition, and his troubles have always been kind of flukish. Maybe not having to catch Joe Niekro's knuckler will help end the mystery of his misery."

HITTING:

Mark Bailey made tremendous strides as a hitter in 1985, improving noticeably from both sides of the plate. His .265 average represented a jump of more than 50 points over his previous season.

He has a lot of raw power from both sides of the plate and his 10 home runs in 332 at-bats are not bad totals for a man playing half his games in Houston.

Without question, Bailey hits fastballs best and he will kill the pitch if it is in his power zone (about belt-high and over the plate). It is not advisable to get behind in the count to him.

A pitcher can throw curveballs, sliders, screwballs, forkballs or anything else except fastballs. Keep the ball down, and he will likely strike out.

He is primarily a straightaway hitter from both sides, but the best bet is to give him the lines and bunch him toward the middle. He likes to pull the ball into the alleys but will go to the opposite field, too.

For a young hitter, Bailey has surprising discipline. In his two seasons with Houston, he has ranked among the team leaders in walks.

BASERUNNING:

Bailey does not run well--he knows it, though. He is not overly aggressive on the bases and is no threat to steal.

FIELDING:

While making tremendous strides offensively, Bailey seemed to go backwards defensively last season. He is a converted infielder who had caught fewer than 100 games before his promotion to the major leagues two seasons ago. For one so inexperienced, he showed brilliant mechanics then. He gave a good, low target and set up well to throw.

For whatever reason, though, he now appears completely out of synch with his throwing. He comes out of his crouch too soon. He stands straight up and has

MARK BAILEY
C, No. 6
SL, 6'5", 195 lbs.
ML Svc: 2 years
Born: 11-4-61 in
    Springfield, MO

1985 STATISTICS											
AVG	G	AB	R	H	2B	3B	HR	RBI	BB	SO	SB
.265	114	332	47	88	14	0	10	45	67	70	0

CAREER STATISTICS											
AVG	G	AB	R	H	2B	3B	HR	RBI	BB	SO	SB
.238	222	676	85	161	40	1	19	79	120	141	0

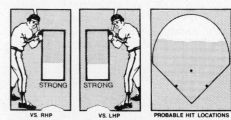

VS. RHP   VS. LHP   PROBABLE HIT LOCATIONS

a tendency to be high with all his throws. He doesn't have any kind of zip on his throws, either.

He is a strong competitor around the plate and is not at all hesitant about blocking incoming runners.

OVERALL:

Bailey was among the Astros' biggest surprises two years ago. He continues to develop as a hitter.

Campbell: "I think that one of the reasons the Astros got rid of Joe Niekro was that Bailey had all sorts of problems catching the knuckleball. This team is counting on Bailey for the future, so do not look for the Astros to be signing any more knuckleball pitchers.

"Bailey has a bright future, too. I'm impressed with him as a hitter. But he may have to go back to work on the defensive side. Maybe it came a little too easy for him. It usually takes a number of years to become a good defensive catcher."

HITTING:

Kevin Bass was particularly impressive early last year when injuries to regulars Jerry Mumphrey, Terry Puhl and Jose Cruz allowed him to start on almost a regular basis. Though never firmly in control of any position, Bass played in 150 games and batted 539 times, third on the team only to Bill Doran and Cruz.

For a long period, Bass led the team in home runs and eventually finished with a more-than-respectable 16, second highest on the team. He emerged as one of Houston's best hitters.

Traditionally, Bass has been much more effective from the left side, and that has made it tough for him to crack the lineup because Puhl and Cruz bat lefty and switch-hitter Mumphrey is at his best lefthanded, too.

Bass did improve last season as a righthanded hitter and that is a big reason why he played so much.

He has improved every year with the bat. He is primarily a straightaway hitter, though he pulled more often last season than before. There is no sure-fire defense against Kevin, but the best idea is probably to bunch the alleys in the outfield.

Bass doesn't scare in clutch situations and his speed helps him get a few infield hits.

One negative is that Bass rarely draws a walk. Only time will tell if he will become a more disciplined hitter.

BASERUNNING:

Bass is among Houston's fastest and most aggressive runners. His 19 steals last season were second only to Bill Doran's 23. This marked considerable improvement over the previous year, when a more conservative Bass attempted only 10 thefts.

FIELDING:

Although he was highly inconsistent

KEVIN BASS
RF, No. 17
SR, 6'0", 180 lbs.
ML Svc: 4 years
Born: 5-12-59 in
Redwood City, CA

1985 STATISTICS

AVG	G	AB	R	H	2B	3B	HR	RBI	BB	SO	SB
.269	150	539	72	145	27	5	16	68	31	63	19

CAREER STATISTICS

AVG	G	AB	R	H	2B	3B	HR	RBI	BB	SO	SB
.253	389	1098	136	278	51	13	20	116	44	156	26

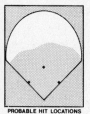

VS. RHP   VS. LHP   PROBABLE HIT LOCATIONS

until last season, Bass showed a lot of improvement defensively. His increased playing time had a great deal to do with that. He plays all three outfield spots.

Good range is his chief asset as a defensive player. His throwing arm is adequate. Bass still misjudges an occasional fly ball, but he is learning.

OVERALL:

Kevin was among the most improved Astros last year at the plate, on the bases and in the field. Considering he wasn't expected to start, he quietly emerged into a solid big league player.

Campbell: "The verdict has been out on Kevin and pretty soon the Astros are going to have to decide whether he is going to be a regular or their fourth outfielder. He certainly played enough that people can evaluate his talent.

"My feeling is he has a good career ahead of him. Only time will tell if it will be great. But he is a darn good prospect."

NEEDS ANOTHER PITCH

PITCHING:

In his first full season in the major leagues, Jeff Calhoun emerged as the most effective lefthanded reliever in the Astros' bullpen (taking the title from Frank DiPino). As the year progressed, then-manager Bob Lillis wasn't hesitant to use Calhoun in any pressure situation.

Calhoun's chief asset is his ability to get out lefthanded hitters. He has a three-quarters delivery and his fastball sinks down and in to lefthanders and it tails away from righthanders. He has a sharp-breaking slider, too, but is basically a two-pitch pitcher. He does not show much of a curve or change-up.

Calhoun is tough to hit, having given up only 56 hits in 64 innings last year, and he has good control. He walked only 24 and struck out 47.

From the beginning, Calhoun indicated that he isn't afraid of pressure. He was a starter in the minors and has adapted well to pitching in relief. He could easily go back to being a starter if he had to.

FIELDING, HITTING, BASERUNNING:

Calhoun is a good athlete who fields his position well. His move to first base is average. He gets few opportunities to hit or run the bases and, like most relief pitchers, he isn't much of a threat in those areas.

JEFF CALHOUN
LHP, No. 49
LL, 6'2", 190 lbs.
ML Svc: 1 year plus
Born: 4-11-58 in
LaGrange, GA

1985 STATISTICS												
W	L	ERA	G	GS	CG	SV	IP	H	R	ER	BB	SO
2	5	2.54	44	0	0	4	63.2	56	21	18	24	47
CAREER STATISTICS												
W	L	ERA	G	GS	CG	SV	IP	H	R	ER	BB	SO
2	6	2.28	53	0	0	4	79	61	24	20	26	58

OVERALL:

Every staff needs a lefthander who can consistently get out one or two lefthanded batters in tight situations. Based on one year, Calhoun seems to be that guy for the Astros. On a team that has a Dave Smith, a Jeff Calhoun can be particularly effective.

Campbell: "Jeff pitched well almost every time I saw him. He has a promising future, although I think it would be a good idea for him to come up with another pitch. If he develops something off-speed, it will make his hard stuff seem that much faster."

JOSE CRUZ
LF, No. 25
LL, 6'0", 185 lbs.
ML Svc: 15 years
Born: 8-8-47 in
  Arroyo, PR

1985 STATISTICS
AVG	G	AB	R	H	2B	3B	HR	RBI	BB	SO	SB
.300	141	544	69	163	34	4	9	79	43	74	16

CAREER STATISTICS
AVG	G	AB	R	H	2B	3B	HR	RBI	BB	SO	SB
.288	2048	6993	932	2014	350	86	143	960	815	872	310

  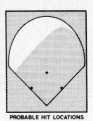

VS. RHP   VS. LHP   PROBABLE HIT LOCATIONS

HITTING:

Jose Cruz has been a .300 hitter throughout his Houston career and it is apparent that he will remain a .300 hitter until Father Time catches up to him.

Jose continues to follow the pattern of starting slowly each year, then getting better as the season goes along. He is a good RBI man, one who drives the ball hard with men on base. Though Cruz isn't a pure home run hitter, don't make a mistake or he'll drill you deep.

Cruz is extremely tough to defense because he learned several years ago to go with the pitch. He will pull the inside pitch with power and he will take the pitch up and away to left field. He isn't greedy. He takes what you give him, and that's smart hitting.

Cruz likes the ball up, but he is unpredictable. You can make him look very bad on one pitch, for example a slow curve, then he will hit that same pitch the next time for a single.

He is a zone hitter. He looks for the ball in a certain spot, and when he gets it there, he doesn't often miss. Cruz is a chop-chop-type hitter, too, one who swings down on the ball. He hits a lot of line drives.

Cruz will swing at an occasional bad pitch, but he usually has good patience. He is among the league leaders in walks every year.

BASERUNNING:

His baserunning is the one area where Cruz's age may be a telling factor. His stolen base output declined to 16 last year. In fairness to Cruz, though, then-manager Bob Lillis didn't stress the running game as much as Bill Virdon had when he managed the club.

Cruz still will take the extra base on hits. Pitchers have been known to catch him leaning too far off first base.

FIELDING:

Cruz always has been regarded as a good outfielder by some observers because of his speed and range, and a bad outfielder by others, because of his inconsistency. To sum it up, he's an average left fielder. He doesn't go into the alley quite as well as in the past and his throwing arm is not strong.

OVERALL:

Cruz remains a model of consistency at the plate. In the past 10 seasons, he's hit .300-plus six times and was at .299 another year.

Campbell: "Cruz is a guy who knows his body is his business, and so he takes care of that body. He plays baseball all year here and in Puerto Rico, and yet he never seems to tire.

"He did have some nagging injuries last year, a rarity for him. With older players, you never known when injuries will become a factor, but he will probably have at least two or three more good years."

HITTING:

Glenn Davis has awesome power. He played only about half of the season, hit 350 times and yet logged 20 home runs, which is remarkable for someone who has to play half of his home games in the Astrodome.

He likes the ball about thigh-high and takes a bit of an uppercut swing. He is not partial to where he hits the ball either, having taken pitches out of the park in right-center field, left-center, right field and down the line in left.

He prefers fastballs and likes the pitch out over the plate. But Davis has made enough strides against the curve that he can't be pitched only one way anymore. Pitchers can get inside on him, but anything inside has got to be good or Davis will send it to the bleachers.

High fastballs will get him occasionally and he will also go after breaking balls out of the strike zone with two strikes on him. A change-up can be effective, but must be down.

Davis has a lightning-quick bat. But he is not a disciplined hitter. He needs to cut down on his strikeouts. It would appear, however, that if he plays on an everyday basis and has the opportunity to know the pitchers better, Davis will cut down on his whiffs.

BASERUNNING:

Davis has little speed and is no threat to steal. He is strictly a station-to-station runner. Fortunately for him, many of his hits land where he can trot around the bases.

FIELDING:

Davis is a defensive liability at first base. He does not have good hands, a good arm or good instincts. Even so, he was better by the end of last season than he was the previous year.

GLENN DAVIS
INF, No. 27
RR, 6'3", 210 lbs.
ML Svc: 1 year plus
Born: 3-28-61 in
Jacksonville, FL

1985 STATISTICS

AVG	G	AB	R	H	2B	3B	HR	RBI	BB	SO	SB
.271	100	350	51	95	11	0	20	64	27	68	0

CAREER STATISTICS

AVG	G	AB	R	H	2B	3B	HR	RBI	BB	SO	SB
.263	118	411	57	108	16	0	22	72	31	80	0

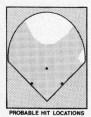

STRONG — VS. RHP   STRONG — VS. LHP   PROBABLE HIT LOCATIONS

Davis handles the batted ball better than the thrown ball. Low throws from infielders prove disastrous: he does not save them from many errors. Experiments with him in right field failed.

OVERALL:

Davis has enormous potential as a hitter. No Houston rookie has shown more power. As he gains experience, his consistency should improve. Because of his other deficiencies, he will have to produce runs on a big-time basis.

Campbell: "Glenn's one major asset is swinging the bat. He may be in the wrong league--he would probably make a great designated hitter. But since there is no DH in the National League, the Astros are going to have to work hard with him on his defense."

PITCHING:

Bill Dawley's 1985 season mirrored the performance of another Houston reliever, Frank DiPino.

As a rookie in 1983, Dawley pitched in the All-Star Game. The next season, after a slow start, he won 11 games and had a 1.94 earned run average. But like DiPino, Dawley fell on hard times last year, saving only two games and winning five. His ERA ballooned to 3.56.

Also like DiPino, Dawley's main problem seemed to have little to do with his talent. He still throws hard, has a good fastball and slider, and his three-quarters delivery makes righthanded batters weak at the knees.

Dawley used to keep his fastball and slider down consistently, but suddenly last season he had all sorts of trouble with location. His pitches appeared live, but he threw too many of them in the middle of the plate from the belt up. Unless a pitcher has magnificent stuff like Dwight Gooden, it is certain death to hand such fat pitches to a hitter. It explains the unusually high number of extra-base hits and line drives Dawley gave up last season.

He did have some arm discomfort early in the season, and when that subsided after the All-Star break, Dawley's performance improved. He can only hope now that the trend continues.

FIELDING, HITTING, BASERUNNING:

At 6'4" and 240 pounds, Dawley would not figure to be a good fielder. But he is. He has quick reflexes for a big

BILL DAWLEY
RHP, No. 46
RR, 6'4", 240 lbs.
ML Svc: 3 years
Born: 2-6-58 in
   Norwich, CT

1985 STATISTICS
W	L	ERA	G	GS	CG	SV	IP	H	R	ER	BB	SO
5	3	3.56	49	0	0	2	81	76	35	32	37	48

CAREER STATISTICS
W	L	ERA	G	GS	CG	SV	IP	H	R	ER	BB	SO
22	13	2.71	157	0	0	21	258.2	209	85	78	94	155

man and is always alert. His move to first base is adequate.

Dawley seldom gets opportunities to hit, but he enjoys taking his cuts and even has a chance of getting a hit. He is an average bunter and not a bad runner for such a big man.

OVERALL:

Dawley has lost his status as the Astros' number one reliever to Dave Smith. Dawley needs a good early season this year if the Astros are to depend on him at all in the key spots. He has one advantage: there will be lots of Houston relievers trying to prove themselves in 1986, and everyone will get a chance.

Campbell: "I don't know whether his main problem was mechanical, mental or an injury, but Dawley was one of the biggest disappointments on the Astros' pitching staff in 1985. He needs to get the ball down again to be effective."

PITCHING:

Frank DiPino had put together two good seasons before last year, but he was one of the Astros' biggest disappointments in 1985. The team had expected DiPino and righthanders Bill Dawley and Dave Smith to to give them one of the National League's deepest relief corps. But only Dave Smith was consistently effective.

DiPino's main problem is not with his stuff, which is good. His delivery is between three-quarters and overhand and he has both a solid fastball and curve. In the past, DiPino was able to throw both pitches over the plate. Last season, however, he was having trouble finding the strike zone and put far too many people on base.

DiPino began the season as the team's number one late-inning stopper. But he saved only six games, his record was 3-7 and his ERA was a fat 4.03.

The encouraging aspect is that DiPino still throws hard and remains an intense competitor. If he regains his control, there is no reason why he cannot become dependable again.

The discouraging part is that over the past three seasons he has been on a downward trend.

FIELDING, HITTING, BASERUNNING:

His quick reactions make DiPino a good fielder. He has worked to improve his move to first base but still doesn't hold runners well for a lefthander.

Though he seldom bats, DiPino isn't an automatic out. He takes healthy cuts.

FRANK DiPINO
LHP, No. 11
LL, 6'0", 180 lbs.
ML Svc: 4 years
Born: 10-22-56 in
   Syracuse, NY

1985 STATISTICS

W	L	ERA	G	GS	CG	SV	IP	H	R	ER	BB	SO
3	7	4.03	54	0	0	6	76	69	44	34	43	49

CAREER STATISTICS

W	L	ERA	G	GS	CG	SV	IP	H	R	ER	BB	SO
12	22	3.62	172	6	0	40	253	227	117	102	113	209

He is an above-average baserunner for a pitcher.

OVERALL:

At times last season, DiPino seemed mystified by the problems that beset him. The Astros' bullpen, a close-knit group, took considerable heat from management, fans and the media as the number one disappointment. For DiPino, and several others, it was a new experience and only added to the pressure. But he wants the baseball and that is a reliever's vital sign.

Campbell: "Early in 1985, most teams that talked trade with the Astros wanted to discuss DiPino. They wanted him more than any other pitcher on the staff. After last season, however, I'm not sure how many requests will be made for him.

"DiPino needs to find his control again in order to resume his role as a bullpen ace."

HITTING:

A switch-hitter, Bill Doran has surprising power from both sides of the plate considering his lack of size. He hit 14 home runs for the Astros last year, and if a pitcher gets behind in the count and makes a mistake with the fastball, he will take him deep. Fifty-nine of his 166 hits were for extra bases.

Doran is a patient, disciplined hitter. He hits straightaway. He will take a walk or do whatever the club needs. Because of his discipline, he is a challenge for any pitcher, whose best chance for success is to keep the ball down and change speeds on him. Doran won't chase bad pitches.

He is a better hitter from the left side, but he has hit some balls a long distance from the right side, too.

Until last year, Doran's only problem was that his season seemed to start in mid-May. The month of April was usually a washout for him. In 1985, however, he was able to maintain consistency all season long.

BASERUNNING:

Doran has good speed and is a heady runner. It's somewhat surprising that his speed doesn't always translate into quickness. The Astros may stress speed more in 1986 than they did last year. If so, it will be interesting to see how much Doran takes advantage of his speed. He is fast enough to develop into a 30 or 40 stolen bases player.

FIELDING:

The more you see Doran around second base, the better you like him. He has excellent hands and is good on the pivot. His range is good. He may not be spectacular, but he is extremely steady. Doran's arm is strong enough that he has even played shortstop in an emergency.

BILL DORAN
2B, No. 19
SR, 6'0", 175 lbs.
ML Svc: 4 years
Born: 5-28-58 in
   Cincinnati, OH

1985 STATISTICS
AVG	G	AB	R	H	2B	3B	HR	RBI	BB	SO	SB
.287	148	578	84	166	31	6	14	59	71	69	23

CAREER STATISTICS
AVG	G	AB	R	H	2B	3B	HR	RBI	BB	SO	SB
.274	475	1758	257	481	64	24	26	145	227	216	61

  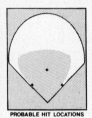

STRONG   STRONG   PROBABLE HIT LOCATIONS
VS. RHP   VS. LHP

OVERALL:

Beyond his obvious overall ability as a hitter, fielder and runner, Doran is an intense competitor, always hustling, always leaping for anything he can get. Watch Doran closely: by the second or third inning, his uniform is almost always dirty from diving or sliding.

Campbell: "Bill has had to learn to harness his competitiveness to overcome occasional fits of anger at himself for not meeting his own standards. And he does set high standards.

"For the most part, Doran is turning his competitive nature into a big advantage. As he matures, he is becoming a team leader and is highly respected by teammates and management. Among all the Houston Astros, Bill Doran impressed me most in 1985."

HITTING:

Not too long ago, Phil Garner's future with the Astros seemed in doubt. But he continues to provide the team with an adequate bat at most times and an even more potent stroke in clutch situations. His nine game-winning RBIs tied Jose Cruz for the team lead.

Garner is a high-ball hitter, uses a closed stance and likes to dive into pitches. Primarily a pull hitter, he has enough power to drive the ball into left-center field.

His main asset is that he is a battler, someone who becomes tougher under pressure. He doesn't give in. He is disciplined and willing to draw a walk. He is a good bunter and is among the best Astros at the hit-and-run.

He played more than was originally expected in 1985 and nothing indicates a change is in store.

Garner has hit in every spot in the order, from leadoff to cleanup to the number eight spot. With Glenn Davis, Bill Doran and Kevin Bass now on hand to take some home run pressure off Jose Cruz, Garner is not needed as much for the long ball, and that could help his consistency. He was once regarded as the National League's best eighth-place hitter.

BASERUNNING:

Garner is not the basestealing threat he once was, but if the Astros put new emphasis on running, he should get more than the four steals he totaled in 1985.

His small number of stolen bases is misleading in terms of his overall value as a runner. Garner is aggressive, takes the extra base, slides hard, breaks up double plays. He never gives less than his best effort.

FIELDING:

Garner's best position is second base, but with Bill Doran on hand that spot is taken. At third base, his re-

PHIL GARNER
3B, No. 3
RR, 5'10", 177 lbs.
ML Svc: 12 years
Born: 4-30-49 in
   Jefferson City, TN

1985 STATISTICS

AVG	G	AB	R	H	2B	3B	HR	RBI	BB	SO	SB
.268	135	463	65	124	23	10	6	51	34	72	4

CAREER STATISTICS

AVG	G	AB	R	H	2B	3B	HR	RBI	BB	SO	SB
.242	1625	5572	708	1460	276	79	95	673	505	750	207

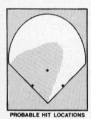

VS. RHP   VS. LHP   PROBABLE HIT LOCATIONS

flexes aren't good, though he handles the balls hit at him, has a fairly accurate arm and played better last year than in the previous two seasons.

If the situation demanded (and Garner were willing), he would make an excellent utility infielder. However, he is not yet ready to yield a starting job.

OVERALL:

Garner is a valuable player. He is a good team man and a proven winner. If the Astros get in a championship race, his experience would be critical.

Campbell: "He has to continue to produce or the Astros may find themselves in a tough spot. Garner's hitting is not as consistent as it once was, though he gives the team some key hits and experience. But one problem is that his salary may be too large for the club to carry him. I wouldn't be surprised to see him move to a club which can afford his salary and use his knowledge."

PITCHING:

Only two years ago, Jeff Heathcock was considered the best pitching prospect in the Astros' organization. Good stuff, good control, good poise--Jeff had it all.

Then, pitching for Houston's Triple-A club in April 1984, Heathcock suffered a freak leg injury while covering first base. He had ligament, tendon and bone damage. He didn't pitch again that year and was approaching full recovery only as the 1985 season ended.

Heathcock pitched last year both in the minors and with Houston. While he still had some trouble with his leg--it affects his drive off the mound--he had enough effective outings that the Astros are counting on him as a probable starter this season.

Heathcock's stamina and the speed of his fastball were slowed by the injury, but both improved throughout last year.

He is primarily a fastball/sinker pitcher, with the sinker being his specialty. Heathcock needs to keep the ball low to maintain consistency. His margin for error isn't the same as that of a Nolan Ryan. Fortunately, though, his control is usually good.

FIELDING, HITTING, BASERUNNING:

Heathcock is a good athlete with excellent reflexes, but his mobility was hurt badly by the leg injury. Assuming he can move well enough, he can field his position well. His move to first base is adequate. He isn't a good hitter

JEFF HEATHCOCK
RHP, No. 31
RR, 6'4", 195 lbs.
ML Svc: 1 year plus
Born: 11-18-59 in
　　Covina, CA

1985 STATISTICS

W	L	ERA	G	GS	CG	SV	IP	H	R	ER	BB	SO
3	1	3.36	14	7	1	1	56.1	50	25	21	13	25

CAREER STATISTICS

W	L	ERA	G	GS	CG	SV	IP	H	R	ER	BB	SO
5	2	3.32	20	10	1	2	84	69	39	31	17	37

or bunter yet and his speed on the bases was negated by the injury.

OVERALL:

Heathcock had a satisfying 1985 season in that he pitched all year in an effort to overcome his misfortune. Now comes the big test.

Last year was one of patience for the pitcher, but this season he is primed to make the rotation. If he's healthy and keeps the ball down, Heathcock can become the dependable winner the Astros anticipated prior to the injury.

Heathcock has yet to spend a full season in the majors, but he has been close enough to the Astro scene that he seems like a veteran. He is a strong competitor with a good attitude. He could make the starting rotation this year.

PITCHING:

This huge righthander had a rocky season last year, but Charlie Kerfeld ended the season on a high note with several good outings for the Astros over the final month.

He began spring training with a good chance at earning a fifth starter's job but was unimpressive. Demoted to the minors, Kerfeld then allowed his weight to balloon to a blimp-like 270 pounds, irritating Houston management to no small degree.

Given a mid-year cup of coffee with the Astros, Kerfeld lasted only a brief time. His control was off, he was hit hard and opponents and fans alike rode him unmercifully about his bulk.

But to his credit, Kerfeld returned to the Triple-A level, worked to improve his consistency and, with a chance to start for Houston in September, drew attention away from his midsection and instead to his talented arm.

And he is talented, having been a top prospect throughout his minor league career. Kerfeld's main weapon is a fastball clocked in the low-to-mid 90s. His fastball has excellent movement. His size and the fact that he is just wild enough make him intimidating to right-handed batters.

Kerfeld's best performances come when he gets his curveball over the plate, though he didn't do that too often last year. Improving his consistency with his curve is a main priority. Over the winter, he will also probably work on a change-up.

FIELDING, HITTING, BASERUNNING:

Moreso than with his pitching, his weight hindered him in all these areas. Defensively, however adroit, he didn't

CHARLIE KERFELD
RHP, No. 37
RR, 6'6", 225 lbs.
ML Svc: less than 1 year
Born: 9-28-63 in
  Carson City, NV

```
1985 STATISTICS
W  L  ERA  G  GS CG SV IP    H   R  ER BB SO
4  2  4.06 11 6  0  0  44.1  44  22 20 25 30
CAREER STATISTICS
W  L  ERA  G  GS CG SV IP    H   R  ER BB SO
4  2  4.06 11 6  0  0  44.1  44  22 20 25 30
```

have the quickness to make tough plays. Until he does trim down, opponents are likely to bunt on him.

At the plate, Kerfeld takes healthy enough cuts to serve as a threat, but occasionally last year he fell down on the ground because of his awkwardness. He is not a fast runner.

OVERALL:

If Kerfeld loses about 30 pounds, he has a chance to become an excellent big league pitcher. The Astros are eager to give him a chance and hope he will fit into the starting rotation this season.

His weight problem, while it does not hinder his stuff, seems to affect his stamina. He has promised to be in better condition this year.

Campbell: "Kerfeld is a solid competitor, loves to win and has the tools to become a winner. He's young, too, and is still maturing as a pitcher and as a person. His attitude improved noticeably as 1985 progressed and the betting in Houston is that Kerfeld will lose weight and become a high quality pitcher."

PITCHING:

Bob Knepper continues to be a solid major league starting pitcher. He has won 15 games in each of the past two seasons, and you can always count on him to go to the post. He is durable and dependable. He would be a good number three or four starter on any ball club.

This lefthander has a fastball which on any given day may reach 90 MPH. It has good movement and can tail up and away or sink down and away. He doesn't hurt himself by a lack of control.

Knepper has a good curveball, especially to lefthanded batters, who have a lot of trouble with its big, sweeping break. He also will throw a straight change-up.

If he has a problem, it is that he gives up a lot of home runs, even in the spacious Astrodome. But that's partly because he throws strikes.

FIELDING, HITTING, BASERUNNING:

Knepper has never had a good move to first base, but he has cut way down on what was a high leg kick during the last couple of years. That gives his catcher a much better chance to throw out runers. At one point, they stole easily on him. Not any more.

As a batter, Knepper isn't consistent but neither is he an automatic out. He got several big hits last year, and when a pitch is in his zone, he's been known

BOB KNEPPER
LHP, No. 39
LL, 6'2", 210 lbs.
ML Svc: 9 years
Born: 5-25-54 in
Akron, OH

```
1985 STATISTICS
W   L ERA   G  GS CG SV IP    H    R   ER BB  SO
15  13 3.55  37 37  4  0 241   253  119 95 54  131
CAREER STATISTICS
W   L ERA   G  GS  CG SV IP     H    R   ER  BB  SO
97 106 3.47 298 284 65  1 1887.2 1877 844 729 580 1063
```

to drive a home run. He is an average bunter and runner.

OVERALL:

Knepper's career has been marked by a good season followed by a bad year followed by another good year. Now, however, he has put two solid seasons back-to-back and his confidence is high. Nobody ever doubted his ability.

Campbell: "The only question about Bob continues to be his competitiveness, I guess because of his milquetoast image off the field. But I think he's the type of guy any staff would like to have. He doesn't miss starts because of injuries, and he is consistent."

HITTING:

Both in terms of average and power, Jerry Mumphrey became a better hitter last year. He has always been a more effective hitter from the left side of the plate but last year, batting right-handed, he began to show some improvement.

From the right side, Mumphrey used to go almost exclusively to the opposite field, but he's learned to open up his stance and pull the ball more. The book used to be that you could get him out batting righthanded by throwing hard stuff, but he made some improvement in that area in 1985.

Jerry has a quick bat, especially lefthanded. He prefers the ball up but often handles low pitches, too.

Mumphrey was among Houston's best clutch hitters two years ago. He wore some teams out again last year, especially San Diego and LaMarr Hoyt in particular. His RBI total was down last season, but injuries limited his at-bats. Also, he was shuffled around in the lineup more. He may be a better hitter playing on a daily basis, but with Jose Cruz, Terry Puhl and Kevin Bass available, his days of playing regularly are in question. Overall, his .277 average indicates Mumphrey is still a good hitter.

BASERUNNING:

Mumphrey dipped from 15 to six steals last year, but some upper-leg injuries were a factor. That may also explain why he wasn't as aggressive last season (on the bases or in the field). He is still an above-average runner. Mumphrey studies each pitcher and knows his weaknesses. He is not hesitant to slide hard into second base to break up the double play.

FIELDING:

Mumphrey is an average outfielder who, even taking injuries into consider-

JERRY MUMPHREY
CF, No. 28
SR, 6'2", 200 lbs.
ML Svc: 10 years
Born: 9-9-52 in
Tyler, TX

1985 STATISTICS

AVG	G	AB	R	H	2B	3B	HR	RBI	BB	SO	SB
.277	130	444	52	123	25	2	8	61	37	57	6

CAREER STATISTICS

AVG	G	AB	R	H	2B	3B	HR	RBI	BB	SO	SB
.287	1293	4309	579	1236	185	51	52	490	410	580	170

VS. RHP   VS. LHP   PROBABLE HIT LOCATIONS

ation, appears to have lost a step or two in center field. He doesn't always get a good jump on a fly ball—especially shallow fly balls. He has never had a strong arm.

Defensively, Mumphrey has difficulty maintaining consistency. He was shifted between center field and right field all last season and never really knew what his set position was supposed to be.

OVERALL:

Mumphrey was one of the Astros' best players in 1984, then inexplicably was placed on the back burner for part of last year. He was confused and unsettled and did not like losing his regular role with the club.

Campbell: "This could be a critical for Jerry in terms of determining his future role with the Astros. One thing seems certain, though, he is still a very good hitter. He is a very nice guy who keeps his mouth shut and goes about his job."

HITTING:

A minor leaguer for almost a decade, Jim Pankovits got his first shot with the Astros for part of the 1984 season and impressed the club. He became a fixture as a utility man last year.

Pankovits is an aggressive hitter who prefers the ball up in the strike zone. You can get him out by keeping the ball down and by jamming him.

Primarily, he is a straightaway hitter, but Pankovits has shown occasional power and will pull a mistake down the line or to left-center field. Even many of his outs are line drives.

At times last year, he was Houston's best pinch-hitter. He seems to thrive on pressure situations. Unlike many players, he is able to come off the bench cold and produce.

His average was only .244, however, and the Astros are going to need more consistency from his bat.

BASERUNNING:

Pankovits has slightly above-average speed and his good hustle aids his running ability. He is no a threat to steal, but he'll take an extra base on hits. His instincts are good and he's an intelligent player.

FIELDING:

Without question, Pankovits's best defensive position is second base. He has good range, good hands and handles himself well on the pivot--but Bill Doran plays there, and Doran is the team's reigning MVP.

So, Pankovits plays a utility role and he played it well last year. He saw considerable action in left field and

JIM PANKOVITS
PH/INF, No. 20
RR, 5'10", 174 lbs.
ML Svc: 1 year plus
Born: 8-6-55 in
   Pennington Gap, VA

1985 STATISTICS											
AVG	G	AB	R	H	2B	3B	HR	RBI	BB	SO	SB
.244	75	172	24	42	3	0	4	14	17	29	1
CAREER STATISTICS											
AVG	G	AB	R	H	2B	3B	HR	RBI	BB	SO	SB
.257	128	253	30	65	3	0	5	28	19	49	3

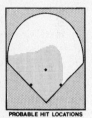

VS. RHP — STRONG   VS. LHP — STRONG   PROBABLE HIT LOCATIONS

didn't hurt the Astros there. His arm and range are only average, but he makes all of the routine plays.

OVERALL:

With Doran at second base, Dickie Thon and Craig Reynolds at shortstop, Jose Cruz in left field and Terry Puhl in right field, even a man who plays all those positions--and Pankovits does--is not likely to find a spot in the starting lineup.

Campbell: "I think he is a good utility player. His attitude seems good. He always hustles and seems to enjoy playing the game. He probably appreciates it more than some others because he spent so many years in the minors."

HITTING:

Terry Puhl's 1985 season was kind of a washout, first when a severe hamstring injury disabled him a couple of times, then because Houston management decided not to take a chance on the injury and kept him out almost the entire second half.

Puhl hit .284 but he played in only 57 games, batting only 194 times.

The injury came at a bad time, too, because both the Astros and Puhl were looking forward to 1985. Puhl was a strong advocate of moving in the Dome's fences, and one reason Houston management made that move was to benefit him. In the past, he had hit countless drives to the warning track. Puhl must wait until this year to see how the new size fits his swing.

Presumably, nothing has changed about Puhl. He likes the ball belt-high, maybe a little above. He sprays the ball to all fields and has good power down the right field line.

A notorious streak hitter, Puhl has stretches where he is all but impossible to get out with any consistency. He has endured bad slumps in the past, as well. In his last full season (1984), Puhl stayed away from prolonged bad periods and hit .301.

BASERUNNING:

Puhl is an excellent runner, and only time will tell if the severe hamstring injury has any lasting effects. When he is healthy, he can steal 20-30 bases. He is a smart runner and moves from first to third well.

FIELDING:

For many years, Puhl has been among the league's best right fielders, lacking only a strong arm. His range is good, his hands superb and his arm,

TERRY PUHL
RF, No. 21
LR, 6'2", 200 lbs.
ML Svc: 9 years
Born: 7-8-56 in
    Saskatchewan, CAN

1985 STATISTICS

AVG	G	AB	R	H	2B	3B	HR	RBI	BB	SO	SB
.284	57	194	34	55	14	3	2	23	18	23	6

CAREER STATISTICS

AVG	G	AB	R	H	2B	3B	HR	RBI	BB	SO	SB
.283	1074	3914	562	1108	188	50	54	349	399	389	181

  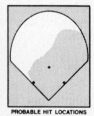

VS. RHP   VS. LHP   PROBABLE HIT LOCATIONS

while hardly a rocket, is accurate. He rarely makes bad throws.

Prior to Puhl's injury, the Astros were toying with the idea of moving him to center field. Don't be surprised if that plan comes up again. Again, his only limitation would be Puhl's arm.

OVERALL:

This is a critical season for Puhl because he must prove that the hamstring injury has completely healed.

Campbell: "There is no questioning his talent. Offensively and defensively, he has been mong the Astros' best players for many years. They missed him last year.

"It will be interesting to see how much a healthy Puhl takes advantage of the shorter Astrodome fences. And if so, will his average suffer?"

HITTING:

His hitting approach seems all wrong: his stance appears awkward, his swing is highly unorthodox--a slapping-type of stroke which resembles an uppercut but produces few fly balls.

But don't quarrel with success. Craig Reynolds remains a respectable hitter, batting .272 last year while sharing time at shortstop with Dickie Thon.

He is basically a pull hitter, but he will take the outside pitch to left field. He will occasionally bunt for base hits and he is a good bet to sacrifice.

He does not have good power, but every so often Craig will surprise a pitcher by hitting a mistake a long, long distance. Pitchers should not hang a breaking ball to him.

Reynolds is an aggressive hitter, one who likes to hack and is difficult to walk.

Last season, he hit mostly against righthanded pitchers, yielding to Dickie Thon against lefthanders.

BASERUNNING:

Craig never has been a big basestealing threat, despite what was once above-average speed and probably is average now. He is not an especially aggressive runner, but he is intelligent, has good instincts and will take an extra base.

He still gets an occasional infield single, too, because of his ability to break quickly out of the batter's box.

FIELDING:

He doesn't have brilliant range or a brilliant arm, but he is very steady. He makes the plays he should make, is good around second base on the double play and is simply a solid major league shortstop.

In a pinch, Reynolds could play second or third base and not be a defensive liability.

CRAIG REYNOLDS
SS, No. 12
LR, 6'1", 175 lbs.
ML Svc: 10 years
Born: 12-27-52 in
Houston, TX

1985 STATISTICS
AVG	G	AB	R	H	2B	3B	HR	RBI	BB	SO	SB
.272	107	379	43	103	18	8	4	32	12	30	4

CAREER STATISTICS
AVG	G	AB	R	H	2B	3B	HR	RBI	BB	SO	SB
.259	1063	3429	377	890	108	59	29	280	158	290	46

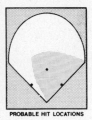

VS. RHP   VS. LHP   PROBABLE HIT LOCATIONS

OVERALL:

It's hard not to be impressed by Reynolds. He lost the starting shortstop job to Dickie Thon four years ago, then got it back when Thon suffered a serious eye injury in the first week of the 1984 season.

Through it all, Reynolds has never complained. He has been used in all sorts of capacities and has remained an asset to the Astros.

Campbell: "I've always been very impressed with this young man both as a player and a person. I don't think any club would be embarrassed to have Craig Reynolds in the lineup on a daily basis. He has worked to make himself as good as he can be.

"The Astros were extremely fortunate to have someone as reliable as Craig when Thon was hurt. And with the Thon situation still up in the air, Reynolds should remain a fixture on the Astros this season."

PITCHING:

Last year, for the first time in many years, Nolan Ryan did not have a good season. Over the years, he has experienced a series of thigh, groin and hamstring injuries; it could be that they have taken a toll. In addition, Ryan also had a shoulder injury at one point last season.

Much of Ryan's success over the years has been attributed to his excellent physical condition. He works hard 12 months a year at staying in top shape. But a rash of nagging injuries can offset even the hardest work.

When he is healthy, Ryan remains awesome. His fastball was clocked as high as 99 MPH last year, a remarkable accomplishment for a man 38 years old. When he has command of his curveball, as well, Ryan can be all but unhittable.

He didn't always have that command last year, though. Ryan allowed only 205 hits in 232 innings--an excellent ratio for most pitchers, but well below his career average. Combined with 95 walks, Ryan put a lot of people on base, although he still got his share of strikeouts.

An interesting development for Ryan—one with both plus and minus effects--is that he has now come up with a change-up. The plus is that he used it effectively early last season, when he was winning. It is a good pitch, one which tails down and away from lefthanded batters. The pitch has outstanding motion. The minus is that Nolan may have fallen too much in love with his new pitch. It may have distorted the rest of his pitches because he was ineffective the second half of the season.

Another trend is that whereas Ryan used to be the best closer in the game, almost never losing a late lead, he has more trouble finishing now.

NOLAN RYAN
RHP, No. 34
RR, 6'2", 210 lbs.
ML Svc: 18 years
Born: 1-31-47 in
Refugio, TX

1985 STATISTICS

W	L	ERA	G	GS	CG	SV	IP	H	R	ER	BB	SO
10	12	3.80	35	35	4	0	232	205	108	98	95	209

CAREER STATISTICS

W	L	ERA	G	GS	CG	SV	IP	H	R	ER	BB	SO
241	218	3.14	581	547	202	2	3937.1	2871	1571	1374	2186	4083

FIELDING, HITTING, BASERUNNING:

Nolan is an average fielder. He does not have a good move to first base and runners can steal on him often. He is not a good hitter and is only an average bunter.

OVERALL:

During the last two seasons, Ryan has gone through periods where he was as good as any pitcher in the league. He has not maintained the consistency, perhaps because of injuries. He slacked off noticeably late last year.

He is still an intense competitor and doesn't beat himself with mental mistakes. He has lost little or nothing in terms of velocity.

Campbell: "This is going to be a make-or-break year for Nolan. He needs to come back and have a more consistent season if he expects to continue his career, or at least to continue it as a high-salaried player."

PITCHING:

Mike Scott was one of baseball's biggest success stories last season. In 1984, at the age of 30, he was hanging on by just a thread. He was allowing baserunners everywhere and had all but abandoned what had once been his best pitch, the slider.

Things were not looking good for Mike Scott. Then he took a little 10-day working vacation in San Diego and turned his entire career around. He went to the split-finger guru, Roger Craig, and became one of the league's best pitchers and almost won 20 games in 1985.

The split-finger is an off-speed pitch which breaks sharply: Scott caught on to it quickly. He already had a good fastball, one which gets up in excess of 90 MPH at times, but when his slider stopped sliding, hitters were able to sit on the fastball and send it sailing out of the park.

The split-finger pitch changed all that. Batters took some feeble swings against Scott last year and appeared to have trouble picking up the rotation on the ball. The off-speed pitch made his fastball seem so much quicker.

The result: Scott's strikeouts were up, his hit ratio was down and his record was 18-8 for a team which finished barely above .500. Scott might have won 20, too, except that he tired in late September after pitching far more innings than in any other season.

FIELDING, HITTING, BASERUNNING:

Scott is an ordinary fielder who does not hurt himself. A big asset is that he has one of the quicker moves to first base among righthanders. Every year, he catches several runners off guard.

As a hitter, Scott has worked hard.

MIKE SCOTT
RHP, No. 33
RR, 6'3", 215 lbs.
ML Svc: 7 years
Born: 4-26-55 in
   Santa Monica, CA

1985 STATISTICS

W	L	ERA	G	GS	CG	SV	IP	H	R	ER	BB	SO
18	8	3.29	36	35	4	0	221.2	194	91	81	80	137

CAREER STATISTICS

W	L	ERA	G	GS	CG	SV	IP	H	R	ER	BB	SO
47	52	4.16	175	148	9	3	884.2	930	468	409	291	444

And it shows. He takes good, healthy cuts with the bat and helped the Astros several times with run-scoring hits. He has good power, too. Scott's hitting ability is another reason for his overall success, because when a manager knows a pitcher is likely to make contact, he isn't as quick to pinch-hit for him. That can mean three or four more victories over the season.

OVERALL:

In a rotation which included Nolan Ryan, Joe Niekro (for most of the year) and Bob Knepper, Mike Scott hardly figured to become the ace. But he did.

Campbell: "He was at a crossroads entering the season, but without question, Scott went in the right direction. The contrast between his 90 MPH fastball and his split-finger pitch makes him extremely effective.

"Scott was easily the most improved player on the Astros last season. It may be fair to say, considering Sutter's off-year, that Mike has the best split-finger pitch in the league."

GOOD CONTROL

PITCHING:

Dave Smith's career has been like a roller coaster ride. In his first two seasons in the major leagues (1980 and 1981), he teamed with Joe Sambito to give the Astros one of baseball's best bullpens. Then, for two years (especially in 1983), Smith struggled badly. He began to bounce back in 1984; and last season, he reached new careeer highs, by saving 27 games and winning nine others.

One of the reasons for Smith's latest rise to the top is that his control has improved remarkably over the past two years. Some time ago, he was struggling with the mechanics of his delivery (probably because of several nagging injuries) and he was unable to spot the ball where he wanted. But last year, he had everything in order: he walked only 17 batters in 79 innings.

Simply: he doesn't beat himself with wildness, and he's got good stuff.

Smith's primary weapon is an excellent forkball. When he is able to control it, its sharp, downward movement can be devastating. His fastball is 86-87 MPH at best and his slider is ordinary. But when he uses them to set up his forkball, the fastball looks faster and the slider suddenly appears to have a big drop.

Another key to Smith's recent success is that he is among the league's toughest competitors. His name is not a household word, but he has been in late-inning relief for six years now, so the pressure of the game is nothing new to him. He never scares.

FIELDING, HITTING, BASERUNNING:

Overcoming several injuries and losing some excess weight has aided Smith's mobility and helped him to become a better fielder. He has seen almost every situation and reacts well under pressure.

DAVE SMITH
RHP, No. 45
RR, 6'1", 195 lbs.
ML Svc: 6 years
Born: 1-21-55 in
San Francisco, CA

1985 STATISTICS												
W	L	ERA	G	GS	CG	SV	IP	H	R	ER	BB	SO
9	5	2.27	64	0	0	27	79.1	69	26	20	17	40

CAREER STATISTICS												
W	L	ERA	G	GS	CG	SV	IP	H	R	ER	BB	SO
34	22	2.60	307	1	0	67	470.2	414	160	136	159	291

His move to first base is average, but Smith watches runners closely. If they pick the forkball to run on, and if it dips sharply, their success ratio is high because the pitch is tough for a catcher to handle.

Smith's one asset as a hitter is that he enjoys taking his hacks. He doesn't bat often and isn't any good, but unlike most late-inning pitchers, Smith is trying. His baserunning is average.

OVERALL:

For the second consecutive year, he made noticeable improvement. Entering this season, he has to rank among the league's best relievers. He has regained a stopper's best friend, his confidence, after suffering through two poor years.

Campbell: "He picked a good time to blossom into a premier reliever. Dawley and DiPino were having their problems, and the Astros turned to Smith. He did not let them down.

"He is able to be an effective reliever without the type of power pitches most short men have. His forkball is so good that he doesn't need anything else except good control."

HITTING:

Last year was a comeback season for Dickie Thon as a hitter. He didn't make it all the way back, but he did make some strides.

Dickie had missed almost all of the 1984 season after being hit in the head by a Mike Torrez pitch in the first week of the season. The accident caused him to have vision problems which still continue.

The Astros were careful to bring him back slowly into the everyday lineup last season, playing him mostly against lefthanded pitchers and keeping him out of the game against the harder-throwing righties.

At first, the results were not encouraging. But Thon began to hit with more consistency and more authority as the summer progressed. He stood in well against lefthanders and took good hacks. Against righthanders, particularly those who drop down in their delivery, he appeared tentative.

Thon is a high-ball hitter who likes pitches where he can extend his arms. He is pretty much a straightaway hitter.

From a power standpoint, Thon is not what he used to be, though that is probably attributable to his eye trouble at this point. Before getting hurt, he killed the high breaking pitch.

BASERUNNING:

In his only full season in the major leagues (1983), he stole 34 bases and projections then were that Thon could eventually steal 50 bases or more as he matured. The injury has left that in doubt. He does have good speed and aggressiveness, though, and if he plays, he will run.

FIELDING:

If Thon's vision affected him defensively, it rarely showed. He has a good

DICKIE THON
SS, No. 10
RR, 5'11", 175 lbs.
ML Svc: 7 years
Born: 6-20-58 in South Bend, IN

1985 STATISTICS

AVG	G	AB	R	H	2B	3B	HR	RBI	BB	SO	SB
.251	84	251	26	63	6	1	6	29	18	50	8

CAREER STATISTICS

AVG	G	AB	R	H	2B	3B	HR	RBI	BB	SO	SB
.275	543	1801	234	496	86	23	29	171	133	226	92

  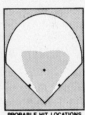

VS. RHP — VS. LHP — PROBABLE HIT LOCATIONS

hands, good range and a good arm. He made some spectacular plays last year. Thon and Bill Doran are an excellent double play combination.

OVERALL:

Prior to the injury, Thon was one of the best hitters in the league. Perhaps he will be one again in time. He did make progress last year, though offensively it was slow progress.

Campbell: "The Houston management has a tough decision to make about Dickie Thon. He says his eyesight still is not what it should be. The Astros are fortunate to have Craig Reynolds to fill in but their two salaries combined are probably more than any club is paying for the shortstop position except for St. Louis with Ozzie Smith.

"There is no question, though, that when he is healthy, Dickie has excellent ability."

HITTING:

Denny Walling is a solid major league hitter, a man who could average in the .270-.280 range and provide some power if he played on an everyday basis. He could probably double his home run output if his home stadium was anyplace but the Astrodome.

But Walling doesn't play regularly and he does play in the Dome. Even so, his average last year again was a creditable .270 in 345 at-bats and he drove in 45 runs with seven homers.

He makes contact and is disciplined enough to take a walk, but Walling will also drive the ball hard to right field and right-center. He is primarily a first-ball, fastball hitter, but he will occasionally surprise a southpaw here and there with his success against a lefthander's breaking ball. In certain situations, Walling is willing to slap that breaking pitch to left field.

After years as the Astros' best pinch-hitter, Walling isn't fazed by any pressure situation. He is one of the club's most feared clutch hitters.

BASERUNNING:

Walling is an average runner, maybe not quite as fast as in his early years, but if opponents ignore him, he still has enough speed to steal a base. He is not particularly aggressive but doesn't make a lot of mistakes on the bases.

FIELDING:

Walling's career has taken on a jack-of-all-trades flavor. He has handled all three outfield positions as well as first base. Most recently, he has split time with Phil Garner at third base.

He has worked hard to improve himself as a third baseman and it shows. Denny is never going to remind anybody of Brooks Robinson, but he will make an occasional good play and hasn't hurt the Astros at third.

DENNY WALLING
3B, No. 29
LR, 6'1", 185 lbs.
ML Svc: 8 years
Born: 4-17-54 in Neptune, NJ

1985 STATISTICS

AVG	G	AB	R	H	2B	3B	HR	RBI	BB	SO	SB
.270	119	345	44	93	20	1	7	45	25	26	5

CAREER STATISTICS

AVG	G	AB	R	H	2B	3B	HR	RBI	BB	SO	SB
.271	773	1751	233	475	72	23	28	236	193	188	38

  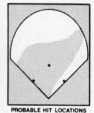

VS. RHP   VS. LHP   PROBABLE HIT LOCATIONS

At one time, he looked like a fairly decent fly-hawk in the outfield, but it now appears he has lost a step. His arm, while good at third base, is not strong for an outfielder.

His best defensive position is first base, and even last year when he started at third, he frequently shifted to first in the late innings to relieve regular first baseman Glenn Davis.

OVERALL:

Walling is a valuable player because of his versatility. He has helped the Astros at five positions through the years.

Campbell: "He's worked to become a good defensive player and won't embarrass his team at first or third base. But I still think Walling's best role on a good ball club would be as a pinch-hitter and part-time fill-in player."

TY GAINEY
OF, No. 24
RL, 6'1", 190 lbs.
ML Svc: less than 1 year
Born: 10-25-60 in
    Cheraw, SC

HITTING, BASERUNNING, FIELDING:

Ty Gainey received two brief trials with the Astros during the 1985 season after impressing then with his bat in spring training. In Florida, he gained attention by belting line drives to all fields and over the walls. ·The only question mark seemed to be his fielding ability.

But with the Astros during the regular season, he was only 6 for 37 and none of those hits was for extra bases. He should be the type of hitter who makes contact regularly; instead, he took prodigious swings and too often met only air.

He likes the fastball down and, when he is in form, Gainey sprays the ball hard to every field.

As a runner, the plus is that he has excellent speed. The minus is that he has yet to learn how to utilize it on the bases.

Defensively, Gainey has a problem. Judging fly balls, using his speed and throwing are all areas in which he needs improvement. The Astros tried him in center field and during one game, he broke in for a ball that traveled over his head and broke back for a ball that landed 20 feet in front of him.

OVERALL:

Maybe Gainey needs only more playing time to relax and become the same good hitter in the major leagues he has been in the minors. But unless he does find that form, he won't stick at the top level. He needs to improve defensively, but he does have good speed, good desire and a hustling nature; improvement could come.

HARRY SPILMAN
C/1B, No. 16
LR, 6'1", 190 lbs.
ML Svc: 7 years
Born: 7-18-54 in
    Albany, GA

HITTING, BASERUNNING, FIELDING:

Harry Spilman is primarily a fastball hitter who likes the ball out over the plate. He has been a good line drive hitter in the past, but Spilman had a terrible season for Houston in 1985 and the Astros didn't try to persuade him from declaring free agency.

He is not a patient hitter and will chase the low breaking ball. He got only line drive hits in 66 at-bats last year, only two of which were for extra bases.

He will pull a mistake hard down the line, but the best defense is to give him the lines and bunch the alleys.

Spilman is a slow runner but is a tough competitor who will break up the double play.

Defensively, he is an adequate first baseman, can play left field or right field and has filled in at catcher. He worked hard at the latter role in Houston and it could enhance his value, even keep him in the big leagues.

OVERALL:

Two years ago, when he was slapping line drives in every direction, Spilman seemed on the verge of earning a starting job with the Astros. But then he suffered a major leg injury.

Campbell: "Now, his career is on the line. His main value is as a lefthanded pinch-hitter; his versatility is another asset."

TIM TOLMAN
OF, No. 18
RR, 6'0", 195 lbs.
ML Svc: 3 years
Born: 4-20-56 in
  Santa Monica, CA

HITTING, BASERUNNING, FIELDING:

Until the final weeks of the 1985 season, it appeared this righthanded pinch-hitter would go the entire year without getting a base hit.

Then, with the Astros out of contention, he was given an opportunity to play occasionally. Then Tim Tolman showed why he was in Houston in the first place. He quickly hit two home runs and had six RBIs.

Tolman was always a solid hitter in the minors, but he has never received a full-time opportunity in the majors. He appeared so seldom last season that it was understandable that his swing was awkward and his production almost nil.

He is a fastball hitter who likes the ball over the plate. He has good power. And until last season, he showed excellent discipline as a hitter.

His speed is average to below average and he has no stolen base potential.

Defensively, Tolman is adequate at first base and in left field.

OVERALL:

Tolman has not had a lot of major league opportunities. There are a lot of holes in his game, but he has shown flashes of power. He may become a good choice as a pinch-hitter once he knows he has the job.

LOS ANGELES DODGERS

HITTING:

After hitting .343 in the minors in 1982, Dave Anderson was named the number one prospect in the Pacific Coast League. He appeared to be on track to fulfilling his promise in 1984 when he displaced Bill Russell as the Dodgers' starting shortstop, but a recurrence of chronic back problems in 1985 not only cost Anderson his job, they cast his major league future in doubt.

Because of Anderson's back problems, he went on the disabled list twice in 1985 and spent three weeks rehabilitating in the minors (at Albequerque).

When he returned, Anderson appeared overmatched by big league pitching and his average never got above .213 before landing with a crash at .199. He had almost as many strikeouts (42) as hits (44).

Last season, it looked as though he didn't have enough bat speed to be a successful hitter at the major league level. How much his back problems contributed to his hitting woes is uncertain, but Anderson was indeed fair game at the plate.

He bats out of a very slight crouch and is a straightaway, singles hitter who likes balls up in the strike zone. He is one of the better bunters on the team.

BASERUNNING:

Anderson has good speed, but again, his back problems limited him to just five stolen bases in nine attempts last season.

FIELDING:

Anderson has good speed but, again, smooth infielder, though he has an annoying habit of muffing routine plays at shortstop. His back also appeared to

DAVE ANDERSON
SS, No. 10
RR, 6'2", 185 lbs.
ML Svc: 3 years
Born: 8-1-60 in
Louisville, KY

1985 STATISTICS

AVG	G	AB	R	H	2B	3B	HR	RBI	BB	SO	SB
.199	77	221	24	44	6	0	4	18	35	42	5

CAREER STATISTICS

AVG	G	AB	R	H	2B	3B	HR	RBI	BB	SO	SB
.221	259	710	87	157	26	4	8	54	92	112	26

VS. RHP

VS. LHP

PROBABLE HIT LOCATIONS

cause him some trouble in getting to balls that were within his reach.

With the emergence of Mariano Duncan as an outstanding shortstop, the Dodgers tried Anderson at third base and he did well there. He also can play second base and not do too much damage.

OVERALL:

Anderson ostensibly is too young to be cast as a utilityman, but his back problems may not allow him the opportunity to be more than a fill-in. His injury also reduces his value in a trade—and he still has to prove he can handle big league pitching.

Campbell: "Dave was Bill Russell's heir apparent, but now he cannot be counted on to play 130 games in a season. His future is very much in question."

HITTING:

Since coming to the Dodgers in a 1983 trade with the Mets, Bob Bailor has spent as much time on the disabled list as he has on the field.

Last spring, Bailor was projected as the Dodgers' top utility player. In a bit of roster shuffling, Bailor began the season on the 21-day disabled list with a minor shoulder injury. He went on the DL again with a pulled right hamstring in June. Just the year before, Bailor had suffered a dislocated shoulder and underwent arthroscopic surgery on his right knee.

The injuries limited Bailor to just 118 at-bats in 1985, his fewest since 1981. The inactivity showed in his average, which dipped to as low as .194 before he finished strongly.

Bailor is a line drive hitter who hits to all fields. He had a four-hit game against the Phillies in August, but never played enough last season to get comfortable at the plate. He is a very patient hitter and struck out only five times.

BASERUNNING:

Bailor stole just one base for the Dodgers after once stealing 20 for the Mets (1982). He has just average speed, but seldom makes a mistake on the basepaths.

FIELDING:

Bailor may be the best-fielding third baseman on the Dodgers, even though his throwing arm is just average. He is also adept at second base and in the outfield and is a better outfielder than he is an infielder. Bailor has caught and

BOB BAILOR
INF, No. 21
RR, 5'10", 160 lbs.
ML Svc: 10 years
Born: 7-10-51 in
    Connellsville, PA

1985 STATISTICS

AVG	G	AB	R	H	2B	3B	HR	RBI	BB	SO	SB
.246	74	118	8	29	3	1	0	7	3	5	1

CAREER STATISTICS

AVG	G	AB	R	H	2B	3B	HR	RBI	BB	SO	SB
.264	955	2937	339	775	107	23	9	222	187	165	90

STRONG
VS. RHP

STRONG
VS. LHP

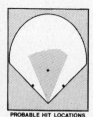

PROBABLE HIT LOCATIONS

even pitched on three occasions (with Toronto in 1980). He is a pro who will not embarrass himself at any position.

OVERALL:

Injuries have kept Bailor from making the contribution the Dodgers have expected from him. Still, his versatility makes him a valuable performer, although he found his lack of playing time last season discouraging.

Campbell: "When Bob is healthy, he is a good hitter who makes contact with the ball and puts it in play. He will do a good job in any field position asked of him. You cannot ask for more from a utility player."

HITTING:

Greg Brock appeared to have arrived as a major league hitter last July when he carried the Dodgers, in the absence of an injured Pedro Guerrero, by hitting .324, smacking five home runs and driving in 24 runs.

But during the last two months, he struggled again. He hit .198 with no home runs in August and hit .237 in September.

Brock stands fairly upright at the plate, his legs wide apart in a slightly closed stance, a fair distance from the plate. He has a habit (which is maddening to the Dodgers) of taking too many pitches for strikes. He should be more aggressive at the plate. Brock might also do well to hit to the opposite field more often as he has the power to go deep to all fields.

The way to pitch Brock is to continually pound him inside, jamming him.

Despite hitting 20 or more home runs for the second time in three seasons with the Dodgers, Brock continues to fall short of the potential projected for him by the Dodgers after his tremendous minor league career.

He is one of the most notorious streak hitters on the team, capable of hitting two home runs and five RBIs in a game, as he did against the Mets last May, then looking totally helpless on other occasions.

Brock's performance at the plate was not helped, either, when manager Tom Lasorda began platooning him with Enos Cabell.

BASERUNNING:

Brock has little speed, but has managed to steal 12 bases in 14 attempts over the last two seasons.

FIELDING:

Brock does not have great range, but

GREG BROCK
1B, No. 9
LR, 6'3", 205 lbs.
ML Svc: 3 years
Born: 6-14-57 in
    McMinnville, OR

1985 STATISTICS

AVG	G	AB	R	H	2B	3B	HR	RBI	BB	SO	SB
.251	129	438	64	110	19	0	21	66	54	72	4

CAREER STATISTICS

AVG	G	AB	R	H	2B	3B	HR	RBI	BB	SO	SB
.232	381	1181	162	275	40	2	55	167	177	195	17

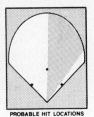

VS. RHP   VS. LHP   PROBABLE HIT LOCATIONS

he has pretty sure hands and is gradually showing improvement in his ability to dig low throws out of the dirt. He has a good throwing arm and is particularly adept at charging a bunt and wheeling to throw out the lead runner, either at third base or second base.

OVERALL:

For the moment, Brock is the Dodger first baseman, but until he shows more consistency, the Dodgers will continue to contemplate alternatives.

Campbell: "It could be Brock is a late bloomer; it's also quite possible that he will remain a streaky performer throughout his career. But as long as he continues to produce at least 20 homers a season, the Dodgers are not likely to give up on him."

HITTING:

Enos Cabell is one of the more notorious bad-ball hitters in the league. He'll swing at a pitch over his head, then golf one down at ankle level. He can be made to look pretty bad on a pitch, especially breaking stuff away, and then jump all over the same pitch on his next at-bat.

Obtained by the Dodgers from the Astros last July, Cabell had two hits in each of his first three starts in Dodger Blue. He wound up hitting .292 for the Dodgers after batting .245 for Houston. Cabell hit .329 against southpaw pitching for the Dodgers.

Cabell doesn't have power, but when he does try for extra bases, he exaggerates his crouch and both of his feet nearly come off the ground when he swings. He makes good contact, is excellent on the hit-and-run and will hit to all fields. Pitchers have to change speeds constantly on him.

BASERUNNING:

Cabell no longer has the speed he once had, but he is an excellent baserunner (the Astros even used him as a baserunning instructor during spring training). He still goes from first to third well.

FIELDING:

The Dodgers played Cabell at both third and first last season; he is much more comfortable at first, where his lack of range and erratic throwing do not hurt him as much as they do on the other side of the diamond.

ENOS CABELL
1B, No. 23
RR, 6'5", 185 lbs.
ML Svc: 13 years
Born: 10-18-49 in
Fort Riley, KS

1985 STATISTICS

AVG	G	AB	R	H	2B	3B	HR	RBI	BB	SO	SB
.272	117	335	40	91	19	1	2	36	30	36	9

CAREER STATISTICS

AVG	G	AB	R	H	2B	3B	HR	RBI	BB	SO	SB
.278	1581	5675	726	1576	252	56	58	567	252	617	227

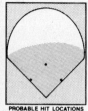

VS. RHP — STRONG VS. LHP — STRONG PROBABLE HIT LOCATIONS

OVERALL:

Cabell's future with the Dodgers is uncertain; he exercised his right to demand a trade after the 1985 season. But he made a significant impact on the Dodgers last year, not only on the field but in the clubhouse, where his biting wit and usual good cheer brought life and levity to a ballclub that was in need of both.

At one time, Cabell had been mentioned as managerial material after his playing days are over. That, of course, remains to be seen.

Campbell: "How do you defense Enos Cabell? It's a mystery to me."

PITCHING:

Bobby Castillo, the man credited with teaching Fernando Valenzuela the screwball, spent five seasons in the Dodger bullpen before being traded to the Minnesota Twins in 1982. He came back to the Dodgers last season as a free agent and worked as a long reliever and spot starter.

In his second go-round with the Dodgers, righthander Castillo continued to struggle in his attempt to come back from the rotator cuff surgery which had been performed while he was with the Minnesota Twins during the 1983 season.

Castillo, a compact 5'10", 180 lbs., began the season on the disabled list with a sore right shoulder. In his first start since returning to the Dodgers, he combined with Tom Niedenfuer to throw a shutout against Pittsburgh, but that was the highlight of an otherwise downbeat season.

In addition to the screwball, he throws a fastball, a slider and a curveball. To make his screwball effective, Castillo must throw his other pitches for strikes. His screwball breaks down and inside on righthanded hitters, but if he is having trouble controlling it, hitters will sit on it. When he hangs a screwball, Lasorda hangs his head and reaches for the phone.

Last season, Castillo pitched constantly with runners on base, allowing 59 hits and 41 walks in just 68 innings, reminiscent of former Dodger reliever Don (Full Pack) Stanhouse.

Castillo's earned run average of 5.43 was the worst on the staff.

BOBBY CASTILLO
RHP, No. 37
RR, 5'10", 180 lbs.
ML Svc: 8 years
Born: 4-18-55 in
  Los Angeles, CA

1985 STATISTICS

W	L	ERA	G	GS	CG	SV	IP	H	R	ER	BB	SO
2	2	5.43	35	5	0	0	68	59	42	41	41	57

CAREER STATISTICS

W	L	ERA	G	GS	CG	SV	IP	H	R	ER	BB	SO
38	40	3.42	250	59	9	18	688.2	623	327	302	327	434

FIELDING, HITTING, BASERUNNING:

His fielding is adequate at best, and he has a mediocre move to first base.

Castillo, who batted .444 (4-for-9) in 1981 (the year before he was traded by the Dodgers), had just one hit in 10 trips last season.

OVERALL:

At age 30, Castillo is, at best, the 10th man on the Dodger staff. His future is in question.

Campbell: "Last season, the Dodgers were willing to take a chance that Castillo would recover from his rotator cuff problems. At one time, the injury caused him to be placed in a cast for nearly 10 weeks. It's not clear whether the Dodgers are willing to take the same chance this season."

PITCHING:

Carlos Diaz is a slender six-footer who pitches with a three-quarters delivery and throws primarily two pitches: a fastball and a slow curve. His curveball is his out pitch. In order for his curveball to be effective, he must show his 80-85 MPH fastball.

Diaz has a tendency to fall behind in the count, but last season, he was able to cut down on his walks and struck out twice as many batters as he had in 1984. He averaged almost one strikeout per inning (73 Ks in 79 1/3 IP).

Manager Tom Lasorda has confidence in Diaz in spot situations,--to get a lefthanded batter or two in the sixth or seventh innings. But you won't see Lasorda going to Diaz with a game on the line, which is one reason the Dodgers have made the acquisition of another lefthanded reliever their number one priority in the off-season.

The fact that Lasorda feels that he can't rely on Diaz in a tight spot was made clear when he had Tom Niedenfuer pitch to Jack Clark in the deciding game of the National League playoffs last year, when lefthanded-hitting Andy Van Slyke was on deck.

FIELDING, HITTING, BASERUNNING:

Diaz has an adequate move to first base, but his slow breaking stuff leaves him open to the stolen base. Otherwise,

CARLOS DIAZ
RHP, No. 27
RL, 6'0", 170 lbs.
ML Svc; 4 years
Born: 1-7-58 in
   Honolulu, HI

1985 STATISTICS

W	L	ERA	G	GS	CG	SV	IP	H	R	ER	BB	SO
6	3	2.61	46	0	0	0	79.1	70	28	23	18	73

CAREER STATISTICS

W	L	ERA	G	GS	CG	SV	IP	H	R	ER	BB	SO
13	6	3.10	160	0	0	4	232.2	216	93	80	90	189

he fields his position adequately.

Diaz has had only 13 major league at-bats and he is still looking for his first hit.

OVERALL:

The Dodgers gave away Sid Fernandez, now a mainstay of the Mets' starting rotation, to bring Diaz to Los Angeles. Tommy Lasorda has said that that trade would never have been made if Steve Howe hadn't been suspended because of drug problems.

Campbell: "Diaz's future with the Dodgers hinges on his continued effectiveness as a long reliever. That, however, is in question."

HITTING:

Last season, the Dodgers found themselves a new leadoff man. Mariano Duncan was supposed to have started the season in Triple-A, but he received an emergency summons when Steve Sax was injured in the last exhibition game of the spring. Duncan's first major league at-bat was inauspicious: he struck out on three pitches from Houston flamethrower Nolan Ryan. But the next night, Duncan had two hits off Joe Niekro and was here to stay.

The switch-hitting Duncan, who stands close to the plate and bats in a crouch, hit .244 as a rookie. The Dodgers would have been satisfied if he'd hit that high in Triple-A, since he only began switch-hitting three years ago. He hit .286 from the right side of the plate, just .224 from the left, and his 110 strikeouts are testimony to the difficulty of getting an education at the plate.

Duncan showed surprising flashes of power with six home runs, four more than he had hit in Double-A. But his development as a hitter will revolve around his ability to swing down on the ball and his improvement as a bunter. His most amazing feat was that he bunted four times for doubles last year.

BASERUNNING:

Duncan is the fastest runner on the team. He stole 38 bases last season, ending the season with a streak of 14 in a row, and was caught just eight times. Duncan got the green light in September and he showed the potential to steal 50 bases when set loose over the course of an entire season.

FIELDING:

Even though he committed 30 errors, Duncan evoked comparisons to Ozzie Smith with his play at shortstop. He started the season at second base when Sax was hurt, but moved to short in May and displaced the injury-ridden Dave Anderson as the Dodgers' shortstop of the future.

MARIANO DUNCAN
SS, No. 12
SR, 6'0", 160 lbs.
ML Svc: 1 year
Born: 3-13-63 in
   San Pedro de Macoris, DR

1985 STATISTICS

AVG	G	AB	R	H	2B	3B	HR	RBI	BB	SO	SB
.244	142	562	74	137	24	6	6	39	38	113	38

CAREER STATISTICS

AVG	G	AB	R	H	2B	3B	HR	RBI	BB	SO	SB
.244	142	562	74	137	24	6	6	39	38	113	38

  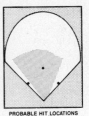

VS. RHP   VS. LHP   PROBABLE HIT LOCATIONS

Duncan has tremendous range, a strong throwing arm, and exceptionally quick feet. He is equally adept at going into the hole or cutting across second base to make a play. A smart, instinctive player Duncan occasionally has a tendency to showboat a little when he charges a ball, opting to throw on the run when he really doesn't have to. But he made enough spectacular plays to make his own personal highlight film.

OVERALL:

The Dodgers, who led the league in errors last season, were a defensive mess until Duncan took over at shortstop. He is only 22 years old and great things are expected of him--especially if he can master the art of switch-hitting.

Campbell: "Unless the notoriety goes to his head, Duncan could be a great player. He is an enormous young talent. The only thing that can stop him is himself."

HITTING:

Pedro Guerrero missed 23 games last season due to back and wrist injuries and still had an MVP-type season. He tied Steve Garvey's LA Dodger record for most home runs (33), a record he undoubtedly would have broken if he hadn't banged his wrist chasing a foul fly hit by Darryl Strawberry in early September.

Guerrero's swing was drastically affected by his injured wrist and he was not able to hit even one home run after his return to the lineup. The Dodgers missed his power punch during the NLCS.

Guerrero crowds the plate in an upright stance and likes the ball up. When he's hot, he will hit anything: fastball, breaking stuff, change-up—all the pitch has to be is up in the strike zone. Occasionally, he'll reach down and golf a pitch as if he were swinging a one iron. At times, he will chase fastballs up and in or breaking stuff down and away. But for the most part, he has an excellent knowledge of the strike zone.

He is a streak hitter who had one of baseball's hottest streaks ever last season: he tied a major league record with 15 home runs in June while driving in 26 runs and scoring 27. In July, he batted .460 despite having to come out of the lineup with back spasms.

Guerrero struggled through the first two months last year, but when Lasorda moved him from third base to the outfield, his bat exploded: from that point on, he hit .348 with 29 home runs and 69 RBIs.

On the advice of batting coach Manny Mota, Guerrero also made a slight adjustment in the way he held the bat. Instead of holding it on his shoulder, with the barrel parallel to the ground, he moved the bat to a more upright position, which seems to have eliminated a slight hitch in his swing.

BASERUNNING:

Guerrero can no longer run because of his injuries. He severely fractured his ankle in 1977 and won't slide feetfirst;

PEDRO GUERRERO
OF, No. 28
RR, 6'0", 195 lbs.
ML Svc: 7 years
Born: 6-29-56 in
  San Pedro de Macoris, DR

1985 STATISTICS

AVG	G	AB	R	H	2B	3B	HR	RBI	BB	SO	SB
.320	137	487	99	156	22	2	33	87	83	68	12

CAREER STATISTICS

AVG	G	AB	R	H	2B	3B	HR	RBI	BB	SO	SB
.306	794	2781	441	850	134	21	134	451	316	474	75

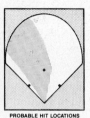

VS. RHP | VS. LHP | PROBABLE HIT LOCATIONS

he won't slide headfirst because of his his past shoulder problems.

FIELDING:

At one time, the Dodgers hoped that one day Guerrero would be as good at third base as Mike Schimdt used to be. In reality, as a third baseman, Guerrero was, as one scout said, "brutal." His poor fielding there also affected his hitting.

Guerrero is much more at home in the outfield. At best, he is an average fielder who doesn't charge balls well and has a below-average throwing arm.

OVERALL:

At the age of 29, Guerrero is just approaching his prime. He could have a 40 HR/125 RBI season any time now.

Campbell: "I've heard that Pedro marches to the beat of his own drum, but when a manager has a talent like him, I guess you go along with the program."

PITCHING:

Early in the 1984 season, Hershiser was a struggling relief pitcher on the verge of being sent to the minors. Manager Tommy Lasorda, fearing that Orel Hershiser was too intimidated by big league hitters, summoned him into his office for a pep talk. Lasorda took to calling the young pitcher "bulldog," and almost overnight, Hershiser became a tenacious battler who gives quarter to no one. Lasorda's speech now is referred to in jest as "The Sermon on the Mound."

Last year, Hershiser had the kind of year last season no one would have expected from a 17th round draft choice. He ended just one victory shy of becoming the Dodgers' first 20-game winner since Tommy John in 1977.

Hershiser, who began his rookie season in the bullpen, was undefeated at Dodger Stadium last year, going 12-0, including a win in the second game of the playoffs, before taking a no-decision in the decisive Game 6.

He has two exceptional pitches: a sinking fastball and a hard curveball that breaks so sharply that other, more jealous pitches have suggested it might be a spitball. When Hershiser has his control, he is virtually unhittable. In the span of one week last season, he threw a one-hitter and a two-hitter agaisnt the San Diego Padres, and then threw another one-hitter against the Pittsburgh Pirates later in the season. He also throws an extraordinary breaking pitch, one that is completely ruinous to righthanded hitters.

He is not physically imposing (it has been said he is built like an X-ray), but he has an easy, fluid motion and is overcoming his tendency of occasionally trying to make every pitch perfect.

OREL HERSHISER
RHP, No. 55
RR, 6'3", 190 lbs.
ML Svc: 2 years
Born: 9-16-58 in
Buffalo, NY

1985 STATISTICS

W	L	ERA	G	GS	CG	SV	IP	H	R	ER	BB	SO
19	3	2.03	36	34	9	0	239.2	179	72	54	68	157

CAREER STATISTICS

W	L	ERA	G	GS	CG	SV	IP	H	R	ER	BB	SO
30	11	2.32	89	54	17	3	437.1	346	143	113	124	316

FIELDING, HITTING, BASERUNNING:

Hershiser is not a good fielding pitcher. He recorded seven errors last year, more than twice as many as any other Dodger pitcher. His pickoff move could still use work.

At the plate, Hershiser makes good contact. He had three hits in one game against the Braves last season and he has developed into one of the best bunters on the team. He doesn't embarrass himself on the basepaths.

OVERALL:

When Hershiser first arrived in the major leagues, he was in awe of the big league hitters. The tables have since turned and the big league hitters now marvel at his ability.

Dating back to 1984, he has won 22 of his last 25 decisions, and has thrown a slew of one-, two- and three-hit games.

Campbell: "How he didn't get a no-hitter last year, I'll never know. With the exception of Dwight Gooden, Orel has the best stuff in the league."

PITCHING:

Rick Honeycutt is a lefthanded control pitcher whose fastball would leave most windowpanes intact but whose sinker can be lethal.

When he is right, Honeycutt gives his infielders a workout. He forces the batters to hit ground ball after ground ball.

Honeycutt also mixes in a slider that is especially effective against lefthanded hitters.

However, Honeycutt has a shoulder ailment which has curtailed his overall effectiveness. He hurt his shoulder when he fell while he was jogging and had surgery performed prior to last year. He pitched in pain all season. The injury caused him to drop his release point, which in turn flattened out his sinker. It became a very hittable pitch.

He has enjoyed a history of fast starts, but last year, he won only two of his first seven decisions. He was unable to attain a .500 level. For a time, he was dropped from the starting rotation and made six appearances out of the bullpen. His eight wins last year were his fewest since he went 5-17 for the Rangers in 1982.

FIELDING, HITTING, BASERUNNING:

Honeycutt is a good fielder with an average move to first base.

He is an excellent all-around athlete

RICK HONEYCUTT
LHP, No. 40
LL, 5'11", 192 lbs.
ML Svc: 9 years
Born: 6-29-54 in
Chattanooga, TN

1985 STATISTICS

W	L	ERA	G	GS	CG	SV	IP	H	R	ER	BB	SO
8	12	3.42	31	25	1	1	142	141	71	54	49	67

CAREER STATISTICS

W	L	ERA	G	GS	CG	SV	IP	H	R	ER	BB	SO
76	96	3.81	243	216	46	1	1391.1	1454	679	590	408	549

and prides himself on his hitting. In the minors, he hit .301 one season, but last season, he had only five hits in 38 at-bats.

OVERALL:

Honeycutt must overcome his physical problems and regain the form that allowed him to compile the lowest earned run average (2.42) in the AL in 1983. He is signed through the 1987 season, but it's possible that he may be challenged for his number five spot in the rotation by rookie Dennis Powell, another lefthander.

Campbell: "He's never had a consistent full season, but is the kind of guy that probably would be a fifth starter on any team for which he pitches."

90+ FASTBALL

PITCHING:

Ken Howell, who made the jump from Class A ball to the big leagues in less than a year and a half, had such an impressive rookie season in 1984 that the Dodgers were quickly comparing him to the best of the big league short relievers. Last spring, the Dodgers indicated that he was better than Tom Niedenfuer.

Howell has the best fastball on the team (he has been clocked in the mid-90s) and a good slider, but he had a lot of trouble controling both pitches last season. His 1985 performance was alternately brilliant and awful; Niedenfuer wound up as the bullpen anchor.

Howell, who had issued just five unintentional walks in 51 1/3 innings in 1984, walked 35 batters in 85 innings last season. It's possible that Howell's quick rise through the Dodger system caught up with him. Minor league pitching instructors Larry Sherry and Sandy Koufax had worked with Howell in the minors to correct his mechanical flaws. Howell needed to learn how to pace himself; he had the tendency to rush his pitches, open up his hip too soon and not follow through properly in his delivery. He was just a young, raw flame-thrower with a lot of problems--Sherry and Koufax had to do a lot with him in very little time.

When Howell went for extended periods of time without much work last year, his mechanics were thrown off again and as a result, he had trouble with his control. For most of the season, Howell and Niedenfuer alternated as the short man, but by the end of the season, Howell was the set-up and Niedenfuer, the closer.

KEN HOWELL
RHP, No. 43
RR, 6'3", 200 lbs.
ML Svc: 2 years
Born: 11-28-60 in
Detroit, MI

1985 STATISTICS

W	L	ERA	G	GS	CG	SV	IP	H	R	ER	BB	SO
4	7	3.77	56	0	0	12	86	66	41	36	35	85

CAREER STATISTICS

W	L	ERA	G	GS	CG	SV	IP	H	R	ER	BB	SO
9	12	3.61	88	1	0	18	137.1	117	62	55	44	139

FIELDING, HITTING, BASERUNNING:

Howell is an adequate fielder who needs more work on his move to first base.

He is hitless in his only nine major league at-bats and isn't going to hurt anyone with his hitting.

OVERALL:

Howell is a bright, sensitive player and appears to have an outstanding future, though he needs to have his confidence restored. By its nature, bullpen work is magnified; a reliever can quickly be the hero or the goat. Winning did not come easily to Howell last year and he now has a lot to prove.

Campbell: "It would behoove Howell to come up with a slower breaking pitch or a straight change-up. There are games during which he is untouchable: he just comes in and blows hitters away. But he has not been doing it on a consistent basis."

HITTING:

Ken Landreaux bounced back from a sub-par 1984 season, though in order to do it, he had to overcome a miserable start in 1985. Landreaux suffered through a .167 April (9-for-54) and a .250 May before coming to life in the summer months, which were highlighted by a .351 July. Landreaux got his average as high as .283 before tapering off the last three weeks of the season, then was one of the Dodgers' best hitters during the playoffs.

Landreaux stands upright at the plate and has one of the quickest and smoothest swings in baseball (he uses the same stroke today as he did when he had a 31-game hitting streak with Minnesota in 1980). He rarely strikes out but he doesn't walk much, either. He is a free-swinger.

Landreaux continues to be a streak hitter--he hit seven straight pop-ups in one miserable stretch early last season. He is a dead pull hitter, although when he's going well, he will go the other way.

Landreaux is a line drive hitter who will hit the occasional home run (he had 12 in 1985). Sinkerball pitchers seem to give him the most trouble. Last season, he improved his hitting against left-handed pitching.

BASERUNNING:

Landreaux stole 30 bases in 1983, but he doesn't run as much anymore. He still has good speed (he stole 15 last year), but his exploits on the basepaths tend to be erratic.

FIELDING:

Landreaux is a defensive liability. He does not charge balls well, he does

KEN LANDREAUX
CF, No. 44
LR, 5'11", 190 lbs.
ML Svc: 9 years
Born: 12-22-54 in
   Los Angeles, CA

1985 STATISTICS

AVG	G	AB	R	H	2B	3B	HR	RBI	BB	SO	SB
.268	147	482	70	129	26	2	12	50	33	37	15

CAREER STATISTICS

AVG	G	AB	R	H	2B	3B	HR	RBI	BB	SO	SB
.271	1046	3636	471	988	163	43	81	427	261	354	130

  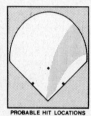

VS. RHP	VS. LHP	PROBABLE HIT LOCATIONS

not get a good jump, he seems to have trouble with line drives hit right at him and his throwing arm is weak. The Dodgers shifted him to right field for a while in 1984, but he was back in center in 1985.

OVERALL:

The Dodgers still would like to see more productivity out of Landreaux, who has two more years left on his contract. This is one position the team really believes could use some improvement.

Campbell: "To me, last season was the best Landreaux has played in the last two or three years. His attitude and enthusiasm appeared much better than in the past and it showed at the plate."

HITTING:

Just as he did when he was traded to the Pirates from the Giants in 1979 and helped Pittsburgh to a World Championship, Bill Madlock was an instrumental part of the Dodgers' stretch drive toward the division title after he was acquired on August 31, 1985.

Madlock, who hit just .251 for the Pirates, went wild with the bat and hit .360 for the Dodgers. He had a 17-game hitting streak with Los Angeles, which matched the longest of his career. And in the playoffs, when Tom Lasorda placed Madlock in the cleanup spot behind Pedro Guerrero, Madlock responded with three home runs off Cardinal pitchers.

Madlock is one of the finest hitters of his generation and appears to have lost little at the plate. He still has that classic short stroke with which he hits line drives to all fields and with extra-base power.

He thrives on fastballs, but will go the other way with breaking pitches. No pitcher has yet been able to figure out a pattern with which to get Madlock out the same way twice.

BASERUNNING:

Seemingly revitalized in Los Angeles, Madlock ran the bases like a man 10 years younger, stealing seven bases in eight attempts (he had stolen only three bases in each of the previous three seasons with the Pirates). Madlock is not as fast as he once was, but he ran with abandon when he moved to the West Coast. He still moves well from first to third and breaks up double plays aggressively.

FIELDING:

Madlock's elbow and shoulder were so weak at the end of spring training last season, he had trouble throwing the ball across the diamond. His arm is still not what it was.

BILL MADLOCK
3B, No. 5
RR, 5'11", 206 lbs.
ML Svc: 13 years
Born: 1-12-51 in
Memphis, TN

1985 STATISTICS

AVG	G	AB	R	H	2B	3B	HR	RBI	BB	SO	SB
.275	144	513	69	141	27	1	12	56	49	53	10

CAREER STATISTICS

AVG	G	AB	R	H	2B	3B	HR	RBI	BB	SO	SB
.309	1587	5828	821	1800	313	34	136	743	541	417	167

STRONG

VS. RHP

STRONG

VS. LHP

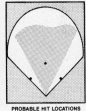

PROBABLE HIT LOCATIONS

His range at third base is limited; he will make the play on balls hit right at him, though not too much else.

OVERALL:

Madlock expects to play for at least another three or four years for the Dodgers. It remains to be seen whether the series of injuries that bedeviled him the last couple of years in Pittsburgh will come back to haunt him, but it is obvious that a winning atmosphere brought him out of his stagnation as a Pirate. Madlock is a proven winner whose leadership qualities had an immediate impact on the Dodgers.

Campbell: "This may be a last hurrah for Madlock, although if he stays healthy and can play every day for the Dodgers, they should be set for the next couple of years."

HITTING:

A major disappointment in 1985, Candy Maldonado was once rated as one of the top prospects in the Dodger organization. He has yet to prove, however, that he can be anything more than a utility player in Los Angeles.

He plays primarily against lefthanders but hit just .229 against southpaw pitching in 1985--a drop of 74 points from the year before.

Maldonado uses an exaggerated uppercut swing which frequently causes him to pop up--and out. He chases bad pitches, especially high fastballs. He bats in a closed stance and is a dead pull hitter, despite the efforts of batting coach Manny Mota to teach him to go the other way.

BASERUNNING:

Maldonado has below-average speed. He has stolen just one base in 296 games with the Dodgers.

FIELDING:

Maldonado improved defensively while platooning with Ken Landreaux in center field last season. He has one of the best arms in the league, but is slow to unload the ball and overthrows the cutoff man or throws to the wrong base. He exercises poor judgment in the field.

OVERALL:

Candy Maldonado has always been a fa-

CANDY MALDONADO
OF, No. 20
RR, 5'11", 195 lbs.
ML Svc: 3 years
Born: 9-5-60 in
  Humacao, PR

1985 STATISTICS

AVG	G	AB	R	H	2B	3B	HR	RBI	BB	SO	SB
.225	121	213	20	48	7	1	5	19	19	40	1

CAREER STATISTICS

AVG	G	AB	R	H	2B	3B	HR	RBI	BB	SO	SB
.237	296	545	50	129	22	2	11	53	44	90	1

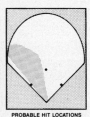

VS. RHP   VS. LHP   PROBABLE HIT LOCATIONS

vorite of Dodger VP Al Campanis, but the romance may be fading. The Dodgers nearly traded Maldonado after the 1984 season to Houston and it's quite possible they may try to package him again in another deal.

Campbell: "The Dodgers thought that as an everyday player, Maldonado would be capable of hitting .280, with 20 home runs and 75 RBIs. But his numbers as a role player don't warrant that kind of projection now."

HITTING:

Mike Marshall is the most aggressive hitter on the Dodgers. Last September, he showed what he is capable of when he batted .340, hit 11 home runs and drove in 37 runs, just four short of Frank Howard's team record of 41 RBIs in one month.

Marshall is constantly tinkering with his stance; he bats in a slight crouch and sort of "wades" into pitches. On the fourth day of the 1983 season, he was seriously beaned by a pitch from Expo Jeff Reardon. Still, Marshall shows no fear at the plate.

He likes his pitches up--he's murder on anything from the belt to the letters. He can be jammed with hard stuff inside, which leaves him prone to chasing breaking stuff low and away.

Marshall strikes out a lot (he fanned 137 times last year) and is usually among the league leaders. In an effort to help him with his perception of the strike zone, this spring the Dodgers are thinking of using a technique they once used with Duke Snider: stand him at the plate without a bat and have him act as the umpire, watching pitch after pitch after pitch, calling balls and strikes.

But the Dodgers don't want to do anything to blunt Marshall's aggressiveness, which usually has him primed to jump on any mistake a pitcher makes. His great power to the opposite field has been likened to that of Atlanta's Dale Murphy. If Marshall had not missed 27 games after undergoing an appendectomy in June, he probably would have cracked the 30 HR/100 RBI level.

BASERUNNING:

Marshall has average speed and is not a basestealing threat. He was thrown out in 10 of his 13 stolen base attempts last year.

FIELDING:

He is a natural first baseman and has had to work hard to improve himself as

MIKE MARSHALL
RF, No. 5
RR, 6'5", 220 lbs.
ML Svc: 5 years
Born: 1-12-60 in
   Libertyville, IL

1985 STATISTICS

AVG	G	AB	R	H	2B	3B	HR	RBI	BB	SO	SB
.293	135	518	72	152	27	2	28	95	37	137	3

CAREER STATISTICS

AVG	G	AB	R	H	2B	3B	HR	RBI	BB	SO	SB
.275	472	1598	200	439	77	3	71	235	134	384	16

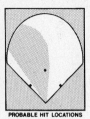

STRONG | STRONG | PROBABLE HIT LOCATIONS
VS. RHP | VS. LHP |

an outfielder. He played in left field in 1984 and last season he played in right field, a spot he prefers.

His lack of speed limits his range, but he has shown a willingness to dive after balls or go into walls after them. He saved a game in Philadelphia by crashing into the wall to make a ninth-inning catch.

OVERALL:

Marshall's development as a hitter parallels that of Atlanta's Murphy. At the age of 26, he is on the verge of crossing into superstardom. He is an extemely intense young man who is learning to take a more even-handed approach to the game: after striking out six times in a row last year, he rebounded in the next game to collect four hits.

Campbell: "His value to the Dodgers is at the plate. Once he gets a better idea of the strike zone and starts to lay off bad pitches, he should become an awesome hitter."

PITCHING:

Tom Niedenfuer, who was actively shopped around the major leagues without success by Dodger VP Al Campanis before the start of the 1985 season, was the savior of the Dodger bullpen last year. Yes, that's true, in spite of the fact that he will probably be remembered best for the home run pitch he served to Jack Clark which clinched the National League pennant for the Cardinals last season.

Niedenfuer combines an imposing physical build (his Goose Gossage-like body inspired the nickname, "Buffalo") with a rising fastball that is clocked consistently in the low-to-mid-90s. He also has an outstanding slider and has developed a split-finger fastball as his off-speed pitch. Look for him to become more comfortable with the split-finger pitch this season and to throw it more frequently.

His delivery is from three-quarters to just below; his motion is unorthodox enough to give hitters something to keep them off stride. He saved 19 games for the Dodgers last season (the most since Terry Forster saved 22 in 1978) and notched seven wins. Niedenfuer's strike-outs-to-walks ratio was exceptional in 1985: 102 Ks/24 walks, for a better than 4-to-1 ratio in 106 1/3 innings pitched.

After experiencing arm trouble in 1984, Niedenfuer had a relatively pain-free season last year; however, Lasorda still must be careful not to overuse him.

FIELDING, HITTING, BASERUNNING:

His move to first base is, at best, average and his delivery to the plate is slow. But when someone suggested to manager Tom Lasorda that runners could take liberties against Niedenfuer, Lasorda

TOM NIEDENFUER
RHP, No. 49
RR, 6'5", 225 lbs.
ML Svc: 5 years
Born: 8-13-59 in
    St. Louis Park, MN

1985 STATISTICS

W	L	ERA	G	GS	CG	SV	IP	H	R	ER	BB	SO
7	9	2.71	64	0	0	19	106.1	86	32	32	24	102

CAREER STATISTICS

W	L	ERA	G	GS	CG	SV	IP	H	R	ER	BB	SO
23	22	2.53	235	0	0	52	344	276	101	97	107	285

said with a snort: "They said the same thing about Koufax."

Niedenfuer rarely gets the opportunity to bat and he collected his first major league hit in 19 trips last year. The hit brought his lifetime batting average up to a whopping .053. His base-running ability is not a factor in a game.

OVERALL:

Niedenfuer overcame some physical ailments in 1984 (the most serious was a series of three separate injuries to his right elbow) to emerge as the stopper in the Dodger bullpen last year. And most likely, he will overcome the aftershock of the nightmare he suffered at the hand of Jack Clark in Game Six of the 1985 playoffs. He has the "easy come, easy go" demeanor a short reliever needs: two days after delivering the fateful pitch, Niedenfuer was on the links playing golf with Koufax.

Campbell: "Tom has a great heart and is a challenge-type pitcher. But he needs another pitcher to share the load with him in the bullpen. The logical candidate appears to be Ken Howell."

PITCHING:

Lefthander Jerry Reuss was in a transitional stage as a pitcher last year, relying more on finesse than the power he pitched with in the past.

Judging by the results, the change has to be regarded as smooth. Reuss won 14 games last season--his most victories since going 18-11 in 1982; it was also nine more wins than he had in his injury-filled year in 1984.

Before last season, there were doubts that Reuss would ever be able to pitch again. In January 1984 he had surgery to remove a bone fragment from his pitching elbow and in October he had surgery to remove bone spurs from both heels.

But he came back in 1985 feeling healthy for the first time in over a year. His fastball started to look good and he was able to keep it low. He changed speeds more often than in the past, but his number one pitch was still his fastball.

Reuss throws a sinking fastball and a slow, overhand curveball. It is easy to tell when he is on his game: opposing hitters will beat the ball into the ground. When he is off, his sinker doesn't stay down and he can't get his curveball over for a strike; hitters will take him deep.

Last season, Reuss was feeling so good, he had three shutouts and took four others into the ninth inning.

FIELDING, HITTING, BASERUNNING:

Reuss is a better fielder than he looked to be last season, when he made

JERRY REUSS
LHP, No. 41
LL, 6'5", 225 lbs.
ML Svc: 16 years
Born: 6-19-49 in
   St. Louis, MO

1985 STATISTICS

W	L	ERA	G	GS	CG	SV	IP	H	R	ER	BB	SO
14	10	2.92	34	33	5	0	212.2	210	78	69	58	84

CAREER STATISTICS

W	L	ERA	G	GS	CG	SV	IP	H	R	ER	BB	SO
192	157	3.44	518	455	123	10	3145.1	3110	1381	1203	1001	1715

errors that belied his considerable experience. He has a good move to first base.

At the plate, Reuss has not had a season to approach 1983, when he batted a stunning .282, but he usually makes contact. He is not a good bunter.

OVERALL:

Over the last six years, Reuss leads the major leagues with an ERA of 2.87. With his health now restored, he figures to continue as a dependable starter in the Dodger rotation. He is signed through the 1987 season, and barring further injury problems, sees no reason why he can't pitch until he is 40.

Campbell: "He used to throw his sinker in excess of 90 MPH, but he has had to learn to win with considerably less velocity. Obviously, he has done that. Jerry is a total professional who has given the Dodgers consistently good work."

HITTING:

Steve Sax, whose average hovered near .230 until July, lost his leadoff spot last year to rookie Mariano Duncan. Sax thrived as the number eight hitter, however, and hit .279, a increase of 36 points over his slump-ridden .243 average in 1984. He missed the first month of the season after the Angels' Bobby Grich fell on his leg on an attempted pickoff play in the last exhibition game of the spring. That injury forced the Dodgers to summon Mariano Duncan up from the minors; Duncan played second until Sax's return. Sax, whose average was .226 on July 2, hit .311 in his last 84 games.

He stands upright at the plate and chokes up on the bat a little. He is notoriously impatient at the plate. He will swing at absolutely anything-- which is one reason he has so few walks and is not an ideal leadoff hitter.

Both Tommy Lasorda and batting coach Manny Mota worked for hours and hours with Sax to get him to swing down on the ball more: Sax has improved a bit. They would also like to see him hit to the opposite field more than he does.

The best way to pitch Sax is to get him to chase something out of the strike zone. He likes fastballs up and away.

BASERUNNING:

Sax's stolen base totals have steadily declined since he swiped 56 in 1983. He stole fewer than half that total in 1985 (27) and has yet to take to the extensive instruction he has received, which has most recently been from all-time great Maury Wills. With his speed, Lasorda said, Sax is capable of stealing 75 to 80 bases; he has yet to come close. He is not an instinctive baserunner and is often thrown out attempting to take a poorly timed extra base.

FIELDING:

A hyperactive sort, Sax is anything but smooth afield and at times will take a step the wrong way when a ball is hit.

STEVE SAX
2B, No. 3
RR, 5'11", 185 lbs.
ML Svc: 5 years
Born: 1-29-60 in
 W. Sacramento, CA

1985 STATISTICS

AVG	G	AB	R	H	2B	3B	HR	RBI	BB	SO	SB
.279	136	488	62	136	8	4	1	42	54	43	27

CAREER STATISTICS

AVG	G	AB	R	H	2B	3B	HR	RBI	BB	SO	SB
.272	617	2437	329	662	75	20	13	174	215	236	171

STRONG — VS. RHP STRONG — VS. LHP PROBABLE HIT LOCATIONS

But he also is exceptionally aggressive and will dive at any ball he thinks he has a chance to reach. He is adequate at the pivot.

Sax has been called the worst-fielding second baseman in the league. Part of that undoubtedly stems from the reputation he gained from his mysterious throwing problems which began in 1983, when he couldn't even make a simple 40-foot toss to first without throwing it away. To a large extent, his throwing problems are history, but now on most plays he holds the ball and won't take the risk of throwing it away.

OVERALL:

Sax is a reckless, emotional player who still has a tendency to play out of control.

Campbell: "Steve is still young, he is only 26, and with maturity and experience, he may be able to channel his excess energy into fulfilling the promise he showed in his first two seasons."

HITTING:

Mike Scioscia caught a career high of 141 games for the Dodgers last season and came within four percentage points of becoming the first Dodger catcher in 30 years to hit .300 (Roy Campanella was the last). His dramatic improvement at the plate was a continuation of a remarkable recovery from a career-threatening rotator cuff injury (1983) which happened when he blew out his shoulder attempting to throw out Alan Wiggins at second base.

Scioscia is an aggressive hitter who makes good contact. He struck out just 21 times in 429 at-bats last year. He hits line drives to all fields and is the Dodgers' most accomplished practitioner of the hit-and-run. He is also an excellent bunter who will use the bunt as a surprise tactic to get on base.

Scioscia's drawback as a hitter is his lack of power, although Dodger batting instructor Ben Hines said Scioscia has improved in his ability to drive the ball and eventually may be good for 10 to 15 home runs a year.

He also hits well with men on base, and rates as one of the Dodgers' best clutch hitters.

Most lefthanded hitters prefer pitches that are from the belt level to the thigh; Scioscia, on the other hand, likes pitches from the belt level to the letters.

BASERUNNING:

The 6'2", 220-pound Scioscia is one of the slowest players in baseball, a fact he sometimes forgets when running the bases, which he tends to do aggressively.

FIELDING:

Scioscia is the premier plate-blocker in the league, immovable and fearless. In one of the season's most memorable collisions, Scioscia was knocked unconscious by Jack Clark of the Cardinals,

MIKE SCIOSCIA
C, No. 14
LR, 6'2", 220 lbs.
ML Svc: 6 years
Born: 11-27-58 in
   Upper Darby, PA

1985 STATISTICS

AVG	G	AB	R	H	2B	3B	HR	RBI	BB	SO	SB
.296	141	429	47	127	26	3	7	53	77	21	3

CAREER STATISTICS

AVG	G	AB	R	H	2B	3B	HR	RBI	BB	SO	SB
.267	543	1594	145	425	73	5	21	173	226	107	8

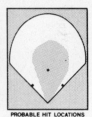

VS. RHP   VS. LHP   PROBABLE HIT LOCATIONS

but somehow still he held onto the ball.

He has the full confidence of his pitching staff, who respect his style of calling a game.

He suffered through a throwing slump for about six weeks early last season, but grew stronger as the year went on. During the NLCS, Scioscia neutralized the speed of the St. Louis Cardinals, who were successful in just five of twelve stolen base attempts.

OVERALL:

Scioscia has emerged as one of the finest catchers in the league. With his outstanding work habits, his willingness to play hurt and his tremendous competitiveness, he also has become a leader by example.

Campbell: "If not for the presence of Pedro Guerrero, Mike Scioscia would be the most valuable player on this team. He definitely has a chance to hit .300 in the future and is the most fearless catcher in the league."

PITCHING:

Fernando keeps coming close.

Each season, he pitches his heart out and still he hasn't won 20 games. Last year, it was a five-game winless streak in September, which was due in part to a sore left ankle, that was the reason for him coming up short.

Nevertheless, Valenzuela finished sixth in the league in ERA, third in innings pitched, tied for second in complete games, tied for third in shutouts and fourth in strikeouts. In his first five starts, Valenzuela allowed only one earned run in 42 innings, that on a home run by San Diego's Tony Gwynn.

Valenzuela throws five pitches for strikes: a fastball, a slider, a curveball and two types of screwballs—a hard one that fades away from righthanded hitters and an off-speed one he uses as his change of pace. Some teams believe that, contrary to the usual percentages, a lefthanded hitter has as good a chance as a righthanded hitter against Fernando because they might have a slight advantage in handling his screwball.

Valenzuela's throws his fastball consistently in the mid- to high-80s. He will throw any of his five pitches at any time in the count, although he gets the majority of his strikeouts with his fastball.

His tendency to be a little fine accounts for his high number of walks (101 last season), which hurts him on occasion. But if he has his control early, forget about beating him.

FIELDING, HITTING, BASERUNNING:

Valenzuela is one of the finest athletes on the Dodgers. An exceptional fielder, he has been known to go behind his back to spear ground balls between his legs. His follow-through always leaves him in position to field and he is nimble coming off the mound.

Valenzuela's pickoff move is one of the most dangerous in the league. Last

FERNANDO VALENZUELA
LHP, No. 34
LL, 5'11", 195 lbs.
ML Svc: 5 years
Born: 11-1-60 in
    Navajoa, Sonora, MEX

1985 STATISTICS

W	L	ERA	G	GS	CG	SV	IP	H	R	ER	BB	SO
17	10	2.45	35	35	14	0	272.1	211	92	74	101	208

CAREER STATISTICS

W	L	ERA	G	GS	CG	SV	IP	H	R	ER	BB	SO
78	57	2.89	176	166	64	1	1285.1	1069	485	413	455	1032

season, he nailed the Cardinals' Terry Pendleton during the NLCS in a particularly fine display of well-timed, sneaky perseverence.

Valenzuela is one of the league's best-hitting pitchers. He is a line drive hitter with flashes of power. He had just one home run last season, but it was a long one off Atlanta's Steve Bedrosian. Valenzuela is also an accomplished bunter. He likes to cross up the defense by first showing the bunt, then slashing the ball past the charging infielders. He is an excellent baserunner with surprising speed.

OVERALL:

Fernando is only 25 years old, yet he already ranks sixth in shutouts among active National League pitchers with 23 (and that figure does not include the epic duel he had with Dwight Gooden of the Mets, in which Valenzuela pitched 11 scoreless innings and Gooden went nine).

Campbell: "It's been said many times, but he is a 25-year-old man who pitches like he's been in the big leagues for 20 years. He'll do everything possible to help himself win. In my opinion, he is the best lefthanded pitcher in the National League."

GOOD CONTROL

PITCHING:

Suffering from a sore right elbow, Bob Welch was able to pitch only five innings during the first two months of the 1985 season before being sent to the Dodgers' spring training complex in Vero Beach, Florida, for rehabilitation.

At the time, it was feared that surgery might be necessary after the season. Instead, Welch made a remarkable comeback. He put together a career-best eight game winning streak, won 13 of his last 16 decisions, threw three shutouts and posted an ERA of 2.31, which was the fifth lowest in the National League.

Welch is a classic over-the-top power pitcher. He added the notorious split-finger fastball to his repertoire last year after its guru, Roger Craig, demonstrated it to Dodgers pitching coach Ron Perranoski. Perranoski taught the technique to Welch.

"It came so naturally," Perranoski said. "He picked it right up, and the bottom just fell out of it. Bobby now has confidence in all three pitches, and it's made his fastball that much better."

Welch, a former number one draft pick, also seems to have overcome the lapses in concentration which have prevented him from being the 20-game winner the Dodgers had predicted. He walked only 35 batters in 167 1/3 innings, the fewest walks he has issued since joining the Dodger rotation.

FIELDING, HITTING, BASERUNNING:

Welch has a quick move to first and is apt to throw over to the bag from a

BOB WELCH
RHP, No. 35
RR, 6'3", 190 lbs.
ML Svc: 8 years
Born: 11-3-56 in
    Detroit, MI

1985 STATISTICS

W	L	ERA	G	GS	CG	SV	IP	H	R	ER	BB	SO
14	4	2.31	23	23	8	0	167.1	141	49	43	35	96

CAREER STATISTICS

W	L	ERA	G	GS	CG	SV	IP	H	R	ER	BB	SO
93	64	3.09	224	199	34	8	1333.1	1200	513	459	424	913

variety of set positions. He is a good fielding pitcher.

He is not a good hitter, but he actually helped himself at the plate in 1985, batting .180 while driving in four runs, the most RBIs he's ever had in a season.

OVERALL:

Welch is 29 games over .500 for his career (93-64) and if his elbow holds up, he may just be entering his prime this season. Problems with his elbow (a bone spur which may someday require surgery) will remain an annual concern for both him and the Dodgers.

Campbell: "Everybody says Guerrero was the key to the Dodgers' success last season, but I'd have to say that Welch played a significant role when he came back from his injury. He's a courageous pitcher, one who isn't afraid of the big games."

HITTING:

Last year in his second season since returning from a three-year hitch of playing ball in Japan, Terry Whitfield emerged as one of the better lefthanded pinch-hitters in the league.

Whitfield led the Dodgers with 14 pinch-hits, one short of the team's club record, and hit two pinch-homers, including a game-winner off Atlanta's Bruce Sutter.

Whitfield was rather streaky in 1985: he was hitting .400 through mid-May, but then went hitless in his next 21 at-bats. He ran off an 8-for-17 streak before tapering off again, with just five hits in his last 31 at-bats.

Whitfield hits the off-speed stuff better than he handles the fastball. He has a long arc in his swing that should enable the hard throwers to tie him up with fastballs and sliders inside. But Whitfield comes out swinging.

BASERUNNING:

Whitfield has average speed at best and is not a threat to steal--he did not have a stolen base in 1985.

FIELDING:

Whitfield plays sparingly in the field and is not a good outfielder. He has limited range, a below-average arm and does not get a very good jump on the balls.

OVERALL:

Initially, Whitfield was a disap-

TERRY WHITFIELD
OF, No. 45
LR, 6'1", 200 lbs.
ML Svc: 6 years
Born: 1-12-53 in
Blythe, CA

1985 STATISTICS

AVG	G	AB	R	H	2B	3B	HR	RBI	BB	SO	SB
.260	79	104	8	27	7	0	3	16	6	27	0

CAREER STATISTICS

AVG	G	AB	R	H	2B	3B	HR	RBI	BB	SO	SB
.282	713	1899	233	536	93	12	33	179	133	286	18

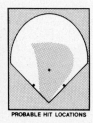

VS. RHP   VS. LHP   PROBABLE HIT LOCATIONS

pointment, as Dodger vice-president Al Campanis had projected him as an everyday player when he signed Whitfield out of Japan. Tommy Lasorda tried platooning Whitfield in right field with Candy Maldonado, an experiment Lasorda quickly abandoned in 1984. But Whitfield is a tireless worker and has since become skilled at the difficult art of coming off the bench for a single at-bat that can decide a game.

Campbell: "Terry is one of the best hustlers in the league, a Gary Matthews type of player. He has become a very good pinch-hitter."

HITTING:

Steve Yeager appeared in only 53 games last season, the fewest he's ever played in his career (the strike-short-ened 1981 season notwithstanding). His inactivity showed at the plate, where he was homerless for the first time in his career and had just nine RBIs.

Yeager was coming back from a serious knee injury, suffered in a home plate collision with Cincinnati Red's Dave Concepcion in September 1984. The surgery left Yeager with screws holding the tibia in his left knee intact.

The righthanded hitting Yeager is a "cripple" hitter, the kind of guy who will jump all over a 2-and-0 or 3-and-1 fastball. But he can be struck out by a steady diet of slow curves, change-ups and sliders. It is starting to look as if he can no longer get around on the exceptionally hard thrower, either.

He leans over the plate in a slight crouch and if he gets a belt-high fast-ball right over the plate, he can still crush it.

BASERUNNING:

With his knees, Yeager does as little baserunning as possible. When he reaches base, he is replaced by a pinch-runner.

FIELDING:

Yeager still has one of the strong-est throwing arms of any catcher in baseball. He threw out 20 of 39 runners attempting to steal, an outstanding 51% ratio. He is very sound fundamentally and calls an intelligent game. His cour-

STEVE YEAGER
C, No. 7
RR, 6'0", 200 lbs.
ML Svc: 14 years
Born: 11-24-48 in
Huntington, WV

1985 STATISTICS

AVG	G	AB	R	H	2B	3B	HR	RBI	BB	SO	SB
.207	53	121	4	25	4	1	0	9	7	24	0

CAREER STATISTICS

AVG	G	AB	R	H	2B	3B	HR	RBI	BB	SO	SB
.228	1219	3454	347	789	116	16	100	398	330	703	14

VS. RHP·   VS. LHP   PROBABLE HIT LOCATIONS

age has never been called into question, either.

OVERALL:

The Dodgers, obviously believing that Yeager can play an important role, signed the cousin of famed test pilot Chuck Yeager to a two-year contract (one year plus an option) after the 1985 season. Yeager will be challenged this spring for the backup catcher's job by rookie Gilberto Reyes.

Campbell: "Yeager is still one of the best defensive catchers around, a very heady, very aggressive player."

LEN MATUSZEK
1B, No. 12
LR, 6'2", 195 lbs.
ML Svc: 4 years
Born: 9-27-54 in
Toledo, OH

HITTING, BASERUNNING, FIELDING:

Len Matuszek's chance to be an every-day player has progressively been diminished. Last year, he was traded twice. He had a shot at playing at first base regularly for the Phillies at one point, but he dislocated a finger in spring training, didn't play well after returning and was traded to Toronto on the eve of the 1985 season.

The Blue Jays projected Matuszek as their lefthanded designated hitter and were disappointed, as Matuszek batted just .212 in 62 games. That prompted his trade to the Dodgers, who used Matuszek primarily as a pinch-hitter and spare outfielder. He had only 63 at-bats with the Dodgers. In 1984, he had led the National League in pinch-hitting.

Matuszek has an upright, closed stance and is a low-ball, fastball hitter with good power to right and right-center. When Pedro Guerrero was hurt in September, Matuszek filled in at left field and had three home runs and seven RBIs in 11 games.

A natural first baseman, Matuszek was a game but miscast outfielder. He may try his hand at third base this season.

OVERALL:

It's uncertain how Matuszek fits into the Dodgers' plans.

Campbell: "In Franklin Stubbs and Greg Brock, the Dodgers already have enough lefthanded-hitting first basemen. Terry Whitfield is the number one lefty pinch-hitter, a role to which Matuszek isn't quite ready to resign himself."

BILL RUSSELL
INF, No. 18
RR, 6'0", 187 lbs.
ML Svc: 17 years
Born: 10-21-48 in
Pittsburgh, KS

HITTING, BASERUNNING, FIELDING:

An eye injury caused Bill Russell to miss the NLCS last season, a time of year when he has traditionally hit well, as evinced by his .337 lifetime average in league championship play.

Russell had just 169 at-bats last season, the fewest in his 17-year major league career.

He is a contact hitter who goes to all fields and prefers pitches up in the strike zone.

Russell has little power--only seven of his 44 hits went for extra bases in 1985 and he didn't hit a home run. But he is an excellent bunter and an adept hit-and-run man. His experience makes his a valued bat coming off the bench in clutch situations.

Russell, always good for 10-15 stolen bases a season, has slowed down considerably. He remains a clever runner who was successful in all four of his stolen base attempts in 1985. He does not make mistakes on the basepaths.

Russell will fill in at second base, shortstop, third base and in the outfield. His range, of course, isn't what it used to be, and his arm remains erratic. He has overcome an injury to the index finger of his throwing hand, which was shattered by a pitch in 1980.

OVERALL:

Russell continues to serve as a stabilizing factor on a young ballclub. He has accepted his new role as a utility player gracefully.

Campbell: "He is the elder statesman of the Dodgers, a heady player who doesn't scare."

ALEJANDRO PENA
RHP, No. 46
RR, 6'1", 200 lbs.
ML Svc: 5 years
Born: 6-25-59 in
Cambiaso, DR

PITCHING:

Alejandro Pena, who led the National League with a 2.48 ERA in 1984, is attempting to come back from a career-threatening shoulder injury which limited him to only one start in 1985.

Pena underwent rehabilitation for more than six months before he was able to start a game in Cincinnati in early September last season. He pitched less than three innings.

When Pena was right, his fastball blew through the strike zone at 95 MPH. He pitched with a fluid three-quarters-to-overhand delivery and had good control. Pena also sported a good slider. But the shoulder injury will most likely change almost everything. Even with his easy delivery, his 95 MPH fastball could be a thing of the past and continuing to throw a slider might damage his arm further at this point.

One of Pena's greatest assets on the mound has been his professional approach, his cool demeanor under fire. He will need all his mettle to come back to pitch in the majors because, in effect, he will now have to learn to be an entirely different pitcher.

OVERALL:

The prognosis is not a promising one for Pena. But for the Dodgers, this is still the season of hope.

"A lot of people crossed off Tommy John after his operation," said Dodger trainer Bill Buhler in an optimistic tone. "And he went on to pitch another 10 years after his operation."

FRANKLIN STUBBS
INF, No. 22
LL, 6'2", 215 lbs.
ML Svc: 2 years
Born: 10-21-60 in
Laurinburg, NC

HITTING, BASERUNNING, FIELDING:

After rushing Franklin Stubbs to the majors in 1984, the Dodgers kept the first baseman in the minors for a full season last year. It is expected that this season he will once again challenge Greg Brock for the first base job.

The Dodgers really hope that Stubbs will no longer be in over his head, as he was when he struck out nearly once in every three at-bats in 1984. He had tremendous difficulty with off-speed breaking stuff in the past and will now have to prove that he can hit a major league curveball.

Stubbs is a lefthanded hitter who stands upright at the plate and has shown flashes of outstanding power. He also runs very well for a big man and is an agile fielder.

OVERALL:

Stubbs was the Dodgers' number one selection in the June 1982 draft. He appears to have one of the most promising futures of any Dodger prospect. Whether he can supplant Brock or will be traded elsewhere remains to be seen.

MONTREAL EXPOS

HITTING:

Hubie Brooks loves the moment:
two out . . . two strikes . . .
the set . . . the pitch . . .

Brooks seemed to relish the challenge given him in Montreal and his knack for driving in the big run was a welcome sight on a team that has had its share of tight collars in the past few years.

His 100 RBIs--typically, he reached the milestone with a two-out hit (on the final day of the season)--led the Expos in his first season since they acquired him as the key player in the Gary Carter trade. Brooks had 13 game-winning RBIs last year, and most of them were "true" game-winners occurring late in the game.

Brooks has an unusual batting stance, with his rear end turned toward the plate. He likes the pitch high and out over the plate. Pitchers have more success against him if they keep the fastball down and away or bust him up and in.

He uses an inside-out batting stroke and at least half of his hits seem to go to the right side of the diamond. Few of Brooks's hits go down either of the foul lines, so the defensive positioning should be to concede the lines and crowd the middle portion of the field.

Brooks has good extra-base power to the alleys and his liners from time to time will carry over the fence. With runners on base, however, he has the ability to adjust his batting stroke to bring runners in.

BASERUNNING:

Baserunning is not Brooks's strong suit. His attempts to score from second base on a single are usually adventures. Brooks stole six bases last year, but it took him 15 attempts.

FIELDING:

Despite his spring training errors and concerns over his transition from third base to shortstop, Brooks sur-

HUBIE BROOKS
SS, No. 7
RR, 6'0", 188 lbs.
ML Svc: 6 years
Born: 9-24-56 in
   Los Angeles, CA

1985 STATISTICS

AVG	G	AB	R	H	2B	3B	HR	RBI	BB	SO	SB
.269	156	605	67	163	34	7	13	100	34	79	6

CAREER STATISTICS

AVG	G	AB	R	H	2B	3B	HR	RBI	BB	SO	SB
.271	707	2648	263	718	119	18	41	319	162	404	34

  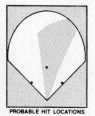

STRONG VS. RHP · STRONG VS. LHP · PROBABLE HIT LOCATIONS

prised almost everyone with his fluidity at short. He still needs work to refine his footwork on the pivot and plays around second base, but he seemed to have caught on quickly last season.

Brooks has a powerful throwing arm: it is his major asset as a fielder. He doesn't have a great deal of range, but he still managed to get to balls that many hitters thought would be through for a hit.

If he had a weakness, it was probably in not holding on to balls where an out couldn't possibly be recorded.

Brooks does not have good range either way, but he has less to his right; however, the presence of Tim Wallach at third compensates.

OVERALL:

Campbell: "Brooks fits in well with the makeup of the Montreal club. They need to stick together if they are to contend and it looks as if Hubie will contribute to the close-knit feeling."

PITCHING:

Nobody gave Tim Burke much of a chance to come north with the Expos last spring--except for Expos manager Buck Rodgers. Burke had pitched for Rodgers in the minors, and the skipper knew what the young pitcher could do. Burke went out and made a prophet of Rodgers by winning a relief job with a sterling spring, and then proceeded to stand major league hitters on their collective ears.

With a style that has been likened to Gene Garber's back-to-the-plate delivery, Burke was the perfect setup man for Jeff Reardon, appearing in 78 games, which tied a league record for a rookie pitcher. Not only did he usually hold things for Reardon, but he also managed to win nine games for himself while allowing only 86 hits in 120 1/3 innings.

Burke's fortes are a sinking fastball and a late-breaking slider. While his aggressive pitching style made many hitters shake in their boots (he led the team by hitting seven batters), his stuff made them shake their heads on the return trip to the dugout.

Since the Expos didn't have much depth in the bullpen last year, Rodgers was forced to use Burke more than he would have liked. As a result, Burke became tired down the stretch and he had difficulty keeping his pitches low.

Even in his fatigue, Burke maintained an edge: his unorthodox delivery continued to cause hesitation in the hitter's timing (he turns his back and hides the ball in his glove until the last possible second).

FIELDING, HITTING, BASERUNNING:

Burke is not a good fielder, but he is a heady player who breaks well toward first base and always seems to be aware of the situation.

His appearances at the plate were

TIM BURKE
RHP, No. 59
RR, 6'3", 205 lbs.
ML Svc: 1 year
Born: 2-19-59 in Omaha, NE

1985 STATISTICS												
W	L	ERA	G	GS	CG	SV	IP	H	R	ER	BB	SO
9	4	2.39	78	0	0	8	120.1	86	32	32	44	87

CAREER STATISTICS												
W	L	ERA	G	GS	CG	SV	IP	H	R	ER	BB	SO
9	4	2.39	78	0	0	8	120.1	86	32	32	44	87

rare, but he was not an automatic out with the bat.

OVERALL:

Jeff Reardon may have been the NL's top fireman, but no one had a better assistant than he did in Burke, whose finest asset is his willingness to take the ball.

There were times when Burke could have easily begged off, citing fatigue, but being the bulldog he is, he appeared in almost half the team's games, even finishing 31 of them to help out when Reardon was sidelined.

If Burke is to be as effective this season, manager Rodgers will have to be more selective in using him. He would probably be an effective starter, but at the moment he is much too valuable in his setup role. There is always the possibility, too, that Burke will be used in short relief to spell Reardon.

Campbell: "This kid has some future ahead of him. He is a fabulous setup man for Reardon, and without a doubt, he could easily take over as the stopper at a moment's notice. He is an all-out type of pitcher who lets the hitter know that he means business."

HITTING:

When Andre Dawson gets into a hot streak, it doesn't matter what a pitcher throws--Dawson is going to hit it. The most scalding of his hot streaks are now fewer and farther between, however.

Every aspect of Dawson's play is--and will always be--affected by his bad knees (his left knee, orignally damaged a high school football accident, has to be periodically drained of fluid).

Dawson's batting stance puts a lot of pressure on the knee and, as a result, he usually isn't able to make a pain-free follow-through on his swing. Even more troublesome for Dawson are the artificial surfaces, which are murder even to healthy knees.

Dawson is an impatient hitter, especially in clutch situations. He lapses into the bad habits of lunging at the ball or overswinging. He can be made to chase a pitch that's out of the strike zone. He likes to flex his muscles when there are no runners on base (most of his home runs are solo).

He can be awesome against high-ball pitchers. His line drives have been known to travel off the bat with the speed of a rocket.

Dawson isn't much on other hitting elements of the game, such as bunting and the hit-and-run, but this may be more a failing of the Expos' system while he was progressing through the minors.

BASERUNNING:

Dawson's knee problems have reduced his basestealing to a game of wits. He may be a smarter baserunner than Tim Raines; even handicapped by weak knees, Dawson stole 13 bases last season. Watching him run from first to third on a single, one would never guess that he's in pain all the way.

FIELDING:

Dawson has earned the respect of many

ANDRE DAWSON
RF, No. 10
RR, 6'3", 195 lbs.
ML Svc: 10 years
Born: 7-10-54 in
Miami, FL

1985 STATISTICS

AVG	G	AB	R	H	2B	3B	HR	RBI	BB	SO	SB
.255	139	529	65	135	27	2	23	91	29	92	13

CAREER STATISTICS

AVG	G	AB	R	H	2B	3B	HR	RBI	BB	SO	SB
.279	1313	5132	763	1434	263	65	205	760	317	817	235

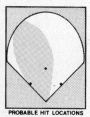

STRONG   STRONG

VS. RHP   VS. LHP   PROBABLE HIT LOCATIONS

runners with his arm strength and pin-point accuracy. A former Gold Glove center fielder, he charges the ball well, which gives the ball more momentum when he throws.

In the field, his knees have caused him to lose maybe a half-step, but he doesn't hold back because of the gimpy wheels. He can still be counted on to make one of those outstanding catches that highlight films are made of.

OVERALL:

Dawson's finest moment last season occurred in September at Chicago's Wrigley Field, when he hit three easy home runs in one game.

Campbell: "His injuries have made him less than the great player he has been in the past, but he is still a good ballplayer--he provides leadership both on the field and off."

HITTING:

Mike Fitzgerald's hitting suffers from his injured knees. The weakness in his knees prevents him from applying too much pressure on his follow-through when swinging. Additionally, he seemed to try to do too much to impress early and fell into some bad habits, such as chasing pitches off the outside part of the plate and failing to fight off the inside pitches.

If a pitcher can consistently work the inside of the plate, keeping the ball down against him, he'll usually be able to get Fitzgerald to hit the ball on the ground at someone.

BASERUNNING:

Fitzgerald is not a lumbering-type of catcher on the basepaths. He is a good athlete, but he was obviously slowed down last season by an unhealthy knee. He still managed to steal five bases, which is something not many catchers can do.

Since Fitzgerald bats at the lower end of the order, he'll probably run even more in 1986 (if he's physically sound) because it might help to set things up for leadoff man Tim Raines.

FIELDING:

The Expos pitchers are unanimous in praising Fitzgerald for the way he calls games. He is a student of opposing hitters. He's a bulldog behind the plate; he blocks the plate well and is agile in scooping up bunts in front of the plate. However, the ups and downs of the position wore even further on his knees and made him slow to react on some plays.

Fitzgerald's throwing arm is below-average, but appeared even worse when compared to his predecessor, the rocket-armed, firebreathing Gary Carter. The Montreal fans and pitching staff were spoiled by Carter's presence behind the plate for so many years; the fans were used to his bullet throws and the pitch-

MIKE FITZGERALD
C, No. 21
RR, 6'0", 185 lbs.
ML Svc: 2 years
Born: 7-13-60 in
    Long Beach, CA

1985 STATISTICS

AVG	G	AB	R	H	2B	3B	HR	RBI	BB	SO	SB
.207	108	295	25	61	7	1	5	34	38	55	5

CAREER STATISTICS

AVG	G	AB	R	H	2B	3B	HR	RBI	BB	SO	SB
.222	228	675	46	150	22	2	8	69	65	132	6

  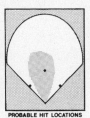

VS. RHP   VS. LHP   PROBABLE HIT LOCATIONS

ing staff had become lax about holding runners on base.

OVERALL:

Fitzgerald is probably more ideally suited to being a platoon catcher than a regular. When healthy, he'll get his share of hits against southpaw pitching. A platoon situation would not only help share the workload, but would also remove him from the scrutiny of the Montreal media and fans as the man who replaced Gary Carter.

Although Fitzgerald never complained, it was obvious last season that as his misfortunes mounted he tried too hard and it only made such things as his throws on steal attempts even worse.

Campbell: "If Montreal has a weakness right now, I'd say it's in the catching department. Fitzgerald is going to have to improve a lot with the bat and with his throwing to become a solid, everyday catcher."

HITTING:

Wind up the Terry Francona doll and it sprays base hits to all parts of the field. Pitchers have discovered there's no sure-fire method to get Francona out because when he's in a groove he hits just about everything.

A player who brings boyish enthusiasm to the game, Francona just loves to hit and he usually doesn't take too many pitches. He likes to swing away; any pitcher who likes to dangle bait on the outside of the plate will find a willing fish in Francona.

Francona's problem, however, is finding a permanent spot in the lineup. He stayed healthy enough last season to get the most at-bats of his career (281), but he still was reduced to being a platoon player when the season ended.

If Francona had more success pulling the ball, he'd be an excellent number two hitter behind Tim Raines. His on-base percentage makes him attractive in that spot, but he has to be able to open up the right side with Raines on base, giving the Expos the added dimension of the hit-and-run.

Because of his free-swinging ways, he is not, in general, a good pinch-hitter. His enthusiasm, however, has worked in his favor a few times in the past and he has had some key hits off the bench. He does not do it consistently enough to earn that role on a regular basis.

BASERUNNING:

Francona's scarred knees limit his mobility on the basepaths, but even before his surgery he was never a very good baserunner. What he lacks in speed he makes up for with hustle, however.

FIELDING:

Francona's best position is first base (knee surgery has made him a risk in the outfield), but he does not hit with enough power for that position on an everyday basis.

TERRY FRANCONA
OF/1B, No. 16
LL, 6'1", 175 lbs.
ML Svc: 5 years
Born: 4-22-59 in
    Aberdeen, SD

1985 STATISTICS

AVG	G	AB	R	H	2B	3B	HR	RBI	BB	SO	SB
.267	107	281	19	75	15	1	2	31	12	12	5

CAREER STATISTICS

AVG	G	AB	R	H	2B	3B	HR	RBI	BB	SO	SB
.290	365	951	83	276	48	5	7	89	36	61	8

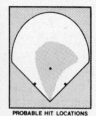

VS. RHP	VS. LHP	PROBABLE HIT LOCATIONS
STRONG	STRONG	

He is not a natural first baseman, yet he has good enough instincts that he is able to make the big glove play as it arises.

His arm is average to below average. As an outfielder, he can catch what comes his way and hustle on others, but his range has been greatly reduced because of his battered knees.

OVERALL:

As long as he remains with Montreal, he will not get the kind of playing time he is looking for and will not be able to shake his tag as a part-time player. One gets the impression that he is ripe for a trade.

Campbell: "Although he may not like it, I think Terry is going to have to be a platoon player. You have to get sock out of your man at first base and he's not going to provide a lot of that, though he will get on base quite a bit. He is entering what should be his peak years and is struggling to stay in the lineup."

PITCHING:

His name was once synonymous with power pitching, but even by his own admission, Bill Gullickson is now more of a finesse pitcher.

His fastball, which earlier in his career sailed toward the batter at more than 90 MPH, currently cruises in the 87-88 MPH range. With two speeds on his curveball, however, Gullickson remains an effective pitcher. He seems able to work the corners of the plate with it much more effectively than in the past.

Batters who frequently used to sit on Gullickson's fastball have found they can no longer do so. In 1985, Gullickson yielded only eight home runs in 181 1/3 innings, a vast improvement on the league leading 27 he allowed in 1984.

Along with developing finesse, he has worked hard on his control, reducing his walks per nine innings ratio to just over two.

Previously a workhorse-type pitcher, Gullickson showed a tendency to be injury prone last season, twice going out with a pulled hamstring.

Entering his seventh season, he seems to be a more mature pitcher than the one who was once chastised for calling the press box in Atlanta over a scoring decision that inflated his ERA.

FIELDING, HITTING, BASERUNNING:

Gullickson now works more quickly than he used to, but he still has to refine his pickoff move, especially with catcher Gary Carter no longer around to compensate for huge jumps frequently taken by baserunners.

BILL GULLICKSON
RHP, No. 34
RR, 6'3", 220 lbs.
ML Svc: 6 years
Born: 2-20-59 in
 Marshall, MN

1985 STATISTICS
W	L	ERA	G	GS	CG	SV	IP	H	R	ER	BB	SO
14	12	3.52	29	29	4	0	181.1	187	78	71	47	68

CAREER STATISTICS
W	L	ERA	G	GS	CG	SV	IP	H	R	ER	BB	SO
72	61	3.43	176	170	31	0	1186	1149	494	453	288	678

Fielding has never been a problem for Gullickson, and at the plate, he is capable of coming through with a key hit, including opposite field doubles down the right field line.

OVERALL:

To this point, Gullickson is one of those pitchers with loads of potential who, because of one thing or another, hasn't become the 20-game winner so many have expected him to be. There isn't a team in the league, though, which would not be interested in acquiring his services.

Campbell: "Gullickson has become a good prospect as opposed to the great one he was a few years ago. What he has lost in his arm, he has made up for by learning how to pitch. Cutting down the home run ball is evidence of that."

PITCHING:

Joe Hesketh was well on his way to at least a 15-win rookie season when disaster struck last August. While trying to hurdle Dodgers catcher Mike Scioscia on a play at the plate, Hesketh's lower leg was broken when it got caught against Sciocia's shin guard. His rookie season ended at a time when he had won 10 games and allowed an impressive 125 hits in 155 1/3 innings.

While a complete recovery is expected in time for the 1986 season, there is still cause for some concern because at 170 pounds, Hesketh is one of the lightest players in baseball. He is frequently ribbed in the clubhouse about his slight size, with teammates nicknaming him "Fungo," as in the thin-shaped bat.

Hesketh says he's just one of those people who can eat without putting on much weight, but it's a fact that many scouts have questioned whether he has the stamina to be a 200+ innings pitcher because of his lean frame.

Overcoming adversity, as he now must, is not something new for Hesketh, who missed more than a year earlier in his minor league career following elbow surgery.

Expos manager Buck Rodgers, for one, says that when Hesketh encounters trouble on the mound, it is usually because he is too tentative. Hesketh must learn to be consistently aggressive against big league hitters. He has a tendency to let down, and, because he is a relative newcomer to the league, he must be reminded of that bad habit.

When Hesketh keeps his slider down, he can be devastatingly effective, as his strikeout ratio of better than 6.5 per nine innings attests. He has excellent poise for a rookie. On several occasions, he pitched against the opposition's ace pitcher and won.

FIELDING, HITTING, BASERUNNING:

His tall, slender body is agile, an

JOE HESKETH
LHP, No. 38
LL, 6'2", 170 lbs.
ML Svc: 1 year plus
Born: 2-15-55 in
Lackawanna, NY

1985 STATISTICS
W	L	ERA	G	GS	CG	SV	IP	H	R	ER	BB	SO
10	5	2.49	25	25	2	0	155.1	125	52	43	45	113

CAREER STATISTICS
W	L	ERA	G	GS	CG	SV	IP	H	R	ER	BB	SO
12	7	2.33	36	30	3	1	200.1	163	64	52	60	145

asset in his fielding of bunts and covering first base on balls hit to the right side of the infield.

His pickoff move is the best on the team, although at times it borders on a balk. Bob Rodgers made a point of explaining the legality of the move to umpires early last season, trying to avoid having Hesketh get called for it.

When he is at the plate and gets a hit, it's a bonus. He's an adequate bunter, but not much of a runner.

OVERALL:

You have to like a pitcher with the promise displayed by Hesketh in 1985. Still, he is almost back at square one because of the severity of his injury. His gung-ho attitude toward the game was clearly evident when he had the nerve to try to shove Scioscia, one of the most notorious plate-blockers in baseball.

Campbell: "The Expos, who have long moaned about a shortage of lefthanded pitching, really need Hesketh to recover. It was no small coincidence that the team's nosedive last season occurred just when he was injured."

HITTING:

Without much flair or fanfare, Vance Law usually does everything anyone could ask of him. There is nothing exceptional about him: he has no brilliant tools, no extraordinary power or speed, but he is a scrappy player who has mastered a lot of the little things well enough to hurt you in any phase of the game.

The Expos needed a second baseman who could provide them with some offensive punch. So, Law went out and had the second-best on-base percentage on the club with a .369 average (trailing Raines's .405).

A disciple of the Charlie Lau school of hitting, Law has a keen eye, as his 86 walks will attest. About the only pitch you can get him to chase is the one that's up around the shoulders. He has cut down considerably on his strike-outs because of his discipline at the plate.

One of Law's finest assets is his adaptability. He can get a single when you need it or use his extra-base power when you're a few runs behind. Again, that is the Lau approach to hitting.

His 17 homers for the Chicago White Sox two years ago were a big surprise. He hit 10 for Montreal last season, many of them coming in the second half after he started to feel comfortable with his move to a new team.

BASERUNNING:

Simply because his head is always in the game, Law will steal the odd base. He doesn't have much raw speed, but he's a perceptive baserunner. He is a student of the game and will rarely be thrown out making a poorly-timed attempt to stretch a base hit or an error of judgment.

FIELDING:

Law doesn't have that much range but he's sure-handed when he can get to the

VANCE LAW
2B, No. 2
RR, 6'2", 190 lbs.
ML Svc: 6 years
Born: 10-1-56 in
  Boise, ID

1985 STATISTICS											
AVG	G	AB	R	H	2B	3B	HR	RBI	BB	SO	SB
.266	147	519	75	138	30	6	10	52	86	96	6

CAREER STATISTICS											
AVG	G	AB	R	H	2B	3B	HR	RBI	BB	SO	SB
.254	612	1908	242	485	91	17	36	213	209	295	20

STRONG

VS. RHP

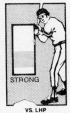

STRONG

VS. LHP

PROBABLE HIT LOCATIONS

ball. He seems to have more trouble going to his left than to his right. His knowledge in positioning himself for each hitter compensates for his limited range. Law has worked overtime with infield instructor Ron Hansen, especially on making the pivot at second base. By the end of last season, he and shortstop Hubie Brooks, another newcomer, had made great strides as a double play tandem.

OVERALL:

Law has a tremendous attitude and is always willing to face a challenge, such as the one he had when he arrived in Montreal. He had spent most of his career at third base, but he was determined to become a decent second baseman. He succeeded.

Campbell: "Law is the type of player who can get taken for granted very easily. He isn't flashy, doesn't complain or boast--he just gets the job done."

PITCHING:

Patient hitters have been known to give Gary Lucas problems. They force him to get the ball up--and Lucas isn't the type who can overpower anyone with a high strike.

Last season, he was used primarily to neutralize lefthanded batters, but he was not as effective in that role as he has been in the past. Part of that can be charged to missing much of the early season with an injury to his back.

Lucas is a gangly man who uses a lot of arm and leg movements in his attempt to confuse the hitter. He found it difficult to maneuver comfortably without his back at 100% flexibility.

He has always been the type who will not carry the misfortunes of a past outing onto the mound in his next appearance. Last season, however, as his failures mounted and fan displeasure increased, he approached each game with apprehension. When he was with the Padres, some observers questioned whether Lucas had the makeup to be the number one man in the bullpen. At this point, that is not a concern, however, as the Expo bullpen is well stocked with Tim Burke and Jeff Reardon.

FIELDING, HITTING, BASERUNNING:

In spite of his back ailments, Lucas is one of the league's better fielding pitchers. He has always worked hard on the fundamentals, and his 6'5" frame enables him to spear the high bouncers that get past other pitchers into center

GARY LUCAS
LHP, No. 25
LL, 6'5", 200 lbs.
ML Svc: 6 years
Born: 11-8-54 in
Riverside, CA

1985 STATISTICS
W	L	ERA	G	GS	CG	SV	IP	H	R	ER	BB	SO
6	2	3.19	49	0	0	2	67.2	63	29	24	24	31

CAREER STATISTICS
W	L	ERA	G	GS	CG	SV	IP	H	R	ER	BB	SO
24	38	2.92	334	18	0	59	548.2	507	214	178	186	335

field for a hit. His pickoff move is above average.

Hitting and baserunning are almost foreign to Lucas these days because of his brief relief outings.

OVERALL:

Lucas is a better pitcher than the two saves he recorded in 1985 indicate, but one has to wonder how much his confidence has been eroded by both his own performance and the fans' reaction. And, because of his tender back, he must pitch with the insecurity of knowing that it threatens his career at any time.

Campbell: "He's an illusionary type of pitcher. He tries to make pitches that look like strikes, but when they get to the strike zone they dip out of it because of the sinker or slider effect. When Lucas has everything working look for a lot of ground ball outs."

PITCHING:

David Palmer pitched more innings last season than in any other in his career, but by the time the season ended, he was reduced to being a spot starter because manager Buck Rodgers felt Palmer had a tired arm.

Since 1980, when he first had elbow surgery, Palmer's medical record has been longer than his career statistics. The promising career that once was Palmer's is gone, but he can still help a team which needs an occasional starter and long reliever.

Palmer throws from three-quarters, relying largely on a slider and sinking fastball which can tail in or away from the hitters. His pitches often do tricks because Palmer lost part of a finger on his pitching hand in a childhood accident and it has an effect on the flight of the ball at his point of release.

Once a superb control pitcher, Palmer issued the most walks of his career in 1985, allowing an average of one walk for every two innings pitched. His uncharacteristic wildness constantly put him behind batters, who simply waited for him to groove a pitch.

If determination was the lone criterion, Palmer would be a Cy Young Award candidate. He is a bulldog on the mound. He isn't blessed with tremendous natural ability, but he challenges hitters as well as any pitcher in the league.

FIELDING, HITTING, BASERUNNING:

Palmer is one of the Expos' faster workers, but not one of their better pitchers at holding on baserunners. He tends to be over-exuberant in the field, which sometimes leads to errors.

DAVID PALMER
RHP, No. 46
RR, 6'1", 205 lbs.
ML Svc: 7 years
Born: 10-19-57 in
    Glens Falls, NY

1985 STATISTICS												
W	L	ERA	G	GS	CG	SV	IP	H	R	ER	BB	SO
7	10	3.71	24	23	0	0	135.2	128	60	56	67	106

CAREER STATISTICS												
W	L	ERA	G	GS	CG	SV	IP	H	R	ER	BB	SO
38	26	3.25	122	86	7	2	577.2	532	237	209	209	270

He works hard at his hitting and doesn't get cheated in an at-bat. He's the type of player who wouldn't hesitate to stick his arm out to get it hit if it meant reaching base in a crucial situation.

OVERALL:

What Palmer needs more than anything else is a clean bill of health. Given his past medical history, however, don't bet the mortgage on it.

If ever someone needed a run of good fortune, it's Palmer; he has accepted all of his hardships with a touch of class. He has spent his entire pro career with the Expos' organization and would prefer to remain with the club, but he would have a better chance at a starting job with another team.

Campbell: "Palmer continues to be an enigma for Montreal management year after year. He's a pitcher with quality stuff and every ball he throws moves, whether it sinks or sails."

HITTING:

After finishing in the league's top three in four major offensive categories, Tim Raines said he would rate his 1985 season as the third-best of his career. In other words, there is still room for improvement.

The switch-hitting Raines is a better hitter for average from the left side, perhaps because Montreal sees a steady diet of righthanded pitching. But he also has excellent power from the right side, getting six of his 11 homers that way last season.

He rarely passes up the chance to hit a first-ball fastball, yet he also has the patience to draw a lot of walks despite his habit of falling behind in the count. There really doesn't seem to be any pitch that gives Raines more difficulty than any other. He can go 0-for-4 one day and 4-for-4 the next day when a pitcher tries to get him out with the same stuff.

Raines is the kind of catalyst every team is looking for; he is the type of player who can simply dominate a game.

BASERUNNING:

Raines was a distant second to Vince Coleman in stolen bases last year, but he was hampered by a tender hamstring early in the season. He seemed to hold back, possibly in light of what less-than-top form would do to his stolen base percentage. He vowed, however, to spend the winter ensuring that his leg muscles would be in peak condition this spring.

Raines also seems to have a self-imposed red light on the bases when Andre Dawson is batting, possibly so as not to disrupt Dawson's hitting.

FIELDING:

Any ball that Raines can get to he usually catches. He made only two errors last season. His speed enables him to track down a lot more balls than an average outfielder. He plays the diffi-

TIM RAINES
LF, No. 30
SR, 5'8", 178 lbs.
ML Svc: 5 years
Born: 9-16-59 in
Sanford, FL

1985 STATISTICS

AVG	G	AB	R	H	2B	3B	HR	RBI	BB	SO	SB
.320	150	575	115	184	30	13	11	41	81	60	70

CAREER STATISTICS

AVG	G	AB	R	H	2B	3B	HR	RBI	BB	SO	SB
.299	731	2792	513	834	145	45	39	252	391	316	391

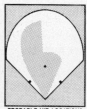

VS. RHP   VS. LHP   PROBABLE HIT LOCATIONS

cult corners at Olympic Stadium well and neatly handles most caroms off the wall.

Raines doesn't jump well for balls at at the fence that are over his head and considering his small size, that probably accounts for a few home runs each year.

His throwing arm was once mediocre, but it's improved in recent years. While he still doesn't have a powerful arm, it's now semi-accurate on throws to the plate.

OVERALL:

The sky's the limit for Raines, who, at 26 years old, still has his peak seasons ahead of him. He comes the closest to fulfilling the role of team leader on the Expos and sets an example by playing the game with sandlot enthusiasm.

Campbell: "He makes things happen and when a spark is needed to ignite a rally, Raines is usually the one who provides it. He continues to be a superb leadoff man. If he puts his mind to it, he could easily steal 100 bases."

PITCHING:

Jeff Reardon has long been looking for respect. And in 1985, he got it. Statistically, he was the NL's premier reliever last season.

Reardon spent all of last spring working to perfect his curveball; the effort paid off. Ironically, though, he developed a tender right elbow last season, the result of an over-reliance on the curve as well as of overwork in the early months.

When he returned from the DL, he was not the same overpowering pitcher he had been in the first half of the year.

Reardon's second-half dropoff was largely the result of his decreasing the number of curveballs he would throw in a game. It is the curveball which sets up his 93 MPH fastball; without the set up, both pitches were less deadly.

A catch-22 situation appears to have developed: Reardon prefers a lot of work to remain effective, but because the tenderness in his elbow makes him ineffective, Expos manager Buck Rodgers really can't afford to have him throwing as frequently as he did last season. Questions about the pain in his elbow, caused by throwing the curveball, are now being raised.

Reardon is currently working to perfect a change-up. It is a pitch that would decrease the strain on his arm and would enable him to handle the kind of workload asked of a short man.

FIELDING, HITTING, BASERUNNING:

Reardon will never win a Gold Glove for his fielding, nor will he gain recognition for doing the little things in the field required by a pitcher. He is often out of position to field sharp drives back to the mound.

In his bullpen role, he doesn't get much of a chance to swing a bat, though it's clear he needs to work on bunting.

JEFF REARDON
RHP, No. 41
RR, 6'1", 195 lbs.
ML Svc: 7 years
Born: 10-1-55 in
Dalton, MA

1985 STATISTICS
W	L	ERA	G	GS	CG	SV	IP	H	R	ER	BB	SO
2	8	3.18	63	0	0	41	87.2	68	31	31	26	67

CAREER STATISTICS
W	L	ERA	G	GS	CG	SV	IP	H	R	ER	BB	SO
35	37	2.62	394	0	0	127	576.2	468	184	168	220	470

OVERALL:

Reardon has the demeanor of a feared reliever. Not only does he fire a blinding fastball, but his beard and menacing eyes are, by his own admission, part of the repertoire he uses to intimidate the opposition. When he comes sidearm with his curve, batters can be made to look hopelessly overmatched, a familiar sight in the first half of last season.

If Reardon has any drawback, it may be that he is an emotional person and allows things such as fan reaction to bother him. Lately, however, he has shown more restraint than he used to.

It may be too much to expect Reardon to duplicate his save total of 1985, but he remains a dependable reliever. In fact, Reardon has saved 20 games or more for the last four years, something few of his peers can claim.

Campbell: "Reardon was called upon at every possible opportunity last season. He's certainly one of the better relievers in the league, but his numbers are a bit inflated because he was called on when other teams might not have felt the need to bring in their short man."

PITCHING:

It seems as though Dan Schatzeder begins every season in Montreal having to work his way out of the bullpen. He would much rather be in the starting rotation from Opening Day on. Last season, just as he was given a starting job and things were going smoothly, Schatzeder developed a tender shoulder, went on the DL and saw limited duty in the rotation upon his return.

Schatzeder is curious in that he is a lefthanded pitcher who has had more success against righthanded batters than the lefthanded swingers he should neutralize more easily.

Earlier in his career, Schatzeder bordered on being a power pitcher, but arm miseries have taken several yards off his fastball. He now uses a mixed bag of pitches including a fastball, a curveball and a slider, with the occasional change-up.

There is some question as to just how much Schatzeder can rely on his curve and slider following the latest ailment in his shoulder. Considering his past history of trouble, he may have to learn the knuckleball to battle hitters with the soft stuff if he wants to survive.

FIELDING, HITTING, BASERUNNING:

Schatzeder is a hyper sort of pitcher, though he was not that way earlier in his career. He was tossed in the scrap heap in San Francisco in 1982, and viewed his chance in Montreal as an opportunity to become more aggressive.

Now, the games in which he pitches are among the Expos' quickest. He takes little time between pitches and wants to go right at the hitter all the time. His delivery to the plate, however, is a bit slow, giving his catcher little chance to throw out potential basestealers.

A former college outfielder, he has good instincts for the position but is frequently out of position on balls hit

DAN SCHATZEDER
LHP, No. 43
LL, 6'0", 200 lbs.
ML Svc: 8 years
Born: 12-1-54 in
    Elmhurst, IL

1985 STATISTICS

W	L	ERA	G	GS	CG	SV	IP	H	R	ER	BB	SO
3	5	3.80	24	15	1	0	104.1	101	52	44	31	64

CAREER STATISTICS

W	L	ERA	G	GS	CG	SV	IP	H	R	ER	BB	SO
52	54	3.61	273	117	18	4	988.1	897	430	397	343	537

up the middle. He does not appear to be a good clutch thrower, often having difficulty on the do-or-die throws to first after he has fielded the ball. Most of his fielding errors occur on this type of play.

Schatzeder gives his team another bat in the order. He can usually be counted on to hit better than .200 and will get an occasional extra-base hit, usually pulled down the right field line. He is a decent baserunner and is likely to be the first pitcher asked to pinch-run.

OVERALL:

On a team which has long coveted lefthanded pitching, the Expos are looking elsewhere for help in the middle and long relief roles. If another club wants complete games, they should shop elsewhere; since Schatzeder developed his arm troubles (with Detroit in 1981), he has gone the distance only three times. When he's pitching, the bullpen should be ready in the sixth inning.

Snider: "Dan's value has slipped because his arm trouble has limited the jobs he can fill. If he could adapt to a short relief role, he might be a good pickup."

PITCHING:

Batters never know quite what to expect from Bryn Smith. The uncertainty is a big part of his success.

Smith throws the fastball, curveball and slider--seldom at the same speed--then completely gets hitters off stride with a palmball, an effective version of a change-up.

He uses the palmball often; it is a pitch that does not put a great strain on his arm. As a result, he is a very durable, usable pitcher, who can be counted on to go for seven or eight innings per start, or more than 200 per season.

Few pitchers in the league do more advance preparation before an appearance. Combine his game strategy with his outstanding control (an average of one walk every six innings) and there are ample reasons for his emergence as one of the league's top pitchers.

Smith is the type of pitcher who normally gives unequivocal signs when he's not on his game. When he falls behind hitters early, it is a billboard-size signal that it is just not going to be his day.

FIELDING, HITTING, BASERUNNING:

Before home games, Smith can sometimes be found driving golf balls toward the outfield fence. An accomplished golfer who probably could have made the pro tour, Smith prides himself on his all-around athletic ability.

Defensively, his quick reflexes make

BRYN SMITH
RHP, No. 28
RR, 6'2", 205 lbs.
ML Svc: 4 years
Born: 8-11-55 in
   Marietta, GA

1985 STATISTICS
W	L	ERA	G	GS	CG	SV	IP	H	R	ER	BB	SO
18	5	2.91	32	32	4	0	222.1	193	85	72	41	127

CAREER STATISTICS
W	L	ERA	G	GS	CG	SV	IP	H	R	ER	BB	SO
39	33	3.07	163	73	13	6	649	608	255	222	161	388

him a solid fielder, and he's one of the team's better righthanders in holding on baserunners, although that's sometimes negated by the speed with which his pitches are delivered to the plate.

The golf swing seems to help him as a hitter and he is usually able to put the bat on the ball.

OVERALL:

Anyone who wasn't sold on Smith's ability as a starter entering the 1985 season has undoubtedly had a change of heart. He has become the ace of the Montreal staff through intelligence and hard work.

Campbell: "He is the type of pitcher who does not scare easily. He come right after you. He is a smart pitcher who gets the most out of his ability."

HITTING:

For several seasons, many scouts have been expecting Tim Wallach to bust out with one of those 35 homer, 100+ RBI seasons. That may happen yet. Wallach is giving it everything he's got and he has even changed his hitting style trying to get more.

Prior to the 1985 season, Wallach was an uppercutting power hitter who hit primarily to right field. Now, he has modified the lift in his swing, which enables him to hit to all fields. The change also gives him additional extra-base power and the ability to drive more home runs.

Wallach has a habit of staying off the plate and often takes the inside pitch. At the same time, he has a remarkable ability to get a lot of inside pitches that appear to be strikes called balls by the umpire.

Nevertheless, the best way for a pitcher to beat him is to pound away on the inside corner of the plate. He is always looking for a pitch that is from thigh- to belt-high and out over the plate. He can still be made to look bad on a slider or curve that misses the outside corner.

Wallach is still a streaky hitter, prone to hot and cold spells but he has cut down on his strikeouts over the past several years.

BASERUNNING:

When he steals a base, it's usually through the element of surprise. His strength lies more in breaking up double play threats at second base.

FIELDING:

Two years ago, Wallach was, at best, an average third baseman. But he has spent long hours taking daily infield practice and has absorbed the teachings of Bill Mazeroski, the former slick-fielding infielder. Wallach has improved tremendously as a defensive player. He

TIM WALLACH
3B, No. 29
RR, 6'3", 200 lbs.
ML Svc: 5 years
Born: 9-14-58 in
Huntington Park, CA

1985 STATISTICS

AVG	G	AB	R	H	2B	3B	HR	RBI	BB	SO	SB
.260	155	569	70	148	36	3	22	81	38	79	9

CAREER STATISTICS

AVG	G	AB	R	H	2B	3B	HR	RBI	BB	SO	SB
.258	705	2551	288	659	134	14	92	355	195	318	18

  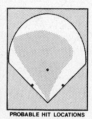

STRONG vs. RHP   STRONG vs. LHP   PROBABLE HIT LOCATIONS

is outstanding at snatching grounders to his left, an important facet especially at this point because Hubie Brooks is still refining his fielding at short.

Wallach's release to first base is strong and accurate and his reflexes on sharply hit balls are, at times, eye-popping. At the crack of the bat, he breaks instinctively toward foul pop-ups down the left field line and is fearless of anything that might get in his way.

OVERALL:

Olympic Stadium is a tough park for righthanded hitters. Wallach's power is more suited to a home park with a more inviting left field porch.

Campbell: "In looking at the other third basemen in the National League, I would have to say that Wallach is in a class by himself. Graig Nettles can still have an occasional good day, Bill Madlock is slowing down and Mike Schmidt has moved on to first. Wallach has taken over at the top of the list."

HITTING:

On the surface, there is nothing that stands out about Mitch Webster, yet last season, he gave indications that he may be in the big leagues to stay. Webster blossomed in the second half of the year when he joined the Expos. He had spent his minor league career with the Dodgers and Blue Jays (he has been in pro ball since 1977).

Webster is a switch-hitter who has more success swinging from the right side, although power-wise, he is a better hitter from the left side of the plate. His home run power came as a bit of a surprise last year. In one stretch, he homered in four straight games and by the end of the season, his home run ratio was one in every 19 at-bats, better than any of the Expos' other sluggers.

Strangely, his home runs seem to be hit quite by accident. He has a compact swing, the kind that does not generate much power, but rather produces line drives into the gaps. The difference with Webster, however, is that he has strong wrists which enable him to get a lot out of a little.

Webster seems to be more patient at the plate than might have been expected: he rarely swings at bad pitches and when he does start slumping, it's because he is swinging up on the ball rather than maintaining his fluid, level stroke.

BASERUNNING:

Webster's speed on the bases is also deceptive. He doesn't appear to be fast but when you look up from your scorecard he's standing safely at second base. He does, however, need to improve the jump he gets against opposing pitchers; he has not learned to read pitchers' pick-off moves.

FIELDING:

Webster has good instincts for playing center field. He does not get a good jump on the ball, but is able to use his speed to compensate for any problem he might have in judgment. His throwing arm

MITCH WEBSTER
OF, No. 23
SL, 6'1", 185 lbs.
ML Svc: 1 year plus
Born: 5-16-59 in
  Larned, KS

1985 STATISTICS

AVG	G	AB	R	H	2B	3B	HR	RBI	BB	SO	SB
.274	74	212	32	58	8	2	11	30	20	33	15

CAREER STATISTICS

AVG	G	AB	R	H	2B	3B	HR	RBI	BB	SO	SB
.265	111	245	43	65	10	3	11	34	22	41	15

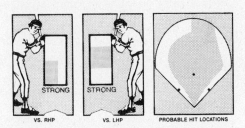

VS. RHP   VS. LHP   PROBABLE HIT LOCATIONS

is average, but he rarely misses a cut-off man and has no fear of fences.

OVERALL:

Webster could be one of those late bloomers who don't realize their full potential until their late 20s. He says that he feels stronger each year.

If the Expos decide to bring Herman Winningham along more slowly this year, Webster may get his opportunity to challenge for the job.

Campbell: "From a manager's point of view, Webster is a model player, going about the job, whatever it may be, without a gripe. He could be a good outfielder; he catches what he gets to and keeps his head in the game.

"New hitters coming into the league in the second half of a season don't get their true test until the following year when the pitchers have had time to figure them out. Who is going to beat whom will be the question for Webster in 1986."

HITTING:

In his first full season as a major leaguer, Herman (please don't call him Herm) Winningham exposed some youthful flaws that need correction. Most scouts feel he has a world of potential, but he will not go far in his present state.

Winningham has an uppercut swing, which causes him to hit far too many balls in the air. He does not have the physical strength to be a power threat; consequently, his fly balls to the out-field are often routine outs.

He wastes too much time swinging up at the ball, defeating his purpose as a hitter: he needs to slap the ball right through the holes in the infield and lay down the odd bunt to keep the infielders honest. With his speed, he could get a lot more bunt singles than he does.

Pitchers can handle Winningham by throwing him up and in—he'll chase any pitch in that spot. With his uppercut swing, he doesn't have much of a chance, however. Winningham also has to be more selective at the plate. He walked only 28 times last year and if he could work more bases on balls, he might be a good number two man to hit behind Tim Raines. Winningham's extra advantage is being a lefthanded hitter who can push the ball into left field to advance Raines.

BASERUNNNING:

Winningham said he planned to match Raines steal for steal in 1985. He had an early lead, but it was all downhill after that and Raines beat him 70-20. Winningham does have fine speed and could steal 50-60 bases if he becomes a keener observer of pitchers and can improve his concentration.

FIELDING:

Winningham was dealt to the Expos by the Mets in the Carter trade; at that time, several scouts felt he should have another year of minor league seasoning. But the Expos needed a center fielder

HERMAN WINNINGHAM
CF, No. 3
LR, 6'1", 170 lbs.
ML Svc: 1 year plus
Born: 12-1-61 in
    Orangeburg, SC

1985 STATISTICS

AVG	G	AB	R	H	2B	3B	HR	RBI	BB	SO	SB
.237	125	312	30	74	6	5	3	21	28	72	20

CAREER STATISTICS

AVG	G	AB	R	H	2B	3B	HR	RBI	BB	SO	SB
.251	139	339	35	85	7	6	3	26	29	79	22

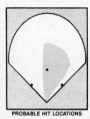

VS. RHP   VS. LHP   PROBABLE HIT LOCATIONS

and wanted to justify the trade, so he was given his baptism by fire.

Winningham covers a lot of ground be-cause of his speed, but his throwing arm is marginal and the better runners will take full advantage of it. He sometimes misses the cutoff man.

He suffers from a rookie's timidity in taking charge in the outfield. There were times last season when he was not authoritative enough on fly balls hit to right- and left-center field.

OVERALL:

This season, Winningham will platoon against righthanded pitchers; he has not been very effective against lefthanders.

Campbell: "He has a great attitude for the game. He'll do whatever work is necessary. That's good, because he has some work ahead of him.

"I think it is imperative that the Expos get him to a hitting instructor who can really break down his swing, change a lot of things and get him to hit the ball on the ground a lot more."

PITCHING:

A full season at the Triple-A level would have helped Floyd Youmans in 1985, but when the Expos staff was depleted by injuries, the righthander was forced to learn at the major league level.

For a young pitcher who was pitching in Class A ball just one year ago, he handled himself very well. Still, he is only 21 years old and needs considerable work to refine his craft. The Expos sent him to the Instructional League in Florida at the end of last season.

When the two were high school teammates, Youmans was considered to be on a par with, if not better than, Dwight Gooden. Gooden, of course, has simply exploded, but what made scouts consider Youmans in the same breath with Gooden is the velocity of his fastball--Floyd's heater consistently clocks in at 92-93 MPH.

At this point, it is the velocity of his fastball that is the problem: he tries to overpower each hitter. Part of his refinement in Florida over the winter was to work on taking some of the speed off his fastball.

Youmans must also improve his control, the lack of which led to an average of more than six walks for every nine innings pitched.

There is much about this young man to like: he struts about with a positive kind of cockiness about him. When he was trimmed from the spring training roster last year, Youmans predicted--correctly--that he would be on the club by mid-season. And he has a friendly competition going with Gooden, with whom he often has telephone conversations after his starts.

Youmans also seems to be a keen competitor. When an opposing pitcher threw at one of his teammates last season, he was quick to retaliate when he returned to the mound, earning immediate respect from the older players.

FLOYD YOUMANS
RHP, No. 33
RR, 6'2", 180 lbs.
ML Svc: 1 year
Born: 5-11-64 in
Tampa, FL

1985 STATISTICS

W	L	ERA	G	GS	CG	SV	IP	H	R	ER	BB	SO
4	3	2.45	14	12	0	0	77	57	27	21	49	54

CAREER STATISTICS

W	L	ERA	G	GS	CG	SV	IP	H	R	ER	BB	SO
4	3	2.45	14	12	0	0	77	57	27	21	49	54

FIELDING, HITTING, BASERUNNING:

As with his pitching, Youmans is still in the process of honing all the parts of his game. His youthful exuberance sometimes forces him into errors on the field. He has to improve on such things as when to break toward first base to cover the bag and how to hold on baserunners effectively.

An outstanding hitter in high school, Youmans goes up to the plate swinging, but he can't be classified as a threat.

OVERALL:

Youmans may turn out to be the key player of the four players Montreal received from the Mets in the Gary Carter trade. A cause for concern is that his desire to fire the ball through a brick wall may cause damage to his young arm.

Campbell: "One of his developments should be to learn to get his breaking ball over more consistently. That would prevent the hitters from sitting on his fastball. This kid looks good--very good. The only chink in his armor so far appears to be his control."

SAL BUTERA
C, No. 11
RR, 6'0", 190 lbs.
ML Svc: 5 years
Born: 9-25-52 in
   Richmond Hill, NY

HITTING, BASERUNNING, FIELDING:

Sal Butera is a backup catcher who enjoyed a little spree with the bat last year. One shouldn't get the impression that he has suddenly become fearsome at the plate. Like most hitters, he can do something with a pitch that's up and out over the plate.

Otherwise, his hitting is suspect. Play him straightaway and don't do him any favors by throwing lollipop curveballs or change-ups. If a pitcher goes after Butera with good, hard stuff and keeps the ball down, he shouldn't be too much trouble.

Butera does not run well.

His throwing arm is adequate for a backup catcher, especially if the pitcher gives him a chance by holding a baserunner close.

OVERALL:

For a player who entered 1985 mainly as an emergency backup in the Montreal farm system, Butera did a commendable job. He won't set a game on fire with his bat, but he will chip in here and there. He executes fundamentals well and since he's had his share of long bus rides, he has an appreciation for the game at the major league level.

He's a good man to have around a team. Butera is a battler who will do whatever is required of him. It's not unusual to see him help out by throwing batting practice.

Campbell: "He appears to be an excellent backup catcher. The pitchers like to work with him, and he, in turn, helps them a lot with his calls behind the plate."

ANDRES GALARRAGA
INF, No. 52
RR, 6'3", 209 lbs.
ML Svc: less than 1 year
Born: 6-18-61 in
   Caracas, VEN

HITTING, BASERUNNING, FIELDING:

There's a marked resemblance between Andres Galarraga and the young Orlando Cepeda--and the Expos are hoping that Galarraga has some of the power the Baby Bull had when he starred as a big leaguer. Galarraga certainly has impressive minor league statistics, but it was obvious during his brief major league stint last year that he must learn the strike zone better.

Most of Galarraga's home runs in the majors came during an early season rampage, but pitchers seemed able to neutralize him with the curveball as the season progressed.

In the field, Andres is surprisingly smooth for his 6'3", 209-pound size. He flags down the sharp ground balls to his left with more agility than those hit to his right and he's good at scooping low throws out of the dirt.

He isn't a threat on the bases, but his physique is intimidating when it comes to breaking up double plays.

OVERALL:

Listed by some scouts as among the league's top 10 prospects at the Triple-A level, Galarraga is undoubtedly better than the overmatched slugger he appeared to be when he joined the Expos last September.

He's still the finest prospect in the Montreal system and since he'll soon be 25 years old, this season looms as make or break for going beyond the "promising" stage.

He is a classic streak hitter who will go through some miserable slumps before breaking out with some big-time hitting.

BERT ROBERGE
RHP, No. 42
RR, 6'4", 190 lbs.
ML Svc: 5 years
Born: 10-30-54 in
    Lewiston, ME

PITCHING, FIELDING:

Bert Roberge has developed a forkball (or split-finger fastball) and it has helped him to become a respectable middle reliever. The pitch seemed to take its toll on his arm, however; Roberge is frequently bothered by a tender elbow.

Considering his history of periodic arm problems, Roberge seems to be most effective when he's spotted an inning here and there. He has good control, poise under pressure and uses the fork-ball as an out pitch, which works out well when a double play is needed.

In the field, he's an average performer, although his pickoff move is pitiful. He led the league by being called for five balks--and he had no pickoffs in 1985.

OVERALL:

Roberge is a journeyman pitcher who can be a definite asset to a club if he can stay healthy for an entire season.

A good team player, Roberge accepts his role quietly and just goes about his job.

Campbell: "He's bounced around for the last couple of years. He is another pitcher who adds depth to an already good Montreal bullpen. His split-finger pitch is slower than most, but he has good control and won't hurt you that way by putting men on base."

RANDY ST. CLAIRE
RHP, No. 51
RR, 6'3", 190 lbs.
ML Svc: 1 year
Born: 8-23-60 in
    Glens Falls, NY

PITCHING, FIELDING:

Randy St. Claire hasn't really had much of an opportunity to get settled in the majors because he's been treated like a yo-yo, shuttling back and forth from the minors to fill a spot on the Montreal roster.

He has always excelled at the minor league level, but has yet to find consistency in the majors.

St. Claire's role is basically as the mop-up man. He relies mainly on the slider and sinking fastball, but lacks a trick pitch or an overpowering pitch to get a big out in clutch situations.

In his favor, St. Claire isn't prone to yielding the home run ball and his innings pitched to hits allowed ratio has almost always been superb.

His most outstanding skill seems to be his fielding ability. He helped himself more than once last season by turning a double play and, on one occasion, he fearlessly blocked the plate and applied the tag to a runner trying to score on a passed ball.

OVERALL:

St. Claire is getting lost in the shuffle in Montreal; a change of scenery might be his best bet; he has been in the Expo organization since 1979 with no significant advancement.

Campbell: "He's such a good-fielding pitcher that it's like having an extra infielder out there. Randy is not a strikeout pitcher; he's a sinker/slider pitcher who has to keep the ball down."

SCOT THOMPSON
INF, No. 41
LL, 6'3", 195 lbs.
ML Svc: 6 years
Born: 12-7-55 in
   Grove City, PA

HITTING, BASERUNNING, FIELDING:

Early in his baseball career, there were scouts who felt that Scot Thompson had the potential to be a batting champion one day. Thompson has never fullfilled that promise, but he's still a useful pinch-hitter, even though his statistics didn't glowingly reflect that in 1985.

The Expos have always seemed to have a shortage of quality pinch-hitters from the left side; after they got Thompson from the Giants in the second half of the season, he pulled through with some key pinch-hits for them.

He's a good low-ball hitter who always seems to know how to find a hole in the infield. He is patient at the plate and able to extend a pitcher to the limit. He does not have much power.

Defensively, Thompson can play both first base and the outfield. His range is limited at both positions, but he can handle smoothly anything hit in his direction. His arm in the outfield is a little below average.

Thompson won't hurt his club on the basepaths. He has above-average speed, although his legs may be a little tight because he doesn't get a chance to play very often.

OVERALL:

Campbell: "Thompson looks as if he will give the Expos some timely pinch-hits. He can be useful if he is used sparingly as a pinch-hitter and as a late-inning defensive replacement."

U.L. WASHINGTON
SS, No. 1
SR, 5'11", 175 lbs.
ML Svc: 8 years
Born: 10-27-53 in
   Stringtown, OK

HITTING, BASERUNNING, FIELDING:

In his first 114 at-bats last season, U.L. Washington hit .333. After he went on the disabled list for the second time with a pulled hamstring (near midseason), both his appearances and his production declined drastically. He had 79 at-bats the rest of the way and finished with a .249 batting average.

A switch-hitter, Washington has more power from the right side of the plate. He is late-swinger and has some extra base power. As a lefthanded hitter, he likes the ball up and away, frequently spraying hits to the opposite field.

Washington is a utility infielder who can play second base, shortstop or third base. He is erratic in the field, and despite his reduced range, can still surprise hitters with what he can get to. His arm is strong and his release is quick. Of the three positions, he is better and more comfortable at shortstop, but it is unlikely he will get much time there with Montreal.

The frequent hamstring pulls have more than taken their toll on his baserunning. It is the weakest part of his game not only because of his legs, but because he makes judgment errors as well.

OVERALL:

Washington's biggest challenge is to convince his club that he is not injury-prone.

Campbell: "He can make contact from the both sides of the plate to put the ball in play, but his once he gets on base, his poor baserunning can negate anything he has done with the bat."

JIM WOHLFORD
OF, No. 5
RR, 5'11", 175 lbs.
ML Svc: 13 years
Born: 2-28-51 in
    Visilia, CA

HITTING, BASERUNNING, FIELDING:

Pinch-hitting specialists sometimes follow a curious good year/bad year pattern: last season was the latter for Jim Wohlford, who pounded lefthanded pitching in 1984.

The highlight of Wohlford's 1985 season was a decisive home run in the home opener--but he never hit another one all last season. Still, Wohlford made his pinch-hits count, driving in six runs with five hits.

Wohlford needs to play a stretch of games periodically to stay sharp and he didn't do as much of that in 1985 as he did the previous year.

A high-ball, line drive-type hitter, Wohlford has been around long enough to force pitchers to come to him.

He is unspectacular in the field, but he's adequate in every defensive category. He can produce a big catch or make a good throw with the game on the line.

On the bases, he is not much of a threat, although he runs well from second to home, and won't take calculated risks.

OVERALL:

The experience that Wohlford brings to the ballpark is invaluable to a team, especially one such as the Expos, who are rebuilding with younger players.

He struggled in the first half of the season, but seemed to closer to his previous form in the second half. The only question is whether, at the age of 35, he's starting to lose it.

NEW YORK METS

PITCHING:

Because of an injury to Bruce Berenyi and the demands of the schedule and pennant race, Rick Aguilera reached the major leagues earlier than he would have if the Mets still were a developing team. Even though his debut was made earlier than planned, Aguilera responded well. By the end of last season, the Mets had to look back and wonder where they might have been without him.

He was recalled May 21, but his first appearance was postponed due to rain. He was returned to the minors. Then, up he came on June 10 and two days later gained a victory in relief. From that point on, Aguilera became a part of the regular rotation and was a major contributor for the rest of the season.

He is a four-pitch, ground ball pitcher who can strike out any batter when his slider is biting. He throws just hard enough to complement his control of the slider, curve, change-up and fastball. And his location is better than average.

Aguilera's control is so good that it suggests he is more experienced than he is. It is, however, his composure which most belies his age: Aguilera does not get rattled. In that regard, he is comparable to teammate Dwight Gooden.

Aguilera does not give in to hitters and lefthanded hitters are not happy to face him because of the slider.

He appears to have "ninth-inning heart" and the ability and stamina to close out a game.

FIELDING, HITTING, BASERUNNING:

Aguilera is a good athlete and is a

RICK AGUILERA
RHP, No. 66
RR, 6'5", 193 lbs.
ML Svc: 1 year
Born: 12-31-61 in
    San Gabriel, CA

1985 STATISTICS

W	L	ERA	G	GS	CG	SV	IP	H	R	ER	BB	SO
10	7	3.24	21	19	2	0	122.1	118	49	44	37	74

CAREER STATISTICS

W	L	ERA	G	GS	CG	SV	IP	H	R	ER	BB	SO
10	7	3.24	21	19	2	0	122.1	118	49	44	37	74

more-than-adequate fielder.

He is an accomplished hitter (last season he hit .278 in 36 at-bats). He makes contact and hits the ball with authority. He has extra-base power (two of his 10 hits were doubles) and takes pride in his offense. He is adequate as a baserunner.

OVERALL:

Aguilera has the potential to rank behind Gooden within the next two years. He does not have overpowering stuff, but his slider is excellent and his composure could carry him a long way.

Snider: "The Mets keep coming up with these great young arms--Rick is a prime example. Last season, he was asked to pitch a bit earlier than the club wanted, but he didn't waste his pitches."

HITTING:

Because of an injury to and poor production by Kelvin Chapman, Wally Backman was afforded the opportunity to play regularly through much of the second half of last season. However, Backman did not perform as well as the Mets had hoped he would.

Backman continues to be a good left-handed hitter, but leaves much to be desired as a righthander. When faced with lefthanded pitching last year, Backman reminded everyone why he had been platooned with Chapman in the first place.

Backman's work righthanded was such that, in the middle of the pennant race in September, he abandoned switch-hitting altogether for 10 days and batted lefthanded against southpaw pitching.

He is more of a pull hitter and does show some power when he bats righthanded. But he is far more productive batting lefthanded.

Defenses have tried to take away his favorite lefthanded-hitting area (between shortstop and third base) by pitching him inside, but without much success. He has become more adept at hitting the ball through the middle of the field and occasionally pulling pitches to right.

At the urging of since-departed coach Bobby Valentine, Backman has improved his bunting. He prefers batting leadoff but does well as the number two man and is a good bet to get on base in the late innings when a baserunner is essential.

BASERUNNING:

That he has stolen 62 bases in the last two seasons as a platoon player demonstrates his basestealing prowess. He accelerates quickly (particularly out of the batter's box) and he rarely grounds into double plays.

Backman will always try for the extra base and do what is necessary to get there.

WALLY BACKMAN
2B, No. 6
SR, 5'9", 160 lbs.
ML Svc: 4 years
Born: 9-22-59 in
   Hillsboro, OR

1985 STATISTICS

AVG	G	AB	R	H	2B	3B	HR	RBI	BB	SO	SB
.273	145	520	77	142	24	5	1	38	36	72	30

CAREER STATISTICS

AVG	G	AB	R	H	2B	3B	HR	RBI	BB	SO	SB
.275	448	1388	205	382	59	11	5	98	158	211	73

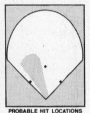

STRONG   STRONG   PROBABLE HIT LOCATIONS

VS. RHP   VS. LHP

FIELDING:

Backman's greatest improvement has been in his defensive ability as a second baseman. His arm, once a liability because of injury, has now become an asset: it helps him to compensate for his average range. His hands are not not great, but they are good enough.

Over the past two seasons, Backman has also worked to improve his footwork and his ability at making the DP pivot.

OVERALL:

If statisticians could develop a means to gauge how much production each player squeezes out of his given ability, Backman's name would surely be at the top of the list. He is not a gifted athlete, but he is diligent, resourceful and motivated.

Snider: "Backman is the kind of guy who has to do all of the little things to be successful. Each season, he seems to find a new skill to improve upon."

PITCHING:

Bruce Berenyi's 1985 season was almost a complete washout. Rotator cuff surgery limited him to just three game appearances in April and 13.2 innings pitched. The Mets originally hoped that he would be ready to return by mid-September, but his shoulder became inflamed and he was unable to pitch.

One of his starts was a seven-inning one-hitter against the Cincinnati Reds, which demonstrated that Berenyi can still be more effective than most when he is sharp and confident.

In his time with the Mets (beginning in June 1984) Berenyi has improved his control and become more willing to throw his fastball than he had been in the past. When he was with the Reds, he had fallen in love with his slider, but, with a better mix of pitches and greater control within the strike zone, Berenyi was just beginning to fulfill his potential when the shoulder problems began.

However, if a result of his surgery is a reduction of his fastball's velocity, he could be in trouble.

FIELDING, HITTING, BASERUNNING:

Berenyi is a good athlete (he is the Mets best golfer next to Ray Knight), but he is not a good fielder, hitter or baserunner.

His defense is ordinary and his move to first base is mediocre. He is an

BRUCE BERENYI
RHP, No. 31
RR, 6'3", 215 lbs.
ML Svc: 6 years
Born: 8-21-54 in
  Bryan, OH

1985 STATISTICS
W	L	ERA	G	GS	CG	SV	IP	H	R	ER	BB	SO
1	0	2.63	3	3	0	0	13.2	8	6	4	10	10

CAREER STATISTICS
W	L	ERA	G	GS	CG	SV	IP	H	R	ER	BB	SO
42	53	3.90	128	124	13	0	742.1	683	362	322	403	577

easy out as a hitter and should never be used as a pinch-runner.

OVERALL:

Berenyi always appears to be on the brink of something special when something interferes, be it injury or his own inconsistency. Before the surgery, he had the equipment to be a big winner.

Snider: "I've liked his stuff and, before the surgery, pitching coach Mel Stottlemyre was helping him to overcome his control problems and making him into more of a pitcher. If Bruce can rebound from this setback and be a strong pitcher, the Mets will improve on one of the best rotations in the league."

HITTING:

Gary Carter remains among the elite players in the game. Without question, he is the best catcher in the National League. The trade which brought Carter to New York from the Montreal Expos was one of the most important moves the Mets have made in years.

Carter is almost the classic number four hitter. Pitchers can keep him honest with pitches up and in and occasionally may get him to fish on breaking balls away. But there is no one way to pitch Carter, no glaring weakness to exploit.

An aggressive hitter, Carter often swings at the first pitch. He does not step up to the plate thinking that he might draw a walk; if a pitcher falls behind in the count, Carter sees it as an open invitation for the downtown express.

Unlike the classic slugger, Carter does not strike out often; witness his 46 Ks in 555 at-bats with 32 home runs. Equally unlike the prototype is his relentless style of running out balls in trying to eke out a base hit.

Most of his extra-base hits are to left-center field, but he will pull the ball sharply if he is pitched inside and will go to right-center with outside stuff. Some clubs use an overshift defense on the left side against him.

BASERUNNING:

Running the bases is not the raison d'etre for any catcher and Carter is no exception. However, he does appear to enjoy his time on the basepaths. Double play pivotmen, on the other hand, don't.

FIELDING:

Carter's arm is not the best in the league. He is not number one at calling a game. But he is the number one catcher once the ball is in play. He is the best at making sure both he and the ball are where they should be as quickly as possible.

GARY CARTER
C, No. 8
RR, 6'2", 210 lbs.
ML Svc: 11 years
Born: 8-8-54 in
 Culver City, CA

1985 STATISTICS											
AVG	G	AB	R	H	2B	3B	HR	RBI	BB	SO	SB
.281	149	555	83	156	17	1	32	100	69	46	1

CAREER STATISTICS											
AVG	G	AB	R	H	2B	3B	HR	RBI	BB	SO	SB
.273	1557	5573	766	1521	273	24	247	894	618	702	35

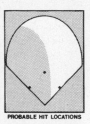

VS. RHP — STRONG   VS. LHP — STRONG   PROBABLE HIT LOCATIONS

In general, the position of catcher lends itself to few spectacular plays other than those at the plate. By his aggressive bulldog style, Carter creates sensational plays. (Last April, he was hitless in the Mets' 18-inning game with the Pirates yet received a standing ovation for his defensive brilliance.)

He both takes and dishes out more punishment than most catchers; there are not many ballplayers in the league who can knock him off his feet. Wild pitches are a rarity when he is behind the plate and few runners steal off him.

OVERALL:

Even on a team loaded with All-Stars, Carter was labeled the most valuable player by manager Davey Johnson in 1985.

Snider: "Carter was made for New York--he has a flair for the spectacular. However, his weak knee is a source of real concern; last year, he almost had to leave the lineup a few times. But you always get everything he's got--he does what he has to do to get the job done."

PITCHING:

Last season, Ron Darling stepped out of the shadow of Dwight Gooden and established himself as a formidable pitcher in his own right. Whatever doubts there might have been about Darling's ability to overcome adversity were erased in the second half of 1985. And if there was a question about his ability to pitch in big games, it was answered when he shut out the Cardinals in a September showdown, allowing only four hits and three walks over nine innings.

Darling's fastball can be devastating, but when he mixes it with his excellent curve, he becomes much more effective.

Few pitchers are as effective after the sixth inning as Darling. Few are as smart.

Darling needs to develop more consistent control. Last season, he walked 114 batters in 248 innings. However, the bases-on-balls don't hurt him as much as they might another pitcher because Darling has a knack of pitching his way out of trouble.

FIELDING, HITTING, BASERUNNING:

A gifted athlete, Darling excels in the field and is fleet on the bases. He looks as if he is the type who should produce at the plate, but thus far he hasn't.

Darling is exceptionally quick off the mound and when teamed with Keith Hernandez and Gary Carter gives the Mets an effective defense against bunts.

His pickoff move is among the best in the league even though he is righthanded. A Gold Glove almost certainly is in his future.

He has been used as a pinch-runner on

RON DARLING
RHP, No. 12
RR, 6'3", 195 lbs.
ML Svc: 2 years
Born: 8-19-60 in
    Honolulu, HI

1985 STATISTICS

W	L	ERA	G	GS	CG	SV	IP	H	R	ER	BB	SO
16	6	2.90	36	35	4	0	248	214	93	80	114	167

CAREER STATISTICS

W	L	ERA	G	GS	CG	SV	IP	H	R	ER	BB	SO
29	18	3.28	74	73	7	0	489	424	201	178	235	326

several occasions, but he has not hit enough--or at least as much as he thinks he should--to take advantage of his good speed. He will steal a base, and has. He is the most efficient bunter among the Mets' pitchers.

OVERALL:

After experiencing trouble early last season and then again following the All-Star break, he continued to develop into a reliable pitcher who almost always gave his team a chance to win.

With his talent, personality, good looks and education, Darling could be a number one starter with many other clubs. He handles his number two status well and even seems to enjoy the relative privacy it affords him.

Snider: "The only thing I question is his control. But then, Robin Roberts made the Hall of Fame and you didn't see his best stuff until he was in trouble. I like Ron's attitude and the way the fur on his neck stands up when he has runners on base."

HITTING:

Pesky. Feisty. Scrappy. These are words everyone uses to describe Lenny Dykstra. He is not a key man in the lineup, but during his abbreviated exposure in the major leagues last season, he demonstrated that he can be an effective presence.

As far as the opposition is concerned Dykstra is a constant irritation, like a fly inside a spacesuit. He has a defiant attitude and refuses to give in.

Almost out of necessity, Dykstra is a contact hitter. He knows how to draw a walk and will gladly accept it as a way of getting on base. Once on first, the little fly in Dykstra tries to steal second base; he has all the qualities of a good leadoff hitter.

He is a line drive hitter with good bat control and would benefit from hitting the ball on the ground more often. He can deliver an occasional extra-base hit, but mostly because outfielders play him shallow.

An inordinately high percentage of his strikeouts came on called third strikes, but that percentage will drop when he learns the pitchers and when the NL umpires finish their initiation with him.

He strikes out most often on breaking balls; he knows what to do with a fastball and changes in speed don't appear to affect him.

BASERUNNING:

Dykstra runs with daring, speed and aggressiveness. He enjoys every running opportunity and takes advantage every time. He usually gets a good lead and, despite his ignorance of most of the pitchers, a good jump. He accelerates quickly, slides headfirst more often than not and proudly wears the dirt on his uniform. Unlike some fleet-footed runners, he wants to steal bases. The extra base is standard fare for him.

FIELDING:

Dykstra wears an oversized glove that

LEN DYKSTRA
OF, No. 4
LL, 5'10", 160 lbs.
ML Svc: 1 year
Born: 2-10-63 in
    Santa Ana, CA

1985 STATISTICS

AVG	G	AB	R	H	2B	3B	HR	RBI	BB	SO	SB
.254	83	236	40	60	9	3	1	19	30	24	15

CAREER STATISTICS

AVG	G	AB	R	H	2B	3B	HR	RBI	BB	SO	SB
.254	83	236	40	60	9	3	1	19	30	24	15

 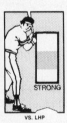 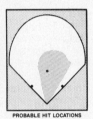

VS. RHP   VS. LHP   PROBABLE HIT LOCATIONS

looks even bigger than it is because his hand is barely inside it. He plays deep in center field--some think too deep. But he charges the ball well; if he breaks in the wrong direction at all, it is usually when he is going back on the ball.

He has no fear of fences, though he could be quicker to the gaps. His arm is extraordinarily strong considering his small build. He doesn't show off the arm and prefers to keep it as something of a secret weapon. It won't be secret for long, however.

OVERALL:

Snider: "Dykstra is an ideal leadoff man/center fielder. His presence at the top of the order can help establish an extra degree of aggressiveness for his team. I like what I saw of him last season—he knows how to get the most out of his ability."

PITCHING:

Sid Fernandez cannot throw a baseball straight. On one day, his pitches may go like this:

Or another day, perhaps like this:

SID FERNANDEZ
LHP, No. 50
LL, 6'1", 220 lbs.
ML Svc: 2 years
Born: 10-12-62 in
  Honolulu, HI

1985 STATISTICS

W	L	ERA	G	GS	CG	SV	IP	H	R	ER	BB	SO
9	9	2.80	26	26	3	0	170.1	108	56	53	80	180

CAREER STATISTICS

W	L	ERA	G	GS	CG	SV	IP	H	R	ER	BB	SO
15	16	3.11	43	42	3	0	266.1	189	100	92	121	251

Hitters simply do not know where the ball is going when he sets to pitch. And until last season, he didn't know either.

Fernandez lost weight, revised his follow-through and suffered through a horrid spring training in 1985 until he finally found the kind of control he had lacked for most of his professional career. The results were magnificent—even if his won-lost record wasn't.

The National League managed to bat just .170 against him last year, lending credence to the evaluations offered earlier in his career that his stuff well above average.

His fastball is good, but not over-powering; it usually is in the 88-91 MPH range. What makes it so difficult to hit are its movement and the slight pause which occurs in his delivery of the pitch. Fernandez seems to stop for an instant just before moving his arm forward, making it difficult to time and track his pitches: they appear to move faster than the measured speed. He also throws a slow curveball which makes his fastball seem faster than it is.

FIELDING, HITTING, BASERUNNING:

Fernandez's delivery is slow and be-cause his move to first is almost non-existent, he is not a good pitcher to pit against the league's running teams. Because he is a slow worker, his defense is not as alert as it would be if he pitched more quickly.

He is a decent-hitting pitcher, but despite his weight loss, he is not a fast runner.

OVERALL:

For all of the improvement Fernandez made last season, his development is as yet incomplete. There are times when he can be the cause of his own undoing. He continues to get rattled when things go wrong and has not developed the maturity to take the game's frustrations in stride--he pouts too much.

Snider: "Fernandez needs to prove that he can be consistent over the entire season. He may need to develop another pitch, perhaps a split-finger fastball, to turn to when he has trouble controling his fastball or curve."

HITTING:

For the past three seasons, George Foster has not been able to find his stroke until July. And each year, he finds his groove progressively later and his summer surges become shorter and shorter. The questions have to be asked: Is this the year George Foster does not have his July renaissance? Is this the year his production falls to the point where he is no longer afforded the benefit of the doubt? Is this season his last chance?

The benefit of the doubt is afforded because when Foster gets going at the plate, he is a dangerous hitter who can decide a game with one swing of the bat. His 21 home runs and 77 RBIs in 452 at-bats is a feat of some note, but those numbers pale in comparison to what he has achieved in the past.

His hitting style has not changed through the years: he takes forever to position himself in the batter's box, still takes too many good pitches and swings at too many pitches out of the strike zone. At times, Foster's bat appears to be weighted with an anvil. But then, there are times when he can pull a Nolan Ryan fastball.

The majority of his extra-base hits are into the gaps. He is successful when he goes to the opposite field but starts off each season trying to pull everything out of the park until he remembers his stroke in July.

BASERUNNING:

Foster is a one-base-at-a-timer. He never sprints except in situations when he can beat out an infield ground ball or avoid a double play. He is an unaggressive slider--when he slides.

FIELDING:

His defense has improved as the Mets' chances for a pennant have improved, prompting one to wonder what he was thinking in 1982 and 1983. He now plays a bit more aggressively than in the past

GEORGE FOSTER
LF, No. 15
RR, 6'1", 198 lbs.
ML Svc: 15 years
Born: 12-1-48 in
Tuscaloosa, AL

1985 STATISTICS

AVG	G	AB	R	H	2B	3B	HR	RBI	BB	SO	SB
.263	129	452	57	119	24	1	21	77	46	87	0

CAREER STATISTICS

AVG	G	AB	R	H	2B	3B	HR	RBI	BB	SO	SB
.276	1890	6739	956	1861	301	44	334	1197	642	1358	50

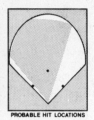

VS. RHP   VS. LHP   PROBABLE HIT LOCATIONS

and will dive for a ball or crush his back against the wall on occasion. His arm will always be weak.

OVERALL:

If Foster was not getting paid such an exorbitant salary--$1.8 million for last season (over $15,000 per hit or over $23,000 per RBI), teammates and fans might not be so quick to snarl. If expectations were not so high based on his achievements with the Reds, Foster might be forgiven for his lack of aggressiveness. But the fact is that he was a .285 hitter in over ten seasons with the Reds and hit a home run every 18 times at bat and has been a .255 hitter and has spaced his home runs to one in every 25 at-bats while with the Mets.

Snider: "Certainly there are questions about his motivation and lack of hustle, but he still has power in his bat and can pour it on. If Foster could put up the kind of numbers he did a few years ago, the Mets might not be bridesmaids this season."

PITCHING:

The difference between the Dwight Gooden of 1984 and the Gooden of 1985 is simple. He got better.

It didn't have to be that way. His composure could have slipped, his fame could have gone to his head, he could have become carried away with his own talent and pitched last season content to rest on the laurels of a fastball that can reach 95 MPH. Instead, he decided to do everything right.

One of his most impressive developments is his ability and concern for pitching to spots. In his rookie season, Gooden was a thrower, a purebred power pitcher who fired pitch after pitch over the plate. Last season, he began to dissect the strike zone. In his mind's eye, the strike zone has become quarters, or sixths or eighths. He thinks about placement, he thinks about location.

Gooden also thinks about his arm. He pitches almost effortlessly with a fluid delivery that puts little strain on his arm. But looking ahead, he has added a change-up as his third pitch and has secured the confidence in his curveball that enables him to throw it when he is behind in the count (a situation he does not find himself in very often).

Gooden starts throwing heat from the first inning on and can keep the fire burning under his fastball if that's what it takes to complete a game. He can be in the late innings of a game, throwing 91-92 MPH, and then increase the velocity to 95 MPH if that is what it will take to get the batter out.

FIELDING, HITTING, BASERUNNING:

Gooden has worked to reduce his delivery time and, as a result, picked off more than his share of runners last season. Baserunners have stopped taking liberties with him. He still is not quick to the plate, but not many batters reach base when he is pitching.

He fields his position well and is

DWIGHT GOODEN
RHP, No. 16
RR, 6'3", 198 lbs.
ML Svc: 2 years
Born: 11-16-64 in
Tampa, FL

1985 STATISTICS

W	L	ERA	G	GS	CG	SV	IP	H	R	ER	BB	SO
24	4	1.53	35	35	16	0	276.2	198	51	47	69	268

CAREER STATISTICS

W	L	ERA	G	GS	CG	SV	IP	H	R	ER	BB	SO
41	13	2.00	66	66	23	0	494.2	359	123	110	142	544

quick to cover first base.

He is proud of his hitting--he hit his first home run of his major league career last season--and says he wants to bat lefthanded, which is his natural side. He is a fleet runner but ankle trouble prevents him from running as hard as he can.

OVERALL:

Mild-mannered and composed, Gooden also proved that he is not afraid to protect his teammates or to move any batter in the league off the plate. He continues to impress in every phase of the game. Rookie of the Year: 1984, Cy Young Award: 1985, the league leader in strikeouts both seasons. Last year, he became the youngest pitcher to win 20 games.

What's next? For starters, he will likely be working to perfect his change-up, though at last look, it was faster than most other pitchers' best fastball.

Snider: "They say that there is a certain number of pitches in an arm. Dwight will see to it that he has a lot left. He could become the best pitcher of all time and he wouldn't have to improve much to do that."

HITTING:

Danny Heep fills an unglamorous but necessary role for the Mets. He is a reserve outfielder who is most effective against righthanded pitching. Last season, he was given the chance to play regularly when Darryl Strawberry was disabled due to a broken thumb. Heep performed well when given his opportunity, but once Strawberry returned, Heep returned to the bench to await the next outfielder's injury. Or slump. Or rest.

Heep takes a big swing at the ball and tries to pull more often than he should; his best shots usually fall in the gaps. Because he tries to pull the ball, pitchers should keep everything away from him. He does not like to dig under low pitches and generally lets pitches below his thighs go by. But he can hit a ball thrown high in the strike zone very well.

He is a streaky hitter who, when hot, will get his fair share of home runs and is fast enough to stretch a single into a double. But during the six-week span last season when he was playing regularly, there were times when he showed his reserve status as prominently as one would a name tag at a convention.

At one time, it appeared as though he might have the ability to jump off the bench and become a consistently productive pinch-hitter. That is not the case.

BASERUNNING:

Heep could be a better baserunner and basestealer than he is. He is faster than he probably thinks he is and is too tentative on the bases. He will rumble on the double play but could use an overall more aggressive approach on the bases.

FIELDING:

Heep is a defensive asset to the Mets because he can play all three outfield positions in addition to first base. He

DANNY HEEP
OF/PH, No. 25
LL, 5'11", 185 lbs.
ML Svc: 6 years
Born: 7-3-57 in
   San Antonio, TX

1985 STATISTICS

AVG	G	AB	R	H	2B	3B	HR	RBI	BB	SO	SB
.280	95	271	26	76	17	0	7	42	27	27	2

CAREER STATISTICS

AVG	G	AB	R	H	2B	3B	HR	RBI	BB	SO	SB
.253	474	1118	120	283	63	3	20	116	123	144	8

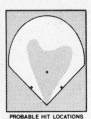

VS. RHP   VS. LHP   PROBABLE HIT LOCATIONS

is adequate at all of them, though he does not often get the chance to play backup to first baseman Keith Hernandez.

Heep's arm and range are acceptable enough to spell Strawberry in right, George Foster in left or even Mookie Wilson in center if Lenny Dykstra is unavailable, but he does not do anything well enough in the field to offset his inability to hit southpaw pitching and be used as a regular.

OVERALL:

Heep is a player who has realized that he has a specific but restricted value to the club.

Snider: "Heep is the type of player that every team has to have and he did a good job replacing Strawberry last year. But his role has narrowed over the past year as he has not been able to produce as a pinch-hitter. He's got his streaks but he's also got some power to show when he's in as a replacement."

HITTING:

Keith Hernandez is the best situation hitter in the National League. There is no other batter who forces the pitcher to throw "his" pitch as many times as Hernandez does. And when he gets it, he knows what to do with it. If the Mets need an RBI double, Hernandez provides it. A leadoff single, it's done. The old sac fly, no problem.

Hernandez is an ideal number three hitter. If there is a way to pitch to him, NL pitchers are still looking for it. There are some lefthanded pitchers—a very select few—who give Hernandez a hard time. But even when he is challenged by a pitching strategy, he can outmaneuver the battery with an opposite field stroke: he can pull a lefty when he has to. In general, however, he uses the entire field and will only pull the ball in rare situtaions.

For a finely tuned hitting machine such as Hernandez, even a short body twist, a lowered elbow or standing an inch farther off the plate can be the difference between a slump and a hot streak. Last season, he was in the midst of a frustrating cold spell when his sharp-eyed father (who watches every Mets game on TV via cable reception from a satellite dish) urged him to close his stance. The obedient son went on a five-week tear.

BASERUNNING:

Baserunning is the only phase of the game in which Hernandez is average. He would rather steal a base hit than a base. He does not try to steal often and when he does attempt a theft, there is a 50/50 chance that he will be successful.

FIELDING:

Hernandez has reset the standards for defensive style at first base. His technique is so athletically brilliant that there is no other first baseman who can match it. His range to his right is

KEITH HERNANDEZ
1B, No. 17
LL, 6'0", 195 lbs.
ML Svc: 11 years
Born: 10-20-53 in
   San Francisco, CA

1985 STATISTICS

AVG	G	AB	R	H	2B	3B	HR	RBI	BB	SO	SB
.309	158	593	87	183	34	4	10	91	77	59	3

CAREER STATISTICS

AVG	G	AB	R	H	2B	3B	HR	RBI	BB	SO	SB
.301	1572	5539	875	1669	338	57	115	817	823	726	94

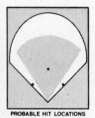

VS. RHP   VS. LHP   PROBABLE HIT LOCATIONS

phenomenal—you often wonder why a second baseman is necessary. Ground balls that elude most other first basemen Hernandez turns into force outs at second base or even double plays.

His glove is as big as the satellite dish in his father's yard and helps him save other infielders from making innumerable errors. He's the best at the 3-6-3 double play. He "cheats" as well as any first baseman.

OVERALL:

Hernandez is a pro's pro. He bore the weight of his testimony at the Pittsburgh drug trial last season without any effect on his performance on the field.

Snider: "One of the most amazing things about Keith is his sixth sense in bunt situations. He seem to know exactly when the bunt is on and precisely where the hitter will lay it down. He charges the hitter and you know that he's ready to smother the ball. Single-handedly, he takes that weapon right out of the manager's hands."

HITTING:

Howard Johnson can get around on the league's best fastballs. A righthanded pitcher is making a big mistake if he throws HoJo anything high and hard. But then there are breaking balls . . . Despite coming to the predominantly fastball National League from the predominantly breaking ball American League, Johnson has a lot of trouble hitting anything other than the fastball.

Some of his problems at the plate could be attributed to his adjustment to the new league. Yet there were encouraging signs. He made good contact against pitchers he had previously faced in the American League during the first half of the season and became a much more conconsistent hitter after the All-Star break.

Last year, the switch-hitting Johnson was clearly a superior hitter as a lefthander. He is a low-ball hitter that way, a fact the pitchers quickly caught onto. He has an almost classic stroke lefthanded and it is from that side that his power lies. He is not as weak a hitter against lefthanded pitching as he appeared to be last season.

Still, Johnson was able to settle down late in the season and provide some critical hits for the Mets. The club is anticipating more from him this season and hopes that he will be a more patient hitter this year.

He is an able bunter who can beat out a bunt when he gets the early break as a lefthanded hitter.

BASERUNNING:

Johnson likes to run and is good at it. He goes in hard to second base on double play attempts. He is an intelligent enough baserunner, with the good speed to back it up, that he could steal 20-25 bases if he were to become an everyday player.

FIELDING:

Johnson's defense was brilliant early in the 1985 season, but he began to fail

HOWARD JOHNSON
3B, No. 20
SR, 5'10", 175 lbs.
ML Svc: 4 years
Born: 11-29-60 in
Clearwater, FL

1985 STATISTICS

AVG	G	AB	R	H	2B	3B	HR	RBI	BB	SO	SB
.242	126	389	38	94	18	4	11	46	34	78	6

CAREER STATISTICS

AVG	G	AB	R	H	2B	3B	HR	RBI	BB	SO	SB
.254	323	965	115	245	37	5	30	115	97	185	23

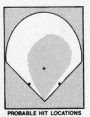

VS. RHP   VS. LHP   PROBABLE HIT LOCATIONS

in June. After that point, it seemed as though he simply couldn't catch a thing.

He is aggressive and willing to put his face in front of a hard ground ball. The Mets even tried him at shortstop, but he seemed out of place there. His arm is good enough for shortstop but his hands are only good enough for third base.

OVERALL:

Johnson is a positive addition to the the Mets. He is only 25 years old and seems to have a lot of natural talent but is rough around the edges. He is an extremely coachable player and has a great attitude.

Snider: "The Mets are specialists at molding young players. Getting Johnson to settle down as a fielder and to learn more about selectivity and patience at the plate will be one of the club's projects. For a relatively small player, he shows good power and should improve this season."

HITTING:

There's not much baseball left in Ray Knight. His body has slowed down in a hurry and has sabotaged his career. There is very little that comes natural- ly and easily to him now--he has to force almost every aspect of his play.

Knight knows the game and knows what has to be done, but his body won't coop- erate to execute the moves. Pitchers don't have to make many concessions to him any longer; his bat has slowed and he has lost the ability to foul off a pitcher's best stuff.

Knight continues to stand far off the plate, which has made him more suscepti- ble than ever to breaking stuff from righthanders, whom he rarely sees. There are not many, but a home run or two still lingers in his bat; with that in mind, pitchers should continue to keep the ball low.

BASERUNNING:

This is the last place one could ex- pect to see a rejuvenation. If you think his bat is slow, watch his legs.

FIELDING:

Knight never did have great range, but now he has none. He is adequate at fielding balls hit at him and can still charge bunts and slow rollers well, but as far as lateral movements and covering the line, it's not even close. He has had surgery on his elbow and his shoul- der, but there has been little improve- ment in his ability to throw the ball to first quickly or accurately.

RAY KNIGHT
3B, No. 22
RR, 6'2", 190 lbs.
ML Svc: 9 years
Born: 12-28-52 in
   Albany, GA

1985 STATISTICS

AVG	G	AB	R	H	2B	3B	HR	RBI	BB	SO	SB
.218	90	271	22	59	12	0	6	36	13	32	1

CAREER STATISTICS

AVG	G	AB	R	H	2B	3B	HR	RBI	BB	SO	SB
.275	1103	3481	359	957	206	23	56	421	244	396	11

STRONG VS. RHP   STRONG VS. LHP   PROBABLE HIT LOCATIONS

OVERALL:

Just when Knight appeared to be com- ing around last season following opera- tions on his shoulder and elbow, a leg injury interrupted his season. He never regained the touch and became one of the favorite targets of the Shea Stadium boo birds last year.

Snider: "Ray's skills are on the down side of the hill. He's about had it as a ballplayer."

PITCHING:

Last season, it appeared as though Ed Lynch had the same stuff he has always had. There is nothing special about his pitching--he needs impeccable control to do well. Yet last season that's exactly what he had and that's exactly what he did.

Instead of merely surviving, Lynch prospered and, at times, tamed batting orders that had abused him in previous seasons.

Rigorous off-season training allowed him to remain stronger later in each start and later into the season. But he still is a nibbler, a pitcher who must have his control.

Lynch needs to be a strategist, to outthink each hitter. As he has gained more experience, he has found the game plan he had been looking for. Opponents batted .325 against him in 1984 but .256 last season.

His most effective pitch is what some consider a slurve and he is improving the use of his change-up each year. He spots his fastball well. His fastball is not overpowering, but his location is usually very good. He does not walk many batters and doesn't give in too often, a practice which often leads to yielding home runs--he gave up 19 in 191 innings last season.

FIELDING, HITTING, BASERUNNING:

Lynch helps himself with his glove and his quick delivery to the plate. He doesn't have a particularly good move to first base, but he receives his sign with his back leg bent to facilitate a quick delivery. Only the more accomplished basestealers run on him without reservation.

ED LYNCH
RHP, No. 36
RR, 6'5", 207 lbs.
ML Svc: 5 years
Born: 2-25-56 in
Brooklyn, NY

1985 STATISTICS

W	L	ERA	G	GS	CG	SV	IP	H	R	ER	BB	SO
10	8	3.44	31	29	6	0	191	188	76	73	27	65

CAREER STATISTICS

W	L	ERA	G	GS	CG	SV	IP	H	R	ER	BB	SO
38	40	3.83	166	98	7	4	728	813	348	310	158	258

He is almost no threat with the bat, though he can bunt. On those rare occasions when he does reach base, Lynch tries to do as much as possible; his enthusiasm on the basepaths can sometimes lead to overaggressiveness and poor judgment.

OVERALL:

Lynch has to prove himself each spring against a steady flow of young phenoms. Still, he always seems to find a way to win a spot on the roster.

Hitters used to look forward to facing him, and while some still do, it is not with the same eagerness.

Snider: "Ed has got moxie. He does a pretty good job considering that he really doesn't have very good stuff.

"Last season, he was able to pitch to locations better than he had in the past. If he can maintain his control, he ought to have a pretty good season again this year."

PITCHING:

Roger McDowell was the most pleasant surprise on the Mets last season. His ability was not the eye-opener, mind you; no, that was never a concern--the Mets had been gushing over McDowell's sinker for a year. But there was uncertainty as to how well and how quickly he would recover from his 1984 elbow surgery. McDowell came back well enough to be the team's saving grace, if not their saving ace. When Doug Sisk was disabled late in the season, McDowell showed his elbow could withstand regular abuse.

He was the talk of the league early in the season, when Davey Johnson, at the urging of general manager Frank Cashen, "nursed" him. He was quite effective until an ankle injury interrupted his season on June 7. He received his Wrigley Field baptism later that month. But by September, he seemed to have regained his early-season touch and developed the composure necessary for late-inning work.

McDowell's pitches just naturally drop, it's as if they "fall off the table." The drop may be as little as one-half an inch, but it is enough to prevent a hitter from getting the good part of the bat on the ball. His stuff always dropped, but since the surgery, the break has been more pronounced and has led to more strikeouts.

If his ball doesn't drop, however, McDowell is in big trouble.

FIELDING, HITTING, BASERUNNING:

McDowell is an exceptionally mobile fielder--and it's a good thing because his sinker forces so many ground balls. His delivery is such that he is in good

ROGER McDOWELL
RHP, No. 42
RR, 6'1", 175 lbs.
ML Svc: 1 year
Born: 12-21-60 in
Cincinnati, OH

1985 STATISTICS
W	L	ERA	G	GS	CG	SV	IP	H	R	ER	BB	SO
6	5	2.83	62	2	0	17	127.1	108	43	40	37	70

CAREER STATISTICS
W	L	ERA	G	GS	CG	SV	IP	H	R	ER	BB	SO
6	5	2.83	62	2	0	17	127.1	108	43	40	37	70

position to cover his area and he appears to know what to do with the ball when he handles it.

He moves quickly to cover first but is not as swift to back up the plate.

He shows little promise as a hitter, but in his role as a late-inning reliever, that is not a source of concern.

OVERALL:

As he learns more about major league hitters and adjusts to their tendencies, McDowell should become a more consistent reliever. With his kind of stuff, consistency is all that is necessary for him to take his place among the game's more elite short men.

Snider: "The bottom just falls out of his sinker; as a matter of fact, it looks as though everything he throws drops. If he has a good defense behind him since he gets a lot of ground balls, he's especially tough."

PITCHING:

Last season, it was difficult to tell which Jesse Orosco would emerge from the bullpen. There are two: one has a hard slider which absolutely freezes opposing batters and renders them helpless and often hitless, while the other throws a lazy slider that can reverse its direction before it reaches the catcher's mitt.

One is a winner, the other is not.

Orosco's problems are related to his elbow. When his elbow is feeling good, he throws hard and gets batters out, but when his elbow feels tender, he is flat out ineffective, a shadow of the Orosco who came into his own in the second half of 1983.

When he is right, of course, Orosco's slider is one of the best in the business; it is so good that his fastball sometimes is forgotten by the batter. Last season, Orosco tried to develop a "backup" slider, slightly off-speed, one which would take some of the strain off his elbow. The new pitch, however, did nothing to relieve the pressure.

His failures and frustrations notwithstanding, Orosco's temperament remains that of a good short reliever. His confidence is high and he does not unravel in tight siutations. If the Jesse Orosco with the hard slider is on the mound, lefthanded hitters are in for a grueling at-bat: Orosco will even drop to sidearm on occasion to keep a lefty even further off-balance. Righthanded hitters don't get much of a break either if Orosco's slider is dropping.

FIELDING, HITTING, BASERUNNING:

Orosco is a remarkable athlete--he can make some incredibly acrobatic plays on bunts and balls hit back to him. His hands are soft and he knows the respon-

JESSE OROSCO
LHP, No. 47
RL, 6'2", 185 lbs.
ML Svc: 5 years
Born: 4-21-57 in
    Santa Barbara, CA

1985 STATISTICS

W	L	ERA	G	GS	CG	SV	IP	H	R	ER	BB	SO
8	6	2.73	54	0	0	17	79	66	26	24	34	68

CAREER STATISTICS

W	L	ERA	G	GS	CG	SV	IP	H	R	ER	BB	SO
36	32	2.51	256	4	0	70	437.1	338	143	122	174	366

sibilities of his position. His move to first base is adequate, and is helped because he doesn't have much of a kick in his delivery, which makes him quick to the plate.

He seldom is called on to bat or run the bases. However, he is a good hitter.

OVERALL:

Orosco's effectiveness is clearly tied to his elbow: if it is sound, the Mets have a relief pitcher with the nasty stuff to complement his "ninth-inning" character.

He is a determined pitcher who always wants the ball. Unfortunately, there were several occasions last season when he took the ball and his arm wasn't well enough to withstand the strain. His enthusiasm to pitch, while admirable, did nothing for either his injury or the team.

Snider: "Orosco's arm has grown old in a hurry. There were times last year when he would have no movement on his pitches. He needs help, maybe even a new pitch. Or, perhaps he should be used three times a week instead of five."

HITTING:

When the Mets look at Montreal and see former Met shortstop Hubie Brooks and his 100 RBIs, and then look to Shea Stadium and see his replacement, Rafael Santana, they don't feel cheated.

Santana is not the so-called American League shortstop Davey Johnson would like in his batting order--but he is the National League-type shortstop Johnson wants handling a double play ball in extra innings.

Santana can be handled by most top pitchers, but he occasionally will hurt a careless or inexperienced pitcher. He has little extra-base power and almost no home run power, but when he finds his groove, he can string together singles that will start or extend rallies.

He strikes out too often for someone with such little power, though batting eighth doesn't help. Breaking balls confuse him, and a good--not necessarily great--fastball can overpower him.

BASERUNNING:

Santana is not as fast a runner as one might expect; his speed is ordinary, but his instincts are good. He does, however, tend to have baserunning lapses and is a prime pickoff target.

FIELDING:

Santana provides the Mets with competent, although rarely flashy play at the most important defensive position on the field. His arm is better than average and his throws are generally well-targeted. His errors do not seem to come at clutch moments.

Santana never shows off his arm. If anything, he times the baserunner's arrival and releases the ball so that it barely beats the runner to the bag. His feeds to second base on DP balls are always perfect. He makes Wally Backman's job easier.

RAFAEL SANTANA
SS, No. 3
RR, 6'1", 160 lbs.
ML Svc: 2 years
Born: 1-31-58 in
  La Romana, DR

1985 STATISTICS

AVG	G	AB	R	H	2B	3B	HR	RBI	BB	SO	SB
.257	154	529	41	136	19	1	1	29	29	54	1

CAREER STATISTICS

AVG	G	AB	R	H	2B	3B	HR	RBI	BB	SO	SB
.260	235	695	56	181	30	2	2	43	40	73	1

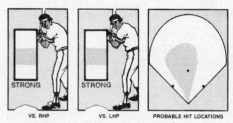

Santana's range is better to his right than his left; though neither is wide, both are adequate.

But Santana gets the job done. He is adept at handling balls chopped over the mound and at plays in the short outfield.

OVERALL:

The Mets would like more offense from their shortstop, but are satisfied with the defense Santana provides.

Snider: "Rafael is an adequate shortstop--nothing acrobatic, but smooth. Once in a while, he might deliver a key hit or drive in a big run. He needs to develop a better eye for the strike zone and to learn to lay off bad pitches. He is never going to hit for power, but he needs to get himself on base and into the action more often."

PITCHING:

Poor Doug Sisk.
First he lost his sinker.
Then he lost his confidence.
Then he lost his job.
And late-season elbow surgery may prove to the most costly loss yet.

Sisk was the relief pitcher nobody wanted to face in the second half of 1983 and the first half of 1984. Hitters don't like to look foolish and Sisk had such good movement on his pitches that he could make them look downright silly. He couldn't throw the ball straight even if he wanted to.

But that knack became a double-edged sword for him last season. His sinker stayed up and his control stayed away, prompting the crowds at Shea Stadium to boo him unmercifully and, eventually, the Mets to option him to Triple-A.

Even after he returned, the results were not encouraging. When Sisk finally began to pitch effectively, his long-lasting elbow trouble worsened.

FIELDING, HITTING, BASERUNNING:

Sisk is not a gifted fielder, but he knows what to do with the ball when his sinker elicits a double play ground ball, as it often does when he is pitching effectively. He has a quick move to first base and a fast delivery.

DOUG SISK
RHP, No. 39
RR, 6'2", 210 lbs.
ML Svc: 3 years
Born: 9-26-57 in
    Renton, WA

1985 STATISTICS

W	L	ERA	G	GS	CG	SV	IP	H	R	ER	BB	SO
4	5	5.30	42	0	0	2	73	86	48	43	40	26

CAREER STATISTICS

W	L	ERA	G	GS	CG	SV	IP	H	R	ER	BB	SO
10	13	3.00	167	0	0	29	263.2	236	111	88	157	95

His baserunning and hitting talents--if they exist--are well hidden.

OVERALL:

Even if Sisk recovers from surgery, there still is the question of regaining his lost form and some of his control. He never had a lot to begin with. This probably will be a tough year for Sisk.

Snider: "He was a tough guy to hit for a while, but I think he became very tentative last year. His control was never great, but last year it was really atrocious."

HITTING:

There are times when Rusty Staub appears capable of simply willing a ground ball through the middle of the infield. He is strong enough to pull any pitch and has enough power to reach the fence in right field. Still, he usually tries to hit to the opposite field or through the middle.

Only a few hitters have as good an idea of what a pitcher is going to throw as Staub has. He studies pitchers and detects minor tendencies that others can't find or don't know how to look for.

He has some trouble against lefthanders, but no pitcher "owns" him. Every pitcher in the league wants to see him hit the ball on the ground.

BASERUNNING:

It would be highly unusual if Rusty were not lifted for a pinch-runner once he was safely on base.

FIELDING:

In a game that will be treasured by Mets fans, Staub and Clint Hurdle flip-flopped between left and right field for six innings of an 18-inning game against Pittsburgh last April. That was done to keep Staub away from the ball since he does not field often, he is slow, he has no range and not much of an arm; but he proved that he still had what it takes

RUSTY STAUB
PH, No. 10
LR, 6'2", 230 lbs.
ML Svc: 24 years
Born: 4-1-44 in
    New Orleans, LA

1985 STATISTICS
AVG	G	AB	R	H	2B	3B	HR	RBI	BB	SO	SB
.267	54	45	2	12	3	0	1	8	10	4	0

CAREER STATISTICS
AVG	G	AB	R	H	2B	3B	HR	RBI	BB	SO	SB
.279	2950	9720	1189	2716	499	47	292	1466	1255	888	47

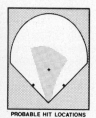

VS. RHP   VS. LHP   PROBABLE HIT LOCATIONS

when he made a game-saving running catch near the right field foul line.

OVERALL:

Snider: "If a team can afford to carry Rusty as a one-dimensional player, it should. In his case, age makes no difference. He is as good a hitter now as he has ever been. If I had room on my club for him, I'd have him--but I would ask him to lose some weight."

HITTING:

A scouting report written in 1980 on an 18-year old Darryl Strawberry read: ". . . tall, lanky, long arms and legs, great body . . . just might be that superstar of the very near future . . . no faults . . . hard to visualize how much he will become . . . " That report is still applicable.

He comes equipped with everything it takes to be a premier hitter and run producer--he has extraordinary skill and power. He can steal a base out from under a fielder's nose and his fielding is beginning to fulfill his promise.

A pitcher can embarrass Strawberry three times up, start feeling pretty content, then render a 450-foot home run the fourth time this beanpole of a hitter faces him. And he's getting better. Strawberry is a more accomplished pull hitter now and has creamed some monstrous home runs to straightaway center.

He has learned to deal with off-speed stuff and with the pitches that are high and inside. He can be happy with a single to left on an outside pitch and then hit a similar pitch well over the left field wall in his next at-bat.

BASERUNNING:

Strawberry is fast: he cruises his 6'6" body from from first to third. His speed is most evident when he has a chance for an infield hit. He steals bases on his speed alone--he does not get a good jump or take a long lead.

His weakness as a baserunner is his occasional overzealousness, indicated when he attempts to steal third with two outs. He does not slide into home with abandon; he can be timid on plays at the plate.

FIELDING:

Poor work habits and nonchalance in the field have been a source of criticism in the past. Last year, however, Strawberry began to take his defense more seriously and the result was a

DARRYL STRAWBERRY
RF, No. 18
LL, 6'6", 190 lbs.
ML Svc: 3 years
Born: 3-12-62 in
   Los Angeles, CA

1985 STATISTICS

AVG	G	AB	R	H	2B	3B	HR	RBI	BB	SO	SB
.277	111	393	78	109	15	4	29	79	73	96	26

CAREER STATISTICS

AVG	G	AB	R	H	2B	3B	HR	RBI	BB	SO	SB
.261	380	1335	216	348	57	15	81	250	195	355	72

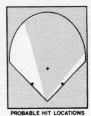

VS. RHP   VS. LHP   PROBABLE HIT LOCATIONS

dramatic improvement.

He had fewer lapses of concentration last year. Though he continues his habit of stepping back as his first reaction to a batted ball, he has become more adept at charging ground ball base hits. His gait is deceiving, but he covers ground. His arm is well above average. Another rap on his defense was his unwillingness to dive and climb walls. Last May, he dove to make a catch, tore ligaments in his right thumb and didn't play again for six weeks.

OVERALL:

Strawberry is one of the few players who can dominate a game offensively with one swing of the bat and do it more than two or three times a year.

Snider: "Darryl appeared more appreciative of his job and took it more seriously after the injury forced him from the game for six weeks. He became a clutch performer down the stretch. He is impossible to replace: the Mets are a different team without him."

HITTING:

Mookie Wilson is not the ideal lead-off hitter. He has excellent speed and he switch-hits, but he strikes out too often, walks too infrequently and his on-base percentage is comparable with Dave Kingman's. Still, Wilson gets the job done and when he is in top form, the entire Mets lineup is more productive.

Last season, a shoulder injury and subsequent surgery forced Wilson out of the lineup and afforded Lenny Dykstra an opportunity to show his considerable leadoff skills. But once Wilson was healthy, he won back his job and helped push the Mets through September.

Time spent on the DL last year did not alleviate Wilson's primary problem as a leadoff man: poor judgment of the strike zone. Though he walked more frequently than ever last season, he still offered at ball four more often than he took it, especially when he was batting righthanded.

Wilson likes high pitches he can drive as a righthanded hitter and prefers low pitches as a lefthander. He has surprising power from the left side (his natural side is the right) and can golf a ball into the stands even at Shea Stadium.

To the amazement of some and the consternation of the Mets, Wilson does not bunt nearly as often as other leadoff batters.

BASERUNNING:

No Mets player is faster. His speed is in the class of Willie McGee, Tim Raines, Rickey Henderson and Willie Wilson. However, Mookie's low on-base percentage last year (.331) prevented him from using his speed very often. He has the speed which can disrupt a defense and force fielders to hurry their throws and make foolish plays.

The majority of his triples would be doubles for those with equal speed but less aggressiveness--he reaches maximum speed almost instantly. His slides are usually hands-first, a technique the club wants him to change.

MOOKIE WILSON
CF, No. 1
SR, 5'10", 168 lbs.
ML Svc: 6 years
Born: 2-9-56 in
Bamberg, SC

1985 STATISTICS

AVG	G	AB	R	H	2B	3B	HR	RBI	BB	SO	SB
.276	93	337	56	93	16	8	6	26	28	52	24

CAREER STATISTICS

AVG	G	AB	R	H	2B	3B	HR	RBI	BB	SO	SB
.275	677	2634	390	724	107	44	31	204	136	425	213

  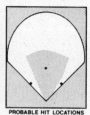

VS. RHP   VS. LHP   PROBABLE HIT LOCATIONS

FIELDING:

Wilson still has trouble with balls hit directly over his head as well as with any ball hit during a day game. He began wearing tinted sunglasses last year both in the field and at the plate to try to alleviate the problem.

His speed helps him track down a lot of balls which might otherwise be hits. He covers a lot of ground in the gaps, particularly in left-center when George Foster is playing in left field.

Wilson's trouble in the field, however, is his throwing. Even if his arm is full strength this season, it will still be considered weak.

OVERALL:

Snider: "Mookie has to continue to work on his judgment of the strike zone and should be a more selective hitter. The bunt would be a great way for him to get on base--if only he would use it."

RON GARDENHIRE
SS, No. 19
RR, 6'0", 174 lbs.
ML Svc: 4 years
Born: 10-24-57 in
  Butzbach, GER

HITTING, BASERUNNING, FIELDING:

At one time, the Mets considered Ron Gardenhire to be the ideal reserve middle infielder. Several problems have changed that view, however.

He is physically fragile, he has not developed enough as a hitter and his defensive abilities, especially at shortstop, have become suspect.

Gardenhire struggles; he can be overmatched by a good fastball and fooled by a good righthanded breaking ball. Lefthanders try to jam him.

He can bunt and knows how to advance a runner. Gardenhire has extra-base but not home run power.

He still is regarded as primarily a reserve second baseman, though he has not hit enough to warrant being platooned with Wally Backman.

When Gardenhire plays shortstop, he seems to make errors at the least opportune moments. His arm is better suited for second base.

Gardenhire has better-than-average speed, but his delicate hamstrings have caused him to miss much of the last two seasons. He is an aggressive runner with good baserunning instincts.

OVERALL:

Gardenhire's demeanor is a positive influence on a ballclub, but his days seem to be numbered. He doesn't do any one thing well enough to carry him on the club, particularly since he often is not healthy.

TOM GORMAN
LHP, No. 29
LL, 6'4", 200 lbs.
ML Svc: 3 years
Born: 12-16-57 in
  Portland, OR

PITCHING, FIELDING,
HITTING, BASERUNNING:

For most of 1984, Tom Gorman was one of the Mets' most effective offensive weapons. He would be summoned to pitch and invariably, the Mets would score. Some of Gorman's 6-0 record of 1984 can be attributed to his being in the right place at the right time.

He was not quite as fortunate last season; Gorman's big pitch is his forkball and when it is not right, neither is Gorman. There are occasions when he

also throws what looks as though it may be a fastball, and a change-up peeks in from time to time, but Gorman lives and dies by his forkball.

Last season, his forkball was not working porperly and his mistakes began to catch up with him. His other pitches are simply not good enough to keep him out of trouble when the forkball fails to drop.

Gorman developed an unwanted habit of yielding home runs last year: he gave up 8 in 52 innings pitched and watched 2 sail through the sky in 6 innings last July 4th in the Mets' 16-13, 19-inning victory. Gorman was the winning pitcher in that Independence Day marathon.

OVERALL:

Snider: "It is all very simple for Tom: when his forkball drops the way it should, he is going to do well. When it doesn't, it is the hitters who are going to do well."

CLINT HURDLE
C, No. 13
LR, 6'3", 195 lbs.
ML Svc: 5 years
Born: 7-30-57 in
Big Rapids, MI

HITTING, BASERUNNING, FIELDING:

Time and inactivity have taken the pop from the stroke that made Clint Hurdle a "can't miss" prospect with the Royals in 1977. Now he is a catcher/pinch-hitter with a positive outlook on a career that has lost so much of the luster it once held.

Hurdle's bat still can sting the best fastballs, but last year it was given little opportunity to do so. As a hitter, he often looked rusty from lack of use (he batted only 82 times last year) and did not produce as a pinch-hitter. The rust seemed to wear off after his first at-bat in games in which he started. He is a low-ball hitter and can be jammed.

Hurdle has a strong arm which makes right field his best outfield position. The Mets continue to work with Hurdle to develop his skills as a catcher and have been delighted with his progress. Still, with Gary Carter ahead of him, he will see extremely limited action at that position. Hurdle can also fill in at first base or third base.

OVERALL:

Hurdle's career has seen its highs and lows. He now approaches the game with an extremely good attitude and his clubhouse personality keeps the team loose. He has proven that he can learn a new position and would make a fine addition to a club looking for a left-handed-hitting catcher.

TERRY LEACH
RHP, No. 48
RR, 6'0", 205 lbs.
ML Svc: 2 years
Born: 3-13-54 in
Selma, AL

PITCHING, FIELDING,
HITTING, BASERUNNING:

For a pitcher who had been released twice, Terry Leach certainly made the most of his third major league tour—all of them with the Mets. Using his sidearm, almost submarine, delivery, Leach won two of the four games he started and pitched a three-hit shutout in one of them.

The sidearm pitch, of course, makes him more effective against righthanded hitters than against lefthanded hitters. In fact, Leach is something of a liability against predominantly lefthanded lineups, which explains why is used mainly as a spot reliever. His stuff is ordinary (he throws an average fastball and curveball)—it is only his delivery which makes him effective.

Leach is an adequate fielder. He considers himself a good bunter, but he failed in three bunt attempts in his shutout.

OVERALL:

Given the course Leach's career has taken, he is happy to be in the major leagues and is willing to do whatever is necessary to remain there. Hitters can learn how to hit him, though, once they become accustomed to his delivery.

BOB OJEDA
LHP, No. 19
LL, 6'1", 190 lbs.
ML Svc: 4 years
Born: 12-17-57 in
    Los Angeles, CA

PITCHING, FIELDING:

Bob Ojeda--and the Mets--are hoping that a change of scenery might be the best medicine for him. Ojeda's six-year career with the Red Sox was marked by mediocrity; he was an in-and-out pitcher who blamed both the Boston fans and the media for his own poor performance as well as the overall unsatisfactory play of the team.

Ojeda's problem has always been control. He has a good fastball and an excellent change-up. But his mind would often wander and his failure to fully concentrate would get him into trouble.

Last year may have been his worst as a starter. Between June 10 and September 22, he started 16 times and won only 3. At one point, he failed to win in 7 straight games and won only once in 13 starts.

Ojeda is the type of pitcher who, when he's on, will get everyone out--no one can hit him. But when he's off--and obviously that was quite often--even the hot dog vendor could get a hit.

As a lefthander, he has an excellent pickoff move. The rest of his fielding is a disaster. Every time he goes for a ground ball, it is an adventure. One never knows what he is going to do after he fields a bunt.

OVERALL:

Robinson: "Ojeda has been too inconsistent for me. He'll pitch one good game, but then is liable to have three bad ones. He rarely takes the same stuff to the mound with him two games in a row."

PHILADELPHIA PHILLIES

HITTING:

Without any fanfare, Luis Aguayo had himself some kind of year last season. He set career highs in virtually every offensive category.

Notoriety did not accompany his fine season because Aguayo is the quintessential utility infielder and the Phillies went nowhere last year. He is a bench guy who does his work in the shadows of the starters.

He is a small man with a surprising amount of pop in his bat. Aguayo is a high-ball, fastball hitter who drives the ball.

He uses an upright, closed stance and crowds the plate. He was hit by pitches six times last season, tying Juan Samuel for the team lead in getting drilled.

He developed patience at the plate last year. He likes to hit early in the count but can now work a pitcher better than he ever did before. In the past, he was a notorious first-ball, fastball hitter. The selectivity and patience has made him into a better hitter.

Pitchers can beat him by throwing him breaking balls down and away and off-speed stuff. Aguayo can drive fastballs and hanging sliders deep into the outfield. He's a far cry from being an automatic out, but pitchers can get him if they're willing to finesse him rather than challenge him.

BASERUNNING:

Aguayo has average speed and is not a threat to steal. He can bunt, but is rarely called upon to do so. When he gets on base, he's careful not to make a mistake.

FIELDING:

Defensively, Aguayo is a jack-of-all-trades with the ability to play third, second and short. His best position is

LUIS AGUAYO
INF, No. 16
RR, 5'9", 190 lbs.
ML Svc: 6 years
Born: 3-13-59 in
Vega Baja, PR

1985 STATISTICS

AVG	G	AB	R	H	2B	3B	HR	RBI	BB	SO	SB
.279	91	165	27	46	7	3	6	21	22	26	1

CAREER STATISTICS

AVG	G	AB	R	H	2B	3B	HR	RBI	BB	SO	SB
.264	266	428	72	113	17	7	14	54	44	69	4

STRONG — VS. RHP   STRONG — VS. LHP   PROBABLE HIT LOCATIONS

second base; his weakest one is third.

He is an adequate second baseman with decent range and a strong, accurate arm. His range as a shortstop is limited and his arm is not strong enough for him to play third every day.

OVERALL:

Aguayo is not an everyday player. His success last year came not only from his ability, but from the fact that he was used correctly. His future remains on the bench, where he is a valuable commodity.

Snider: "Over the past several seasons, Luis has been carving out a nice niche for himself. He is always there and I think that his new-found patience at the plate is a tribute to his desire to do the best he can with what he has to work with."

PITCHING:

Andersen is a sinker-slider pitcher who makes his living in the anonyminity of middle-inning relief. Maybe that should be made his living. For from the All-Star break on, Andersen was a non-person in the Phillies' bullpen, and by the end of 1985 there was every reason to believe Andersen would not be returning to Philadelphia for another turn.

Basically, there were two reasons why the personable Andersen fell on such hard times. One had to do with his performance. In early July, he simply did not get enough hitters out to inspire confidence from his manager. The other had to do with the Phillies' philosophy. The club embarked on a youth movement in 1985 and much of that youth was centered in the bullpen. Felske used his corps of young relievers to find out what they could do.

This made Andersen the odd man out. He was having difficulty getting his ball to sink and his slider, which had previously made him tough on righthanded hitters, had lost some of its bite.

He had trouble with his lower back in spring training and wasn't bending properly. Then he tried to change his basic stand-up, three-quarters sidearm motion for the "rocking chair" delivery favored by pitching coach Claude Osteen. When that didn't work, Andersen went back to slinging the ball without bending his back leg a great deal. The back injury was not the entire problem, but it was a contributing factor.

Andersen did have some successes last season but not enough to offer too much hope for his future with Philadelphia.

FIELDING, HITTING, BASERUNNING:

Andersen did not see enough action to

LARRY ANDERSEN
RHP, No. 47
RR, 6'3", 205 lbs.
ML Svc: 6 years
Born: 5-6-53 in
Portland, OR

1985 STATISTICS
W	L	ERA	G	GS	CG	SV	IP	H	R	ER	BB	SO
3	3	4.32	57	0	0	3	73	78	41	35	26	50

CAREER STATISTICS
W	L	ERA	G	GS	CG	SV	IP	H	R	ER	BB	SO
10	14	3.87	241	1	0	13	374.2	378	187	161	116	209

have taken too many cuts with the bat last season. He is an unremarkable hitter and runner.

OVERALL:

Andersen made a contribution last season. He brought some much-needed laughter into the clubhouse. He is the resident jokester and loved to don wigs and masks to make his teammates break up. No club, however, is going to pay a guy just to do a stand-up routine.

He's at the crossroads of his career. He believes that he can still pitch. The Phillies' decision makers, however, are not so sure.

Snider: "He didn't get much chance to pitch in July and August last year. Larry is like any breaking ball pitcher: his mistakes get hit. He was never overpowering and he might have lost a little off his fastball. I think his main problem last season was location. He just wasn't getting his pitches where he wanted them. I think he can still be a pretty good middle-inning guy."

PITCHING:

Steve Carlton's decline continued at a rapid pace last season. He has already relinquished his title as "The Dominant Lefthander" and has now become a pitcher trying to battle a serious injury for the first time in his career.

According to physicians, Carlton must have been pitching in pain for quite some time. He virtually abandoned his lethal slider two seasons ago and still won 13 games that year with essentially a curve, a change-up and a fastball. But his fastball, which has never been a killer, was timed at 75 MPH last season. And his slider, which has frustrated so many hitters for so long, does not have the nasty break of its former years.

He was barely able to last seven innings last year and missed a turn in the rotation for only the seventh time in his career. He was later placed on the disabled list for the first time in his incredibly long career.

When he returned in early September, his fastball had picked up to the mid-80s. But that was after 72 days of rest and offers no indication as to what to expect in 1986.

FIELDING, HITTING, BASERUNNING:

As a fielder and a baserunner, he remains below average. Carlton is not quick off the mound, so any ball bunted to the left or right side has a chance to be a hit; he seldom is quick enough to stab ground balls up the middle.

He is a good enough hitter to help himself in a game and he likes to hit. But he's not nuts about running the bases. He is a ponderous baserunner who does not run hard on ground balls, and when he does get on, he advances one base at a time. The only hit that will

STEVE CARLTON
LHP, No. 32
LL, 6'5", 210 lbs.
ML Svc: 21 years
Born: 12-22-44 in
   Miami, FL

1985 STATISTICS

W	L	ERA	G	GS	CG	SV	IP	H	R	ER	BB	SO
1	8	3.33	16	16	0	0	92	84	43	34	53	48

CAREER STATISTICS

W	L	ERA	G	GS	CG	SV	IP	H	R	ER	BB	SO
237	153	3.00	483	483	185	0	3613.1	3122	1384	1213	1207	2969

score him from first is a home run.

OVERALL:

Carlton holds the major league record for most consecutive games by a pitcher without a relief appearance. His greatest strengths remain his superb physical condition and his excellent powers of concentration. His weaknesses are his age (41) and his wounded shoulder.

Both physically and contractually, Carlton is near the end of his career. He may or may not be able to pitch this season, but if he does, it may not be with the Phillies.

Snider: "I don't think that he is out of it. He has a program of physical conditioning that keeps him levels and levels above the rest. Physical strength or not, however, there are some injuries that just cannot be overcome.

"Carlton wants to keep going. He has developed a pitch he can turn over, and a shade of the slider is still there, although it doesn't come in at its former velocity. All eyes will be on him this spring."

PITCHING:

Don Carman came from nowhere to become one of the more reliable members of a generally unreliable Phillies' bullpen. During spring training of 1985, He was just another lefthander--until the team watched him strike out batter after batter after batter. He had control of himself on the mound and, suddenly, had command of all his pitches. For this pitcher, staying away from winter ball had kept his arm resilient.

Carman was brought along slowly but gradually; manager John Felske began to trust him and he was given more responsibility. He throws a fastball in the mid-80s as well as a slider. He uses each pitch about half the time.

By season's end, Carman had shown himself to be excellent in tie games but not so good in save situations. He had earned himself a spot in the bullpen for 1986, but not as a late-inning closer. He seems better suited as the tablesetter, a guy who could go in in the seventh or eighth inning and hold the fort for the closer.

Carman spent almost the entire 1985 season working on his delivery and his slider. He has been working on the "rocking chair" approach on the mound: bending his back leg and using it as a plant to drive toward the hitter. Tom Seaver has used that style of pitching with great success over the years. It takes a great deal of concentration on mechanics. Carman is working on being consistent with it.

If he gets it all together, he could be awesome. When something goes awry, however, he tends to be wild and away from righthanded hitters.

FIELDING, HITTING, BASERUNNING:

Carman has an average move to first for a lefthander but doesn't let baserunners distract him. He is always in position to make a play in the field and covers first well. Carman didn't hit or

DON CARMAN
LHP, No. 42
LL, 6'3", 190 lbs.
ML Svc: 1 year plus
Born: 8-14-59 in
  Oklahoma City, OK

1985 STATISTICS

W	L	ERA	G	GS	CG	SV	IP	H	R	ER	BB	SO
9	4	2.08	71	0	0	7	86.1	52	25	20	38	87

CAREER STATISTICS

W	L	ERA	G	GS	CG	SV	IP	H	R	ER	BB	SO
9	5	2.51	83	0	0	8	100.2	66	34	28	44	103

run the bases enough for a judgment to be formed.

OVERALL:

He has the chance to become the Phillies' premier closer in the future. Despite the number of years he spent in the minors, Carman is just beginning to learn how to pitch. He's shown he can get out major league hitters. What he hasn't shown is an ability to get them out consistently with a game on the line. That could come with more experience.

The key to his future lies in his mental toughness. Does he possess the makeup of a late-inning reliever? Or is he more suited to the less glamorous, less pressurized role of pitching in the middle innings?

Snider: "He comes right at you and as a reliever that's what he has to do. He has developed a good deal of poise. He will need to get even more ice in his veins, however, if he is going to be successful in the long haul.

"Carman does not have a great fastball but he's done a lot of work with his slider. When he goes out there, he has a good idea of what he wants to do. He should be a good one."

HITTING:

There's bad luck, rotten luck and the kind of luck Tim Corcoran had last year. Statistics don't lie but they never tell the whole story. Looking over his lines, he had a bad season: .214 overall and .125 as a pinch-hitter. What you cannot see is that Corcoran may have set a club record for most line drive outs in a season. Corcoran hit the ball hard last year. Unfortunately, those hard-hit balls landed in the fielder's glove too often.

Corcoran is a low-ball, opposite field hitter with minimal power to right and right-center field. Most of his hits are to center or left-center field. He likes the ball away from him; pitchers can beat him by throwing him up and in.

He is a selective, patient hitter who has a good knowledge of the strike zone. He takes the outside pitch to left and will drill the inside pitch to center. Corcoran is a good breaking ball hitter and isn't often fooled by off-speed pitches. Pitchers can overpower him with high fastballs and hard sliders.

BASERUNNING:

Corcoran has below-average speed on the bases and is not a threat to steal. He rarely makes mistakes on the bases, though, and goes hard into second to break up the double play.

FIELDING:

Corcoran has the ability to play both the outfield and first base but was used almost exclusively at first last year. He is an excellent defensive first baseman with good range to either side. He digs balls out of the dirt well. His arm is average but his throws are accurate.

He fields bunts well. As an outfielder, Corcoran is well schooled in the fundamentals. It is hard, however, to teach great range. He goes to his left

TIM CORCORAN
OF/1B, No. 22
LL, 5'11", 180 lbs.
ML Svc: 7 years
Born: 3-19-53 in
   Glendale, CA

1985 STATISTICS
AVG	G	AB	R	H	2B	3B	HR	RBI	BB	SO	SB
.214	103	182	11	39	6	1	0	22	29	20	0

CAREER STATISTICS
AVG	G	AB	R	H	2B	3B	HR	RBI	BB	SO	SB
.271	503	1043	119	283	46	4	12	128	128	102	4

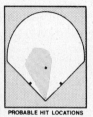

VS. RHP   VS. LHP   PROBABLE HIT LOCATIONS

and right equally well but his lack of speed limits him. He charges balls better than he backpedals.

OVERALL:

For the most part, Corcoran is not an everyday player and knows it. At 33, he has been on the fringes for a long time and is probably near the end of his baseball career. He is a role player whose greatest contribution is sitting on the bench without complaining. He can be a handy pinch-hitter.

Snider: "He has not done badly; not everyone can be a star. If Mike Schmidt had not proved to be such an incredible first baseman, Tim might have seen more playing time last season. As things have turned out, however, Mike's good play was bad news for Corcoran in terms of his future. He may spell Mike a bit this season and continue to pinch-hit."

DARREN DAULTON

Defensively, Darren Daulton is already a major league catcher. Offensively, however, he is a big question mark.

Two years ago, Daulton developed tendinitis in his right shoulder. He was leading his club in most offensive categories when the injury ended his season that July. Last season, he spent three months on the disabled list with the same problem.

Although Daulton insisted that his shoulder was fine, the Phillies took no chances. As it turned out, the rest did Daulton a world of good. When he was activated late in 1985, his arm was (finally) fine.

The time off the field took its toll at the plate, however. He became entirely too passive. Because he has so many fine natural tools, it is expected that he will become more relaxed and aggressive in 1986.

Daulton has excellent power to right and right-center field. Like most left-handed hitters, he is a low-ball hitter.

One of the worst things that a catcher can do when he is at the plate is to try to think like one. It is a guessing game that Daulton tried to play--and lost--too often last season. He must learn this lesson and learn it fast. When you have a bat in your hands, you are a hitter. So . . . hit the ball.

BASERUNNING:

Daulton runs extremely well for a catcher.

FIELDING:

When he is healthy, Daulton's arm is above average. He is a fine receiver and shows a keen ability to set up the hitters. The Philadelphia staff has a history of being very finicky about their backstops and they love to throw to Daulton. Happy battery-mates are a big advantage.

DARREN DAULTON
C, No. 10
LR, 6'2", 190 lbs.
ML Svc: 1 year plus
Born: 1-3-62 in
   Arkansas City, KS

1985 STATISTICS

AVG	G	AB	R	H	2B	3B	HR	RBI	BB	SO	SB
.204	36	103	14	21	3	1	4	11	16	37	3

CAREER STATISTICS

AVG	G	AB	R	H	2B	3B	HR	RBI	BB	SO	SB
.208	38	106	15	22	3	1	4	11	17	38	3

VS. RHP

VS. LHP

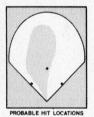
PROBABLE HIT LOCATIONS

OVERALL:

Daulton is the catcher of the Phils' future. Given the amount of time that he has missed over the last two seasons, it is difficult to judge exactly when his day will come. The organization is high on his potential. If Daulton can improve at the plate and if his shoulder remains healthy, the future could be very soon.

Snider: "I like the way he catches and I like the way he throws. I also think that, with a lot of work, he can hit. Last season, he was too tentative at the plate. At times, it appears as though he is feeling for the ball instead of looking to drive it. It is almost as if he is afraid of striking out.

"He should know that big league pitching is just flat out tough to hit. It takes time."

PITCHING:

On the surface, John Denny was the same pitcher he had always been, using an abbreviated windup and a three-quarters delivery. He continues to mix up his fastball with a huge roundhouse curveball. While the fastball saunters to the plate at a pedestrian 80 MPH or so, the curveball is easily his best pitch.

Denny has lost something off his fastball. He never ripped the pitch, so it was not velocity that he lost as much as it was movement. For a pitcher who lives and dies with his control, it was enough to make him become that much finer with his pitches.

He keeps his curveball away from righthanded hitters and throws it high and tight to lefthanders. He moves his fastball up and down, in and out, around the strike zone. When he's on, he gets a lot of ground-ball outs. When he's not, he struggles to throw his curve for strikes.

Denny has an excellent change-up but hardly used it until last August. When he finally returned the change-up to his repertoire, he said that he regretted having overlooked it for so long. Which is a shame because it is a good, effective pitch. It complements his fastball well. He rarely throws his change for strikes, using it most often to fool hitters when he's ahead in the count.

Early in the year, Denny experimented with a forkball. He had trouble throwing it for strikes and needs a lot more work with it before it becomes a pitch he can depend on.

FIELDING, HITTING, BASERUNNING:

Denny is an excellent fielder with good range to either side of the mound. His compact windup and abbreviated follow-through leave him in an excellent position to field grounders hit back up

JOHN DENNY
RHP, No. 40
RR, 6'3", 190 lbs.
ML Svc: 11 years
Born: 11-8-52 in
   Prescott, AZ

1985 STATISTICS

W	L	ERA	G	GS	CG	SV	IP	H	R	ER	BB	SO
11	14	3.82	33	33	6	0	230.2	252	112	98	83	123

CAREER STATISTICS

W	L	ERA	G	GS	CG	SV	IP	H	R	ER	BB	SO
112	98	3.53	298	295	61	0	1978.1	1914	878	776	722	1031

the middle. He covers first consistently. He has an above-average move to first and holds runners well.

He is also a good hitter who can help himself at the plate. Denny is a deceptive baserunner who is capable of stealing a base if the pitcher doesn't pay him at least cursory attention.

OVERALL:

His greatest strength is his knowledge of pitching. He can be an artist on the mound, painting the corners with deft precision. His greatest weakness is his perfectionism. If every pitch is not exactly where he wants it, if his fielders miss a play or if the umpire blows a call, he loses his concentration.

Snider: "His best years are behind him but he certainly has several good seasons to look forward to. It appears as though he has lost that little extra edge on his fastball. He has been pinpointing his pitches even more than ever. That makes his effectiveness on any given day that much more difficult to attain. If he can develop the forkball to the point that he can get it over and keep the hitters off balance, it might help him in the long run."

TOM FOLEY

Tom Foley is a low-ball, fastball hitter. He can pull pitches that are down and in and has some power to right field. Primarily, however, he is an opposite field hitter who sprays the ball from center to left-center field.

Foley has trouble with pitches up and away. He tends to get on top of them and pound them into the ground. A pitcher can beat him by staying up in the strike zone. Foley can be jammed up and in and can be overmatched up and away. He is a patient hitter with the ability to be selective. He is also an excellent bunter.

He improved dramatically last season as a situation hitter while remaining a good clutch hitter. As the No. 8 hitter in the lineup, Foley was not offered too many fat pitches to hit.

BASERUNNING:

Foley is an excellent baserunner. Although he does not have great speed, he gets out of the box well and will not make mistakes. He is willing to sacrifice his body to break up the double play.

FIELDING:

Foley is steady in the field and will make all of the routine plays. He goes to his left well and gets to a lot of balls hit up the middle. However, he is not good at going to his right. He will not go into the hole to take a hit away. He takes charge on pop-ups, although he has not demonstrated great range in this area. His arm is accurate, though it is not strong.

His strength lies in his consistency.

OVERALL:

Manager John Felske said that Foley

TOM FOLEY
INF, No. 10
LR, 6'1", 175 lbs.
ML Svc: 3 years
Born: 9-9-59 in
  Columbus, GA

1985 STATISTICS										
AVG	G	AB	R	H	2B	3B	HR	RBI	BB	SO	SB
.240	89	250	24	60	13	1	3	23	19	34	2

CAREER STATISTICS										
AVG	G	AB	R	H	2B	3B	HR	RBI	BB	SO	SB
.240	263	625	57	150	25	5	8	59	56	87	6

  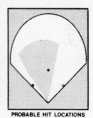

VS. RHP   VS. LHP   PROBABLE HIT LOCATIONS

is his man at shortstop in 1986. His hitting against lefthanders is questionable, as is his lack of range in the field. If Foley does play every day, he should be able to play positional shortstop to compensate for that weakness.

He needs time to mature and has the makeup to become a good everyday player. Foley is not going to forge a career on talent alone.

Snider: "Sometimes, I think that people underestimate how important it is to have a player at short who can make all of the routine plays. You don't have to do backflips to be good.

"Tom is a good guy to have on a club: he loves to play the game. He won't make the spectacular play but he will get the job done and that's more important for a shortstop. Given the chance, I think that he can play every day."

HITTING:

Greg Gross is a low-ball, opposite field hitter who likes the ball away from him. He is a patient, selective hitter who knows the strike zone, and more importantly, knows what pitches he can and can't handle.

Gross is a prototypical bench player who knows and accepts his role. The Phillies use him primarily as a pinch-hitter, a job he usually performs with great success. He also can play in left or right field and at first base without embarrassing himself.

Most often, Gross hits pitches down and away to left field. He takes inside pitches up the middle and rarely, if ever, pulls the ball. He lays off anything else until he has two strikes, and then he simply puts the ball in play.

Pitchers can beat him by mixing up their pitching patterns: pitch him inside one at-bat, up and away the next. If a pitcher keeps the ball up and away, Gross will hit the ball in the air. He doesn't have enough power to hit it out, so his fly balls are usually outs. He is an excellent bunter to the left side of the mound and can move runners and occasionally bunt for a base hit.

Gross did not have a good year. Like almost everyone else on the team, he struggled early.

BASERUNNING:

Gross has below-average speed, but is an intelligent baserunner who is careful not to make mistakes.

FIELDING:

Defensively, Gross is as solid in fundamentals as any player in the game. He charges the ball extremely well and gets rid of it quickly. He goes to his left and right well, but has minimal range. His arm is average, but extremely accurate. Gross picks up several outfield assists a year simply by executing the fundamentals: getting to the ball quickly, getting it out of his glove and getting it to the cutoff man.

Gross is a sound player wherever he's put defensively. He doesn't have the

GREG GROSS
OF/1B, No. 21
LL, 5'11", 175 lbs.
ML Svc: 12 years
Born: 8-1-52 in
York, PA

1985 STATISTICS

AVG	G	AB	R	H	2B	3B	HR	RBI	BB	SO	SB
.260	93	169	21	44	5	2	0	14	32	9	1

CAREER STATISTICS

AVG	G	AB	R	H	2B	3B	HR	RBI	BB	SO	SB
.293	1450	3303	412	968	120	45	6	279	450	218	38

  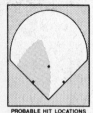

VS. RHP   VS. LHP   PROBABLE HIT LOCATIONS

range for center field or the arm for right field, but on any given day he can be put in either one of those positions and will do a solid job.

In an emergency, he can be used at first base. He brings to that position the same qualities that make him a sound player in the outfield. He anticipates well, gets to the ball and knows exactly what to do with it.

OVERALL:

When taken in context, Gross's bad start wasn't all that surprising. He is not capable of carrying a team and once he remembered that last season, he began to hit.

Snider: "Greg is a good guy to have on the bench; I like the way he goes about his business. He has a history of bouncing back after bad years and should do better this season. Last season, the entire team was out of synch early in the year. Greg got caught up in it, too, but I don't think it will happen again.

"He needs to stay sharp as a pinch-hitter and needs to get in his swings regularly--the Phillies usually see to it that he gets them."

BIG, BREAKING CURVEBALL

PITCHING:

Kevin Gross needed to be convinced that he had a good fastball. Now that he sort of believes it, he's become the Phils' most reliable righthanded starter. He has four pitches: fastball, slider, curve and change-up. He can throw all of them for strikes. His best pitch is his curveball, which has been both a blessing and a curse in his brief career. He is breaking himself of the habit of his breaking stuff. He can use his fastball to set up his other three pitches.

Gross uses a smooth delivery with a high leg kick. He uses the kick to his advantage. He will throw either his breaking pitch or his new-found friend, the fastball, when behind in the count.

When Gross becomes tired, his breaking pitches get lazy and become eminently hittable. At this point, he hasn't learned how to win without his best stuff. He can get hit hard and early.

He could help himself in this respect if he learned the benefits of game preparation and concentration. The stakes are high in the big leagues and Gross has the potential to be a 20-game winner. The missing ingredient might be developing more mature working habits. That does not mean pre-game tosses.

FIELDING, HITTING, BASERUNNING:

Gross' move to first is less than average. He tends to ignore baserunners and, with his high leg kick, that makes him easy prey for basestealers. His solution is to keep the rabbits off base when he can. Gross is an excellent athlete and a capable, if unspectacular, fielder. He is quick to cover first and gets to the bag consistently.

Gross is a dangerous hitter because he has some power. He loves to hit and will tell anyone willing to listen how good a hitter he was in his amateur days

KEVIN GROSS
RHP, No. 46
RR, 6'5", 203 lbs.
ML Svc: 3 years
Born: 6-8-61 in
Downey, CA

1985 STATISTICS

W	L	ERA	G	GS	CG	SV	IP	H	R	ER	BB	SO
15	13	3.41	38	31	6	0	205.2	194	86	78	81	151

CAREER STATISTICS

W	L	ERA	G	GS	CG	SV	IP	H	R	ER	BB	SO
27	24	3.66	99	62	8	1	430.2	434	198	175	160	301

as a second baseman. Gross is a nondescript baserunner.

OVERALL:

The key to Gross' future lies directly under his cap. He has the physical tools and all the pitches to become one of the game's steadiest righthanded pitchers. But he has to learn how to prepare himself for the weak as well as the strong teams. He must also learn to concentrate in every inning of every start. His greatest strength is his physical ability; his greatest weakness is overestimating his ability.

Snider: "He knows how to pitch and has some of the best breaking stuff in the league. Still, he needs more. He still throws too many breaking balls and a guy who throws a lot of slow stuff is going to make some mistakes. He gets the ball up where it's hittable.

"If Gross can get the hitters looking for the breaking ball, his fastball will seem to pick up a foot or two. Most importantly, he needs to develop better control without taking anything off the pitches; he cannot start aiming the ball."

HITTING:

Von Hayes squirrels away his failures and carries them around with him until he cracks under their collective weight. He gets angry when he fails at the plate. The angrier he gets, the more he presses. He spent all of last season trying to learn how to avoid that trap.

Through the first six weeks of the 1985 season, Hayes was hitting .340, while the rest of the team was in a huge slump. He tried to carry them but could not; his sweet stroke went sour. Hayes stopped contributing.

Hayes is a low-ball, straightaway hitter. When he is swinging well, he hits to all fields, taking the outside pitch to left and pulling the down-and-in pitch to right. He has good power to right and right-center field. Now and then, he will pop a ball out to the opposite field.

Hayes is a patient hitter who has a good idea of the strike zone. He can be selective and is an excellent breaking ball hitter on a team composed primarily of first-ball, fastball hitters. He is a fair bunter who will lay down a drag bunt once in a while.

BASERUNNING:

On the bases, Hayes has above-average speed but below-average presence of mind. He gets out of the box quickly and gets down the line well. He really is a threat to steal--but he could steal more by studying the pitchers.

He takes too many chances on the basepaths and ran the Phillies out of more than one inning last year.

FIELDING:

Hayes can improve in all phases of his defense. In center field, he has great range but doesn't get a good jump on the ball. He does not charge balls well and is average going both to his left and to his right. He is at his best when going back for balls and will make spectacular catches at the wall. When he comes in, he has the habit of going for

VON HAYES
OF, No. 9
LR, 6'5", 185 lbs.
ML Svc: 5 years
Born: 8-31-58 in
    Stockton, CA

1985 STATISTICS

AVG	G	AB	R	H	2B	3B	HR	RBI	BB	SO	SB
.263	152	570	76	150	30	4	13	70	61	99	21

CAREER STATISTICS

AVG	G	AB	R	H	2B	3B	HR	RBI	BB	SO	SB
.268	621	2118	292	567	99	20	50	268	212	311	129

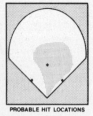

VS. RHP   VS. LHP   PROBABLE HIT LOCATIONS

the diving catch when he should be playing the ball on one hop.

He does not get rid of the ball quickly: he tends to wind up, almost as a pitcher would, before throwing the ball. His arm is accurate but not very strong.

Hayes has a habit of taking his last at-bat with him to the field; he should learn (as Mike Schmidt has) to leave it behind. His offense definitely affects his defense.

OVERALL:

He has not come into his own as a player but the time is at hand. The potential to become an excellent all-around player is there. He has a lot to learn and a lot to live up to.

Snider: "Hayes is a good low fastball hitter but it has come to the point now where pitchers can get him with that fastball in a little more. He has great potential but needs to mature a bit. Many of his problems should straighten out if he develops a more positive mental approach."

PITCHING:

Charlie Hudson: resident enigma
Diagnosis: lack of motivation
Treatment: a kick in the butt

CHARLIE HUDSON
RHP, No. 49
SR, 6'3", 185 lbs.
ML Svc: 3 years
Born: 3-16-59 in
   Ennis, TX

This patient has the potential to be one of the best young righthanders in the National League. He is having difficulty, however, getting his head to work in tandem with his arm.

He will occasionally flash the form that made him one of the game's most exciting rookie pitchers in 1983. These days are rare. Instead of progressing, this case is regressing at an alarming rate. His vital signs are stable but his ERA is way too high. His overall record last season took a severe downward trend and he became a below-.500 pitcher. His strikeouts-to-walks ratio is not good and does not appear to be improving. His hits-to-innings pitched ratio is distressing for an alleged power pitcher.

The "young-and-inexperienced" pass which many pitchers get in this situation is about to expire.

In spring training of 1985, the Phils experimented with turning Hudson into a late-inning reliever. The patient did not agree with this type of treatment and complained more than once. He showed his displeasure by being unimpressive out of the bullpen.

His fastball has been clocked in the high 80s and he likes to run it in on righthanded hitters. His second-best pitch is his slider. Ninety-five percent of his pitches are fastballs and sliders. He uses the change-up the rest of the time.

When he is throwing strikes with his two primary pitches, Hudson can be effective. When he's not, he gets hit hard. He gave up a massive 21 home runs in his first 22 starts.

1985 STATISTICS												
W	L	ERA	G	GS	CG	SV	IP	H	R	ER	BB	SO
8	13	3.78	38	26	3	0	193	188	92	81	74	122

CAREER STATISTICS												
W	L	ERA	G	GS	CG	SV	IP	H	R	ER	BB	SO
25	32	3.72	94	82	7	0	536	527	266	222	179	317

FIELDING, HITTING, BASERUNNING:

Hudson has virtually no move to first and is easy prey for basestealers. He does cover first quickly and consistently. He is a good athlete, lithe and quick, but a lot of balls hit up the middle get past him.

Hudson is a switch-hitter. He is much better lefthanded than righthanded. He could help himself more if he learned how to bunt. He is a deceptively fast baserunner and knows what he's doing when he gets on.

OVERALL:

Prognosis: Outlook remains positive but patient will have to improve his powers of concentration.

Snider: "The key to his future lies in his ability to take advantage of the hitters' weaknesses--that's what power pitchers are supposed to do. I classify him more as a thrower, not a pitcher. He must improve his location. He grooves too many fastballs and hangs too many sliders. He still has the stuff but what he really needs to improve is his mental approach."

HITTING:

Is there room in the game for good-field, no-hit shortstops? Steve Jeltz is having trouble hitting major league pitching well enough to play every day. Even in the minor leagues, Jeltz was never a good hitter, so the no-hit tag should not have been a surprise.

He is a physically small player who swings with an uppercut. Little men with uppercuts tend to pop up, fly out routinely and strike out often. The Phils wanted Jeltz to abandon his thin-handled bat and his uppercut. They wanted him to choke up on a thick-handled bat and hit down on the ball. Jeltz tried to change; he listened to all kinds of advice but it served only to confuse him.

As a low-ball, fastball hitter, Jeltz had trouble with any pitch up in the strike zone. Pitchers worked him in the generic method of throwing him breaking balls away and fastballs up. They did this with great success. Jeltz can lay down a bunt for a sacrifice but doesn't know how to bunt for a base hit, another weapon that might have helped save his job last season.

BASERUNNING:

Jeltz is an excellent baserunner with above-average speed. He gets out of the box quickly and gets down the line well. Once on base, he is a heads-up runner. He has enough speed to be a basestealing threat but, batting eighth, he did not get the call.

FIELDING:

As a fielder, Jeltz has a tendency to make the occasional spectacular play but then turn around and botch the routine play. He is much better going into the hole than behind second base for a ball. He is a much better fielder on artificial turf than on grass. When playing on grass, he tends to stay back and wait for the ball to come to him instead of charging it. He backhands even balls hit right at him. Jeltz has a strong, accurate arm and his throws generally are good.

STEVE JELTZ
SS, No. 30
RR, 5'11", 170 lbs.
ML Svc: 2 years
Born: 5-28-59 in
  Paris, FR

1985 STATISTICS

AVG	G	AB	R	H	2B	3B	HR	RBI	BB	SO	SB
.189	89	196	17	37	4	1	0	12	26	55	1

CAREER STATISTICS

AVG	G	AB	R	H	2B	3B	HR	RBI	BB	SO	SB
.191	130	272	24	52	4	3	1	20	34	68	3

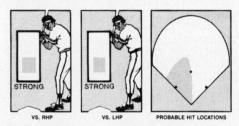

STRONG — VS. RHP   STRONG — VS. LHP   PROBABLE HIT LOCATIONS

There's a lot to like about Jeltz in the field. He has the tools to play shortstop every day. However, he continues to suffer lapses in concentration, such as forgetting to cover second on a stolen base. He also makes mistakes at crucial times. In 1985, he committed more than half of his errors while playing at home.

OVERALL:

Last season, it was surprising that Jeltz seemed unwilling to make whatever changes were necessary to keep his job. After a dazzling 1984 season, he showed an alarming lack of consistency last year. He may have proved himself to be a marginal player. The September weight-lifting program he began might be a day late and a dollar short.

Snider: "There's no question he was a disappointment. Because he didn't hit, it affected his fielding. But he is going to have to get over that because he is never going to be much of a hitter. It looked as if he was stabbing at the ball instead of being that vacuum-cleaner-type guy."

PITCHING:

An arthritic left knee brought Jerry Koosman's season to an early conclusion last year and has cast a shadow of doubt on what remains of his career. He had surgery performed in May but was able to return in June. All seemed well. He was the Koosman of recent vintage, using control and guile to outsmart hitters. He continued to use an economical rock-and-throw windup and four pitches: fastball, cut fastball, curve and change-up. His curve is his best pitch. The others he uses to set up hitters. While by no means overpowering, he still has the ability to sneak his fastball by the hitters.

Koosman is a master pitcher with the ability to throw all of his pitches for strikes at any time in the count. He mixes his change-up and off-speed curve in extremely well, throwing them at any point in the count, except 0-2 or 1-2, and to all types of hitters. His out pitch is his curveball or fastball, depending on how he sets up the hitter. He changes his pitching pattern on hitters from at-bat to at-bat, making it extremely difficult for them them to sit on any of his pitches. His concentration is superb in all kinds of situations.

In order for Koosman to be effective, he must keep his pitches down in the strike zone. When he's tiring or just doesn't have it, his pitches are up and he gets hit hard. It's also vital for him to pitch ahead in the count. Even though he's more than willing to throw a 3-1 change-up, like most pitchers he tends to challenge hitters when he's behind in the count. If he's up in the strike zone, his fastball is going to get hit.

FIELDING, HITTING, BASERUNNING:

Koosman has an above-average move to

JERRY KOOSMAN
LHP, No. 24
RL, 6'2", 220 lbs.
ML Svc: 18 years
Born: 12-23-43 in
Appleton, MN

1985 STATISTICS

W	L	ERA	G	GS	CG	SV	IP	H	R	ER	BB	SO
6	4	4.62	19	18	3	0	99.1	107	56	51	34	60

CAREER STATISTICS

W	L	ERA	G	GS	CG	SV	IP	H	R	ER	BB	SO
222	209	3.38	612	527	140	17	3829	3631	1608	1433	1199	2556

first. He keeps runners close and throws over often. He is an excellent fielder who is always in position to make the play and who covers first consistently. Koosman is a good hitter and an above-average bunter. As a baserunner, however, he does not scare anybody.

OVERALL:

From June until August of last year, Koosman was able to pitch effectively. He was on the disabled list at both ends of the season. Because of his knee problems, it might be the time to put him in long relief. His future with the Phils is very much in doubt. What is for certain, however, is that, barring further knee ailments, Koosman can still pitch.

Snider: "Jerry is the consummate pitcher. He has been able to make the transition from power pitcher to control pitcher. He sets up the hitters well and spots his pitches as well as anyone. There is nothing wrong with his arm."

HITTING:

Unquestionably, Joe Lefebvre could have helped the Phillies last year. But he didn't.

Their lineup, which is dominated by young, overly aggressive righthanded hitters, cried out for a lefthander with some experience. Lefebvre would have fit the bill nicely had he not been spending the year rehabilitating his right knee.

The Phillies know that he will be back this year. They were sure enough of that to sign Lefebvre to a one-year contract at the end of last season. What they do not know, and what no one knows, is how much Lefebvre is going to be able to play. It is uncertain how much pounding his reconstructed right knee will be able to take.

Lefebvre is a line drive, alleys hitter with good power to left-center and right-center. He helped the Phillies reach the World Series in 1983. Unfortunately, in June 1984, he tore both cartilage and ligaments in his right knee while going for a fly ball on the warning track at Wrigley Field.

He tried to come back without surgery but succeeded only in worsening his condition. In August 1984, he underwent reconstructive surgery. Since then he has twice undergone arthroscopic surgery to remove adhesions, most recently in May of 1985.

BASERUNNING:

Lefebvre's baserunning will undoubtedly be affected by his knee injury. Even if he is able to run, he is not likely to be foolishly over-aggressive.

FIELDING:

By the end of last year, Lefebvre had progressed to the point where he was running, but he had not attempted to make the quick starts and stops and the lateral moves demanded of an outfielder.

More than likely, he'll begin this

JOE LEFEBVRE
OF, No. 23
LR, 5'10", 180 lbs.
ML Svc: 6 years
Born: 2-22-56 in
Concord, NH

1985 STATISTICS

AVG	G	AB	R	H	2B	3B	HR	RBI	BB	SO	SB
DID NOT PLAY IN 1985											

CAREER STATISTICS

AVG	G	AB	R	H	2B	3B	HR	RBI	BB	SO	SB
.260	433	1073	139	279	52	13	31	130	136	199	11

VS. RHP

VS. LHP

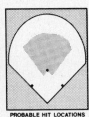

PROBABLE HIT LOCATIONS

year on the bench and will be used primarily as a lefthanded pinch-hitter.

There is nothing wrong with his defense. When he was healthy, he was a sound defensive outfielder with a strong and accurate arm. After missing more than a year and a half, it would be foolish to expect him to play in the field more than occasionally.

OVERALL:

If healthy, he can almost definitely be a contributor. It may be in everyone's interest, however, for him to find a team in the American League where the DH rule would make him more likely to play more regularly.

Snider: "Lefebvre will play this year, although he'll never be the player he was before the injury. There's no reason why he won't be able to hit."

HITTING:

The Phillies continued to phase out Garry Maddox last season. After spending most of his career as their regular center fielder, Maddox had been relegated to their bench, where he was a luxury. His $750,000 salary may have made him the highest-paid defensive replacement in baseball.

His approach to the game has not changed much. He is a first-pitch, low-ball hitter with the ability to drive fastballs to center and left-center field and to turn on breaking balls down and in. He uses an exaggerated-spread stance and does not move his front foot much when he swings. Instead, he relies on his wrists and bat speed to generate pop.

A pitcher can beat him by keeping the ball up in the strike zone and varying pitching patterns. Maddox can be jammed up and in. He can be fooled by off-speed pitches. He is a hacker who goes to the plate looking for something to hit and doesn't walk very often. When Maddox was a regular, his disregard for drawing walks was an issue. But as a bench player, Maddox's traditional lack of selectivity was not critical to the team.

BASERUNNING:

Maddox no longer has the speed that once made him a threat on the bases. Chronic knee problems and a bad back have reduced him to an average runner. He does not know how to slide and is not aggressive at breaking up the double play.

FIELDING:

Defensively, he remains one of the best in the business. He covers a lot of territory, although not quite as much as he did in his prime. His ability to go back on fly balls allows him to play very shallow, which in turn helps him

GARRY MADDOX
CF, No. 31
RR, 6'3", 190 lbs.
ML Svc: 14 years
Born: 9-1-49 in
  Cincinnati, OH

1985 STATISTICS

AVG	G	AB	R	H	2B	3B	HR	RBI	BB	SO	SB
.239	105	218	22	52	8	1	4	23	13	26	4

CAREER STATISTICS

AVG	G	AB	R	H	2B	3B	HR	RBI	BB	SO	SB
.284	1743	6324	776	1799	337	62	117	753	321	780	248

STRONG   STRONG

VS. RHP   VS. LHP   PROBABLE HIT LOCATIONS

get to many pop-ups that would otherwise fall in.

His arm is neither strong nor accurate but he compensates for this by getting rid of the ball quickly and hitting the cutoff man.

OVERALL:

It took some time, but Maddox was able to make the mental adjustment from being an everyday player to being a reserve. He can no longer play regularly but would contribute more if he were used more often.

Snider: "He's still one of the best defensively. The Phillies are going with their younger guys and that has left Garry out. He has been around for a while, but I believe that he can be of some help to a team that can afford him.

"He hasn't changed much as a hitter, still uses that unorthodox stance, still isn't very patient. But he gets the job done."

PITCHING:

It appears that Shane Rawley is finally able to shake his reputation as a seven-inning guy. What his stats don't tell is that he posted four complete games in August, a month when starters for losing teams begin to look to the bullpen around the sixth inning.

Rawley's development has come on two levels. One is the emergence of a good slider and the other is increased stamina. Rawley embarked on a grueling martial arts type of workout program under the same man who has taken care of Steve Carlton.

The addition of a good slider has taken a lot of the burden off his fastball. Until last season, Rawley relied heavily on his fastball and threw it almost exclusively.

Over the past two seasons, Rawley has had to make the change from being used as a reliever to being strictly a starter. It is an adjustment that not only takes time, but also needs more tricks. His fastball got him along well enough when he came out of the bullpen, though it was never up to the calibre of a top reliever's. His curve and change-up have always been just mediocre; it made sense to work on breaking his slider more to make it his number two pitch.

Rawley has above-average velocity on his fastball, but he does not get a great deal of movement on it. His slider, a pitch he was rarely able to throw for strikes before, now has a bigger break to it. He is not afraid to throw it when he is behind in the count.

Still, he is a much better pitcher when he's ahead in the count. Even though the slider made Rawley less predictable at 2-0 or 3-1, he continued to have a tendency to groove pitches. It is a problem he has had for a few seasons, though last year he was grooving his pitches less and did not give up as many home runs as he had in the past.

SHANE RAWLEY
LHP, No. 48
RL, 6'0", 180 lbs.
ML Svc: 8 years
Born: 7-27-55 in
Racine, WI

1985 STATISTICS

W	L	ERA	G	GS	CG	SV	IP	H	R	ER	BB	SO
13	8	3.31	36	31	6	0	198.2	188	82	73	81	106

CAREER STATISTICS

W	L	ERA	G	GS	CG	SV	IP	H	R	ER	BB	SO
70	72	3.83	351	114	25	40	1140.1	1131	611	486	460	640

FIELDING, HITTING, BASERUNNING:

Rawley has an average move to first for a lefthander. A lot of times he pays only casual attention to baserunners. He fields his position well, however, and covers first base quickly and consistently.

As a hitter, he is of the average-pitcher variety, but he is a better baserunner than most. Most pitchers have trouble getting over to third on a single to right, but Shane can do it.

OVERALL:

Rawley is cruising at peak speed now. He will never be a great pitcher, but he is capable of winning 15-18 games. He should remain in the rotation and can be counted on to pitch well every turn.

Snider: "His slider improved dramatically; it was easy to see the new downward break he was able to give it. The slider has given him more options as a pitcher and the hitters more to watch. At this point, Rawley might consider working on his change-up. A good third pitch could make even more of a difference."

PITCHING:

Last season, Dave Rucker was used all over the place: long relief, middle innings, late innings and in the starting rotation.

Rucker uses a three-quarters sidearm motion to deliver fastballs and sliders. He began to develop an off-speed breaking ball during last season. He'll need it if plans to convert him to a full-time starter are carried through.

Rucker has excellent movement on his fastball. His fastball comes in at the mid-80 MPH range. His slider is average and breaks in to righthanded hitters without much drop. The off-speed breaking ball was a pitch he used only on rare occasions. His out pitch is his fastball and he will throw it 70% or more of the time.

Rucker's problem is control. When he is throwing strikes, he can be effective. But he didn't throw strikes often enough last year to inspire the confidence of his manager. Thus, Rucker was one of the forgotten men of the bullpen, making only 35 relief appearances before getting his first start since 1983 in mid-September. By then, the Phillies were seriously looking at Rucker as a possible starter for 1986 and he was more than willing to give it a try.

As a reliever, Rucker tends to pitch himself into jams whenever he has trouble throwing strikes. He walks too many batters. When he gets behind in the count, he grooves his pitches and batters are able to hit them on a sharp line toward the outfield.

He is a better pitcher when the game is not on the line.

When Rucker struggles, he falls behind in the count. When he's behind in the count, he falls back on his fastball. Hitters know this and sit on it.

Rucker is not shy about working inside, a trademark of the Philadelphia staff. He likes to jam lefthanders by throwing them up and in. He doesn't come inside as often to righthanders, though

DAVE RUCKER
LHP, No. 36
LL, 6'1", 190 lbs.
ML Svc: 4 years
Born: 9-1-57 in
San Bernardino, CA

1985 STATISTICS
W	L	ERA	G	GS	CG	SV	IP	H	R	ER	BB	SO
3	2	4.31	39	3	0	1	79.1	83	42	38	40	41

CAREER STATISTICS
W	L	ERA	G	GS	CG	SV	IP	H	R	ER	BB	SO
16	16	3.67	156	10	1	1	266.1	264	126	109	124	607

he will try to get them down and in with his slider.

FIELDING, HITTING, BASERUNNING:

Rucker is a good fielder to either side of the mound and hustles to cover first on grounders to the right side. His move to first is below average for a lefthander, although he does try to keep runners close by throwing over often.

He is no threat at the plate. He runs the bases rarely, but when he does get on, he is cautious and doesn't make mistakes.

OVERALL:

Rucker is still developing. The possibility of his conversion to a starter will be, in part, tied to his stamina.

Snider: "He will need to add something off-speed this season. He has to find himself on the mound; it seems to take him an inning or two to find his rhythm. Being a starter will afford him that luxury.

"He seems especially prone to walking the early batters and that is deadly for a reliever. If he starts, he should develop the confidence to create his own game and to get the big outs."

POWER POTENTIAL

HITTING:

Over the course of a misbegotten season, Russell showed just enough power to keep Philadelphia interested. Maybe.

He hit poorly and struck out often; part of the blame lies with his early-season handling. Part. His swing is the other piece to the pie.

He is a classic arms-extended power hitter who doesn't generate enough bat speed to turn on inside pitches. Get a fastball out over the plate to him and he'll put it in the upper deck. Bust him inside and you've got a very good chance of jamming him because whether the pitch is inside or outside, Russell extends his arms and swings from the heels.

Pitchers are able to tantalize him with a mysterious pitch known as the slider. Bust him up and in with a fastball, give him a slider down and in, then throw the same pitch a foot outside and Russell will go for it every time.

BASERUNNING:

As a baserunner, Russell has below-average speed. He's not going to beat anybody with his legs. He breaks up the double play well, but is strictly a one-base-at-a-time runner.

FIELDING:

If he is going to play left field in the big leagues, Russell has a lot of work to do. He doesn't get a good jump on the ball in any direction: right, left, up or back. His arm is mediocre at best. Still, you don't have to have a great arm to play left field. All you need is the ability to get to the ball quickly and hit the cutoff man.

OVERALL:

Russell was handled badly last season. He got caught in the Phillies'

JOHN RUSSELL
OF, No. 29
RR, 6'0", 200 lbs.
ML Svc: 1 year plus
Born: 1-5-61 in
Oklahoma City, OK

1985 STATISTICS

AVG	G	AB	R	H	2B	3B	HR	RBI	BB	SO	SB
.218	81	216	22	47	12	0	9	23	18	72	2

CAREER STATISTICS

AVG	G	AB	R	H	2B	3B	HR	RBI	BB	SO	SB
.238	120	315	33	75	20	1	11	34	30	105	2

right field/first base/left field shuffle. When he lost the right field job to Wilson, the team told Russell that he was their man at first base. He had never played that position before at any level. He was eaten alive. He made a bunch of errors and couldn't get going at the plate. He was platooned, and when the team decided to move Mike Schmidt to first base, Russell was sent to the minors--to play in left field, of course. He should have stayed in the minors.

It would be a shame to write him off based on his 1985 performance. The mistreatment, however, was not responsible for the holes in his game. It exposed them rather clearly. Still, he deserves the chance to show what he can do at a familiar position.

Snider: "Sometimes, you have to wait longer for power hitters than you do for singles and doubles hitters. They take a little bit longer to get it together. You cannot give up on a guy like Russell who has shown some power.

"With a lot of work on his swing and if he can take a different approach on the ball with two strikes on him, he could turn into a valuable commodity."

HITTING:

It is generally acknowledged that Juan Samuel has the ability to become one of the game's dominant offensive players. In 1985, he became the first player ever to reach double figures in doubles, triples, home runs and stolen bases in his first two seasons.

But in his second year, he remained the same hitter he was in his rookie season: totally undisciplined at the plate. He is trying not to be a first-ball, fastball hitter. Most of his hits come off pitches down, in or out of the strike zone. He pulls the down-and-in pitch and will take the low-and-away pitch to right.

Pitchers beat him by not throwing him strikes. He's an easy bet for an eye-high fastball, a pitch he invariably chases when behind in the count. The pattern to him: breaking balls and then make him fish for the high fastball.

Samuel is a low-ball hitter, a fact that everyone except him seems to know. Basically, he is an alleys hitter, although he does pull the ball on occasion and does have some power to the opposite field.

Samuel's blazing speed makes him a natural leadoff hitter but his wildly swinging ways will keep him out of that spot for a while.

BASERUNNING:

Samuel is fast enough not to have to be a smart baserunner. Which is a shame because he's not. He has no idea when it's good to steal a base and when he should stay put. The Phillies should take the green light away from Samuel in certain situations.

FIELDING:

Samuel has made dramatic improvements in the field. In 1984, he led all NL second basemen in errors with thirty-three. His footwork would have made Ginger Rogers bleed. His first baseman needed a shovel.

All that has changed. While he con-

JUAN SAMUEL
2B, No. 8
RR, 5'11", 170 lbs.
ML Svc: 2 years
Born: 12-9-60 in
  San Pedro de Macoris, DR

1985 STATISTICS

AVG	G	AB	R	H	2B	3B	HR	RBI	BB	SO	SB
.264	161	663	101	175	31	13	19	74	33	141	53

CAREER STATISTICS

AVG	G	AB	R	H	2B	3B	HR	RBI	BB	SO	SB
.269	339	1429	220	384	68	34	36	148	65	325	128

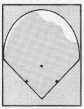

VS. RHP   VS. LHP   PROBABLE HIT LOCATIONS

tinues to play ground balls a bit too much to the side, his footwork has vastly improved. He has worked to learn to plant his foot and to get his body set before throwing the ball. He has cut down on his sinking sidearm throws. While he is still too slow and deliberate on the double play pivot, he has improved there as well.

OVERALL:

Snider: "In many ways, Juan is still a diamond in the rough. To his credit, he is willing to take the time to learn how to do things correctly. He is several years away from being at his peak and has the potential of becoming one of the most exciting players in the game.

"He must hold himself back on that first pitch or his speed will be wasted. The Phillies have a few options with him because he has got some good power and doesn't really have to bat leadoff. Defensively, he has turned himself into a reliable second baseman. His steady progress will be watched with interest."

HITTING:

For a dozen years, Mike Schmidt made a very nice living as a low-ball, fastball hitter. But the style of pitching has changed in the National League. The sinker-slider pitchers who dominated the league in the late 1970s and the early part of this decade have been replaced by high-ball, fastball pitchers such as Dwight Gooden, Mario Soto and Joaquin Andujar. Schmidt has had to adjust.

His uppercut has been replaced by a more level swing, while his stance remains unchanged. Now, he will swing down on a pitch, rolling his top hand to produce backspin to lift the ball.

During the early part of last season Schmidt wasn't able to hold himself back from swinging at the waist-high fastball. Pitchers were able to work him with breaking stuff away and then get him to swing at a fastball up in the strike zone.

His early-season problems were, to some extent, attributed to his fifteen-pound weight loss over the winter. However, that theory was tossed the minute he began to hit around the time of the All-Star break.

Hitters such as Mike Schmidt just don't stop. He simply needed the time to fine-tune his swing. The move to first base helped his hitting.

BASERUNNING:

Mentally, he is an excellent baserunner, but physically, because his legs are so fragile, he is not exactly a weapon on the bases.

FIELDING:

It was headline news when Schmidt was asked to play first base last season. He went along with it, though he made it clear that he felt it was a poor move. Schmidt showed everyone just how great an athlete he is. He turned out to be the best first baseman the Phillies have ever had.

His range to either side is excellent. He digs balls out of the dirt and starts the 3-6-3 double play as well as

MIKE SCHMIDT
1B, No. 20
RR, 6'2", 203 lbs.
ML Svc: 13 years
Born: 9-27-49 in
Dayton, OH

1985 STATISTICS

AVG	G	AB	R	H	2B	3B	HR	RBI	BB	SO	SB
.277	158	549	89	152	31	5	33	93	87	117	1

CAREER STATISTICS

AVG	G	AB	R	H	2B	3B	HR	RBI	BB	SO	SB
.266	1947	6740	1250	1794	323	56	458	1273	1265	1660	168

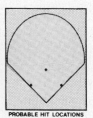

VS. RHP   VS. LHP   PROBABLE HIT LOCATIONS

any first baseman in the league. He is capable of throwing to third when a runner tries to advance on a ground ball to the right side. He says that he "thinks more" about throwing to third than most first basemen do.

OVERALL:

One of Schmidt's biggest problems has always been that he "over analyzes" each play in the field and each pitch thrown to him. Being placed at first base kept him busier in the field than he had ever been before and it appeared to help him with his hitting. He was not able to spend as much time thinking and was able to just do what came naturally.

Snider: "Mike tried to carry the team early in the year and, as a result, he is the one who suffered. I don't think that he will fall into the same trap this season.

"He surprised everybody with how well he played first base. If Keith Hernandez wasn't in the league, Schmidt would be the best, and that's amazing."

HITTING:

Rick Schu is a high-ball, fastball hitter who likes the ball away from him. He is basically a straightaway hitter but occasionally pulls the ball down the line.

He can hit the fastball to either alley but has a tendency to pull off breaking pitches thrown down and away. Pitchers can beat him by jamming him and working him with breaking balls away. Hard throwers can overmatch him; control pitchers can finesse him. As a rookie last year he lived and died on pitchers' mistakes. Schu is a patient hitter with an excellent concept of the strike zone, something that can only help to make him a better hitter in the future.

Schu has not shown the kind of power the Phillies are used to getting from their third baseman. It was not an easy act to follow (slugger Mike Schmidt had been at third for 12 years), but Schu handled himself well. Now that he has had the chance to play almost an entire season and see National League pitching, he should be able to drive in more runs. His off-season weightlifting program should help him develop more strength.

BASERUNNING:

Schu has good speed and gets out of the box well. He is fast enough to steal an occasional base and doesn't ground into many double plays. On the bases, he remains alert and rarely makes mistakes.

FIELDING:

Schu has excellent reflexes but he tends to lunge at every ball hit his way. He makes the charge play and goes to his left well but has a severe weakness to his right. Schu has an accurate arm that should get stronger as he matures. Schu's quickness is an asset: the rest will come with experience.

RICK SCHU
3B, No. 15
RR, 6'0", 170 lbs.
ML Svc: 1 year plus
Born: 1-26-62 in
  Philadelphia, PA

1985 STATISTICS

AVG	G	AB	R	H	2B	3B	HR	RBI	BB	SO	SB
.252	112	416	54	105	21	4	7	24	38	78	8

CAREER STATISTICS

AVG	G	AB	R	H	2B	3B	HR	RBI	BB	SO	SB
.254	129	445	66	113	23	5	9	29	44	84	8

STRONG — VS. RHP   STRONG — VS. LHP   PROBABLE HIT LOCATIONS

OVERALL:

Schu is expected to develop further and to eventually hit 10-12 homers a year. He is several years away from his peak as a player. Schu is a gutty player who plays hurt and wants to make it in the big leagues. He will.

Snider: "I like his defense. He does a good job at third base. I did think, however, that he would show more sock in his bat. He tries to go to right with the inside pitch too often.

"He has to go on a strength program to build up his hands and forearms. That would enable him to get the front end of the bat out more quickly. When he sees that inside pitch coming, he needs to be quick enough to get the big end of the bat through the strike zone to pop the ball a bit better."

PITCHING:

One thing Dave Stewart doesn't lack is confidence. Before he was traded to the Phillies last season, Stewart was told by Texas Rangers pitching coach Tom House that he had one of the top five arms in baseball. "Is that right?" he replied. "I can't think of who the other four could be."

Stewart's problem during most of his time with the Rangers, his great arm simply couldn't get batters out consistently. The Rangers experimented with him almost everywhere: they tried him as a starter; they tried him as a short reliever; they tried him as a long man.

When in doubt Stewart always goes back to his fastball and he always throws it at the same speed. In spring training last year, he showed a wicked forkball and a much-improved change-up, but he was reluctant to use them in game situations once the regular season began. Not only that, despite the advice of the Rangers coaching staff, he continued to throw all of his pitches at the same velocity. His explanation was that, if he missed his spot, he wanted to miss with his best stuff.

Batters were able to time his stuff; if the ball didn't have movement on it (as it too frequently didn't), they were able to get good wood on the ball. He also had trouble hitting his spots inside the strike zone and often fell behind in the count.

FIELDING:

Stewart is a good athlete, but he has lapses of concentration in fielding situations. For example, in one game for the Rangers he made a good play to get to first and take a relay throw from second. Then he rolled the ball back to the mound, forgetting that there were only two outs. He scrambled to recover once he realized his mistake, but while he did, the winning run scored.

DAVE STEWART
RHP, No. 48
RR, 6'2", 200 lbs.
ML Svc: 5 years
Born: 2-19-57 in
Oakland, CA

1985 STATISTICS
W	L	ERA	G	GS	CG	SV	IP	H	R	ER	BB	SO
0	6	5.42	42	5	0	4	81.1	86	53	49	37	64

CAREER STATISTICS
W	L	ERA	G	GS	CG	SV	IP	H	R	ER	BB	SO
30	35	3.94	206	55	5	19	600	574	287	263	237	371

He also has to be more conscious of holding runners on base. He has a wide-open delivery and takes a long time to unload the ball to the plate. Runners can often get a good jump on him. He needs improvement in both his pickoff move and the frequency with which he uses it.

OVERALL:

Stewart still has a lot of potential but, after some down years, is nearing the point in his career where he needs to prove that he can translate potential into the ability to get people out. He may be the victim of too much advice, much of it contradictory. First he is told to pitch inside, then to pitch outside. He has been told to rely on his fastball, then to use an assortment of pitches.

Killebrew: "The key for the Phillies will be to refine Stewart's control and to convince him to change speeds with his fastball. That will set up his curve. He also should continue to work on his forkball and change-up until he feels comfortable enough to use them in crucial situations."

PITCHING:

It's never pretty when a closer can't shut the door anymore. For Kent Tekulve, who made a pretty good living for the better part of ten years as a bullpen stopper, the door kept swinging open in 1985, signaling that he was getting closer to stepping through it and leaving the game.

Tekulve throws a sinker and a slider with a submarine motion. He has lost quite a bit off his fastball over the years and consequently his mistakes are hit harder. His submarine motion causes his slider to rise rather than drop, making him particularly tough on right-handed hitters. Lefthanders, though, find him easy pickings. Since most left-handers are low-ball hitters, Tekulve's sinker plays right into their hands. He invariably pitches around lefthanders.

His inability to get out lefthanders has dramatically undercut his effectiveness as a late-inning reliever. If he enters a game with runners on base, opposing managers simply send up a parade of lefthanded pinch-hitters.

As a ground-ball specialist, Tekulve is much more effective on grass than on artificial turf. Since turf grounders tend to pick up speed as they move along and choppers tend to bounce higher, one of the approved methods of hitting against Tekulve is to beat his sinker into the turf and get a grounder through the infield. The other is to be patient and force him to throw his sinker higher in the strike zone.

FIELDING, HITTING, BASERUNNING:

Tekulve has a below-average move to first but keeps runners close by paying strict attention to them. He is meticulous about holding runners on. He is a good fielder who is quick off the mound and covers first consistently.

He is not much of a hitter but that

KENT TEKULVE
RHP, No. 27
RR, 6'4", 185 lbs.
ML Svc: 11 years
Born: 3-5-47 in
Cincinnati, OH

1985 STATISTICS
W	L	ERA	G	GS	CG	SV	IP	H	R	ER	BB	SO
4	10	3.57	61	0	0	14	75.2	74	35	30	30	40

CAREER STATISTICS
W	L	ERA	G	GS	CG	SV	IP	H	R	ER	BB	SO
74	71	2.70	780	0	0	172	1089.1	967	384	327	392	588

is not very important for someone in his role. On the rare occasions that he runs the bases, Tekulve is conservative.

OVERALL:

In all likelihood, Tekulve will retire at the conclusion of the 1986 season. His job for this year will be more specialized than ever. He won't be the big stopper any longer and cannot be used in long relief because he cannot pitch for more than two innings at a stretch.

What he can do is get righthanders to hit ground balls and pitch for short stretches almost every day. This makes him almost perfectly suited to coming into a game in the middle innings, when he's sure to face righthanded hitters: an opposing manager might be more reluctant to use a lefthanded pinch-hitter in the sixth inning than in the ninth.

Snider: "He has had a good career and has taught a lot of young pitchers some valuable lessons along the way. There continues to be a job for him because he is still tough on righthanded hitters. While he is certainly not as quick as he once was, his sinker can be an effective pitch."

HITTING:

For the second year in a row, Ozzie Virgil hit a ton in the first half, not a lick in the second. What's going on here? It appears as though he gets easily burned out.

He is a low-ball, fastball hitter with very little patience. Pitchers like to work him up and in with fastballs and down and away with sliders. Virgil has excellent power to left and left-center and some power to right and right-center. He rarely goes to the opposite field, although in the past he has been able to do that.

Toward the latter half of the season, he tried to pull every pitch he saw. Consequently, he grounded out a lot. No Philadelphia player was more prone to grounding into double plays than Virgil.

He had spent much of 1984 learning to lay off the breaking ball but that lesson was lost last season. Virgil was not as disciplined as in the past. Pitchers were able to get him to chase whatever breaking pitches they chose to throw him.

He is not a good defensive hitter and must remain ahead in the count. Because he drives the ball, he must have the edge to get anywhere.

BASERUNNING:

He is slow and not a threat to steal. Virgil is careful not to make a mistake when he's on the bases.

FIELDING:

On the surface, Virgil continued to improve his defense, which had traditionally been the weakest part of his game. He made only four errors in his first 121 games. He has a strong, accurate arm. He has worked to improve his footwork and has developed a quicker release. The more finely-tuned catching did not go unnoticed by the opposition.

His biggest problem, however, is his inability to keep his pitching staff happy. He does not block balls in the

OZZIE VIRGIL
C, No. 17
RR, 6'1", 205 lbs.
ML Svc: 4 years
Born: 12-7-56 in
Mayaguez, PR

1985 STATISTICS

AVG	G	AB	R	H	2B	3B	HR	RBI	BB	SO	SB
.246	131	426	47	105	16	3	19	55	49	85	0

CAREER STATISTICS

AVG	G	AB	R	H	2B	3B	HR	RBI	BB	SO	SB
.246	383	1134	131	279	51	5	46	154	112	239	1

VS. RHP   VS. LHP   PROBABLE HIT LOCATIONS

dirt well and has trouble holding on to foul-tip third strikes. He does not "think" along with the pitcher and much of the staff does not like to throw to him.

OVERALL:

He has room for improvement in the areas of consistency and game-calling. If he can maintain his first-half levels into the second half of a season, he will always be a valuable player to have around.

Snider: "The Phillies are taking a long, hard look at their young catcher, Darren Daulton. Virgil is going to have his hands full convincing the team that he is their number one guy. As a hitter, Virgil seems to fall into a common trap, that is, pressing when he's not hitting well, and not hitting well because he's pressing.

"As the season wears on, it gets really tough on everyday catchers. He is not an ironman and needs to rest on a regular schedule."

HITTING:

All it took for Glenn Wilson to see the light was a pair of glasses. He was fitted for glasses to correct an astigmatism during spring training 1985. Once he finally tackled the problem and got his glasses, it was amazing what a difference it made. The first thing he noticed was that he was in Philadelphia and the next thing he did was whack the ball all over the place.

He also worked hard on his hitting during the winter, finding a stance he was comfortable with and learning to level off his swing. He opted for an upright one, closed, with his hands held higher than ever before. He remains a high-ball, fastball hitter, an alleys hitter with most of his power to left-center and right-center field.

He likes the ball away from him and up in the strike zone and is susceptible to inside fastballs and breaking pitches down and away.

He is not a very patient hitter and strikes himself out a lot. It is not his style to go to the plate too relaxed: he feels that he must remain keyed up to be effective. While that is admirable, it often serves to overexcite him and he will hack at the first thing that looks good.

Pitchers beat him by working him down and in with fastballs and down and away with breaking pitches. Wilson also can be induced into chasing high fastballs out of the strike zone. A pitcher who keeps the ball down on Wilson can get him to hit a ground ball; he led the Phillies in grounding into double plays last year.

BASERUNNING:

Wilson gets out of the box quickly and runs well. He doesn't offer much distraction when he takes his lead off first, but is a good baserunner who is fast enough to steal a base once in a while and go from first to third on a single to right.

FIELDING:

He became a fine right fielder last

GLENN WILSON
RF, No. 27
RR, 6'1", 190 lbs.
ML Svc: 4 years
Born: 12-22-58 in
Baytown, TX

1985 STATISTICS

AVG	G	AB	R	H	2B	3B	HR	RBI	BB	SO	SB
.275	161	608	73	167	39	5	14	102	35	117	7

CAREER STATISTICS

AVG	G	AB	R	H	2B	3B	HR	RBI	BB	SO	SB
.269	521	1774	195	478	100	15	43	232	92	303	10

  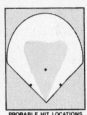

VS. RHP   VS. LHP   PROBABLE HIT LOCATIONS

season and led the league in assists. He is extremely aggressive in the field. He charges every ball hard and is absolutely fearless of walls. He gets to the ball quickly and has an outstanding arm.

He rarely, if ever, has a lapse of concentration and doesn't let what he did in his last at-bat affect his fielding.

OVERALL:

Wilson has finally blossomed into the player the Phillies thought he could be. He showed up last season a much more confident player than he had ever been. He has not yet reached his potential and should have an even better year in 1986.

Snider: "It was easy to see that he had learned the strike zone much better last season. Even still, there is room for more selectivity there. He should learn to let the pitchers pitch around him once in a while.

"I like the way he plays. He has a great arm, and is getting more accurate. He's much more aggressive with it."

ROCKY CHILDRESS
RHP, No. 50
RR, 6'2", 195 lbs
ML Svc: less than 1 year
Born: 2-18-62 in
    Santa Rosa, CA

PITCHING:

Rocky Childress is a righthanded sinker/slider pitcher. Oddly enough, the Phillies did not use him in the style to which he had become accustomed at he minor league level.

In both Double-A and Triple-A, Rocky was used as a late-inning reliever. The 1985 Phillies, however, had all of those rooms booked. Although none of their short men were particularly noteworthy last year, Childress was used in long relief.

At Portland, he was 5-2 with a 1.27 ERA and six saves, sharing the late-inning chores with Dave Shipanoff. With Philadelphia, he was hardly used at all. He spent two weeks with the Phillies in May and made just four appearances, pitching all of 5 2/3 innings. He spent six more weeks with the major league club from June to August and made four more appearances, rolling up 13 1/3 innings. When Childress was optioned to Portland in August, his ERA was a disastrous 6.63.

Finally, he was recalled for the September "surge," making eight more appearances, including one emergency start against Pittsburgh on the next-to-last day of the season. He strung together four appearances in which he did not allow a run, but then was lit up in successive appearances against the Cubs and Cardinals.

In his lone start he pitched well, allowing six hits and two runs with one walk in six innings.

OVERALL:

Based on 1985, it's impossible to judge Childress. It appears, however, that the best thing for him would be to spend one more complete season in Triple-A.

DAVE SHIPANOFF
RHP, No. 33
RR, 6'1", 185 lbs.
ML Svc: less than 1 year
Born: 11-13-59
    in Edmonton, CAN

PITCHING, FIELDING,
    HITTING, BASERUNNING:

Dave Shipanoff is a long, lean righthanded power pitcher with a major league fastball, a good, hard slider and control problems.

He was one of three minor leaguers acquired from the Toronto organization for first baseman Len Matuszek in an early-season trade last year. Shipanoff spent four months in Triple-A before being recalled in August.

When he first arrived in the major leagues, he had a great deal of success and the Phillies were considering him as a member of their bullpen in 1986. In his first 13 appearances, Shipanoff went 1-0 with three saves and a 1.47 ERA. More importantly, he walked only three and struck out 13 in his first 18 1/3 innings.

The Phillies were mildly concerned about his fastball because he had shown more velocity (low 90s) in the minors. But pitching coach Claude Osteen worked with him on his delivery, teaching him to get the ball out of his glove sooner and the problem seemed to iron itself out.

But over his last 13 appearances, Shipanoff was inconsistent. He walked 12 and struck out 12 in his final 18 innings, lost two games and finished with a 3.22 ERA.

OVERALL:

The Phillies like his arm and hope to give him a job in the bullpen. They'll probably use him as a tablesetter for lefthander Don Carman.

DERRELL THOMAS
INF, No. 13
SR, 6'0", 160 lbs.
ML Svc: 14 years
Born: 1-14-51 in
    Paris, FRANCE

HITTING, BASERUNNING, FIELDING:

The most recent stop on the much-traveled path of Derrell Thomas was in Philadelphia. He has been a man without a team, a guy with a reputation as a clubhouse lawyer who was toiling in the purgatory of the Class A Miami Marlins when the Phillies resurrected him last May.

He helped them. He didn't bowl anyone over with his average (.207) or his defense (seven errors at various positions) but he gave them a switch-hitting pinch-hitter and kept a very low profile in the locker room. By the end of the season, the Phillies were talking to him about signing him for this year.

Offensively, Thomas was used primarily as a lefthanded pinch-hitter. He showed some pop, hitting three of his four homers and driving in nine of his twelve runs from the left side last year. From the left side, he's a low-ball hitter with power to right field. He can drive pitches down and in. Pitchers can beat him by keeping the ball away from him. From the right side, Thomas likes the ball away a little more. He can be jammed up and in. Pitchers also can get him with breaking balls down and away. He has good knowledge of the strike zone and knows what pitches he can handle.

Defensively, he's a butcher. He can play all eight positions, none of them particularly well. Last year, he caught, played second, third, short, left and center field. Primarily, though, he was used at short and in left.

OVERALL:

Snider: "He may have resurrected a dead career last year. The main thing for him will be to remain low-key."

FRED TOLIVER
RHP, No. 30
RR, 6'1", 170 lbs.
ML Svc: less than 1 year
Born: 2-3-61 in
    Natchez, MS

PITCHING:

Fred Toliver has got the tools but has Fred Toliver got what it takes?

The tools include a 94 MPH fastball, a hard slider and a change-up. But so far, Toliver has not been able to live up to the potential his fastball says he possesses. He is a thrower, not a pitcher.

Control is his problem. He has a history of having trouble throwing strikes. In his first six minor league seasons, he walked an inordinate number of batters. While he has since cut that as-tronomical proportion, he continues to issue too many free passes.

Still, Philadelphia management is high on him. When you see a guy who zings it in at 94 MPH, you tend to give him every chance imaginable. The Phils feel that they can tame him.

He has been auditioned him for two seemingly disparate roles: as a starter and as a late-inning relief pitcher. Considering Toliver's background is as a starter and considering the Phillies were shopping for a fifth starter at the end of last season, Toliver might best fit in as a starter. He shows a live arm and a gritty demeanor.

OVERALL:

Toliver is nowhere near his potential. Despite his extensive minor league experience, he is still quite young. The key to his future lies in his control. If he learns to throw strikes, he could be an effective pitcher.

PITTSBURGH PIRATES

HITTING:

Bill Almon refound his glory days in his utility role with the Pirates. He teamed with Jim Morrison & Lee Mazzilli to give the Pirates one of the best benches in baseball.

A high fastball hitter, Almon has changed his hitting style over the past several years. He now hits standing straight up and goes for more power, especially when the situation calls for it. He is a smart hitter who can bunt, hit-and-run or drive the ball.

He is a notorious streak hitter who can really help a team when he's on one of his hot streaks. Since he can play a number of defensive positions, he can remain in the lineup when he is hot, giving a variety of players a day or two off.

BASERUNNING:

His days as a basestealer are over, although he can still surprise the opposition and take a base on occassion. A graduate of Brown University, he is an extremely intelligent baserunner. He is also aggressive and is not afraid to go in and break up the double play.

FIELDING:

The rap on Almon is that he is an erratic fielder, but he did a better than adequate job when called on to play shortstop on a regular basis for the Pirates. His major value is that he can play a number of positions well. Last season he started 31 games at shortstop, 21 in left field, four at third base, three at first base and two in center field.

BILL ALMON
INF/OF, No. 34
RR, 6'3", 190 lbs.
ML Svc: 9 years
Born: 11-21-52 in
    Providence, RI

1985 STATISTICS

AVG	G	AB	R	H	2B	3B	HR	RBI	BB	SO	SB
.270	88	244	33	66	17	0	6	29	22	61	10

CAREER STATISTICS

AVG	G	AB	R	H	2B	3B	HR	RBI	BB	SO	SB
.258	1046	3034	347	783	125	23	29	263	208	566	116

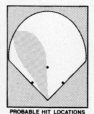

STRONG — VS. RHP | STRONG — VS. LHP | PROBABLE HIT LOCATIONS

With all of that, he made only five errors.

OVERALL:

Just when it appeared as though his career might be nearing the end, Almon was born again with the Pirates. He was once the nation's number one draft pick out of college and is now considered to be one of the game's top utility players (he has done everything but pitch).

Snider: "Bill surprised me with his power. He has changed quite a bit since he first came to the big leagues and seems to have created a niche for himself with the Pirates."

PITCHING:

Mike Bielecki was one of the major disappointments of the 1985 season for the Pittsburgh Pirates. He was coming off a 19-3 season in Hawaii and had been named Player of the Year in the minor leagues by a national publication.

A power pitcher who depends on a 90 MPH fastball and an explosive forkball, Bielecki was thrust into the starting rotation last season, which enabled John Candelaria to be moved to the bullpen.

Bielecki, however, began to have control troubles. He walked more batters than he struck out and was 1-3 with a 5.40 ERA before he was returned to the minors.

One of his problems was that he seemed to be intimidated by major league hitters and was trying to be too fine. He often fell behind in the count, and the more trouble he got in, the worse his control became.

After his return from Hawaii, he was more relaxed, but he still finished with more walks than strikeouts.

FIELDING, HITTING, BASERUNNING:

Bielecki is a competent fielder. He needs work holding runners close to first base and his move is only average.

As a hitter he is below average, victimized some by the designated hitter rule in the minors that keeps young pitchers from ever getting to bat.

MIKE BIELECKI
RHP, No. 34
RR, 6'3", 200 lbs.
ML Svc: 1 year plus
Born: 7-31-59 in
Baltimore, MD

1985 STATISTICS

W	L	ERA	G	GS	CG	SV	IP	H	R	ER	BB	SO
2	3	4.53	12	7	0	0	45.2	45	26	23	31	22

CAREER STATISTICS

W	L	ERA	G	GS	CG	SV	IP	H	R	ER	BB	SO
2	3	4.14	16	7	0		50	49	26	23	31	23

He is an average runner who has not been on base enough to have acquired any skills.

OVERALL:

Bielecki is still considered one of the prime prospects the Pirates have. Part of a season in the big leagues should have helped to settle him down. He has to improve his control if he is to become the pitcher predicted for stardom.

Snider: "Bielecki is the kind of pitcher who, once he matures, can become a star. He needs to figure out how to blow his fastball by the hitters, and once he does that, look out."

HITTING:

Sid Bream came to the Pirates late in the 1985 season from the Los Angeles Dodgers in exchange for Bill Madlock. In Pittsburgh, Bream was given the opportunity to play at first base when Jason Thompson underwent knee surgery, and performed so well that the Pirates think he might be their starting first baseman this spring.

A power hitter with a big, looping swing, Bream could benefit from cutting back on his stroke; his big stroke prevents him from being a consistent performer. He showed a lot of strength in the minor leagues and has the potential to develop into a power hitter in the big leagues.

Bream is a pull hitter who likes to hit the high and inside fastball. He does not have good bat control, but when he hits the ball, he usually hits it hard.

The trade to Pittsburgh looks as though it may be a good one for both Bream and the Pirates; he hit .313 in his last 20 games with 3 home runs and 14 RBIs. He also had a 10-game hitting streak.

BASERUNNING:

Bream has no speed to speak of and is conservative in his approach to running the bases. He does not get thrown out taking silly chances. He stole only one base in 135 games last year.

FIELDING:

Bream does not have much range at first base and has a lot of trouble with throws in the dirt. He seems to be unsure of himself in the field but may im-

SID BREAM
1B, No. 33
LL, 6'4", 215 lbs.
ML Svc: 2 years
Born: 8-3-60 in
  Carlisle, PA

1985 STATISTICS

AVG	G	AB	R	H	2B	3B	HR	RBI	BB	SO	SB
.230	50	148	18	34	7	0	6	2	18	24	0

CAREER STATISTICS

AVG	G	AB	R	H	2B	3B	HR	RBI	BB	SO	SB
.216	92	208	20	45	10	0	6	29	26	35	1

  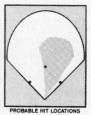

VS. RHP — STRONG   VS. LHP — STRONG   PROBABLE HIT LOCATIONS

prove with more playing time in the big leagues.

OVERALL:

Bream was buried in Los Angeles behind Greg Brock and got his chance with his trade to Pittsburgh. A good minor league hitter, Bream showed late last year that he might be ready to approach his minor league figures as a big league hitter if he gets the opportunity to play.

Snider: "Sid needs to settle down a bit as a hitter, but if he can develop more consistency with the bat, the Pirates might decide to make him their starter at first base instead of Jason Thompson."

HITTING:

One of the top hitters to come out of the Angels' farm system, where he hit for power, average and run production, Mike Brown found the National League's style of pitching to his liking. With the Angels, he was buried behind Reggie Jackson and was unable to get a chance to play regularly despite those top minor league credentials.

Brown possesses gap power and should develop into a 20-25 home run hitter. He is not a traditional pull-hitting power hitter and actually went to right field a lot after his trade.

A fastball hitter, he is intense and takes every at bat seriously. He can go 3-for-5 and be unhappy about the two at bats where he failed.

Brown proved to be a consistent batter, having hit in streaks of seven, eight (twice) and 11 games after being traded.

BASERUNNING:

Brown is one of the league's most aggressive baserunners, a guy who seems to like to go into second base hard and take out the pivotman on the double play. He isn't fast and won't steal many bases, but he will challenge an outfielder's arm by going from first to third. His mistakes will be those caused by being overly aggressive.

FIELDING:

Brown came to the Pirates with the reputation of being a strong defensive player, but he was unable to live up to that billing in Pittsburgh. He made six errors, many attributed to his being unaccustomed to playing on Astroturf. He also developed tendinitis in his throwing shoulder--the result of playing everyday, something he was not accustomed

MIKE BROWN
RF, No. 27
RR, 6'2", 175 lbs.
ML Svc: 3 years
Born: 12-29-59 in
　San Francisco, CA

1985 STATISTICS

AVG	G	AB	R	H	2B	3B	HR	RBI	BB	SO	SB
.268	60	153	23	41	9	1	4	20	7	21	0

CAREER STATISTICS

AVG	G	AB	R	H	2B	3B	HR	RBI	BB	SO	SB
.264	153	405	44	107	22	5	14	51	27	64	1

STRONG

VS. RHP

STRONG

VS. LHP

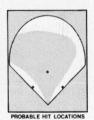

PROBABLE HIT LOCATIONS

to. That rendered his normally strong arm null and void. He is an aggressive outfielder who enjoys playing defense.

OVERALL:

Given the opportunity to play everyday for the Pirates, Brown did not disappoint them, providing them with a .300 bat and RBI power. He figures to get better with experience. He is often compared with Tom Brunansky, who also came out of the Angels' farm system and became a hitting star with the Minnesota Twins.

Snider: "I think this kid is going to get better and better. He uses the whole ballpark and is going to be tough to defense. I really think the Pirates have something here."

PITCHING:

The Pirates had high hopes last year that Jose DeLeon would be a 20-game winner in 1985. Instead, they had to send him to the bullpen and then to the minor leagues just to prevent him from becoming a 20-game loser. Instead of progressing, DeLeon regressed and finished with a record of 2-19 with a 4.70 ERA.

Most hitters who face DeLeon come back to the bench wondering how anyone hits him. His hits to innings pitched ratio is good (138 hits in 162.2 innings pitched) and he struck out enough batters to finish 12th in the league in strikeouts despite spending a month in the minors.

DeLeon lost his last 11 decisions of the season. He did pitch in some tough-luck games, being shut out seven times and the team averaged only 2.32 runs in games he started.

Mostly, however, he beat himself with mistakes. He would throw a ball away, walk a hitter to open an inning or fail to hold a runner close at first base.

DeLeon is a power pitcher with a fastball, slider and a nearly unhittable forkball. It is the forkball, however, that has gotten him into trouble most often--he tends to overuse it. When batters lay off that pitch, it is usually called a ball and quickly puts him behind in the count.

DeLeon's natural ability should carry him a long way once he learns to harness it. For the moment, however, he is a thrower, not a pitcher. He needs to listen to advice and to pitch to the hitters' weaknesses, rather than challenge everyone who comes to the plate.

FIELDING, HITTING, BASERUNNING:

DeLeon is weak in all three of these areas. He worked hard on holding runners close and showed some improvement in this regard last year, but he is still a

JOSE DeLEON
RHP, No. 25
RR, 6'3", 219 lbs.
ML Svc: 3 years
Born: 12-20-60 in
LaVega, DR

1985 STATISTICS

W	L	ERA	G	GS	CG	SV	IP	H	R	ER	BB	SO
2	19	4.70	31	25	1	3	162.2	138	93	85	89	149

CAREER STATISTICS

W	L	ERA	G	GS	CG	SV	IP	H	R	ER	BB	SO
16	35	3.86	76	68	9	3	463	360	215	199	228	420

below-average fielder. He is slow off the mound and becomes rattled when he fields a crucial bunt. He also needs to cover first base more quickly.

De Leon is one of the game's weakest hitters, collecting only two singles in 36 trips to the plate in 1985. He often misses pitches by laughable margins and strikes out more than half the time he bats. He did show a great deal of improvement as a bunter this past season, but he is still below average in that department as well.

OVERALL:

DeLeon has all of the equipment to become a superstar pitcher, yet he had one of the game's worst records last year.

Snider: "Give Jose a chance. I don't care if he was 2-19--I'll still take him. Tony Pena tells me that Jose is the toughest pitcher he ever had to catch because his forkball breaks like a knuckleball. DeLeon has control problems, but Sandy Koufax was very wild for several years, too. Koufax had to learn not to throw the ball through the umpire to simply relax and pitch. Jose should try to do the same."

HITTING:

Once again last season, injuries cut into Steve Kemp's career. Traded to the Pirates and expected to be their every-day left fielder, he showed up at spring training and revealed that over the winter he had undergone surgery to repair a torn rotator cuff.

That forced him to spend the majority of spring training rehabilitating the shoulder instead of preparing to play. He opened the year on the disabled list and did not begin to get into the groove until August, hitting .328 after the All-Star break.

An aggressive, line drive hitter, Kemp has survived a serious eye injury and the rotator cuff tear to continue his career.

He attacks every pitch. Pitchers try to offset that by working him up and in or down and in. He can also be fooled by off-speed pitches as he is usually looking fastball. Kemp spent most of his time as a pinch-hitter and adjusted to the role well, batting .333, although he maintains that he is still capable of playing regularly and will be given a chance to win the left field job.

BASERUNNING:

Kemp runs the bases the way he hits: all out. He hustles hard on every ball that is hit, even little taps back to the mound. He is not fast, but his hustle will often get him an extra base.

FIELDING:

The rotator cuff tear made what was one of the weakest throwing arms in baseball even weaker. When Kemp came to spring training he could not throw a ball 30 feet. Courageously, Kemp worked every day on strengthening the arm. By the season's end he could get the ball

STEVE KEMP
OF, No. 13
LL, 6'0", 190 lbs.
ML Svc: 9 years
Born: 8-7-54 in
San Angelo, TX

1985 STATISTICS
AVG	G	AB	R	H	2B	3B	HR	RBI	BB	SO	SB
.250	92	236	19	59	13	2	2	21	25	54	1

CAREER STATISTICS
AVG	G	AB	R	H	2B	3B	HR	RBI	BB	SO	SB
.279	1139	4006	578	1117	179	25	129	631	570	590	37

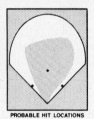

VS. RHP — STRONG   VS. LHP — STRONG   PROBABLE HIT LOCATIONS

back into the infield well enough, although he still lacked any zip on his throws.

He catches everything he gets to, although he doesn't look very graceful doing it.

OVERALL:

If anyone can come back from the injuries he has suffered, Kemp can. He is the ultimate team player, a hustler and still a good hitter. But no one knows if the arm will ever come back enough so that he is not a defensive liability.

Snider: "If he can come back and throw a little bit, the Pirates might have something. He's too good a competitor to give up on and he's one of the most willing players in baseball. When he's healty, he can hit."

HITTING:

When Sammy Khalifa first came to the big leagues, there was some thought that good big league pitching might be able to knock the bat out of his hands. At 21 years old, he did not seem ready for the majors. He fooled a lot of people.

He hit well and even showed some power by hitting a couple of home runs. He is going to get bigger and stronger and that can only help him.

Khalifa struck out far too often, however, and is going to have to work on making better contact this year. He looks as though he could mature into a good number two hitter in the batting order as he is capable of both bunting and delivering on the hit-and-run play.

He likes the ball out over the plate and has a little bit of trouble with fastballs, so pitchers try to crowd him.

BASERUNNING:

Although a shortstop, Khalifa is not extremely fast. He seems to be well schooled in the fundamentals and doesn't make a lot of mistakes. On the bases, he could afford to take a larger lead.

FIELDING:

Khalifa can only get better and better on defense. He has soft, sure hands. His range is average and he does not yet go into the hole well on Astroturf. His arm is average. At times, he lacks concentration on defense and makes errors on routine balls.

OVERALL:

The Pirates organization—except for then-manager Chuck Tanner—originally scheduled Khalifa to play the entire

SAM KHALIFA
INF, No. 58
RR, 5'11", 170 lbs.
ML Svc: 1 year
Born: 12-5-63 in
Fontana, CA

1985 STATISTICS

AVG	G	AB	R	H	2B	3B	HR	RBI	BB	SO	SB
.238	95	319	30	76	14	3	2	31	34	56	5

CAREER STATISTICS

AVG	G	AB	R	H	2B	3B	HR	RBI	BB	SO	SB
.238	95	319	30	76	14	3	2	31	34	56	5

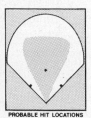

VS. RHP   VS. LHP   PROBABLE HIT LOCATIONS

1985 season in the minors. Tanner wanted him to play everyday almost from the start. Instead, what Tanner got last year was a parade of shortstops (Tim Foli, Rafael Belliard, Jerry Dybzinski, Bill Almon and Johnnie LeMaster) until Khalifa was called up.

A former number one draft pick, he showed surprising power and looked as though he might be capable of hitting .260 or .270 once he learns the National League pitchers.

Snider: "If he could go on a bit of a body building program to get a little stronger, I think you would see a pretty good shortstop. He is quick and has the potential to develop into a consistent hitter."

HITTING:

The nicest thing that can be said about Johnnie LeMaster's hitting last year is that he hit a home run off Cincinnati's Ron Robinson. That covers the highlights.

In 1985 LeMaster managed to bat almost 100 points below his lifetime batting average. He has long been known as a weak hitter: pitchers do not hold meetings to cover how to pitch to him. Fastballs down usually do the trick.

LeMaster was the Pirates' starting shortstop--despite his hitting problems--until he injured his left knee last season. He underwent arthroscopic surgery on July 7 and played in only three games after that as rookie Sammy Khalifa took over the starting role.

BASERUNNING:

For someone who doesn't spend a lot of time on base, LeMaster is a good baserunner. In his one good offensive season, he proved himself to be a decent basestealer, getting 39 steals. He has better-than-average speed.

FIELDING:

LeMaster is a big leaguer because of his defensive abilities. Former Pirates manager Chuck Tanner feels that LeMaster is just a notch beneath Ozzie Smith defensively. He goes into the hole well and has a strong throwing arm.

JOHNNIE LeMASTER
SS, No. 10
RR, 6'2", 180 lbs.
ML Svc: 11 years
Born: 6-19-54 in Portsmouth, OH

1985 STATISTICS

AVG	G	AB	R	H	2B	3B	HR	RBI	BB	SO	SB
.128	45	94	5	12	0	0	1	8	6	23	1

CAREER STATISTICS

AVG	G	AB	R	H	2B	3B	HR	RBI	BB	SO	SB
.223	1019	3167	317	707	109	19	22	228	240	560	94

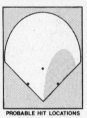

VS. RHP — STRONG   VS. LHP — STRONG   PROBABLE HIT LOCATIONS

OVERALL:

LeMaster managed to play for three last place clubs last season: Cleveland, San Francisco and Pittsburgh. He will be given a shot to beat out Sammy Khalifa at shortstop this year, but will probably be relegated to a backup role.

Snider: "LeMaster's glove will keep him in the big leagues, but he is probably through as a starting player. He will have to fight just to make the club this year."

HITTING:

Sixto Lezcano looks like a hitter. He stands crouched in the back of the batter's box like a coiled snake ready to strike. When he swings there's no holding back--it's all or nothing.

Last year it was mostly nothing. Used sparingly by the Pirates, he drove in only eight runs and hit .207. Employed mostly as a pinch-hitter, he seldom saw the fastballs he loves to hit. Unwilling to wait for them, he often chased bad breaking balls and got himself into trouble.

Lezcano was supposed to platoon in left field at the beginning of the season but started only 29 games and never was able to get into any kind of groove and recapture the previous success that had led to a .275 lifetime average with 145 home runs.

BASERUNNING:

Lezcano is an average baserunner with below-average speed. He is no threat to steal and is not aggressive breaking up the double play.

FIELDING:

Lezcano is one of the better right fielders in the game; his arm was once considered one of the best in the NL. While it no longer qualifies for that distinction, it is far above average and draws the respect of baserunners. He'll take a chance diving for balls and is aggressive in charging ground balls.

SIXTO LEZCANO
OF, No. 28
RR, 5'10", 190 lbs.
ML Svc: 12 years
Born: 11-28-53 in
  Arecibo, PR

1985 STATISTICS

AVG	G	AB	R	H	2B	3B	HR	RBI	BB	SO	SB
.207	72	116	16	24	2	0	3	9	35	17	0

CAREER STATISTICS

AVG	G	AB	R	H	2B	3B	HR	RBI	BB	SO	SB
.271	1291	4134	560	1122	184	34	148	591	576	768	37

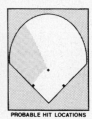

VS. RHP   VS. LHP   PROBABLE HIT LOCATIONS

OVERALL:

He went through what was basically a wasted year and there has to be some question about his skills decaying on the bench. He is with his sixth big league team in six years.

Snider: "He gets into a groove I've seen a lot of ballplayers experience. Deep down inside himself, he thinks that he can turn his skills on and off anytime--but baseball is not that way."

HITTING:

Lee Mazzilli has finally accepted the role the Pirates have in mind for him, that of a veteran pinch-hitter.

Over the last couple of seasons, he had fought off the designation of being a pinch-hitter, thinking that at 30 years old he was at the prime of his career. However, as last season wore on and he saw his only playing time would be off the bench, he responded with eight hits in his last 20 pinch-hitting appearances--a .400 clip. He finished the season with a .286 pinch-hitting average built on 16 hits in 56 trips. The 16 pinch-hits were the most by a Pirate since Manny Mota in 1969.

Mazzilli has a better-than-average eye for the strike zone and great patience at the plate. He walked 29 times in addition to his base hits to give him the team's highest on-base percentage at .425.

A switch-hitter, Mazzilli stands erect with his feet parallel to the plate. He has more power from the left side and tries to pull more from the left side. He is also a better hitter lefthanded than he is righthanded.

BASERUNNING:

Once blessed with excellent speed, Mazzilli now has to do with his head what he used to do with his legs. He has good baserunning habits and is a master of the hook slide, either to the left or to the right. Once a basestealing threat, he stole only four bases last year.

FIELDING:

An outfielder for most of his career, Mazzilli was given the opportunity to try his hand at first base last year. He started only five games in the outfield while playing 19 at first base for the often-injured Jason Thompson.

Mazzilli was a capable center fielder

LEE MAZZILLI
OF/1B, No. 16
SR, 6'1", 190 lbs.
ML Svc: 10 years
Born: 3-25-55 in
Brooklyn, NY

1985 STATISTICS

AVG	G	AB	R	H	2B	3B	HR	RBI	BB	SO	SB
.282	92	117	20	33	8	0	1	9	29	17	4

CAREER STATISTICS

AVG	G	AB	R	H	2B	3B	HR	RBI	BB	SO	SB
.263	1143	3607	486	950	171	22	81	391	537	526	179

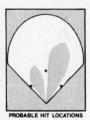

STRONG VS. RHP — STRONG VS. LHP — PROBABLE HIT LOCATIONS

early in his career and can still catch anything he gets to. However, he has one of the weakest throwing arms in baseball, so he should not play center field or right field. His only possible outfield spot would be in left field, but if he ever becomes an everyday player again, it will most likely be as a first baseman.

OVERALL:

Mazzilli still believes he can be an everyday player with better-than-average offensive statistics, but he is aware, too, of the importance of being a pinch-hitter. Learning to play first base has increased his value to a team and gives him some added versatility.

Snider: "Lee seems to have come to accept that a pinch-hitter's role is as important as any to a team. A club has to have reliable hitters off the bench and it looks as if he will be one of them."

PITCHING:

A sore arm, caused by tendinitis of the shoulder, turned Larry McWilliams into only a shadow of what he had been over the past few seasons, that being one of the better lefthanders in the league. He found his way onto the disabled list twice during the season and was forced into the bullpen because of his ineffectiveness as a starter.

McWilliams's career was saved four years ago when it appeared he was about to disappear from the major league scene forever. He credits Johnny Sain, then his pitching coach in Richmond, with turning his career around. Sain gave McWilliams a herky-jerky, no-windup delivery, much as Sain did to prolong the career of Jim Kaat, another left-hander, a number of years back.

McWilliams now often quick-pitches the batter and seems to be jumping at him as he delivers the ball. As a result of his unorthodox way of pitching, hitters are kept off balance, often stepping out of the box to regain their composure and to slow McWilliams down.

When healthy, McWilliams relies mostly on his fastball and forkball. He will also mix in a curveball, but the fastball/forkball combination is what he uses to get most of his outs. When he is healthy, he is a strikeout pitcher, not a power pitcher, which is something of a rare breed.

FIELDING, HITTING, BASERUNNING:

One of McWilliams's strengths is his ability to keep runners close. They seldom even try to run on him. Only four of 10 potential basestealers were safe last year.

He is a good athlete who fields his position well. He gets off the mound quickly to cover first base.

LARRY McWILLIAMS
LHP, No. 49
LL, 6'5", 181 lbs.
ML Svc: 7 years
Born: 2-10-54 in
  Wichita, KS

1985 STATISTICS

W	L	ERA	G	GS	CG	SV	IP	H	R	ER	BB	SO
7	9	4.70	30	19	2	0	126.1	139	70	66	62	52

CAREER STATISTICS

W	L	ERA	G	GS	CG	SV	IP	H	R	ER	BB	SO
65	56	3.78	209	169	29	2	1118	1100	523	469	375	692

As a hitter, he is only adequate, batting .130 lifetime, but he is above average as a bunter and helps himself in that area. He is a smart enough and fast enough runner that he is often used as a pinch-runner.

OVERALL:

An injury-free McWilliams can be counted on for 15 victories or more on a team with any kind of offense. He does all the little things that can help a pitcher win and is a good man to have around the clubhouse.

He was used 11 times in relief last season, and if the Pirates believe they have enough starting pitching, he could become the Pirates' lefthanded short reliever.

Snider: "The players say that his ball moves a lot and is tough to figure out because of his unorthodox delivery. Last year, the running fastball did not move as quickly, however, and it seemed a little lazy. It must have been the arm trouble. You can't give up on a guy like this."

HITTING:

One of the toughest things to do in baseball is to hit consistently while playing sporadically. Jim Morrison has made a career out of doing this.

Usually one of the finest reserve players in the game, Morrison did not have a good year last season. His batting average and power output fell, probably because he was hitting on a team where pitchers could afford to work around hitters.

He seemed to lack his normally patient approach at the plate, walking only 8 times in 244 appearances.

Because of his lack of patience, he was hitting the pitcher's pitch more often than usual. He was swatting at good breaking balls instead of waiting for the fastball or the hanging curveball that he has devoured throughout his career.

Another reason for Morrison's impatience probably was that he felt the Pirates, who needed power, wanted him to try and hit home runs.

BASERUNNING:

Morrison has average speed, but is a smart runner. Although he stole only three times last season, he made it each time he tried. He is seldom thrown out trying to take an extra base.

FIELDING:

Morrison is a utility player because he does everything well enough to remain in the major leagues, but nothing well enough to be a starter. He filled in at third base and second base last year, starting 43 times at third and 12 times at second. Used for short periods of time at either position, he can be an asset, but if forced to play on a regu-

JIM MORRISON
INF, No. 2
RR, 5'11", 185 lbs.
ML Svc: 8 years
Born: 9-23-52 in
Pensacola, FL

1985 STATISTICS											
AVG	G	AB	R	H	2B	3B	HR	RBI	BB	SO	SB
.254	92	244	17	62	11	0	4	22	8	44	3
CAREER STATISTICS											
AVG	G	AB	R	H	2B	3B	HR	RBI	BB	SO	SB
.264	730	2207	244	583	106	10	74	263	126	322	30

STRONG

VS. RHP

STRONG

VS. LHP

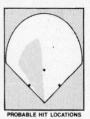

PROBABLE HIT LOCATIONS

lar basis, he would hurt the club defensively. He has also worked on playing left field and first base. He has good hands but not much range and only an adequate throwing arm.

OVERALL:

Morrison is one of those overlooked players of value, the kind who allows the team to rest a tired or injured infielder without losing much in the short run. He is the type of role player every team has to have.

Snider: "He is a fine utility player who seems to come up with that key extra base hit. He is a great guy to have around in the clubhouse; the players like him and he is their player representative."

HITTING:

Joe Orsulak surprised everyone by developing into a .300 hitter as a rookie. He and Mark Salas of Minnesota finished at .300 to lead all rookie hitters in 1985.

Orsulak is a contact hitter who slaps the ball around and bunts frequently. He finished the season with 14 bunt hits. He struck out only 27 times in 387 at bats, which is exceptional for a rookie who is adjusting to big league pitching.

While most players would be happy with one four-hit game, Orsulak had six of them. Most pitchers try to get him out with high fastballs and breaking balls down and out of the strike zone. They don't fear him hitting the ball out of the park as he went the entire season without a home run.

If Orsulak is to be the center fielder that the Pirates are looking for, he will have to hit for more power. He drove in only 21 runs out of the leadoff spot.

BASERUNNING:

Orsulak showed that he could develop into an outstanding basestealer, being successful on 24 of 35 attempts. He is a hustler who runs out everything full speed and who is not afraid to go hard into second base to break up a double play. Sometimes he's overly aggressive and runs himself into outs.

FIELDING:

Orsulak is a better-than-average center fielder who will dive for balls and challenge walls to make a catch. His aggressive style sometimes creates problems in the outfield, where he gets in the way of the other outfielders, but that will be corrected the more they play together.

JOE ORSULAK
OF, No. 11
LL, 6'1", 185 lbs.
ML Svc: 1 year plus
Born: 5-31-62 in
   Glen Ridge, NJ

1985 STATISTICS

AVG	G	AB	R	H	2B	3B	HR	RBI	BB	SO	SB
.300	121	397	54	119	14	6	0	21	26	27	24

CAREER STATISTICS

AVG	G	AB	R	H	2B	3B	HR	RBI	BB	SO	SB
.290	160	475	66	138	15	8	0	25	27	36	27

VS. RHP — STRONG   VS. LHP — STRONG   PROBABLE HIT LOCATIONS

Orsulak has a strong, accurate arm. He may be more suited to right field than center because of his arm, especially if the Pirates obtain a power-hitting center fielder.

OVERALL:

Orsulak is a player who doesn't mind getting his uniform dirty. He plays the game much as Pete Rose does, going into walls and headfirst into bases. His attitude is outstanding and he could become a fine player if he can develop some power.

Snider: "He showed me he can play the game of baseball. The more he gets to know National League pitching, the better he's going to get. I'm very impressed with every aspect of his performance. He's not afraid to put his nose into the dirt."

HITTING:

With the Pirates struggling to score runs, Tony Pena took it upon himself to try and provide a remedy. As a result of trying to do too much, he suffered his first bad season at the plate. A .296 career hitter, he slipped to .249 with 10 homers and 59 RBIs last year.

Pena has never met a pitch he didn't like. A free-swinger, he is an excellent bad-ball hitter who looks like the best hitter in the world when he's on a hot streak--and one of the worst when he's in a slump.

Pena's power is mostly to left field, usually on a hanging breaking ball up and in. He seldom takes a strike and often swings so hard that he has to take a long walk away from the plate to put his head and body back together.

Pena does not like to walk and did so only 29 times in 1985. Pitchers had success last year making him chase pitches that were further and further out of the strike zone. Being so eager to produce, he refused to hold back and swung himself into a hole.

BASERUNNING:

Tony Pena's baserunning can be summed up in one word: aggressive. He'll take chances, sometimes foolish chances, in an effort to make something happen. On one trip around the bases last year against Montreal, Pena stole third, escaped two rundowns, wound up at third base along with another runner, came home on a ground ball and then was called out while sitting in the dugout for missing home plate.

FIELDING:

No catcher in the National League has a stronger throwing arm or a quicker release than Pena. He loves to throw and will try to pick runners off base five to 10 times a game. He catches as he hits and runs the bases--aggressively. He is excellent on pop-ups, but still needs a lot of work on calling a game.

TONY PENA
C, No. 6
RR, 6'0", 181 lbs.
ML Svc: 5 years
Born: 6-4-57 in
   Montecristi, DR

1985 STATISTICS

AVG	G	AB	R	H	2B	3B	HR	RBI	BB	SO	SB
.249	147	546	53	136	27	2	10	59	29	67	12

CAREER STATISTICS

AVG	G	AB	R	H	2B	3B	HR	RBI	BB	SO	SB
.285	657	2362	251	674	114	13	53	288	121	303	33

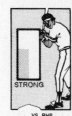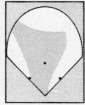

VS. RHP   VS. LHP   PROBABLE HIT LOCATIONS

There are those who believe that Jose DeLeon's failures are in part his refusal to shake off some of Pena's signs.

Pena is excellent at handling pitches in the dirt, but he does not block the plate well. He has a style all his own when catching with the bases empty, stretching out one leg and sitting back on the other. His reasoning is that it gives the pitcher a lower target to aim for. This unusual position does not hinder his ability to jump out after bunts or foul pops.

OVERALL:

Snider: "Tony is one of the most fun players in the league to watch; he is always smiling, talking and enjoying the game. He is also one of the most exciting.

"He probably would be a better player if he were given some more days off or were to play at first base occasionally, just for a rest. Playing first is like a day off for a catcher."

PATIENT HITTER

JOHNNY RAY
2B, No. 3
SR, 5'11", 185 lbs.
ML Svc: 5 years
Born: 3-1-57 in
Chouteau, OK

HITTING:

Johnny Ray struggled at the plate last season, dropping his average to a career low .274, which should say something about how good a hitter the man is. It was obvious, however, why his average fell.

Throughout most of the season, the switch-hitting second baseman was troubled by a painful groin pull which refused to go away. It was especially painful when he was batting lefthanded or was trying to run. Add that to the fact that the Pirates called upon him to provide power, often batting him in the number three spot in the order, and you can see why he struggled.

Ray's overall season, however, was not a bad one. He led the Pirates in RBIs with 70 and matched his career high with 7 home runs.

Always a patient hitter, Ray was the most difficult batter in the big leagues to strike out last season. He struck out just 24 times in 652 plate appearances, an average of once every 27.2 trips to the plate. He never struck out twice in a single game. Ray also developed into a clutch hitter. He batted .294 with runners in scoring position.

He is basically a contact hitter who drives a lot of balls into the gaps, which accounts for his 109 doubles over the past three seasons. Once a far better hitter lefthanded than he was righthanded, Ray has worked hard to become more adept as a righty; his diligence is evident in his .277 average as a righthanded hitter over the past two seasons.

BASERUNNING:

Ray does more with his baserunning than his speed would indicate. For a second baseman he has below-average speed but he is smart and seldom makes a mistake. He gets a better-than-average lead and goes from first to third and second to home well.

FIELDING:

Ray had a fielding slump late last

1985 STATISTICS											
AVG	G	AB	R	H	2B	3B	HR	RBI	BB	SO	SB
.274	154	594	67	163	33	3	7	70	46	24	13
CAREER STATISTICS											
AVG	G	AB	R	H	2B	3B	HR	RBI	BB	SO	SB
.285	653	2474	299	706	150	23	25	259	160	124	58

VS. RHP — STRONG | VS. LHP — STRONG | PROBABLE HIT LOCATIONS

year and struggled through a period when he had trouble catching many routine ground balls. He finished the season with 18 errors, which was 50% more than he made the prior season. Normally, he is a sure-handed second baseman who seldom makes a bad throw.

Last year, Ray made dramatic improvement in his ability to make the double play pivot. And when one considers that he had to work with six different shortstops last season, Ray's improvement at the pivot is even more impressive.

OVERALL:

Ray is a solid player who has become a better all-around player since coming to the big leagues. He is not a superstar, but he is one of the league's better second basemen.

Snider: "He did not have as good a year as he is capable of, but I have to think that something to do with it was the frustration of playing for a last place team. It gets to you."

PITCHING:

Rick Reuschel became one of the great comeback stories in baseball history last season as he was named Comeback Player of the Year.

A one-time 20-game winner for the Chicago Cubs, Reuschel fought his way back from rotator cuff surgery. He spent time rehabilitating in the low minor leagues, was unwanted when he became a free agent and signed with the Pirates in 1985 as a last resort.

He opened the season in Hawaii, where he was 6-2, earning himself a promotion to the major leagues, where he had what was arguably his best season.

Reuschel throws harder now than he did when he was a 20-game winner. He still relies on a sinker that makes hitter after hitter bounce into easy ground ball outs.

A control pitcher, Reuschel walked two or fewer batters in 22 of his 31 games.

Not only did he win 14 games, but he pitched nine complete games, which was more than the rest of the Pirate staff combined.

FIELDING, HITTING, BASERUNNING:

Even though Reuschel has lost 30 pounds, he is still a large man. His size is deceiving because he is both quick and graceful on the mound. Last year, he led National League pitchers in fielding and did not make an error in 64 opportunities. He is exceptionally quick on bunt plays and covering first and has one of the best pickoff moves in the league.

Reuschel also knows what he is doing

RICK REUSCHEL
RHP, No. 47
RR, 6'3", 205 lbs.
ML Svc: 13 years
Born: 5-18-49 in
   Quincy, IL

1985 STATISTICS
W	L	ERA	G	GS	CG	SV	IP	H	R	ER	BB	SO
14	8	2.27	31	26	9	1	194	153	58	49	52	138

CAREER STATISTICS
W	L	ERA	G	GS	CG	SV	IP	H	R	ER	BB	SO
153	139	3.38	401	380	77	4	2556	2.593	1089	961	702	1527

with the bat--he even shows flashes of power. His abilities in these three often-overlooked areas make him one of the game's most complete pitchers.

OVERALL:

Reuschel is a clear example of what drive, desire and determination can do for a player. Once down and out, he fought his way back into the majors, not just to make the team, but to become a winning pitcher for a last place team.

Reuschel was rewarded with a three-year contract by the Pirates, who now believe that he can be effective until he is 40 years old.

Snider: "When I first learned that Rick was in the Pirates rotation last year, I thought, 'I hope he pitches against the Expos. We'll beat him.' He sure made a fool out of me and I'm happy he did. He really overcame a lot of disappointments. You can't help but admire his accomplishment last year."

HITTING:

R.J. Reynolds came to the Pirates as the key man in the trade that sent Bill Madlock to the Los Angeles Dodgers and immediately provided a flair that the club had previously lacked.

Since he was often injured while with the Dodgers (the victim of many leg muscle pulls), Reynolds was caught behind a number of Dodger outfielders without having much chance of becoming anything but a reserve--until he was rescued by the Pirates. He was given the left field job and did well in the 31 games in which he played for Pittsburgh.

A switch-hitter with some power, Reynolds seems to have learned to hit the fastballs that gave him trouble in his Dodger days.

BASERUNNING:

Reynolds has excellent speed and knows how to use it. He's a daring runner who will try to take an extra base on a sleeping outfielder and who will slide hard into second base to break up the double play. He goes from first to third well and stole 12 bases in 14 attempts for the Pirates.

FIELDING:

At times, Reynolds looked a bit uncertain in left field: he seems to have trouble seeing in Three Rivers Stadium's lighting. His speed allows him to run down mistakes. His throwing arm is above average.

OVERALL:

Reynolds won the left field job and

R.J. REYNOLDS
OF, No. 23
SR, 6'0", 190 lbs.
ML Svc: 3 years
Born: 4-19-60 in
    Sacramento, CA

1985 STATISTICS

AVG	G	AB	R	H	2B	3B	HR	RBI	BB	SO	SB
.282	104	337	44	95	15	7	3	42	22	49	18

CAREER STATISTICS

AVG	G	AB	R	H	2B	3B	HR	RBI	BB	SO	SB
.269	201	632	72	170	27	9	7	77	39	98	30

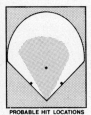

VS. RHP   VS. LHP   PROBABLE HIT LOCATIONS

the Pirate fans' support with his play in the final month of the season. He has to prove he can play an entire year the same way while staying injury-free. If he can, the Pirates have themselves a player who will add speed and offense to their lineup.

Snider: "He was one of those guys who was probably caught in the frustration of the Dodgers. They rush a lot of guys to the big leagues and put a lot of pressure on them. R.J. relaxed when he came to Pittsburgh and played flat-out good baseball. He could be a fixture in the Pirates' outfield."

PITCHING:

Rick Rhoden followed the best year of his career with the worst, slipping to a 10-15 record with a 4.47 ERA last season. A control pitcher, he complained of a tired shoulder during the season, which may have robbed him of his best stuff.

Evidence of his decline was that in 1984 he averaged 7.22 innings pitched per start, a figure that fell to 6.10 innings in 1985. Rhoden is a fastball/slider pitcher who, in the past, has been accused of scuffing up the baseball, although nothing has ever been proved. Last year, when he was losing, there were very few queries.

Rhoden works to get ahead in the count, then make the batter hit his pitch, which is usually a slider. He is not a strikeout pitcher but has always been able to get the job done.

He learned most of his pitching while he was with the Los Angeles Dodgers, patterning himself after Don Sutton. Like Sutton, Rhoden is capable of winning when he doesn't have his best stuff because of his intelligence and his guts.

He likes to finish what he starts and knows how to close out a game.

FIELDING, HITTING, BASERUNNING:

For the second straight year, Rhoden won the Silver Slugger award as the National League's best hitting pitcher even though his average dropped to .189, a tribute to his reputation as a hitter. He struck out only seven times in 78 plate appearances.

Unable to run faster than a trot due to a childhood ailment, he is not a good

RICK RHODEN
RHP, No. 29
RR, 6'4", 203 lbs.
ML Svc: 11 years
Born: 5-16-53 in
  Boynton Beach, FL

1985 STATISTICS

W	L	ERA	G	GS	CG	SV	IP	H	R	ER	BB	SO
10	15	4.47	35	35	2	0	213.1	254	119	106	69	128

CAREER STATISTICS

W	L	ERA	G	GS	CG	SV	IP	H	R	ER	BB	SO
106	85	3.56	299	270	48	1	1864.2	1897	821	738	567	1018

baserunner, yet he is an outstanding fielder and always wins the race to cover first base.

He has one of the best pickoff moves among righthanders in baseball, last year picking off five runners. Opposing runners managed to steal 19 bases in 31 attempts.

OVERALL:

One of the game's most courageous athletes, Rhoden had osteomyelitis as a youth and it left him with a withered left leg. He has, however, become an All-Star pitcher who can do all of the little things necessary to win. He should just be reaching the peak of his career.

Snider: "He still has quality stuff and is a battling type of pitcher. No one with the Pirates really had a good year, so you can probably throw 1985 out for him. I don't think that last year indicates his abilities."

PITCHING:

Big, raw-boned Don Robinson is looking forward to this, an even-numbered year, for it probably means that he can avoid surgery. It seems that in every odd-numbered year he has had the doctor cut into him. Last year was no exception when, following the season, he underwent arthroscopic surgery on his right knee. In other odd-numbered years Robinson had elbow surgery (1977), shoulder surgery (1979), shoulder surgery (1981) and shoulder surgery again (1983).

Most players would have quit from the adversity Robinson has faced, but it has just made him more determined to prove he can remain an effective pitcher.

Used mostly in relief in a Pirate bullpen which spent most of the year in turmoil, he slipped to a record of 5-11 with a 3.87 ERA. The injured knee was one reason and another was that he never really had his job defined, sometimes pitching long, sometimes short relief while also starting six times.

A hard thrower who loves to challenge hitters, Robinson has a big curve and has come up with a palmball that he uses as an off-speed pitch. When healthy, he is a strikeout pitcher.

The Pirates are thinking of using him as their number one righthanded short reliever, a role he covets.

FIELDING, HITTING, BASERUNNING:

One of the best hitting pitchers in baseball, Robinson is also one of the most dangerous as a power hitter. He owns a .261 career batting average with six homers. When he was having trouble with his shoulder, the Pirates sent him

DON ROBINSON
RHP, No. 43
RR, 6'4", 225 lbs.
ML Svc: 8 years
Born: 6-8-57 in
Ashland, KY

1985 STATISTICS
W	L	ERA	G	GS	CG	SV	IP	H	R	ER	BB	SO
5	11	3.87	44	6	0	3	95.1	95	49	41	42	65

CAREER STATISTICS
W	L	ERA	G	GS	CG	SV	IP	H	R	ER	BB	SO
56	59	3.88	251	126	22	17	1067.2	1028	511	461	392	719

to the Instructional League to see if he could be converted to an outfielder.

Pitchers pitch him as if he were another hitter, seldom giving him a fastball unless it is up and in and has a lot on it.

Robinson is an excellent fielder and has a fine move to first base. He is a bit slow coming to the plate due to a high leg kick. As a baserunner, he is just ordinary but doesn't make mistakes.

OVERALL:

A healthy Don Robinson could develop into the kind of strikeout pitcher every team needs out of the bullpen in the late innings. He is a blue-collar, hard-working pitcher with a lot of talent and even more guts.

Snider: "He is still a 'thrower'--I don't classify him as a 'pitcher' yet. He is not afraid to go right after the hitters with everything he's got."

HITTING:

Jason Thompson underwent knee surgery before the end of last season to correct a problem which has plagued him for the past two seasons. Because a hitter's power is generated mostly from his legs, Thompson's knee miseries probably had as much to do with his lack of power last season as anything else. The aches and pains in his legs kept him from really turning on the ball.

Thompson's swing is big and complicated, making him look very bad on occasion. Like many power hitters, he is streaky and can look very, very good or very, very bad. For most hitters, patience is a virtue, but Thompson carries it to the extreme. He seems almost content to walk in situations where he must be aggressive, allowing pitchers to pitch around him in key situations. Over the past two seasons, he was the only legitimate power threat in the Pirate lineup, yet he was more than willing to take a walk.

Thompson has hit 30 homers in two different seasons, but last year, he finished with just 12, partially because of the knees and partially because he was an island of power in the tranquil sea that was the Pirates' lineup.

Thompson stands straight at the plate and takes a big swing at the ball. For a power hitter, he gets a great many hits to left field although his home run power is as a pull hitter.

BASERUNNING:

Thompson is one of the slowest runners in baseball even when he's healthy. His knee ailments have aggravated that problem. His lack of speed actually causes him to clog up the bases so much that pitchers do not fear walking him, knowing it still takes two hits to drive him home. He seldom takes a chance, however, and is rarely thrown out on the bases.

JASON THOMPSON
1B, No. 30
LL, 6'3", 218 lbs.
ML Svc: 10 years
Born: 7-6-54 in
  Hollywood, CA

1985 STATISTICS

AVG	G	AB	R	H	2B	3B	HR	RBI	BB	SO	SB
.241	123	402	42	97	17	1	12	61	84	58	0

CAREER STATISTICS

AVG	G	AB	R	H	2B	3B	HR	RBI	BB	SO	SB
.261	1388	4751	634	1243	200	12	208	778	798	850	8

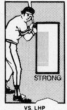
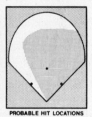

VS. RHP   VS. LHP   PROBABLE HIT LOCATIONS

FIELDING:

Thompson is, at best, an average fielder. He has literally no range going either to his left or right. He handles foul pops well and is good on throws in the dirt, but his arm is average and he is hesitant to throw the ball except when he has a sure out.

OVERALL:

Snider: "Thompson's lack of aggressiveness at the plate really hurts him as he often waits for a perfect pitch to hit. When a cleanup batter hits .241 with just 61 RBIs, something must be changed.

"Sometimes it's hard to find the home runs in your bat. You can't just push a button and have one pop out. He might do better if he were on a team where he was not the only legitimate power hitter. It might take some of the pressure off him and he could concentrate more on what he can do naturally."

PITCHING:

Lee Tunnell was given a chance to be a regular in the starting rotation when the 1985 season opened, but wound up having to return to the minors to get himself straightened out. Back in the majors during the final month of the season, Tunnell seemed to find the key to success as he won three in a row in the first two weeks of September.

Not overpowering, Tunnell relies on mixing his pitches. His best pitch is a curveball but he also throws a fastball, a slider and a forkball as a change-up. He has to be a thinking pitcher who relies on fooling the hitters.

Tunnell's biggest problem has been a lack of control. Not that he necessarily walks a lot of hitters, but he often either falls behind in the count and has to challenge with the fastball, or he is wild and high in the strike zone, presenting the hitter with a pitch he can drive.

Tunnell's mental approach to the game could probably be improved. He is a worrier who has done well when he has been given surprise starts, which does not allow him time to think about the upcoming game.

FIELDING, HITTING, BASERUNNING:

Tunnell has one of the best moves to first base on the Pirates' staff, and last year, he used it to pick off five runners. He is a good fielder but not a good hitter. He batted only .085 and did not successfully bunt anyone over.

LEE TUNNELL
RHP, No. 22
RR, 6'1", 180 lbs.
ML Svc: 3 years
Born: 10-30-60 in
Tyler, TX

1985 STATISTICS

W	L	ERA	G	GS	CG	SV	IP	H	R	ER	BB	SO
4	10	4.01	24	23	0	0	132.1	126	70	59	57	74

CAREER STATISTICS

W	L	ERA	G	GS	CG	SV	IP	H	R	ER	BB	SO
17	24	4.06	90	57	5	1	396.2	391	203	179	160	224

OVERALL:

Lee Tunnell must start if he is to pitch in the big leagues and he must be used regularly. However, it's up to him to prove that he can handle that assignment. He has shown flashes of brilliance but has lacked the consistency necessary to be assured a spot in the starting rotation.

Snider: "If Tunnell gets the ball over the plate, he can be tough. It seems that he was one of those guys who was in awe of the big leagues when he first came up and tried too hard to prove himself. Then, all of a sudden last year, he really started to become a pitcher."

PITCHING:

Sometimes it takes a pitcher a while to mature and that might be the case with Bob Walk, who has been with Atlanta, Philadelphia and now the Pirates. Always a free-spirit off the field, his attitude has always been what was questioned most.

Put a player in the minor leagues for a while and make it look as though his big league career might be over and you can sometimes get him to reach the heights he should. This may have been what happened with Walk in 1985--he had a big season at Hawaii.

Walk has always been his own worst enemy. He has good stuff, but until last season he was forever fighting his control. When he gets the ball over the plate, he is a good pitcher. His good stuff won't get him anywhere when he can't throw the ball where he wants to.

His fastball is above average and he throws a nasty curveball that is really his out pitch. When they are thrown for strikes, he is tough to hit.

FIELDING, HITTING, BASERUNNING:

Walk is not a good hitter but is capable of helping himself with the bunt. As a fielder, he is only average, with just a fair move to first base. Runners can take liberties with him when he goes to the plate. He has average speed and is no threat on the bases.

BOB WALK
RHP, No. 18
RR, 6'4", 208 lbs.
ML Svc: 4 years
Born: 11-26-56 in
Van Nuys, CA

1985 STATISTICS

W	L	ERA	G	GS	CG	SV	IP	H	R	ER	BB	SO
2	3	3.68	9	1	1	0	58.2	60	27	24	18	40

CAREER STATISTICS

W	L	ERA	G	GS	CG	SV	IP	H	R	ER	BB	SO
26	24	4.54	83	66	6	0	432	458	243	218	177	248

OVERALL:

Walk is probably at a crossroads in his career. He was once thought of highly enough that the Phillies started him in the opening game of the 1981 World Series, but his stock slipped and he wound up in the minor leagues.

He probably has a better chance of getting back to the big leagues through a trade than with the Pirates.

Snider: "It appeared when he came up from Hawaii at the end of the season that he is starting to learn how to pitch. He has always had great potential, but he needs to get really serious about baseball. It looks as though he might be on his way to doing just that."

HITTING:

Just when it appeared Marvell Wynne was ready to become the Pirates' center fielder for a long time to come, he lost his job to Joe Orsulak. Injuries played a part in his decline; he sprained both of his ankles during the season, and each time the injury caused him to go on the disabled list. His ankles never were 100% and that hurt his game, which is based on speed.

Being in and out of the lineup made it difficult for Wynne to correct any of his hitting weaknesses, the most glaring being that he has trouble handling a big league breaking ball. He also has had tremendous difficulties learning to bunt for a base hit, which limits how much he can use his speed.

Wynne lacks power, last year ending a spell of 794 at-bats without a home run by hitting one off Houston's Bob Knepper --an inside-the-park home run.

BASERUNNING:

For three years, the Pirates have tried to make Wynne into a basestealer. If he could turn his speed into a dangerous weapon on the bases, his overall offensive value to the club would increase. However, he remains unable to grasp the fine points of basestealing. In almost three major league seasons, he has stolen just 46 bases despite having above-average speed.

Other than basestealing, Wynne is a capable baserunner who will go from first to third and score from second on a single.

FIELDING:

Along with a decline in his hitting, Wynne's fielding suffered last season. Perhaps because of the ankle injuries, he was not getting to balls in the gaps

MARVELL WYNNE
CF, No. 36
LL, 5'11", 169 lbs.
ML Svc: 3 years
Born: 12-17-59 in
  Chicago, IL

1985 STATISTICS

AVG	G	AB	R	H	2B	3B	HR	RBI	BB	SO	SB
.205	103	337	21	69	6	3	2	18	18	48	10

CAREER STATISTICS

AVG	G	AB	R	H	2B	3B	HR	RBI	BB	SO	SB
.245	360	1356	164	332	46	16	9	83	98	181	46

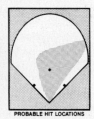

VS. RHP   VS. LHP   PROBABLE HIT LOCATIONS

which he had caught in previous seasons.

Wynne has one of the most accurate throwing arms in baseball, although he throws with an unorthodox motion.

His arm strength is slightly above average, but because of his accuracy, runners seldom challenge him.

OVERALL:

Wynne finds himself without a job and will have a lot of trouble winning back his old one unless he improves in the areas of his game that are lacking, most importantly his ability to steal bases. The Pirates would also like to see him hit with a bit more authority.

Snider: "He had a very disappointing year. I thought he went backwards as far as outfield play was concerned. He's going to have to shake off this year and start the 1986 season fresh."

DENNY GONZALEZ
INF, No. 24
RR, 5'11", 184 lbs.
Ml Svc: 1 year plus
Born: 7-22-63 in
    Sabana Grande
    Boya, DR

HITTING, BASERUNNING, FIELDING:

Denny Gonzalez has big shoes to fill, replacing four-time batting champion Bill Madlock at third base. A fastball hitter who will often chase a bad pitch, Gonzalez must learn patience and discipline before he will become a solid major league hitter. He has extra base power and has been hitting 10 to 15 home runs in the minor leagues but will have to pull more than he does now before he becomes a home run threat.

Gonzalez is an aggressive, quick baserunner who has averaged 40 stolen bases a year in three seasons at the Pirates' Hawaii farm team. He slides hard and will go from first to third or score from second on a hit.

The jury is out on Gonzalez as a fielder. The Pirates have bounced him around from position to position in his minor league career, trying to find a spot for him. He's played second base, the outfield and third base. Third base, however, seems to be the position he is best suited to play, though he is still far from good there.

OVERALL:

Snider: "I was in the same boat Denny Gonzalez was in, being sent to the minors twice before I got my feet on the ground in the big leagues. A few base hits here, a key base hit there and he'll get his confidence. It usually takes a young hitter who comes into the major leagues three or four years before he gets established."

CECILIO GUANTE
RHP, No. 47
RR, 6'3", 200 lbs.
ML Svc: 4 years
Born: 2-2-60 in
    Jacagua, DR

PITCHING, FIELDING
HITTING, BASERUNNING:

Cecilio Guante has a live arm and comes at the hitter from every possible angle. His fastball has been clocked at better than 90 MPH.

He is really tough on righthanders, coming sidearm and throwing not only a strong fastball but a slider as well. Lefthanded hitters find him easier to handle.

The Pirates have tried him in both long relief and in short relief. He has performed far better in the long role. It seems that in close games he has had trouble holding the lead, but when called upon to pitch three runs up or three runs down he's been nearly unhittable.

Guante is a below-average fielder who has trouble on bunt plays and on balls hit back at him. He is not as good at holding a runner close as a reliever should be.

As a hitter, he is not much to look at and he strikes out more than half his times at bat. He doesn't bunt well and is a terrible baserunner.

OVERALL:

Someday, Guante may put all of his pitching talent together and become one of the game's premier relievers. To date, however, all efforts to put him into any kind of position that carries responsibilty has failed.

Snider: "If I were playing today, I'd be glad he is righthanded. He can put a little fear in a righthander."

JUNIOR ORTIZ
C, No. 26
RR, 5'11", 175 lbs.
ML Svc: 4 years
Born: 10-24-59 in
    Humacao, PR

league home run.

But Ortiz's strength is his defense, not his offense. He is almost a clone of Pena in that he loves to throw and has a strong arm. His throwing style mimics that of Pena as well and he is not reluctant to try a pickoff at any moment.

Ortiz runs like a catcher, which means he won't steal bases or challenge an outfielder's arm.

HITTING, BASERUNNING, FIELDING:

Used sparingly behind Tony Pena, Junior Ortiz proved himself to be a competent backup. Never considered much of a hitting threat (even though he led the Eastern League in batting in 1980), Ortiz had his finest season in 1985. He closed with a six-game hitting streak to hit .292, and even added his first big

OVERALL:

Ortiz is adequate as a backup catcher. He has the makeup to sit for long periods and still do the job when called upon.

Snider: "Ortiz can do the job for a short period if Pena is out with an injury, but he will never be a number one catcher."

JIM WINN
RHP, No. 41
RR, 6'3", 210 lbs.
ML Svc: 1 year plus
Born: 9-23-59 in
    Stockton, CA

feel comfortable with himself.

Winn is an average fielder who is not particularly quick off the mound. He has trouble holding runners close and his pickoff move is just average. He is not terrible as a hitter but he'll never make a living with his bat. A slow runner, he is no threat to do anything once he gets on base.

PITCHING, FIELDING,
HITTING, BASERUNNING:

Jim Winn is a number one draft pick who has come along slowly. He is a sinkerball pitcher who is not overpowering, but who relies on his own control and his team's defense.

The Pirates have shuffled him back and forth between starting and relievving and are going to have to make a decision whether or not he's a starting pitcher or a reliever so he can begin to

OVERALL:

Winn is reaching the point in his career where he is going to have settle in with the Pittsburgh organization or go somewhere where he can discover if he is of big league quality.

Snider: "The first time I saw him last season he was a little nervous but later he pitched well. The thing to do is wait and see. He needs the chance to pitch and might just turn out to be a good pitcher."

PAT CLEMENTS
LHP, No. 54
RL, 6'0", 175 lbs.
ML Svc: 1 year
Born: 2-2-62 in
McCloud, CA

PITCHING, FIELDING,
HITTING, BASERUNNING:

Pat Clements came to the Pirates from the California Angels in the John Candelaria-George Hendrick trade. He had jumped from Double-A ball to the big leagues and, as a relief pitcher, was unbeaten in five decisions when the deal was made. In both his pitching style as well as his physical makeup, Clements is similar to the Cardinals' lefthander John Tudor.

Clements is a sinkerball pitcher who keeps the ball down. When he has trouble, it is with his control. He will leave the ball too high in the strike zone.

He is still kind of young to be used as the number one stopper out of the bullpen, but he could mature into that role.

Clements is a solid fielder. He gets off the mound quickly both to field bunts and cover first base. His move to first base is average for a lefthander.

He has not hit enough to be a good hitter and did not get on base enough to judge his baserunning ability.

OVERALL:

The Pirates have gotten themselves one of the rarest of commodities in baseball, a talented, young lefthander with control. Working in a deep bullpen he could be of value this year.

Snider: "Any time you can get a lefthanded pitcher with ability, you jump at the chance, and the Pirates, in the trade with the Angels, got two promising young ones in Clements and Bob Kipper."

ST. LOUIS CARDINALS

PITCHING:

Joaquin Andujar is a mystery man wrapped in an enigma.

He had 20 wins with six weeks to go in the season last year yet finished with only 21. There are various theories which attempt to explain his inability to win more than one game in six weeks, and the most prevalent are that he lost the location with his wicked slider, refused to develop his change-up and was distracted by the publicity centering on the Pittsburgh drug trial.

Andujar is extremely sensitive to anything written or said about him and the fact is that after August 23rd, which was just shortly before the drug trial began, his earned run average was 6.35.

Andujar throws both straight overhand and sidearm but his sidearm deliveries often are very predictable. He will invariably come sidearm to a right-handed hitter when the hitter has a two-strike count.

He is a challenging pitcher in that he pitches straight at the hitters, although for whatever his reasons he was not doing that in the final two months last year. As it became more apparent that he was not himself, hitters began to look forward to facing him, feeling that they would surely get something good to hit. It is also clear that when Andujar is distracted--by umpires' calls or other matters--he is not as sharp. His temper is the monkey on his back.

Andujar is a thrower, not a pitcher. He is not the type of pitcher for whom a catcher can set a target and expect it to be hit exactly. But he has tremendous talent and has the pitches to pull off a good performance.

FIELDING:

A Gold Glove-winner in 1984, Andujar

JOAQUIN ANDUJAR
RHP, No. 47
SR, 6'0", 180 lbs.
ML Svc: 10 years
Born: 12-21-52 in
  San Pedro de Macoris, DR

1985 STATISTICS

W	L	ERA	G	GS	CG	SV	IP	H	R	ER	BB	SO
21	12	3.40	38	38	10	0	269.2	265	113	102	82	112

CAREER STATISTICS

W	L	ERA	G	GS	CG	SV	IP	H	R	ER	BB	SO
110	101	3.46	341	256	60	8	1858.2	1720	799	715	628	893

is cat-quick off the mound and is not afraid to take chances by throwing to second or third on bunts instead of taking the automatic out at first. His move to first is among the best in baseball for righthanders.

OVERALL:

After ten seasons of being in the NL, this year could be Andujar's most interesting yet. The factors to consider are: a) he begins the season under a 10-game suspension for his outrageous behavior in the 1985 World Series; b) as a member of the Oakland A's, he will be pitching to a new stream of batters who can be just as hotheaded as he; c) umpires in the AL have a slightly different perception of the strike zone than NL umpires. Andujar did not like the calls he got in the NL; it will be curious to see how his views match those of the American League umpires.

Snider: "He is very proud of the fact he is the only active pitcher to have won 20 games in each of the two previous seasons and he has enough stuff to make it three if he can get a better hold on himself and his emotions."

HITTING:

Just when most people thought he was through, Cesar Cedeno may have resurrected his major league career last season with a torrid six-week performance after the Cardinals acquired him from the Cincinnati Reds for a minor league player. Cedeno hit more than .400 during that time as he played on a fairly regular basis. He was an important contributor to the Cardinals' clinching of the National League title.

He was the old Cedeno as he hit with power and with an aggressive style that had not been seen from him in quite a while.

Cedeno holds the bat high and drives into everything, especially pitches up in the strike zone. He basically is a pull hitter although he showed an ability to hit the outside pitch to the opposite field.

The pitching pattern to Cedeno is to force him off the plate with the fastball and then work the breaking ball on the outside portion.

At age 36, Cedeno no longer has the blazing speed to beat out any bunts, but he still can be a productive player as an extra man at first base or in the outfield.

BASERUNNING:

As the years go along, Cedeno is more and more susceptible to leg injuries; the injuries have taken away his base-stealing game. He still is one of the game's best, though, at taking the extra base on balls hit into the outfield gaps.

FIELDING:

Cedeno has good enough speed and his arm remains strong enough to enable him

CESAR CEDENO
OF, No. 28
RR, 6'2", 195 lbs.
ML Svc: 16 years
Born: 2-25-51 in
Santo Domingo, DR

1985 STATISTICS

AVG	G	AB	R	H	2B	3B	HR	RBI	BB	SO	SB
.291	111	296	38	86	16	1	9	49	24	42	14

CAREER STATISTICS

AVG	G	AB	R	H	2B	3B	HR	RBI	BB	SO	SB
.286	1969	7232	1079	2069	426	51	199	970	657	925	549

  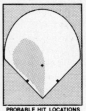

STRONG   STRONG

VS. RHP   VS. LHP   PROBABLE HIT LOCATIONS

to play all three outfield positions. In all likelihood, however, he will be seen at first base as much as anyplace else. His arm never has been much above average, but he has always compensated for that with a quick release.

OVERALL:

Cedeno must adapt to being a utility player. As he showed late last season, he is still capable of putting together a hot streak for several weeks.

Robinson: "Buried on the Cincinnati bench, Cedeno put on his best display in several years at precisely the right time--when many major league scouts were watching."

HITTING:

Jack Clark was just what the Cards needed last season--a power hitter in the middle of the lineup. Had he not been sidelined for two stretches (totaling 36 games) because of injuries to his left side last season, and continued to hit at the same pace, Clark might have hit 30 home runs with 100 RBIs.

Nonetheless, Clark played enough to hit 22 homers and drive in 87 runs. He provided the hammer in the order after pitchers had tortured themselves worrying about the baserunning exploits of Vince Coleman and Willie McGee.

Clark looks for the fastball at all times and makes no bones about it. He feels that if he's looking for a fastball and gets a breaking ball, he has time to adjust. He can look bad on a breaking ball, especially one down and out of the strike zone, but he rarely lets a fastball pass by untended.

He likes the ball belt-high and away and never gets cheated in his swings. Swinging too hard is one of the reasons he got hurt but, by the end of the World Series, he was feeling almost up to par.

The problem the Cardinals now face is finding someone to hit behind Clark, who drew 83 walks last year (14 of which were intentional). Clark often had to chase balls out of the strike zone, assuming they were the best pitches he was going to get. The intentional walk to Clark is a strategy Dodger manager Tommy Lasorda won't soon forget.

BASERUNNING:

Clark doesn't steal many bases but he knows how to run the bases. He was much better last year than in previous years, when his mind would occasionally wander.

FIELDING:

Clark made the transition from the outfield to first base last year and he played adequately. He handles thrown balls well enough but will make errors in judgment on batted balls, often cov-

JACK CLARK
RF, No. 22
RR, 6'3", 205 lbs.
ML Svc: 10 years
Born: 11-10-55 in
    New Brighton, PA

1985 STATISTICS

AVG	G	AB	R	H	2B	3B	HR	RBI	BB	SO	SB
.281	126	442	71	124	26	3	22	87	83	88	1

CAREER STATISTICS

AVG	G	AB	R	H	2B	3B	HR	RBI	BB	SO	SB
.277	1170	4173	668	1158	223	33	185	682	490	656	61

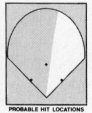

STRONG VS. RHP   STRONG VS. LHP   PROBABLE HIT LOCATIONS

ering what should be the second baseman's territory. The result is often that there is no one to cover first on time for the throw. He has a good arm, but does not get the chance to show it off as a first baseman.

In all likelihood, he will be a better first baseman this season with a year's experience under his belt.

OVERALL:

Prior to 1985, Clark spent his entire major league career with the Giants. In those ten seasons, they never fielded a club as balanced and as strong as the Redbirds of 1985, leading one to think that at age 30 Clark still may have his most productive years ahead of him.

Snider: "The only thing standing between Jack Clark and a .300 average is a good hitter behind him in the order. He has got a good club all around him now and he hit well even though he saw some bad pitches last year. But to take full advantage of him in the lineup, he must see more pitches he likes."

HITTING:

Vince Coleman hit far better than anyone had dreamed he would last year. The Cardinals probably would have been happy if he hit .220, but found his .267 average to be the icing on the cake.

Coleman is a switch-hitter who has an unusual swing in which he sort of flings the bat at the ball. It doesn't look very effective--but it is. If he keeps the ball on the ground, he can amass a staggering total of infield hits by his speed alone. More than one-fourth of Coleman's hits last year were infield hits.

At first, when he was recalled from the minors, Coleman was feeling for the ball and seemed intimidated by major league pitching. He got on-the-job training and while he learned a lot of lessons about hitting at the big league level, he still has to learn to cut down on his high strikeout total (115 last season).

Coleman had particular trouble hitting breaking balls, especially first-pitch breaking balls from lefthanded pitchers.

BASERUNNING:

It seems entirely possible that he will break all of baseball's basestealing records and then hold them for a long time.

He has the nerve to take the longest lead in baseball--often having both feet off the dirt surface. His only real problem is stealing first base because he certainly does not have any trouble with the other three (he stole third base more than 20 times last season).

A hard worker, Coleman likely will get even better and it is interesting to speculate how many bases he would have stolen if he batted .300, considering that he stole 110 as it was.

Coleman is not expected to be affected by the freak injury he suffered to his right leg during the playoffs last year when the automatic tarpaulin rolled

VINCE COLEMAN
LF, No. 29
SR, 6'0", 170 lbs.
ML Svc: 1 year
Born: 9-22-61 in
     Jacksonville, FL

1985 STATISTICS

AVG	G	AB	R	H	2B	3B	HR	RBI	BB	SO	SB
.267	151	636	107	170	20	10	1	40	50	115	110

CAREER STATISTICS

AVG	G	AB	R	H	2B	3B	HR	RBI	BB	SO	SB
.267	151	636	107	170	20	10	1	40	50	115	110

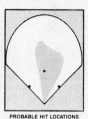

VS. RHP   VS. LHP   PROBABLE HIT LOCATIONS

over his leg.

FIELDING:

Coleman plays rather shallow as an outfielder but his great speed enables him to run down balls in the gaps. His arm is much stronger than was anticipated and he can play any of the three outfield positions with equal ability.

OVERALL:

Snider: "I thought I had seen the fastest in Maury Wills and then along came Lou Brock. Then it was Tim Raines and Rickey Henderson. Now it's Coleman.

"He doesn't look as though he's finished developing his body and will probably get stronger.

"He is going to have a lot more years ahead of him to break his own mark and should take time to work on his hitting. He needs to be more patient and perhaps bunt more often than he does--anything to help him get on base!"

PITCHING:

Danny Cox won 18 games last season despite being troubled with tendinitis in his right elbow.

He throws almost straight over the top, and like other Cardinals pitchers, he is most effective because of his change-up. At 6'4" and 230 pounds, it would seem that he could throw a ball through a brick wall. But he is not as as overpowering as his size would suggest and his fastball is not much above average.

When he gets his slider over, he can be very, very tough. But the hard slider may be the most demanding pitch on a pitcher's arm and there is some concern about Cox being injured again and not having the success that he could have.

When Cox gets behind in the count, he does not give in to the hitters, but rather will throw his breaking ball or change-up. His biggest problems occur when he tries to overthrow in compensation for his merely-average fastball. He has to be careful and blend all three of his pitches.

Cox's arm may not have the endurance to pitch in Whitey Herzog's four-man rotation; he would do better if he had the extra day's rest a five-man rotation would give him. Cox was able to pitch very well early in the season on only three days' rest, but then the tenderness began and Herzog gave him longer periods of rest between starts.

FIELDING, HITTING, BASERUNNING:

Cox's follow-through often carries

DANNY COX
RHP, No. 34
RR, 6'4", 230 lbs.
ML Svc: 3 years
Born: 9-21-59 in
Northhampton, UK

1985 STATISTICS
W	L	ERA	G	GS	CG	SV	IP	H	R	ER	BB	SO
18	9	2.88	35	35	10	0	241	226	91	77	64	131

CAREER STATISTICS
W	L	ERA	G	GS	CG	SV	IP	H	R	ER	BB	SO
30	26	3.31	76	74	11	0	480.1	489	210	177	141	237

him past the normal ending point for a pitcher, leaving him vulnerable to balls hit up the middle. For a big man, he is quick in pursuit of a batted ball and his move to first is above average.

At bat, Cox has made strides, especially in his ability to bunt runners over. His size is also deceptive when he is at the plate; he has not shown the power one would suspect from a man of his size. He is a good athlete and runs the bases well.

OVERALL:

Snider: "When a pitcher has the kind of straight change that Cox has, it is one of the most valuable weapons in baseball--if the pitcher has a good fastball to go with it. Cox's fastball is not great, but it is good enough.

"If he stays healthy, I can see Danny Cox as a 20-game winner or better."

PITCHING:

It's been said that confidence is everything. For Ken Dayley, that's his life's story. A bust as a starter, he had to regain his confidence before he became one of the game's premier left-handed relievers last year. Only 14 of the 51 runners he inherited managed to score against him.

Dayley is the reverse of a pitcher such as Montreal's Bryn Smith, who was awful as a reliever but last year became one of the league's best starters. When Dayley was a starter with Atlanta (1982-84) and with St. Louis (1984), he could only occasionally pump his fastball up to 90 MPH. Most often, he threw his fastball at around 83 MPH (below the major league average) and had only a rolling curveball. He couldn't get lefthanded batters out, let alone righthanders. Dayley had little confidence in his own ability.

But in spring training last season, pitching coach Mike Roarke helped put the snap back in Dayley's curveball. Once the curveball was right, his confidence returned, at first gradually, and then by leaps and bounds. His exuberance and self-assuredness fairly bubbled out of him as he trotted in from the bullpen saying, "Give me the ball!"

With confidence, Dayley's fastball appeared to pick up speed. And he also felt strongly enough about his curveball that he was not afraid to throw it even when he was behind in the count.

Prior to last season, Dayley seemed to have trouble putting his last hitter or last inning behind him, but now he seems to have the ability to forge ahead and forget about any of his previously unfavorable performances.

He also isn't "squeezing" the ball any more nor looking over his shoulder.

KEN DAYLEY
LHP, No. 46
LL, 6'0", 171 lbs.
ML Svc: 4 years
Born: 2-25-59 in
Jerome, ID

1985 STATISTICS

W	L	ERA	G	GS	CG	SV	IP	H	R	ER	BB	SO
4	4	2.76	57	0	0	11	65.1	65	24	20	18	62

CAREER STATISTICS

W	L	ERA	G	GS	CG	SV	IP	H	R	ER	BB	SO
14	23	4.33	108	33	0	11	265	288	150	127	93	176

He no longer expects to go to the minor leagues if he has a bad outing.

FIELDING, HITTING, BASERUNNING:

Dayley is a good all-around athlete and makes all the fielding plays he should. He also swings a potentially dangerous bat, as his 2-for-5 record as a hitter last year attests.

OVERALL:

Dayley, who was considered a longshot to make the team last year, seized his opportunity and didn't let go all year long. At age 27, his best years are ahead of him--and there may be many.

Snider: "He was Atlanta's first-round draft choice in 1980 and was used almost exclusively as a starter for five seasons. He finally found out what his best role was last year. Dayley is very tough, his curveball is a great pitch now and he seems to love the pressure of his position. Look for more accomplishments as he enters this season secure in his assignment for the first time in his career."

PITCHING:

Last season, Bob Forsch bounced back well enough from back surgery to win nine more games than many had thought he would. Three of this veteran's triumphs were during the final month of the season when the Cardinals pulled away to win the National League Eastern Division title.

Forsch's playoff and World Series starts were spotty but it would have been hard for anyone not to pitch for eight or ten days and then be thrown into the fire.

Once a power pitcher, Forsch now has to have pinpoint control to set up the hitters. He must keep the ball down and needs a good defense behind him. He does not do well pitching from behind in the count.

When the Cardinals went to a five-man rotation, Forsch was their fifth starter although he supplanted struggling Kurt Kepshire as the Cardinals' number four starter later in the season.

Forsch has long been regarded as one of the Cardinals' most intense competitors. He is not afraid to pitch inside if he has to.

FIELDING, HITTING, BASERUNNING:

He uses a slow, deliberate delivery and is an accomplished fielder. He has a quick move to first, made faster by a little kickstart with his leg.

BOB FORSCH
RHP, No. 31
RR, 6'3", 215 lbs.
ML Svc: 12 years
Born: 1-13-50 in
   Sacramento, CA

1985 STATISTICS

W	L	ERA	G	GS	CG	SV	IP	H	R	ER	BB	SO
9	6	3.90	34	19	3	2	136	132	63	59	47	48

CAREER STATISTICS

W	L	ERA	G	GS	CG	SV	IP	H	R	ER	BB	SO
129	106	3.66	359	326	61	3	2141.2	2091	997	871	629	846

For a pitcher, he is a great hitter; last season, he had two doubles, one triple and a home run while batting .244.

OVERALL:

This season, Forsch is on the last year of a $500,000 a year contract and must pitch well to give himself a chance to continue in baseball.

Snider: "He still might be able to do the job. I don't think what happened in the playoffs and World Series was any reflection on what kind of year he had. There's not too much he can't do. He is one of the most intense competitors in the game and never beats himself."

HITTING:

Tommy Herr had one of the most remarkable seasons in baseball history last year, driving in 110 runs with only eight home runs. He had never driven in more than 49 runs before, but once manager Whitey Herzog installed him as the Cardinals' third-place hitter last year, Herr performed as if he should have been there all along.

An extremely patient and selective hitter, Herr took advantage of every fastball he saw last season. And with speedsters Vince Coleman and Willie McGee on base ahead of him, he saw lots of them. Herr had 60 hits in 175 at-bats with runners in scoring position and, given the speed ahead of him, he could even log three RBIs with one single.

Previously a good hitter, last year Herr became a feared one (although it surely didn't hurt to have the already-ferocious Jack Clark coming up behind him) from both sides of the plate. He hit .313 lefthanded and .282 as a righthander.

In 1985, his righthanded hitting was the most improved part of his game--previously, he had never been above .230 as a righty.

BASERUNNING:

Previous knee surgery has not affected Herr's basestealing ability. He is a sneaky runner who stole 31 bases in 34 attempts last year. He reads pitchers well and gets a good jump.

FIELDING:

Herr underwent several knee operations between 1982-83 and seems to have regained most of his range. His forte, however, is positional ball--he puts himself in just the right spot.

TOM HERR
2B, No. 28
SR, 6'0", 185 lbs.
ML Svc: 7 years
Born: 4-4-56 in
Lancaster, PA

```
1985 STATISTICS
AVG   G    AB    R    H    2B  3B  HR  RBI  BB   SO   SB
.302  159  596  97   180  38  3   8   110  80   55   31
CAREER STATISTICS
AVG   G    AB    R    H    2B  3B  HR  RBI  BB   SO   SB
.281  721  2603 373  733  120 18  24  288  286  247  108
```

VS. RHP   VS. LHP   PROBABLE HIT LOCATIONS

No other second baseman stands in tougher on the double play and he never misses the routine play.

OVERALL:

Herr does everything a ballplayer should do and plays uncomplainingly despite injuries. He played a team-high 159 games last year and seemed to tire in the second half.

Snider: "It is exciting for me to see a guy have the kind of season Tommy had last year. Sometimes, you never know what a player can do until he finds the ideal circumstances. Herr was always thought of as a number one, two, seven or eight hitter until last year. But he really changed that!"

PITCHING:

Though he does not throw hard, Rick Horton is among the most sought-after lefthanders in the league because of his ability to both start and relieve.

Last year, he relieved 46 times out of 49 appearances but his three starts in September were, in general, quality ones as he helped the Cardinals to the National League title.

Horton doesn't have great stuff but he is good enough to get hitters out. He must remember that his fastball is not really his out pitch and he must not try to overthrow with something that is not there.

What he does well is establish the corners with his breaking stuff and he has been especially effective against predominatly lefthanded-hitting teams such as Houston.

FIELDING, HITTING, BASERUNNING:

Horton finishes in perfect position after his follow-through and is an excellent fielder. The word got around last year about his good move to first so his number of runners picked off dropped but his move remains one of the league's best.

Horton had only one hit in 16 at-bats

RICK HORTON
LHP, No. 49
LR, 6'2", 195 lbs.
ML Svc: 2 years
Born: 7-30-59 in
  Poughkeepsie, NY

1985 STATISTICS

W	L	ERA	G	GS	CG	SV	IP	H	R	ER	BB	SO
3	2	2.91	49	3	0	1	89.2	84	30	29	34	59

CAREER STATISTICS

W	L	ERA	G	GS	CG	SV	IP	H	R	ER	BB	SO
12	6	3.22	86	21	1	2	215.1	224	83	77	73	135

last year, but he can make contact and he helps himself by bunting.

Among the Cardinals' pitchers, he is the fastest runner and can be used for occasional pinch-running assignments.

OVERALL:

Snider: "I don't see Horton as ever being a big winner but he seems to be a reliable middle reliever who has a lot of good qualities. He often goes unnoticed because of the somewhat anonymous nature of his role, but he keeps his club in the ballgame."

PITCHING:

Kurt Kepshire was the Jekyll & Hyde pitcher on the Cardinals' staff last year. He was very good when he was good and very bad when he was bad. For a while, Kepshire alternated such performances but then, to everyone's astonishment, he lost all of his control in September.

After one start in which he threw 13 balls in 14 pitches at Chicago, Kepshire was removed from the rotation, never to return again. Furthermore, he was left off the Cardinals' post-season roster.

Kepshire possesses an above-average fastball and adequate curveball although he could use an off-speed pitch. He spent time in the Florida Instructional League after the season working on a change-up.

But when he had trouble throwing strikes, Kepshire began aiming the ball and his velocity dropped to the low 80s, making him very hittable.

At times, he was devastating but he just never seemed to relax. He assumed (correctly as it turned out) that he might be out of the rotation if he did not do well on a particular day. It may be that being omitted from the post-season roster will be the best thing for him, offering him the winter to analyze his ineffectiveness.

FIELDING, HITTING, BASERUNNING:

Kepshire's control lapses are compounded by the fact he has a very slow move to the plate when runners are on

KURT KEPSHIRE
RHP, No. 50
LR, 6'1", 180 lbs.
ML Svc: 2 years
Born: 7-3-59 in
   Bridgeport, CT

1985 STATISTICS												
W	L	ERA	G	GS	CG	SV	IP	H	R	ER	BB	SO
10	9	4.75	32	29	0	0	153.1	155	89	81	71	67

CAREER STATISTICS												
W	L	ERA	G	GS	CG	SV	IP	H	R	ER	BB	SO
16	14	4.15	49	45	2	0	262.1	255	136	121	115	138

base. He is an average fielder.

His problems extended themselves to the plate, where he hit just .118. He did, however, improve his bunting and sacrificed seven times.

OVERALL:

Kepshire does have major league talent and did win 10 games last year. What he does not have is major league consistency.

Snider: "He was squeezing the ball a little bit last season; it's an insecurity you see in a lot of young pitchers. They figure if they do badly, they won't be out there five days later.

"I don't believe that there is anything wrong with his arm. He could be a winner if he can keep his lack of control in check."

PITCHING:

Jeff Lahti came into his own last year. He was the Cardinals' top right-handed reliever while notching 19 saves in 22 opportunities, maintaining a 1.84 earned run average.

Lahti's value to the club was enhanced by the fact that just 15 of the 45 runners he inherited came in to score last year. He retired the first hitter he faced in 40 of 52 appearances.

He favors a hard-breaking slider which complements his above-average fastball. Like many other pitchers, he can be hurt if he falls behind in the count because hitters can then sit on his fastball.

That slider, however, took its toll on his shoulder sometimes and Lahti found periods when he had tenderness or could not get loose while warming up in the bullpen.

He really does not have an off-speed pitch, but a reliever rarely needs more than two pitches, particularly if he can get them both over as Lahti can. Any pitcher becomes doubly effective if he can mix his two pitches and get both of them over.

FIELDING, HITTING, BASERUNNING:

Lahti is generally in good position to field balls hit at him although his follow-through is a powerful one and can take him off target once in a while. He

JEFF LAHTI
RHP, No. 32
RR, 6'0", 180 lbs.
ML Svc: 4 years
Born: 10-8-56 in
    Oregon City, OR

1985 STATISTICS

W	L	ERA	G	GS	CG	SV	IP	H	R	ER	BB	SO
5	2	1.84	52	0	0	19	68.1	63	15	14	26	41

CAREER STATISTICS

W	L	ERA	G	GS	CG	SV	IP	H	R	ER	BB	SO
17	11	3.15	201	1	0	20	283.2	249	109	99	110	134

is alert in covering first base and he has at least an average move to first.

OVERALL:

After several years in the shadow of Bruce Sutter, Lahti got his chance to be a savior and became a good one. With the emergence of Todd Worrell and Ken Dayley in the bullpen, though, the Cardinals don't have to depend entirely on Lahti and he can get rest when he needs it.

Snider: "Jeff waited a few years for his big chance and he capitalized on it. He has increased his knowledge of pitching and should have several good years as a reliever."

HITTING:

Tito Landrum, who had excelled in post-season play before (at Baltimore in 1983), became a nationwide item last year with his lusty hitting in the World Series and National League playoffs.

During the season, Landrum had been one of the best extra men in baseball, hitting .280 with four home runs, and he continued on that tack once the play-offs began.

Previously a dead fastball hitter, Landrum was able to make adjustments last season which enabled him to handle breaking pitches better than he had in the past. He is a fanatic about keeping his body in shape, and he also has much more power now than he had when he first joined the Cardinals' organization more than a decade ago.

Landrum is most effective against lefthanded pitching and is platooned with Andy Van Slyke in right field. He is also one of baseball's top pinch-hitters, hitting .333 in that role last year.

FIELDING:

Landrum can play any of the three outfield positions and is more than ade-quate at all of them. He is an excellent defensive replacement and has made just three errors in his six-year big league career. His arm is not exceptional, but it is above average.

BASERUNNING:

For all his natural speed, Landrum is not a good basestealer although he can take the extra base on hits.

OVERALL:

As his late-season play indicated, he

TITO LANDRUM
OF, No. 21
RR, 5'11", 175 lbs.
ML Svc: 6 years
Born: 10-25-54 in
Joplin, MO

1985 STATISTICS

AVG	G	AB	R	H	2B	3B	HR	RBI	BB	SO	SB
.280	85	161	21	45	8	2	4	21	19	30	1

CAREER STATISTICS

AVG	G	AB	R	H	2B	3B	HR	RBI	BB	SO	SB
.271	417	649	81	176	29	10	10	82	51	119	12

  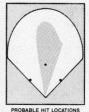

STRONG   STRONG

VS. RHP   VS. LHP   PROBABLE HIT LOCATIONS

is one of those players who seems able to rise to the occasion. There is little that is flashy about him; rather, he is a good, hard-nosed player who is not in awe of his surroundings.

Landrum should be satisfied being one of baseball's best reserves. He likely would not be as effective if he played 150 games.

Manager Whitey Herzog gives Landrum enough playing time so that he is an ef-fective pinch-hitter. Landrum returns the favor by doing a good job at what-ever he's been asked to do.

Snider: "There are few bench players who have as much versatility as Tito does. In any game, he might be called on as a defensive replacement, a pinch-runner or a pinch-hitter. He is one of the best professional replacements in the business."

HITTING:

According to manager Whitey Herzog, the best thing about Willie McGee is that no hitting coach has ever tinkered with him. Nobody would want to teach anyone to hit like McGee--he swings at a lot of bad pitches and looks futile when he flails at a curveball in the dirt, only to drive the same pitch for an extra-base hit later in the game. McGee, the league's MVP last year, is not ahead in the count when it is 2-0 and he is not behind when it is 0-2. He is highly unorthodox and terribly effective.

As a righthanded hitter (his natural side) McGee has more extra-base pop than he does as a lefty. Last season, he hit seven homers righthanded in 210 at-bats and three lefthanded in 402 trips. He is likely to chase more bad balls righthanded and he is more likely to feel for the ball lefthanded, where he can get an infield hit on the artificial surface. Nonetheless, his averages were almost identical: .356 lefty and .348 righty.

Ideally, McGee should be more patient at the plate and, indeed, his discipline was better last season. On the other hand, no one wants to tamper with his aggressive style at the plate. So many pitches that McGee hits are not strikes but who can argue when he hit .353?

McGee benefits considerably from hitting behind Vince Coleman, whose threat to run at any time means that McGee is more likely to see fastballs from over-anxious pitchers.

In addition to being the league's top hitter last season, McGee was also one of its best hitters in the clutch: he hit 17 game-winning RBIs.

BASERUNNING:

McGee does not get a good jump on the ball, does not have a good knowledge of pitchers' moves and will never slide headfirst. He runs the bases on instinct and is fast enough to outrun the ball. He stole 56 bases in 72 attempts last

WILLIE McGEE
CF, No. 51
SR, 6'1", 175 lbs.
ML Svc: 4 years
Born: 11-2-58 in
  San Francisco, CA

1985 STATISTICS

AVG	G	AB	R	H	2B	3B	HR	RBI	BB	SO	SB
.353	152	612	114	216	26	18	10	82	34	86	56

CAREER STATISTICS

AVG	G	AB	R	H	2B	3B	HR	RBI	BB	SO	SB
.308	467	2206	314	679	79	45	25	263	101	322	162

  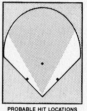

VS. RHP — STRONG   VS. LHP — STRONG   PROBABLE HIT LOCATIONS

season, but his biggest high comes from running out a triple. He had a league high of 18 in 1985.

FIELDING:

McGee's speed helps give him what is probably the best range of any center fielder in the National League. He is able to play more deeply than others at that position because he is so good at racing in on a ball (he is better coming in than going back). Sometimes, he shows a fear of crashing into walls and pulls up short to avoid contact.

His arm is strong and very accurate.

OVERALL:

Snider: "It will be interesting to see what pitchers might have learned last year about pitching to McGee. It isn't likely he will hit .353 again but his great speed and the artificial turf at Busch Stadium will make it hard for him not to hit .300."

HITTING:

Tom Nieto got the most out of a .225 average with no home runs by driving in 34 runs. Aware of his limitations as far as power and speed go, he helped himself greatly last season on offense by being able to bunt. On several occasions, manager Whitey Herzog put on the suicide squeeze with Nieto, including a successful attempt in post-season play.

Nieto hits from a low crouch, which may cut down on his power but gives him a better look at the ball. He is more of a right field hitter than a pull hitter and because of his lack of speed, opposing infields can play him very deep.

When Darrell Porter was hurt and then when he was slumping, Nieto turned in a solid month of offense from mid-May to mid-June. When Porter resumed a platoon with Nieto in the second half of the season, Tom's offense dropped considerably. He likely could be a .245 or .250 hitter with regular duty, although he would not contribute much power.

BASERUNNING:

Like many catchers, Nieto is not fast. This poses a problem when pitchers try to bunt him to second base because it takes a perfect bunt on artificial turf to accomplish the feat.

FIELDING:

Nieto has gained the respect of the Cardinals' pitching staff for the manner in which he calls a game. He spends a lot of time with each pitcher discussing strategy and can think along with each one.

He moves around behind the plate and will come inside and outside with the

TOM NIETO
C, No. 23
RR, 6'1", 193 lbs.
ML Svc: 1 year plus
Born: 10-27-60 in
Downey, CA

1985 STATISTICS

AVG	G	AB	R	H	2B	3B	HR	RBI	BB	SO	SB
.225	95	253	15	57	10	2	0	34	26	37	0

CAREER STATISTICS

AVG	G	AB	R	H	2B	3B	HR	RBI	BB	SO	SB
.239	128	339	22	81	14	2	3	46	31	55	0

  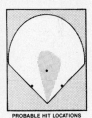

VS. RHP   VS. LHP   PROBABLE HIT LOCATIONS

glove, giving the pitcher a better target, a tactic Darrell Porter has never employed.

Nieto's throwing is sub-par, his release is slow and his mechanics are not as finely tuned as they should be. The Cardinals staff does not help him much holding the runners on base.

OVERALL:

Given that the Cardinals won 101 games, it can be said that Nieto, for whatever his deficiencies, is a winner.

Snider: "He won't embarrass you. He is a good guy to have on the ball club. He seems to be in the game all the time and he might be a better player if he had the opportunity to play more often."

HITTING:

After an impressive rookie season in 1984 when he hit .324, Pendleton saw the other side of the coin in 1985 and skidded to a .240 average. He did, however, have 69 RBIs, including 11 game-winners during the second half of the season. By that time, he had come to accept the fact that he wasn't going to have good offensive numbers and just tried to do the best he could.

Last season was a learning experience for Pendleton, who endured frustration at the major league level for the first time. He began to get back on track in the second half and became a more selective and better hitter.

Given his continued willingness to work hard, Pendleton should improve this year and settle in at the .275-.280 range. That was the average the club originally thought he would produce; they were not expecting him to maintain his .324 pace.

A lot of players today have to learn at the major league level because they are briefly force-fed in the minors, and Pendleton may be one of these. What he still has to learn is how to bat when he is ahead in the count. Too often, he would be at 2-0 and then swing at a high, outside pitch which he simply couldn't handle.

Pendleton resembles the Dodgers' Bill Madlock and, when he is going right, Pendleton's short, compact swing resembles Madlock's, too.

BASERUNNING:

Pendleton isn't tremendously fast but he has stolen 37 bases in a season and a half. He is reliable on the bases and rarely makes an error in judgment.

FIELDING:

Pendleton is not cat-like at third base but he is very aggressive and plays with flair. He has good hands and is not afraid to knock a ball down to keep it in front of him.

TERRY PENDLETON
3B, No. 9
SR, 5'9", 180 lbs.
ML Svc: 2 years
Born: 7-16-60 in
  Los Angeles, CA

1985 STATISTICS

AVG	G	AB	R	H	2B	3B	HR	RBI	BB	SO	SB
.240	149	559	56	134	16	3	5	69	37	75	17

CAREER STATISTICS

AVG	G	AB	R	H	2B	3B	HR	RBI	BB	SO	SB
.267	216	821	93	219	32	6	6	102	53	107	37

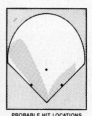

After such initial success, Pendleton may have lapsed into a period of over-confidence and laziness. He seemed to brood a bit early and it affected his performance in the field, but in the second half of the season, he was a defensive dynamo.

He could be a Gold Glove-winner in years to come and is the perfect left-side complement to shortstop Ozzie Smith, after whom he has patterned himself greatly.

OVERALL:

Pendleton has a good head on his shoulders and will continue to learn. One improvement he needs to make on offense is to hit with more authority. He had just 16 doubles last season in 559 at-bats and he should have more in spacious Busch Stadium.

Snider: "There's no substitute for experience and confidence and now Terry has both. I don't see any reason why he should not be able to hit 40 points higher this year."

HITTING:

Ozzie Smith, improving all the time on offense, became a real threat last year when he hit .276 with six home runs and 54 RBIs. His timing last season could not have been better: he hit his first-ever home run lefthanded last season, a game-winning blast off the Dodgers' Tom Niedenfuer in the fifth game of the National League playoffs.

The most notable change in Smith's lefthanded hitting last season was his ability to pull the ball. He drove many doubles and triples past some very surprised first basemen. Smith had a much quicker bat than ever before from the left side last year, partially the result of constant wrist-strengthening exercises and other drills that he tirelessly went through between games.

Nonetheless, most of his power comes from the right side, where he has hit all 13 of his regular-season home runs. But Smith's new potency lefthanded may keep defenders more honest.

This season, Smith has to be careful not to swing too hard. His best skill as a hitter is that he rarely strikes out (he fanned just 27 times in 537 at-bats last season) and he must remember that getting on base is everything.

BASERUNNING:

Smith is one of the smartest baserunners in the game. Traditionally, he has one of the highest ratios for thefts in the business. Last season, he stole 31 bases in 39 attempts (a 79.4% success ratio). He rarely steals a base unless his team needs it.

He is almost peerless in taking the extra base.

FIELDING:

Last season, Smith won his sixth consecutive Gold Glove. He is good enough to be the flashiest shortstop in baseball. His spectacular fielding may save the Cardinals as many as 100 runs a

OZZIE SMITH
SS, No. 1
SR, 5'10", 150 lbs.
ML Svc: 8 years
Born: 12-26-54 in
Mobile, AL

1985 STATISTICS

AVG	G	AB	R	H	2B	3B	HR	RBI	BB	SO	SB
.276	158	537	70	148	22	3	6	54	65	27	31

CAREER STATISTICS

AVG	G	AB	R	H	2B	3B	HR	RBI	BB	SO	SB
.243	1164	4225	516	1025	160	34	13	320	449	246	272

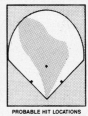

VS. RHP   VS. LHP   PROBABLE HIT LOCATIONS

year. He never misses a routine play and makes the difficult ones appear simple.

His arm, which is barely above average, was hurt last season but he compensated for the injury by using a quicker release.

His diving stops and quick moves have made his defensive play a difficult standard for others to meet.

OVERALL:

Snider: "Much of Ozzie's talent is natural, but there is also a lot he has had to work for. His diligence in trying to improve his lefthanded hitting is one example and it paid off for him last season.

"Defensively, he is still the best to have come along in a long time and his natural abilities as a shortstop will make it hard for anyone to play the position with his kind of style.

"If he can continue to put together the kind of offensive numbers he produced last year, he'll head right for the Hall of Fame."

PITCHING:

Until 1985, there were many who questioned whether John Tudor had enough stuff to be a 20-game winner. Last year, Tudor took full advantage of the National League's number one defense and the league's most productive offense to have the best season of his career.

While he had been an effective pitcher in previous years (he has never had a losing season), Tudor was simply overwhelming in 1985. He started off the season poorly; in early June his record was 1-7. Then a high school friend who had been following Tudor on cable television noticed that he wasn't freezing his front leg long enough before delivering the ball to the plate, thus causing his leg to arrive well before his arm released the ball. Tudor corrected the problem.

After that, hitters in the league agreed: Tudor's 1985 fastball was faster than it had ever been before.

He is able to pitch with only a semblance of a breaking ball because his change-up is so outstanding and because he actually throws two kinds of fastballs, both of which move.

This lefthander rarely throws harder than 85 MPH, which is barely average for a major league pitcher, but his change-up makes his fastball seem even faster. He is the type of pitcher whom hitters don't mind batting against at first because he is not overpowering. Then they wind up going back to the bench while wondering, "Why didn't I hit that guy?"

Tudor's fastball/change-up combination means that hitters can't sit on his change-up. And, as he demonstrated last year in post-season play, he can make

JOHN TUDOR
LHP, No. 48
LL, 6'0", 185 lbs.
ML Svc: 7 years
Born: 2-2-54 in
   Schenectady, NY

1985 STATISTICS												
W	L	ERA	G	GS	CG	SV	IP	H	R	ER	BB	SO
21	8	1.93	36	36	14	0	275	209	68	59	49	169
CAREER STATISTICS												
W	L	ERA	G	GS	CG	SV	IP	H	R	ER	BB	SO
72	51	3.31	174	162	41	1	1123.2	1054	463	414	313	668

lefthanded hitters looks particularly helpless.

FIELDING:

Tudor's delivery leaves him in perfect position to make plays on balls hit back at him. His move to first is only average.

He is a first-rate competitor at the plate and is able to help himself by being able to bunt and by putting the bat on the ball.

OVERALL:

Snider: "He has such command of his pitches; it's very difficult to hit against a pitcher who can get more than one pitch over at a time. He has just become a quality pitcher. If he can do this year what he did the last three-quarters of last season, he shouldn't have any problems."

HITTING:

Still a player with considerable potential, Andy Van Slyke is running out of chances. The Cardinals expect him to be more than a .260 hitter and, unfortunately, that is what he has been for the last three years.

Van Slyke has everything going for him--size, speed, throwing arm, power--but all too often he finds himself hitting behind in the count after taking a couple of fastballs down the heart of the plate while he's been looking for a breaking ball.

Perhaps he puts too much pressure on himself or perhaps he is "thinking" too much when he is at bat. But it is clear that he takes pitches he just is not ready to hit.

Van Slyke has been platooned for most of his time in St. Louis, having had a rough time against lefthanded pitching. He can, however, take care of a pitch in his wheelhouse when he is ready for it; his 13 home runs last year were the second highest total on the club.

At this point, what he needs to do is relax. He squeezes the bat too much out of anxiety and he worries about each appearance. Van Slyke might try to have some fun. He has a good eye, but he's got to realize that there are pitches coming in that are meant for hitting and he cannot continue to fall behind 0-2 or 1-2 every time he's at the plate.

BASERUNNING:

As unaggressive as Van Slyke is at bat, he is just the opposite on the bases. He is among the top percentage basestealers in the league, having stolen 34 in 40 tries last year.

FIELDING:

Van Slyke has one of the strongest,

ANDY VAN SLYKE
INF/OF, No. 18
LR, 5'11", 175 lbs.
ML Svc: 3 years
Born: 12-21-60 in
Utica, NY

1985 STATISTICS

AVG	G	AB	R	H	2B	3B	HR	RBI	BB	SO	SB
.259	146	424	61	110	25	6	13	55	47	54	34

CAREER STATISTICS

AVG	G	AB	R	H	2B	3B	HR	RBI	BB	SO	SB
.255	384	1094	157	279	56	15	28	143	156	189	83

VS. RHP

VS. LHP

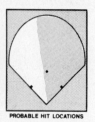
PROBABLE HIT LOCATIONS

most accurate right field arms in the game and closes off gaps with his great speed. He finally settled into one position last year after bouncing around for two years, although he could probably be one of the best center fielders in baseball, too.

OVERALL:

The time for Van Slyke to improve is now. The Cardinals certainly have given him enough chances.

Snider: "It is up to him to make use of his opportunity. He's got to be himself at the plate. It looks as though he is pressing, trying too hard to shake home runs out of his bat and somehow afraid there aren't any. If a player has power, then it will come through."

ST. LOUIS CARDINALS

PITCHING:

Last season, from the depths of the Cardinals minor league system, stepped a tall, dark, handsome, mild-mannered flamethrower. This former Bible student turned tiger threw one overhand fastball after another past the Kansas City Royals in the fifth game of the World Series to strike out all six hitters he faced.

Todd Worrell was unsuccessful as a starting pitcher for nearly three years in the minors. But once converted to a reliever by his minor league manager Jim Fregosi, the sting was on. His fastball has been clocked as high as 94-95 MPH and he routinely throws at 92 MPH.

Worrell also throws a hard slider, although that pitch is not nearly as effective as his fastball. It probably wouldn't hurt him to have an off-speed pitch as a third pitch, but that will come later.

There isn't a whole lot of mystery to Worrell. No matter what the count, he will throw his fastball. His attitude and poise seem uncommon for a man with just a month of major league experience. He so impressed Whitey Herzog that the manager was quick to project him as the next Lee Smith. Herzog went so far as to compare him with Rich Gossage.

There is little doubt that the Cards are hoping that Worrell is their main man in the bullpen this season, ahead of Jeff Lahti.

FIELDING, HITTING, BASERUNNING:

Worrell is reasonably agile for a tall man, witness his play on a bunt in the sixth game of the World Series. He has batted just once in professional baseball, so it is difficult to get a

TODD WORRELL
RHP, No. 38
RR, 6'5", 200 lbs.
ML Svc: less than 1 year
Born: 9-28-59 in
   Arcadia, CA

1985 STATISTICS

W	L	ERA	G	GS	CG	SV	IP	H	R	ER	BB	SO
3	0	2.91	17	0	0	5	21.2	17	7	7	7	17

CAREER STATISTICS

W	L	ERA	G	GS	CG	SV	IP	H	R	ER	BB	SO
3	0	2.91	17	0	0	5	21.2	17	7	7	7	17

handle on him there.

OVERALL:

Worrell's progress will be watched under a magnifying glass this season. With so little experience as a reliever, there is simply no way of knowing how effective he can be over a stretch. Of course, based on what the Royals saw during the World Series, the projection would have to be extremely positive.

Were he not to succeed, however, he would not be the first flash-in-the-pan in baseball nor the first name buried in its lore. But somehow one gets the feeling that it will not be that way for Todd Worrell.

Snider: "After last October, I really can't wait to see him pitch again. He was simply brilliant and it is going to be fun to see how he does this year.

"It would be a fast learning experience for him to get a little touched up once in a while. Baseball can be a humbling game and it doesn't matter whether you are a newcomer or an old-timer."

STEVE BRAUN
INF/OF, No. 26
LR, 5'10", 180 lbs.
ML Svc: 15 years
Born: 5-8-48 in
    Trenton, NJ

HITTING, FIELDING, BASERUNNING:

Steve Braun was the Cardinals' top lefthanded pinch-hitter last year, although his statistics weren't up to his usual standards. Batting almost exclusively against righthanded pitching, he was 11-for-45 as a pinch-hitter and he hit just .239 for the season.

Beginning his sixth season with the Cardinals, Braun comes to the park early almost every day for extra batting practice. In the past, he also has engaged a hypnotist to keep his thoughts along positive lines.

Braun is tough to strike out because he doesn't have a big swing. He has a good batting eye and draws his share of walks. He is one of the better students of the game and knows what to expect.

For the most part, he is a straightaway hitter although he can pull a ball if the occasion demands it.

He is not fast although he knows how to run. Manager Whitey Herzog routinely replaces him with a pinch-runner when he gets on base. Braun will start a half-dozen or so games in the outfield every year as Herzog seeks to keep him sharp.

OVERALL:

His pinch-hit, game-winning homer at Los Angeles just after the All-Star break might have been one of the biggest hits of the Cardinals' season. Braun hit .313 in the second half of the season to cement his job for yet another year.

Snider: "I marvel at guys like Braun who can come off the bench and do what he does."

IVAN DeJESUS
SS, No. 11
RR, 5'11", 185 lbs.
ML Svc: 11 years
Born: 1-9-53 in
    Santurce, PR

HITTING, BASERUNNING, FIELDING:

Ivan DeJesus, who was acquired by the Cardinals as insurance for Ozzie Smith last season, got to the plate only 72 times. After having been a full-time player for eight years, he produced very little as a part-timer.

When he did have the opportunity to play, it was clear that he was rusty. It is possible that he could still be a valuable player if he ever regains his regular status.

DeJesus has trouble with hard stuff and with breaking balls away. In his prime, DeJesus was one of baseball's best number eight hitters.

DeJesus is what is known as a contact hitter and is adept at the hit-and-run.

He is not a fast runner, although he is sure and steady when on base and rarely runs into an out.

DeJesus' defensive skills dropped off steadily in 1984 and he rarely got the chance to play his normal position (shortstop) last year because Ozzie Smith played in 158 games. DeJesus was tried at third base but did not seem particularly well suited there and he got in no work at second base.

OVERALL:

If DeJesus is to finish his career as an extra man, he will have to learn to play second and third base better.

Snider: "Ivan can still be a hitter with pop in his bat--especially against lefthanded pitchers. He is a hard worker who would be a valuable addition to any ballclub."

BRIAN HARPER
OF, No. 25
RR, 6'2", 195 lbs.
ML Svc: 4 years
Born: 10-16-59 in
    Los Angeles, CA

HITTING, FIELDING, BASERUNNING:

Brian Harper was one of the most effective Cardinals against lefthanded pitching last season and delivered several critical hits even though he batted just 52 times. His most memorable hit was the pinch-single which put the Cards in position to win the sixth game of the World Series--before the Royals rallied for two runs in the ninth inning.

On some teams, Harper would be a platoon player, but he gets little chance to play in a solid St. Louis lineup. He is one of the most versatile Cardinals as he can play third base, first base, left field and right field, in addition to his original position as catcher. He is only adequate at all these positions, however.

OVERALL:

Harper is gradually learning how to be a major league bench player. He is one of the hardest workers on the club. He is always in shape and is considered a good "role" player in that he accepts the fact he will play little but doesn't complain about his fate.

TOM LAWLESS
INF, No. 20
RR, 5'11", 170 lbs.
ML Svc: 3 years
Born: 12-19-56 in
    Erie, PA

HITTING, BASERUNNING, FIELDING:

Tom Lawless is a light-hitting veteran (of the Cincinnati and Montreal organizations) in spite of his having two game-winners among the 12 hits he had last year in limited duty. He probably is best-known as the player Cincinnati traded to get Pete Rose from Montreal.

Lawless' value is his speed. He was the Cardinals' primary pinch-runner last year and scored several important runs.

He can play second base or third base with above-average skill and may have a lengthy career as a utilityman if he can improve his hitting a bit. He is most effective against lefthanded pitching and is overmatched against some righthanders.

OVERALL:

Many utility players chafe and complain that they should be playing regularly. Lawless is not like that and accepts his role, though it is a small one in the Cardinals' scheme.

Snider: "It's a rude awakening for some players to be classified as utility players--but it's either that or the minor leagues. Lawless is not going to be a regular. He's not that type of player."

SAN DIEGO PADRES

HITTING:

Kurt Bevacqua became an instant celebrity with a .417 average in the 1984 World Series, but his excellence as a pinch-hitter waned last year. In fact, he hit better (.250) as a position player than he did in the pinch. As a pinch-hitter, he hit below .200.

Age may be taking its toll on this popular veteran, but Bevacqua's value goes beyond what he can do in clutch situations. While it may not get him too many extra seasons on the roster, he is a team leader and can keep the clubhouse loose.

He is a good fastball hitter who is especially proficient on the high heaters. Successful pitchers keep the ball low and make him chase breaking balls. Kurt is not a home run hitter but he has good power to the alleys. For years, he was more effective off the bench than in any other role. His 80 career pinch-hits have him knocking on the Top 20 list, but he was 5-for-26 as a pinch-hitter last season.

BASERUNNING:

Bevacqua uses veteran savvy to be an effective baserunner, but he is not blessed with speed and is no threat to steal a base. In fact, he didn't even try last year.

FIELDING:

Bevacqua won't hurt you at first base, but as an outfielder or a third baseman, his arm is barely adequate. He is strictly a fill-in player and is not for defensive purposes. He is adequate, at best.

KURT BEVACQUA
INF/PH, No. 7
RR, 6'2", 190 lbs.
ML Svc: 15 years
Born: 1-23-48 in
   Miami Beach, FL

1985 STATISTICS

AVG	G	AB	R	H	2B	3B	HR	RBI	BB	SO	SB
.239	71	138	17	33	6	0	3	25	25	17	0

CAREER STATISTICS

AVG	G	AB	R	H	2B	3B	HR	RBI	BB	SO	SB
.236	970	2117	214	499	90	11	15	275	221	329	12

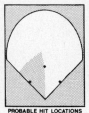

STRONG | STRONG | PROBABLE HIT LOCATIONS
VS. RHP | VS. LHP |

OVERALL:

Bevacqua has managed to log a lot of time in the majors without really doing anything well. He's made a career of it by being a strong team man and, until last year, a valuable pinch-hitter. It seems like his days are numbered because he is keeping a promising youngster off the roster.

Snider: "It's difficult to keep a guy around exclusively to be a pinch-hitter, but Kurt has done a good job at it over the years. He slipped a bit last year, but it's good to have him around for morale purposes. He accepts his role and has a lot of fun. The Padres need to do some reshuffling and Kurt's card may be in the deck."

PITCHING:

Pitching greatness has been predicted for Dave Dravecky, who did nothing last year to dissuade that notion. He has excellent stuff and should be better than a 13-11 pitcher. There are those who feel that he is best-suited for relief.

He is definitely one of the better lefthanders in the league, yet his record doesn't show it. Dravecky has the repertoire and the staying power to be an effective starter and a durable arm that would serve him well in the bullpen. He has an improved fastball, good breaking pitches and control.

Dravecky's fastball and slider make him tough on righthanders as well. He is especially difficult for lefthanders because he is a smart pitcher with a variety of pitches.

His strength is getting ahead of the hitters. If anything, he could improve on his change-up. But that isn't critical because he has so much movement on his other pitches and good command on the mound.

FIELDING, HITTING, BASERUNNING:

Dave is a decent fielder because he's a good athlete with sharp reflexes. He has a good move to first and is above average as a fielder.

He is not an automatic out at the plate, belting a double and a triple last year. He could help himself by working on his bunting.

DAVE DRAVECKY
LHP, No. 43
RL, 6'1", 193 lbs.
ML Svc: 4 years
Born: 2-14-56 in
   Youngstown, OH

1985 STATISTICS
W	L	ERA	G	GS	CG	SV	IP	H	R	ER	BB	SO
13	11	2.93	34	31	7	0	214.2	200	79	20	57	105

CAREER STATISTICS
W	L	ERA	G	GS	CG	SV	IP	H	R	ER	BB	SO
41	32	2.37	143	83	19	10	660	592	247	224	185	309

OVERALL:

Dravecky is the type of pitcher who is in demand around the league--a lefthander who can get the ball over the plate. There is every indication that he could blossom into a big winner. The Padres think so, too, making him almost exclusively a starter last year after he served primarily as a reliever in 1984. His 2.93 ERA suggests it wasn't a mistake.

Snider: "Dave should be a good starter for years once he settles into the role. Right now, he's young enough and strong enough to keep you in it until Goose can take over. I regard him as one of the best pitchers on the staff because he's a good competitor with a gung-ho attitude for baseball you like to see. He has good instincts for the game."

HITTING:

The departure of Alan Wiggins provided more playing time for Tim Flannery last season. He pounced on the opportunity with his best major league season at the plate. He always had a reputation for being better suited to a part-time role, yet Flannery played in more games and had more at-bats last year than ever before. He seems to have responded well to regular duty.

Flannery is a spray hitter who likes the good, high fastball. Because his bat speed is slow, flamethrowers bother him. It also makes Flannery vulnerable to the inside pitch.

He has become a much better pull hitter than he had been, and can keep the outfielders honest. In the past, he hit exclusively to left field with the fastball, which enabled left fielders to play him shallow.

After all these years of sitting and learning, he has become an intelligent hitter. He is especially adept at belting breaking balls. He also has a good eye and has the patience to wait out a pitcher for a walk.

BASERUNNING:

Flannery is no threat to steal a base but is an aggressive runner who likes to break up double plays. He knows what he can and can't do.

FIELDING:

His fielding can best be described as unspectacular and efficient. He is best-suited to second base because his arm is not strong. He worked at his fielding to become average defensively. His glove is dependable. He is not good at turning the double play.

OVERALL:

Tim is a player who plays up to his

TIM FLANNERY
2B/3B, No. 11
LR, 5'11, 176 lbs.
ML Svc: 7 years
Born: 9-29-57 in
Tulsa, OK

1985 STATISTICS

AVG	G	AB	R	H	2B	3B	HR	RBI	BB	SO	SB
.281	126	384	50	108	14	3	1	40	58	39	2

CAREER STATISTICS

AVG	G	AB	R	H	2B	3B	HR	RBI	BB	SO	SB
.255	580	1529	159	390	51	18	6	134	144	150	12

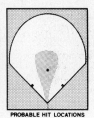

VS. RHP   VS. LHP   PROBABLE HIT LOCATIONS

potential. He got more mileage out of his ability last year than anyone could have expected. A good guy to have around as a jack-of-all-trades, he is probably better suited to a utility role over the long haul. He will stay in the majors by refining that role, but he played well enough last season to make some people change their minds about his ability as a regular. He topped the club in on-base percentage and combined with Jerry Royster to give the Padres more production out of the position than they enjoyed with Wiggins. He definitely bears consideration as a regular.

Snider: "He didn't look all that good when I saw him, but he obviously performed well over the course of a season. I don't know that he is an everyday man, but he's a self-made player who uses all of the talent he's got. I like to see that."

HITTING:

Steve Garvey concluded the 1985 season with a rush which salvaged the year for him. As consistent as he has been, 1985 was not a good one by Garvey standards. Everyone has come to expect so much from him.

Garvey showed some power in his swing and was able to drill more home runs than he had since 1980. In swinging for the long ball, his average dropped and it took a nine-game hitting streak at the conclusion of the season to lift his mark to .281.

Garvey remains an aggressive, productive hitter, one who always thrives on pressure situations. He is confidence personified at the plate and can hit any pitch and any pitcher when he's in a groove.

The age factor (he is 37 years old) comes up now when he is in a slump. The cold periods seem to occur more frequently, especially when those around him aren't keeping pitchers honest. When he dips into a slump, Garvey will chase low and outside breaking pitches, making him the antithesis of the disciplined hitter that he is.

BASERUNNING:

He's aggressive on the basepaths but absolutely no threat to steal. He knows how to avoid trouble, always pays attention and is alert to sense the break up of the double play.

FIELDING:

Garvey has always had a high fielding percentage and holds the major league record for consecutive games without an error at first base. Still, he cannot be labeled as a great fielder.

His arm is notoriously average and Garvey has difficulty stretching for the high throws (he's more stumpy than slender). One of the precious commodities of an infield is a first baseman who can dig out low throws and can be counted on

STEVE GARVEY
1B, No. 6
RR, 5'10", 190 lbs.
ML Svc: 16 years
Born: 12-22-48 in
Tampa, FL

1985 STATISTICS
AVG	G	AB	R	H	2B	3B	HR	RBI	BB	SO	SB
.281	162	654	80	184	34	6	17	81	35	67	0

CAREER STATISTICS
AVG	G	AB	R	H	2B	3B	HR	RBI	BB	SO	SB
.298	2150	8202	1080	2441	415	43	250	1218	455	921	82

  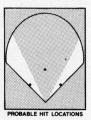

VS. RHP   VS. LHP   PROBABLE HIT LOCATIONS

to catch what he is thrown. Garvey does all of that.

OVERALL:

Players like Mr. Consistency (Garvey) and and Mr. October (Reggie Jackson) tend to be judged harshly because of the high standards which they have set over the years. Steve Garvey comes to the ballpark every day to play baseball. He was the only National League player to start in all 162 games last season. It might have been an off-year for him, but it would have been a great one for most.

Snider: "In particular, his average was down. That may have something to do with who was hitting behind him. He was pitched around very often last season. When that happens, a hitter begins to chase bad pitches. A guy like Garvey, who knows that he can carry a team for a stretch, may have felt some of the burden for the Padres.

"His determination and intensity, however, never waver."

PITCHING:

It was not a great year for the San Diego Padres, but you couldn't judge it from Goose's statistics. He missed more than a month following arthroscopic knee surgery last August, yet he ended the year with one more save than he had in the Padres' pennant-winning 1984 season. Sure, he's lost some zip off his fastball, but he is 34 years old and he can still throw heat with the best of them. Actually, the best of them try to throw heat like him.

He may not pop the fastball with the 96 MPH consistency he once did, but he remains one of the more imposing and intimidating pitchers in the game. He is still very much a power pitcher, but his curve is effective enough against right-handed batters to make his fastball look even better.

Goose still rares back and throws, daring batters to hit the ball. The man thrives on pressure and has the stats to prove it. If he has lost something, he is sure fooling a lot of people. However, he does seem much more effective when he inherits a tough situation than when he starts an inning from scratch and has time to think about it.

FIELDING, HITTING, BASERUNNING:

The Goose's strong suit is pitching, period. He was hitless in 11 trips last year and he never has been regarded as cat-like off the mound. He is below average as a fielder because he's so off-balance after his release. This gives batters the inspiration to bunt on him, and they do.

His pickoff move is no threat, so you can run on him if you reach base. Getting on base: that's the secret. The velocity of his pitches allows him a poor move and he will throw to first base often to compensate further. But

RICH GOSSAGE
RHP, No. 54
RR, 6'3", 220 lbs.
ML Svc: 14 years
Born: 7-5-51 in
    Colorado Springs, CO

```
1985 STATISTICS
W  L  ERA  G  GS CG SV  IP    H    R   ER  BB  SO
5  3  1.82 50  0   0 26  79    64   21  16  17  52
CAREER STATISTICS
W  L  ERA  G   GS  CG SV  IP     H    R   ER  BB   SO
96 82 2.80 680 37  16 257 1417.2 1127 495 441 572 1212
```

runners aren't fooled. They know he's not serious about it.

OVERALL:

Goose was the glue that held the 1984 champions together. Not only because of his stout relief, but because of his presence. The Padres felt a lot more confident when they took the field. It also worked wonders with the starting pitchers knowing he was there to back them up. The starting pitching flourished again last year and Goose was his usual ominous self, so they or he can't be faulted for the collapse of the 1985 Padres.

Snider: "Consistency is hard to come by in a reliever, but he has been remarkable, posting an ERA under 2.90 and at least 18 saves the last nine years.

"He can still bring it with the best. In recent years, he's lost a little off his fastball, but he remains one of the few guys who can remain consistently effective by being a thrower. He had surgery last year, yet still came back and did a job. If he had a partner or two in the bullpen, it would take a lot of pressure off him, though he seems to handle it well."

HITTING:

Tony Gwynn was in a slump last season. He hit only .317. When you compare that to his .351 of the previous year, it's easy to see that even when in a slump, Tony Gwynn has a magic wand.

Nobody believes Tony was a lesser hitter last year. If anything, respect for him has grown. He hit even though the batting order the Padres used last season just wasn't the same as it was during their banner year--it did not click as well without Alan Wiggins. Gwynn also managed to hit .317 after facing pitchers who had learned their lessons in 1984; they were much more cautious with him last year. Gwynn finished fast by batting .364 over the final month and belting a career high in doubles and home runs.

He's a straightaway hitter with a slight crouch. He hits the fastball as well as anyone, using his tremendous bat speed to bring his bat snapping through the strike zone. Gwynn is a marvel at smashing a hanging breaking ball.

His vast improvement into becoming one of the league's premier hitters has been attributed to learning how to handle the low breaking stuff. He has a keen eye and has the discipline not to go after bad pitches. He waits for a good pitch and he usually hits it.

Tony also has shown an improvement in handling lefthanders and in toughening up with two strikes. He is a notorious line drive hitter who uses all fields and could develop into power hitter.

Like most great hitters, he could hit the long ball more, but he prefers to go for the high average and get on base for the big boys behind him.

BASERUNNING:

Considering his decent speed, Gwynn is not a good basestealer and is caught more often than he is successful. He runs well to first and gets some infield hits that way.

TONY GWYNN
OF, No. 19
LL, 5'11", 206 lbs.
ML Svc: 4 years
Born: 5-9-60 in
  Los Angeles, CA

1985 STATISTICS											
AVG	G	AB	R	H	2B	3B	HR	RBI	BB	SO	SB
.317	154	622	90	197	29	5	6	46	45	33	14

CAREER STATISTICS											
AVG	G	AB	R	H	2B	3B	HR	RBI	BB	SO	SB
.325	452	1722	245	559	74	19	13	171	141	93	62

  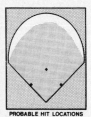

VS. RHP   VS. LHP   PROBABLE HIT LOCATIONS

FIELDING:

Gwynn is a careful and improving fielder; he isn't a typical right fielder insofar as he lacks a strong throwing arm. His arm is merely average, but he compensates for it by being accurate and by getting a good jump on balls. He plays the walls well.

OVERALL:

Gwynn's accomplishments at the plate in only two full years as a regular have been astounding. He figures to be a threat for the batting title for many years. If he adds a power dimension, look out.

Snider: "Tony is about as consistent a hitter as you can be. People expected a big dropoff after his .351, but I think that he actually became a better hitter last year. Pitchers just got a lot more careful with him, and he did not have a lot of support, yet he was still able to do well. He's only going to get better."

PITCHING:

In THE SCOUTING REPORT: 1985, it was reported that there are many who believe that Andy Hawkins "will explode into one of the greatest pitchers in the game." He came close last season, at least for half a season. He raised eyebrows by going 11-0 at the start of the season. He showed tenacity in overcoming the mounting early-season pressure to continue winning with a fluid motion, a sinking fastball and an improved slider.

And whereas he was a nibbler in the past, he started to make the best use of his ample stuff by challenging hitters in 1985. It seemed that all he needed for success was confidence, and he got that late in 1984. His development made it easy to forget Ed Whitson.

FIELDING, HITTING, BASERUNNING:

Hawkins improved considerably as a fielder last year, making only one error during the entire season and being more aggressive on difficult chances.

He is not a good hitter, but he can help himself with the bat because he bunts well. In fact, Andy topped the Padres with 13 sacrifice hits. A lumbering runner, he's more of a detriment on the bases than an asset.

OVERALL:

Hawkins blossomed from a prospect to a standout last year, so the next step is to have two great halves instead of only one. There is every reason to be-

ANDY HAWKINS
RHP, No. 40
RR, 6'3", 205 lbs.
ML Svc: 4 years
Born: 1-21-60 in
Waco, TX

1985 STATISTICS

W	L	ERA	G	GS	CG	SV	IP	H	R	ER	BB	SO
18	8	3.15	33	33	5	0	228.2	229	88	80	65	69

CAREER STATISTICS

W	L	ERA	G	GS	CG	SV	IP	H	R	ER	BB	SO
33	29	3.61	105	84	12	0	558	544	261	224	212	230

lieve that will happen because he progressed more quickly than he was expected to once he got a full-time job in the rotation.

A blister and a circulatory problem contributed to 40 days without a victory in the second half, so staying healthy is also vital to his emergence as a star. He became a competitor in 1985 and that should serve him well in the future.

Snider: "I feel his experience in the post-season games of 1984 made him a better pitcher last year. You could see the confidence, especially early in the season when the club was doing well. His second-half dropoff was more or less indicative of how the team went: it can be infectious. But he's a tough kid with a good makeup who will quietly take his place among the league's top starters."

SAN DIEGO PADRES

PITCHING:

It appears that LaMarr Hoyt has finally found his control. He has always
had control of his pitches; in fact, it
is his trademark. What he really needed
was control of his appetite. He managed
to trim down considerably for the 1985
season and was so happy with his pitching at the lighter weight that he has
vowed to show up this spring even
thinner.

Pinpoint control is his main ally. He
walked only one batter every ten innings
last year, giving him a large margin for
error in yielding hits.

Although he has an overpowering presence on the mound, Hoyt's stuff isn't
overwhelming. His strength over the
years has been the ability to master all
of his pitches, and he has quite a few.

Good movement on his fastballs and
sliders coupled with impeccable control
and determination make him a an effective pitcher.

Somewhat streaky, LaMarr won 14 in a
row at the end of his Cy Young season
and tied Andy Hawkins's club record with
11 straight last summer. At the end of
1984, the White Sox were contemplating
bullpen duty for the heavy hurler, but
the trade to San Diego took care of that
idea, and last year he made the NL even
more of a pitcher's league.

FIELDING, HITTING, BASERUNNING:

Hoyt has never been a good fielder,
and he never had to worry about running
and hitting until last year. Well, the
big guy didn't scare anyone with his
presence on the basepaths and his hitting was nothing to brag about. But he

LaMARR HOYT
RHP, No. 31
RR, 6'2", 244 lbs.
ML Svc: 6 years
Born: 1-1-55 in
Columbia, SC

1985 STATISTICS
W	L	ERA	G	GS	CG	SV	IP	H	R	ER	BB	SO
16	8	3.47	31	31	8	0	210.1	210	85	81	20	83

CAREER STATISTICS
W	L	ERA	G	GS	CG	SV	IP	H	R	ER	BB	SO
90	57	3.83	209	147	47	10	1152.1	1243	537	491	211	596

helped the Padres by learning how to put
down a bunt. In fact, his dozen sacrifice hits ranked second on the club.

OVERALL:

The Padres felt they pulled a coup by
wrestling Hoyt from the White Sox, and
he proved them accurate by thriving in
new surroundings. He and Hawkins gave
the club a new one-two punch, and there
is no reason to believe LaMarr will not
hold up his end of the bargain for years
to come. The McDonald's people know all
about quality beef.

Snider: "Hoyt has good low stuff, so
changing leagues didn't make a difference. He's a pitcher who knows what he
is doing all the time, so he can win
anywhere. If anybody had known Hoyt and
Hawkins would win 34 games, they would
have expected the Padres to repeat. But
the long relievers were so ineffective
that the ball didn't get to the Goose in
enough winning situations."

HITTING:

The number of home runs Terry Kennedy hit dipped last year, but his average and RBI total climbed on the heels of a disappointing 1984 season. Catching too much may be a factor in his inconsistency. If he's still with the Padres this year, he could someday succeed Garvey at first base, where he could concentrate on offensive production.

He crouches in a slightly closed stance, and when he is hitting well, anything can be pulled with authority. But he's only a shadow of the hitter who was so productive in 1982-83, totaling 195 RBIs those two years as compared to 131 the last two. He is simply not as aggressive at the plate. Part of that may be attributed to his overall unhappiness in San Diego.

BASERUNNING:

Kennedy is a liability on the basepaths because of his ponderous size and a history of knee problems. He is a throwback to the catchers of old: lumbering and powerful.

FIELDING:

While he is showing some improvement, Kennedy is not strong defensively. His footwork is not good and his release is too slow.

Runners test him frequently even though he has a strong arm. He can't get rid of the ball fast enough. The Padres' pitching staff does not hold runners on well, and that does not help him. He has, however, shown considerable improvement in calling a game.

OVERALL:

"Teke" might benefit from a change of

TERRY KENNEDY
C, No. 16
LR, 6'4", 224 lbs.
ML Svc: 7 years
Born: 6-4-56 in
    Euclid, OH

1985 STATISTICS

AVG	G	AB	R	H	2B	3B	HR	RBI	BB	SO	SB
.261	143	532	54	139	27	1	10	74	31	102	0

CAREER STATISTICS

AVG	G	AB	R	H	2B	3B	HR	RBI	BB	SO	SB
.273	821	2941	301	802	155	9	70	420	201	491	3

  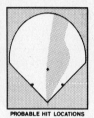

VS. RHP   VS. LHP   PROBABLE HIT LOCATIONS

scenery. He has been a workhorse catcher for the Padres, but he doesn't seem to be enjoying his job in San Diego. It is difficult enough to be a catcher without being unhappy as well.

He simply has been having far too many dry spells for a catcher once touted as the next Johnny Bench. He's good, but perhaps all those expectations have contributed to his decline.

Snider: "Something is holding him back, but he is a tough player who has the ability to bounce back. Offensively, he has been held back by an uppercut swing which he should work on. He just pops up too much.

"But he's a hard worker and he knows what he has to do to become a better hitter."

PITCHING:

Craig Lefferts did not allow even one run in 10 post-season innings in 1984, so big things were expected of him in 1985. There were no big things happening for him, however.

Lefferts is a one-pitch pitcher. The screwball, which had brought him attention the previous season, was not being thrown consistently for strikes last year. He also had elbow trouble in the spring of 1985 which made him lose some zip on his fastball, and without that, hitters sat back and waited for his inconsistent off-speed stuff.

His specialty pitch had taken him a long way. The screwball had turned him from a journeyman pitcher to an untouchable star in the NLCS and World Series two years ago. For that week in October, Lefferts was elevated from obscurity to a quality middle reliever. Last season, he took the train back to Obscurityville.

Manager Dick Williams still had enough confidence in him to use him in 60 games, and in return, Lefferts won seven.

Overall, though, Lefferts and the other middle relievers provided a convenient excuse when the Padres failed to live up to expectations last year.

FIELDING, HITTING, BASERUNNING:

As a middle reliever, Lefferts seldom bats. He's an adequate fielder, nothing more.

CRAIG LEFFERTS
LHP, No. 37
LL, 6'1", 196 lbs.
ML Svc: 3 years
Born: 9-29-57 in
  Munich, W.GER

1985 STATISTICS

W	L	ERA	G	GS	CG	SV	IP	H	R	ER	BB	SO
7	6	3.35	60	0	0	2	83.1	75	34	31	30	48

CAREER STATISTICS

W	L	ERA	G	GS	CG	SV	IP	H	R	ER	BB	SO
13	14	2.81	178	5	0	13	278	243	98	87	83	164

OVERALL:

When hurlers come up with a specialty pitch, they can fool some of the hitters some of the time. That luck ran out for Lefferts last season, but then again, he raised expectations with his flawless post-season performances in 1984.

If he can continue to baffle hitters with his screwball, there's no reason why he can't be an effective pitcher for many years. The key, however, is to regain his premium fastball because one-pitch pitchers seldom survive.

Snider: "Here's a guy who got hit a lot early in his career, so he came up with a pitch to save his major league life. He reminds me of my own former teammate Joe Black, who came up with a slider to become an effective reliever with Brooklyn. Lefferts has got to keep his scroogie in a non-hittable zone, something he wasn't able to do very much last season."

POWER POTENTIAL

HITTING:

Carmelo Martinez continued to fool the experts last year. It was originally thought the Cubs made a mistake by letting Martinez get away after he showed flashes of power in 1984. Then he was terribly inconsistent in post-season performance, in the NLCS and the 1984 World Series (he hit .176 in both) and he again raised doubts.

But Martinez rallied from an early-season injury last season to lead the Padres in home runs and game-winning RBIs, so he's doing something right.

Martinez has a long, looping swing that usually results in a lot of strike-outs. He cut down on those last year by becoming more disciplined at the plate, though he is still more or less a free-swinger.

Martinez is generally going for the fences when he is at the plate; pitchers should know that breaking pitches drive him crazy, and they would be crazy to send him a fastball down the middle of the plate.

The Padres have had so many disappointments in other areas of the team that they have to be careful not to become too impatient with Martinez. This year represents his third major league season, and he has clearly shown the potential to develop into a legitimate power hitter.

BASERUNNING:

Martinez is a poor baserunner who cannot steal and is prone to judgment mistakes on the basepaths. He lumbers and doesn't run with confidence.

FIELDING:

Martinez is a butcher in left field and does not throw well. His natural position is first base, but waiting for that position to become available in San Diego is like waiting for Dick Clark to give up American Bandstand.

CARMELO MARTINEZ
OF, No. 14
RR, 6'2", 210 lbs.
ML Svc: 3 years
Born: 7-28-60 in
Dorado, PR

1985 STATISTICS

AVG	G	AB	R	H	2B	3B	HR	RBI	BB	SO	SB
.253	150	514	64	130	28	1	21	72	87	82	0

CAREER STATISTICS

AVG	G	AB	R	H	2B	3B	HR	RBI	BB	SO	SB
.252	328	1091	136	275	59	3	40	154	159	183	1

VS. RHP

VS. LHP

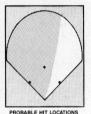

PROBABLE HIT LOCATIONS

OVERALL:

The advantages of playing Martinez are not outweighing the drawbacks. If he is not hitting home runs and driving them in, he is too weak a player in other aspects to be carried. On the other hand, if he can find his groove, he could become a hitter who gets 30 home runs in a season. He may be a candidate for the American League as a designated hitter.

It may serve him well to lose about 15 pounds. He is not a natural athlete, but he seems to get the most of his ability.

Snider: "He strikes out too much. But his poor defense is an even bigger problem. He has raw power and a good home run swing, reminding me a little of Orlando Cepeda. You have to remember that power hitters take a little longer to develop."

HITTING:

By the end of last season Kevin McReynolds did not look like the same player he had been just a year before. He was a confident, determined and aggressive hitter as a star on the 1984 pennant-winning Padres, but by September of last year, he was glad it was all over. Many feel that his problems were as much mental as they might have been physical; he had difficulty dealing with manager Dick Williams's gruff demeanor.

Apparently, McReynolds is a player who needs to be stroked. He did not get the kind of support he needs and began to handle the pressure of not producing by falling deeper and deeper into a rut as the season progressed. In fact, he fell behind Carmelo Martinez in most offensive categories after being regarded as a hotter prospect.

BASERUNNING:

McReynolds is not slow, but his knee problems make him a lesser basestealing threat than most center fielders. With more experience and certainly more confidence, he could be more than an average runner on the basepaths. Increased confidence would also lead to a more aggressive overall approach.

FIELDING:

After showing progress as a fielder during his rookie year, Kevin slipped badly last year. He goes to his left and right well, but is atrocious at judging balls hit directly at him. Consequently, he played a lot of outs into extra-base hits last year and now is merely average at his position.

OVERALL:

Expectations have run high for Kevin. He was an awesome minor league hitter

KEVIN McREYNOLDS
OF, No. 18
RR, 6'1", 207 lbs.
ML Svc: 3 years
Born: 10-16-59 in
Little Rock, AK

1985 STATISTICS

AVG	G	AB	R	H	2B	3B	HR	RBI	BB	SO	SB
.234	152	564	61	132	24	4	15	75	43	81	4

CAREER STATISTICS

AVG	G	AB	R	H	2B	3B	HR	RBI	BB	SO	SB
.251	338	1229	144	309	53	11	39	164	89	179	9

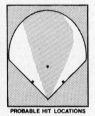

VS. RHP — STRONG   VS. LHP — STRONG   PROBABLE HIT LOCATIONS

and broke in solidly as a rookie two years ago. He was targeted as an excuse for the club's demise last season. That may not be the entire case.

He appears to need the managing of a sensitive skipper, something he got little of in San Diego in 1985.

But the good players overcome such obstacles and rise to the top. Kevin would be better off giving it 100% and making good things happen instead of brooding over adversity and waiting for luck.

Snider: "I was not alone in expecting constant improvement from Kevin. It was clear that something wasn't right for this talented young player last year. He was very unhappy and when things kept going bad, he probably put too much pressure on himself. It can be unnerving to try to recapture the glow of a good season."

HITTING:

At age 41, Graig Nettles is a productive player on a limited basis. With this in mind, the Padres signed him to a one-year contract for this season. His celebrated trade from the Yankees to San Diego proved to be an elixir in 1984 and may have added an extra year or two to his career. He responded well to San Diego.

Nettles will not produce a high average but he will provide some pop. He has not been a disppointment with his ability to hit home runs and to produce RBIs.

Nettles is a classic, lefthanded pull hitter who used that to his best advantage at Yankee Stadium. He is a low-ball hitter and can pull the ball with authority. He continues to be a dangerous hitter against an exclusive diet of righthanded pitching.

BASERUNNING:

His years on the basepaths have brought him savvy. He's an alert runner who doesn't clog the bases.

FIELDING:

Nettles is no longer the glove whiz he was in his younger days, but that's no insult because he used to be great. He is not as quick as he used to be and his range has decreased. He compensates with an accurate arm and good hands.

Nettles has trouble bending over, which makes a lot of plays at third difficult. He no longer charges bunts well and won't make diving catches with the reckless abandon of his earlier days. Defense is no longer his strong suit.

GRAIG NETTLES
3B, No. 9
LR, 6'0", 189 lbs.
ML Svc: 19 years
Born: 8-20-44 in
San Diego, CA

1985 STATISTICS

AVG	G	AB	R	H	2B	3B	HR	RBI	BB	SO	SB
.261	137	440	66	115	23	1	15	61	72	59	0

CAREER STATISTICS

AVG	G	AB	R	H	2B	3B	HR	RBI	BB	SO	SB
.250	2382	8362	1136	2095	307	27	368	1212	1175	1165	32

  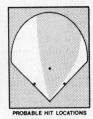

VS. RHP VS. LHP PROBABLE HIT LOCATIONS

OVERALL:

The Padres aren't being charitable. They signed Nettles because he's still a valuable spot player who doesn't hurt a team in the field and can provide an occasional longball.

Snider: "Oddly enough, I think that he had a better year offensively in 1985 than he did when the Padres won the pennant in 1984. He only dropped off in home runs.

"He is just a great influence on young players because he's done it all. He's been a quality player for many years. His leadership contribution cannot be minimized."

HITTING:

Now that he's accepted his role as a utility player, Jerry Royster has become one of the best in the majors in that role. After his figures began to slip during his two previous years with the Atlanta Braves, Royster had to make a good debut with the Padres in 1985.

Royster shared second base duty with Tim Flannery when former second base regular Alan Wiggins was given his walking papers. Royster and Flannery were effective at getting on base.

Royster's biggest problem is a lack of consistency at the plate, though sometimes this is gently referred to as being a streaky hitter. He does have the ability to get hot with the bat, which leads a manager to scratch his head and wonder if Royster should be given the everyday job.

He can cool off considerably and quickly. Pitchers get ahead of him in the count without much effort by throwing him inside and by changing speeds.

BASERUNNING:

Jerry holds a lot of the Braves' stolen base marks and was a very good base-stealer in his earlier years.

He does not attempt to steal much when he is on base, though his good speed is still rated above-average.

FIELDING:

A jack-of-all-trades and a master of none, Royster got more exposure at second last year after playing more third base in the past. His hands are average and he has shown poor judgment in diving for balls, being overly aggressive when caution would suffice. He does have a

JERRY ROYSTER
INF/OF, No. 3
RR, 6'0", 165 lbs.
ML Svc: 10 years
Born: 10-18-52 in
    Sacramento, CA

1985 STATISTICS											
AVG	G	AB	R	H	2B	3B	HR	RBI	BB	SO	SB
.281	90	249	31	70	13	2	5	31	32	31	6

CAREER STATISTICS											
AVG	G	AB	R	H	2B	3B	HR	RBI	BB	SO	SB
.250	1169	3653	487	913	137	32	28	298	300	441	182

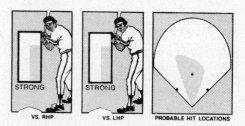

good arm, but at no point should he be in the lineup everyday.

OVERALL:

Royster is a solid role player who would be an asset on any team because he does a lot of things well and can play several positions. There was a time when he brooded over his utility status, yet he has discovered that he has made a nice career of it.

Snider: "He's always a great guy to be around and to have around. I managed against Jerry in the minors and I liked him then. He has a great attitude and is exactly what you'd want in a utility player."

PITCHING:

The Padres' workhorse in 1985, Eric Show should be better than a .500 pitcher. He has all of the pitches it takes to be a 20-game winner, but he is still more of a thrower than a pitcher.

He makes enough mistakes to hold himself back. He has good movement on his above-average fastball, a hard sinker and a good, quick slider. He gets burned by the longball because he will groove his pitches when he is behind in the count. He continues to have periods of control trouble.

Show, who has a degree in physics, is as intelligent as they come among baseball players. His critics are quick to point out that he "thinks" too much on the mound and that his mind retards his arm.

But it is his arm, not his brain, that sends his pitches too high in the strike zone. He gets his pitches up too high too often and batters begin to tee off. He cannot be successful throwing breaking stuff that hangs. Once Show cures his control problems, his intelligence should work well for him on the mound. To a certain extent, he suffers from a lack of run support, but it is not the whole story.

FIELDING, HITTING, BASERUNNING:

For a pitcher who extracts a lot of grounders out of his sinker, Eric would do well to improve his fielding. But he compensates with a great move to first base; his move is in the running for the best righthander's move in the National League.

ERIC SHOW
RHP, No. 30
RR, 6'1", 175 lbs.
ML Svc: 5 years
Born: 5-19-56 in
Riverside, CA

1985 STATISTICS

W	L	ERA	G	GS	CG	SV	IP	H	R	ER	BB	SO
12	11	3.09	35	35	5	0	233	212	95	80	87	141

CAREER STATISTICS

W	L	ERA	G	GS	CG	SV	IP	H	R	ER	BB	SO
53	41	3.35	164	114	14	6	813.1	722	338	303	306	475

He uses a quick delivery, which gives his catcher a bit of a break on potential basestealers.

Show is improving as a hitter, and last year he led the Padres' staff with one homer and six RBIs. He is a below-average bunter and merely average on the basepaths.

OVERALL:

Show has the stuff and ability to be the ace of the staff. His so-so record belies his ability; better run support could have made him 15-8 instead of 12-11 last year and there would be less concern.

Snider: "At times he's a very good pitcher, but at other times he looks too much like a thrower. Once in a while, he starts aiming the ball and that hurts him. But when you have a guy with so much stuff, you nurse him along and wait for the good things to happen."

PITCHING:

After pitching over his head with the Cubs in 1984, the big guy came crashing back to earth last year. Tim Stoddard can still throw good heat, but it's a straight fastball and very hittable.

Stoddard is the epitome of a thrower, not a pitcher. He is fearless and will rebound nicely from a poor outing. But his need to rebound has become common-place. He might be fighting for his baseball life were it not for a long-term contract.

A lack of control has been his problem when things aren't going well. Without control, he is a hitter's delight. When he is going good, at 6'7" and 250 lbs., he is intimidating and overpower-ing on the mound.

Stoddard has thrived on being just wild enough to be effective, a reputa-tion he has had since his career began. The fact remains, however, that he would be a much better reliever if he could develop something off-speed. He doesn't have the good control of his hard stuff, is prone to making mistakes and would benefit if he had a reliable slow pitch.

FIELDING, HITTING, BASERUNNING:

His size is a deterrent to impres-sive fielding. He is weak in handling bunts or anything hit back toward the mound. His defensive shortcomings com-bine with first baseman Steve Garvey's lack of range to make a weak right side of the infield when Stoddard is on the mound.

He has a slow delivery and is easy to

TIM STODDARD
RHP, No. 49
RR, 6'7", 250 lbs.
ML Svc: 7 years
Born: 1-24-53 in
   East Chicago, IN

1985 STATISTICS

W	L	ERA	G	GS	CG	SV	IP	H	R	ER	BB	SO
1	6	4.65	44	0	0	1	60	63	35	31	37	42

CAREER STATISTICS

W	L	ERA	G	GS	CG	SV	IP	H	R	ER	BB	SO
30	26	3.83	332	0	0	65	465.2	436	214	198	235	378

steal against.

His above-average pitcher's style of hitting was not evident in 1985. His size also affects his baserunning in a negative way.

OVERALL:

Stoddard will have to bounce back quickly and impressively or the Padres might have to think about eating his contract. He was acquired to complement the Goose in the bullpen last year, but he kept bringing kerosene to the mound. At age 33, he may be nearing the twi-light of a mediocre career.

Snider: "He was very effective for the Cubs in 1984, but he really didn't show much last season. He's a workhorse with a big heart, but he suffers from control problems and makes too many mistakes."

HITTING:

Last year was Garry Templeton's best season with the Padres. He was voted club MVP as a tribute to his consistency last season. In the past, Templeton had been regarded as a better power hitter from the right side of the plate, but he has improved in all phases from the left side. He hit .292 with five homers left-handed and only .261 with one homer from the right side. As a lefty, Templeton hits line drives and grounders up the middle or to the opposite field. As a righty, he is more of a pull hitter. He likes the ball down and over the plate as a lefthanded batter, having most difficulty with inside fastballs and sliders. From the right side, he prefers fastballs up and over the plate.

An aggressive hitter who lacks discipline, Templeton could be more effective if he were more selective. He's a first-ball hitter who disdains the base on balls. He is not an effective bunter but doesn't have to be.

BASERUNNING:

With Alan Wiggins gone, Templeton became more of a basestealing threat and posted 13 more thefts than in 1984. He was a much better runner before his arthritic knees reduced his overall effectiveness. He is as good on the bases as his knees are on a given day.

FIELDING:

Templeton has been a solid, dependable shortstop for years. His range is excellent and he has helped his fielding by releasing the ball more quickly and by improving his accuracy.

He is terrific on pop flies and, like so many infielders, has the tendency to make mistakes on the easier plays.

He has become a steadier and less spectacular shortstop since his younger days with the Cardinals.

GARRY TEMPLETON
SS, No. 1
SR, 5'11", 170 lbs.
ML Svc: 10 years
Born: 3-24-56 in
Lockey, TX

1985 STATISTICS

AVG	G	AB	R	H	2B	3B	HR	RBI	BB	SO	SB
.282	148	546	63	154	30	2	6	55	41	88	16

CAREER STATISTICS

AVG	G	AB	R	H	2B	3B	HR	RBI	BB	SO	SB
.287	1276	5052	661	1452	219	84	42	475	221	688	205

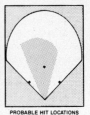

VS. RHP   VS. LHP   PROBABLE HIT LOCATIONS

OVERALL:

Templeton made a great turnaround in his career last year, regaining what he'd lost ever since his well-publicized falling out in St. Louis. A solid post-season performance in 1984, perhaps, was all that was needed to return him to star status. While much of San Diego burned around him, Garry took advantage of everything that came his way.

Snider: "It was a great year and I'm happy for Garry because he has had to battle injuries and the inevitable comparisons with Ozzie Smith. He really turned it on last year, and I do not think the Ozzie thing bothers him anymore.

"He looks nonchalant at times, but that's only because he's relaxed. He comes to play."

PITCHING:

Mark Thurmond was the most disappointing of the Padres' starters last year. He has merely average stuff, so the margin of error is not very large when he is not running on all cylinders. Last season, almost nothing went right for the lefthanded surprise of the 1984 pennant drive.

He relies on location, and when it is not there he will get hit hard. His stuff includes a fastball, curveball, slider and change-up. He must keep his pitches low, but was unable to do that for much of 1985.

The hits-to-innings ratio was poor, but he was as effective as any of the Padres' starters in keeping the ball in the park. He is at his best when working against teams with lots of lefthanded power.

After being a starter for most of the 1984 season, Thurmond's ineffectiveness leaves no choice but bullpen duty. He needs to regain his control; the relative obscurity of long relief will be his suit until he does.

FIELDING, HITTING, BASERUNNING:

Thurmond is a better-than-average fielder who holds runners on base well.

An absolutely awful hitter, Mark can still help himself with the bunt. Since he seldom reaches base, running is not a part of his game.

MARK THURMOND
LHP, No. 38
LR, 6'0", 193 lbs.
ML Svc: 3 years
Born: 9-12-56 in
    Houston, TX

1985 STATISTICS

W	L	ERA	G	GS	CG	SV	IP	H	R	ER	BB	SO
7	11	3.97	36	23	1	2	138.1	154	70	61	44	57

CAREER STATISTICS

W	L	ERA	G	GS	CG	SV	IP	H	R	ER	BB	SO
28	22	2.79	89	70	4	2	432.1	432	180	154	132	165

OVERALL:

He must throw low.

He should lose a few pounds.

Thurmond's advantage is that he is a lefthander, the game's most precious commodity (with the exception perhaps of consistent third basemen). As a result, he will get a longer look.

Snider: "There's a fine line between his being an effective pitcher or just another arm. He just doesn't keep the ball down consistently, and given his merely pretty good stuff, Mark cannot afford to get his pitches in the strike zone or he will be hammered like he was last year."

BRUCE BOCHY
C, No. 15
RR, 6'4", 229 lbs.
ML Svc: 7 years
Born: 4-16-55 in
Landes de Boussac, FR

HITTING, BASERUNNING, FIELDING:

There could be more playing time this year in store for Bruce Bochy. He has begun to show signs that he can handle more responsibility. He has the best home run ratio on the Padres and might be able to hit 30 over the course of a full season.

Bochy does a lot of things well; he has shown the abiltiy to hit some pretty good fastballs and is getting the knack of handling even the better breaking balls in the National League.

He is not a good baserunner. Very few catchers run the bases with any kind of speed; Bochy is no exception and may be on the low end of the scale in the speed and judgment department.

Defensively, he is average, though he is surely no worse than regular catcher Terry Kennedy behind the plate. He handles the pitching staff well and has an adequate arm.

OVERALL:

From all indications, Kennedy could use more rest from his backup chores and Bochy's development might accelerate the process. It's too early to tell whether Bruce would profit from more playing time, but there's a good chance we'll find out this summer because the Padres like what they've seen of him.

Snider: "He's an adequate backup guy who keeps improving. I'm sure that he would like a more prominent role, but he has handled his situation well. He is a solid team man who may have a good career ahead of him."

BOBBY BROWN
OF, No. 20
SR, 6'1", 231 lbs.
ML Svc: 7 years
Born: 5-24-54 in
Turbeville, VA

HITTING, BASERUNNNING, FIELDING:

Bobby Brown fell on hard times last year. A switch-hitter, he was supposed to be the club's top pinch-hitter from the left side, taking the job away from Champ Summers, but Brown failed in that role and was a mere 8-for-44 off the bench and 5-for-40 otherwise.

Earlier in his career, there were those who felt Bobby would develop into a solid regular. Such expectations were never realized, as the Padres have been content to use him as a dependable, but little-playing reserve.

Now, even that part-part-time role is in question because of his dismal 1985 showing, which included no positive stats except, errorless defense.

Brown has the reputation as a streak hitter. Last year, he looked undisciplined and anxious at the plate.

His fine baserunning has always been one of his strengths, especially going from home to first when batting from the left side, but he only batted .115 as a southpaw last year so that talent was wasted. His best defensive asset in the outfield is his speed because the other facets of his play are merely average or below-average.

OVERALL:

One year ago, Brown's prospects looked good for steady employment as a part-time outfielder, but his poor 1985 season will have him fighting for a job in the spring. He may be running out of teams--and time.

Snider: "There was quite a dropoff in his play from 1984. There was a time when it was thought he'd be more than a role player, but now I don't know. He has some value because he switch-hits and runs well, but there's no question last year set him back."

AL BUMBRY
OF, No.
LR, 5'8", 175 lbs.
ML Svc: 13 years
Born: 4-21-47 in
Fredricksburg, VA

HITTING, BASERUNNING, FIELDING:

Al Bumbry is a veteran outfielder who found life harsh in the National League in 1985. His problem is more the effects of advancing age than the usual inter-league adjustment period.

Known as a bad-ball hitter during his career with the Orioles, Bumbry was just a bad hitter with the Padres. While his younger teammates cavorted in the outfield, Bumbry's primary job was as a pinch-hitter. He made 46 trips to the plate in that role and managed just five hits (.106). He hit .200 overall.

He likes low fastballs and will chase high ones, but was not very successful against anything last year.

Once a decent basestealer, leg injuries and a .200 average tell the story of his 1985 baserunning attack.

When he was with the O's, he was known a weak-armed center fielder who played his position well otherwise. With the Padres, he did not play much in the field.

OVERALL:

From all indications, Bumbry reached the end of the line in 1985. It was a massive plunge from his platooning success (.270) at Baltimore in 1984, but there simply was nothing positive about his work off the bench in San Diego.

JERRY DAVIS
OF, No. 28
RR, 6'0", 180 lbs.
ML Svc: 1 year
Born: 12-25-58 in
Trenton, NJ

HITTING, BASERUNNING, FIELDING:

Jerry Davis looks like the man most likely to replace Bobby Brown as the Padres' fourth outfielder. Davis was the best of the club's backup outfielders last season, batting .293 in his first full season as a major leaguer.

Throughout his minor league career, Jerry showed the ability to reach base. He did a decent job in that area last year and performed well when he had a chance to play, batting .333 when he wasn't pinch-hitting.

As a fielder, Davis's strength is a strong arm which produced 17 assists in 129 games for Las Vegas in 1984. His excellent speed also served him well as a fly-chaser, but that same swiftness was not evident on the bases last year.

After swiping 35 bases for Las Vegas in 1984, he didn't attempt even one stolen base in the major leagues. But he seems to have the ability to get on base, so more running can be expected from him in the future.

OVERALL:

Davis played briefly last year, but he was at least adequate in all phases of the game. He seems perfectly suited for a reserve outfield role, especially on a club where so many of the other spare outfielders struggled in 1985.

Defensively, he can do no worse than Carmelo Martinez and Kevin McReynolds. With Miguel Dilone and Al Bumbry on their last legs, Davis could be in the right place at the right time.

LUIS DeLEON
RHP, No. 35
RR, 6'1", 159 lbs.
ML Svc: 4 years
Born: 8-19-58 in
        Ponce, PR

PITCHING, FIELDING, HITTING,
BASERUNNING:

Arm injuries over the last two years have drastically affected the career of Luis DeLeon. He was a budding bullpen superstar in 1982. However, since the arm injuries, he has fallen out of favor with the Padres following a poor start last year and he may now be phased out of the club's plans.

When he was right, Luis dazzled batters with a three-quarters delivery and great stuff: he had an exceptional slider and a hard sinker. But the arm woes have taken something from his fastball, which now leaves his other pitches more vulnerable.

Luis has suffered from concentration lapses in the past, and now a lack of confidence has to be a problem following two mediocre sessons.

In the past, he had been very successful against righthanded batters. He has since fallen short in that claim.

Rangy and graceful, DeLeon fields his position well and can run the bases, but he is not a good hitter and doesn't bunt well. His recent pitching problems have affected his entire game.

OVERALL:

The fact that DeLeon has lost some zip from his fastball may prevent him from ever regaining his form. There's no question a change of scenery would help, but the most important thing is staying healthy.

Snider: "Luis had the chance to pitch early in the season but was never heard from again. I would like to find out what's the matter. It seems like the Padres feel they can't depend on him, so he'd be better off elsewhere."

LANCE McCULLERS
RHP, No. 50
SR, 6'1", 186 lbs.
ML Svc: less than 1 year
Born: 3-8-64 in
        Tampa, FL

PITCHING, FIELDING,
    HITTING, BASERUNNING:

Lance McCullers has the potential to be a great pitcher. His debut with the Padres last year was impressive enough to earn him the club's Rookie of the Year honors even though he only joined the club in mid-August.

Lance is nicknamed "Baby Goose" because his fastball is hot and hard, and is similar to his notorious teammate. He gets good movement on the fastball and loves to challenge the hitters with his best stuff. He appears to have a lot of poise for such a young pitcher.

When Rich Gossage was sidelined, Lance picked up the slack and finished with five saves, all in his first eight big league appearances. His innings-to-hits ratio (35-23) was excellent.

His fielding looks as if it could use some work. His brief duty coupled with his role as short man did not afford the opportunity to judge his hitting and baserunning. It does appear, however, that he knows his future lies with his pitching and not his hitting.

OVERALL:

McCullers looks as if he might have the ability to come in and slam the door in the late innings. The Padres needed the boost he provided in 1985.

Snider: "I was very impressed with McCullers and Gene Walter down the stretch last year. Both are fine prospects. I like the way McCullers goes after the hitters. He has exceptional poise and ability."

MARIO RAMIREZ
INF, No. 12
RR, 5'9", 173 lbs.
ML Svc: 4 years
Born: 9-27-57 in
    Yauco, PR

HITTING, BASERUNNING, FIELDING:

Mario Ramirez is not much more than a solid backup player. He can make a nice career for himself out of being a caddy for the durable Garry Templeton at shortstop.

Ramirez added a new dimension to his role last year by proving that he is not an automatic out. In his previous four major league seasons, Ramirez never hit above .196. Last year, though, he found the right combination and batted .283. On a team where pinch-hitters combined for a sub-.200 average, Ramirez belted three hits in five trips.

He runs well and could be even better if he weren't overweight. His fielding has vastly improved over his early minor league days. He's capable of playing at third base, second base and shortstop. Ramirez has good hands, a good arm and decent range.

OVERALL:

Ramirez has potential as a journeyman reserve infielder, nothing more. Until last year, he never batted above .252 at any professional level, so it remains to be seen whether 1985 was a fluke. He's the type of player who won't help or hurt you much, a role player who comes inexpensively.

SAN FRANCISCO GIANTS

PITCHING:

Juan Berenguer won 20 games over the 1983-84 seasons for the Detroit Tigers and found himself dispatched to the bullpen at the outset of last year. Juan cannot pitch in relief. He is a "feel" pitcher who must rely on an 88-92 MPH fastball before he gains command of his breaking pitches. That requires two or three innings to heat up, something that no reliever can afford.

Berenguer is now re-united with former Tiger pitching coach Roger Craig, who spent countless hours diligently working with the sensitive Panamanian in 1983-84. Berenguer could achieve a moderate degree of success with the Giants. He depends on his fastball to a great extent and occasionally can get by without throwing too many breaking pitches.

The break on his curve is good, but his control is erratic. The same is true of his split-finger fastball.

Berenguer relies on power to escape jams. He can do this against some clubs, but requires control of all three of his pitches to fare well against the majority of teams.

Issuing walks upsets him. His concentration level is not high and he needs constant encouragement. He is headed for the shower if his control is bad.

Berenguer rarely brushes back hitters on purpose, but they are reluctant to dig in because of his erratic control.

FIELDING:

Berenguer's follow-through does not

JUAN BERENGUER
RHP, No. 44
RR, 5'11", 215 lbs.
ML Svc: 8 years
Born: 11-30-54 in
  Aguadulce, PAN

1985 STATISTICS

W	L	ERA	G	GS	CG	SV	IP	H	R	ER	BB	SO
5	6	5.59	31	13	0	0	95	96	67	59	48	82

CAREER STATISTICS

W	L	ERA	G	GS	CG	SV	IP	H	R	ER	BB	SO
28	38	4.18	139	82	5	1	571.1	495	301	265	291	426

leave him in the proper fielding position. He falls off the mound toward first base. He was once hit in the head by a line drive off the bat of Al Bumbry because he couldn't protect himself with his glove hand.

His move to first is quick and is very nearly a balk because he dips his front (left) knee.

OVERALL:

Berenguer is blessed with an outstanding arm. He must watch his weight and improve command of his curve and split-finger fastball.

Robinson: "Juan's great arm will keep him in the big leagues, but he's as good now as he will ever be. He's just too inconsistent."

PITCHING:

Vida Blue made a strong comeback last year after not pitching since August 5, 1983. He went to the Giants training camp as a non-roster player and earned a job by showing that he still could throw heat.

His biggest problem was a lack of control, which may be traced to the way he was used last year. It was late in the season until he was given a regular turn in the rotation; before that, he was shuttled back and forth from the bullpen. When Blue had the chance as a regular starter, his control took a turn for the better.

The famous Blue Blazer is still an above-average fastball. Vida actually throws two fastballs: one which he grips across the seam that is more effective against righthanded batters; the other is held on the seam and tails away from lefthanded batters.

He added to his repertoire last year by developing a slider and a change-up. Though neither is a great pitch, they do complement his fastball well and keep the batters honest. If Blue can perfect either the slider or the change-up, he would be more successful.

FIELDING, HITTING, BASERUNNING:

Blue is a hard worker in these phases of the game, more so last year than in the past because he had something to prove. Still, he is nothing more than an average fielder and his move to first base is not good for a lefthander.

As a hitter, he doesn't get cheated, but he also doesn't connect often. On the bases, Blue knows what to do.

OVERALL:

Vida was one of the few bright spots

VIDA BLUE
LHP, No. 14
SL, 6'0", 200 lbs.
ML Svc: 15 years
Born: 7-28-49 in
Mansfield, LA

1985 STATISTICS

W	L	ERA	G	GS	CG	SV	IP	H	R	ER	BB	SO
8	8	4.47	33	20	1	0	131.1	115	70	65	80	103

CAREER STATISTICS

W	L	ERA	G	GS	CG	SV	IP	H	R	ER	BB	SO
199	191	3.26	474	445	143	2	3187.2	2802	1292	1156	1108	2075

in a dismal season for the club. He was eligible for free agency but expressed hope at the end of the year the Giants would sign him so he would be near his Bay Area home.

He proved he still could pitch on the major league level and that his fastball is still big league calibre. He is being driven, in part, by his burning desire to win 200 games. Entering the 1986 season, he is one victory from attaining that goal.

Blue is no longer the ace of a staff, but he can provide a pitching staff with versatility.

Campbell: "Blue made a remarkable comeback from all of his personal problems. He still has a better-than-average major league fastball. If he can come up with a quality breaking ball, I think he would be a heckuva relief pitcher--a guy who could come in and blow you away for a couple of innings. He can still get it up there and doesn't get hit often. The only question is his control."

HITTING:

Bob Brenly slumped badly last year and seemed unable to find his groove at all. He continued to give the Giants the long ball--his 19 home runs led the club--but the problem was that his home runs did little to help the club.

Brenly spent almost every at-bat trying to drive the ball out of the park. His season started off poorly, so he resigned himself to a low average early on and was trying to salvage something by looking for home runs.

He likes pitches up and has become more of a pull hitter recently after being a straightaway hitter in the past. The most effective way to keep away from his ample power is to keep the ball down and to change speeds. Brenly is not a selective hitter; he tends to chase anything out of the strike zone, especially when he's not going well. But, still, Brenly is at the plate just waiting to crunch a mistake--a pitcher really can't afford to make many to him.

BASERUNNING:

He won't steal a base, but he has above-average speed for a catcher. In fact, he's not your prototypical sluggish backstop, which is one reason he has been used at third base as well as the outfield.

FIELDING:

After fumbling his chance with a poor 1985, Brenly's days as the club's regular catcher may be numbered. The Giants acquired defensive specialist Bob Melvin from the Detroit Tigers in the off-season, so that tells you what they think of Brenley's glovework.

Brenly has a fairly quick release, but his accuracy is suspect. Last year, he tried to become more of a take-charge guy behind the plate, but he didn't pull it off. He is still regarded as below average defensively. That would apply to his third base play as well.

BOB BRENLY
C, No. 15
RR, 6'2", 210 lbs.
ML Svc: 4 years
Born: 2-25-54 in
    Coshocton, OH

1985 STATISTICS

AVG	G	AB	R	H	2B	3B	HR	RBI	BB	SO	SB
.220	133	440	41	97	16	1	19	56	57	62	1

CAREER STATISTICS

AVG	G	AB	R	H	2B	3B	HR	RBI	BB	SO	SB
.257	466	1452	182	373	62	9	51	189	166	192	23

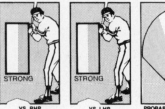
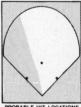

VS. RHP   VS. LHP   PROBABLE HIT LOCATIONS

OVERALL:

It's difficult to evaluate his future with the club. Roger Craig has indicated he likes Brenly's aggressiveness and leadership potential, but at the same time, Craig has hinted that Melvin would get every chance to catch.

With a pitching-minded manager like Craig, defense is a high priority behind the plate, so Brenly's biggest contribution may be as a jack-of-all-trades.

Campbell: "Bob was a better hitter back in 1984 when he was being more selective. Everything fell into place for him then and he was expected to improve. But then, so were the Giants. Brenly was never able to regain his touch after a terrible start last year.

"He gave up a lot of passed balls and his pitchers were charged with a lot of wild pitches, so you have to wonder about his defense. One thing you have to respect, however, is his power."

TOP PROSPECT

CHRIS BROWN
3B, No. 35
RR, 6'0", 185 lbs.
ML Svc: 1 year plus
Born: 8-15-61 in
   Jackson, MS

HITTING:

Chris Brown, an injury-prone rookie, had a bittersweet season in 1985. He was easily the most effective clutch hitter on the Giants, surpassing all spring training expectations with his bat and his glove, yet he was never able to gain the respect of his teammates for a job well done: his physical brittleness kept him out of 31 games and caused his teammates to point a collective finger in his direction.

Chris is a high-ball hitter with a slightly closed stance. He hits out of a crouch and is basically a straightaway hitter. He grounds into a lot of double plays, but compensates for this by being tough in the clutch.

Brown is a confident hitter and seems to thrive with men on base. He improved his average by hitting a very respectable .307 in the second half of the season. He is a good prospect for future stardom--if he can remain healthy.

BASERUNNING:

Brown is below average on the basepaths. A rash of nagging injuries have restricted his running; nevertheless, he has a reputation for not hustling on the bases. A more determined and less casual approach on the bases is required.

FIELDING:

Overlooked because of his annoying tendency toward being injury-prone and his lax attitude on the bases is his fine defensive ability. Brown played third base as well as anyone in the NL. His 10 errors were the fewest among regulars at third base and his .971 fielding percentage was the league's best since Ken Oberkfell's .972 in 1982.

Brown has adequate range, good hands and a strong and accurate arm. He is the best defensive third baseman for the Giants since Jim Davenport in the 1960s.

1985 STATISTICS

AVG	G	AB	R	H	2B	3B	HR	RBI	BB	SO	SB
.271	131	432	50	117	20	3	16	61	38	78	2

CAREER STATISTICS

AVG	G	AB	R	H	2B	3B	HR	RBI	BB	SO	SB
.273	154	516	56	141	27	3	17	72	47	97	4

STRONG

VS. RHP

STRONG

VS. LHP

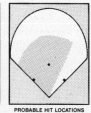

PROBABLE HIT LOCATIONS

OVERALL:

Giants' management is going batty trying to discover what makes Brown tick and his woeful teammates often used him as an excuse for the entire club's troubles. The numbers indicate, however, that he was not the cause for the club's shoddy year.

Campbell: "Chris was the best rookie hitter in the National League and a nice surprise for the club. He doesn't scare in clutch situations and is certainly a bright prospect.

"During spring training last year, he appeared to be too cocky for his own good, yet he went out and did a fine job, so you can't say much against him.

"He missed a lot of games with injuries and ailments; he might have a low threshold for pain or else it's that Lady Luck is not in his corner."

HITTING:

Chili Davis had a respectable season at the plate last year, though it paled in comparison to his outstanding performance in 1984 when he hit .315.

Davis maintained an acceptable average, but dropped off considerably in home runs and run production. There are some who feel that Davis has power from both sides of the plate, yet 12 of his 13 home runs last year were hit from the left side (31 of his last 34 home runs have been as a lefthanded hitter). He has worked so hard to improve his hitting against righthanders that now his righthanded hitting has suffered.

As a lefthanded hitter, he pulls the ball more than as a righty and is a low-ball hitter. He can be jammed by hard stuff inside.

He has become more disciplined and has reduced his strikeouts considerably. Davis will take a walk more often now, though he suffered as the number three hitter when the two hitters in front of him failed to reach base.

BASERUNNING:

Chili is not really a basestealing threat at this stage, but he can turn on the basepaths and would steal more if he were higher in the batting order. He really doesn't take advantage of all his ability on the basepaths.

FIELDING:

Perhaps affected by the club's slide, Chili became a little careless afield last year following a solid 1984. He uses his speed well in right field and his arm is strong, though it is not accurate. He has a tendency to miss the cutoff man.

OVERALL:

The Giants have been predicting superstardom for Davis for three or four years. Yet Davis has shown too much

CHILI DAVIS
RF, No. 30
SR, 6'3", 195 lbs.
ML Svc: 4 years
Born: 1-17-60 in
Kingston, JAM

1985 STATISTICS

AVG	G	AB	R	H	2B	3B	HR	RBI	BB	SO	SB
.270	136	481	53	130	25	2	13	56	62	74	15

CAREER STATISTICS

AVG	G	AB	R	H	2B	3B	HR	RBI	BB	SO	SB
.268	572	2122	281	569	94	16	64	272	205	373	63

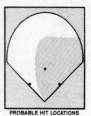

VS. RHP   VS. LHP   PROBABLE HIT LOCATIONS

inconsistency to make any kind of bold statements regarding his future. He has blown hot and cold, doing well in the even numbered years and faltering in the odd.

There is the possibility of a motivational problem, playing for a weak team which has been forced to play in what has been acknowledged as the worst park in the major leagues.

Chili was affected by the Jack Clark trade in 1985 and, for the first time, revealed a desire to move elsewhere. He was not a happy player last year and his play often reflected his mood. At one time, it seemed like he could become the next Eddie Murray, but he will soon become just another major leaguer if he does not make the best of his situation.

Campbell: "He's the type of guy with a world of talent and he's certainly done a bunch of damage against the San Diego Padres over the years, but he remains unable to put it all together for more than just a flash."

PITCHING:

Mark Davis has an awesome curveball. It enabled him to strike out 39% of the first batters he faced in relief last year and gave him a strikeout ratio of 10.31 per nine innings, second in the majors to Lee Smith's 10.32.

Davis, whose 128 strikeouts out of the bullpen topped all major league relievers, has a good fastball to complement his devastating curve. And he is working to develop the most potentially devastating pitch of all, the dreaded split-finger fastball. He is now under the tutelage of its guru, manager Roger Craig.

Davis was unsuccessful as a starter in 1984, but his ability as a reliever has made him a hot property.

What he needs to improve the record and the ERA is mental toughness, which could come with experience. After all, last year was his first as a full-time reliever.

FIELDING, HITTING, BASERUNNING:

Mark is an excellent athlete, a fact reflected by his ability in the other areas of baseball. He batted .250 last year on a club which collectively hit .233 and he belted a triple. Davis appeared in 77 games, yet didn't make an error and he runs the bases well.

OVERALL:

Considering his abundant stuff, Mark should be more successful. There's no reason he should lose one dozen games

MARK DAVIS
LHP, No. 13
LL, 6'4", 195 lbs.
ML Svc: 3 years
Born: 10-19-60 in
   Livermore, CA

1985 STATISTICS

W	L	ERA	G	GS	CG	SV	IP	H	R	ER	BB	SO
5	12	3.54	77	1	0	7	114.1	89	49	45	41	131

CAREER STATISTICS

W	L	ERA	G	GS	CG	SV	IP	H	R	ER	BB	SO
17	37	4.61	154	58	3	7	450.1	436	252	231	174	372

or have an ERA above 3.00. He's had a problem dealing with pressure and he is well aware of it; wilting in tight situations is one thing he must rectify to fulfill his potential . . . Dr. Craig may have the remedy.

The fact that the Giants had so many winter inquiries regarding Davis' availability suggests what baseball people think of his overwhelming talent.

Campbell: "I think Mark has the best curveball of any lefthander in the NL. He may have the best curveball of any pitcher in the league, for that matter.

"His hits-to-innings and strikeout figures were outstanding last year. The only knock I have is that he needs to get more confidence and to become tougher with a game on the line. He needs a better mental makeup, but he's learning. If he only realizes how good he is, how good his stuff is, I think he can go a long way."

HITTING:

Dan Driessen arrived in San Francisco last season with the hope of providing the Giants with some much-needed left-handed hitting. He was only able to provide too little, too late. He managed only three homers in 54 games with the Giants and now appears destined for spot duty and pinch-hitting.

Dan likes the ball up and over the plate and has a quick bat. When he is hot, he is a difficult hitter to jam, though he was not hot enough last season to make that the case.

Driessen gets fooled on pitches more often now than ever before. The best way to strike him out is by keeping the ball down. In the past, Driessen has proved himself to be a smart hitter who could adjust to almost anything a pitcher threw him and could hit to the entire field. But his numbers have been on the decline for a few seasons and not much of his former hitting abilities are now very apparent.

Driessen had been a remarkably steady hitter over the years--nothing spectacular, but highly efficient. His career appears to be on the decline; given every opportunity to produce in recent seasons, he has been unable to put anything together.

BASERUNNING:

At one time, Dan ran as well as any first baseman in the league and was capable of stealing over 20 bases. Age has taken its toll; he no longer looms as a threat to steal nor does he run the bases with his past abandon.

FIELDING:

If there's one area where Dan has remained consistent, it has been as a reliable first baseman. He made only one error in 49 games with his new club and finished the season with a .997 field-

DAN DRIESSEN
1B, No. 22
LR, 5'11", 200 lbs.
ML Svc: 13 years
Born: 7-29-51 in
   Hilton Head, SC

1985 STATISTICS

AVG	G	AB	R	H	2B	3B	HR	RBI	BB	SO	SB
.243	145	493	53	120	26	0	9	47	50	51	2

CAREER STATISTICS

AVG	G	AB	R	H	2B	3B	HR	RBI	BB	SO	SB
.268	1676	5379	734	1440	277	23	151	749	745	705	154

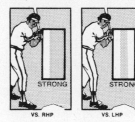

VS. RHP   VS. LHP   PROBABLE HIT LOCATIONS

ing percentage. He plays a steady but never-flashy first base. He's better than average with his glovework.

OVERALL:

If the Giants don't acquire a new first baseman over the winter, Driessen will likely survive as a semi-regular for one more year, perhaps platooning with either David Green or Bob Brenly. Dan obviously can't do it over the long haul any longer, so he's probably a stop-gap first baseman against right-handers until rookie phenom Will Clark emerges from the minors.

Campbell: "Like Manny Trillo, Dan is approaching the twilight of his career--but I think that Driessen can still be useful to a club. I think Dan's role at this point would have to be as a spot player and pinch-hitter, though he did not do well in that role last year."

PITCHING:

Scott Garrelts burst upon the scene as a potential bullpen superstar last year, and his success relegated Greg Minton to secondary status. Garrelts teamed with Mark Davis to form a one-two punch for the Giants which should serve the club well for years to come.

A failure as a starter in 1984, Scott switched to the bullpen last season and had his big chance when Minton was injured in spring training. Garrelts took full advantage of the opportunity and exceeded all expectations as a stopper.

He has three quality major league pitches: an above-average fastball, a good slider and a forkball which is particularly devastating to lefthanded batters when they are behind in the count. He doesn't throw the forkball very much; he uses it as a surprise and it is quite effective that way.

If there is one knock against him, it is that he will occasionally get hurt by a lack of control. When he begins to issue walks, he will do it in bunches. But his hits-to-innings ratio was great last season and he struck out an average of one batter per inning.

Like Mark Davis, Garrelts needs to acquire more mental toughness, he made greater strides in this area last season than Davis did: Scott's new-found bulldog determination was clearly reflected in his flashy statistics and successful performance.

FIELDING, HITTING, BASERUNNING:

In sharp contrast to his pitching development, Garrelts' work in other areas is far from special. Defensively, he is somewhat atrocious. Every time he bends over for a batted ball, it is an adventure, especially when he has to throw hurriedly. His fielding is a liability.

On the other hand, his hitting is acceptable, although he does need to learn

SCOTT GARRELTS
RHP, No. 50
RR, 6'4", 195 lbs.
ML Svc: 2 years
Born: 10-30-61 in
 Urbana, IL

1985 STATISTICS

W	L	ERA	G	GS	CG	SV	IP	H	R	ER	BB	SO
9	6	2.30	74	0	0	13	105.2	76	37	27	58	106

CAREER STATISTICS

W	L	ERA	G	GS	CG	SV	IP	H	R	ER	BB	SO
13	11	3.28	101	8	1	13	186.2	157	84	67	113	158

how to bunt. He is an adequate baserunner.

OVERALL:

Garrelts gets nothing but applause for having been a spring training question mark who blossomed into the bullpen answer. It was his rookie year as a short reliever and he was just short of phenomenal--his performance landed him an All-Star berth last year. His 9 wins topped the staff, as did his 2.30 ERA and 13 saves. He was responsible for 22 of the club's 62 victories and had an ERA under 2.00 for most of the season.

Garrelts is a pressure pitcher on a club which doesn't handle adversity well, so it appears the sky's the limit for him.

Campbell: "I would have to say that he is the brightest new relief pitcher to appear in this league in the last couple of years. His fastball exceeds 90 MPH and he has a great arm.

"What is interesting is that he is just learning how good he can be. If he can believe a little more in himself, I feel he will be among the elite relief pitchers in the National League for many, many years."

HITTING:

Greatness was predicted for Dan Gladden when he batted .351 for half a season in 1984. Last season, however, his on-base percentage barely reached .300 and this leadoff hitter's year was a confusing disaster.

Gladden is the player best-suited to lead off on the Giants, yet his mere 40 walks indicate he had trouble discerning a strike last year. He also developed delusions of grandeur and fancied himself a power hitter, swinging for the fences when he should have been concentrating on contact.

Gladden is not a good clutch hitter; his occasional home runs do not take away from the fact that he must be a pesky hitter who gets on base to be truly valuable to the club. In 1985, he was a detriment. He did not do his job and needs to have a solid offensive year this season to prove that his 1984 numbers were not a fluke.

BASERUNNING:

In spite of all his problems at the plate, Gladden is able to exploit his excellent speed when he does get on base. Last season, he stole 32 bases. Still, for all his talent, he will have concentration lapses on the basepaths. He must also learn to judge his theft opportunities better--he was caught 15 times in 1985.

If he can clean up his hitting problems and get on base as often as a lead-off hitter should, Gladden should be able to steal more than 50 bases.

FIELDING:

Gladden can fool you into thinking that he is good defensive player by coming up with a spectacular catch. But he won't do it every day and is otherwise, not very good in the outfield. His speed gives him good range and he can get to a lot of balls others miss, but his arm is not strong and he

DAN GLADDEN
CF, No. 32
RR, 5'11", 180 lbs.
ML Svc: 3 years
Born: 7-7-57 in
   San Jose, CA

```
1985 STATISTICS
AVG  G   AB   R   H   2B  3B HR  RBI BB  SO  SB
.243 142 502  64  122 15  8  7   41  40  78  32
CAREER STATISTICS
AVG  G   AB   R   H   2B  3B HR  RBI BB  SO  SB
.282 246 907 141  256 34 10 12   81  78 126  67
```

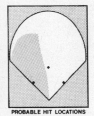

will misread the plays developing in the infield.

OVERALL:

It will be interesting to see which Dan Gladden shows up in 1986: he might come as the bright prospect of 1984 or he may continue to be the player who falls into bad habits and does not always exercise his best judgment either at the plate or in the field.

He may benefit by the presence of the new Giants' skipper, Roger Craig. There are questions, however, that if he manages to make a good first impression, will he then be able to maintain it?

Campbell: "At one point, it looked as though he would be a fixture in the outfield for the next ten years but everything fell apart for him last year. He goes for a stretch when he can look brilliant, but that is not on an every-day basis.

"His biggest goal for this season has to be to get on base and make things happen for the Giants offense."

PITCHING:

Jim Gott missed the final three weeks of last season due to a sore shoulder, but until that time, he was a respectable fifth starter. He made a quick adjustment to the National League, going 3-2 with a 2.25 ERA after his first 10 starts.

Gott is a pitcher who gets the most out of his pitches and his ability. Other than a 90 MPH fastball, his stuff is merely ordinary, which is one reason he has been a sub-.500 pitcher in the majors.

Gott throws an average major league curveball and slider. He has a change-up, though it is not very good. He suffers from spotty control and, like most pitchers with just average pitches, he will get hammered when he starts to lose his control and gets his pitches up in the strike zone. His fastball does not have great movement, therefore it is very important that he keep his pitches low.

FIELDING, HITTING, BASERUNNING:

Although Gott did not make an error last seaon, he is not regarded as a good fielder. He is not quick off the mound and he doesn't hold runners on base well.

As a hitter, Gott rates as one of the best--and most surprising--of pitchers. Last year, in his first full season as a hitter, he belted three home runs, including two in one game, a first for a Giants pitcher since 1949.

JIM GOTT
RHP, No. 46
RR, 6'4", 210 lbs.
ML Svc: 4 years
Born: 8-3-59 in
    Hollywood, CA

1985 STATISTICS

W	L	ERA	G	GS	CG	SV	IP	H	R	ER	BB	SO
7	10	3.88	26	26	2	0	148.1	144	73	64	51	78

CAREER STATISTICS

W	L	ERA	G	GS	CG	SV	IP	H	R	ER	BB	SO
28	40	4.33	125	91	10	2	571	566	306	275	234	354

OVERALL:

Gott is about as good a pitcher as one could expect from a fifth starter, but he has the chance to improve under Roger Craig's tutelage. Gott kept the Giants in most of the games he pitched and was a victim of tough luck.

Despite troublesome blisters, he had some good starts. Since the Giants are pushing some young arms, his future more than likely will be long relief.

Campbell: "There was nothing special he did last year except hit three home runs. I consider him an average major league pitcher. If the Giants staff was better, his best role would be as a long reliever."

HITTING:

The Giants had a lot of disappointments in 1985 and David Green was right up there with the biggest of them. He is generally regarded as an enormous talent, but where that talent was anyone's guess as he hit a minuscule .080 in his first 21 games. That proved to be a critical slump because Jack Clark, for whom he was traded, was off to a great start for St. Louis. Green overcame the slow start to bat .318 over the final three months, but the bad taste of his poor start lingered.

Green is not a selective hitter; he draws few walks and is a poor run producer for a hitter who bats in the middle of the order. There are some who feel that Green has power potential, but there was no pop in his bat last year; its absence cost him regular duty.

Green likes the ball out and over the plate so he can get his arms extended. When he falls behind in the count, he's vulnerable to bad breaking balls and high fastballs and will chase both of them.

BASERUNNING:

Green is a gifted athlete and can really scoot going from first to third or from second to home, but he is surprisingly ineffective as a basestealer. One reason may be that he didn't have the opportunity or the encouragement last year.

FIELDING:

An excellent fielder, Green is particularly good at picking up ground balls and at scooping throws out of the dirt. He is very agile for his size and was an All-Star outfielder in winter ball before joining the Giants in 1985. While right field is his best position, he is very good at first base.

OVERALL:

Green was truly a mystery last year. His silence with the press, as well

DAVID GREEN
1B, No. 22
RR, 6'3", 165 lbs.
ML Svc: 5 years
Born: 12-4-60 in
Managua, NIC

1985 STATISTICS

AVG	G	AB	R	H	2B	3B	HR	RBI	BB	SO	SB
.248	106	294	36	73	10	2	5	20	22	58	6

CAREER STATISTICS

AVG	G	AB	R	H	2B	3B	HR	RBI	BB	SO	SB
.267	475	1368	164	366	46	17	30	179	82	273	68

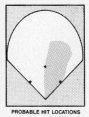

STRONG   STRONG

VS. RHP   VS. LHP   PROBABLE HIT LOCATIONS

as his poor start, accentuated by Jack Clark's quick dash from the starting gate in St. Louis, highlighted Green's 4-for-50 introduction to San Francisco.

He did settle down and hit .283 the rest of the way, but there is no question that he was hurt by the controversy surrounding the trade. Green finished the year with fewer RBIs than Clark had homers and Green's own lack of production only added fuel to the fire. By the time Green began to hit, he had already lost his job to Dan Driessen. Nevertheless, David Green is too much of a natural talent to be denied a second chance.

Campbell: "He appears to be an excellent athlete, so the reasons for his problems are unclear. It does seem, however, that there are some off-field problems which may be affecting his play. He must get his personal problems worked out--it is the only chance for him to reach his potential. If he does not improve this season, however, it could just be that he can't."

PITCHING:

Neither his record nor ERA were much to brag about, but Atlee Hammaker regarded 1985 as a winning season because he was able to pitch the entire year with a minimum of arm trouble. He only pitched in six games in 1984 due to arm surgery.

Hammaker throws a below-average fastball in terms of speed, but because he gets good movement on it, it is an effective pitch. His breaking pitch is more like a rolling slurve. However he doesn't get the same kind of bite he used to get on his breaking stuff--he throws it differently now because he is afraid of reinjuring his arm.

His biggest asset is his control; he thrives on moving the ball in and out and keeping the hitters off balance. His control helped make him the league leader in ERA in 1982, but his arm trouble has made him just a shadow of his previous self.

Atlee is a tough competitor, one whose record would have been much better last year if he had more run support. The Giants scored only 13 runs while he was pitching in his last 16 starts; his record was a meager 3-6 despite a 2.98 ERA in his first 13 starts.

FIELDING, HITTING, BASERUNNING:

Hammaker doesn't help himself off the mound. He is not a good fielder, he doesn't hold runners on base well (especially for a lefty) and he has an awful move to first base. Roger Craig should be able to help him improve his move.

He is not much of a threat at the plate and he doesn't run the bases well. Hammaker is a gifted athlete who has not applied himself to any aspect of baseball except pitching.

ATLEE HAMMAKER
LHP, No. 14
LL, 6'2", 195 lbs.
ML Svc: 5 years
Born: 1-24-58 in
Carmel, CA

1985 STATISTICS
W	L	ERA	G	GS	CG	SV	IP	H	R	ER	BB	SO
5	12	3.74	29	29	1	0	170.2	161	81	71	47	100

CAREER STATISTICS
W	L	ERA	G	GS	CG	SV	IP	H	R	ER	BB	SO
30	32	3.45	97	91	13	0	589.2	573	258	226	128	364

OVERALL:

Hammaker proved he could go the distance last year, but whether he'll ever be as effective as he was in his pre-surgery days remains to be seen. It is also difficult to determine if Hammaker has the makeup to overcome the frustrations of the rehabilitation proccess. His exterior appearance often suggests indifference which may be an result of his preoccupation over the last two years with taking his progress one step at a time.

Campbell: "If Atlee is going to be an effective starting pitcher again, he must start to throw his hard breaking ball. If he still has pain in his elbow and cannot throw it, then he will become just a very average big league pitcher.

"Two years ago, I thought he had better stuff than any lefthanded pitcher in the National League. The elbow problems have taken their toll and I think he's reluctant to throw breaking pitches like he used to."

PITCHING:

A bruised thumb forced Mike Krukow to miss a month of the season last year, but pitching in less-than-perfect health is not a new experience for him. Limited to just 28 starts, he was the Giants' most effective and consistent starter last year. He recorded a career high in strikeouts and was seldom chased from a game early. In tribute to his fierce competitiveness, Krukow was named the Most Inspirational Player by his teammates last season.

Krukow's best pitch is an above-average fastball; he can make it look better than it really is because he is able to throw it with good control. He also has a decent slider, but he stopped using his slow curveball because he was not able to control it as well as he would have liked.

The key to Krukow's success is his control. When he's on, he can pitch as well as the best pitchers in the league (in April 1985, he was 2-0 with a 0.53 ERA). When he's hitting the corners, he is extremely effective.

FIELDING, HITTING, BASERUNNING:

Krukow fields his position well because he is always alert to game situations and he knows what each batter is capable of. But his high kick makes him vulnerable to the steal and he does not hold runners on base well--though he did show improvement in this area last year.

Teammate Jim Gott may have caught the home run bug last season, but Krukow is the most consistent hitter on the club among the pitchers. Last season he hit .218 with four doubles--not bad considering his two catchers didn't do much better.

MIKE KRUKOW
RHP, No. 39
RR, 6'4", 205 lbs.
ML Svc: 9 years
Born: 1-21-52 in
    Long Beach, CA

1985 STATISTICS

W	L	ERA	G	GS	CG	SV	IP	H	R	ER	BB	SO
8	11	3.38	28	28	6	0	194.2	176	80	73	49	150

CAREER STATISTICS

W	L	ERA	G	GS	CG	SV	IP	H	R	ER	BB	SO
88	95	3.96	277	275	27	1	1613.1	1664	810	711	617	1103

OVERALL:

Krukow has not been able to shed the ".500 pitcher" label, perhaps because he has been miscast as a staff ace when he is better suited to a complementary role. He has the kind of stuff that makes people wonder why the results are not any better than they are. At times, he can be untouchable.

Mike is a hard-nosed competitor and a leader who would likely flourish as part of a better pitching staff instead of worrying about being the best the Giants can send to the mound.

Campbell: "Mike had some pretty good numbers as the Giants' best starter last year. He is the best strikeout man among the starters and has become a dependable pitcher. I think he came to the Giants with the reputation of not being the most competitive of pitchers, but from all indications that's changed. The Giants like his spirit and expect big things from him--though they must give him better run support."

HITTING:

There are just some days when you get out of bed and you know it's going to be a bad day. Jeff Leonard, a righthanded power hitter, just couldn't get anything going most days during last year. He had a poor start, was hampered by injuries down the stretch, couldn't make any solid contact with the ball, increased his strikeout totals and became a prime target for hissing and booing by the few cold fans who showed up at Candlestick last season.

Leonard likes the ball low and inside, especially from lefthanders. It is the pitch he can drive for home runs. He is a better hitter against a breaking ball than he is with a fastball. Righthanders who throw three-quarters to sidearm can throw Leonard off stride. Pitchers such as Eric Show and Rich Gossage can just about strike him out by throwing him mean looks.

He hates to walk his way on base; he goes up to the plate swinging and hacking away. However, he was not able to hack with much power except in batting practice last year.

BASERUNNING:

Jeff has the ability to steal 20 or more bases, however, his basestealing was not a matter of high priority last season. He has above-average speed and can really motor on the bases, but he has not yet taken the time to learn the fine points of successful basestealing technique.

FIELDING:

Despite all of his problems at the plate last year, Leonard continued his development into becoming one of the better outfielders in the league. He picks up assist after assist with his strong and accurate arm. He charges the ball well, uses good judgment (especially in a tough park like Candlestick) and could easily shift to center field if

JEFF LEONARD
LF, No. 20
RR, 6'4", 200 lbs.
ML Svc: 8 years
Born: 9-22-55 in
Philadelphia, PA

1985 STATISTICS

AVG	G	AB	R	H	2B	3B	HR	RBI	BB	SO	SB
.241	133	507	49	122	20	3	17	62	21	107	11

CAREER STATISTICS

AVG	G	AB	R	H	2B	3B	HR	RBI	BB	SO	SB
.272	773	2623	331	713	116	28	75	386	208	566	104

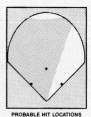

STRONG   STRONG

VS. RHP   VS. LHP   PROBABLE HIT LOCATIONS

the Giants are serious about their second base experiment with Dan Gladden in 1986.

OVERALL:

Leonard is a complex individual whose gruff demeanor has caused him to be unpopular with his teammates. Last season, he was embarrassed by his involvement in the Pittsburgh drug trial, which very likely distracted him at the plate.

This season, his challenge will be to march to new manager Roger Craig's beat.

Campbell: "I don't know how well Jeff fits into the team concept of baseball because he is an individualist. Roger Craig has laid down some new rules which Leonard will have to adjust to.

"He was named team captain, but he doesn't seem to be a leader-type player whom the other guys can turn to. Still, he has a lot of natural ability and is the best defensive left fielder in the National League."

HITTING:

Bob Melvin's future is brighter now that he has escaped backup duty to All-Star Tiger catcher Lance Parrish. Melvin was the key acquisition for the Giants in an October 1985 trade that sent Dave LaPoint to Detroit.

Giants' fans shouldn't expect lusty hitting from Melvin. He's a low fastball hitter with straightaway power, which won't produce many home runs. His selection is reasonably decent for an inexperienced major leaguer. He has trouble pulling the trigger on off-speed pitches from righthanded pitchers and is vulnerable to fastballs and sliders on his fists.

Melvin's stock will rise if he learns to pull with power.

BASERUNNING:

Melvin's speed is above average for a catcher. He is not, however, a threat to steal and usually advances one base at a time on singles.

FIELDING:

Melvin's arm strength and release time both are above average, which is important in the National League. He does have a couple of mechanical flaws that can be straightened out.

He has a tendency to rise straight up from his crouch before releasing the ball, rather than moving out at an angle to accept the pitch. It is a time-consuming extra step that can make the difference between a stolen base and an out. He also rotates his glove 180 degrees just prior to the pitcher's release.

BOB MELVIN
C, No. 12
RR, 6'4", 205 lbs.
ML Svc: 1 year
Born: 10-21-61 in
Palo Alto, CA

1985 STATISTICS

AVG	G	AB	R	H	2B	3B	HR	RBI	BB	SO	SB
.220	41	82	10	18	4	1	0	4	3	21	0

CAREER STATISTICS

AVG	G	AB	R	H	2B	3B	HR	RBI	BB	SO	SB
.220	41	82	10	18	4	1	0	4	3	21	0

  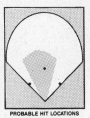

VS. RHP   VS. LHP   PROBABLE HIT LOCATIONS

That habit can disturb the concentration of some pitchers.

OVERALL:

Melvin has the tools to be an adequate catcher. He needs to gain confidence and iron out his mechanical flaws. His bat probably will not contribute a lot to the Giants' offense.

Robinson: "Melvin does everything pretty well except hit. My best bet is that he will always be a backup catcher because of his weak offensive skills."

PITCHING:

Last year Greg Minton did not register a save until June. He was in the
manager's doghouse and was demoted to a
backup role in the bullpen behind Scott
Garrelts. At one point, Minton was in
such bad stead with then-skipper Jim
Davenport that it seemed a trade was inevitable. Minton should get a reprieve
as new manager Roger Craig advocates
bullpen depth and would like to have him
around.

Minton has one of the better sinkers
in baseball when it's dropping properly,
but it has been erratic the last couple
of years. His inconsistency paved the
way for both Scott Garrelts and Mark
Davis to displace him as the bullpen
stoppers. Greg did not like playing second (and even third) fiddle and pleaded
for more work. His aggressiveness is an
asset, but not when his sinker doesn't
sink.

Minton wants the ball and his sinker
is obviously his meal ticket; but when
it's not working, all he eats is home
runs. His occasional slider is average,
his change-up is just an afterthought.

This season, if Minton can get it--
and keep it--together, he could be used
along with Garrelts as the Giants stoppers. This would keep Mark Davis out of
the tight spots.

FIELDING, HITTING, BASERUNNING:

Minton would probably be a better
fielder and baserunner if he shed a few
pounds--he will have no choice but to
get into better shape under Roger Craig.
Minton is a good athlete who fields his
position well, but he does not have a
good move to first.

GREG MINTON
RHP, No. 38
SR, 6'2", 190 lbs.
ML Svc: 8 years
Born: 7-29-51 in
Lubbock, TX

1985 STATISTICS

W	L	ERA	G	GS	CG	SV	IP	H	R	ER	BB	SO
5	4	3.54	68	0	0	4	96.2	98	42	38	54	37

CAREER STATISTICS

W	L	ERA	G	GS	CG	SV	IP	H	R	ER	BB	SO
40	48	3.15	489	7	0	110	778.2	764	318	273	334	309

At the plate, he has flashed some
power in the past, but no one saw any
sparks last season.

OVERALL:

Minton has seen better days. He has
not been the same pitcher since signing
a fat contract, one which makes it difficult to trade him. This season, if his
sinker sinks and his attitude is right,
he could provide insurance for the
club's younger relievers if he accepts
the fact he is not Numero Uno.

Campbell: "Greg has recently been
struggling with his control more than he
ever did before. When his sinker is
right, Minton gets the hitters out because he makes them hit the ball on the
ground. If the Giants can do it, he
would make great trade bait because he
has the kind of personality that really
needs to be the big man in the bullpen.
That, however, is not likely to happen
with the Giants this season."

HITTING:

A pleasant surprise last year, Ron Roenicke joined the club at mid-season. He hit .286 as a regular and gave the Giants much-needed lefthanded hitting off the bench.

Roenicke's switch-hitting is an asset, though the Giants used him primarily from the left side. Roenicke is a selective hitter who was able to get on base often last season. He waits for a pitch and will not hit it unless it is right where he wants it. He hits with good power to the alleys.

BASERUNNING:

Ron is an above-average baserunner who compensates for a lack of blazing speed with savvy on the basepaths. He was successful in six of eight attempts last year; he picks his spots well.

FIELDING:

Roenicke made only one error in 65 games and was able to play all three outfield positions. A solid outfielder who has good judgment and an accurate arm. He will not embarrass himself regardless of where he plays because he's developed into a sound ballplayer who's survived with an intelligent approach to the game.

Roenicke is the man most likely to become the fourth outfielder this year if Joel Youngblood's desire to play elsewhere is accommodated.

OVERALL:

Roenicke's dependable performance last year showed the Giants he deserves a job. The fact that he switch-hits and plays several different positions makes him extremely valuable. He gets the most

RON ROENICKE
OF, No. 41
SL, 6'0", 180 lbs.
ML Svc: 5 years
Born: 8-19-56 in
    Covina, CA

1985 STATISTICS

AVG	G	AB	R	H	2B	3B	HR	RBI	BB	SO	SB
.256	65	133	23	34	9	1	3	13	35	27	6

CAREER STATISTICS

AVG	G	AB	R	H	2B	3B	HR	RBI	BB	SO	SB
.246	336	666	82	164	33	1	10	60	109	115	21

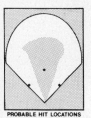

VS. RHP   VS. LHP   PROBABLE HIT LOCATIONS

out of his ability and last year was a dependable part-time player.

Surely, the Padres made a mistake by releasing him last spring, given the mediocrity of their bench and their defensive problems in the outfield.

While it is possible that Roenicke maintained his hustling attitude because he was not with the lackluster Giants from Opening Day, he realized that his opportunity in San Francisco might be his last in the majors. He gave it his best shot and was impressive.

Campbell: "Ron is a fundamentally sound player who can help a club in many ways. He is the type of guy I would want on my club. He could have definitely helped the Padres last year. He is not an everyday player, but a manager likes to have him around because he can do so many things."

HITTING:

The Giants haven't had much luck with good-hitting shortstops since Chris Speier was traded away, but this rookie is an improvement over Johnnie LeMaster and is expected to get better.

Uribe is a switch-hitter, though it is curious that he continues to hit righthanded as he hit only .216 from that side last year. He is a decent hitter from the left side (.245 last season) and batted .264 over the last three months, which is an indication of his gradual improvement at the plate.

He seems to like the ball up and away from the left side and hits it to the opposite field. From the right side, he often looks lost and does not have a very good stroke. He could help himself by being more selective.

BASERUNNING:

Jose has shown indications he will be a more dangerous basestealer as he gains more confidence. He was nailed only twice in 10 attemps last year, which isn't bad. He had good theft marks in the minors.

Uribe has good speed, but is still learning to become more efficient on the basepaths.

FIELDING:

Uribe was a star second baseman in winter ball. In fact, he kept Mariano Duncan (who is now with the Dodgers) on the bench. But the Giants needed a shortstop and he played the position well until arm trouble cropped up in September.

Uribe's arm was definitely tired by then. He played in more games than any other Giant player last season (147), including 70 games in a row. Until the soreness developed in his arm, his arm was accurate, though not overly strong.

His quickness enables him to cover a lot of ground. He wasn't as good as

JOSE URIBE
INF, No. 23
SR, 5'10", 165 lbs.
ML Svc: 1 year plus
Born: 1-21-60 in
  San Cristobal, DR

1985 STATISTICS
AVG	G	AB	R	H	2B	3B	HR	RBI	BB	SO	SB
.237	147	476	46	113	20	4	3	26	30	57	8

CAREER STATISTICS
AVG	G	AB	R	H	2B	3B	HR	RBI	BB	SO	SB
.236	155	495	50	117	20	4	3	29	30	59	9

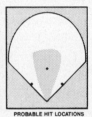

VS. RHP   VS. LHP   PROBABLE HIT LOCATIONS

LeMaster in the hole, but he handled himself well going toward second base. If his arm stays sound, Uribe has the potential to become a solid shortstop in time.

OVERALL:

The fact he had to play so much last year makes it obvious that the club's spare infielders cannot play shortstop. Jose was judged a little harshly by outsiders, but he was a blessing after years of LeMaster's lightweight hitting and chronic moping. As they say, it's all relative.

Campbell: "Jose was not impressive when I saw him in September, when the soreness in his arm was affecting his throwing. I would think that if the Giants could get a good shortstop, Uribe would be an adequate backup at short or at second base Based on what I've seen, he's not a front-line major leaguer."

HITTING:

Joel Youngblood was not a happy player in 1985. He struggled in the first half of the season and was around the .200 mark before hitting .310 during the second half. The trouble started just when he began to get hot with the bat. He was as effective as any other hitter on the club and then was inexplicably benched. Denied earning incentive money, Youngblood got hot under the collar and was quickly eager for a change of scenery.

Youngblood is a good contact hitter who shows surges of power. He responds well in clutch situations and is a hard worker. He doesn't strike out much, so he can be of value as a pinch-hitter.

BASERUNNING:

Joel is a heady baserunner, but he hasn't been much of a basestealer since his days with the New York Mets (1979-80). He is alert on the basepaths and is not prone to mistakes because his head is always in the game.

FIELDING:

Youngblood is versatile enough to play just about everywhere except third base. The outfield is where his strength lies--especially in right field. In fact, his strong throwing arm makes him an above-average outfielder, one who seemingly could be a starter on another club.

Youngblood had the chance to be the Giants' regular third baseman in 1984, but a rash of errors convinced people that chasing flies is his forte. He also played at second base for a spell in 1983, was better there than at third, but still, he belongs in the outfield.

OVERALL:

Joel is a high-strung, cerebral sort

JOEL YOUNGBLOOD
OF/PH, No. 8
RR, 5'11", 175 lbs.
ML Svc: 10 years
Born: 8-28-51 in
Houston, TX

| 1985 STATISTICS | | | | | | | | | | | |
AVG	G	AB	R	H	2B	3B	HR	RBI	BB	SO	SB
.270	95	230	24	62	6	0	4	24	30	37	3

| CAREER STATISTICS | | | | | | | | | | | |
AVG	G	AB	R	H	2B	3B	HR	RBI	BB	SO	SB
.268	1083	3143	398	843	156	23	69	354	286	504	57

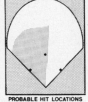

STRONG VS. RHP   STRONG VS. LHP   PROBABLE HIT LOCATIONS

who has been accused of "thinking" too much instead of simply letting his natural talent flow. There's no question he's a worrier, which makes it tougher for him to snap out of the doldrums.

Last year's extended slump drove him bananas and he was extremely disgruntled when he was benched after he finally got into a groove. Youngblood is a player who needs to move to a team that could appreciate his talents--and he is talented. There aren't many utilitymen who can hit well and play good defense.

Campbell: "Joel is a darn good hitter and a very good right fielder.

"At one time, it looked as though he had the chance to be one of the game's best utilitymen, but his lack of consistency in the infield reduced some of that value. I don't think he's going to play regularly on an outstanding team, but he can do an awful lot of things well and could definitely be a valuable addition to a lot of other clubs."

ROB DEER
OF, No. 45
RR, 6'3", 210 lbs.
ML Svc: 1 year plus
Born: 9-29-60 in
    Orange, CA

HITTING, BASERUNNING, FIELDING:

Rob Deer's problem has been finding enough playing time to show what he can do. His power potential is enormous, but so are the strikeout totals. His three pinch-homers tied for the league lead in 1985, but he also fanned 71 times in 162 at-bats. But home run hitters, like lefthanded pitchers with control and third basemen who can hit, are worth waiting for.

Deer seems to be the type of hitter who will do one of two things at the plate: either hit the ball out of the park or miss it completely. He will never develop into a high-average hitter, but the Giants are willing to live with 150+ strikeouts if Deer shows consistent long ball ability.

His baserunning is below average because he prefers the home run trot.

OVERALL:

It is about time for the Giants to fish or cut bait with this promising talent. If there is a major shakeup on the roster this season, Deer may get his chance to play, but he is a definite risk because of his strikeouts.

Campbell: "I think the Giants have to give him a shot as a full-time player--they need a franchise-type player who can hit 30-35 homers and Deer could do that. The trick, of course is to keep the strikeouts down. He might benefit from some visual acuity work by an optometrist. It has helped a lot of athletes, including George Brett, so it may be worth a try in Deer's case."

BILL LASKEY
RHP, No. 19
RR, 6'5", 190 lbs.
ML Svc: 4 years
Born: 12-20-57 in
    Toledo, OH

PITCHING, FIELDING,
HITTING, BASERUNNING:

The Giants are wondering which Bill Laskey will show up at spring training this season. A streaky pitcher throughout his career, he is capable of winning five or six in a row then losing just as many. Prior to his swap to Montreal last August, Laskey won four in a row. The trade stunned him and he proceeded to go 0-5 with a 9.44 ERA for the Expos, which prompted them to virtually give him back to the Giants.

Laskey has the four basic pitches and has good control, but he does not have the stamina to pitch more than five innings at a time. He uses a herky-jerky delivery which may be placing a strain on his arm.

As a hitter, Laskey isn't an automatic out, but his hitting has waned over the last couple of years. Baserunning is not his forte.

His move to first base is terrible and he doesn't field particularly well.

OVERALL:

Laskey is a prime reclamation project for Roger Craig. He enters this season as a bit of an unknown whose spring performance will determine his role on the club.

Campbell: "The thing that impresses me most about him is that he's a good competitor and isn't afraid of a challenge. None of his pitches are above average, so he could use another pitch."

ROGER MASON
RHP, No. 15
RR, 6'6", 215 lbs.
ML Svc: 1 year plus
Born: 9-18-58 in
Bellaire, MI

PITCHING, FIELDING, HITTING, BASERUNNING:

Roger Mason is a rangy righthander who has the best chance of any newcomer to have an impact on the Giants pitching staff. Roger Craig likes him from their days together in Detroit and the youngster's strong finish last season virtually guarantees him a spot in the club's "new-look" rotation.

Mason has a very effective tailing fastball and a small slider which acts as a cut fastball. He also is learning the split-finger fastball from the guru. Craig hopes that the split-finger will do for Mason what it did for Houston's Mike Scott.

Mason has outstanding potential. He was an immediate hit when he joined the Giants' organization last year, going 12-1 for Phoenix (AAA) and firing a four-hit shutout against Atlanta in his last major league start.

Because of his size, he is not known for a good move to first or holding runners on base well.

Since his background is in the AL, it hasn't been determined if he can hit or run.

OVERALL:

Mason should be a breath of fresh air to a stagnant starting rotation this year. Being reunited with Craig will increase Mason's chances for success.

Campbell: "Mason is big and strong and has outstanding capabilities. It's no secret that the split-finger fastball will be dancing in San Francisco this season and Mason looks like he may take the lead."

ALEX TREVINO
C, No. 29
RR, 5'11", 170 lbs.
ML Svc: 7 years
Born: 8-26-57 in
Monterrey, MEX

HITTING, BASERUNNING, FIELDING:

Just when it looks as though Alex Trevino is about to have difficulty holding onto his job (he doesn't do any one thing very well), he'll do something to surprise you. Last year, for example, he hit a career high six home runs after collecting only five in his previous six major league seasons. He also batted .289 after the All-Star break when he had a chance to spell the slumping Bob Brenly.

Trevino can hit the ball down both lines, so defenses should give him the alleys and protect the lines. He pulls slow stuff down the line in left and hammers high pitches to right. He seems to be a stronger hitter now, so pitchers should keep the ball down and change speeds on him to induce grounders.

He runs very well for a catcher; as a matter of fact, he may be the fastest-running catcher in the league.

Defensively, however, Trevino is a liability. He is below-average in most aspects of the position, and though his release is quick, his throws are not always accurate.

OVERALL:

Campbell: "Every time I see Trevino play, I change my mind about his abilities. One day he does nothing but hit balls to the right side with an inside-out stroke, then, all of a sudden, he does nothing but pull the ball to left. He's hard to figure, but he does a few things well enough to be a backup."

MANNY TRILLO
2B, No. 9
RR, 6'1", 164 lbs.
ML Svc: 12 years
Born: 12-25-50 in
Caritito, VEN

HITTING, BASERUNNING, FIELDING:

Once an All-Star performer, Manny Trillo no longer has any of the skills that made him a standout second baseman for years.

He hit a career-low .224 last year, was an anchor on the basepaths and, most importantly, lost his luster as a gloveman. As a number two hitter, his success often depended on what the leadoff man did, so Dan Gladden's 1985 slump did not help.

In fact, Trillo has been an offensive zero ever since a broken bone in his right hand shelved him for two months in 1984. The best way to get him out in the past was to throw hard low stuff, but last year he had trouble with almost everything, so the end apparently is near.

His notoriously wide range has been reduced to almost nothing, though he still is sure-handed and his off-balance throws remain accurate. Trillo hasn't lost his smoothness; he plays with a grace other second basemen only dream about.

OVERALL:

Trillo would have been phased out of the Giants' plans sooner if the club had a respectable replacement. But Brad Wellman and Mike Woodard have proved unacceptable. The Giants cannot patch second base with Trillo much longer.

Campbell: "I think the end of the line has come for Manny. His average is way down, he has no running speed whatsoever, he does not hit in key spots and his range is gone."

FRANK WILLIAMS
RHP, No. 47
RR, 6'1", 180 lbs.
ML Svc: 2 years
Born: 2-13-58 in
Seattle, WA

PITCHING, FIELDING,
HITTING, BASERUNNING:

Frank Williams has merely average stuff; he is not the big stopper in the bullpen, but he can be especially effective against a righthanded hitter. He uses a sidearm--almost submarine--style of delivery that confuses righthanded hitters and can almost freeze them.

Williams has an average sinking fastball, a very average change-up and a slurve that is a great big breaking pitch. It is kind of flat though it rises if he gets underneath it. His strength is that his pitches arrive at different angles, which make them tough for the righthanders to pick up.

One of Williams' problems last year was inconsistency. Because the starters were pitching well early in the season, there was little work for long relievers like Frank. He withered from inactivity, was optioned and really didn't hit his stride until the last few weeks of the season following his recall from the minors.

Williams is a pitcher--his hitting and fielding are atrocious. His sidearm motion makes his throwing very erratic when he fields a batted ball.

OVERALL:

Williams likely will be fighting for his pitching life this year, but would profit from regular work.

Campbell: "It seems to me that he can be valuable to a club in two ways: he has a rubber arm and always seems ready to pitch and he can be very effective against teams loaded with righthanded hitters."

PLAYER INDEX

C

D

E

I

J

K

L

M

N

O